HIDDEN ®
New England

HIDDEN®

New England

SIXTH EDITION

Ulysses Press®

BERKELEY, CALIFORNIA

Published by:
ULYSSES PRESS
P.O. Box 3440
Berkeley, CA 94703-3440
www.ulyssespress.com

ISSN 1090-6894
ISBN 1-56975-205-2

Printed in Canada by Transcontinental Printing

20 19 18 17 16 15 14 13 12 11 10

UPDATE AUTHOR: Richard Harris
AUTHOR: Susan Farewell
MANAGING EDITOR: Claire Chun
PROJECT DIRECTOR: Lynette Ubois
COPY EDITORS: Steven Zah Schwartz, Lily Chou
EDITORIAL ASSOCIATES: Melissa Millar, Marin Van Young, Aimee
    Benedict, Cathy Chun, Natasha Lay
TYPESETTERS: Jennifer Brontsema, David Wells
CARTOGRAPHY: Pease Press
HIDDEN BOOKS DESIGN: Sarah Levin
COVER DESIGN: Leslie Henriques
INDEXER: Sayre Van Young
COVER PHOTOGRAPHY
    FRONT: Pat and Chuck Blackley (The Jenny Farm, South
    Woodstock, VT)
    CIRCLE: Pat and Chuck Blackley (Nobska Point Light,
    Woods Hole, MA)
    BACK: Markham Johnson (Cycling in Nantucket, MA)
ILLUSTRATOR: Timothy Carroll

Distributed in the United States by Publishers
Group West, in Canada by Raincoast Books,
and in Great Britain and Europe by World
Leisure Marketing

HIDDEN is a federally registered trademark
of BookPack, Inc.

Ulysses Press 🐢 is a federally registered
trademark of BookPack, Inc.

Write to us!

If in your travels you discover a spot that captures the spirit of New England, or if you live in the region and have a favorite place to share, or if you just feel like expressing your views, write to us and we'll pass your note along to the author.

We can't guarantee that the author will add your personal find to the next edition, but if the writer does use the suggestion, we'll acknowledge you in the credits and send you a free copy of the new edition.

ULYSSES PRESS
P.O. Box 3440
Berkeley, CA 94703-3440
E-mail: readermail@ulyssespress.com

Acknowledgments

Ulysses Press would like to thank the following readers who took the time to write in with suggestions that were incorporated into this new edition of *Hidden New England*:

Mrs. Dorothy Broekhuizen of Portage, MI; Linda Fowler of Maineville, OH; Pauline Tom of Buda, TX; Jean C. Pegg of E. Freetown, MA; David Rutigliano of Derby, CT; Anuradha Vaitheswaran of Des Moines, IA. By e-mail: Gary B. Gaines; L.A. Hoffman.

What's Hidden?

At different points throughout this book, you'll find special listings marked with a hidden symbol:

◄ *HIDDEN*

This means that you have come upon a place off the beaten tourist track, a spot that will carry you a step closer to the local people and natural environment of New England.

The goal of this guide is to lead you beyond the realm of everyday tourist facilities. While we include traditional sightseeing listings and popular attractions, we also offer alternative sights and adventure activities. Instead of filling this guide with reviews of standard hotels and chain restaurants, we concentrate on one-of-a-kind places and locally owned establishments.

Our authors seek out locales that are popular with residents but usually overlooked by visitors. Some are more hidden than others (and are marked accordingly), but all the listings in this book are intended to help you discover the true nature of New England and put you on the path of adventure.

Contents

Maps

OUTDOOR ADVENTURE SYMBOLS

The following symbols accompany national, state and regional park listings, as well as beach descriptions throughout the text.

Camping

Hiking

Biking

Horseback Riding

Downhill Skiing

Cross-country Skiing

Swimming

Snorkeling or Scuba Diving

Surfing

Waterskiing

Windsurfing

Canoeing or Kayaking

Boating

Boat Ramps

Fishing

ONE

New England Sojourn

There is no more instantly recognizable scenery in the American landscape—or the American mind—than the picture-postcard image of a New England village: the white-steepled church on an emerald green, ringed by white clapboard houses, the whole of it haloed by forests aflame with fall reds and golds.

No wonder people come hoping, wanting, expecting to find this metaphor for New England life. And this place of centuries past still exists, in many small towns scattered throughout the six states.

But New England is stunningly heterogeneous, possessed of countless rich dimensions. In just one state, you find old textile and industrial cities, rivers and lakes, and towering spruce forests whose denizens are moose and black bear. Visitors will discover miles and miles of white sand beaches fringed with dunes and marsh grasses; thriving metropolises like Boston and Providence; mountain ranges with hiking and skiing trails; fishing villages hundreds of years old; Indian burial grounds; and coastal resorts where elegant yachts bob in the harbor. Standing fast before time, New England's old wooden saltbox houses have weathered into the colors of the very ground that made them.

Bounded on the north by Canada, on the east by the Atlantic Ocean, on the south by Long Island Sound, and on the west by New York, New England sits squarely in the northeastern corner of the United States. Five states border the ocean, which is never far from anyone's mind. Fishing blessed all who settled here, from the Indians and the Pilgrims to the 19th-century whalers and today's fishermen of Gloucester, New Bedford and Plymouth. New Englanders have always been premier shipbuilders and sailors, and today one of the greatest pleasures is to ride a Maine windjammer, an excursion boat or a tiny sailboat.

The ocean also tempers the weather, making summers cooler and winters less fierce. The seasons pull out all the stops here, parading four kinds of memorable variety every year. In warmer, more monotonous climes, the passing of time recedes to a blur.

New Englanders love and revere their covered bridges, their Revolutionary War–era, Federal and Greek Revival homes, and their chowder made with milk, not tomato juice, thank you. To a real New Englander, there's nothing quite like the first cider of the fall, real native maple syrup or a clambake on the beach.

To give them credit, many dour old Yankees have expanded their tastes to include the flowers, glass arcades and gourmet restaurants of Quincy Market and whimsical things like balloon festivals.

Still, there is little of glitz about this region. New England simply is what it is, without apology. It's not an invented attraction but a real place, one that stands on the legitimacy and integrity of its origins.

This book was designed to help you explore this wonderful area. Besides leading you to countless popular spots, it will also take you to many off-the-beaten-path locales, places usually known only by locals. The book will tell the story of the region's history, its flora and fauna. Each chapter will suggest places to eat, to stay, to sightsee, to shop and to enjoy the outdoors and nightlife, covering a range of tastes and budgets.

The book sets out in Connecticut, taking visitors in Chapter Two through the rural outlying areas and along its pretty coastline. Chapter Three outlines tiny little Rhode Island's greatly unspoiled topography and gorgeous beaches, as well as elite Newport and historic Providence. Because of its dense population and diversity, Massachusetts is presented in four chapters. Quintessential Boston is explored in Chapter Four, from its Revolutionary War–era sites to Beacon Hill and Back Bay. Chapter Five covers all of Cape Cod, as well as the islands of Martha's Vineyard and Nantucket. Chapter Six moves along the Massachusetts Coast, from the North Shore to Plymouth and New Bedford on the South Shore. In Chapter Seven, you'll discover the Pioneer Valley and the Berkshires of central and western Massachusetts.

Chapter Eight covers Vermont, with its Green Mountains and covered bridges. Chapter Nine is dedicated to New Hampshire, land of sparkling lakes, the White Mountains and majestic Mount Washington. Last but by no means least, you'll explore the stately pine forests and rugged coast of Maine in Chapter Ten.

Wherever you choose to go, whatever you choose to see and do, you're bound to find something to like in this infinite variety. Generations of travelers have enjoyed New England's coast and mountains, forests and lakes, in all kinds of weather.

▼▼▼▼▼▼▼▼▼▼▼▼▼▼▼▼▼▼▼

The Story of New England

GEOLOGY

Geology is destiny, you might say. Certainly this is true in the case of New England. Some of the region's most famed symbols, from stone walls, mill towns and rivers, to Bunker Hill, Walden Pond, Cape Cod and the White Mountains, sprang from geologic events.

New England is one of the oldest continuously surviving land masses on earth. In Cambrian times, half a billion years ago, New England was covered by a vast inland sea. When the earth's crust buckled and rose, it pushed up mountainous masses—the ancestors of the Berkshires and the Green Mountains. During the same era, a mass of hot molten rock gave birth to the White Mountains from deep within the earth.

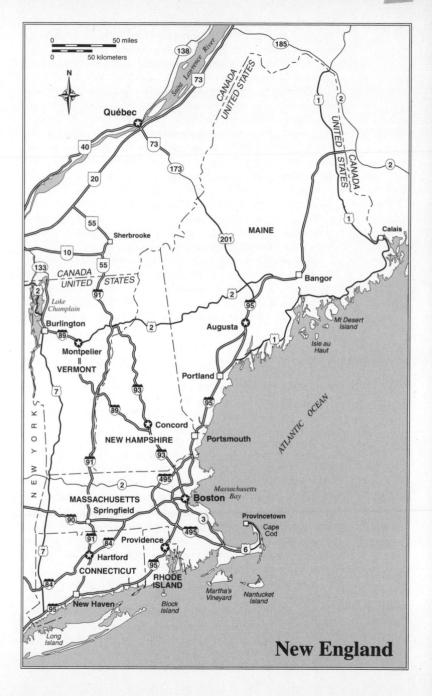

New England

Even while the mountains were rising, running water began to wear away at the land, leveling it and washing sediments down from the uplands. Finally all New England was reduced almost to sea level, like a flat plain. But some of the mountains survived, particularly those in the north, which was less completely leveled.

The earth's crust stirred again, 200 million to 300 million years later, but gently this time. The land rose just enough to give altitude to the slow-moving rivers of the plains, causing them to flow more swiftly, and set them off to carving out valleys. Eventually New Englanders would find these fast-flowing, powerful rivers and build mill wheels on them to run their factories and mills, which you can still see today.

The Ice Age seized the region in a frozen grip about a million years ago, gradually spreading and growing. The mass of ice finally became so vast and heavy that its own weight pushed it down and outward, and it began to move. For thousands of years, the ice cap grew, engulfing all of New England.

As it moved, the ice cap picked up boulders, some as large as houses, and carried them along with it. Fields of boulders, filled with rocks of all sizes, are common in New England. Farmers had to clear their fields of countless rocks before they could plant, and they used them to make stone walls, which still line the landscape today.

The ice moved in a southerly direction, from Canada to Long Island, paring off hills and ledges as it went. Some of the glacial till was clay, which sticks to itself more readily than to ice. Deposited clay formed into low-lying, oval-shaped hills called drumlins, many a mile or more long and a hundred feet high. Some of the region's most famous drumlins are Bunker Hill and World's End in Hingham, Massachusetts.

The glaciers came and went four times, retreating and advancing for over a million years, finally leaving New England about 10,000 to 12,000 years ago. The last glacial advance formed Cape Cod, Martha's Vineyard, Nantucket, Block Island and the Rhode Island shore. At the front of the advancing ice sheet, released rock debris built up a terminal moraine—a ridge of rubble. These islands and coasts are what remains of the morainal ridges. Watch Hill, Rhode Island, has been called by geologists "one of the finest examples of glacial dumping ground" in the eastern United States.

Large blocks of melting glacial ice formed kettle-hole lakes, deep bodies of water with a rounded shape, of which Walden Pond is a good example. It might also be said that kettle lakes make for fine ice-skating and ice-fishing.

HISTORY   New England is America's scrapbook, the memorabilia of a nation conceived on hardship and perseverance, faith and dreams.

It is a riveting story of high adventure and the push for freedom, of ingenuity and despotism, of victory over adverse conditions.

The opening pages tell of Pilgrims who charted a course to Greenland but were blown far southward by violent winds. The year was 1000 A.D., and, according to Norse legend, Norseman Leif Ericsson landed in a strange place, probably along Maine's rocky coast. Discovering friendly Indians and fertile land where grapes and wheat grew wild, he dubbed his find Vinland the Good and returned to Norway with tales of a fascinating world.

More than 450 years would pass before European explorers would again call on the intriguing land. Navigator John Cabot, on assignment from England's King Henry VII and seeking a Northwest Passage to the East, explored the coasts of Maine and Massachusetts in 1497. He found no pass but claimed a considerable chunk of the New World—everything north of Florida and east of the Rockies—for the British crown.

Italian explorer Giovanni da Verrazano staked out the same coast some 27 years later, claiming the territory for his employer nation, France. Just prior to his visit, navigator Miguel Corte Real had been checking out the terrain for Portugal.

Dutch sailor Adriaen Block launched a coastal investigation in 1614, calling a Narragansett Bay island "Roodt Eyland," or Red Island, a likely precursor to Rhode Island. That same year, English captain John Smith mapped the Massachusetts coast and was taken by its beauty. A soldier of fortune, Smith wrote a glowing report of the intriguing land, describing its "sandy cliffes and cliffes of rock" planted with cornfields and gardens.

Though captivated by the new region, none of these adventurers did what seemed the most logical thing: settle the place. Of course, this white man's frontier had been inhabited at least five centuries by Algonquin tribes. A peaceful people who dwelled in wigwams, they were expert growers of corn, tobacco, pumpkins and other crops. They hunted forests plentiful with moose, deer, turkey and goose, and fished the streams and ocean for bass, salmon, lobster and clams, throwing the area's earliest clambakes.

A CORNUCOPIA OF HISTORY

It would be almost impossible to find another place in the United States so densely packed with history. You can barely take a step without stumbling over a Colonial battlefield, a historic site or monument, or an 18th-century house. All that you learned in school about the birth of the United States will come to life before your eyes. And every year or so, another New England town celebrates its 350th anniversary.

The Algonquins were not populous. Small tribes, sometimes with as few as 200 Indians, were scattered among the forests and along the coast. The Pennacook tribe resided in what would become New Hampshire and Massachusetts; the Abenaki favored the New Hampshire area, too, as well as Maine. The Narrangansetts were natives of today's Rhode Island. All told, New England's Indians numbered about 25,000 when they welcomed the first permanent European settlers in 1620.

> By the mid-1660s, Rhode Island received New England's first Jews and several hundred French Huguenots and Quakers.

Religious asylum, not adventure or fortune, is what those first real settlers were seeking. The Puritans, cut off from Anglican England because of their strict Protestant beliefs, read with interest John Smith's glowing report on the New World. Could it be their Utopia? They were anxious to find out.

In the spring of 1620, the Puritans struck a deal with the Plymouth Company to finance a settlement in the New World. By summer's end, 102 Puritans boarded the *Mayflower* for a rigorous, two-month journey to America. They first sighted land at Cape Cod, then cruised the coast for a month and landed at Plymouth Rock. On December 21, the Plymouth Colony was born.

That first winter proved brutal for the colonists as they fought scurvy, pneumonia and other diseases that killed nearly half their group. But springtime brought relief and the opportunity to plant crops, thanks to help from the Indians who were hospitable to their new neighbors. To celebrate the first anniversary of their friendship, the Pilgrims and Indians feasted together for three days that fall.

As word of the successful colony trickled back to England, more Puritans set out for the New World. In 1630, about 1000 Puritans on 11 ships landed at Salem during the "Great Migration." Drawn by a vast harbor filled with sea life, settlers moved southward and declared Boston their main colony. Fur-trading posts were established in Maine, and small villages sprang up in New Hampshire, Connecticut and Rhode Island.

By 1636, another 12,000 immigrants had arrived. Puritan ministers, sensing the need to train future leaders, founded Harvard College and set up a general court to govern the colonies. Local matters were dealt with by town leaders at regular meetings, the forerunners of today's town council sessions.

Ironically, those same Puritans who sought the New World for religious freedom would not tolerate other beliefs. In 1651, a visitor from the Rhode Island colony was publicly whipped for being a Baptist. Victims of English persecution, Quakers fleeing the Old World were arrested on ships in Boston Harbor before they ever set foot on the new land. Additionally, in 1659, two men and a woman were hanged in Massachusetts for espousing Quaker beliefs.

Religious dissidents fled to Rhode Island, which Puritans dubbed "the sewer of New England" and "Rogue's Island." But the tiny colony held fast to religious and social freedoms.

It was Puritan fanaticism that caused the untimely end of several other unfortunate New England souls. Witches, the Puritans said, were lurking about, possessed by demons and casting spells on innocent minds.

The accusations led to witch trials in Charlestown in 1648 and in Boston in 1655, but the most hideous ordeal occurred in Salem in 1692. After hundreds of people were imprisoned in a "Witch House," 19 were executed, including 80-year-old Giles Corey, who was pressed to death when he pled no-contest.

The Puritans were also a nightmare for the Indians. Determined to "save" them from their pagan ways, missionaries translated the Bible into Algonquin and set about converting new Christians. By the 1670s, nearly one-fourth of the Indian population had officially accepted the imposed faith. But it was not enough. The Puritans wanted not just mental converts but a race that would abandon its centuries-old customs, its very mode of existence.

As colonies expanded, the Indians got in the way. Several skirmishes ensued, but it was King Philip's War, from 1675 to 1676, that spelled the beginning of the end for the New England Indians. Pressured by colonists to abandon his land, chief Metacomet (King Philip) led a series of battles against his encroachers. He lost a decisive engagement, the "Great Swamp Fight" near Kingston, Rhode Island, when Massachusetts and Connecticut colonists burned wigwams, killing hundreds of women and children and disorganizing Indian forces.

Betrayed by a fellow Indian, King Philip was captured soon thereafter, his body beheaded and quartered. His head was displayed on a gibbet in Plymouth for 20 years as a reminder of white victory. Just four decades after the Indians had welcomed the first Puritans into their home, the Puritans had decimated them.

Eighteenth-century New England was a place of social, economic and political growth. Life centered around the ocean and rivers, as shipbuilding thrived in towns such as Portsmouth in New Hampshire, Groton in Connecticut, Kittery in Maine and, of course, Boston. Coopers, potters and furniture makers plied their trades along the waterfront, and coastal and international trade boomed.

Colleges and universities that today rank among the nation's best were established: Yale University, New Hampshire's Dartmouth College, and Rhode Island College, now Brown University. The influx of non-Puritans created a greater cultural and religious mix, and politics flourished as colonists demanded more autonomy from Mother England.

Determined to subdue its wayward child, England in 1764 imposed the Revenue Act, which levied duties on silk, sugar and some wines. Colonists rebelled and promptly boycotted the tariffs.

England didn't flinch. One year later, it slapped colonies with the Stamp Act, taxing commercial and legal papers such as newspapers and licenses. Outraged, colonists denounced the tax and refused to buy European goods. "No taxation without representation," they cried. Every Colonial stamp agent resigned, and before the law could take effect November 1, Parliament repealed the act.

But England insisted on political and economic control. Several months later Parliament passed the Townshend Acts, imposing heavy taxes on paper, glass and tea. Colonists again rebelled, and England sent troops to squelch rioting in Boston.

By 1770, hoping to rid the city of "Redcoats"—the colonists' name for the British militia—Bostonians gathered at the Customs House and began taunting the sentry. Troops arrived, and after a series of violent skirmishes, they fired shots into the crowd. When the Boston Massacre was over, five colonials lay dead on King Street, present-day State Street.

England repealed most of the Townshend taxes, leaving duties on imported tea—then the most popular drink in America. New Englanders retaliated by buying smuggled tea. In 1773, when England's Tea Act flooded the market with cheap tea, agents would not accept deliveries—except for Governor Thomas Hutchinson in Boston.

When three tea-filled ships sailed into Boston Harbor, the Committees of Correspondence and Sons of Liberty—pre-revolutionary activists—blocked the piers. Governor Hutchinson refused to let the ships return to England, so protesters invited him to a little tea party.

Disguised as Indians, 60 Sons of Liberty boarded the ships on the night of December 16, 1773 and dumped 342 chests of tea into the harbor. It was a defiant move and an ominous portent of what lie ahead: revolution was in the air.

On April 19, 1775, a single musket discharge set off America's first full-scale war. "The shot heard 'round the world" was fired at the Battle of Lexington and Concord, an effort by the Redcoats to crush revolutionary uprisings around Boston.

Forewarned by Paul Revere that the "British are coming," 77 Minutemen crouched in early morning darkness, waiting for the Redcoat attack. The British advanced, killing eight rebels and wounding ten on the present-day Lexington Green before continuing to Concord. There they destroyed a cache of arms and were finally driven out.

The colonies rallied together. Vermont's Green Mountain Boys, led by Ethan Allen and Benedict Arnold, captured Fort

Ticonderoga on Lake Champlain, blocking a British invasion from Canada. On June 17, 1775, New Englanders fought the war's first major engagement—known as the Battle of Bunker Hill although it was really fought on nearby Breed's Hill—on the Charlestown peninsula near Boston. After enduring two British attacks, the Americans ran short of ammunition and retreated.

Though a technical victory for England, Bunker Hill cost the crown more than 1000 troops—over twice the Colonial losses. More important, it proved that the Minutemen volunteers were a match for the better-trained British army.

On July 4, 1776, the Declaration of Independence was adopted by the Continental Congress. The war raged on in surrounding states for six years, but New England was free.

Economic depression followed the war. Paper money was scarce, loans difficult to obtain and court foreclosures commonplace. When their new state government levied high taxes, Massachusetts farmers rose up in anger. Shays' Rebellion, which lasted from 1786 to 1787 but was unsuccessful at stopping the taxes, proved that democracy was still an elusive concept.

New England heralded the 19th century with a burgeoning shipping industry, though the War of 1812 temporarily halted matters with stiff trade embargoes. With the advent of the cotton mill in Pawtucket, Rhode Island, weavers no longer had to work at home, though their 12-hour workdays and paltry wages led to the nation's first labor strike in 1800. Eli Whitney's cotton gin revolutionized the wool industry, and mills sprang up across New England. By the 1830s, Providence alone produced 20 percent of the country's wool.

As New England grew and the railroad headed west, settlers starting moving into the interior. Wilderness areas of northern Maine, Vermont and New Hampshire were slowly penetrated, and pioneers established small farms. But unforgiving soil and unpredictable weather squelched any hopes of real agriculture, and by 1860 farming as serious business ceased to exist in these states.

AMERICAN INGENUITY

Hundreds of inventions put New England at the forefront of the industrial age. Yale graduate Samuel Morse masterminded the telegraph and his own code, Elias Howe crafted the world's first sewing machine, and Charles Goodyear developed a type of commercial rubber, though he died $200,000 in the red. In Hartford, Samuel Colt opened a munitions factory and Francis Pratt and Amos Whitney manufactured machine tools and interchangeable parts.

The Industrial Revolution sparked a mass immigration of Europeans, with hundreds arriving from England, Scotland, Italy and Portugal. Victims of the 1845 Great Potato Famine, thousands of Irish sailed to Massachusetts with dreams of a new life. By 1850, one of every ten New Englanders was foreign born. Only ten years later, 61 percent of Boston residents had been born abroad.

Not all New Englanders welcomed so many immigrants with open arms. During the 1850s, several political monsters reared their ugly heads. The Know-Nothing Party blatantly opposed all immigrants, particularly the Irish. Together with virulent anti-Roman Catholic factions in Maine, the party burned several Catholic churches. The powerful Know-Nothings managed to control governorships in several states.

At the same time, the abolition movement gripped New England. Connecticut's Harriet Beecher Stowe raised public consciousness in 1852 with *Uncle Tom's Cabin*. A fervent opponent of slavery, William Lloyd Garrison published his *Liberator* newspaper for 34 years in Massachusetts, despite being dragged through streets by angry mobs and threatened constantly.

New England was also experiencing a cultural renaissance. The great "Flowering of New England" was centered in Boston. Now called the "Athens of America," the city saw the founding of such eminent institutions as the Museum of Fine Arts, the Boston Symphony Orchestra and the Boston Pops.

Great minds thrived across the region. Artists, thinkers and literary geniuses would set the dynamic tone in New England for centuries to come. People like Nathaniel Hawthorne and Oliver Wendell Holmes, Henry David Thoreau and Julia Ward Howe, Ralph Waldo Emerson and Emily Dickinson made New England an intellectual mecca.

By the turn of the century, an ethnic and political metamorphosis had taken place. The long-time bastion of Yankee Protestantism was now being run by Roman Catholics. In 1900, a majority of New England legislators were Catholic.

At the same time came a wave of corruption that would last for several decades. In Rhode Island, Republican "Boss" Charles R. Brayton built his regime by exchanging bought votes for "judgeships and other political jobs," charged journalist Lincoln Steffens. Brayton even paid "yellow dog" Democrats to be loyal to the machine. Iniquity reached its height in Boston's James Michael Curley, elected mayor four times between 1914 and 1950 and state governor from 1935 to 1937. The "Irish Mussolini" perfected ward politics, handing out jobs, favors and money to those who guaranteed his return to office.

The Depression crushed New England. Between 1929 and 1950, more than 149,000 textile workers lost their jobs as the manufacturing industry fell prostrate. Wages were slashed in half for those lucky enough to work, and hundreds of thousands lost their homes.

New England never fully rebounded from those difficult years. During the 1960s and early 1970s, foreign imports dealt a blow to most of the manufacturing left in the area. Void of natural resources such as oil and coal, the area was especially hard hit by the 1970s recession.

But today's New England has seen a rebirth of industry and technology. Modern enterprises have flourished, producing such far-reaching wonders as missile and space systems, jet aircraft engines, computers and computer equipment, and biomedical and photographic instruments. The new businesses circle Boston around Route 128 and spill over into Hartford, southern New Hampshire, Rhode Island and even Vermont's Burlington area.

Massachusetts and Connecticut boast one of the nation's largest pools of capital, with Boston claiming more than 50 insurance companies and about 35 percent of U.S. mutual fund holdings. The greater Boston metropolitan area is home to some 21 newspapers, 8 television stations, 31 radio stations and many libraries and museums of national stature.

Progressive New Englanders were among the first to push environmental issues to the national front, passing stringent air pollution and zoning laws. As early as the 1960s, rural Vermont banned billboards and nonreturnable bottles. Massachusetts passed the nation's earliest wetlands act.

Higher education is itself a leading "industry" of Massachusetts, the site of some 121 colleges and universities—47 in Boston alone. And New England's immense beauty and rich history make tourism the number two industry, second only to manufacturing.

Today, beyond the high-tech centers and tourist attractions resounds the inescapable presence of New England's colorful past: Revolutionary War monuments, 18th-century covered bridges and statehouses, steepled churches that held this country's first congregations.

One need only explore Paul Revere's House, the Bunker Hill Monument and the Granary Burial Ground in the Boston area to recognize the sites of this country's genesis. For New England's past is America's past. And the region remains a vital part of the nation's present and future.

The glorious flaming reds, oranges and yellows of a New England fall come from changes in its thick stands of hardwood trees, which cover more than three-quarters of the region. The most colorful displays are put on by sugar and red maples, beech, oak, birch, hickory and red oak (see "Fall Foliage: Nature's Kaleidoscope" in this chapter).

FLORA

Text continued on page 14.

Fall Foliage:
Nature's Kaleidoscope

Like nature's last fling before a long slumber, the changing hues of New England's fall foliage precede winter with a fantastic display of color gone wild. Meadows are splashed with orange and purple, lakes appear ringed with fire and whole mountains turn from green to gold.

Better than any fireworks show, this phenomenon draws at least 2.8 million visitors to New England each year. Arriving by car, train, bus and bicycle, they pitch tents in forests, settle into cabins and resorts and pack the roadways everywhere. They come not just to marvel at the scenery but to be part of an all-encompassing experience.

The show starts up around mid-September with a few hints of scarlet and gold, as if the mountains were blushing. Then slowly, the blush becomes a sea of reds and orange and purples that melt together like rivers of shimmering watercolors. Each day brings new colors, new perspectives.

What makes it all happen? Prodded by cool nights and shorter autumn days, tree leaves abandon their green veneer to reveal hues ranging from crimson and sunburst to mahogany, violet and bronze.

Of course, each tree has its own brand of color. Maples flash a brilliant red leaf. Shagbark hickory leaves turn yellow and resemble hammered gold, while witch hazel's flaxen leaves camouflage small yellow flowers. The sumac sports purple saw-toothed leaves and fuzzy twigs resembling antlers. Thin and dainty, cherry leaves go from bright purple to bright yellow.

Then there's the clever speckled alder, a swamp dweller that doesn't change color at all. Its broad green leaves provide a nice contrast to all those reds and yellows and purples.

The farther north you are, the earlier the show starts. Northern areas of Maine, New Hampshire and Vermont set things off, sending waves of color southward as fall advances. The show usually winds down around mid-October, or after the first few frosts.

Though you can "see the leaves" change almost anywhere in New England, the best leaf-peeping exists in mountain areas. Reputed as one of the best fall-foliage spots in the world, New Hampshire's White Mountain National Forest offers 763,000 acres of uninterrupted timberland that explodes with continuous color.

Next door, Vermont's Green Mountain National Forest has miles of dense woods, gentle mountains and rushing streams that form a spectacular foliage backdrop. In Maine, head for the area around Machias known as **blueberry barrens**. A vast sweep of blueberry fields, the barrens turn flaming red in the fall and stretch as far as the eye can see. Maine's rock-lined coast also provides extraordinary foliage pageantry, with spiraling scarlet trees set against a sea of aquamarine.

Connecticut's foliage beauty lies in its diverse forests that provide the entire spectrum of colors. Travel from the pastel-colored oaks and birches along the coast to the deep red pepperidge trees in the southwest. Then cut up to the yellow and vermilion maple trees in the northwest corner.

Tiny Rhode Island is all ablaze with fall color, though it is most concentrated in the uplands. Located on the north and west corridors, the uplands are a picture of amber rolling hills, thick timbers and nearly 300 lakes and reservoirs rimmed with rainbow hues.

For a special foliage treat, head for Massachusetts' South Shore, where **cranberry bogs** stretch just south of Boston to Bristol. During October harvests, farmers flood the bogs, forcing the berries to the top of the marsh and creating a sea of bright crimson (see "Exploring Cranberry Country" in Chapter Six).

If you'd like to take home more than photographs, gather an assortment of your favorite leaves and branches. While they're still supple, press the leaves between layers of cardboard, then secure between heavy boards or books and tie tightly with rope. Store in a warm, dry place for ten days, making sure the rope is always snug.

Branches make beautiful bouquets once preserved. Simply split the stems at the base and cover with a solution of two parts water and one part glycerine. Store in a cool, well-ventilated area until leaves show a slight change in color. Remove and hang upside down until dry.

To get the scoop on leaf-peeping conditions, call the foliage hotlines (during fall months only) sponsored by each state: New Hampshire, 603-271-6870, 800-258-3608; Vermont, 802-828-3239; Maine, 800-777-0317; Connecticut, 800-282-6863; Rhode Island, 401-222-2601; Massachusetts, 800-227-6277. Some states supply foliage guides with tips on picture-taking and leaf identification.

A word of advice: fall-foliage season is the most popular vacation time in New England, so it's important to make travel arrangements far in advance—at least six months ahead of time.

Vast and stately pine forests blanket much of the north, creating its characteristic wild and rugged look. Among them are spruce, balsam fir and hemlock. Southern New England, too, has conifers throughout, the most common being white pine. Among the tallest of eastern trees, the sun-loving white pine may live 400 years or more.

New England grows some 2000 species of flowering plants and ferns. Wildflowers bloom in colorful profusion along the roadsides and in parks and forests. The leader of the wildflowers is the long-stemmed goldenrod, which occurs almost everywhere, as do black-eyed Susans, lupine, purple asters, daisies and Queen Anne's lace. Shady, moist habitats foster several species of orchids, with the pink lady's slipper being the showiest and most common.

Three of the most spectacular wildflower displays are given by the rhododendron, flowering dogwood and mountain laurel, the state flower of Connecticut, which occurs in southern New England. The mountain laurel's lustrous, dark green leaves and six-sided, pink-and-white blossoms form a dense, impenetrable thicket in the forest, sometimes up to 13 feet high.

At the shore grow miles and miles of shrubby wild beach roses with delicate scent and fragile petals of pink, white and fuchsia. Also along the shore grow beach peas, pitch pine, huckleberry, lowbush blueberry, sheep laurel and bayberry, from which the colonists made candles.

Wetlands are prevalent throughout New England, left by glacial action. Swamps, marshes and bogs all have their own little communities of plants, specially adapted to float on the water or emerge from it. Two very characteristic swamp plants are the purplish green skunk cabbage, with a strong odor like a skunk's, and Jack-in-the-Pulpit, which looks like a miniature preacher in a covered pulpit.

In the soft, dark muck and highly organic environs of marshes grow grasses, reeds and sedges such as cattails. Purple loosestrife now covers huge expanses of marsh and wet meadows. Other common marsh plants include duckweed, the smallest flowering plant known; blue flag, a kind of native iris; Joe-pye weed and yellow pond lily.

Sphagnum moss and sedges are partial to bogs, as are knee-high evergreen shrubs, bog laurel, bog rosemary and Labrador Tea, reputedly brewed as a substitute for tea in Colonial times. In low-lying, sandy-floored bogs thrive cranberries, a mainstay of the Massachusetts economy.

FAUNA

No single animal is more ubiquitous in New England than the gray squirrel, which flirts its bushy tail as it races along telephone wires, up and down trees in city parks and through backyards. A close second is the dramatically colored eastern chipmunk. Though they are pests to the gardener and the householder, rabbits and woodchucks are numerous, too.

The black bear, New England's only bear, and the moose claim title to being the region's largest land mammals, favoring wilder woodland areas in the north. The homely moose, believe it or not, is a member of the deer family and lives in the deep cover of northern forests in Maine, New Hampshire and Vermont. Another large mammal favored by hunters is the white-tailed deer, which has a bushy white tail, big ears and long legs.

The fallow deer, a native of Asia Minor, was released on Nantucket and Martha's Vineyard. The deer became so numerous that they overran the islands and had to be thinned.

Smaller mammals include beaver, red foxes, raccoons, porcupines, skunks and possums. Pity the poor possum: he is poorly adapted to the cold, and many New England possums lose pieces of their paper-thin ears and bare tails to frostbite.

Off the rocky shores in northern coastal waters, harbor seals cavort, hauling out to sun themselves on islands and rocky shores. The coast is also home to the Atlantic white-sided dolphin and several species of whales, best seen up-close on whale-watching trips.

The arrival of spring in New England is announced vociferously by spring peepers, tiny frogs measuring little more than an inch long that climb trees to sing their lyrical nocturnal chorus.

Other native amphibians include the spotted salamander, green frog and bullfrog, a giant of native frogs, sometimes over eight inches long. Reptiles are represented by snapping turtles, painted turtles, box turtles, garter snakes and black racers. New England also has two poisonous snakes, the timber rattlesnake and the northern copperhead, although you will almost surely never see one, so rare and retiring are they.

Situated as it is right along the Atlantic Flyway, New England is a premier place for birding, especially during spring migration. More than 400 species have been sighted in New England, although more than half are transient migratories, shorebirds that rarely come ashore or accidentals carried in by storm winds. The single most characteristic bird is the gull, found everywhere along the coast.

Canada geese and cormorants have increased their range and numbers, as have ospreys, after being given special nesting platforms on Martha's Vineyard. The handsome loon rules the northern lakes. There are many species of ducks, in both fresh water and salt water.

Endangered species include the piping plover, roseate tern, peregrine falcon, upland sandpiper, short-eared owl and bald eagle, now nesting in the Quabbin Reservoir in central Massachusetts.

▼▼▼▼▼▼▼▼▼▼▼
Where to Go

As with Europe, deciding what to see and where to go in New England is a tough choice. The good news is, you'll just have to keep coming back to get to know the real New England.

To help you with your decisions, we'll entice you with some brief descriptions of each state. To get the whole story, read the introductions to each chapter, then the more detailed material on the regions that appeal to you.

Connecticut packs several very different regions into its compact space. We first visit the southeastern part of the state, neighbor to New York. Failing in their effort to annex this corner, New Yorkers have nonetheless succeeded in remaking it in their own image: brimming with the fancy gourmet stores and chichi boutiques so vital to Manhattanites. The state's northwest corner offers historic villages and picturesque lakes. The capital city is Hartford, also known as the insurance capital of the world. South along the coast stands the city of New Haven, an urban industrial center whose main claim to fame is Yale University. From New Haven to the Rhode Island border, coastal Connecticut strings together one pretty fishing and sailing village after another: Essex, Old Saybrook, Mystic and Stonington. Connecticut's rural northeastern corner is the least known and developed area.

With two feet in the ocean, **Rhode Island** boasts miles of sandy beaches with rolling surf rivaling those of the Cape. The coastal villages of South County have a quiet, antique charm, while Victorian Block Island is a little island lost in time. Newport's fabled elegance still shines today in the extravagant summer "cottages" built by Gilded Age multimillionaires. Providence, a revitalized urban center, stands tall with one of the nation's finest historic districts, showcasing restored 18th- and 19th-century period houses. Farther north, the Blackstone Valley, stretching from Pawtucket to Woonsocket and west, is known as the "birthplace of American manufacturing."

With its quaint, cobblestoned streets, old-fashioned neighborhoods and big-city charms, **Boston** delights all who visit. Here is where America's most iconographic history lives on, at such sites as Paul Revere's House and the Old North Church in the North End. Much of Boston sparkles with new polish, especially the waterfront. Perennial favorites include Quincy Market, the diminutive brick townhouses and sprightly gardens of Beacon Hill, the imposing brownstones of Back Bay and the soaring architecture of Copley Square. Across the Charles River sits Harvard Square, the thriving nexus of intellectual Cambridge. Rural Lexington and Concord are known for their Colonial history.

Cape Cod and the Islands explores some of the most famous and popular areas of the state. Cape Cod is a favored spot for summer vacations. The North Cape is known for its quaint historical villages, the South Cape for Hyannis, home of the Kennedy clan, the Outer Cape for its beaches and sand dunes and Provincetown for its gay life. South of the Cape lie the islands of Martha's Vineyard and Nantucket, both prosperous whaling ports in their day and now drenched in the natural beauty of windswept moors, weathered cottages, pine woods and intimate beaches.

Wending its way hundreds of miles from Boston's North Shore to New Bedford in the southeast corner of the state, the **Massachusetts Coast** is studded its entire length with lovely resorts, fine sandy beaches and small fishing villages. Gloucester, Rockport and Salem are the highlights of the exclusive North Shore. The Plymouth area is rich in Colonial history and lined with attractive fishing and farming villages with neat clapboarded 18th- and 19th-century sea captains' homes. New Bedford and Fall River have troves of whaling and textile history lore, respectively, as well as oodles of discount outlet stores.

Central and western Massachusetts includes a vast part of the state, from the old industrial city of Worcester west of Boston to the resort-oriented Berkshires on the western border. Rural hamlets, wildlife sanctuaries and state parks ring central Massachusetts, where Old Sturbridge Village re-creates the farming life of the 1840s. The Pioneer Valley stretches up the Connecticut River, through another large city with a rich industrial past, Springfield. A summer capital of music, dance and drama, the Berkshires are serene and sylvan settings of mountains, forests and lakes. Here Norman Rockwell made the streetscapes of Stockbridge famous. The Berkshires have produced a lovely commingling of luxurious resorts, charming inns, gourmet restaurants and ski havens.

No single New England state is more rural than **Vermont**, with its miles of open farmland, covered bridges, maple sugarhouses and small towns with classic village greens and general stores. Some of the best skiing in America is here, as is some of the best cheddar cheese you'll ever eat. Lying on Vermont's western border with New York is the magnificent Lake Champlain, named for explorer Samuel de Champlain and popular with boaters, swimmers and ice fishers. The most rugged region is the Northeast Kingdom, three northern counties bordering Canada that make up a realm of tiny townships, mountains, forests and isolated farms.

Though **New Hampshire**'s tiny seacoast measures a mere 18 miles, along it lies Portsmouth, a jewel of a town that is one of the most handsome refurbished antique settlements on the East Coast. Old textile mills and factories sprawl along the Merrimack River, while outlet stores and other commerce thrive in the state's prosperous, booming southern half. The northern half is a wilderness of lakes, mountains and evergreen forests. Large and beautiful bodies of water like Lake Sunapee and Lake Winnepesaukee, and the White Mountains offer sports enthusiasts numerous choices, as well as plentiful resorts. Weathered barns and country towns complete the scenery in the Monadnock Region.

Maine, the land of Downeast, has sent its most famous delicacy, Maine lobster, all over the world. In this state's wilderness and waterways live thick spruce forests, moose, black bear, loons and deer. More developed than the north, the southern coast presents low-key resort towns and outlet stores, as well as the city of Portland, a restored maritime Victorian jewel. North of Portland is the rugged, rockbound coast, the real Downeast, with its independent-minded towns of Damariscotta, Wiscasset, Camden and Castine. Out on Mount Desert Island, the old-money resort of Bar Harbor reigns, alongside the splendid Acadia National Park. Maine is also Andrew Wyeth country, as seen in the turn-of-the-20th-century world of Monhegan Island, just one of hundreds of islands in Casco Bay. To the north, the Maine woods offer an unparalleled wilderness experience, where visitors can travel for a hundred miles without spotting any sign of civilization. The lakes region provides scenic splendors and water sports galore.

When to Go

SEASONS

A constant battle wages here in New England between bristling battalions of cold, dry Canadian arctic air and laid-back, warm, humid air from the tropics. When these two mix it up, which is frequently, you have New England's legendary changeable weather. The morning may dawn fine and sunny, afternoon turn cold and foggy and nightfall bring a raging northeaster.

More than you might think, the weather varies from south to north. Weather in southeastern New England, tempered by ocean winds, is warmer. While mean temperatures for Connecticut range from 27°F in January to 73°F in July, in Vermont they go from 16° in January to 70° in July. And at the top of New Hampshire's Mount Washington, it may as well be Antarctica.

No matter how you slice it, winters are long and cold here, and the overall effect has been described as "nine months of winter and three of rough sledding." Winters are invariably colder in Vermont and Maine, where temperatures range from -10°F to 10°F and sometimes drop to -30°F. In southern New England, temperatures are more likely to hover in the 20s and 30s in winter.

In the north, snow arrives as early as Thanksgiving and stays on the ground into mid-April, but near the coast in the southeast, it's indecent of snow to put in an appearance until Christmas and subzero weather is almost unheard of. But don't be deterred by the long winter; that's what puts plenty of white stuff on the northern ski slopes.

And, inevitably, there comes the spring thaw, which in the northern country goes by the popular name of "mud season." When the frozen ground starts melting, the result is a muddy morass. Spring is a little less messy in the south, where by mid-March the songbirds are chirping away, followed by greening in another few weeks.

Summer sets in around about mid-June. Days are quite warm, with temperatures ranging from 70 to 90°F, turning to slightly cooler evenings, especially along the shore and in the mountains. Despite the tempering ocean breezes, summer can be humid, as well as foggy and rainy. The weather is hottest in central Massachusetts, in the dry valley of the Connecticut River.

Autumn may be the most wonderful season of all to visit, and certainly the most popular one. Fall colors are at their peak, and all the fall harvests of apples, cider, cranberries and pumpkins are in. Sunny days often warm up to "Indian summer" comfort, energized by cool, crisp nights. In the southeast, autumn lasts right into November.

Both autumn and winter are substantially drier than in other locales. Still, it manages to rain, snow or sleet about one day out of three, making for an annual precipitation of 42 inches and an annual snowfall in the mountains of 90 to 100 inches.

Tourists flock to New England for fall-foliage season (mid-September through October), when it can be very difficult to get reservations. High summer (July through Labor Day) is also a busy time, especially along the coast. You might want to consider a visit to a seaside resort in the spring or fall, when rates are lower. Christmas, New Year's and ski season (late January through March) are other popular times with tourists. During the low

WHAT ABOUT HURRICANES?

Hurricanes, which can occur in subtropical waters any time from late June through September, occasionally veer up the Atlantic coast all the way to New England—but not often. In the 20th century, disastrous hurricanes struck in 1938, when entire coastal towns were swallowed by the sea, and 1991, when then-President George Bush's family home in Maine was demolished. Most recently, Hurricane Floyd ravaged the Carolinas in 1999 and continued up the coast to Boston, but by the time it got there it had been downgraded to a mere tropical depression. In fact, researchers at Brown University have found that only six hurricane-force storms have struck New England since 1400 A.D.

seasons of April, May and late October to late December, you'll have a much less crowded vacation and a much easier time getting reservations.

CALENDAR OF EVENTS

Each year, New England celebrates its Colonial past by reenacting historic events that took place in all six states. Other annual observances celebrate the wonderful largesse of this region: apples, maple sugar, blueberries, scallops, clams. The list of merrymaking goes on, with art, music and dance festivals, and occasions honoring many New England traditions, such as shipbuilding, quiltmaking, sheep shearing and Shaker craftsmanship.

JANUARY
   Boston   The **Chinese New Year** is celebrated in January or February, with three weeks of festivities.
Vermont   Sled dog races, parades and downhill and cross-country skiing events comprise the **Stowe Winter Carnival**.

FEBRUARY
   Boston   The **New England Boat Show**, one of the largest on the East Coast, brings out the latest and fanciest in power and sail. Four of the city's biggest hockey-playing colleges (Harvard, Northeastern, Boston University and Boston College) face off in the **Beanpot Hockey Tournament**.
New Hampshire   The **Dartmouth College Winter Carnival** is an exuberant expression of fun during the winter doldrums.

MARCH
   Boston   The **New England Spring Flower Show** has been running for more than 100 years, giving a lift to winter-weary Bostonians. The **St. Patrick's Day Parade** thrown by the Irish of South Boston is one of the largest and most festive in America.
Maine   Appropriately, the **Sled Dog Races** take place in the frontier town of Fort Kent.

APRIL
   Boston   The nation's premier running event, the **Boston Marathon** is only one of several signal events on **Patriot's Day**. Other activities commemorating Revolutionary War events include a parade plus reenactments of Paul Revere's famous ride and the Battle of Lexington and Concord.
Cape Cod and the Islands   During Nantucket's **Daffodil Festival**, hundreds of these sprightly blooms decorate shop windows.
Vermont   At the **Vermont Maple Festival** in St. Albans, sample maple products, watch contests and enjoy the entertainment.

MAY
   Connecticut   Picnic-style lobster dinners, naturally, are the main event at the **Lobster Festival** at Mystic Seaport.
Rhode Island   **Gaspee Days** in Warwick, which sometimes run into June, commemorate the colonists' burning of Britain's H.M.S.

Gaspee in 1772—one of the first acts of hostility leading to the Revolution—with historic reenactments, a parade, arts and crafts, food and entertainment.

Boston **Lilac Sunday** at the Arnold Arboretum finds 400 varieties of lilacs in bloom, and the Franklin Park Zoo hosts a colorful **Annual Kite Festival.**

Cape Cod and the Islands Sandwich's **Heritage Plantation Rhododendron Festival** features blooms as far as the eye can see, plus lectures and plant sales.

Central and Western Massachusetts The **Brimfield antique shows**, also held in July and September, draw more than 1000 dealers for week-long events in the small town of Brimfield.

Vermont Stowe's annual **Basketry Festival** hosts more than 20 instructors teaching over 35 workshops.

Connecticut Celebrate the blooming of over 15,000 rose bushes at the Greater Hartford **Rose Festival** held in the Elizabeth Park Rose Garden.

JUNE

Rhode Island Providence's historic east side is on view during the **Festival of Historic Houses.**

Boston The **Bunker Hill Day Re-enactment and Parade** features contemporary patriots dressed in Revolutionary uniforms fighting the famous battle again.

Cape Cod and the Islands At Hyannis' **Cape Cod Chowder Festival,** you can vote for the best chowder and enjoy live entertainment.

Massachusetts Coast Anything made with fresh strawberries can be served at the **Annual Strawberry Festival** in Ipswich.

Central and Western Massachusetts Wine and cheese on the lawn while listening to the Boston Symphony Orchestra is the attraction of the **Tanglewood Music Festival.** One of the Northeast's best-known dance festivals takes place at **Jacob's Pillow** in the Berkshires.

Vermont Hot-air balloons light up the scenery at the **Hot Air Balloon and Crafts Festival** in Quechee.

New Hampshire Local and national acts heat up the summer at the **Portsmouth Jazz Festival.**

Maine The **Old Port Festival** brings the historic part of Portland to life with a street fair of arts and crafts, music, jugglers, kids' events and ethnic foods. **Windjammer Days** in Boothbay Harbor show off these classic schooners under full sail in a dress parade.

Connecticut The **Columbus 500 Summer Concert Series,** held in Milford, features four days of performances by the Subway Regional Symphony Orchestra throughout the month.

JULY

Boston The **U.S. Pro Tennis Championship** draws thousands of tennis fans to the Longwood Cricket Club. Every weekend in July and August, **Italian street festivals** honor patron saints with colorful parades and festivities. The **Boston Harborfest** offers nearly a hundred activities celebrating the harbor at 30 sites, highlighted by a chowderfest and wingfest. Local restaurants serve up heaping samples of clam chowder as they battle for the tastiest bowl of "chowdah" as determined by popular vote at the **Chowderfest** on City Hall Plaza. The **Boston Pops Fourth of July Concert** on the Esplanade's Hatch Shell promises an evening of free music and glorious fireworks.

Cape Cod and the Islands In early July, the People of the First Light's **Mashpee Pow-Wow** is held at the Heritage Ballfield in Mashpee. The pow-wow attracts American Indians from all over the United States, as well as from Canada, Mexico and some Central and South American countries. In Sandwich, book lovers delight in the **Cape Cod Antiquarian Book Fair**, with more than 40 dealers, rare and out-of-print books, manuscripts and collectibles. The **Edgartown Regatta**, held on Martha's Vineyard, is one of New England's best and most serious yacht races. The **Cape Cod Antique Market**, a large gathering of antique and collectible dealers, takes place in Falmouth at the First Congregational Church Village Green.

Massachusetts Coast In Gloucester, the **Hammond Castle Annual Renaissance Faire** has magic shows, music and merriment. **Race Week** in Marblehead includes sailboat races, parades and concerts.

Maine Celebrate that incredibly edible food in Pittsfield during the **Central Maine Egg Festival**. There are parades, fireworks, dances, and, of course, lots of breakfast.

AUGUST **Connecticut** The **Pilot Pen Tennis Women's Championships** showcases top women tennis stars in world-class play at Yale University. You'll find more than 400 antique and classic cars, parts, refreshments and even a hula-hoop contest at the **Antique Auto Show and Swap Meet** in Goshen.

Rhode Island Some of the world's best jazz musicians entertain the thousands sprawled out on the green lawns of Fort Adams State Park in Newport at the JVC **Jazz Festival**. B. B. King, Randy Newman and Leon Redbone have all performed at **Ben & Jerry's Newport Folk Festival**. A haven for independent filmmakers, the **Rhode Island International Film Festival** screens more than 60 titles in Providence.

Cape Cod and the Islands The **Falmouth Road Races** is the event of the year on the lower Cape, where the seven-mile race is run along the Shining Sea Path. On Nantucket, the **Annual An-**

tique **Show** offers quality antiques. Imaginations go wild at the **Sandcastle Contest** at Jetties Beach on Nantucket. Also on Nantucket, the **Annual Billfish Tournament** is a big event where anglers compete for the biggest catch of each species. In Oak Bluffs, on Martha's Vineyard, **Illumination Night** is pure magic, with hundreds of paper lanterns strung between the Gothic homes.

Massachusetts Coast   New Bedford's **Annual Feast of the Holy Ghost**, the largest Portuguese feast in America, features terrific ethnic food at budget prices.

New Hampshire   Thousands flock to Louden for the **New England 200**, an Indy car race at the New Hampshire International Speedway.

Maine   Hundreds of performers from around the world enliven Brunswick at the **Maine Festival** with music, dance, crafts, demonstrations and food. An all-you-can-eat blueberry pancake breakfast starts off the week for the **Union Fair** in Union, noted for its blueberry festival.

Connecticut   The South Norwalk **Oyster Festival** has something for everyone: oysters galore, seafood and ethnic foods, nationally known singers and bands, arts and crafts, tall ships and marine skills demonstrations.

SEPTEMBER

Boston   The **Boston Film Festival** is held at the end of the month and includes feature-length movies by major studios as well as more unusual films from independent producers, students and foreign filmmakers.

Cape Cod and the Islands   The **Harwich Cranberry Festival** includes ten days of parades, contests, fireworks and exhibits. Wellfleet holds **Bygone Days**, a nostalgic weekend including a children's parade, a Cape Cod Shore dinner, fashion shows, church suppers, nature walks, quilt raffles and the Saturday Harvest Moon Dance. **Tivoli Day** is usually held on the second Saturday of the month in Oak Bluffs, on Martha's Vineyard, where there's a street fair and a 62-mile bike race.

Massachusetts Coast   At the **Gloucester Schooner Festival**, you can watch races, a boat parade and other maritime activities. **Plimouth Plantation Muster Day** includes antique militia weapons and defense displays, tactical moves, feasting and recreation.

Central and Western Massachusetts   The **Big E**, or the **Eastern States Exposition**, in West Springfield is the East's largest annual fair, strong on agricultural and animal exhibits, horse shows and rides and food galore. King Kielbasa, "the world's biggest kielbasa," sets the tone for the **World Kielbasa Festival** in Chicopee.

New Hampshire   The **Scottish Highlands Games** draw thousands of people to Lincoln; some show up in kilts for highlander games and music.

Maine   In Unity, the **Common Ground County Fair** celebrates the rural Maine life with homegrown foods and locally produced crafts.

OCTOBER   **Boston**   More than 3000 oarsmen compete in the **Head of the Charles Regatta**, now a two-day rowing spectacular. **Lowell Celebrates Kerouac** stages poetry readings and organizes "beat" tours in honor of '50s literary giant Jack Kerouac who lived and worked in Lowell

Massachusetts Coast   If ever a place looked haunted, it would be Hammond Castle in Gloucester during the **Eight Nights of Halloween**, where ghosts and ghouls spook and delight you as you tour this romantic castle. **Haunted Happenings**, Salem's citywide Halloween festival, includes haunted-house tours, costume parades, parties, magic shows, psychics and candlelight tours with, of course, witches. Mysterious legends of Essex County are recounted by costumed storytellers in historic houses at Salem's Peabody Museum **Essex Eerie Events**.

Central and Western Massachusetts   The **Topsfield Fair** is another vintage event, with sheep dog trials, ethnic foods and midway rides.

Maine   Held since the mid-1800s, the **Fryeburg Fair** sticks close to its agricultural roots during week-long festivities.

NOVEMBER   **Massachusetts Coast**   A **Sea Captain Celebrates Thanksgiving**, an 18th-century banquet in Salem's House of Seven Gables, also includes discussions on meal preparation, dining customs and music of the time (reservations required). Have a traditional turkey dinner with all the trimmings in America's hometown, Plymouth, during its annual **Thanksgiving Dinner**.

Central and Western Massachusetts   Cascade mums, standard varieties and new hybrids are shown at the week-long **Chrysanthemum Show** at Smith College in Northampton.

DECEMBER   **Connecticut**   Lantern light tours and a **Carol Sing** mark Christmas at the Mystic Seaport Museum.

Boston   Staged by the Center of Afro-American Artists, Langston Hughes' **Black Nativity** is a holiday spiritual tradition. Hundreds of events mark **First Night**, an alcohol-free New Year's Eve celebration held throughout the city. There's a huge pageant, plus choral groups, ice sculptures, storytellers, acrobats, puppeteers and art and drama presentations. The **Boston Tea Party Re-enactment** finds patriots dressed as Indians throwing chests of tea into Boston Harbor one more time.

Cape Cod and the Islands   Main Street looks like something out of Dickens when the **Nantucket Christmas Stroll** takes place, with a weekend of carolers and other Yuletide festivities.

Massachusetts Coast   **Salem Holiday Happenings** includes fairs, crafts, house tours, auctions, concerts, ballet and more. Elaborate Christmas displays and a train ride through acres of colored lights are part of Edaville's **Christmas Festival of Lights** in South Carver.

New Hampshire   The **Candlelight Stroll** at Strawbery Banke illuminates three centuries of houses.

As well as large cities, many small towns have chambers of commerce or visitor information centers that provide detailed information about the area you wish to visit; a number of these facilities are listed in *Hidden New England* under the appropriate state or region.

▼▼▼▼▼▼▼▼▼▼▼
Before You Go

VISITORS CENTERS

Travel information on Connecticut is available from the **Vacation Center.** ~ Department of Economic Development, 505 Hudson Street, Hartford, CT 06106; 860-270-8081, 800-282-6863, fax 860-270-8077; www.ctbound.org.

For Rhode Island, contact the **Tourism Division.** ~ 1 West Exchange Street, Providence, RI 02903; 401-222-2601, 800-556-2484, fax 401-222-2102.

For Massachusetts information, contact the **Massachusetts Office of Travel and Tourism.** ~ State Transportation Building, 10 Park Plaza, Boston, MA 02116; 617-727-3201, 800-227-6277, fax 617-973-8525; www.massvacation.com.

For more detailed information on Boston, contact the **Greater Boston Convention and Visitors Bureau.** ~ 2 Copley Place, Suite 105, Boston, MA 02116; 617-536-4100, fax 617-424-7664; www.bostonusa.com.

For information on vacationing in Vermont, write the **Vermont Department of Tourism and Marketing.** ~ 6 Baldwin Street, Montpelier, VT 05602; 802-828-3237, 800-837-6668, fax 802-828-3233; www.travel-vermont.com or www.1-800-vermont.com.

In New Hampshire, the contact the **Office of Travel and Tourism** for travel information. ~ Box 1856, Concord, NH 03302; 603-271-2666, 800-386-4664; www.visitnh.gov.

In Maine, write the **Maine Publicity Bureau.** ~ Tourism Association, 33 Stone Street, Augusta, ME 04333; 207-623-0363, 800-782-6419, 888-624-6345.

PACKING

Packing for a visit to New England is a little trickier than for other destinations. What you must take is dictated by the fickle Yankee weather, which might change at any minute. A warm, sunny day can turn cool and foggy without so much as a by your leave. The best bet is to bring layers of clothing that can be added or subtracted as needed. Even in the summer, bring some long-sleeved shirts, long pants and lightweight sweaters and jackets, along with your T-shirts, jeans and bathing suit.

Fall and spring call for a full round of warm clothing, from long pants and sweaters to jackets, hats and gloves. While fall days are often sunny and warm, fall nights can turn quite crisp and cool. Bring your heaviest, warmest clothes in winter: thick sweaters, knitted hats, down jackets and ski clothes.

No spot in New England is more than a day's drive from any other.

Boston Brahmins notwithstanding, most of New England is a pretty casual place, especially in summer, when everyone has sand in his shoes. No one will look askance if you wear your deck shoes and L. L. Bean pants to dinner at most restaurants, particularly in coastal resort areas like Kennebunkport. New England is less casual, however, than a warm-weather resort, and you can't get into most restaurants or bars without a shirt or shoes, or if you're wearing a bathing suit.

Boston is the most conservatively dressed place you'll visit. Some downtown Boston restaurants have dress codes, requiring men to wear jackets and ties and women to be "appropriately attired."

New Englanders are used to rolling up their car windows every night in summer, knowing it may rain any night. Rain, though not usually heavy, is a big part of every season, so be sure to bring an umbrella and a raincoat, even in the summer.

Some of the streets are almost as old as New England itself. In many areas such as Boston, on these rough, cobblestone ways you need sturdy, comfortable shoes that can take this kind of beating and be kind to your feet. Women should never attempt to navigate cobblestone streets in high heels. Likewise, some New England shores can be rocky. A pair of rubber shoes or old sneakers for swimming is sometimes advisable.

Though New England is not the Caribbean, you can get just as impressive a sunburn here. Bring a good sunscreen, especially to the beach, where sand and water reflect the sun's rays more intensely. Bring insect repellent in the summertime as insurance against the greenhead flies at the shore and blackflies in the mountains.

For the northern woods of Maine and other out-of-the-way places, you'll have far fewer stores to rely on, so come prepared with whatever gear you'll be using. It's wise to consult a backpacking or camping supply store before you leave about what to bring for the weather conditions likely at the time of your travels.

When you come here, you'll need nothing but the best street and road maps. Many roads in New England are winding, poorly marked or not marked at all, following an age-old philosophy that if you live here, you know where you're going, and if you don't, you have no business being here anyway.

You may want to toss in an antique guide along with your other reading; the country's oldest antiques are for sale here. Bring your camera for capturing quintessential New England vistas of lighthouses and white-steepled villages, and for heaven's sake, don't forget your copy of *Hidden New England*!

LODGING

Visiting New England is your opportunity to stay in some of the most historic lodgings this country has to offer. A number of them date to the 18th century, such as Longfellow's Wayside Inn in Sudbury, Massachusetts. Randall's Ordinary in North Stonington, Connecticut, dates to the 17th century.

New England is where the bed-and-breakfast movement gained ground in this country, and the region is thick with historic farmhouses and sea captains' homes turned into bed and breakfasts. These are often rambling, cozy affairs complete with fireplace, bookshelves and resident cat. But bed-and-breakfast booking agencies, especially in urban areas, also list host homes with a spare room, which isn't quite the same thing. Be sure to ask whether a bed and breakfast is a real inn or not.

In addition, accommodations include mom-and-pop motels, chain hotels and rustic seaside cottages where you'll awaken to the sounds of surf and crying gulls. Cities have the most deluxe highrise hotels, but outside urban areas, lodgings are generally casual and lowrise.

Whatever your preference and budget, you can probably find something to suit your taste with the help of the individual chapters in this book. Remember, rooms are scarce and prices rise in the high season, which is summer, fall-foliage time and Christmas throughout New England, and ski season in northern areas.

There are lots of special weekend and holiday packages at the larger hotels, and off-season rates drop significantly, making a week- or month-long stay a real bargain.

Accommodations in this book are organized by state or region and classified according to price. These refer to high-season rates, so if you're looking for low-season bargains, be sure to inquire about them.

Budget lodgings generally cost less than $60 a night for two people and are satisfactory and clean but modest. *Moderate*-priced lodgings run from $60 to $120; what they offer in terms of luxury will depend on their location, but in general they provide larger rooms and more attractive surroundings. At *deluxe*-priced accommodations, you can expect to spend between $120 and $175. In hotels of this price you'll typically find spacious rooms, a fashionable lobby, a restaurant or two and often some shops. *Ultra-deluxe* facilities, priced above $175, are a region's finest, offering all the amenities of a deluxe hotel plus plenty of luxurious extras, such as jacuzzis and exercise rooms, 24-hour room service and gourmet dining.

If you've got your heart set on a room with a water view, be sure to pin that down. Be forewarned that "oceanside" doesn't always mean right on the beach. If you want to save money, try lodgings a block or so away from the water. They almost always offer lower rates than rooms within sight of the surf, and the savings are often worth the short stroll to the beach.

DINING

Succulent native seafood stars at legions of New England restaurants, from lobster in the rough and tender bay scallops to codfish, mussels, steamers and milky clam chowder.

Besides seafood and traditional Yankee foods, New England restaurants also serve up ethnic cuisines of every stripe, plus gourmet foods and fast food. No matter what your taste or budget, there's a restaurant for you.

Within each chapter, restaurants are organized geographically. Each entry describes the cuisine and ambience and categorizes the restaurant in one of four price ranges. Dinner entrées at *budget* restaurants usually cost $9 or less. The ambience is informal, service speedy, the crowd often a local one. *Moderate*-priced eateries charge between $9 and $18 for dinner; surroundings are casual but pleasant, the menu offers more variety and the pace is usually slower. *Deluxe* restaurants tab their entrées above $18; cuisines may be simple or sophisticated, but the decor is plusher and the service more personalized. *Ultra-deluxe* establishments, where entrées begin at $24, are often the gourmet gathering places; here cooking is (hopefully) a fine art, and the service should be impeccable.

Some restaurants, particularly those that depend on the summer trade in coastal areas, close for the winter.

Breakfast and lunch menus vary less in price from one restaurant to another. Even deluxe establishments usually offer light breakfasts and luncheons, priced within a few dollars of their budget-minded competitors. These smaller meals can be a good time to test expensive restaurants.

TRAVELING WITH CHILDREN

New England is a wonderful place to bring children. Besides many child-oriented museums, the region also has hundreds of beaches and parks, and many nature sanctuaries sponsor children's activities year-round.

Quite a few New England bed and breakfasts don't accept children, so be sure of the policy when you make reservations. If you need a crib or cot, arrange for it ahead of time.

Travel agents can help with arrangements; they can reserve airline bulkhead seats where there is plenty of room and determine which flights are least crowded. If you are traveling by car, be sure to take along such necessities as water and juices, snacks and toys. Always allow extra time for getting places, especially on rural roads.

A first-aid kit is a must for any trip. Along with adhesive bandages, antiseptic cream and something to stop itching, include any medicines your pediatrician might recommend to treat allergies, colds, diarrhea or any chronic problems your child may have.

At the beach, take extra care with your children's skin the first few days, even though this is not the Caribbean. Children's tender young skin can suffer severe sunburn before you know it. Hats for the kids are a good idea, along with liberal applications of a good sunscreen. Never take your eyes off your children at the shore. If you are traveling in winter, never leave a child alone near a frozen lake.

All-night stores are scarce in rural areas, and stores in small towns often close early. You may go a long distance between stores that can supply you with essentials, so be sure to be well stocked with diapers, baby food and other needs when you are on the go. But all-night stores such as Store 24 and Christy's are plentiful in urban areas.

To find specific activities for children, consult local newspapers. The *Boston Globe Thursday Calendar* has especially comprehensive listings that cover a good part of New England.

The **Travelers Aid Society of Boston, Inc.** is a resource for any traveler in need and maintains booths at the major transportation terminals. Volunteers can arrange to meet young children who are traveling alone. ~ 17 East Street, off of Atlantic Avenue, Boston, MA 02111; 617-542-7286, fax 617-542-9545.

Traveling solo grants an independence and freedom different from that of traveling with a partner, but single travelers are more vulnerable to crime and should take additional precautions.

WOMEN TRAVELING ALONE

It's unwise to hitchhike and probably best to avoid inexpensive accommodations on the outskirts of town; the money saved does not outweigh the risk. Bed and breakfasts, youth hostels and YWCAs are generally your safest bet for lodging, and they also foster an environment ideal for bonding with fellow travelers.

Keep all valuables well-hidden and hold onto cameras and purses. Avoid late-night treks or strolls through undesirable parts of town, but if you find yourself in this situation, continue walking with a confident air until you reach a safe haven. A fierce scowl never hurts.

These hints should by no means deter you from seeking out adventure. Wherever you go, stay alert, use your common sense and trust your instincts. For more hints, get a copy of *Safety and Security for Women Who Travel* (Travelers Tales, 1998).

If you are hassled or threatened in some way, never be afraid to scream for assistance. It's a good idea to carry change for a phone call and to know the number to call in case of emergency. Most areas have 24-hour hotlines for victims of rape and violent crime. In the Boston area, call the **Boston Area Rape Crisis Center**. ~ 617-492-7273. In New Hampshire, contact **Sexual Assault Support Services**. ~ 603-436-4107. In Rhode Island, **Sexual Assault Trauma Resource Center** provides assistance. ~ 401-421-4100.

GAY & LESBIAN TRAVELERS

While New England is generally not known for its progressive attitudes, the people who live here tend to be very independent minded and not apt to stick their noses in other people's business. This allows gay or lesbian travelers to feel comfortable here. Whether you're interested in exploring the scenic rural backroads or sightseeing in the region's cities, New England has much to offer. The region also boasts several gay and lesbian hot spots to which this guidebook dedicates special "gay-specific" sections.

The first of these sections covers Boston's gay neighborhood in the city's South End. Both Boston and nearby Cambridge are home to large gay communities, with the South End area of Boston offering the greatest concentration of gay-friendly bars, nightclubs and restaurants (see "Boston Gay Scene" in Chapter Four).

Located at the tip of Cape Cod and attracting gay and lesbian travelers from all over the world is the well-known resort mecca of Provincetown (see "Provincetown" in Chapter Five).

Hidden New England lists gay-friendly lodging, dining and nightlife scattered throughout the six states. You can look in the index under "gay-friendly travel" to find these listings.

The bucolic Pioneer Valley in central Massachusetts, which includes the college towns of Amherst and Northampton, is more commonly known in the gay community as "The Happy Valley," and has one of the largest lesbian communities in the United States (see "The Happy Valley" in Chapter Seven).

Gay and lesbian publications providing entertainment listings and happenings are available in many of the region's towns. *The Metroline*, a free bi-monthly that you can find in cafés, covers Connecticut, Rhode Island and Massachusetts. ~ 860-233-8334, fax 860-233-8338; www.metroline-online.com. In Northampton, Massachusetts, pick up a copy of *The Lesbian Calendar* at area bookstores to get an update on local happenings. ~ 413-586-5514, fax 413-586-1890; e-mail tlcprods@ crocker.com.

In Boston, you can get the weekly *Bay Windows* for entertainment listings. ~ 617-266-6670, fax 617-266-5973. The quarterly *Gay Community News* is available at bookstores for $4.95.

~ 617-262-6969. Boston also has the free *IN Newsweekly*, available at cafés and bookstores. ~ 617-426-8246, fax 617-426-8264; e-mail innews@tiac.net.

New England is a hospitable place for senior citizens to visit; countless museums, historic sights and even restaurants and hotels offer senior discounts that cut a substantial chunk off vacation costs. And many golden-agers from hotter climes flock to New England for its cool summers. **SENIOR TRAVELERS**

The **American Association of Retired Persons** offers membership to anyone over 50. AARP benefits include travel discounts. ~ 601 E Street Northwest, Washington, DC 20049; 800-424-3410, fax 202-434-7688; www.aarp.org, e-mail member@aarp.org.

Elderhostel offers many educational courses in a variety of New England locations that are all-inclusive packages at colleges and universities. ~ 75 Federal Street, Boston, MA 02110; 877-426-8056, fax 617-426-0701; www.elderhostel.org.

Be extra careful about health matters. In New England's changeable and sometimes cold weather, seniors are more at risk of suffering hypothermia, especially during prolonged exposure to wind. Older travelers should be very careful when walking to beware of falls. Sidewalks may be poorly paved or buckled in places, and cobblestone streets are easy to lodge an ankle in.

Out-of-state prescriptions are not filled so try to bring extra of whatever medications you use. Or consider carrying a medical record with you, including your history and current medical status as well as your doctor's name, phone number and address. Make sure that your insurance covers you while you are away from home.

The **Travelers Aid Society of Boston, Inc.** can provide emergency financial assistance and medical and social service referrals, help find low-cost accommodations, give directions and information and assist with banking and check cashing, and train, plane and bus connections. Volunteers can arrange to meet travelers who have special needs. ~ 17 East Street, off Atlantic Avenue, Boston, MA 02111; 617-542-7286, fax 617-542-9545.

New England has made real strides toward making its many attractions and services handicapped-accessible. Parking spaces for the handicapped are provided at most services and attractions, although few buses are handicapped-accessible. **DISABLED TRAVELERS**

Special escorted group tours are offered by **The Guided Tour**. ~ 7900 Old York Road, Suite 114-B, Elkins Park, PA 19027; 215-782-1370, 800-783-5841, fax 215-635-2637; www.guidedtour.com.

There are many organizations offering general information. Among these are:

The Society for the Advancement of Travel for the Handicapped. ~ 347 5th Avenue, Suite 610, New York, NY 10016; 212-447-7284, fax 212-725-8253; www.sath.org, e-mail sathtravel@aol.com.

The Travel Disabilities Information Service. ~ 1200 West Tabor Road, Philadelphia, PA 19141; 215-456-5995, fax 215-456-5994; www.mossresoucenet.org, e-mail rosenbam@aehn2.einstein.edu.

Flying Wheels Travel. ~ P.O. Box 382, Owatonna, MN 55060; 800-535-6790, fax 507-451-1685; e-mail thq@LL.net.

Also providing information for travelers with disabilities is Travelin' Talk, a networking organization. ~ P.O. Box 1796, Wheat Ridge, CO 80034; 303-232-2979; www.travelintalk.net, e-mail info@travelintalk.net.

The Spaulding Community Access Line helps people find handicapped-accessible family activities, restaurants and cultural events in the greater Boston area. ~ 125 Nashua Street, Boston, MA 02114; 617-573-7000, fax 617-573-7009; www.spaulding rehab.org.

The Travelers Aid Society of Boston, Inc. can arrange for volunteers to meet handicapped travelers. ~ 17 East Street, off Atlantic Avenue, Boston, MA 02111; 617-542-7286, fax 617-542-9545.

Access-Able Travel Source has worldwide information online. ~ 303-232-2979; www.access-able.com.

FOREIGN TRAVELERS

Passports and Visas   Most foreign visitors are required to obtain a passport and tourist visa to enter the United States. Contact your nearest United States Embassy or Consulate well in advance to obtain a visa and to check on any other entry requirements.

Customs Requirements   Foreign travelers are allowed to carry in the following: 200 cigarettes (one carton), 100 cigars or two kilograms (4.4 pounds) of smoking tobacco; one liter of alcohol for personal use (you must be 21 years of age to bring in alcohol); and US$100 worth of duty-free gifts that can include an additional quantity of 100 cigars. You may bring in any amount of currency, but must fill out a form if you bring in over US$10,000. Carry any prescription drugs in clearly marked containers. (You may have to produce a written prescription or doctor's statement for the customs officer.) Meat or meat products, seeds, plants, fruits and narcotics are not allowed to be brought into the United States. Contact the United States Customs Service for further information. ~ 1300 Pennsylvania Avenue Northwest, Washington, DC 20229; 202-927-6724; www.customs.treas.gov.

Driving   If you plan to rent a car, an international driver's license should be obtained *before* arriving in New England. Some rental companies require both a foreign license and an international-al driver's license. Many car rental agencies require a lessee to be 25 years of age; all require a major credit card. Seat belts are mandatory for the driver and all passengers. Children under the age of 5 or 40 pounds should be in the back seat in approved child-safety restraints.

Currency   United States money is based on the dollar. Bills come in six denominations: $1, $5, $10, $20, $50 and $100. Every dollar is divided into 100 cents. Coins are the penny (1 cent), nickel (5 cents), dime (10 cents), quarter (25 cents). Half-dollars and dollar coins are rarely used. You may not use foreign currency to purchase goods and services in the United States. Consider buying traveler's checks in dollar amounts. You may also use credit cards affiliated with an American company such as Interbank, Visa, Barclay Card and American Express.

Electricity and Electronics   Electric outlets use currents of 110 volts, 60 cycles. To operate appliances made for other electrical systems, you need a transformer or other adapter. Travelers who use laptop computers for telecommunication should be aware that modem configurations for U.S. telephone systems may be different from their European counterparts. Similarly, the U.S. format for videotapes is different from that in Europe; National Park Service visitors centers and other stores that sell souvenir videos often have them available in European format on request.

Weights and Measurements   The United States uses the English system of weights and measures. American units and their metric equivalents are as follows: 1 inch = 2.5 centimeters; 1 foot = 0.3 meter; 1 yard = 0.9 meter; 1 mile = 1.6 kilometers; 1 ounce = 28 grams; 1 pound = 0.45 kilogram; 1 quart (liquid) = 0.9 liter.

Outdoor Adventures

CAMPING

New England offers a rich spectrum of camping experiences, from sites in the deep wilderness of the White Mountains and the Green Mountains and quiet lakeside spots to protected forests and recreational vehicle parks.

For information on camping in the Green Mountain National Forest, contact the **U.S. Forest Service**. ~ RR#1, Box 1940, Manchester Center, VT 05255; 802-362-2307; www.fs.fed.us/r9/gmfl.

Brochures on camping in the White Mountains are available from the **White Mountain National Forest**. ~ North 719 Main Street, Laconia, NH 03246; 603-528-8721; www.fs.fed.us/r9/white.

In Connecticut, quite a few state parks and forests are open for camping. The **Bureau of Parks and Forests** has information on fees and regulations. ~ Department of Environmental Protection, 79 Elm Street, Hartford, CT 06106; 860-424-3200; www.dep.state.ct.us.

The beautiful Acadia National Park in Maine, as well as about half the state parks, permit camping. For information about Acadia, contact **Acadia National Park**. ~ P.O. Box 177, Bar Harbor, ME 04609; 207-288-3338; www.nps.gov/acad. To find out about camping in state forests, contact **De Lorme**. ~ 2 De Lorme Drive, Yarmouth, ME 04096; 207-846-7000; www. delorme.com. Or contact the **Bureau of Parks and Recreation**. ~ 22 State House Station, Augusta, ME 04333-0022; 207-287-3821. The **Maine Campground Owners Association** offers a free camping guide. ~ 655 Main Street, Lewiston, ME 04240; 207-782-5874; www.campmaine.com, e-mail info@campmaine.com. At privately owned campsites, facilities range from rustic basics in wilderness areas to fairly deluxe cabins and cottages. The **Maine Publicity Bureau** offers a current listing of trailer parks and campsites. ~ Tourism Association, 33 Stone Street, Augusta, ME 04333; 207-623-0363, 800-782-6419, 888-624-6345.

For information on camping at Massachusetts state forest sites, contact the **State Division of Forests and Parks**. ~ 100 Cambridge Street, 19th Floor, Boston, MA 02202; 617-727-3180. A free guide, the *Massachusetts Campground Directory*, is published by the **Massachusetts Association of Campground Owners**. ~ P.O. Box 548, Scituate, MA 02066. This guide is also available from the **Massachusetts Office of Travel and Tourism**. ~ 10 Park Plaza, Suite 4510, Boston, MA 02116; 617-727-3201, 800-227-6277; www.massvacation.com. Camping is also permitted on several of the Boston Harbor Islands (see the "Beaches & Parks" sections of Chapter Four).

New Hampshire Loves Campers, a free guide to New Hampshire campgrounds covering private, state and White Mountain National Forest campsites, is published by the **New Hampshire Campground Owners Association**. ~ P.O. Box 320, Twin Mountain, NH 03595; 603-846-5511, 800-822-6764; www.ucampnh.com.

In Rhode Island, the **Tourism Division** provides information on facilities and permits, and offers *The Rhode Island Camping Guide*, which lists state, municipal and private campgrounds. ~ 1 West Exchange Street, Providence, RI 02903; 401-222-2601, 800-556-2484, fax 401-222-2102.

The **Vermont Department of Forests, Parks and Recreation** operates 35 campgrounds with 2200 campsites. ~ Agency of Natural Resources, 103 South Main Street, Waterbury, VT 05671; 802-241-3655; www.vtstateparks.com. The state has about 90 private campgrounds. Write the **Vermont Association of Private Campground Owners and Operators** for a free brochure. ~ c/o Marguerite, 400 Woodstock Road, White River Junction, VT 05001; 802-296-6711.

WILDERNESS PERMITS   Primitive campsites are provided in certain state parks and recreation areas. While wilderness camping away from designated areas is sometimes not allowed, in other cases it is allowable without a permit.

No permit is needed for wilderness camping in either the Green Mountain National Forest or the White Mountain National Forest. But Acadia National Park does not allow camping away from designated areas.

Connecticut allows backpack camping on state lands; a wilderness permit is needed. Contact the **Department of Environmental Protection.** ~ Eastern District Office, 209 Hebron Road, Marlborough, CT 06447; 860-295-9523; www.friendsctstate parks.net. Or get in touch with the DEP's **Western District Office.** ~ 230 Plymouth Road, Harwinton, CT 06791; 860-485-0226; www.dep.state.ct.us.

In Maine and New Hampshire, no permit is required to camp in wilderness areas in state forests.

Rhode Island and Massachusetts do not allow camping outside designated camping areas in state forests.

Groups of more than ten people who wish to camp in wilderness areas in Vermont need a permit; contact the **Vermont Department of Forests, Parks and Recreation** for the location of the appropriate local district office. You can also contact the forestry department for a free brochure, the *Vermont Guide to Primitive Camping on State Lands.* ~ Agency of Natural Resources, 103 South Main Street, Waterbury, VT 05671; 802-241-3655, fax 802-244-1481; www.vtstateparks.com.

Boating is one of the most popular activities in New England. Sailboats, canoes, windjammers, power boats, cruise boats and ferries all ply the coastline and region's large lakes and rivers. You can bring your own boat and get your feet wet doing some New England cruising, or rent or charter a craft here. Each chapter in this book offers suggestions on how to go about finding the vessel of your choice.

BOATING

Charts for boaters and divers are widely sold at marine shops and bookstores throughout New England.

Boating regulations vary slightly from state to state. In Connecticut, for a list of boating regulations and safety information, contact the **Department of Environmental Protection.** ~ Office of Parks and Recreation, Boating Safety Division, P.O. Box 280, Old Lyme, CT 06371; 860-434-8638, fax 860-434-3501.

For Rhode Island regulations, contact the **Department of Environmental Management.** ~ Office of Boat Registration and Licensing, 235 Promenade Street, Room 360, Providence, RI 02908; 401-222-6647, fax 401-222-1181; www.ridem.com.

Massachusetts boating information can be obtained from the **Division of Law Enforcement.** ~ 175 Portland Street, Boston, MA 02114-1701; 617-727-3905; www.state.ma.us.

Vermont boating regulations can be obtained from the **Vermont State Police Headquarters.** ~ 103 South Main Street, Waterbury, VT 05671-2101; 802-244-8775; www.dps.state.vt.us/vsp.

In New Hampshire, contact the **New Hampshire Marine Patrol.** ~ 31 Dock Road, Gilford, NH 03246; 603-293-2037.

For Maine regulations, contact the **Department of Inland Fisheries and Wildlife.** ~ 284 State Street, Station 41, Augusta ME 04333; 207-287-2043; www.state.me.us/ifw.

Canoe trails in Connecticut are described in two free brochures from the **Bureau of Outdoor Recreation**—*Canoe Camping* and *Canoeing in Connecticut.* ~ Department of Environmental Protection, 79 Elm Street, Hartford, CT 06106; 860-424-3014, fax 860-424-4070; www.dep.state.ct.us.

The **Vermont Department of Tourism and Marketing** sends out travel guides with information about canoeing. ~ 6 Baldwin Street, Montpelier, VT 05602; 802-828-3237, 800-837-6668; www.travel-vermont.com or www.1-800-vermont.com.

WATER SAFETY

Even in winter, you'll find diehard surfers and windsurfers riding the waves in their wetsuits. Swimming, waterskiing, jetboating and floating on inflatable rafts are popular activities in the summer.

People have drowned in New England waters, but drownings are avoided when you respect the power of the water, heed appropriate warnings and use good sense.

Wherever you swim, never do it alone. On the ocean or in large lakes like Lake Champlain or Lake Winnipesaukee, always face the incoming waves. They can bring unpleasant surprises even to the initiated. If you go surfing, learn the proper techniques and dangers from an expert before you start out. Respect signs warning of dangerous currents and undertows. If you get caught in a rip current or any tow that makes you feel out of control, don't try to swim against it. Head across it, paralleling the shore. Exercise caution in the use of floats, inner tubes or rafts; unexpected currents can quickly carry you out to sea.

There are some jellyfish that inflict a mild sting, but that is easily treated with an over-the-counter antiseptic. If you go scalloping or musseling, swim in or wade in murky waters where shellfish dwell, wear canvas or rubber shoes to protect your feet.

Remember, you are a guest in the sea. All rights belong to the creatures who dwell there, including sharks. Though they are rarely seen and seldom attack, they should be respected. A wise swimmer who spots a fin simply heads unobtrusively for shore.

Scuba divers should always put out a visible float or flag to warn approaching boats of their presence. On a boat or a canoe,

Facts and Foibles

Population—13.3 million
Square miles—66,608
Miles of coastline—6130
States with no coastline—1 (Vermont)
Square miles of lakes, rivers and streams—3660
Number of farms—23,000
Number of Fortune 500 companies—49
Percentage of college graduates—18
Colleges and universities
    In New England—264
    In Massachusetts—121
    In Boston—47
U.S. presidents born here—7
Percentage of native New Englanders in population—67.8
Inventive inventions—laughing gas, frozen food, sandpaper, snow-
    making machines, basketball, Monopoly, chocolate chip cookies
Gallons of maple syrup produced annually in Vermont—500,000
Covered bridges in Vermont—109
Pounds of Maine lobster caught annually—46 million
Pounds of Maine blueberries picked annually—52.3 million
Bushels of New Hampshire apples picked annually—1.5 million
Miles of stone walls in Connecticut—50,000
Famous cookie named for a Boston suburb—Fig Newton, for Newton
Highest natural point—Mount Washington in New Hampshire (6288 feet)
Highest manmade point—John Hancock Tower in Boston (790 feet)
Nation's first
    Highway—Route 20, Old Boston Post Road, from Boston to New
    York City
    Synagogue—Tuoro Synagogue (1759) in Newport
    College—Harvard (1639) in Cambridge, Massachusetts
    Postage stamp—printed in Brattleboro, Vermont (1846)
    Recipient of Social Security—Ida Fuller of Ludlow, Vermont, in
    1940 received check #00-000-001 for $22.45
    Human Flying Stunt—John Childs (1757), using a half glider/half
    umbrella, jumped from the steeple of Boston's Old North Church

always wear a life jacket; ocean and river currents can be very powerful.

If you're going canoeing or whitewater rafting, always scout the river from land before the first trip, and check the available literature. Rivers have danger areas such as falls, boulder fields, rapids and dams.

FISHING

Ever since the Puritans discovered salt cod, New Englanders have been fishing these waters. In the 19th century, men went down to the sea in ships after bigger fish—whales.

Today many people fish just for fun, casting a line into the surf off a rock jetty for flounder, striped bass or bluefish, or perhaps going out to sea for such deep-water game fish as bluefin tuna or shark.

For tamer activities, try harvesting mussels, scallops, littleneck clams or quahogs. And anyone can throw out a lobster pot or two and bring home a tasty dinner.

Freshwater fishing in streams, lakes and ponds nets rainbow, brook and brown trout, as well as largemouth bass, northern pike, bullhead, perch, sunfish, catfish and pickerel. In cold northern lakes, you can catch lake trout, steelhead, landlocked salmon, smelt, sauger, walleye, largemouth and smallmouth bass, northern pike, muskellunge, yellow perch and channel catfish.

The most common saltwater fish are winter flounder and bluefish. Other saltwater species include striped bass, cod, tautog, mackerel, haddock, pollock, weakfish and smelt.

While all six states require a license for freshwater fishing, no license is needed for saltwater fishing, with a few restrictions.

In Connecticut, freshwater fishing licenses can be bought from town clerks or sporting goods stores. For information on fishing regulations, contact the **Fisheries Division**. ~ Department of Environmental Protection, Room 255, 79 Elm Street, Hartford, CT 06106; 860-424-3474; www.dep.state.ct.us/bunatr/fishing.

In Rhode Island, freshwater fishing licenses can be bought at bait and tackle shops, all town clerks' offices, or from the **Department of Environmental Management**. ~ 235 Promenade Street, Providence, RI 02908; 401-222-3576.

For fishing in Massachusetts, contact the **State Division of Fisheries and Wildlife** and ask for the Abstracts of the Fish and Wildlife Laws. ~ 100 Cambridge Street, Room 1902, Boston, MA 02202; 617-727-3151; www.state.mass.us/dfwele. A saltwater permit is required for tuna or lobster fishing; for this permit, contact the **State Division of Sport Licensing**. ~ 175 Portland Street, 2nd Floor, Boston, MA 02114; 617-727-3900.

Fishing licenses in Vermont may be purchased from any town clerk or at many sporting goods stores, general stores, and state parks. The **Vermont Department of Fish and Wildlife** has details and maps in *The Digest of Fish and Wildlife Laws* and the *Vermont Guide to Fishing.* ~ Agency of Natural Resources, 103 South Main Street, Building 10 South, Waterbury, VT 05676; 802-241-3700; www.anr.state.vt.us/fw/fwhome.

For fishing fees and regulations in New Hampshire, contact the **New Hampshire Department of Fish & Game.** ~ 2 Hazen Drive, Concord, NH 03301; 603-271-3211; www.wildlife.state. nh.us.

TWO

Connecticut

Connecticut is the gateway to New England and it offers, despite its diminutive size, a sampling of everything that makes the region famous. Although it takes no more than two and a half hours to drive across the state, these 5000 square miles hold a surprising variety of riches: 250 miles of jagged shoreline; farms, woodlands, mountains and rolling hills; villages of white-clapboard houses huddled around classic greens; and cities rich in cultural offerings. Three hundred and fifty years of history are reflected in the varied architecture and in countless sites—vintage houses, museums, historical societies—that celebrate the forceful men and women who made Connecticut their home.

Shaped like a rectangle measuring about 90 miles from west to east and 55 miles north to south, Connecticut is bounded by New York State on its western border, Massachusetts to the north and Rhode Island to the east. The southern edge is traced by Long Island Sound, a sheltered arm of the Atlantic Ocean that was formerly a vital avenue of trade and transportation and is now a prime recreational asset. The state's other major waterway is its namesake: the Connecticut River, longest in New England, which roughly cuts the state in half and was the site of the earliest 17th-century settlements.

Indian names grace the rivers Housatonic, Quinnipiac and Naugatuck, as well as towns and villages like Cos Cob, Niantic, Saugatuck and Wequetequock. Most towns, however, bear names that have their roots in Great Britain—Windsor, Bristol, New Britain, Greenwich, Norwich—or in the Bible—Bethel, Goshen, Canaan, Bethlehem.

England, their land of birth, and the Puritan faith were crucial influences on the original settlers, who left the fledgling Massachusetts colony in 1633 to found the communities of Hartford, Windsor and Wethersfield on the Connecticut's fertile banks. A few years later, the three settlements joined together as the Hartford Colony—soon to become the Colony of Connecticut—and adopted the Fundamental Orders of 1639. This document, created as a framework for governing the colony, is regarded by many as the world's first written constitution. That's why the words "Constitution State" are heralded on automobile license plates.

Other, less glorious nicknames include "The Nutmeg State," a reference to the days of the itinerant Yankee peddler who went up and down the Atlantic seaboard door to door, selling anything the householder might need, including imported nutmeg, to add flavor to food. Legend has it that wily peddlers would leave the lady of the house holding a "wooden nutmeg"—a fake.

Be that as it may, few of those households could grow much of their own food, since the state's surface is largely glacial soil, too rocky for successful farming. From the beginning, many of the residents had to turn to other endeavors—commerce, shipping, insurance and, in time, manufacturing, which put the state on the map.

Towns and cities grew up around their factories—you'll see handsome brick or stone mills as you drive along the valleys of the Naugatuck, the Quinebaug and other rivers—and each locality became known by the product it manufactured. Waterbury was the brass city; New Britain was the hardware capital of the world; Danbury's fame was hats; Bristol boasted of its clocks.

As mills and factories grew, so did their need for workers. During the late 19th and early 20th centuries great waves of immigrants entered the state from Ireland, Italy, Germany, Poland—every country in Europe. The makeup of the population changed from a homogeneous nucleus of English Protestant descent to the mosaic of nationalities and ethnic groups that characterizes Connecticut's 3.3 million people today.

Industry continues to remain important to some extent: airplane parts are manufactured in East Hartford, helicopters in Stratford; in Groton, Electric Boat builds submarines. But changing patterns and needs across the nation have led to factory closings throughout the state, and to grave problems for older manufacturing cities. At the same time, a number of national corporations have moved their headquarters to Connecticut, creating new skylines and new work in cities like Greenwich, Danbury and Stamford. As a whole, the state continues to be one of the most prosperous in the country, although substantial segments of the population have been unable to share in the wealth.

Despite the importance of manufacturing, a large proportion of the land has remained rural, with vast acreage set aside for recreation and open space in more than 50 state parks and forests, as well as municipal parks and nature preserves. These peaceful oases are scattered throughout the state: along the shoreline, in the pastoral northern corners, even in the more populated valleys near the three largest cities—Bridgeport, Hartford and New Haven.

The landscape ranges from a level shoreline dotted with small beaches and coves through rolling country to the green-clad mountains of the northwest corner and gentle hills of the northeast. At the center is the Connecticut River Valley, once fertile farmland whose traditional crops, tobacco and corn, have largely given way to suburban growth in recent decades.

The central section of the state is home to several major universities: Yale in New Haven, Wesleyan in Middletown, Trinity College in Hartford. New London, on the southeastern coast, boasts Connecticut College and the Coast Guard Academy, while the University of Connecticut's main campus is in Storrs.

Though distances are short, the climate varies by several degrees from north to south, with snow and ice lasting longest in Litchfield County, the northwestern region. Winter temperatures can go below zero at times, though seldom for long; summer can be occasionally hot and humid. And yet each season brings its own rewards and calendar of attractions. Winter turns the hilly regions into scenes of skating and ice fishing on lakes and ponds, while downhill skiers rush to half a dozen well-equipped areas and cross-country buffs head for countless trails. In spring, the dogwood's snowy blossoms brighten the roadways, and mountain laurel, the state flower, paints hillsides the very palest pink. Summer is the favorite vacation season, a time of festivals and fairs, swimming, fishing and boating, and crowds of visitors at beaches and parks. Fall, some say, shows the state at its best, with maples, oaks, dogwoods, ferns, even the dreaded poison ivy turning the countryside into a symphony of orange, red and gold.

Connecticut can be explored from several points of entry, but chances are that visitors will be coming in from New York state. With this in mind, the chapter has been organized as one lengthy, S-shaped path, going from southwest to northwest; then to the Hartford area, more or less the state's center; south to New Haven; then east along the shore with a brief jog up the Lower Connecticut Valley; finishing up with the scenic, little-known northeast corner. It's a journey that could take a few days, a week or a lifetime spent discovering the treasures of this compact state.

Southwestern Connecticut

Guidebooks tend to dismiss southwestern Connecticut, which roughly corresponds to Fairfield County, as merely a bedroom community for New York City, not worthy of a visitor's time. In fact, it's far more complex—a mix of attractive residential towns with roots in the 17th and 18th centuries, once-thriving industrial cities struggling to find new roles for themselves and clusters of tall, sleek corporate headquarters that have transformed the county's way of life. What's more, although the area is far from rural, a surprising amount of open space has been preserved in state parks and nature preserves.

SIGHTS

A brief tour to sample this variety should start in **Greenwich**, the first town encountered on crossing into the state from the southwest. Famed as an exclusive residential enclave of affluent New York commuters, this community of 60,000 has acquired an additional role as a business center. A host of corporate office buildings draws some 20,000 workers from other towns, as well as hundreds of foreign executives. The old order changeth, even here!

HIDDEN ►

The beauty of the town remains, as does the atmosphere of quiet privilege. Visitors seeking a glimpse of the **great estates** that give Greenwich its special ambience should wander the "backcountry" roads north and immediately south of the Merritt Parkway, along Lake Avenue, North Street, Round Hill Road and smaller, bucolic lanes and drives—as long as they are not guarded by stone gateposts with "No Admittance" signs! It's a world of white churches and manicured country clubs, ancestral trees and lavishly landscaped grounds, with mansions, neo-Tudor or Colonial Revival, barely visible behind iron gates, stone walls and fences.

One former estate that, happily, is open to the public is the renovated **Bruce Museum**, housing American paintings, American Indian pottery and textiles, natural science and geologic displays and frequent exhibitions that reflect the eclectic nature of the holdings. Closed Monday. Admission (free on Tuesday). ~ 1 Museum Drive, Greenwich; 203-869-0376; www.brucemuseum.org.

Putnam Cottage is a late-17th-century tavern and site of General Israel Putnam's 1779 daring escape against the redcoats—a favorite bit of local lore. Open Wednesday, Friday and Sunday. Closed January through March. Admission. ~ 243 East Putnam Avenue, Greenwich; 203-869-9697.

Also worth checking out in Greenwich are the **Cavalier Galleries**, which have a variety of contemporary paintings and more than 30 large-scale, modern figurative sculptures on display. An affiliated sculpture garden in Stamford is open by appointment. Closed Monday. ~ 405 Greenwich Avenue, Greenwich; 203-869-3664.

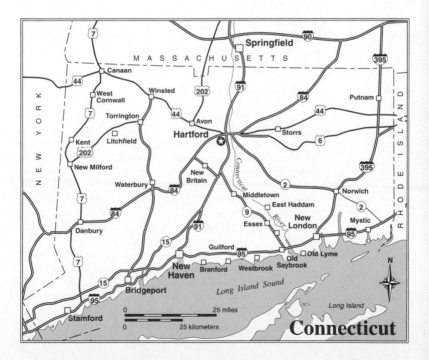

Another nearby attraction is the **Bush-Holley Historic Site and Visitor Center**, devoted to the community's long and colorful history. The 18th-century saltbox house, a boarding house for Connecticut's first art colony in the 1890s, is a National Historic landmark. Closed Monday and Tuesday year-round; closed weekdays from January through March. Admission to the house. ~ 39 Strickland Road, Cos Cob; 203-869-6899.

> Many of the great estates of Greenwich are owned by celebrities—Diana Ross, Victor Borge and Ivana Trump among them.

Driving east from Greenwich on Route 95, you'll spot **Stamford**'s skyline, which appears as a forest of discordant office towers, huge corporate headquarters built since the 1960s that dwarf the few remaining older structures. An enlightened giant, the Champion International Corporation, houses a branch of New York's prestigious **Whitney Museum of American Art**. It's a handsome, sleek gallery space, with exhibits of 20th-century American art. Closed Sunday and Monday. ~ 1 Champion Plaza, at the corner of Atlantic Street and Tresser Boulevard, Stamford; 203-358-7630; www.whitney.org.

Another interesting destination in Stamford is the **First Presbyterian Church**, a unique fish-shaped church that was designed by Wallace K. Harrison. Closed Saturday, and Sunday afternoon. ~ 1101 Bedford Street, Stamford; 203-324-9522.

A few miles north of downtown you'll find the **Stamford Museum and Nature Center**, perhaps the most eclectic institution in the state. Set on more than 118 acres, the center offers, in a number of widely scattered buildings, galleries devoted to art and American and natural history; an auditorium; a planetarium; an observatory; a small New England farm; and nature trails, picnic grounds and a small lake populated by all manner of geese, ducks and swans. This one's truly a treat for the whole family. Special seasonal programs are offered. Admission. ~ 39 Scofieldtown Road, Stamford; 203-322-1646; www.stamfordmuseum.org.

Just east of Stamford is **Darien,** one of Connecticut's most coveted addresses. Take time out to see the **Bates-Scofield Homestead**, a classic 1736 Connecticut saltbox house now used as a museum. All rooms, including the kitchen and the buttery, are fully restored with 18th-century furnishings and artwork. Open only on Thursday and Sunday; call ahead. ~ 45 Old Kings Highway North, Darien; 203-655-9233; www.darien.lib.ct.us.historical/default.htm.

Next stop along the shoreline is **Norwalk**, a city of 80,000 that was settled in 1645 and thrived on the coastal trade and manufacturing, then went into a slump. After years of neglect, the area closest to the harbor, **South Norwalk** (known as SoNo), has been restored, gentrified and listed in the National Register of Historic Places. Its major artery, **Washington Street**, is now a stroller's mecca offering many shops and boutiques, art and craft galleries, restaurants and bars, all set in handsome 19th-century commercial buildings.

Around the corner, on five acres of riverfront, rises one of the state's top three attractions, the **Maritime Aquarium at Norwalk**. It includes an aquarium with myriad tanks that take you from salt marsh into open sea, sharks, harbor seals and all; a maritime museum displaying classic open boats; a touch tank; a stingray petting pool; and a high-tech, 337-seat IMAX theater with a six-story screen that stretches 80 feet. Admission. ~ 10 North Water Street, Norwalk; 203-852-0700; www.maritimeaquarium.org.

From an adjacent dock you can board **The Seaport Island**, an open ferry that goes to the 1868 lighthouse on Sheffield Island. It operates on weekends only from Memorial Day to the second week of June, then daily until Labor Day. Closed Labor Day to Memorial Day. Admission. ~ 132 Water Street, Norwalk; 203-838-9444, 888-701-7785; www.seaport.org.

Other vessels take longer jaunts around all the islands. Information about this and other attractions is available from the **Coastal Fairfield County Tourism Information Center**. ~ 297 West Avenue, Norwalk; 203-854-7825.

The center occupies the gate house to the **Lockwood-Mathews Mansion Museum**. This lavish 62-room residence, built in the 1860s in French Second Empire style, includes work by some of the finest cabinetmakers and craftsmen of the day. Saved from the bulldozer by local preservationists, it has been gradually restored room by room—frescoed ceilings, inlaid woodwork, glassed-in conservatory—and now serves as a museum of Victorian life. Closed Monday; open in January and February by appointment only. Admission. ~ 295 West Avenue, Norwalk; 203-838-1434; www.norwalk.com/mansion.

Continue east and you'll soon come to **Westport**, a popular summer spot as well as a thriving community year-round. Its beaches are a magnet for visitors from inland and other parts of the coast. Take the second Westport exit northbound on Route 95 to reach **Sherwood Island**, a public beach with picnic tables, changing facilities and beachside refreshments.

A more beautiful beach—**Compo Beach**—is for Westport residents and anyone who doesn't mind paying $10 a day for parking ($25 on weekends and holidays). The price is ridiculously high, but that's what keeps the crowds from getting too big.

Westport is home to **The Nature Center for Environmental Activities**, a 62-acre wildlife sanctuary providing habitat for squirrels, birds, deer and other animals native to the region. The museum offers a variety of educational programs and live-animal touch tanks; the center also operates a rehabilitation program for injured animals. ~ 10 Woodside Lane, Westport; 203-227-7253.

HIDDEN ►

From Westport, follow Greens Farms Road to Beachside Avenue, which will turn onto Pequot Avenue and take you right into **Southport**, one of Connecticut's most enchanting villages. Here you will find a stunning collection of houses, churches and public buildings crowding around the tiny Southport Harbor. Drive slowly down Pequot Avenue past the parade of homes in the Federal and Greek Revival style and later ones in all the variations we tend to lump together as Victorian.

After you pass a small cluster of stores and antique shops, take a right to the harbor, the original source of the wealth that created the handsome dwellings. The vessels that traded with Boston and New York from this small, sheltered port have given way to sailboats moored at the yacht club, but the homes built by the ship's owners and captains are still lived in and lovingly maintained. Park if you can, and walk up Harbor Road for a fine view of the watery landscape.

Bridgeport, the next city along Route 95, is the largest in the state and no one's dream of a tourist attraction, but **The Barnum Museum** will delight both children and adults. For Bridgeport, P. T. Barnum was more than the king of hoax and hokum, more than the creator of the legendary Barnum and Bailey Circus. He was a philanthropist and real estate developer, the city's mayor and its favorite son. The museum established in his will in 1891 is as flamboyant as he was, a gargoyled, towered and domed red building in the heart of the city, a reflection of his eclectic interests. Circus buffs will go straight to the third floor with its mementos of General Tom Thumb, the talented midget who achieved world fame; its big top memorabilia; and especially the 1000-square-foot scale model of "The Greatest Show on Earth," complete with over 3000 miniatures of acrobats, clowns, elephants, trains and tents, every tiny detail hand carved by a craftsman from a nearby town. Closed Monday. Admission. ~ 820 Main Street, Bridgeport; 203-331-1104; www.barnum-museum.org.

Bridgeport is also home to **The Discovery Museum**, an interactive art and science museum featuring hands-on exhibits in both disciplines. In the science section explore light, sound, computers, electronics and nuclear energy; in the arts section play with color, line and perspective. The Challenger Learning Center gives you the chance to go on a simulated space mission, and the planetarium offers daily shows on the stars and planets. The museum also has two art galleries with rotating exhibits. Children and adults alike will love this museum. Closed Monday in fall and winter. Admission. ~ 4450 Park Avenue, Bridgeport; 203-372-3521; www.discoverymuseum.org.

In addition to the towns along the shores of Connecticut's southern coast, there are a few villages just inland that merit a visit. These include New Canaan and Ridgefield.

New Canaan is a quiet residential community that was settled in 1731. Throughout the town and along the winding roads that surround it are beautifully maintained New England homes and churches. One worthwhile stop is the **Silvermine Guild Arts Center**, an art center with a school whose galleries have showcased the works of member artists and artisans since 1922. Closed Monday. ~ 1037 Silvermine Road, New Canaan; 203-966-5617; www.silvermineart.org.

Another spot to check out is the **New Canaan Nature Center**, a 40-acre preserve that encompasses a variety of habitats, including woodland, marshes and fields. Its Discovery Center offers interactive, educational exhibits on animal behavior that will intrigue youngsters. The building is closed Sunday but grounds are open from dawn to dusk. ~ 144 Oenoke Ridge Road, New Canaan; 203-966-9577.

Perhaps the most idyllic town in this busy part of the state is **Ridgefield**, a quintessential New England enclave of stately homes, ancient trees and mementos of battles long past. To reach Ridgefield, a bit farther inland than Bridgeport, take Route 123 through a corner of New York State to Route 35. Once a way station on the road from New York to Boston, the town provided inns for

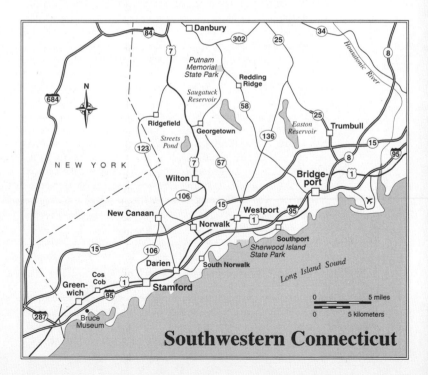

Southwestern Connecticut

weary passengers. The tradition continues, with several old but up-to-date hostelries and one that now acts as a museum, the **Keeler Tavern Museum**, whose most famous feature is a cannonball lodged in its wall since the Battle of Ridgefield, April 27, 1777. Benedict Arnold was a hero on that day! Also on the grounds is a walled garden with a reflecting pool. Open Wednesday, Saturday and Sunday afternoons; tours on other days are available by appointment. Garden is open daily. Closed January. Admission. ~ 132 Main Street, Ridgefield; 203-438-5485.

Not far from the tavern, another 18th-century building (from 1783, to be exact) has been transformed into the **Aldrich Museum of Contemporary Art**. Surrounding the historic main structure and its congenial addition is an outstanding two-acre sculpture garden representing rotating contemporary outdoor pieces. Closed Monday. Admission. ~ 258 Main Street, Ridgefield; 203-438-4519; www.aldrichart.org.

LODGING   Surrounded by extensive, stately homes in an exclusive part of Greenwich known as Belle Haven, **The Homestead Inn** first saw life in 1799 as a farmhouse. It was converted to an inn 50 years later and eventually acquired a jaunty cupola, a Victorian wraparound porch and two outbuildings that also offer accommodations. A million-dollar renovation in 1978 supervised by designer John Saladino brought everything up-to-date, creating a graceful, sophisticated country inn with 23 guest rooms, ample public spaces and a three-star restaurant, all embellished with carefully chosen antiques and reproductions. ~ 420 Field Point Road, Greenwich; 203-869-7500, fax 203-869-7502. ULTRA-DELUXE.

Set proudly among the tall new office towers of downtown Stamford, the **Stamford Marriott** boasts more than 500 elegant rooms and such amenities as an indoor-outdoor pool, racquetball courts, a rooftop jogging track and a revolving restaurant with views of Long Island Sound. It may not be everyone's ideal vacation hideaway, but its proximity to Route 95, the railroad station, cultural offerings and a major shopping mall makes it attractive. Weekends bring lower rates. ~ 2 Stamford Forum, Stamford; 203-357-9555, 800-228-9290, fax 203-324-6897; www.marriotthotels.com. ULTRA-DELUXE.

Silvermine Tavern has a special charm that spells New England, even though it's just a hop from the New York state line. Well-known for its restaurant, this picturesque cluster of rambling, circa-1785 frame buildings offers ten comfortable bedrooms appropriately but not lavishly furnished with country antiques. Overlooking the mill pond and its waterfall, the complex is at the crossroads of a woodsy residential community. Continental breakfast. ~ 194 Perry Avenue, Norwalk; 203-847-4558, fax 203-847-9171. MODERATE TO DELUXE.

Author Picks

CHAPTER FAVORITES

I learned much more than I thought I knew about the 19th century's greatest promoter and the preposterous cast of prodigies, dwarves, elephants, Siamese twins and others he elevated to international stardom at **The Barnum Museum** in Bridgeport. *page 46*

My pick for best dining bet in Connecticut is the dining room of the **Lakeview Inn** on Lake Waramaug, run by the owners of Manhattan's French Culinary Institute, one of the top chefs' schools in the country. Try the lobster. *page 69*

For wildlife viewing, I like to set up camp by bucolic Bantam Lake in the **White Memorial Foundation & Conservation Center**, waking just after dawn to stroll along the network of trails that wends through this 4000-acre refuge teeming with great horned owls, snow geese and more than a hundred other bird species. *page 74*

One of my favorite aspects of traveling in Connecticut is staying at small rural establishments like the early-19th-century **Applewood Farms Inn**, where guests can practice on the putting green or soak away their troubles in the corn crib's hot tub. *page 105*

A clutch of motels lines Route 1, the old Boston Post Road and now the area's crowded commercial strip. For one that's clean, quiet and operated by the same family for over 30 years—they live on the premises—try the **Garden Park Motel**. Their 21 units all have air conditioning, cable television, good bathrooms and firm mattresses; there's even a picnic table under a shady tree for the guests' use. Fancy it's not, but it's cheap in an area that tends to be expensive. ~ 351 Westport Avenue, Norwalk; 203-847-7303. MODERATE.

Situated on the banks of the Saugatuck River in Westport, **The Inn at National Hall** occupies a restored, historic brick building. Its 15 rooms and suites are luxuriously decorated, with lots of trompe l'oeil, handcrafted stenciling and arched ceilings. So exquisite is this small hotel that it was featured in an *Architectural Digest* cover story. On the premises is a pricey restaurant, which hosted President Clinton and Vice President Gore on separate visits to Westport. ~ 2 Post Road, Westport; 203-221-1351, 800-628-4255, fax 203-221-0276; www.innatnationalhall.com. ULTRA-DELUXE.

The Inn at Longshore is an unusual place to stay: a 12-room inn with a ballroom and banquet facilities in the midst of a town-owned golf course and park, with lawns that sweep down to Long

Island Sound. The rooms (three of them are suites that can sleep four) are almost an afterthought, but they're tastefully done, with up-to-date bathrooms and views of white sails dancing on blue water. Guests may use town facilities, such as the golf course, swimming pool and tennis court, on payment of a fee. Continental breakfast. ~ 260 Compo Road South, Westport; 203-226-3316, fax 203-227-5344. DELUXE TO ULTRA-DELUXE.

The **Roger Sherman Inn** is located just outside the center of New Canaan. It's a small inn that dates back to around 1740. All 17 guest rooms are decorated with cherrywood antiques, and several have sitting rooms. There is a restaurant on the premises. ~ 195 Oenoke Ridge, New Canaan; 203-966-4541, fax 203-966-0503; www.rogershermaninn.com. DELUXE.

Right next door is **The Maples Inn**, a 25-room inn that was built back in 1908. It's a grand old hotel with a wraparound porch. The large guest rooms, all with four-poster canopy beds, are furnished with antiques and reproductions. ~ 179 Oenoke Ridge, New Canaan; 203-966-2927, fax 203-966-5003. DELUXE.

Connecticut's largest city is Bridgeport, with 130,000 people, followed closely by Hartford and New Haven.

In serene Ridgefield, set behind a wide lawn and ancient trees, sits **West Lane Inn**, a gracious dowager of a place built as a home in the early 1800s, embellished in the Victorian era and then converted to an inn in the late 1970s. There's a wide porch that wraps around two sides, with colorful hanging baskets and black wrought-iron furniture for lazy summer days. A great carved oak staircase leads up to 20 generous-sized rooms. All show restrained elegance, and each is individually designed with plush carpeting, fine upholstered pieces and period-style furniture. Continental breakfast. ~ 22 West Lane, Ridgefield; 203-438-7323, fax 203-438-7325; www.wetlaneinn.com. DELUXE TO ULTRA-DELUXE.

The **Elms Inn**, operating as an inn since 1799, has been run by only four families in all these years. Today, the famed restaurant occupies most of the main building, with two bedrooms and two suites up a steep, cramped flight of stairs. The annex offers 16 accommodations—three of them suites—which are elegantly carpeted and appointed with attractive stenciled wallpapers and period furniture. Some of the rooms offer four-poster and canopied beds. The rooms over the restaurant are more casual, with rag rugs, hand-stenciled borders on the ceilings and bathrooms sporting a "country" look. In-room continental breakfast. ~ 500 Main Street, Ridgefield; phone/fax 203-438-2541; www.elmsinn. com. DELUXE TO ULTRA-DELUXE.

DINING

For a glimpse of Connecticut dining at its classiest, start with **Restaurant Thomas Henkelmann at The Homestead Inn**. A 1799 farmhouse turned hostelry and exquisitely restored, the inn stands on a knoll in an exclusive residential area—a treat to the eye as well as the palate. In the restaurant, the ambience is classic French and subdued; the fare is French, sophisticated and up-to-date. Tables sparkle with fine glass and unique plates designed in southern France; service is proper. In the summer, you can enjoy the outdoor patio for lunch. Breakfast, lunch and dinner. ~ 420 Field Point Road, Greenwich; 203-869-7500. ULTRA-DELUXE.

Greenwich is also home to **Restaurant Jean-Louis**, a top-drawer French restaurant. Chef-owner Jean-Louis is well known in the culinary world for his masterful food preparation. The prix-fixe menu changes daily and may include such dishes as steamed lobster salad, scaloppine of salmon with parsley coulis, boneless quail stuffed with rice and truffles, and medallions of ostrich. Whatever the menu, everything is made from fresh, seasonal ingredients. The decor is romantic, with mirrors and original French artwork on the walls. The restaurant is small, so reservations are *très* necessary. Dinner only; call for lunch hours. Closed Sunday. ~ 61 Lewis Street, Greenwich; 203-622-8450. ULTRA-DELUXE.

Among the myriad Italian restaurants in this part of the state, **Il Falco** is considered one of the best. Set in the heart of Stamford, this pleasant spot without glitz or pretension serves regional specialties that don't appear on every menu—gnocchi, *vitello tonnato*, fish prepared in the style of various Italian cities—all cooked with imagination and care. Closed Sunday. ~ 59 Broad Street, Stamford; 203-327-0002. MODERATE TO DELUXE.

Siena Ristorante is a noteworthy Tuscan restaurant. Under Chef Eugene Jerome, the kitchen serves up some of the best risotto and pasta (all homemade) you'll find in the county; the menu changes four times a year. The wonderful desserts include crème brulée and a chocolate tart with almonds. Beautifully decorated with stucco walls and a painted mural cloud ceiling, Siena seats just 58 and has a loyal clientele, so be sure to make reservations (especially on weekends). No lunch on Saturday; closed Sunday. ~ 519 Summer Street, Stamford; 203-351-0898. DELUXE.

A great diner to find your way to is **Bull's Head Diner**, which offers such favorites as sandwiches, stir-fry, pasta, filet mignon, seafood and roast chicken 24 hours a day. The diner also serves up Greek specialties like spinach pie, moussaka and savory sampler plates. Breakfast, lunch and dinner. ~ 43 High Ridge Road, Stamford; 203-961-1400. MODERATE.

South Norwalk, or SoNo, a restored 19th-century neighborhood, is a good place to window-shop for lunch or dinner. On rejuvenated Washington Street and the adjoining Main Street, you can read menus in restaurant windows and decide if you're in the mood for Italian, French, Mexican, Chinese, seafood or sandwiches, funky or chic. There's been some turnover among the tenants in this historic district, but **Jeremiah Donovan's** has been a lively meeting place for over a century, a wood-paneled Victorian saloon with unpretentious, inexpensive food—good burgers, salads, sandwiches, their special New England chowder and hearty bowls of chili—and a prodigious selection of beers. A collection of vintage prizefighter photos adorns the walls, legacy of a regional champ who owned the place many decades ago. ~ 138 Washington Street, South Norwalk; phone/fax 203-838-3430. BUDGET.

Barcelona, a Spanish tapas restaurant, attracts a crowd of fanatical regulars nightly. Step inside the stuccoed bar area and you will feel as if you're in Madrid. Elegant-looking diners crowd the bar and high-stooled tables. An outdoor courtyard is enclosed for winter. Moderately priced tapas include grilled baby octopus salad with pickled onions, black-bean dip with pita crisps and a portobella, spinach and mozzarella sandwich. Entrées include pasta dishes, pan-roasted monkfish and, in the summer, a variety of dishes prepared on the outdoor wood-burning grill. ~ 63 North Main Street, South Norwalk; 203-899-0088. MODERATE TO DELUXE.

Silvermine Tavern is a landmark: a country inn, popular for decades, with several antique-filled dining rooms and a romantic terrace for summer dining, overlooking a waterfall and pond. Offerings fit the Colonial atmosphere: roast beef, seafood, poultry and pasta. The Silvermine also serves Sunday brunch and Thursday-night buffet. Closed Tuesday. ~ 194 Perry Avenue, Norwalk; phone/fax 203-847-4558. DELUXE.

Norwalk is home to a Spanish restaurant, **Meson Galicia**. Here you can have reasonably tabbed tapas, or opt for a paella or one of the other northern Spanish specialties, including roasted duckling with dried figs, sautéed veal sweetbreads with pistachios and lingonberries or quail stuffed with sweetbreads, shrimp and mushrooms. The dining room looks and feels like a Spanish country inn, with lots of tiles, woodwork and dim lighting. Closed Monday. ~ 19 Wall Street, Norwalk; 203-866-8800. MODERATE TO ULTRA-DELUXE.

Looking out on Westport's Saugatuck River, the **Bridge Cafe** serves Mediterranean cuisine. The menu changes daily and usually includes a variety of fish, chicken and lamb dishes. It's a festively decorated restaurant with a patio for dining outside during warm weather. ~ 5 Riverside Avenue, Westport; 203-226-4800. MODERATE TO ULTRA-DELUXE.

Nearby at the Westport Inn is chef-owned **Christina's,** a great choice for brunch. Menu offerings are largely country French and Italian—fresh pasta dishes and entrées like braised lamb shank with saffron mashed potatoes and roasted zucchini. For brunch, try the crêpes with fresh fruit. For lunch you'll find salads, sandwiches and pizzas. ~ 1595 Post Road East, Westport; 203-255-8889, fax 203-255-1796. MODERATE TO DELUXE.

Over by Compo Beach is **Allen's Clam & Lobster House.** While it has the look of a tourist establishment, the food is unfailingly good. Choose from steak, chicken or lobster—their specialty—and a variety of other seafood. Located right on the water's edge, this restaurant has a resort feel to it during the summer months. Closed Monday and all of January. ~ 191 Hillspoint Road, Westport; 203-226-4411, fax 203-454-3108. DELUXE.

Donuts don't often merit hymns of praise, but at the **Coffee An' Donut Shop** they are handmade by the owner, with lots of TLC, each morning before 7 a.m. The resulting confections—glazed, sugared, twirled with cinnamon, rolled in thick chocolate or filled with raspberry jelly—have made addicts for miles around and been dubbed best in the country by food critics of national renown. ~ 343 North Main Street, Westport; 203-227-3808. BUDGET.

> Connecticut has more miles of paved highway than Alaska, the largest U.S. state.

In nearby Fairfield, you'll find **Centro**, a popular spot for northern Italian dishes. The menu includes a selection of daily special pastas, house pizzas and fish and chicken dishes. The Caesar salad is done very well, as is the creme brulée dessert. In addition to two main dining areas, there's a tiny bar in the rear and *al fresco* dining May through November. Centro is a festive place, with paper table coverings and a glass of crayons for mid-meal inspirations and explanations. Be prepared to wait on weekend nights—the restaurant does not take reservations and has quite a devoted clientele. No lunch on Sunday. ~ 1435 Post Road, Fairfield; 203-255-1210, fax 203-259-5040. BUDGET TO MODERATE.

Parc 1070 and the hotel that houses it are stepping-stones on the way to the long-awaited renaissance of downtown Bridgeport. The emphasis is on steaks, chicken and lasagna. The food is expertly prepared and served in bountiful portions—good reasons for dining in an area not previously known for its cuisine. Breakfast, lunch and dinner. ~ Bridgeport Holiday Inn, 1070 Main Street, Bridgeport; 203-334-1234. MODERATE.

A Fairfield County grande dame, the **Roger Sherman Inn** stands in the heart of an attractive residential community. Once a classic country inn and restaurant known for American fare, the Roger Sherman has been totally—and tastefully—renovated and is now dedicated to Continental cuisine, with grilled meats high on the list of favorites. No lunch on Monday. ~ 195 Oenoke Ridge, New Canaan; 203-966-4541. ULTRA-DELUXE.

A more casual find is **Tequila Mockingbird**, a Mexican-style restaurant with terra-cotta tiled floors and a festive mural. Menu items include all sorts of Mexican favorites. Dinner only. ~ 6 Forest Street, New Canaan; 203-966-2222. MODERATE.

The **Gates Restaurant** is generally filled with "ladies who lunch" during weekdays and preppie bar-goers at night. The fare is American with a selection of salads, chicken, fish and pasta dishes. Decor is very light and airy, with lots of greenery around. ~ 10 Forest Street, New Canaan; 203-966-8666. MODERATE.

For a festive occasion, try **The Elms Restaurant and Tavern**, which has been greeting travelers since 1799. The handsome old white inn has changed a lot since then, needless to say. Its dining rooms are now gracious and serene, all flickering candles, flowered china and snow white linens, and they serve impeccably prepared American cuisine. Seafood, fowl and steak are featured. Closed Monday and Tuesday. ~ 500 Main Street, Ridgefield; 203-438-9206. DELUXE TO ULTRA-DELUXE.

Thirty Three and a Third is another great dinner choice in Ridgefield. Tucked away in a shopping complex, this small restaurant prides itself on its nonpareil risotto. Honestly, have it here and you'll find yourself holding it up as the model of great risotto for years to come. Of course, there are other alternatives on its seasonally changing menu, including a variety of pasta, fish (try the pecan-crusted Idaho brook trout) and chicken dishes. Thirty Three and a Third tends to fill up early, especially on weekend evenings, so be sure to call ahead. Closed Sunday. ~ 125 Danbury Road, Ridgefield; 203-438-3904. MODERATE TO DELUXE.

For brunch in Ridgefield, choose **Gail's Station House**. It's a funky little restaurant where the servings are huge, healthy *and* delicious—a rare combination. Cuisine is contemporary with foreign and regional American accents. For dinner try the rainforest stir-fry (roasted cashews and brown rice in a ginger sauce) or the salmon phyllo with mushroom duxelles and lemon mayonnaise with capers. Brunch features corn-and-cheddar pancakes and skillet specials. Breakfast and lunch daily, dinner Friday through Sunday. ~ 378 Main Street, Ridgefield; 203-438-9775, fax 203-438-4493. BUDGET TO MODERATE.

Another good choice in Ridgefield is the **Hay Day Country Market**, a gourmet grocery store. Choose from a wonderful selection of salads, pastas and soups, as well as sandwiches such as grilled vegetables on Italian ciabotta bread and a California roll with jack cheese, alfalfa sprouts and avocado. After you've paid, you can eat your purchases at the coffee bar. ~ 21 Governor Street, Ridgefield; 203-431-4400. BUDGET.

HIDDEN ► Run by an energetic local couple, busy **Ciao! Café and Wine Bar** is tucked in an unlikely spot behind Danbury's Main Street, not far from the train station. The decor in this small restaurant is simple, with black chairs, booths and tables and tables. The menu focuses on Italian dishes, with veal and inventive sauces playing major roles. Try to save room for the flourless chocolate cake. ~ 2-B Ives Street, Danbury; 203-791-0404. MODERATE.

Owned and run by the same couple who began Ciao!, **Two Steps Downtown Grille** is just . . . two steps away, though quite different in decor and menu. Here you will find Southwestern fare with Caribbean and Jamaican influences. Count the elaborately painted boots that hang from the ceiling; the owners, customers, staff and their friends decorated them. ~ 5 Ives Street, Danbury; 203-794-0032, fax 203-730-1962. MODERATE.

Greenwich Avenue, the main street of elite Greenwich, and the adjoining blocks on **Putnam Avenue** (Route 1) present a profusion of upscale apparel shops—skiwear to prom gowns, trendy to purest Ivy League. You'll also find gifts, fine china, crystal, furniture and home accessories (check out the exquisite imported ceramics) at **Hoagland's of Greenwich**. Closed Sunday. ~ 175 Greenwich Avenue, Greenwich; 203-869-2127.

SHOPPING

Fairfield County is a shopper's dream come true. Most of the shoreline towns, as well as several major cities, offer such a variety of consumer experiences that people come from far and wide to browse and buy.

In Stamford, now a mini-metropolis, you can find stylish, established department stores such as **Lord and Taylor**. ~ 110 High Ridge Road, Stamford; 203-327-6600.

Another choice is the Cadillac of downtown shopping malls, the seven-level **Stamford Town Center**, which is anchored by **Macy's** (203-964-1500), **Saks Fifth Avenue** (203-323-3100) and **Filene's** (203-357-7373). What more could one wish? Well, there are chic European shops like **Burberry** (203-325-1450); prestigious American labels such as **Abercrombie and Fitch** (203-327-4840); **F.A.O. Schwarz** (203-324-1643) for the finest in toys; even a branch of **New York's Metropolitan Museum of Art Shop** (203-978-0554)—all connected by high-tech escalators and glass-enclosed elevators and serviced by a mammoth parking garage. ~ 100 Greyrock Place, Stamford.

Stamford is also home to a one-of-a-kind shopping experience: **United House Wrecking**. This huge store sells the salvaged remains of demolitions and estate sales—antiques, architectural items, and old lighting and plumbing fixtures. ~ 535 Hope Street, Stamford; 203-348-5371.

Washington Street, the heart of South Norwalk's historic district, is great for browsing through a potpourri of small shops and boutiques devoted to home furnishings, both yesterday's and today's, quirky clothing, jewelry, high-tech lighting fixtures and French ceramics. If stringing beads is something you always wanted to try, **Beadworks** will show you how and sell you all the necessary materials. Beadwork classes are also offered. ~ 139 Washington Street, South Norwalk; 203-852-9194.

For an outlet mall experience, try **The Factory Outlets at Norwalk**, a former hat mill now devoted to 26 stores bursting with designer clothes, shoes and accessories for men, women and children, as well as linens, luggage and gifts. ~ 230 East Avenue, Norwalk; 203-845-8880.

Other discount outlets are located up and down nearby West Avenue, including **Loehmann's**, the grandmother of all off-price designer clothing stores. ~ 467 West Avenue, Norwalk; 203-866-2548.

You can't leave Norwalk without a trip to **Stew Leonard's**, say its fans. "The World's Largest Dairy Store" is a near-supermarket with Disneyland overtones, where bigger-than-lifesize animated displays—cows, dogs, giant milk cartons—sing for your children's pleasure, if not yours. Its success is now legendary, largely because dairy products, meat, fish, fruit, veggies, baked goods and ready-cooked foods are super fresh and reasonably priced. ~ 100 Westport Avenue, Norwalk; 203-847-7214, 800-729-7839.

Back to more traditional shopping: a stroll downtown in Greenwich or in Westport provides a mall's worth of attractive shops and boutiques. On Westport's short but lively Main Street you'll find predictable fashion names like **Ann Taylor** and **Banana Republic**. The street has been called "A Mall without Walls."

Behind Klein's office supply and camera store you'll spot **Uproar Home**, one of Westport's hippest retailers. You'll find a fabulous selection of home furnishings, from small accessories (such as candles and pillows) to oversized couches, flop-into chairs and other furniture. ~ 36 Elm Street, Westport; 203-221-9210.

Westport is also home to **Save the Children**, where you can find all sorts of gifts—pottery, musical instruments, jewelry and neckties designed by kids around the world. Closed Sunday. ~ 54 Wilton Road, Westport; 203-221-4206.

Westport has several children's clothing stores, including **Gymboree** (51 Main Street; 203-226-8337), **Blessings** (closed Sunday from Memorial Day to Labor Day; 1864 Post Road East; 203-255-1122) and **Kidswear** (closed Sunday from Memorial Day to Labor Day; 1045 Post Road East; 203-454-1818), where local Westporters attire their sprouts in the latest, chic-est fashions.

Antique shops are ubiquitous in Fairfield County, as they are everywhere in the state. An extensive list of Connecticut's antique dealers is available from the Connecticut Department of Economic Development. ~ 505 Hudson Street, Hartford, CT 06106; 860-270-8080, fax 860-270-8077; www.ctbound.org.

One of the most attractive spots for viewing yesterday's treasures is **Cannondale Village**, a 19th-century New England village. In the handful of small, picturesque buildings you'll also find an art gallery, gifts, dried floral arrangements, glassware, furniture, antiques and a tiny restaurant in an old schoolhouse. Closed Monday. ~ 30 Cannon Road, just off Route 7, Wilton; 203-762-3432.

Across the way is **St. Benedict Guild**, a cross-cultural shop selling clothing, jewelry and artifacts from around the world. Closed Monday. ~ Cannondale Depot, 22 Cannon Road, Wilton; 203-762-3633.

There are also quite a few consignment stores in Fairfield County, especially on the Post Road, between Greenwich and Southport.

Another in the state's collection of oversized emporiums is **Danbury Fair Mall**. It's huge and glitzy, boasting **Macy's** (203-731-3500), **Filene's** (203-790-4000), a food court and a gaily painted carousel, in memory of the days when this vast site was the beloved Danbury Fairgrounds. ~ 7 Backus Avenue, Danbury.

NIGHTLIFE

The **Stamford Center for the Arts**, which houses the Palace Theater and the Rich Forum, presents a dazzling potpourri: classical music, jazz, folk, musical theater, dance, all performed by nationally known artists on tour. ~ 307 Atlantic Street, Stamford; 203-325-4466.

A cozy night spot called **Brennan's Restaurant** includes a pub and an outdoor patio. On Friday night they feature live R&B. ~ 82 Iroquois Road, Stamford; 203-323-1787.

For music and dancing, follow the crowds to **Shenanigan's**. There's live entertainment every night except Monday and Tuesday. This rustic brick-and-wood dance hall, located in a historic building, offers classic rock-and-roll, R&B and occasional headliners like Bo Diddley and Bonnie Raitt. Cover Thursday through Sunday. ~ 80 Washington Street, South Norwalk; 203-853-0142.

John Harvard's Brew House is a restaurant/pub that attracts well-heeled beer-drinking partiers nightly. The brews on tap change seasonally. Bands play occasionally. ~ 540 Riverside Avenue, Westport; 203-454-2337.

Nearby is **The Black Duck Café**, which has been a magnet for the beer-and-burger crowd since 1978. Located in a barge right on the Saugatuck River, this somewhat cramped bar is famed for its karaoke nights on Monday and Tuesday. ~ 605 Riverside Avenue, Westport; 203-227-7978.

The Cedarbrook Cafe is a popular gay spot with periodic cabaret shows. Downstairs is a disco with dancefloor and loud deejay music, while upstairs is more conducive to quiet conversation and socializing. Gay-friendly. ~ 919 Post Road East, Westport; 203-221-7429.

Downtown Cabaret Theater varies the formula by encouraging patrons to bring along their own picnic. Special children's

Text continued on page 60.

American Indian Connecticut

Connecticut's pre-Columbian inhabitants were a tribe of Algonkian Indians known as the Pequot (the name means "destroyers"). Soon after white settlers arrived in the 1630s, smallpox decimated the tribe, reducing their number from 10,000 to 3000. In 1637, Puritans from Massachusetts declared war on the Pequot, killing more than half the tribe. Most of the survivors were sent to the West Indies as slaves, some were given to New England settlers as "servants," and still others were given to the neighboring Mohegan people, who mistreated them so badly that in 1655 the British gave the Pequot their own reservation. By then, their numbers had declined to 140—about the same as today.

Although New England's American Indian heritage is evident in tongue-twisting place names all over the region, just a few years ago it would have been easy to believe that the native people had vanished and been forgotten. Recently, however, two museums have opened on opposite sides of Connecticut to educate locals and visitors alike about the estimated 60,000 people who lived in New England before the first Europeans arrived.

The **American Indian Archaeological Institute** in the Litchfield Hills contains an authentically reproduced Algonkian village that shows the various types of shelters—wigwams, longhouses and rock shelters—used by Connecticut's native people and illustrates how corn, beans and squash were grown. There's also a simulated archaeological site presenting how archaeologists excavate such sites in Connecticut fields today, as well as a museum of woodsplint baskets, bone combs, pots, art and artifacts from 10,000 years of Algonkian habitation. Native artists and craftspeople offer frequent demonstrations, workshops and storytelling performances. Admission. ~ Curtis Road, Washington; 203-868-0518.

On the Pequot Indian Reservation near Mystic, the **Mashantucket Pequot Museum** has a more elaborate full-size reproduction of a 16th-century village, complete with lifelike human figures and sound stations that describe what life in the community must have been like. Other exhibits at this $130 million tribal museum include simulations of an Ice Age glacier cave and caribou hunt and a gathering space in the cedar swamp where Pequot refugees hid from British soldiers' campaign to exterminate the tribe in the 1630s. The museum also conducts tours of five archaeological sites on the reservation every Tuesday in August and Thursday and Saturday in September. Admission ~ 110 Pequot Trail, Foxwoods; 860-396-6981, 800-411-9671.

The most visible symbol of Indian presence in Connecticut is **Foxwoods**, the controversial site of a modern-day economic miracle. Only two elderly half-sisters lived on a 214-acre remnant of the Pequot Reservation in the 1970s, and it was feared that with their deaths the tribe would cease to exist and its land be forfeited to the state. Indian rights activist Amos George sought out all of the 55 tribal members living and working in New England, and led them in reorganizing the tribe, adopting a new constitution, and filing a successful land claim suit to regain 5000 acres of land that had been taken from the tribe.

In 1992, when the federal government recognized Indian tribes' right to operate gaming casinos, the Mashantucket Pequots were quick to open the original Foxwoods Casino and High Stakes Bingo Parlor. This coincided with federal defense cutbacks that brought massive unemployment to the shipyards of nearby Mystic, making state and local government officials amenable to an ambitious expansion plan for Foxwoods. Today, **Foxwoods Resort Casino** has grown to be the largest casino on earth, with over 4500 slot machines, 233 table games, 75 poker tables and the most technologically advanced sports book in the country, as well as a 1416-room hotel and the Cinetropolis entertainment complex featuring a 360-degree wraparound movie theater, virtual thrill rides, a state-of-the-art game arcade and a high-tech dance club. ~ Route 2, Ledyard; 860-312-3000; www.foxwoods.com.

Though it still has fewer than 100 members, the Mashantucket Pequot tribe is now the largest employer in Connecticut, with more than 12,000 employees and an annual payroll of more than $300 million. Under its revenue-sharing agreement, the casino pays more than $150 million a year to state government and has made multimillion-dollar donations to the Mystic Marine Life Aquarium, the Special Olympics World Games and the Smithsonian Institution's National Museum of the American Indian.

shows are staged on weekends during the school year. ~ 263 Golden Hill Street, Bridgeport; 203-576-1636.

In tiny Georgetown, the unpretentious **Georgetown Saloon** has an acoustic set on Thursday, rock-and-roll and R&B on Friday, country on Saturday, and "family music" on Sunday. On Wednesday from July through September, they feature a Southern pig roast. Cover on Friday and Saturday. ~ 8 Main Street, Georgetown; 203-544-8003.

Ives Concert Park presents an outdoor music festival during the summer that caters to most preferences: classical, pops, jazz, country and classic rock. Closed Labor Day through May. ~ West Side Campus, Western Connecticut State University, Danbury; 203-837-9226.

BEACHES & PARKS

SHERWOOD ISLAND STATE PARK 🏃 🚴 🏊 🐟 🛶 One and a half miles of wide, sandy beach front the calm waters of Long Island Sound, with the coast of Long Island visible on a clear day. Behind the beach are extensive open fields and groves of maples and oaks that shelter picnic tables. Birding is good here; two breakwaters offer fine saltwater fishing for bluefish, striped bass and blackfish. Facilities include a nature center, a pavilion with food concession stands, restrooms, bathhouses and lifeguards (in summer only). Day-use fee (charged weekends only in May and September, daily from Memorial Day to Labor Day), $5 to $12. ~ Exit 18 off Route 95 in Westport; 203-226-6983.

PUTNAM MEMORIAL STATE PARK 🏃 🚴 🎣 🏛 This 183-acre park was the site of the Continental Army's 1776 winter encampment, under the command of General Israel Putnam. Remains of the encampment can be viewed, as well as reconstructed log buildings. A historical museum is open on weekends and holidays from Memorial Day to Labor Day. Hiking trails fan out into the woods; the pond is suitable for fishing and ice skating. There's a picnic area, swings, horseshoe pits and a historical site. ~ Three miles south of Bethel on Route 58; 203-938-2285.

▼▼▼▼▼▼▼▼▼▼▼▼▼▼
Northwest Corner

The northwestern corner of Connecticut is New England, just as you pictured it. There are big old white churches, Colonial houses, covered bridges, stone walls, winding roads and woods all around. To top it all off, there are quite a few fine restaurants, historic inns and an abundance of small shops and galleries. Litchfield County encompasses most of the area and is home to dozens of small villages, including one by the same name.

From southern points the Litchfield area—often referred to as the Litchfield Hills—can be reached by taking Route 684 to

Route 84 east and then following Route 7 north (Exit 7) to New
Milford, or by taking Route 684 north to Route 22 and crossing
over the state line on Route 55, heading into Gaylordsville.

Just north of New Milford, the road turns into a shunpiker's **SIGHTS**
dream, a gentle rollercoaster with views of fields and streams and
vintage houses. Just before Kent, stop at **Bull's Bridge**, one of two
covered bridges in the state that cars can drive through—a most
picturesque spot. Washington crossed it in March 1781, and it's
said that one of his horses fell into the freezing Housatonic River
and had to be pulled out.

The town of Kent boasts the **Sloane-Stanley Museum**, which
contains Early American farm and woodworking tools collected
by Eric Sloane, artist and writer, as well as some of his own oil
paintings. The grounds include the ruins of Kent Iron Furnace,
one of many used for smelting the iron ore that was the mainstay of the northwest corner from the mid-18th century until the
close of the next. Closed Monday and Tuesday and from November to mid-May. Admission. ~ Route 7, Kent; 860-927-3849.

A few miles later, on the right of the road, the 250-foot cascade of **Kent Falls** dominates an attractive state park (see the
"Beaches & Parks" section below).

Then the road splits: Route 45 goes south to **Lake Waramaug**,
a zigzagged, three-mile long body of water that has drawn visitors since the mid-1800s—by train back then. Drive all around
it: the hilly, wooded shores shelter several inns, a state park and
—surprise!—**Hopkins Vineyard**, with a winery housed in a restored 19th-century barn, where you can taste and buy both wines
and various gourmet items. Since the late 1970s, even as dairy
farms have gradually disappeared from the landscape, vineyards
have sprung up, half a dozen at least and more to come. Closed
Monday through Thursday in January and February, and Monday
and Tuesday in March and April. ~ 25 Hopkins Road, New
Preston; 860-868-7954; www.hopkinsvineyard.com.

From Lake Waramaug it's a short drive to **Washington**, a pristine, white hilltop residential village built around a church. Less
than two miles from there, on Route 199, is the **Institute for American Indian Studies**, with excellent exhibits, including a habitat
trail, a simulated archeological site and an outdoor Indian village
—a good way to learn about the region's earliest dwellers. Closed
Monday and Tuesday from January through March. Admission.
~ 38 Curtis Road, Washington; 860-868-0518; www.amerindian.
institute.org.

Litchfield is the most visited spot in the northwest corner, and
its spare, graceful **Congregational Church**, built in 1828, rates
among the finest in New England and is a popular photo subject. ~ Junction of Routes 202 and 118, Litchfield.

Shooting the Litchfield Hills

With its incomparable maze of two-lane highways winding through hundreds of quaint villages and Colonial towns, the possibilities for driving excursions in Connecticut are virtually limitless. Designed especially for travelers seeking to capture a cross-section of classic New England scenes on film, this all-day, 95-mile meander through the Litchfield Hills offers maximum country charm per mile.

LITCHFIELD   Start your tour at Litchfield (page 61), one of New England's best-preserved historic towns, where the **Litchfield Congregational Church** is one of the region's most photographed churches. Nearby **White Flower Farm** (page 64) and **Topsmead State Forest** (page 74) offer great floral shots any time during the summer months.

NORFOLK   From Litchfield, head north on Route 63 for six miles to the village of Goshen, turn east (right) onto Route 4, go about one and a half miles and turn north (left) onto East Street North. This idyllic country lane joins Route 272 at South Norfolk, taking you to **Dennis Hill State Park** (page 65), with one of the best panoramic views in Connecticut from its summit, and to adjacent **Hillside Gardens** (page 65), ablaze with color. In Norfolk (page 65), stately architecture—the Yale School of Music White House, the Norfolk Library (c. 1889), the Norfolk Academy (c. 1840) and the Church of Christ (c. 1814)—surrounds the village green.

SALISBURY   From Norfolk, drive west on Route 44 for half a mile and turn south (left) on Westside Road. At the first stop sign, turn west (right) onto Mountain Road, which takes you past pretty **Wagnum Lake**. Bear left at the fork in the road, then take a right onto Under Mountain Road. Time seems to have bypassed these pastoral farm roads, which take you in about ten miles to Route 7. Turn north (right) and drive three miles on Route 7, then take a sharp left onto Sand Road to continue your sce-

The **Litchfield Historical Society Museum**, which owns a fine selection of 18th-century portraits, houses items of the town's past and present. Closed Monday and from mid-November to mid-April. Admission to the museum also admits you into the Tapping Reeve House and Law School. ~ Located on the corner of East and South streets, Litchfield; 860-567-4501.

Litchfield is home to America's first law school, **Tapping Reeve House and Law School**, founded in 1784 and now an interactive interpretive museum that re-creates the environment of an 18thnic backroad detour. At the first fork in the road, bear right onto Boinay Hill Road, which leads to Route 44. Turn southwest (left) and continue seven miles to **Salisbury Center**, where you'll find another picture-perfect village green flanked by an old academy building, a library, and a Congregational Church (c. 1800) topped by a unique whale weathervane. The Appalachian Trail runs through town, and a hike of less than a mile takes you to the 2010-foot summit of **Bald Peak** for a spectacular 360-degree panoramic view.

CORNWALL   Continue southwest for four miles on Route 44 through Lakeville and past scenic **Wononskopomuc Lake**, turning east (left) onto Route 112 for some of the best landscape views in the Litchfield Hills. At the end of the road, turn south (right) on Route 7, which follows the twists and turns of the Housatonic River, a favorite of canoers and kayakers, to **West Cornwall** (page 64), site of Connecticut's most photogenic covered bridge. Continuing south on Route 7 takes you past **Housatanic Meadows State Park** (page 75) and to **Kent Falls State Park** (page 73), where you'll find a spectacular 200-foot waterfall.

LAKE WARAMAUG   Route 7 intersects Route 341 in Kent. Turn east (left) and follow Route 341 for eight miles to the turnoff to **Lake Waramaug** (page 61). The road goes completely around the lake; we suggest you follow the south shore through **Lake Waramaug State Park** (pages 73–74) and **Mount Bushnell State Park**, turning north (left) on Route 45 at the south tip of the lake. Driving north for five miles, turn east (right) and you're back on Route 341. Just past Woodville, **Mount Tom State Park**'s Tower Trail offers another succession of great vistas. Another seven miles on Route 341 and you're back in Litchfield, where you may wish to climax your visual adventure with a visit to **White Memorial Foundation** (page 64), the state's largest nature center and wildlife sanctuary.

century law student. Closed Monday and from mid-November to mid-April. Admission. ~ 82 South Street, Route 63 South, Litchfield; 860-567-4501.

For a touring map and information on events throughout the county, stop at the seasonal booth (open mid-June to mid-October) on Route 20 maintained on the green by the **Litchfield Hills Visitors Bureau.** ~ P.O. Box 968, Litchfield, CT 06759; 860-567-4506; www.litchfieldhills.com.

Despite its palpable concern for the past, Litchfield is very much alive and offers a variety of attractions, such as **Haight Vineyard and Winery**, with winery tours, tastings and vineyard walks. ~ 29 Chestnut Hill Road, off Route 118, one mile east of Litchfield; 860-567-4045.

Another worthwhile stop is **White Flower Farm**, a nationally known nursery with five acres of display gardens and thirty of growing fields. ~ Route 63, three miles south of Litchfield; 860-567-8789; www.whiteflowerfarm.com.

White Memorial Foundation & Conservation Center, the state's largest nature center and wildlife sanctuary, is an ideal place for lovers of the outdoors. This 4000-acre preserve has a nature museum (admission), gift shop and 35 miles of hiking trails. ~ 80 White Hall Road; 860-567-0857.

In Bristol, southeast of Litchfield, is the **American Clock & Watch Museum**, whose more than 3000 timepieces are displayed in an 1801 house. There is also a sundial garden and museum shop. Closed December through March. Admission. ~ 100 Maple Street, off Route 6, Bristol; 860-583-6070; guest.ccsu.edu/acwm.

In nearby Waterbury, the **Mattatuck Museum** exhibits artifacts such as clocks, novelty watches, art deco tableware and some of the buttons locally produced in this former "brass capital of the world." You can also visit a historic brass mill and a 19th-century boarding house highlighting immigrant memories, or peruse the galleries showcasing 18th-century furniture and American masters who have been associated with Connecticut. Closed Monday year-round, closed Sunday in July and August. ~ 144 West Main Street, Waterbury; 203-753-0381; www.mattatuckmuseum.org.

After enjoying the museum take the self-guided walking tour of the historic downtown district. Many buildings have been renovated thanks to the combined efforts of preservationists and developers. For further information about the Waterbury area, contact the **Waterbury Region Convention and Visitors Bureau**. Also available are self-guided tours of nine other historic towns in the area. Closed Saturday and Sunday. ~ 21 Church Street, Waterbury; 203-597-9527, fax 203-597-8452; www.wrcvb.org, e-mail wrcvb@aol.com.

There's no way to see all the picturesque little towns around these parts, but you should sample the northernmost ones, such as Norfolk, surrounded by mountains and state parks. Along the way, if you go by Route 7, you'll pass the much-photographed **covered bridge** at West Cornwall and the attractive cluster of homes and shops by its side. This section of the Housatonic River is much favored by devotees of kayaks and canoes, which can be rented both here and in **Falls Village**, a few miles to the north.

The **falls** in that town's name are channeled to provide electric power part of the year. In spring you have but to cross the bridge in the middle of town and you'll be rewarded by a dramatic rush of water to rival far more celebrated ones.

◄ HIDDEN

Alternatively, you could opt to drive north via the picturesque towns of Sharon, Lakeville and Salisbury, passing, along the way, some of the richest, most scenic farmland in the state. Either way, when you get to Canaan, just south of the Massachusetts line, stop by to see the unique **Union Station and Depot**, built in 1872 with two wings at right angles to each other, to service the two railroads that used to come this way. In our near-trainless times, the building houses office space and a restaurant. ~ Route 44, center of Canaan.

Heading east along the swift Blackberry River, Route 44 takes you to tiny, serene **Norfolk**. Affluent families have maintained summer homes in this town since the 1880s, drawn by the cool mountain air and by the much-acclaimed **Chamber Music Festival**, held each year from June to August. Bring a picnic dinner and enjoy the grounds before the Friday- and Saturday-night concerts at the Ellen Battell Stoeckel Estate. ~ Routes 44 and 272, Norfolk; 860-542-3000; www.yale.edu/norfolk.

Hillside Gardens, a display garden of perennial flowers with a retail nursery at the home of Frederick and Mary Ann McGourty, is one of the few private residential gardens in America open to visitors on a regular basis. Fred started gardening the five stone-walled acres of this 1780s farmstead on weekends in 1963 while commuting to New York, where he worked as editor of the *Brooklyn Botanic Garden* handbook series. Careful attention has been given to plant combinations that yield a continuous succession of color-coordinated blooms from May to mid-September, with a peak in late July, drawing many horticulture enthusiasts back time after time over the summer months. Visitors can picnic at adjacent **Dennis Hill State Park**, which offers one of Connecticut's finest views. Open daily in season except holidays. ~ 515 Litchfield Road, Norfolk; 860-542-5345.

◄ HIDDEN

From here you can drive to several mountains with stunning views. You have to be on foot to appreciate Norfolk's exquisite green (Route 44), embellished by a fountain designed by Stanford White, eminent architect of the Gilded Age, and surrounded by graceful homes and the Congregational Church, built in 1813.

Each of the inns studded around serpentine Lake Waramaug has a distinct personality, and its own dedicated fans. Here's a selection:

LODGING

More cost-conscious travelers wishing to stay near the lake, yet who loathe roughing it at Lake Waramaug State Park, will find four quiet bed-and-breakfast rooms about a mile up the hill at

Constitution Oak Farm. It's a rambling 1830s farmhouse over-looking ten acres of corn, and its name comes from a majestic oak tree said to descend from the legendary one in which Connecti-cut's Colonial charter was concealed. Two downstairs rooms have baths; the two on the second floor share. Breakfast is in the guests' own living room. The owner collects many and sundry things—a boon to some, but irksome to those who dislike clutter. ~ 36 Beardsley Road, Kent; 860-354-6495, fax 860-354-0861. BUDGET.

Boulders Inn offers 17 rooms, six in the picturesque, turn-of-the-20th-century main house, three in the carriage house and the rest in individual guest houses, all of which are set in the hill that rises immediately behind the inn. The rooms are decorated with flair: those in the stone-and-shingle main house have antique fur-niture and quilts; the carriage-house rooms have antiques and stone fireplaces, while most of the guest houses boast freestand-ing fireplaces. There's hiking on wooded trails and a small private beach with boats for the guests' use. ~ Route 45, New Preston; 860-868-0541, 800-552-6853, fax 860-868-1925; www.boulders inn.com. ULTRA-DELUXE.

The **Hopkins Inn** was named for the family who settled the northern shore of the lake in 1847, built a great rambling clap-board home and took in lodgers who came up from the city in the summer. Today, the graceful yellow bed-and-breakfast inn is best known for its restaurant, but it does rent eleven rooms and two apartments (that sleep up to four) on the second and third floors. The rooms are bright, with country antiques and Colonial-style wallpaper—comfortable, not dramatic. Two share a bath, the others have their own, with old-fashioned tub or stall shower. Downstairs, a shaded terrace high over the lake affords spectac-ular views. The adjoining hillside is owned by Hopkins Vineyards, where visitors can taste and purchase locally produced wines. ~ 22 Hopkins Road, New Preston; 860-868-7295, fax 860-868-7464. MODERATE.

LITCHFIELD'S LEGACY

Litchfield is as prosperous a town today as it was as an outpost and trading center; and, happily, it still centers on the handsome green that was laid out in the 1770s. The wide, maple-lined streets are edged with homes of un-usual distinction, boasting past residents such as Aaron Burr, Ethan Allen and Harriet Beecher Stowe. Burr lived with his brother-in-law, Tapping Reeve; Allen was born on Old South Road, in a small privately owned house; the site on North Street where Stowe was born bears a marker—the house itself was moved some years ago.

The **Lakeview Inn** has been in operation since 1876, when the first tourists arrived at Lake Waramaug and farmer Ben Norris transformed his century-old farmhouse into a boarding house for them. In 1998, local chefs Dorothy and Doug Hamilton bought the inn and renovated it, reducing the number of guest units to five spacious rooms and suites, each individually decorated in a distinctive color scheme and furnished with antiques; all have private baths. A broad sundeck overlooks the lake and a vast expanse of parklike lawn with shade trees. Breakfast and dinner, personally prepared by internationally renowned chef William Lopata, are included in the rates and are among the best parts of a stay here. Two-night minimum stay on weekends. ~ 107 North Shore Road, New Preston; 860-868-1000, fax 860-868-2595; e-mail info@thelakeviewinn.com. ULTRA-DELUXE.

Atha House, a cozy Cape Cod–style home, is convenient to galleries and antique stores. This bed and breakfast has three rooms looking out on a big garden with evergreen, silver birch and dogwood trees as well as a Connecticut stone fence. There's a fireplace and piano in the living room. Dogs can be accommodated. ~ Wheaton Road, New Preston; phone/fax 860-355-7387. MODERATE.

The small village of Washington is home to one of the state's most exquisite inns. The **Mayflower Inn** has 25 lavishly decorated guest rooms filled with English and American antiques from the 18th and 19th centuries, some with four-poster, king-sized canopy beds. All rooms overlook the surrounding gardens and hills. The inn is a Relais & Chateaux property set on 28 acres of lawns and woods, with hiking trails, an outdoor heated pool, a tennis court and a fitness center. The service is bend-over-backwards accommodating. ~ Route 47, Washington; 860-868-9466, fax 860-868-1497; www.mayflowerinn.com. ULTRA-DELUXE.

For visitors who prefer to stay in Litchfield, the area's most visited town, there's a choice of two inns, one old, one new but Colonial in feeling. The **Litchfield Inn**, built circa 1980, works hard at being graciously New England even as it highlights facilities for weddings, conferences and banquets. Its 32 rooms are spacious and well-appointed, with elegant bathrooms. Two units even have a dry bar. A continental breakfast is provided, and there's an elevator—a rare commodity among country inns. ~ Route 202, Litchfield; 860-567-4503, 800-499-3444, fax 860-567-5358; www.litchfieldinnct.com. DELUXE TO ULTRA-DELUXE.

Tollgate Hill Inn, built in 1745, is listed on the National Register of Historic Places as The Captain William Bull Tavern. As befits a tavern, you enter through the bar, and you can feel the pride of place in the fine way paneling and fireplaces have been restored. There's a top-rated restaurant. The 20 bedrooms are stylishly decorated with four-poster and canopied beds, authentic wallpapers and antique tables and chests. Continental breakfast. ~ Route 202, Litchfield; 860-567-4545, 800-445-3903, fax 860-567-8397. DELUXE.

The **Blackberry River Inn**, built in 1763, is also listed on the National Register of Historic Places. Situated on 27 acres in the woodsy Litchfield Hills and complete with its own pool and tennis courts, the inn offers 20 guest rooms, some in the handsome, two-story main building, others in the adjoining carriage house, and a cottage. Most rooms have their own bath, with an occasional clawfoot tub; a few share. The spacious public rooms are comfortable and pleasing to the eye. Complimentary breakfast is served in an attractive dining room. ~ Route 44, Norfolk; 860-542-5100, 800-414-3636, fax 860-542-1763; www.blackberry riverinn.com. MODERATE TO ULTRA-DELUXE.

A bed and breakfast furnished with antiques, **Greenwood's Gate** is a beautifully restored 1797 Colonial home. Each of the four deluxe suites has a luxury bathroom, bedroom and sitting room. Relax in the living room in front of the fireplace or lounge in the library with a book. Full gourmet breakfast. ~ 105 Greenwoods Road East, Norfolk; 860-542-5439; www.greenwoods gate.com. ULTRA-DELUXE.

Just down the road is **Angel Hill Bed & Breakfast**, a two-room two-suite 1880 Victorian inn with a separate carriage house that sleeps up to four. Set on eight acres, it's a five-minute walk from the village with its restaurants, antique shops and museum. Each room is beautifully decorated with antiques and supplied with robes, candles, and picnic baskets to borrow. ~ 54 Greenwoods Road East, Norfolk; 860-542-5920; www.angelhill.com. DELUXE TO ULTRA-DELUXE.

Manor House is a sumptuous bed and breakfast, an 1898 Tudor-inspired Victorian mansion with windows designed by Louis Tiffany, a family friend. Up the handsome, carved cherry wood staircase, nine guest rooms—all with private bath, some with balcony and fireplace—have been done to a turn in period elegance. Two rooms have private jacuzzis. There's even vintage clothing hung here and there, for decoration. A classy touch: breakfast—a very hearty one—can be served in the room, even in bed. ~ 69 Maple Avenue, Norfolk; phone/fax 860-542-5690; www.manorhouse-norfolk.com. MODERATE TO ULTRA-DELUXE.

In Salisbury, which is west of Falls Village and very close to the New York border, is **The White Hart**. This carefully renovated three-story inn began operating in the early 19th century. Furnishings throughout include antiques and Chippendale reproductions. The 26 guest rooms are decorated in Early American style, some with four-poster beds. In winter guests can warm up in front of the fireplace in the Hunt Room, which features dark wood paneling and overstuffed leather couches; in summer the large front porch with wicker furniture is inviting. ~ Village Green at Routes 41 and 44, Salisbury; 860-435-0030, 800-832-0041, fax 860-435-0040; www.whitehartinn.com. DELUXE.

Nearby you'll find **The Under Mountain Inn**, which is housed in an 18th-century farmhouse. A true inn, both breakfast and dinner are included in the tab. The seven guest rooms are named after famous sites in England, the owner's homeland. The Covent Garden room has a Shaker canopy bed and a cast-iron tub; Buckingham Gate is a large, sunny corner room with one king-size canopy bed. One of the two libraries is stocked with books and videos on England, and the pub offers English ales. Breakfast alternates between English and American fare. Dinner features dishes such as steak-and-kidney pie and bread-and-butter pudding as well as American choices. Two-night minimum; three-night minimum in October. ~ 482 Under Mountain Road, Salisbury; 860-435-0242, fax 860-435-2379. ULTRA-DELUXE.

DINING

Le Bon Coin serves French entrées such as dover sole Riviera, sweetbreads with various garnishes, and seasonal game. Located in a Cape Cod–style house, the two small dining rooms are decorated with impressionist paintings à la Toulouse-Lautrec. Closed Tuesday and Wednesday. ~ Route 202, New Preston; 860-868-7763. MODERATE TO DELUXE.

Each of the several inns around Lake Waramaug has its followers, who proclaim it the best. The **Hopkins Inn**, a rambling, many-windowed mid-19th-century house, boasts a unique location, high on a hill overlooking sparkling blue water. On a warm day, sitting under the ancient trees on the terrace would be reason enough for deep content, but the eclectic Continental menu casts its own spell. Austrian and Swiss traditions are emphasized; *wienerschnitzel* is a perennial favorite, as is trout, live from the inn's own tank, prepared *à la meunière* or *bleu*, the Swiss way. Closed Monday and January through March. ~ 22 Hopkins Road, New Preston; 860-868-7295. DELUXE.

The **Lakeview Inn** is a great choice for lunch or dinner, served daily except Tuesday in an antique-furnished sunroom or on the terrace looking out over the lake. The menu, which changes seasonally, focuses on fresh local produce and seafood. Lunch items tend to be inventive, like the wild mushroom and raclette cheese strudel with roasted red peppers and parsnip sauce, served with mixed greens and brown basmati–wild rice, while dinner features more traditional New England fare such as steamed or broiled Maine lobster from the inn's saltwater tank, served with cole slaw, corn on the cob and new potatoes. Each dish is impeccably prepared and presented, as you might expect at this inn run by the owners of Manhattan's prestigious French Culinary Institute. ~

107 North Shore Road, New Preston; 860-868-1000; e-mail info @thelakeviewinn.com. MODERATE TO ULTRA-DELUXE.

Several area places feature both lunch and take-out foods—a pleasant thought on days that call for a picnic. **The Pantry**, which doubles as a cookware shop and small restaurant, serves well-prepared entrées such as ham-and-leek quiche and shrimp-and-goat cheese pizza as part of their ever-changing menu, as well as homemade soups, salads and desserts. Closed Sunday and Monday. ~ Titus Square, Washington Depot; 860-868-0258, fax 860-868-1523. BUDGET TO MODERATE.

The **Mayflower Inn** offers guests and passersby a highly respected restaurant. The cuisine is Continental with a Northeast accent. The salmon is hand smoked and the bacon is home cured. Dine in the garden room adorned with tapestries and feast on specialties like grilled veal with wild-mushroom sauce. Although the decor and food are elegant, dress is informal. ~ Route 47, Washington; 860-868-9466. DELUXE TO ULTRA-DELUXE.

Food doesn't come more traditionally English on this side of the pond than at **G. W. Tavern**, where specialties include fish and chips, roast beef with Yorkshire pudding, and chicken pot pie. The tone of this Colonial-style restaurant is set by a fieldstone fireplace and a large landscape mural. In the summer, food is served on an open-air terrace overlooking the Shepaug River. ~ 21 Bee Brook Road, Washington; 860-868-6633. BUDGET TO MODERATE.

In nearby Woodbury, feast on great food and enjoy great art at **Carole Peck's Good News Cafe & Gallery**. Works by nationally and internationally recognized artists are showcased throughout the restaurant (the exhibitions change every two months). Owned by Carole Peck, who is considered one of the best chefs in the United States, the changing menu includes creative dishes like a crisp risotto cake on a platter of roasted seasonal vegetables. Always on the menu are wok-seared shrimp with green beans, peas, olives, potatoes and garlic aioli and a grilled New York strip steak with mashed potato and crispy onion bundle. Closed Tuesday. ~ 694 Main Street South, Woodbury; 203-266-4663. MODERATE TO ULTRA-DELUXE.

Tollgate Hill Inn is a 1745 tavern restored as an inn in admirably authentic fashion. Two intimate ground-floor dining rooms are most attractive, with dark, wide floor boards and paneling and just a few handsome antiques. Upstairs, the ballroom with its fieldstone fireplace and fiddlers' loft is used for Saturday dinner and Sunday brunch. Meals feature American cuisine with European touches, including many unusual seafood entrées. Closed Tuesday. ~ Route 202, Litchfield; 860-567-4545. DELUXE.

The **West Street Grill** is a good place to people-watch as well as feast on contemporary American dishes. Start with the specialty of the house—peasant bread with parmesan aioli—then move on to the sautéed diver sea scallops with potato shallot cake and wilted watercress in an orange and brown butter sauce, or the pan-flashed Asian shrimp patties served with baby greens and three dipping sauces. The decor is country elegant, with earth tones, terra cotta and wood floors. Closed Tuesday. ~ 43 West Street, Litchfield; 860-567-3885. MODERATE TO DELUXE.

The Bistro East at the Litchfield Inn serves New American cuisine in a country inn atmosphere. Grilled gorgonzola-crusted New York strip steak, truffle-crusted Arctic sea bass and pan-seared pork tenderloin with fresh cranberries and shiitake mushrooms in a bourbon sauce are a few of the specialities. There's always a pasta dish and a variety of fresh fish offerings. ~ 432 Bantam Road, Litchfield; 860-567-9040, 800-499-3444, fax 860-567-0387. MODERATE TO DELUXE.

Set on the shore of Bantam Lake, shaded by woods that dwarf the classic white wayside inn with its towering cupola, **Deer Island Gate Restaurant** specializes in German fare. *Weinerschnitzel, jaegerschnitzel* and sauerbraten share the menu with steak and fresh seafood. Dining here is a special adventure on Sunday, when a German buffet brunch is featured in addition to the regular menu. ~ Route 209, Morris; 860-567-4622. MODERATE TO DELUXE.

Right on Main Street in the historic little town of Salisbury, you'll find the **Ragamont Inn**, where you can dine on a sheltered terrace or in one of two dining rooms. The Swiss-inspired cuisine features veal dishes, with *wienerschnitzel* gaining the most requests. Homemade pasta is another specialty: black pepper fettuccine is one of the chef's creations, served with scallops or shrimp. Closed Monday and Tuesday and November through May. ~ 8 East Main Street, Salisbury; 860-435-2372. MODERATE TO DELUXE.

A welcome addition to good eating at the northernmost edge of the state is **The Cannery Café**, an informal American bistro. Specialties are grilled portobella mushroom salad and eggplant-and-walnut ravioli. Or try the fresh fish, grilled shrimp or pasta. Closed Tuesday year-round and Wednesday in winter. ~ 85 Main Street, Canaan; 860-824-7333. MODERATE TO DELUXE.

◀ HIDDEN

SHOPPING

Every little town in this fashionable rural area hosts a variety of intriguing shops and boutiques, not to mention art galleries, craft studios and antiques of all kinds.

The Silo is an uncommon enterprise, a former barn with silo that combines a handsome art gallery with changing exhibitions, a cooking school and a store that stocks everything the home chef might ever need—all in a warren of quaint little rooms. ~ 44 Upland Road, New Milford; 860-355-0300.

Historic Litchfield is a paradise for lovers of antiques, who might strike gold right in the center of town, at **Thomas McBride Antiques**, for example. Open weekdays and by appointment on weekends. Closed January through March. ~ 62 West Street, Litchfield; 860-567-5476.

Or head a few blocks west on Route 202 to reach **Linsley Antiques**, where English country furniture is the specialty. Closed Wednesday. ~ 499 Bantam Road, Litchfield; 860-567-4245.

For a complete list of antique stores in the area, contact the **Litchfield Hills Visitors Bureau**. From mid-June to mid-October, the council runs an information booth on Route 202. ~ P.O. Box 968, Litchfield, CT 06759; 860-567-4506.

You can window shop for elegant, country-style clothes or home accessories alongside the green, or half a mile west on Route 202 at Litchfield Common, an enclave of attractive shops.

Flower lovers will want to visit **White Flower Farm**, a retail and mail-order nursery known countrywide for its perennials, garden store and five acres of exquisite display grounds. ~ Route 63, Litchfield; 860-567-8789, 800-503-9624.

Alongside the picturesque covered bridge at West Cornwall, you can stroll into **Cornwall Bridge Pottery Store** and purchase attractive pots, lamps and tiles made by Todd Piker. Also for sale are handcrafted items such as clothing and wood products. Closed Tuesday and Wednesday from Memorial Day to Labor Day. ~ Route 7, West Cornwall; 860-672-6545.

Should you wish to watch this fine craftsman at work, you're welcome to visit **Cornwall Bridge Pottery** on Route 7, one-half mile south of the junction with Route 4. Closed Tuesday and Wednesday from Memorial Day to Labor Day. ~ 860-672-6545.

Brass Bugle Antiques offers furniture, primitives, quilts, china, glass and tools. One of the region's finest antique shops, it's located in a 19th-century barn. Closed December to mid-May. ~Warren Hill Road, Cornwall Bridge; 860-672-6535.

Salisbury's pretty Main Street is great for gazing at 19th-century homes and window shopping innumerable small, attractive shops that feature clothes, antiques, gifts and books. There are also exotic teas to buy or sip at tiny tables at **Chaiwalla**. Closed Monday and Tuesday; closed in March. ~ 1 Main Street, Salisbury; 860-435-9758.

In Riverton, traditional home of the celebrated Hitchcock chair, you can purchase recently made reproductions at the **Hitchcock Chair Factory Store**. ~ Route 20, Riverton; 860-379-4826.

In addition to shops, there are vineyards and wineries in the area where you can sample and purchase local wines. Three noteworthy choices include **DiGrazia Vineyards** (closed Monday through Friday from January through April; 131 Tower Road, Brookfield; 203-775-1616), **Haight Vineyard** (29 Chestnut Hill Road, Litchfield; 860-567-4045) and **Hopkins Vineyard** (closed

Monday through Thursday in January and February, and Monday and Tuesday in March and April; 25 Hopkins Road, New Preston; 860-868-7954).

Litchfield County attracts devotees of classical music to its two long-established summer festivals, both of which feature musicians of national and international renown. **Music Mountain** presents chamber music and jazz from June to September. Concerts are Saturday night and Sunday afternoon. Admission. ~ 225 Music Mountain Road, off Route 7, Falls Village; 860-824-7126. The **Norfolk Chamber Music Festival** lasts from June to August, offering Friday- and Saturday-evening concerts. Admission. ~ Battell Stoeckel Estate, Routes 44 and 272, Norfolk; 860-542-3000.

NIGHTLIFE

The **Marbledale Pub** is located five miles north of New Milford, and you'll find it lively every night, summer or winter. Locals, of the young and upscale kind, drop in before or after dinner to meet their friends, play a game of darts or pool, and try their hand at one of the video games. On Sunday, a deejay spins techno, disco and rock. ~ Route 202, Marbledale; 860-868-1496.

MACEDONIA BROOK STATE PARK 🏃 🏕 🎣 Many streams course through the forested 2300 acres of this park, and numerous trails traverse it. One trail reaches the crest of Cobble Mountain, almost 1400 feet, affording splendid views of the Taconic and Catskill Mountains in the adjoining states. Streams in the park are stocked in the spring with brook, brown and rainbow trout. You'll find a picnic shelter and outhouses. ~ Four miles northwest of Kent off Route 341; 860-927-3238.

BEACHES & PARKS

▲ There are 83 tent/RV sites (no hookups); $9 per night; no pets or alcohol allowed. Closed October to mid-April.

KENT FALLS STATE PARK 🏃 🎣 The foaming waterfall that cascades 250 feet here is at its peak in springtime. It's popular in summer as well, when the welcome spray brings relief from the heat, and in the fall, when the surrounding 275 acres of woods turn red and gold. Then there are those who love the waterfall in winter, when frozen rivulets turn the mountainside to glistening abstract sculpture. You can admire it all from a grassy plain at road level, or you can view it from many different angles as you climb a wide, stepped pathway all the way to the head of the cascade. Fishing for trout is allowed at the base of the waterfall. There are picnic grounds and restrooms. Day-use fee (weekends and holidays only), $5 to $8. ~ Four miles north of Kent on Route 7; 860-927-3238.

LAKE WARAMAUG STATE PARK 🚲 🚣 🏊 🚤 🎣 Ninety-five wooded acres front this scenic body of water. Visitors can swim or explore countless hidden coves in paddleboats and canoes that can be rented here. Fishing is good for bass, sunfish and perch. Bicycling along the quiet road around the lake is also popular, as is touring the nearby towns by car. Facilities include a picnic shelter, restrooms, food concession stands and boat and canoe rentals. Day-use fee, $5 to $8. ~ On Lake Waramaug Road, off Route 45; 860-868-0220.

▲ There are 77 sites, 6 are designated for RVs (no hookups); $10 per night. Some sites have lake views.

BURR POND STATE PARK 🏃 🐎 🏠 🏊 🛶 🚤 ⛵ Five miles north of Torrington on Route 8, Burr Pond is the site of Borden's first condensed-milk factory. The 88-acre pond is very clear, and lovely for swimming in summer and skating in winter. The scenic hiking trail surrounding it is great for cross-country skiing come winter. Amenities include restrooms and a snack bar. No pets are allowed. Day-use fee, $8. ~ Located on Burr Mountain Road, five miles north of Torrington; 860-482-1817.

▲ There are 40 primitive campsites; $10 per night.

TOPSMEAD STATE FOREST 🏃 🏠 Bequeathed to the people of Connecticut by Edith Morton Chase upon her death in 1972, this 511-acre forest is located about two miles east of Litchfield atop a 1230-foot knoll. Its main attraction is Miss Chase's summer home, an English Tudor-style cottage designed by Richard Henry Dana, Jr., in 1924. Open to the public the second and fourth weekends of each month from June through October, the house still contains most of its original furnishings. The surrounding grounds include lawns, orchards, stone walls and far-reaching views. The area is perfect for nature walking, and a two-mile trail loops around the cottage. Fires are not permitted. ~ Entrance on Buell Road, Litchfield; 860-567-5694.

WHITE MEMORIAL FOUNDATION & CONSERVATION CENTER 🏃 🚴 🐎 🏠 ⛵ This 4000-acre nature sanctuary bordering scenic Bantam Lake is crisscrossed by 35 miles of trails for hiking, birdwatching, horseback riding or cross-country skiing. The legacy of two visionary residents, this extraordinary preserve is dedicated to conservation education and research as well as recreation. A nature center and natural-resource museum (admission) are open to the public as are the grounds. Facilities include picnic areas, restrooms and a store. ~ On White Hall Road, off Route 202, Litchfield; 860-567-0857.

▲ There are 68 sites in several locations, including waterfront sites at popular Point Folly; $11.50 per night for tents, $13.50 per night for RVs; closed mid-October to mid-May. Tent-only sites are available at Windmill Hill; $8 per night; closed Labor Day to Memorial Day. Reservations required. ~ 860-567-0089.

HAYSTACK MOUNTAIN STATE PARK 🏃 🏠 ⛵ From the stone tower atop Haystack Mountain (1706 feet above sea level) visitors can see south as far as Long Island Sound and north to the Berk-shires' peaks in Massachusetts. You can drive halfway up the mountain, then hike a steep half-mile to the top. Fall foliage is out-standing up there, as is June's show of mountain laurel in bloom. There are picnic grounds and outhouses. Though it's closed to vehicles between the first snow and the spring thaw, the park remains open to foot traffic all year. ~ One-half mile north of Norfolk on Route 272; 860-482-1817.

▲ There is camping nearby at Taylor Brook Campground (Mountain Road off Route 8). The campground includes 44 tent/RV sites (no hookups); $10 per night. Closed October to mid-April.

HOUSATONIC MEADOWS STATE PARK 🏃 🛶 Encompass-ing 451 acres, this park is set on a former flood plain and offers flyfishing for trout and bass in the Housatonic River. Visitors will find miles of hiking trails including Pine Knob Loop Trail, which gives hikers a view of the green valley. Camping is especially good and the fall foliage is fantastic. You'll find picnic grounds and rest-rooms. ~ In Sharon on Route 7; 860-927-3238.

▲ There are 95 sites; $10 per night; no pets or alcohol al-lowed. Closed January to mid-April.

Hartford Area

Practically smack dab in the middle of the state is Hart-ford, its capital. Many people know it only because it's where they send their insurance payments. Indeed, Hart-ford is home to dozens of insurance companies and, in fact, is the insurance capital of the world. But it's not all business in Hartford: the city—and its surrounding towns—offers a variety of histori-cal and cultural attractions.

SIGHTS

Route 44 heads southeast out of Norfolk, leading, some 35 miles later, to Hartford. It's a more scenic road to the state capital than the highways, one that offers the chance to stop at some attrac-tive towns in the **Farmington Valley**. In fact, if you prefer small towns to city bustle, you could overnight there and take day trips into Hartford. For information about them, stop at the office of the **Greater Hartford Tourism District**. ~ 234 Murphy Road, Hartford; 860-244-8181, 800-793-4480, fax 860-244-8180; www.enjoyhartford.com, e-mail ctfuntour@aol.com.

◄ *HIDDEN*

Take a brief detour south on Route 179 to the village of **Col-linsville** for a glimpse of an intact 19th-century mill village—one of hundreds built across the state by the companies that gave them their names. The Collins Company was purveyor of axes and machetes to the world; the **Canton Historical Museum** features a wide array of Victorian collectibles and a charming railroad diorama circa 1900. Closed weekdays from December through

March; closed Monday and Tuesday the rest of the year. Admission. ~ 11 Front Street, Collinsville; 860-693-2793.

Continue on Route 179 into Route 4 as it follows the Farmington River into the residential town of **Farmington**, whose Main Street is a treasure trove of Colonial architecture. Just a few blocks away you'll find a little-known gem: the **Hill-Stead Museum**. Unique in many ways, Hill-Stead is a turn-of-the-20th-century Colonial revival country house built for an art-loving industrialist, Alfred A. Pope. It is furnished as if the Popes had left yesterday, and on its walls hangs a breathtaking collection of impressionist paintings—works by Monet, Degas, Manet and their American contemporaries, Cassatt and Whistler. The residence was designed by the Popes' daughter, Theodate Pope Riddle, in collaboration with an architectural firm. The personality of this pioneering woman, who went on to become an architect at a time when that profession was unheard of for a female, comes through vividly on a guided tour of the house. And there's a fine, short videotape to enlighten one further. The grounds are noteworthy as well, with hiking trails in the woods and a sunken garden designed by landscape architect Beatrix Farrand. Closed Monday. Admission. ~ 35 Mountain Road, Farmington; 860-677-9064 or 860-677-4787; www.hillstead.org.

If you're intrigued by this unusual woman and her work, head north of Farmington by way of Route 10 and take a left onto Old Farms Road. In a few moments you will come to the campus of **Avon Old Farms School**, a boy's preparatory academy founded during the 1920s by Theodate Pope Riddle and designed by her in what is described as Tudor/Cotswold style—cottage-inspired buildings in reddish sandstone and dark timbers. It's private property, but nobody seemed to mind our driving through the picturesque campus. Old Farms Road winds its way north, emerging in the center of Avon, a busy suburban town that was once an agricultural community.

HIDDEN ▶

Not long ago, great **fields of shade tobacco** covered portions of this valley and that of the Connecticut River, a few miles to the west. Suburbanization, highways and, of course, the intense disfavor with which the evil weed is now regarded have cut sharply into this profitable business. Yet there are still some 1800 acres devoted to tobacco in the state. In summer, when the fields are covered by acres of netting, they create a unique, dramatic setting enhanced by the long, narrow red barns used for drying tobacco leaves. Go north on Route 10 through **Simsbury**, noting the many graceful 18th- and 19th-century buildings of this prosperous community. Two miles north of the town center take Hoskins Road, and you'll get a taste of this picturesque, surreal landscape.

From Route 10, as you look to the west, you'll see a ridge of hills topped by a stone tower, the centerpiece of **Talcott Mountain**

Hartford Area

Barkhamstead
Reservoir

0 — 5 miles
0 — 5 kilometers

Granby
Bradley
International
Airport
K
Windsor
Locks

Stratton Brook
State Park
Simsbury

Canton
Avon

Talcott Mtn
State Park

Windsor

Bloomfield

Hartford **C**
O **F**
Farmington Ave

Main St

Farmington **G**

Maple Ave

D
O **H**
A **P**

**Wethers-
field**

Rocky
Hill

**New
Britain**

J

Dinosaur
State Park

Connecticut River

Berlin

N

Downtown
Hartford

Main St
Windsor St
Ann St
Church St
Asylum St
Ford St
Pearl
Trumbull
St

E

Market St
Columbus
Blvd
Bulkeley
Bridge

State St

L
Central
Row
Founder's
Bridge

B
Gold

Jewell St
Bushnell Park
Trinity St
M
Elm St
Capitol Ave
Buckingham
Hudson
Main St

N

Arch
St

Sheldon St

Charter Oak Ave

Commerce St

Connecticut River

Taylor St

Oak St
Lafayette St

POINTS OF INTEREST

A Buttolph-Williams House
B Center Church
C Connecticut Historical Society Museum
D The Cove Warehouse
E Greater Hartford Convention
  & Visitors Bureau
F Harriet Beecher Stowe House
G Hill-Stead Museum
H Hurlbut-Dunham House
I Mark Twain House
J New Britain Museum of American Art
K New England Air Museum
L Old State House
M State Capitol
N Wadsworth Atheneum
O Webb-Deane-Stevens Museum
P Wethersfield Museum

State Park, which can be reached by Route 185. Hartford lies on the other side.

Truth is, **Hartford** suffers the same image problems that afflict other American cities, and there are many well-traveled residents of the state who've never been there. They're missing a lot. Its long and distinguished history—from newborn settlement in 1635 to shipping center throughout the 18th century, industrial leader in the 19th and capital of the insurance business to this day—is reflected in its varied architecture and active cultural life. For easier sightseeing, the city can be subdivided into three separate parts: downtown; the capitol area, on the opposite side of beautiful Bushnell Park; and Asylum Hill, where Mark Twain built his celebrated mansion.

Hartford's venerable Old State House was almost bulldozed, until a vocal group of preservationists came to its aid.

Start at the dignified **Old State House**, designed in 1796 by Charles Bulfinch and used as the seat of the state's government until 1878, years during which Hartford alternated as capital with New Haven. Part of the building is now used as a museum and part as a visitors center. Closed Sunday. ~ 800 Main Street, Hartford; 860-522-6766.

Ask for the walking tour map of the city prepared by the **Greater Hartford Convention and Visitors Bureau**. It will guide you to two dozen landmarks, old and new. (As you've no doubt noticed, the former are being squeezed out by the latter). Closed Saturday and Sunday. ~ 1 Civic Center Plaza, Hartford; 860-728-6789, 800-446-7811, fax 860-293-2365; www.enjoyhartford. com, e-mail ghcub@connix.com.

If the printed itinerary seems overwhelming, here's a shortened list: Walk by the **Richardson**, as it is known today, a massive, handsome brownstone building designed in 1876 by Henry Hobson Richardson in his distinctive Romanesque style. It's just north of the Old State House, on Main Street. A few blocks south, and across the street, stands **Center Church**, built in 1807, whose white portico and ornate white spire contrast with the red brick of the facade. Next to it, the **Ancient Burying Ground** shelters gravestones that date back to 1640. ~ 675 Main Street, Hartford.

Across the street is the **Wadsworth Atheneum**, America's longest continuously operating public art museum, opened in 1844 and later harmoniously enlarged. Walk up the steps of the towered, castlelike original building and turn around before entering. You'll be rewarded with an extensive view of Bushnell Park and the glimmering gold dome of the State Capitol across the park. Inside, you'll find a distinguished collection, strong in paintings of the Hudson River school, Colonial American furniture, African-American art and other works of this century. Also displayed are Greek and Roman art and European works from the 16th through the 18th centuries. Yet the museum doesn't overwhelm you with size and arrogance; it feels friendly, somehow. Closed Monday. Admission. ~ 600 Main Street, Hartford; 860-278-2670; www. wadsworthatheneum.org.

Nestled between the Atheneum and the fine **Municipal Building** of 1915 is **Burr Mall**, a small, endearing open space centered on Alexander Calder's giant sculpture *Stegosaurus*. The two classic buildings and the bright red steel abstract sculpture form a wonderful contrast.

◄ *HIDDEN*

On to the **State Capitol**, a monumental Victorian Gothic structure that can be toured, along with the new legislative office building, in groups led by members of the League of Women Voters. The 1878 capitol is a sight to behold: gold-domed, turreted, mansarded, adorned with statues of Connecticut's greats (including Ella Grasso, the late governor and first woman to be elected to that post in her own right). The soaring, lavishly decorated interior is as exuberant as the facade; clearly Hartford was out to celebrate when it won the designation of sole capital over New Haven in 1875. ~ Tours: Capitol Information Desk and Tour Guide Service, 210 Capitol Avenue, Hartford; 860-240-0222; www.cga.state.ct.us.

The stately building across Capitol Avenue houses the State Library, the Supreme Court and the **Museum of Connecticut History**, which specializes in military, political and industrial history. Exhibits here include a collection of historic Colt firearms and a trove of documents such as the 1662 Royal Charter. Closed Saturday and Sunday. ~ 231 Capitol Avenue, Hartford; 860-566-3056; www.cslib.org.

Asylum Hill is where Mark Twain built his Hartford residence, along with many eminent citizens of the 1870s who fled the downtown area for what was then considered the suburb. His mansion was part of Nook Farm, an enclave of writers and intellectuals that included Harriet Beecher Stowe. The **Mark Twain House** is a super-ornamented extravaganza where he wrote *Huckleberry Finn* and *Tom Sawyer*. Closed Tuesday from October through May. Admission. ~ 351 Farmington Avenue, Hartford; 860-493-6411; www.hartnet.org/twain.

You can visit the **Harriet Beecher Stowe Center**, which features Stowe's discreet Victorian "cottage" along with the Day-Stowe House. Closed Monday from October through May. Admission. ~ 77 Forest Street, Hartford; 860-525-9317.

Located a few blocks away is the **Connecticut Historical Society Museum**, where a variety of lively exhibits will help you place the sights you've seen in historical context. Within the museum is a genealogy library. Library closed Sunday and Monday. Museum closed Monday. Admission. ~ 1 Elizabeth Street, Hartford; 860-236-5621; www.chs.org.

Hartford's surroundings offer varied attractions that can be visited on day trips. Art buffs won't want to miss the **New Britain Museum of American Art**, which features a collection spanning 250 years and is strong on Hudson River school painters and American artists of the 20th century. Closed Monday. Admission. ~ 56 Lexington Street, New Britain; 860-229-0257.

North of the capital, the **New England Air Museum** exhibits 75 aircraft that trace the history of aviation. Admission. ~ Off Route 75, Bradley International Airport, Windsor Locks; 860-623-3305; www.neam.org.

A mere three miles south of Hartford on Route 91, the town of **Wethersfield**, one of the original three settlements on the Connecticut River, is famed for its extensive historic district comprising 150 dwellings built before the mid-19th century. Several old Wethersfield homes are open to the public as house museums:

American Indians knew Connecticut as Quinnetukqut, "long tidal river."

The **Webb-Deane-Stevens Museum** consists of three homes built, respectively, for a wealthy merchant, a diplomat and a craftsman, each representing a different style of 18th-century life. The Webb house was the setting for a conference between General George Washington and his French counterpart, Jean de Rochambeau, that led to the British defeat at Yorktown in 1781. Closed Tuesday; Closed weekdays from November through April. Admission. ~ 211 Main Street, Wethersfield; 860-529-0612; www.webb-deane-stevens.org.

Across the street, the **Hurlbut–Dunham House** is a stylish two-story brick Georgian-style building with Victorian porches and a belvedere. It features early-20th-century collections of the Dunham family, including paintings, glassware, china and ceramics. The house retains its original wallpaper. Closed Monday through Wednesday and from January through March. Admission. ~ 212 Main Street, Wethersfield; 860-529-7656.

The **Buttolph-Williams House** is a late-17th-century "mansion house" with a collection of period furnishings. Its overhanging eaves and small casement windows reflect the medieval character of the pilgrim century. Closed Tuesday and November through April. Admission. ~ 249 Broad Street, Wethersfield; 860-247-8996.

The **Old Academy** is a fine 1804 brick building in the federal style housing a library with genealogy resources and several offices. Closed Sunday and Monday. ~ 150 Main Street, Wethersfield.

Nearby is the **Wethersfield Museum** exhibiting the Wethersfield Historical Society's collection of local history. Closed Monday. Admission. ~ Robert A. Keeney Memorial Cultural Center, 200 Main Street, Wethersfield.

For information on the Old Academy or the Wethersfield Museum, contact the **Wethersfield Historical Society**. Closed Saturday and Sunday. ~ 150 Main Street, Wethersfield; 860-529-7656; www.wethhist.org.

At the north end of Wethersfield's Main Street, right on the Cove, is **The Cove Warehouse**. This 17th-century building is a symbol of Wethersfield's prosperous maritime past. The warehouse was one of six built in 1661. Hanging exhibit panels tell the complete story. Open weekends mid-May to mid-October. ~ North end of Main Street, Wethersfield; 860-529-7656.

For budget lodgings in the Farmington Valley, the place to go is the **Hillside Motel**, 17 miles west of Hartford. It's family owned and operated, and its 15 simple rooms—all with bath, four with cooking facilities—are clean, neat and air-conditioned, though there's nothing fancy. What's more, it's close to that great canoeing and tubing section of the Farmington River known as Satan's Kingdom. ~ 671 Route 44, Canton; 860-693-4951. BUDGET.

LODGING

Avon Old Farms Hotel, once a small motel, has grown gradually into its present role as a major country hotel with 164 guest rooms. This multiwinged hostelry has a dining room, an outdoor pool, an on-site fitness center, well-landscaped grounds and great views over woods and stream. You can choose from inexpensive lodging in the older motel or more expensive options in the three-story main wing, where the rooms are done in old New England elegance and the carpeted staircase in the lofty lobby just begs for Scarlett O'Hara to sweep down. ~ Junction of Routes 10 and 44, Avon; 860-677-1651, 800-836-4000, fax 860-677-0364; www. avonoldfarmshotel.com. DELUXE TO ULTRA-DELUXE.

If a truly exquisite restoration makes your heart sing, then the **Simsbury 1820 House** is a must. Set on a knoll in the center of this historic small town, the three-story, four-chimney brick building was home to generations of distinguished Americans, including Gifford Pinchot, known as the father of the conservation movement. No pains were spared in transforming the graceful grey mansion and the nearby carriage house into a 32-room inn with a fine restaurant. Each room is carpeted and furnished with antiques, with imaginative use made of the nooks, crannies and arched windows. ~ 731 Hopmeadow Street, Route 10, Simsbury; 860-658-7658, 800-879-1820, fax 860-651-0724. DELUXE TO ULTRA-DELUXE.

Behind the ornate 19th-century brick facade of the **Goodwin Hotel** in the heart of downtown, all is brand new. Once a distinguished apartment house, a local landmark, it was entirely rebuilt inside and appointed in a style that would have pleased the Hartford-born financier the hotel honors. Fine reproductions grace the 124 rooms and suites, service is personal and the ambience is gracious and subdued. Public spaces are adorned with works borrowed from the nearby Wadsworth Atheneum, one of the country's finest museums. Rates are expensive but lower on weekends and worth it if a touch of urban elegance fits in your plans. ~ 1 Haynes Street, Hartford; 860-246-7500, 800-922-5006, fax 860-247-4576; www.goodwinhotel.com. ULTRA-DELUXE.

A luxury downtown hotel that offers attractive weekend packages is the **Hilton Hartford**, joined by a bridgeway to the Civic Center's many attractions. The rooms, almost 400 and generous in size, tend toward contemporary furnishings. There's a health club, an indoor pool, a restaurant and, right next door, the award-winning Hartford Stage Company—food for both the body and the soul. ~ 315 Trumbull Street at Civic Center Plaza, Hartford; 860-728-5151, 800-455-8667, fax 860-240-7247; www.hartford hilton.com. DELUXE.

Budget accommodations can be found on the outskirts of Hartford off Route 91 at Exit 27. Of several chain motels, the **Grand Chalet** seemed the most attractive, with an airy lobby, good size outdoor pool and 129 standard motel rooms: clean and small but adequate. ~ 185 Brainard Road, Hartford; 860-525-9306, 800-524-2538, fax 860-525-2990. MODERATE.

DINING   **Apricots** fronts a lively stretch of the Farmington River. You can sit on a riverbank terrace, drink or sandwich in hand, and almost feel the water as it leaps around shiny rocks. The ground floor of the old building, a former trolley stop, is devoted to a popular pub where the "happy hour" boasts a heaping tableful of complimentary food. Upstairs is the restaurant itself, an oasis of fine American cuisine where the deluxe to ultra-deluxe entrées most in demand are rack of lamb and swordfish. ~ 1593 Farmington Avenue, Farmington; 860-673-5405, fax 860-673-7138. MODERATE TO ULTRA-DELUXE.

Avon Old Farms Inn is just what you pictured for dinner at a country inn. Located in an 18th-century stagecoach stop, it serves large portions of traditional American food (including salmon, swordfish, chicken, lamb, lobster and pasta dishes). All the baking is done on the grounds. ~ 1 Nod Road, Avon; 860-677-2818, fax 860-676-0280; www.avonoldfarmsinn.com. DELUXE TO ULTRA-DELUXE.

The restaurant at **Simsbury 1820 House** is in what was once the cellar of the lovely old mansion. Room dividers give the illusion of intimate dining rooms, enhanced by several distinct styles of decor: exposed brick walls with arches in one area; patterned wallpaper for another; traditional prints of hunting scenes highlighting a third. The atmosphere is casual, the cuisine Continental. An additional pleasure is a drink on the spacious wrought-iron-veranda overlooking the gardens. Closed Friday through Sunday. ~ 731 Hopmeadow Street, Route 10, Simsbury; 860-658-7658. MODERATE TO DELUXE.

Max Downtown, popular with the upscale young crowd, serves eclectic American and Continental dishes. The menu, which is written daily, might include grilled swordfish with roasted pepper sauce or roasted New Zealand rack of lamb with herbed couscous crust and harissa sauce. ~ 185 Asylum Street, Hartford; 860-522-2530, fax 860-246-5279. MODERATE TO ULTRA-DELUXE.

If a visit to the Wadsworth Atheneum is on your itinerary, consider staying for lunch at **The Museum Café.** It's an attractive, restful room off the rotunda on the main floor, enhanced by a changing selection of prints or paintings. Open only for lunch, it offers a dozen entrées that include stir-fried vegetables, fresh fish, chicken and sandwiches with a gourmet touch. There is also a Sunday brunch and dinner on Thursday. Closed Monday. ~ 600 Main Street, Hartford; 860-728-5989. BUDGET TO MODERATE.

Another option is the Pavilion at State House Square, a stylish office-and-retail complex whose second floor boasts a dozen eateries. Try **The Natural,** which features healthy soups, salads and Mediterranean dishes like falafel, tabbouleh and hummus. Closed Saturday and Sunday. ~ Food Court in the Pavilion at State House Square, Hartford; 860-247-1627. BUDGET.

SHOPPING

Canton abounds in antique shops. For some competitive shopping, visit the Saturday auction at 7:30 p.m. at **Canton Barn Auctions.** Doors open at 5 p.m. ~ 75 Old Canton Road, off Route 44, Canton; 860-693-0601.

The **Farmington Valley Arts Center** comprises 20 artists' studios, a gallery with changing exhibitions and American contemporary crafts from all over the United States for sale. It's an intriguing complex of handsome brownstone buildings scattered about a landscaped park. Closed Monday and Tuesday. ~ 25 Arts Center Lane, Avon; 860-678-1867.

Riverdale Farms used to provide fresh milk to Hartford County. Today it houses over 50 varied shops and services in 16 buildings, some old, some new but harmonious. There are fashions, gifts, jewelry, clothes, a day spa and special stores for people who like to knit and sew. ~ 124 Simsbury Road, Avon; 860-677-6437.

In downtown Hartford you will find two shopping malls. First, there is the standard but extensive **Civic Center Mall.** ~ 1 Civic Center Plaza; 860-275-6100. The other is the dazzling **Pavilion at State House Square.** ~ 30 State House Square, Hartford; 860-241-0100.

For unusual gifts, you might consider **The Museum Shop** at the Wadsworth Atheneum, which stocks a fine selection of art books, reproductions, prints, cards, elegant wrapping papers as well as games and books for enquiring young minds. Closed Monday. ~ 600 Main Street, Hartford; 860-278-2670.

The shop at the **Old State House** leans more toward things historical, as befits this ancient, still lively institution. Also available are Connecticut-made products. ~ 800 Main Street, Hartford; 860-522-6766.

NIGHTLIFE   **Bushnell Memorial Hall** has been a major performing arts center since 1929. The vast art deco auditorium is where audiences flock for concerts of the Hartford Symphony and other orchestras, the ballet and the opera, and touring dramas and musicals. ~ 166 Capitol Avenue, Hartford; 860-987-5900.

Hartford Civic Center schedules frequent, star-caliber entertainment. ~ 1 Civic Center Plaza, Hartford; 860-727-8080.

A pub and restaurant called **Brew Ha Ha** features comedians from New York City on Friday and Saturday nights. The theme here is very beer-oriented, with eight to ten homebrewed beers on tap nightly and beer decor throughout. Closed Sunday from Memorial Day to Labor Day. Cover for comedy club only. ~ 942 Main Street, Hartford; 860-525-1600.

At **Bourbon Street North** it's rock and alternative music Thursday through Saturday; a deejay also fires up on Friday. Closed Sunday and Monday. Cover on Friday and Saturday. ~ 70 Union Place, Hartford; 860-525-1014.

BEACHES & PARKS   **STRATTON BROOK STATE PARK** An unusual feature of this 148-acre park in the Farmington Valley is a shady bicycle trail built on a former railroad bed. It travels across woodlands and along several scenic brooks, then continues through a town forest. There are also hiking trails and a pleasant pond. Facilities include a picnic shelter, restrooms and changing rooms. The park is completely wheelchair accessible. Day-use fee. ~ Route 305, two miles west of Simsbury; 860-658-1388.

TALCOTT MOUNTAIN STATE PARK Views from this mountain, of the city of Hartford and the valleys of the Farmington and Connecticut rivers, have been favorites of painters for more than 100 years. Atop the mountain stands handsome Heublein Tower, part of a residence deeded to the state by a prominent Hartford family. A one-and-a-half-mile hike leads from the parking lot to the tower, 165 feet high; the ground floor houses a museum of local history, open weekends from mid-April through Labor Day and Thursday through Sunday from Labor Day through October; closed November through mid-April (information, 860-677-0662). Along the trail, you might see people hang-gliding: the mountain is considered a good jumping-off place for this sport. Amenities include picnic grounds, restrooms and a museum and an observation tower. ~ Route 185, three miles south of Simsbury.

▲ There is camping nearby at the American Legion State Forest. The campground includes 30 tent/RV sites (no hookups); $10 per night. Reservations suggested. Closed mid-October to mid-April. ~ West River Road, Pleasant Valley; 860-379-0922.

DINOSAUR STATE PARK 🏃 This 70-acre park, set midway between Hartford and New Haven, boasts a geodesic dome exhibit center enclosing a celebrated exposure of rock. The ancient rock bears some 500 tracks made by dinosaurs of the Jurassic period —185 million years ago. Visitors may make plaster casts of some tracks from May through October, but materials are not provided. Call 860-529-5816 for information about casts. Two miles of nature trails wind through the park, which offers visitors picnic grounds, restrooms and an exhibit center (closed Monday). Day-use fee, $2. ~ On West Street in the Rocky Hill area, one mile east of Exit 23 off Route 91; 860-529-8423; www.dinosaurstate park.org.

New Haven Area

Located just about midway between the borders of New York and Rhode Island, New Haven is the last major hub you reach when heading north on Route 95. The city itself is a fascinating blend of old and new, urban center and university campus—a must on any tour of the state. Just to the east is a handful of towns—including Branford, Guilford and Clinton—that are home to historic homes and museums. Just offshore are the Thimble Islands, a galaxy of tiny islands.

New Haven was founded as an independent colony in 1638, but in 1784 it merged with Hartford to become co-capital of the state, which it remained until 1875. Although it shone as an industrial center in the 19th and early 20th centuries, the special flavor that sets it apart today is due in large part to the presence of Yale University, an institution that has shared the city's fortunes since 1718.

SIGHTS

New Haven was planned around a green at its founding, and happily the 17-acre square with its trio of churches in the center has been proudly maintained as open space and still acts as focus of the downtown area. Yale University forms the backdrop to the green's western edge, along College Street and fanning out across a dozen blocks west and north of it. Most of the cultural and architectural landmarks that define this uncommon city can be seen on a walk around the immediate area.

Yale University offers free guided tours of the campus and a walking tour of the New Haven green. ~ Visitor Information Center, 149 Elm Street, New Haven; 203-432-2300. The **Greater New Haven Convention and Visitors Bureau** provides maps and an outline for a walking tour of campus and civic landmarks. ~ 59 Eve Street, New Haven; 203-777-8550, 800-332-7829, fax 203-782-7755; www.newhavencvb.org, e-mail mail@newhavencvb.org.

Three hundred years of history and architecture can be traced on these rambles. For the earliest structures, start with the three graceful clapboard homes built by late-18th-century gentry at **149, 155** and **175 Elm Street**. The three facades, set among much grander, later buildings, give a glimpse of how the city looked 200 years ago. The only structures on the green itself are the churches —**Trinity, Center** and **United**—erected between 1812 and 1815 in Gothic, Georgian and Federal styles.

HIDDEN ►

Yale's oldest remaining building, **Connecticut Hall**, is part of what is known as the old campus, which can be entered through **Phelps Gateway**, the school's massive front door at 344 College Street. It's a bulky, gambrel-roofed brick structure facing a statue of Nathan Hale, who lived there as a student.

Much of the architecture for which Yale is famous is 19th- and early-20th-century Gothic Revival. By crossing the Old Campus onto High Street, the visitor can wander past **Dwight Chapel** (1842), the first Gothic design; **Harkness Tower** (1917), whose turrets and pinnacles are a symbol of Yale itself; and **Sterling Memorial Library** (1927), a modern Gothic.

York Street, one block west of High, is also lined with Yale-related buildings, including the legendary **Mory's**, a private club celebrated in "The Whiffenpoof Song." ~ 306 York Street, New Haven.

One of the finest contemporary complexes on campus rises just west of York Street: **Morse and Stiles Colleges**, designed in 1960 by Eero Saarinen, contrasting yet in harmony with the older buildings.

HIDDEN ►

Don't miss Claes Oldenburg's powerful sculpture **Lipstick**, an anti-Vietnam War statement that dominates the courtyard of Morse College.

Another renowned 1960s structure is Gordon Bunshaft's **Beinecke Rare Book and Manuscript Library**, a granite and translucent marble landmark that seems to float above a sunken court featuring sculptures by Isamu Noguchi. Step inside to view a Gutenberg Bible, original Audubon prints and other exhibits. Closed Saturday and Sunday. ~ 121 Wall Street, New Haven; 203-432-2977; www.yale.edu.

Down on Chapel Street, you come upon the **Yale University Art Gallery**, known for American, European, African, Asian and pre-Columbian works, as well as a special gallery devoted to American art that includes the historical paintings of John Trumbull, the artist-patriot of the American Revolution. Designed by architect Louis I. Kahn, the gallery is exceptional for its use of interior space and light. One of its most appealing features is its idyllic **outdoor sculpture garden**. Closed Monday. ~ 1111 Chapel Street, New Haven; 203-432-0600; www.yale.edu/artgallery.

HIDDEN ►

Across the street you'll find the **Yale Center for British Art**, which was also designed by architect Louis I. Kahn and is also known for the quality of its collections. It boasts canvases by Turner, Gainsborough and Constable, among other renowned artists. Closed Monday. ~ 1080 Chapel Street, New Haven; 203-432-2800.

New Haven has suffered its share of urban ills, and efforts to upgrade its image have sometimes been ill-advised. Two of the more successful projects are the recent creation of an entertainment district on College Street, centering on the renovated **Shubert** and **Palace** theaters (see "Theater in Connecticut" in this chapter).

Another area that has been successfully restored is **Wooster Square**, between Chapel and Greene streets, six blocks east of the green. This early 19th-century enclave of graceful homes, after years of neglect, is once again a fashionable in-town address.

◄ HIDDEN

Among the many cultural and recreational facilities in New Haven are the **Peabody Museum of Natural History**, with its famed dinosaur collection and a Pulitzer Prize–winning mural entitled *The Age of Reptiles*. Admission. ~ 170 Whitney Avenue, New Haven; 203-432-5050; www.peabody.yale.edu.

Nearby, the **New Haven Colony Historical Society** contains furniture and decorative arts from early New Haven homes, an art gallery, a maritime collection and industrial displays. Closed Monday; in July and August, closed Sunday and Monday. Admission. ~ 114 Whitney Avenue, New Haven; 203-562-4183.

Farther out Whitney Avenue you'll find the **Eli Whitney Museum**, dedicated to the New Haven industrialist who invented the cotton gin and then developed the concept of interchangeable parts, which led to modern mass-production methods. Displays trace 200 years of industrial growth on the site. Closed Monday and Tuesday. Admission. ~ 915 Whitney Avenue, Hamden; 203-777-1833; www.eliwhitney.org.

CONNECTICUT INVENTIONS

Among the products invented, or perfected, by Connecticut Yankees were hats, combs, pins, clocks, seeds, furniture, typewriters, axes, hardware of all kinds, vulcanized rubber, bicycles, textiles—both silk and cotton—silverware and firearms. Samuel Colt developed the Colt 45, "the gun that won the West," at his armory in Hartford. At his firearms factory near New Haven, Eli Whitney, who had previously invented the cotton gin, introduced the concept of interchangeable parts, which led to the flowering of the Industrial Revolution.

On a day that calls for outdoor fun, consider a trip to **Lighthouse Point Park**, with facilities for picnicking and swimming and a classic old-time carousel. Admission. ~ 2 Lighthouse Road, New Haven; 203-946-8005.

Or you may want to head for the **Shoreline Trolley Museum**, where you can ride classic, antique trolleys along a scenic one-and-a-half-mile route. Open daily from Memorial Day to Labor Day; closed January through March; call for other hours. Admission. ~ 17 River Street, East Haven; 203-467-6927; www.bera.org.

East of New Haven, the shoreline is dotted with a string of attractive residential towns that started life as farming and fishing villages. Branford is about six miles east of town on Route 1. It's home to **Harrison House**, which was built in 1724 and is now a house museum filled with 18th- and 19th-century furnishings. Closed Sunday through Wednesday and October through May. ~ 124 Main Street, Branford; 203-488-4828.

Nearby is Bittersweet Farm, where the **Branford Craft Village** is located. The Branford Craft Village is both working farm and perennial crafts fair (see "Shopping" below) on 85 acres. There are more than two dozen shops and studios, a restaurant and a play area for children. Closed Monday. ~ 779 East Main Street, Branford; 203-488-4689.

HIDDEN ▶

Slightly south and just east of Branford is Stony Creek, from which cruises for the Thimble Islands sail. **The Thimbles**, some no larger than a rock that disappears at high tide, others topped by a single elaborate Victorian mansion or two, are an enchanting group of islands. They say Captain Kidd hid stolen treasures on one of these rocky outposts. You'll learn all about that, and other local legends, if you take one of the small **excursion boats** around this miniature archipelago. Seasonal. ~ *Volsunga III*, Town Dock (203-481-3345); *Sea Mist*, Thimble Islands Cruise, Stony Creek dock, Branford; phone/fax 203-488-8905.

Route 146 leads from Stony Creek to Guilford, a town that has preserved many pre-Revolutionary War houses, including the **Henry Whitfield State Museum**. This home of the town's first minister, built in 1639, is said to be both the oldest stone house in New England and the oldest building in Connecticut. The green is special, generous for a town of this size and evocative of an earlier time. The museum is closed Monday and Tuesday year-round; from mid-December through January, visits are by appointment only. Admission. ~ 248 Old Whitfield Street, Guilford; 203-453-2457.

A few miles farther east you might consider a swim at **Hammonasset Beach State Park**. It's Connecticut's largest public beach, over two miles long.

A worthwhile stop in Clinton, a picturesque, little seaside village made up of Colonial Cape Cod homes, is the **Stanton House**, built in 1789. Once a general store, it now exhibits items that would have been sold in that era, such as hardware, yard goods, spices and dishware. Closed Monday and from October through May. ~ 63 East Main Street, Clinton; 860-669-2132.

Located just a block from the Yale campus, the **Three Chimneys**   **LODGING**
Inn is a lovely Victorian mansion (circa 1870) filled with antiques and 19th-century details. The inn also has 20th-century touches, including computer hookups and conference rooms. Its ten guest rooms have canopy beds, oriental rugs and period furnishings; some have fireplaces. ~ 1201 Chapel Street, New Haven; 203-789-1201, fax 203-776-7363; e-mail chimneysnh@aol.com. DELUXE TO ULTRA-DELUXE.

The Colony is a modern, five-story hotel with 86 attractive rooms done in Colonial style. Its convenient location makes it popular with Yale visitors as well as those sampling the city's theaters and museums. The Colony has its own indoor garage, a boon in the busy downtown area, as well as a restaurant and lounge with entertainment on the weekends. ~ 1157 Chapel Street, New Haven; 203-776-1234, 800-458-8810, fax 203-772-3929; www. colonyatyale.com. MODERATE.

The historic **Hotel Duncan**, a landmark since 1894, has probably seen better days, yet it must be the best buy in town. Behind its handsome Romanesque facade rise five floors of neatly furnished rooms with old-fashioned baths. No air conditioning here, just fans to keep you cool on a hot day, and the pleasure of being part of a tradition. ~ 1151 Chapel Street, New Haven; 203-787-1273, fax 203-787-0160. MODERATE.

East of New Haven, the shoreline towns are well stocked with budget- and moderate-price motels close to Route 95. **Holiday Inn Express**, a facility only seven miles from New Haven, has 82 guest rooms, a pool and complimentary breakfast. It's also near Tweed–New Haven Airport and the popular Trolley Museum. ~ 30 Frontage Road Exit 51, East Haven; 203-469-5321, 800-465-4329, fax 203-469-2544; www.schafferhotels.com. MODERATE.

The Chapel Street area is so rich in theaters, museums and sce-   **DINING**
nic vistas of Yale that it's become a spawning ground for restaurants.

You'll find **Scoozzi** down a flight of stone stairs, between the British Art Center and the Yale Repertory Theater. Location is everything, but here the high-tech setting is attractive as well, and the trendy, Italian-inspired fare pleases the customers. ~ 1104

Text continued on page 92.

Theater in Connecticut

Over the past two decades, this small state has been gaining a large reputation for excellent theater. Connecticut theater no longer means merely summer stock or road companies of successful Broadway shows. The state has seen a flowering of professional regional theaters, staging their own productions of classics and new plays and sending them forth into the national arena, where they have garnered many top awards.

New Haven, once known as a venue for New York producers testing out Broadway-bound plays, now boasts two prestigious producing companies of its own.

One is the 487-seat, thrust-style **Long Wharf Theater**. It's found in the heart of the city's wholesale market, adjacent to Route 95—a great location with no parking problems. Its season, from September through June, spans the spectrum of American and European drama and comedy, with an occasional musical—outstanding productions that have gained recognition around the country. ~ 222 Sargent Drive, New Haven; 203-787-4282; www.longwharf.org.

The other one, the prestigious **Yale Repertory Theatre**, is the professional adjunct of Yale University School of Drama, and its artistic director, Stan Wojewodski, Jr., doubles as dean of the drama school. Works such as Lee Blessing's *A Walk in the Woods*, Athol Fugard's *Master Harold . . . and the Boys* and August Wilson's Pulitzer Prize–winning *Fences* made their debut in the attractive church-turned-theater and then went on to fame and fortune around the land. Closed Sunday and June to mid-September. ~ 1120 Chapel Street, New Haven; 203-432-1234.

The state capital is home to the **Hartford Stage Company**, winner of the 1989 Tony Award for Outstanding Achievement in Regional Theater. Housed in a contemporary, 489-seat theater downtown, the company is devoted to innovative, sometimes controversial interpretations of the classics, as well as new works by playwrights of today. The season runs year-round. Closed Monday. ~ 50 Church Street, Hartford; 860-527-5151, fax 860-247-8243; www.hartfordstage.org.

The **Goodspeed Opera House** is dedicated to the American musical—to reviving vintage ones and inspiring the new. The legendary *Annie* as well as *Man of La Mancha* were both seen for the first time in this Victorian jewel box on the Connecticut River, as were numerous song-and-dance gems from the past that went on to Broadway. The season is April to December. Closed Monday and Tuesday. ~ Route 82, East Haddam; 860-873-8668; www.goodspeed.org. A second stage, the **Goodspeed-at-Chester/Norma Terris Theatre**, opened in 1984 to house workshops of new musicals-in-progress. Closed Monday and Tuesday. ~ North Main Street, Chester; 860-873-8668.

The **National Theatre of the Deaf** makes its home in Connecticut, although it travels during most of the year. A professional ensemble of deaf and hearing actors, NTD combines the spoken word with sign language in unique performances that have touched the hearts of audiences in all 50 states and more than two dozen countries for 25 years. On Sundays during summer, they offer free storytelling on the green in Chester. ~ P.O Box 659, Chester, CT 06412; 860-526-4971 voice, or 860-526-4974 TTY; www.ntd.org.

The **Eugene O'Neill Theater Center** is a nationally known play-wrights workshop created on a 90-acre estate overlooking Long Island Sound. Staged readings (fee) or run-throughs of works-in-progress are open to the public in July. Closed Sunday. ~ 305 Great Neck Road, Waterford; 860-443-5378.

These are the big guns on the theater scene, the award winners whose names are recognized by stage buffs around the land. Each year also brings new professional theater groups, such as the **Music Theatre of Connecticut**. Closed Monday through Wednesday. ~ 246 Post Road East, Westport; 203-454-3883.

Other showplaces present national tours of popular dramas and mu-sicals. Foremost among them is New Haven's historic **Shubert Theater**, restored to its stylish 1914 sparkle and offering a varied fall, winter and spring season. ~ 247 College Street, New Haven; 203-562-5666; www.shubert.com.

Connecticut's straw-hat circuit—how quaint that name seems nowa-days—is comprised of numerous theaters, some old, some new, that present generally lightweight fare during the summer. Among them are **Gateway's Candlewood Playhouse**. ~ Junction of Routes 37 and 39, New Fairfield; 203-746-4441. In the Lower Connecticut River Valley, the **Ivoryton Playhouse** offers both summer stock and winter stock. ~ 103 Main Street, Ivoryton; 860-767-8348. In the Northeast Corner the **Connecticut Repertory Theater** performs year-round. ~ 802 Bolton Road, Storrs; 860-486-3969. The **Oakdale Theater**, located north of the New Haven area, also stages works all year long. ~ 95 South Turnpike Road, Wallingford; 203-265-1501; www.oakdale.com. In Southwestern Connecticut, the **Westport Country Playhouse** is one of the oldest summer theaters in the country. Closed Sunday. ~ 25 Powers Court, Westport; 203-227-4177; www.westportplayhouse.org.

Chapel Street, New Haven; 203-776-8268, fax 203-772-2124.
MODERATE TO DELUXE.

Louis' Lunch is one of New Haven's claims to fame—it seems
Louis Lassen was the man who first put ground-up beef between
two halves of a bun, back in 1903. The small brick building is considered a landmark; in fact, it was moved in 1975 to save it from
incoming bulldozers. It's old New Haven, where people talk to
strangers, and the hamburger—a very fine one—is king. No dinner Tuesday or Wednesday. Closed Sunday and Monday; closed
August to mid-September. ~ 261 Crown Street, New Haven; 203-
562-5507. BUDGET.

Pizza on Wooster Street is a must in New Haven—you'll find
no disagreement on that. But whether Pepe's is better than Sally's,
or vice versa, is cause for arguments in this city that is considered
the pizza capital of the state. There are numerous Italian restaurants lining the street, and all of them have lines that are long but
friendly. Here are two favorites. Maybe you'll try them both, and
then decide. One of the most popular is **Frank Pepe Pizzeria**. No
dinner Friday or Saturday. Closed Tuesday. ~ 157 Wooster Street,
New Haven; 203-865-5762. BUDGET TO MODERATE. Another good
spot to try is **Sally's Apizza** a few doors down. ~ 237 Wooster
Street, New Haven; 203-624-5271. BUDGET TO MODERATE.

If you're in the mood for a French meal, be sure to make res-
ervations at the **Union League Café**. Owned by chef Jean-Pierre
Vuillermet, this is one of only a few places you can get authentic
French cuisine in the city. The ever-changing menu may include
Provençal specialties such as salmon with cucumbers and mint.
The dining room is large, open, and surrounded with Tiffany-style
windows. No lunch on Saturday or Sunday. ~ 1032 Chapel Street,
New Haven; 203-562-4299, fax 203-562-6712. MODERATE TO
DELUXE.

Decorated in a turn-of-the-century style, **500 Blake Street** is
a local favorite, specializing in Italian/Continental cuisine. There's
something for everyone, including fish, pasta, chicken, duck and
beef dishes. There's also a piano bar. ~ 500 Blake Street, West-
ville; 203-387-0500, fax 203-387-7578. MODERATE TO DELUXE.

The **Stony Creek Market** has as many enthusiasts as do the
enchanting islands it overlooks. Locals and visitors drop in and
order their favorites—soups, unusual salads, breads, muffins
and cookies still warm from the oven—then take their choices to
a table inside or on the deck. Pizza is available at dinner Tuesday
through Sunday. Food, views and friendly atmosphere vie for the
raves. Closed Monday night and Tuesday during winter. ~ 178
Thimble Island Road, Stony Creek; 203-488-0145. BUDGET TO
MODERATE.

When in New Haven, do as the Yalies do—patronize the **Yale** **SHOPPING**
Co-op, two mammoth floors filled with everything needed by
students—and other humans, too. Glance at the striking, geometric facade—a 1960s design by Eero Saarinen—before you suc-
cumb to temptation inside. Books are the main attraction here,
a most extraordinary selection of titles, but you'll also find men's
and women's dress and casual clothes, records and radios, computers and a travel agency. ~ 924 Chapel Street, New Haven; 203-
772-2200.

Among the bountiful bookstores in this learned city is **Atticus**
Bookstore Café, a great place to start reading that novel you just
bought as you linger over a cappuccino and pastry or a sandwich.
~ 1082 Chapel Street, New Haven; 203-776-4040; e-mail atticus3
@connix.com.

The area around Chapel and College streets, home to theaters,
museums and restaurants, is great for shopping, too. Some of the
stores are multiples—Laura Ashley, The Gap—while others are
New Haven originals. **Endleman Gallery** carries one-of-a-kind
jewelry by over 100 American designers. ~ 1014 Chapel Street,
New Haven; 203-776-2517.

The Endleman Gallery's offspring, **Endleman Two**, presents
uncommon accessories and clothes. ~ 1014 Chapel Street, New
Haven; 203-782-2280.

Branford Craft Village at Bittersweet Farm is quite a delight—a cluster of some 20 workshops carved out of buildings
that were part of a chicken farm. You can watch craftspeople at
their work—woodworker, potter, glass blower, knitter, stained-
glass artist—and order custom-made pieces or select from their
ample stock. ~ 779 East Main Street, near Exit 56 on Route 95,
Branford; 203-488-4689.

New Haven is blessed with an outstanding theater scene (see **NIGHTLIFE**
"Theater in Connecticut" in this chapter), frequent concerts by
the New Haven Symphony and visiting artists and several late-
night spots well worth a visit.

Toad's Place headlines local and national bands. Cover. ~ 300
York Street, New Haven; 203-624-8623.

HAMMONASSET BEACH STATE PARK 🏃 🚲 ⛵ 🎣 **BEACHES**
🚤 ⚓ Largest of Connecticut's shoreline parks, 919-acre Ham- **& PARKS**
monasset offers a two-mile-long, wide sandy beach that's great
for swimming, snorkeling and fishing. Patient anglers often reel
in good-size bluefish, striped bass or blackfish. You can launch
small sailboats on the beach, hike along numerous hiking and
biking trails and visit the nature center, which sponsors interpretive programs. Moreover, the park is ideally located for visiting the

picturesque shoreline towns. Visitors will find picnic grounds with shelter, restrooms, food concession stands, a pavilion with changing rooms and a nature center. Day-use fee, $7 to $12. ~ In Madison, one mile south of Exit 62 on Route 95; 203-245-2785, fax 203-245-9201.

▲ There are 550 tent/RV campsites (no hookups); most are located in open fields, a five-to-ten-minute walk from the beach; $12 per night; for camping information call 203-245-1817.

Lower Connecticut River Valley

The Lower Valley of the Connecticut River—stretching north for some 30 miles from Old Saybrook, where the river empties into Long Island Sound, is a favorite destination for visitors from near and far. The area is studded with small scenic towns once known as shipbuilding and sea-going communities. Also blessed with numerous state parks, and sophisticated restaurants and lodgings, the Lower Valley provides a chance to get close to the longest waterway in New England, a river that was central to the development of the young nation.

SIGHTS

There's a highway information center on Route 95 (northbound) at **Westbrook**. You'd do well to begin this leg of the trip by stopping there, or contacting the **Connecticut River Valley and Shoreline Visitors Council** for information and detailed maps. Closed Saturday and Sunday. ~ 393 Main Street, Middletown, CT 06457; 860-347-0028, 800-486-3346, fax 860-704-2340; www.cttourism.org.

In fact, Westbrook, on Long Island Sound, is a good place to begin your exploration of the valley. Take Route 1 east until it

HIDDEN ►

joins **Route 154**, then ramble with it past salt marshes, causeways and marinas through **Old Saybrook**, a town with shoreline along both Sound and river and many picturesque watery views.

Route 154 (natives call it the Shore Route) leads to **Essex** and points north, as does Route 9, which is speedier and beautiful in its own right, but the older road is best for antiquing and poking; it gives you more of a sense of place. Essex is one of the most visited towns in the state, and with good reason: it's a compact peninsula where the tree-lined streets end at the river and the white houses, set cheek-by-jowl, date back to 18th-century shipbuilding days. Beware of summer weekends, however: Essex's charms have been sung once too often.

At the foot of Main Street, with a river view to make you catch your breath, stands the **Connecticut River Museum**, housed in a restored 1878 warehouse where steamboats used to stop for freight and passengers on their way to Hartford or New York. Exhibits will help you place the river's role into perspective. Closed Monday. Admission. ~ Steam Boat Dock, 67 Main Street, Essex;

860-767-8269, fax 860-767-7028; www.connix.com/~crm, e-mail crm@connix.com.

The **Valley Railroad** is a vintage steam train that winds its nostalgic way through the countryside for about 20 minutes to Deep River, the next town up the line. From there you may continue on by train or hop aboard a riverboat up the Connecticut River—and then climb back on the train to return to Essex. The combination train/ riverboat trip takes about two and a half hours. Open daily April through Labor Day; closed January through March; call for other hours. Admission. ~ 1 Railroad Avenue, Essex; 860-767-0103; www.valleyrr.com.

> When visiting the Connecticut River Museum, be sure to view the full-size replica of the ill-fated *American Turtle* (the world's first submarine), built just before the Revolutionary War.

When you head north from Essex, go right at the turnaround at the head of Main Street and take River Road as far as Deep River—just keep bearing right when the road forks. It's a winding, narrow country road with views of quietly flowing waters and the forested banks across the way. Then back on Route 154 and on to **Chester**, a picture-postcard village with a short main street lined with charmingly eclectic buildings—a few shops, galleries and restaurants, all restored to a fare-thee-well. Should you be there in the summer, you'll want to know about the **Sunday afternoon story-tellings** in words and pantomime held on the green, a present to the community by the award-winning **National Theatre of the Deaf**, a company that tours the world and makes its home in this town. ~ P.O. Box 659, Chester, CT 06412; 860-526-4971 voice, or 860-526-4974 TTY; www.ntd.org.

◀ *HIDDEN*

Since 1769, Chester has been the site of a ferry to the river's east bank. It's a few minutes' drive east of the town center, on Route 148. By all means, take it. The five-minute crossing operates continuously from 7 a.m. to 6:45 p.m. from April through November, at a minimal charge. Looming above you as you stand on deck you'll see what looks like a medieval fortress atop a steep wooded hill. It's **Gillette Castle**, Connecticut's own castle-on-the-Rhine, the creation of a turn-of-the-20th-century actor/playwright who specialized in playing Sherlock Holmes. It took William Gillette five years to build his eccentric dream house, all to his own designs down to the ingenious locks for all 47 doors and the carved oak trim of the mammoth living room. At his death, it was purchased by the state, which made it the centerpiece of a popular state park with wonderful vistas, **Gillette Castle State Park**. Closed January through Memorial Day; open daily from Memorial Day to Columbus Day; open weekends from Columbus Day through December. Admission for castle only. ~ 67 River Road, East Haddam; 860-526-2336.

East Haddam, a few miles south on Route 82, holds what many consider the jewel of the valley: the **Goodspeed Opera House**. Built on the river in the elegant mansard-roofed style of 1876, this petite Victorian beauty was reopened in 1963 and dedicated to reviving American musicals of the past. Tours of the exquisitely restored interior can be taken on Monday and Saturday in July, August and September. (For performances, see the "Theater in Connecticut" feature in this chapter.) Admission. ~ Route 82, East Haddam; 860-873-8668; www.goodspeed.org.

The little town retains many well-kept buildings, reminders of the days when steamboats made regular stops, and sailing ships before them. High on a knoll is the little red schoolhouse where Nathan Hale taught in 1773–74, two years before he was hanged as a spy by the British.

A brief voyage on the Connecticut River gives new perspectives on the picturesque shores. **Camelot Cruises** offers lunch, dinner, Sunday brunch, fall foliage cruises and murder mystery outings along the scenic Connecticut River (call for operating seasons). Also available are all-day trips across Long Island Sound (Memorial Day to Labor Day only). ~ 1 Marine Park, Haddam; 860-345-8591, 800-522-7463; www.camelotcruises.com.

Old Lyme lies due south of East Haddam, at the eastern end of the highway bridge that spans the river as it flows to the sea. The town's wealth, reflected in extraordinarily handsome, spacious homes, was born in the days of clipper ships and the China trade, but at the start of this century Old Lyme became a magnet for artists drawn by its beauty and tranquil setting. They called themselves American impressionists: Childe Hassam, Willard Metcalf, Henry Ranger and others who stayed at "Miss Florence's" boardinghouse. Miss Florence Griswold was a ship captain's daughter and lover of art. Her home, built in 1817, is today the **Florence Griswold Museum**, with period furniture and changing exhibitions. Most interesting is the dining room, where the artists painted local scenes on wall and door panels. A long, humorous vignette over the fireplace represents the group at an imaginary fox hunt, each member in a characteristic pose. Closed Monday. Admission. ~ 96 Lyme Street, Old Lyme; 860-434-5542, fax 860-434-6259; www.flogris.org, e-mail flogris@connix.com.

The imposing **Congregational Church** that appears frequently in the impressionists' paintings stands at Lyme Street's south end. Admired though it is, it is a 1910 copy, faithful in all details, of the original 1816 structure, destroyed by fire. **The Lyme Academy of Fine Arts** continues the town's tradition with a variety of exhibits throughout the year, as do several galleries on Lyme Street. Closed Monday in summer. ~ 84 Lyme Street, Old Lyme; 860-434-5232, fax 860-434-8725; www.lymeacademy.edu, e-mail admissions@lymeacademy.edu.

Westbrook is blessed with that rarest of pearls, a bed and break-fast set right on the sea. At **Talcott House**—an 1890 dormered, shingled home—guests can cross the quiet street and go swimming, or they can sit in the spacious, informal living room and admire the view. The four guest rooms face the sea, have private baths and are all tastefully done with country antiques. Hearty full breakfast included. ~ 161 Seaside Avenue, Westbrook; 860-399-5020. DELUXE.

For accommodations in the moderate range, it would be hard to beat the **Maples Motel**. Forty years of tender loving care by the same family have made it grow into a woodsy, attractive poolside complex of 18 units—some with cooking facilities—and seven "cottagettes" that can be rented by the week. Guests share a picnic area and may use a private sandy beach, minutes away. ~ 1935 Boston Post Road, Westbrook; 860-399-9345. BUDGET.

◄ HIDDEN

For many travelers, the words Connecticut Valley are interchangeable with the **Griswold Inn**. "The Gris" is a legend; a white, rambling landmark on the picture-postcard main street since 1776. Serving as a meeting place for the town, it's Olde New England to its very bones, with a taproom and restaurant, a gallery of vintage marine art and nightly musical jamborees. Four period buildings house 31 guest rooms and suites. Some are remodeled; in others, the floors list to port or starboard, as if to remind you of the town's maritime past and its nautical present as well. Continental breakfast is included. ~ 36 Main Street, Essex; 860-767-1812, fax 860-767-0481; www.griswoldinn.snet.net. DELUXE.

Located within easy reach of the Goodspeed Opera House and Gillette's Castle, **The Inn at Chester** is a 200-year-old homestead with plenty of modern amenities. Its 42 rooms are furnished with antiques; some have canopy beds and some have fireplaces. Other comforts include a tennis court, an exercise room, a sauna, a library and a game room with pool table, darts and plenty of board games. There are also hiking trails, and bikes are loaned free of charge to guests. ~ 318 West Main Street, Chester; 800-949-7829, fax 860-526-4387. DELUXE TO ULTRA-DELUXE.

Copper Beech Inn is a classic: a sedate, gracious country inn with an award-winning French restaurant in what was once the home of a wealthy ivory merchant—the trade that put this little town on the map. Four of the 13 rooms are in the main house, meticulously appointed all, with charming old-fashioned baths. Set back near the woods, the Carriage House has been remodeled with exquisite taste and a sense of romance, and its nine bedrooms all have jacuzzis and doors leading out to a deck with sylvan vistas. Continental breakfast. ~ 46 Main Street, Ivoryton; 860-767-0330; www.copperbeechinn.com. MODERATE TO ULTRA-DELUXE.

Antique lovers won't know where to look first at **Riverwind Country Inn**. This bed and breakfast, in the center of one of the valley's quieter towns, is chockablock with country antiques and folk art—some from the owner's own family, others trophies of forays around the country. Rates for the eight attractively furnished, hand-stenciled rooms, all with bath, include a prodigious breakfast that reflects the innkeeper's Southern background. ~ 209 Main Street, Deep River; 860-526-2014, fax 860-526-0875; www.innformation.com/ct/riverwind. MODERATE TO ULTRA-DELUXE.

What could be more pleasant than to waltz across the street to **Bishopsgate Inn** after enjoying a nostalgic musical at Goodspeed Opera House? Or any time, in fact. The early 19th-century shipbuilder's house stands tall and handsome on a landscaped knoll, and the six guest rooms, all with theatrical names on the door, are done in good taste and have private baths. Breakfast is served in the spacious country kitchen. ~ Goodspeed Landing, East Haddam; 860-873-1677, fax 860-873-3898; www.bishopsgate.com. MODERATE TO DELUXE.

The **Bee and Thistle Inn** is on every list of all-time favorites. A gambrel-roofed, mid-18th-century house, it's right next door to the Florence Griswold Museum on the town's major street, yet it's set back on extensive landscaped grounds that sweep down to the Lieutenant River, a branch of the Connecticut. Most of the ground floor is devoted to the popular restaurant. Eleven tasteful, uncluttered rooms occupy the second and third floors, each with its own decor, all with bath. There's also a one-bedroom "Innkeepers Cottage" featuring a library with fireplace, kitchen and glass-enclosed sitting room. Rooms in the main house are moderate to ultra-deluxe; the cottage is ultra-deluxe. Closed for three weeks in January. ~ 100 Lyme Street, Old Lyme; 860-434-1667, 800-622-4946, fax 860-434-3402; www.beeandthistleinn.com, e-mail info@beeandthistleinn.com. MODERATE TO ULTRA-DELUXE.

The **Old Lyme Inn** is set in a farmhouse that dates back to the 1850s. The 13 rooms, five in the original farmhouse, are furnished with Victorian and Empire antiques. The honeymoon suites have

THE "GRIS"

Historic is a word used lightly around these parts, but surely it applies to the **Griswold Inn**, established in 1776. Go for lunch, dinner, the famous Sunday "Hunt Breakfast" or a drink, so you can view the warren of wood-paneled, evocative rooms that tumble one into the other. Partake of the New England specialties and other Americana on which the "Gris" has built its reputation, it's an experience one shouldn't miss. ~ 36 Main Street, Essex; 860-767-1812, fax 860-767-0481; www.griswoldinn.snet.net. DELUXE.

four-poster beds, Victorian loveseats and marble-topped dressers. Guests can lounge in the library in front of the fireplace and choose from a variety of puzzles and games. A continental breakfast is served every morning. Four rooms on the first floor are wheelchair accessible. Gay-friendly. ~ 85 Lyme Street, Old Lyme; 860-434-2600, 800-434-5352, fax 860-434-5352; www.oldlyme inn.com, e-mail olinn@aol.com. DELUXE.

DINING

Seafood lovers think of Westbrook as the home of **Bill's Seafood Restaurant**. Here at this informal spot, fried-clam aficionados gather inside or on the terrace overlooking the salt marsh. Fish, shrimp and lobster rolls have a place on the menu, as do hot dogs and burgers, but it's the sweet, plump, lightly fried clams that are the attraction. ~ Boston Post Road at the Singing Bridge, Westbrook; 860-399-7224; e-mail bseafood@uconect.net. MODERATE.

Fiddlers is a pleasantly appointed, unpretentious place residents turn to when they want carefully prepared, really fresh seafood—chicken and meat, too. Fish entrées change according to the market and can be ordered to your taste—sautéed, poached, baked, broiled, cajun or mesquite-grilled. Closed Monday. ~ 4 Water Street, Chester; 860-526-3210; www.chester.com. MODERATE TO DELUXE.

The Wheat Market creates gourmet sandwiches, as well as changing entrées, salads, soups and a famed deep-dish pizza to eat at tables or take along on a picnic. With Gillette Castle State Park just a five-minute ferry ride away, that might be just the ticket on a nice day. Closed Sunday. ~ 4 Water Street, Chester; 860-526-9347. BUDGET.

The **Copper Beech Inn** is a landmark, a longtime favorite among followers of fine French cuisine. Set in a tree-shaded, 1890 home, it breathes Old World elegance and charm. Sterling silver, fresh flowers and fine china grace the tables in the three dining rooms. Despite the high prices, you'll have to reserve well in advance, at least on weekends. Closed Monday all year; also closed Tuesday, January through March. ~ 46 Main Street, Ivoryton; 860-767-0330; www.copperbeechinn.com. DELUXE TO ULTRA-DELUXE.

For years, the **Bee and Thistle Inn** has been voted the most romantic restaurant in the state by readers of *Connecticut* magazine. It's true, the rambling rooms and porches exude an air of intimacy and warmth appealing to lovers, and other mortals as well. The offerings are elegantly served and very tasty: seafood, game, poultry, meats, each flavored with fresh herbs shipped in or picked from the sunken garden just outside the windows. Closed Tuesday and for three weeks in January. ~ 100 Lyme Street, Old

Lyme; 860-434-1667; www.beeandthistleinn.com, e-mail info@
beeandthistleinn.com. DELUXE TO ULTRA-DELUXE.

SHOPPING Antiques are what most shoppers seek in this region, and every
little town responds with its own array of specialized offerings.
There's even the **Essex Saybrook Antiques Village**, where no fewer
than 120 dealers hold forth in their own cluster of Colonial-
looking buildings. Closed Monday from late December through
Memorial Day. ~ 345 Middlesex Turnpike, Old Saybrook; 860-
388-0689.

The **Connecticut River Valley and Shoreline Visitors Council**
has compiled a complete listing of antique shops in the area. ~
393 Main Street, Middletown; 860-347-0028, 800-486-3346;
www.cttourism.org.

Window shopping along Essex's lovely Main Street is a pop-
ular pastime—too popular, you might find, on summer weekends.
Many of the stores' names will be familiar; some are originals, like
Swanton Jewelry, experts in jewelry old and new. ~ 1 Griswold
Square, Essex; 860-767-1271.

If herbs intrigue you, drive to the **Sundial Gardens** in tiny Higganum, where you can stroll through an 18th-century-style garden, then browse in the attractive barn-turned-herb-shop stocked
with gourmet items, plants, books, a myriad of herbs and rare
and fine teas for sale. Make reservations for Saturday or Sunday
tea and a tour of the exceptional garden. Admission. ~ Route 81
to Brault Hill Road extension, Higganum; 860-345-4290; www.
sundialgardens.com.

NIGHTLIFE The elegant **Water's Edge Inn and Resort** offers live bands in the
lounge on weekends and outdoor entertainment from Memorial
Day to Labor Day. ~ 1525 Boston Post Road, Westbrook; 860-
399-5901.

The **Griswold Inn** is a favorite meeting place after sundown.
A landmark of this exquisite river town ever since 1776, "the
Gris" boasts an old taproom as fine as any in the state. Nightly
doings range from Dixieland to sea chanteys to traditional ballads
or classic arias, all performed in a warm, friendly atmosphere. ~
36 Main Street, Essex; 860-767-1812; www.griswoldinn.snet.net.

BEACHES **SELDEN NECK STATE PARK** 🏃 🛶 🎣 ⚓ 🚣 ⛴ 🛥 This
& PARKS one is special, a 528-acre island in the Connecticut River accessible only by water—truly a place to get away from it all. You can
hike along woodsy trails that lead to old rock quarries, explore the
shore in your kayak or canoe or contemplate the wide, tranquil
river. Canoes and kayaks can be launched at the ferry slip below
Gillette Castle or anywhere along the Connecticut River. There
are outhouses, picnic tables and fireplaces. ~ The island is located

two miles south of Gillette Castle State Park in East Haddam, which handles information and permits for both parks; phone/fax 860-526-2336.

▲ Four primitive tent sites are available for one-night stops by boaters only; $4 per person.

GILLETTE CASTLE STATE PARK 🏃 🚣 ⛵ One of the most popular destinations in Connecticut, this mountainside park is topped by the picturesque fieldstone structure built at the start of the century by William Gillette, a well-known actor (see the "Sights" section in this chapter). Views of the Connecticut River are spectacular, and you can hike on shady trails to the water's edge and watch the ferry plying its way between Chester and Hadlyme. Picnic grounds, restrooms, food concession stands, a gift shop and horse-drawn carriage rides are all available here. Closed January through Memorial Day; open daily from Memorial Day to Columbus Day; open weekends from Columbus Day through December. ~ Four miles south of East Haddam, off Route 82. From the west bank of the river, take the ferry from Chester to Hadlyme and follow the signs up the mountain; 860-526-2336.

▲ One primitive tent site is available for one-night stops for canoers and kayakers only; $4 per person.

▼▼▼▼▼▼▼▼▼▼
Mystic Area

The easternmost stretch of the Connecticut coast is lined with towns and villages with deep maritime roots. These include New London, home to the U.S. Coast Guard Academy; Groton, the "submarine capital of the world"; Mystic, where the popular Mystic Seaport is located; and Stonington, where you will find an impressive collection of 18th- and 19th-century buildings that were built for ship captains and other seafarers. Several of the east-coast towns were important whaling centers back in the early 1800s, which brought great prosperity to the area.

SIGHTS

The centerpiece of this chunk of the coast is the historic Mystic Seaport, which could keep you happily amused for hours, but you'll find quite a bit to see in the towns surrounding it.

It's best to stop at the information center on Route 95 at North Stonington (southbound) or contact the **Southeastern Connecticut Tourism District** (Mystic and More) to get the lay of the land—and of the water. Closed Saturday and Sunday. ~ P.O. Box 89, 470 Bank Street, New London, CT 06320; 800-863-6569, fax 860-442-4257; www.mysticmore.com.

New London, Groton, Mystic and Stonington grew prosperous as sea and river ports, and today, the recreational uses of this jagged coastline are central to the communities' appeal. Moreover, New London and Groton are home to water-related military facilities, some of which are open to the public. At the **United**

States Coast Guard Academy visitors may tour the grounds, visitors center, museum, the chapel, some of the buildings and, when it's in port, the tall ship *Eagle*, used as a training vessel for the cadets. What a vision, when she sails down the Thames River and out to sea! ~ 15 Mohegan Avenue/Route 32, New London; 860-444-8270, fax 860-444-8289.

HIDDEN ▶

Though the glories of whaling days are New London's main claim to fame—be sure to drive past the four magnificent 1832 temple-front mansions, known collectively as **Whale Oil Row** (105–119 Huntington Street)—the city has many strings to its bow: the lively town pier, with charter boats of all kinds; ferries that ply across the Sound to several island destinations; and some fine historic homes and museums.

Visitors of a literary bent will want to stop by the shorefront **Monte Cristo Cottage**, boyhood home of playwright Eugene O'Neill and the setting for his two autobiographical plays, *Ah! Wilderness* and *Long Day's Journey Into Night*. Closed Monday and from October through May. Admission. ~ 325 Pequot Avenue, New London; 860-443-0051.

The Monte Cristo cottage is part of the **Eugene O'Neill Theater Center**, an organization devoted to developing new works for the stage. Some of the play readings, performances and rehearsals are open to the public. (See the "Theater in Connecticut" feature in this chapter.) Closed Sunday. ~ 305 Great Neck Road, Waterford; 860-443-5378.

Nearby is New London's **Ocean Beach Park**, with a broad expanse of fine sand, a boardwalk and vistas of passing ships, ferries and a handsome lighthouse. Admission. ~ 1225 Ocean Avenue, New London; 860-447-3031, 800-510-7263, fax 860-442-1117.

A river scene great to behold is a submarine being towed by a tugboat to or from the United States Naval Submarine base on the Groton side of the Thames. In Groton, you can tour the **USS Nautilus**, the first nuclear-powered submarine, now a National Historic Landmark, permanently berthed and refitted to receive visitors. Closed Tuesday form November to mid-May. ~ Exit 86 off Route 95, Groton; 860-694-3174, fax 860-694-4150; www.ussnautilus.org.

Alongside is the striking, steel-and-glass **Submarine Force Library and Museum**, with hands-on, up-to-date exhibits that trace the history of the submarine from our friend Bushnell's *Turtle* to the sleek, high-tech models of today. ~ Exit 86 off Route 95, Groton; 860-694-3174, fax 860-694-4150.

Boat tours of the Groton–New London area offer a multitude of choices, including the two-and-one-half-hour educational cruise on the research vessel **Enviro-Lab**, where passengers learn about marine life firsthand. Open from mid-June through Labor Day.

Admission. ~ Project Oceanology, 1084 Shennescossett Road, Avery Point, Groton; 860-445-9007, 800-364-8472, fax 860-449-8008; www.oceanology.org, e-mail info@oceanology.com.

Driving toward Mystic on Route 95, you'll arrive at a scenic overlook where **Mystic Seaport Museum** comes into view. Just for a moment—as you spot the masts of tall ships in the distance and the smaller craft that ply the Mystic River—you might really believe you're entering a 19th-century New England seaport. When you get there, you and thousands of others, a little of the magic wears off. Yet it's unique, this indoor/outdoor museum on 17 riverfront acres. Admission. ~ 75 Greenmanville Avenue, Mystic; 860-572-0711, fax 860-572-5326; www.mysticseaport.org.

Begun in 1929, Mystic Seaport has grown steadily, encompassing a coastal village—church, chapel, schoolhouse, pharmacy, bank, ship's chandlery—several buildings with indoor exhibits of figureheads, marine paintings and ship's models; a lively children's museum; a preservation shipyard where you can watch the craftsmen at work; and a collection of some 300 boats and ships headed by the *Charles W. Morgan* (1841), America's sole surviving wooden whaleship. Crowds or no crowds, you won't want to miss the opportunity to explore its decks, visit the cramped quarters where crews lived for years at a time and watch members of the staff set sails and climb the rigging as they sing traditional chanteys. An ideal time to go is on a drizzly, misty grey day, when visitors are fewer and the atmosphere even more evocative.

Having been transported into the reconstructed past, take time to roam the town of **Mystic** itself, where vessels of all kinds, including whalers, clipper ships and pleasure boats, have been built since the 17th century. You'll find streets, such as Gravel, Clift and High, edged with early- and mid-19th-century homes of ships' owners and captains. The small downtown bustles with visitors, all watching the parade of boats passing under the rare *bascule* bridge (that's French for seesaw) that opens hourly all summer long, while traffic stops dead. There are **windjammers** and all manner of craft available for cruises of an hour or a week. You can help sail, or not, according to the mood of the moment. For details, contact the Southeastern Connecticut Tourism District. Closed Saturday and Sunday. ~ P.O. Box 89, 470 Bank Street, New London, CT 06320; 800-863-6569.

Stonington, the easternmost coastline town in the state, is thought by many to be the most attractive. The densely settled, narrow tongue of land known as Stonington Borough, part of the larger town, is home port to Connecticut's one remaining commercial fishing fleet. Its compact streets are a treasury of architectural styles dating back to the 18th and 19th centuries, when generations of seamen sailed in locally built vessels to trade with China and as far as Antarctica in search of whales and seals. A pleasant walking tour of Main, Water and the short diagonal streets could begin at the **Old Lighthouse Museum**, where the 1823 granite lighthouse (moved to its current location in 1840) displays maritime exhibits and artifacts of early American coastal life. Be sure to climb the stone steps to the top of the tower where there is a wonderful view of three states and Long Island Sound. Closed from November through April (except by appointment) and closed Monday in May, June, September and October. Admission. ~ 7 Water Street, Stonington; 860-535-1440.

UNDERWATER MYSTIC

You'll want to visit Connecticut's most popular attraction, **Mystic Aquarium**. It boasts 34 fine indoor exhibits; outdoor habitats for sea lions, seals and penguins; the World of the Dolphin has hourly demonstrations starring trained dolphins; watch Beluga whales and harbor seals in the Alaskan exhibit; in summer, open classroom programs are available for children, (reservations required); an interactive exhibit, Challenges of the Deep, illustrates the wonder and complexity of deep sea exploration. Admission. ~ 55 Coogan Boulevard, Mystic; 860-572-5955, fax 860-572-5984; www.mysticaquarium.org.

Don't be lulled by the abundance of accommodations around New
London and Mystic; in season, a good room can still be hard to get.
There's a big cluster of motels at Exit 90 off Route 95, ranging
in price from moderate to deluxe (less in winter and spring). Some
other options, all within a few miles of the main attractions:

LODGING

The **Lighthouse Inn** was the summer home of a steel magnate
who decided, in 1902, to build a Spanish-style stucco "cottage"
in the meadows overlooking the sea. The meadows have been re-
zoned residential, but the mansion makes an opulent 52-room inn,
with a fine restaurant and individually designed, generous bedrooms with water views, antique furnishings and unusual details;
a few even have ocean views. ~ 6 Guthrie Place, New London;
860-443-8411, 888-443-8411, fax 860-437-7027; www.light
houseinn-ct.com. DELUXE TO ULTRA-DELUXE.

The cozy **Shore Inne** is a five-room bed and breakfast set
among small homes right on the water—"like being in grandmother's cottage," the owner says. Grandma should consider
new mattresses. Other than that, it's a great place to be: The views
are splendid and you can walk to any of three private beaches
nearby. Closed November through March. ~ 54 East Shore Avenue, Groton Long Point; 860-536-1180. MODERATE.

◄ *HIDDEN*

The Inn at Mystic is a hilltop potpourri of accommodations:
a fine motel and two historic buildings for a total of some 68
rooms. The exquisitely landscaped complex also includes an ex-
emplary restaurant, tennis courts, a pool and a dock with rowboats, kayaks and canoes. Rooms are individually designed and
old-time in feeling, even in the motel. Not so the bathrooms, which
are luxuriously up-to-date. Despite the feeling of elegant seclusion,
you're only a mile away from Mystic Seaport. ~ Routes 1 and
27, Mystic; 860-536-9604, 800-237-2415, fax 800-572-1635.
MODERATE TO ULTRA-DELUXE.

At the **Whaler's Inn** you'll find a variety of rooms housed in
the inn itself and two motor courts. You couldn't be more "downtown": The famed bridge is within a few feet. There are two restaurants attached to the inn and a few rooms with fine views of
the Mystic River and the Seaport, just a half-mile away. ~ 20 East
Main Street, Mystic; 860-536-1506, 800-243-2588, fax 860-572-
1250. DELUXE TO ULTRA-DELUXE.

Two gems lie on the outskirts of Mystic. **Applewood Farms
Inn**, an early-19th-century farmhouse complete with corn crib
(which has a hot tub!) and barn, is a few miles north of Route
95 and the visiting crowds. Set on 33 acres and surrounded by
farms, this is one bed and breakfast that welcomes children (if
prior arrangements are made). The house, a National Historic
Register Landmark, is blessed with magnificent fireplaces, and
the two common rooms and five guest rooms have distinct personalities, highlighted by an eclectic selection of period pieces.

◄ *HIDDEN*

Breakfasts are uniformly bountiful, true country meals. After breakfast, golfers can hone their skills on the U.S.G.A.-designed putting green. ~ 528 Colonel Ledyard Highway, Ledyard; 860-536-2022, 800-717-4262, fax 860-536-6015; www.visitmystic. com/applewoodfarmsinn, e-mail applewoodfarms@yahoo.com. DELUXE TO ULTRA-DELUXE.

The **Palmer Inn** is southern in inspiration, a columned, porticoed mansion built in this captivating little community in 1907. Here all is graciousness and Victorian elegance—carved mahogany paneling, stained glass, Oriental carpets on polished wood floors —in the main hall, the parlor and the sitting room as well as the six spacious bedrooms up the wide, curving stairs. Continental breakfast. ~ 25 Church Street, Noank; 860-572-9000. DELUXE TO ULTRA-DELUXE.

DINING

Lunching at the **Lighthouse Inn,** you'll glimpse an intriguing view of Long Island Sound between two rows of houses. These good-size 20th-century homes seem to be dollhouses, in contrast to the baronial grandeur of the inn's dining room—dark, heavy overhead beams and dark wainscoting, great fireplaces and heavy, almost grotesque chandeliers. Yet, though the dining rooms seat more than 200, business is brisk. And with good reason: the food is well prepared, heavy on seafood—a favorite around these parts. ~ 6 Guthrie Place, New London; 860-443-8411, 888-443-8411, fax 860-437-7027; www.lighthouseinn-ct.com. MODERATE TO DELUXE.

For a meal or snacks at any time of day, the place to go, according to residents of the area, is **G. Williker's!**. It has a popular taproom and a friendly staff, the usual faux-Victorian decor and a variety of excellent burgers, seafood, steak and all-American favorites such as tacos and pizza. ~ 156 Kings Highway, Exit 86 on Route 95, Groton; 860-445-8043, fax 860-445-4082. BUDGET TO MODERATE.

Restaurant Bravo Bravo features cuisine with Italian and French accents. You may choose from entrées like veal medallions stuffed with garlic, spinach and cheese and topped with shiitake mushroom sauce, or garlic and tomato shrimp baked in a casserole. During the summer, enjoy the outdoor café where you can watch the best show in town: The old drawbridge that opens every hour to let boats go through. Closed Monday. ~ In the Whaler's Inn, 20 East Main Street, Mystic; 860-536-3228. MODERATE TO ULTRA-DELUXE.

If you're spending the day at Mystic Seaport, you'll want to know about **The Seamen's Inne**, located next to the Seaport entrance. It's a large, busy place, built to resemble the New England–style structures nearby, and it specializes in the appropriate fare—basically seafood. Portions are ample. ~ 105 Greenmanville Avenue, Mystic; 860-536-9649, fax 860-572-5304; www.seamens inn.org. MODERATE TO DELUXE.

High on a knoll overlooking the harbor sits the **Flood Tide Restaurant**, a favorite with visitors to the town. Part of The Inn at Mystic but set apart on the unusually handsome grounds, this bright, airy dining room offers award-winning Continental cuisine with something for every taste. ~ Routes 1 and 27, Mystic; 860-536-8140. DELUXE TO ULTRA-DELUXE.

And then there's **Abbott's Lobster in the Rough**, a legend in is own time, a place where dining informally means sitting at waterfront picnic tables or in the simple dining room and truly using your hands for all they're worth. There's chowder, steamed clams, mussels and shrimp, but it's the lobster that has made Abbott's famous for 40 years—caught in local waters, steamed to just the right degree of tenderness. On a summer day, you can expect a wait, maybe a long one. But who minds waiting, when there's a harbor full of boats and a picturesque village to delight? Open daily Memorial Day to Labor Day; weekends only from Labor Day to Columbus Day and early May to Memorial Day. ~ 117 Pearl Street, Noank; 860-536-7719. BUDGET TO ULTRA-DELUXE.

In captivating Stonington, the **Water Street Cafe** is a wonderfully casual, yet elegant spot. The cuisine is classic with an Oriental twist. For example, there's a sesame-ginger roasted salmon dish and a seared tuna served with a wasabi dipping sauce. For vegetarians, there's a very tasty vegetable Napoleon. It's a small restaurant—seating just about 30 people—with red walls and crisp white tablecloths. ~ 142 Water Street, Stonington; 860-535-2122. BUDGET TO DELUXE.

Randall's Ordinary is, in fact, unique. Everything on the menu at this inn-with-restaurant—that's what *ordinary* meant in days of yore—is cooked over the fire in authentic Early-American fashion. Guests are invited to stand before the three massive fireplaces and watch dinner cooking; then it's brought to the table by servers in period costumes. The backdrop for this gastronomic journey into the past is a landmark 17th-century country home listed on the National Register of Historic Places. The price includes soup, an entrée of poultry, meat or fish, and dessert. ~ 41 Norwich Westerly Road, North Stonington; 860-599-4540; www.randalls ordinary.com, e-mail info@randallsordinary.com. ULTRA-DELUXE.

Olde Mistick Village is an entire community of Colonial-style structures built in 1973 to house every kind of shop and boutique known to the traveler—60 businesses on 20 landscaped acres. A bit cutesy, but it's an attractive place for browsing, with winding lanes, a stream, benches, wonderful flowers, even an authentic-looking meeting house with slender steeple and bells that soothe

SHOPPING

the weary visitor with music. ~ Exit 90 off Route 95; 860-536-4941, www.visitnewengland.com.

Within Mystic Seaport itself, the vast **Mystic Seaport Museum Stores** emphasize things nautical and traditionally New England: gifts, clothes, jewelry, foods, books, prints, reproductions from the museum's collection. A separate section houses the prestigious Mystic Maritime Gallery. ~ 47 Greenmanville Avenue, Mystic; 860-572-0711, fax 860-572-5326; www.mysticseaport.org.

Stonington's Water Street offers a wealth of pristine buildings to admire, good antiquing and a clutch of interesting boutiques as well. At **Hungry Palette** you'll find exclusive, locally designed fabrics and clothes. ~ 105 Water Street, Stonington; 860-535-2021.

Quimper Faïence imports its traditional, hand-painted dinnerware and accessories directly from France. ~ 141 Water Street, Stonington; 860-535-1712; e-mail mail@quimperfaience.com.

NIGHTLIFE **Ocean Beach Park** presents nightly programs with top entertainment acts performing under a spacious tent close to the sea. Open only in the summer. Parking fee. ~ Ocean Avenue, New London; 860-447-3031, 800-510-7263.

After a heavy day of sightseeing in Mystic, try the bar at the **Captain Daniel Packer Inn**. The cozy, rustic room with its old fireplace is a favorite gathering place for residents of all ages. It features live music Tuesday through Thursday and a relaxing atmosphere seven nights a week. ~ 32 Water Street, Mystic; 860-536-3555.

Located on the Mashantucket Indian Reservation, **Foxwoods Resort Casino and Tower Hotel** is the largest casino in the world. The casino more than 300 gaming tables, 24 restaurants and other entertainment including the Fox Theater. The hotel has 1416 rooms and more than 315,310 square feet designated for gaming. It's open 24 hours a day, year-round. ~ Route 2, Ledyard; 860-312-3000, 800-752-9244; www.foxwoods.com.

BEACHES & PARKS **ROCKY NECK STATE PARK** 🚶 🚴 ⚓ ⛵ The main attraction here is a half-mile sandy beach with excellent swimming and fishing, and a picturesque view of shorefront cottages across the bay. The 700-acre park also encompasses vast salt marshes sheltering a variety of bird life that can be viewed from trails and raised boardwalks. There are picnic grounds, restrooms, bathhouses and food concession stands. Day-use fee, $8 to $12. ~ Three miles west of Niantic on Route 156; 860-739-5471, fax 860-739-9023.

▲ There are 169 campsites, 149 for tents and RVs, 20 for tents only (no hookups); $12 per night.

OCEAN BEACH PARK ⚓ ⛵ This city-owned park has a one-mile-long, crescent-shaped beach of sparkling white sand, backed by an old-fashioned boardwalk for jogging or strolling. The beach has excellent swimming. There's also miniature golf, a gift shop, snack bars, an arcade and nightly entertainment under the stars. Facilities include an olympic-sized pool, beach volleyball, picnic pavilion, restrooms and changing rooms. Parking fee. ~ In New London; from Route 95, take Exit 82A northbound or Exit 83 southbound, then follow signs; 860-447-3031, 800-510-7263.

North of the bustling, at times crowded coastline lies the region that has dubbed itself "the quiet corner": Connecticut's little-known, unspoiled Northeast, rich in scenic and historic interest if not in per capita wealth. You'll find no corporate towers here, no hordes of tourists, but interesting small towns, some of them settled in the 18th century, and a wealth of green pastures, rolling hills, rivers and forests.

Northeast Corner

The **Northeast Connecticut Visitors District** will supply brochures listing accommodations and points of interest. ~ P.O. Box 598, Putnam, CT 06260; 860-928-1228, fax 860-928-4720; www. wcbtravels.com.

SIGHTS

To reach the quiet corner from the coast, the fastest route is 395, which branches off from Route 95 west of New London. If you're in Stonington, however, and don't wish to retrace your steps, a pleasant alternative would be Route 2, which winds its way through unspoiled rural areas to Norwich, a historic city at the head of the River Thames. At the junction of Routes 2 and 169, in Norwich, the old **Leffingwell Inn**, a former Colonial "publique house" and now a museum, served as a meeting place for patriots in the Revolutionary War. Closed Monday and from mid-October to mid-May. Admission. ~ 348 Washington Street, Norwich; 860-889-9440.

From there, Route 169 heads north and passes through the village of Taftville, past an immense, turreted brick construction handsome enough to serve as a king's castle. It's **Ponemah Mill**, a former cotton factory thought to have been the largest in the country and the most beautiful, many say. You won't find it on tourist itineraries—it's privately owned and now home to several companies—but it's an appropriate introduction to an area where the textile industry set the pattern of life from the mid-19th century until recent decades. When the industry moved to the South, it left behind its footprints: imposing riverfront mills, each with its village where the workers lived. Many such complexes—some shuttered and depressed, others used for new purposes—hug the banks of the Quinebaug River, which flows close to Route 169.

◄ HIDDEN

The road also passes graceful Colonial towns like **Canterbury**, with its neat village green, where the **Prudence Crandall Museum**, a National Historic Landmark, pays tribute to the resolute young teacher who dared to open a school for "young ladies of color" in 1833. The ensuing controversy led to imprisonment—happily, brief—and to the school's closing. Fifty years later, as a restitution of sorts, the state legislature granted Crandall an annuity of $400 per year. Closed Monday and Tuesday and from mid-December through January. Admission. ~ Routes 14 and 169, Canterbury; 860-546-9916, fax 860-546-7803; e-mail crndll@snet.net.

The courthouse where Crandall's trial took place is a few miles north, in **Brooklyn**, where it serves as the current town hall. Near it, on Brooklyn's green, is the first **Unitarian Church** in the state, a simple, elegant white structure built in 1771, with a Paul Revere bell in its lofty belfry.

HIDDEN ►

The town is known for its agricultural fair in late August, but it also holds a hidden gem: **Old Trinity Church** (1771), bypassed by time and now open just once a year on All Saints' Day. From the town center, take Route 6 east for one mile, go left on Church Street and you'll find the serene white clapboard structure, with its arched windows and pedimented door, standing next to its ancient graveyard in a leafy grove, surrounded by cornfields.

Eight miles north of Brooklyn is **Pomfret**, site of an elite private school. The community has long been a magnet for affluent city families, who built substantial summer homes and landscaped gardens here.

Woodstock sits high on a hill overlooking a rich agricultural valley. Visitors come from far away to see **Roseland Cottage/Bowen House**, a bright pink Gothic-inspired mansion built in 1846 by Henry Bowen, a local boy who grew rich in business in New York, then turned his energies toward publishing an anti-slavery, staunchly Republican weekly called *The Independent*. The lavish house and gardens, which remained in the family for over 100 years, are intact. Closed Monday and Tuesday and mid-October through May. Admission. ~ 556 Route 169, Woodstock; 860-928-4074, fax 860-963-2208; www.spnea.org.

Across the Quinebaug, and just a few miles from the Rhode Island and Massachusetts lines, the town of **Thompson** boasts a magnificent 19th-century mill fronting the river, as well as a classic residential area on a hilltop—one of the finest. Today, it's as composed and tranquil as any you'll find, with its traditional green —they call it a common here—fine meeting house and white or pale-yellow homes on shady streets. It was a busy crossroads in the past: two major turnpikes intersected there, Boston to Hartford and Providence to Springfield.

The two-story tavern built in 1814 is still operating today, now as **The White Horse Inn at Vernon Stiles**. In its early days, it was a bustling place for stagecoach travelers. It also did a brisk wedding business, as young lovers fled the stringent laws of nearby states. The 19th-century innkeeper, Captain Stiles, administered

The Rose of New England

In the shadow of its more famous—and touristy—neighbors, Mystic and New London, the little town of **Norwich** is a historic gem hidden in plain sight at the mouth of the Thames River. Founded in 1659, the settlement grew to become the second-largest city in Connecticut by the mid-18th century. After the Stamp Act of 1764 brought about a boycott of English imports, Norwich evolved into one of New England's major commercial and industrial centers, eventually boasting the world's largest cotton mill complex. It also gained notoriety by association with the town's most famous native son, traitor Benedict Arnold. Dubbed "the Rose of New England" by author James Lloyd Greene, who compared the surrounding hills to the petals of a rose, Norwich's faded as the area's economic base shifted to the coast. Today the rose remains the symbol of this time-capsule town, and the **Norwich Memorial Rose Garden** (in Mohegan Park on Rockwell Street) is one of its top attractions.

A trip along Broadway, Broad Street and Washington Street reveals a wealth of stately Victorian homes, the graceful neo-Gothic **St. Patrick's Cathedral** (213 Broadway), and the extravagant French Second Empire–style **City Hall** (100 Broadway). The **Slater Museum** (108 Crescent Street; 860-887-2506), with its Richardsonian Romanesque design and landmark round tower, exhibits American Indian artifacts, Victorian furniture, plaster casts of classic sculptures, and works by regional artists. The **Old Norwichtown Burying Grounds** (Old Cemetery Lane, off Norwichtown Green) contains unusual 18th-century tombstone art by eight renowned local stone carvers. The two-mile **Heritage Walkway** makes its way from **Yantic Falls** (the cascade that drove the powerhouse where industrialism got its start in Connecticut), along the riverfront, past the large marina at **American Wharf**, to **Howard T. Brown Memorial Park**, where summer band concerts are held every Wednesday at noon and Friday evening.

As Norwich transforms to a tourism-based economy, antique stores are springing up by the score. Two casinos, operated by the Mohegan and Mashantucket Pequot Indians, now stand on the outskirts of town. and plans have been announced for a new heritage center, Civil War and fire equipment museums, and a 50-acre botanical garden adjoining the rose garden.

the vows. Today's owners merely provide food and drink in a charming setting. Closed Monday and Tuesday. ~ Junction of Routes 193 and 200, Thompson; 860-923-9571, fax 860-923-0291; www.whitehorseinn.com, e-mail whitehorseinn.neca.com.

After this spell of old-time tranquility, you'll be ready for the bustle and bounce of an up-to-date university campus. Route 44 will take you west to Storrs, bordering the town of Mansfield, location of the main campus of the **University of Connecticut**. Closed Saturday and Sunday. ~ Information Center on Storrs Road on Depot Campus; 860-486-2000, fax 860-486-2063.

Now a prestigious university, "UConn" was founded in 1881 as an agricultural school. The sight of emerald pastures dotted with well-fed cows across the street from massive modern buildings makes an intriguing contrast. It also makes for great ice cream, which you can buy at the Dairy Bar, made every day. Refreshed, you'll want to stop at the **William Benton Museum of Art**, where wide-ranging exhibitions are displayed in an attractive, cathedral-ceilinged gallery. The Benton has the honor of being Connecticut's state art museum—a fitting way to finish up a tour. Closed Monday and between exhibits. ~ 245 Glenbrook Road, Storrs; 860-486-4520, fax 860-486-0234.

LODGING   In recent years numerous new bed and breakfasts have sprouted in this little known area, where accommodations were once hard to find. The **Northeast Connecticut Visitors District** will help visitors find one that suits their needs. ~ P.O. Box 598, Putnam, CT 06260; 860-928-1228, fax 860-928-4720; www.webtravels.com.

Several bed and breakfast reservation services will supply additional suggestions for accommodations throughout the state. Try the **Nutmeg Bed and Breakfast Agency**. Closed Saturday and Sunday. ~ P.O. Box 271117, West Hartford, CT 06127; 860-236-6698, 800-727-7592, fax 860-232-7680; www.bnb-link.com, e-mail nutmegbnb@home.com. Another agency is the **Covered Bridge Bed and Breakfast Reservation Service**. ~ P.O. Box 447, Norfolk, CT 06058; 860-542-5944.

The posh place to stay in Norwich is the **Norwich Inn & Spa**, a Georgian-style inn on 40 acres of landscaped grounds, forest and spring-fed ponds. Guest accommodations include 65 spacious rooms in the two-story main house and suites or townhouse-style duplexes with kitchens and fireplaces in 70 luxury villas hidden along wooded roadways fronting the Norwich Golf Course. Spa facilities include a whirlpool, sauna, steam room, indoor pool and fitness center. There are tennis courts, hiking trails and fitness classes including tai chi and yoga. ~ 607 West Thames Street, Norwich; 860-886-2401, 800-275-4772. MODERATE TO ULTRA-DELUXE.

The **King's Inn** makes a handy jumping-off place for exploring the "quiet corner" of the state. In decor, it tries to re-create old-time New England, but what it does best is supply 40 pleasant motel rooms, adding a pool and a restaurant for your convenience. ~ 5 Heritage Road, Putnam; 860-928-7961, 800-541-7304, fax 860-963-2463. MODERATE.

The 1825 **Inn at Woodstock Hill** is a Christopher Wren–style, three-story white building with black shutters. The 22 guest rooms are decorated in Waverly chintz with an assortment of antique cherry and maple furniture. Six of the rooms feature fireplaces and four-poster beds. Guests may linger at the piano in the living room or relax with a book in front of the fireplace in the library. Continental breakfast. ~ 94 Plaine Hill Road, South Woodstock; 860-928-0528, fax 860-928-3236; www.webtravels.com/wood stockhill. MODERATE TO DELUXE.

One bed and breakfast with a faithful following is **Altnaveigh Inn,** a 1734 farmhouse less than two miles from the University of Connecticut. The five well cared for rooms are located above a popular restaurant and are simply furnished. ~ Route 195, Storrs; 860-429-4490, fax 860-429-0371. MODERATE.

DINING

Some people plan a trip to this part of the state just to have a meal at the **Golden Lamb Buttery**. Located in a converted 1860s barn, it's country dining like you've never experienced. The menu generally includes classic American dishes and whatever's ready to be plucked from the garden. There's usually a wonderful soup to start, followed by a choice of entrées: duck, lamb, various seafood and chateaubriand. Throughout the meal a strolling guitarist lightly strums away. The restaurant is open mid-April through New Year's Eve; closed Sunday and Monday. ~ Wolf Den Road at Bush Hill Road, Brooklyn; 860-774-4423, fax 860-774-5225. ULTRA-DELUXE.

In Thompson, **The White Horse Inn at Vernon Stiles** is the latest incarnation of a building that began as a stagecoach tavern back in 1814. After recent major renovations, the restaurant has reopened. It's a rambling two-story structure with several dining areas filled with turn-of-the-20th-century furnishings. The food is American regional with a French influence, including steak, duckling and seafood dishes. Closed Monday and Tuesday. ~ Junction of Routes 193 and 200, Thompson; 860-923-9571, fax 860-923-0291. DELUXE TO ULTRA-DELUXE.

If you're tooling around the region and feel a sudden yen for a real, old-fashioned roadside diner, **Zip's Diner** is the answer to your prayers. It's a legacy from the 1950s with a jukebox at every booth; a true formica-and-stainless-steel classic that serves up pot roast, roast turkey, eggs any way you like, pie and ice cream and lots of hot, strong coffee. ~ Routes 12 and 101, Dayville; 860-774-6335. BUDGET TO MODERATE.

A few miles from the University of Connecticut campus, and a favorite with the "UConn" crowd, is the **The Depot Restaurant**. The simple 1920s structure has been restored with restraint and good taste, in keeping with its origins as a small country station. The atmosphere is warm and comfortable and the food rates raves from faithful followers. It's regional American cuisine, with an emphasis on fresh fish, along with a choice of vegetarian entrées and specials. ~ 57 Middle Turnpike, Route 44, Mansfield; 860-429-3663, fax 860-429-6826. MODERATE TO ULTRA-DELUXE.

SHOPPING The "quiet corner" offers its own array of antique shops on country roads or quiet main streets. Contact the **Northeast Connecticut Visitors District** for a complete list of the region's shops. ~ P.O. Box 598, Putnam, CT 06260; 860-928-1228, fax 860-928-4720; www.webtravels.com.

Each town has its complement of boutiques and stores, but visitors seeking an unusual buying foray often head for one of the region's scenic vineyards: **Nutmeg Vineyard**, located about 20 minutes south of Storrs. Chardonnays and French hybrids are among the offerings here. Open on weekends. ~ 800 Bunker Hill Road, Coventry; 860-742-8402.

Another popular shopping destination is **Caprilands Herb Farm**, most famous of its ilk. On the extensive grounds stand a bookshop, a bouquet and basket shop, a restored 18th-century barn that carries herbs and spices, a greenhouse that sells seeds and plants, and an old farmhouse open for luncheon programs (daily, by reservation only), not to mention 31 different gardens featuring vegetables, herbs and herbal flowers. ~ 534 Silver Street, Coventry; 860-742-7244; www.caprilands.com, e-mail herbs@caprilands.com.

NIGHTLIFE A welcome addition to the area's nightlife scene is **J. D. Cooper's Fine Food and Spirits**. This triple-threat establishment comprises a restaurant, a bar and the Cooper Stadium Sports Bar, where the whole family can enjoy darts, an oversized TV screen and interactive video games. ~ 146 Park Road, Putnam; 860-928-0501.

The **Jorgensen Auditorium** is the University of Connecticut's major performing center, presenting a program of music, dance and theater performed by artists of international renown. Closed June through August. ~ University of Connecticut, 2132 Hillside Road, Storrs; 860-486-4226; www.jorgenson.ct-arts.com.

The **Bidwell Tavern** dates from the 1800s, but the music that fills this rustic spot is up-to-date, contemporary acoustic. Live music nightly except Monday. ~ 1260 Main Street, Coventry; 860-742-6978.

MASHAMOQUET BROOK STATE PARK 🏃 🚲 ⛵ 🛶 Two **BEACHES** major hiking trails lead to the park's most famous feature: a wolf **& PARKS** den where, in 1742, young Israel Putnam shot a wolf that had terrorized the population. Putnam became a local hero and later gained national fame as a Revolutionary War general. The park also boasts a small, clear pond for swimming and a brook for fishing. Located at the entrance is Brayton Grist Mill, last in the area, with its traditional machinery intact and a display of black-smithing tools belonging to three generations of the same family. Facilities include picnic grounds, restrooms, a concession stand and a nature trail. Day-use fee (weekends and holidays), $8. ~ Five miles southwest of Putnam on Route 44; 860-928-6121, fax 860-963-2656.

▲ There are 55 tent/RV sites (no hookups); $9 per night.

Along the coast of Long Island Sound, fishing boats cast off daily with passengers eager to try **Outdoor Adventures** their luck. Popular spots are near Block Island and Alligator Ledge. Common catches inshore (within ten miles of **SPORT-** shore) are bluefish, blackfish, striped bass, cod and tuna. Catches **FISHING** offshore (50–100 miles from shore) include tuna, marlin and mako shark. Tackle can be rented on board. Among the party-fishing boats that sail on specific schedules and can be boarded on a first-come, first-served basis are the following:

MYSTIC AREA In New London, the **Wanderer** and the **Seacure** sail from mid-May to mid-November. Join an inshore or offshore fishing trip or opt for a scenic cruise to Block Island, Greenport or Montauk Point. ~ Thamesport Landing; 860-739-2801. In Niantic, the 65-foot **Black Hawk II** has six-hour trips on Long Island Sound. ~ Niantic Beach Marina; 860-443-3662, 800-382-2824. The 87-foot **Mijoy/Mijoy 747** books half-day tours and more throughout the year. ~ Mijoy Dock, Waterford; 860-443-0663. Half-day fishing trips, as well as lighthouse, nature and whale-watching cruises, are available with **Sunbeam Fleet**. ~ Captain John's Dock, Waterford; 860-443-7259; www.sunbeamfleet. com. In Groton, try the 150-passenger **Hel-Cat II**. At 114 feet, this is the largest party boat in New England. In addition to half- and full-day trips, the *Hel-Cat II* does overnight trips and group charters. ~ Hel-Cat Dock; 860-535-2066.

Charter fishing boats that can be booked by private groups are more numerous. You can call the **Reelin'**, a 41-foot craft that accommodates up to six people. ~ Groton; 860-536-0642. The **Trophy Hunter Sportfishing** runs inshore and offshore excursions from April through November. ~ Noank; 860-536-4460.

LOWER CONNECTICUT RIVER VALLEY The **Sea Sprite** offers five- to eight-hour fishing charters out of Saybrook Point Marina on a 41-foot Hatteras twin diesel in search of trophy bass, bluefish and bonita. Its captain guarantees that you will catch fish or the trip is free. Closed December through April. ~ 113 Harbor Parkway, Clinton; 860-669-9613; e-mail samoreoraj@aol.com.

SAILING & WIND-SURFING

Sailing is a way of life along the Connecticut shoreline. Each harbor, big or small, shelters its own flotilla at the ready, and yet it's hard to find sailboats for rent. Here are a few suggestions:

SOUTHWESTERN CONNECTICUT   Boating is good in the Long Island Sound. The small waves at Cockenoe Island and Compo Beach are great for beginning to intermediate windsurfers. If you need a little instruction, **John Kantor's Longshore Sailing School** offers classes for sailing, kayaking and windsurfing. The school also offers an eight-hour course to obtain the required Connecticut Safe Boating Certificate. Hourly rentals are available for small sailboats, catamarans, canoes, kayaks and sailboards. ~ 260 Compo Road South, Longshore Club Park, Westport; 203-226-4646; www.longshoresailingschool.com.

LOWER CONNECTICUT RIVER VALLEY   Colvin Yachts has sailing lessons and a fleet of six sailboats for rent. For a day trip, take out a 22-foot sloop; for a longer trip, choose a boat up to 36 feet. Captained sailing excursions are also an option. ~ 57 Hammock Dock Road, Westbrook; 860-399-9300.

MYSTIC AREA   Mystic Seaport offers a different maritime experience: a sailing education program for young people aged 15 to 19 on the 61-foot schooner *Brilliant*. Youths act as crew for six- to ten-day trips, under professional supervision. An adult version of the project involves four-day stints, from May to October. ~ 75 Greenmanville Avenue, Mystic; 860-572-0711; www.mystic seaport.org.

CANOEING & KAYAKING

The Connecticut River lends itself to a variety of canoeing experiences, from guided overnight trips to rent-your-own. You can find out about canoe camping at three state parks by writing the **Department of Environmental Protection.** ~ Office of State Parks and Recreation, 79 Elm Street, Hartford, CT 06106; 860-424-3200, fax 860-424-4070; www.dep.state.ct.us.

SOUTHWESTERN CONNECTICUT   Canoeing trips on rivers, lakes and Long Island Sound are arranged by the **Mountain Workshop.** Programs run anywhere from a day to two weeks. ~ P.O. Box 625, Ridgefield, CT 06877; 203-438-3640; www.mt workshop.com.

NORTHWEST CORNER   For explorations of the Housatonic River by canoe, kayak or whitewater raft, contact **Clarke Outdoors.** You can also take a kayak lesson or, in the spring, a guided whitewater rafting trip. ~ Route 7, Box 163, West Cornwall, CT 06796; 860-672-6365.

HARTFORD AREA   You can paddle the waters of the Farmington River in a kayak or canoe by day or on moonlit nights through the services of the **Main Stream Canoe Corporation**. There is a shuttle service available. ~ Route 44, Box 448, New Hartford, CT 06057; 860-693-6791; www.mainstreamcanoe.com.

MYSTIC AREA   **North American Canoe Tours, Inc.** offers tubing on the Farmington River. ~ Niantic; 860-739-0791.

The state's ski areas improve on nature with snow-making machines. Rentals and lessons are available at all the resorts listed.

SKIING

NORTHWEST CORNER   Downhill skiers and snowboarders can hit the slopes day or night at **Mohawk Mountain**, which has a vertical drop of 640 feet. There are five lifts for the 24 trails (20 percent beginner, 60 percent intermediate, 20 percent advanced). ~ Great Hollow Road, off Route 4, Cornwall; 860-672-6100, 800-895-5222, fax 860-672-0117. Another great winter sports complex, **Woodbury Ski Area** has a double chairlift and three rope tows serving 13 trails (30 percent novice, 30 percent intermediate, 40 percent advanced). The first ski area in the country to allow—and promote—snowboarding, it has a specially designed snowboard park including a half-mile trail with jumps and a half-pipe and slalom course with a 20-foot bank turn. There are also 2.5 kilometers of groomed cross-country trails lighted for night skiing, a sledding, tubing and tobogganing park, and an ice-skating rink. ~ Route 47, Woodbury; 203-263-2203.

HARTFORD AREA   You'll find good downhill runs and a 625-foot vertical drop at **Ski Sundown**. They're open for both day and night skiing and snowboarding. Eighty percent of the runs are beginning and intermediate slopes. ~ 126 Ratlum Road, off Route 219, New Hartford; 860-379-9851; www.skisundown.com.

Cross-country aficionados can head to **Winding Trails Cross-country Ski Center**. Twenty kilometers of groomed trails traverse the 350-acre facility. Moonlight ski tours are available. There's even a hill for kids to sled down, but they'll have to bring their own sled. ~ 50 Winding Trails Drive, Farmington; 860-678-9582, fax 860-677-9407; www.windingtrails.com.

LOWER CONNECTICUT RIVER VALLEY   At an elevation of 500 feet, the family-friendly **Powder Ridge** has downhill trails and a separate snowboard park with a full-size half-pipe. There's also a designated area for snow tubing, the largest in New England. Four lifts and three surface tows serve the 17 trails (40 percent beginner, 35 percent intermediate and 25 percent advanced). They have a special ski program for kids ages four through six. ~ 99 Powder Hill Road, Middlefield; 860-349-3454; www.powder ridgect.com, e-mail skiridge@aol.com.

Ski Rentals   You can rent downhill and cross-country skis and snowboards at **Action Sports**. ~ 1385 Boston Post Road, Old Saybrook; 860-388-1291.

GOLF

Golf courses dot the Connecticut landscape like dandelions on a lawn in spring. All these courses have pro shops that rent clubs and carts. Here's a selection of 18-hole courses open to the public:

SOUTHWESTERN CONNECTICUT   In Stamford, the **E. Gaynor Brennan Golf Course** is open year-round. ~ 451 Stillwater Road; 203-324-4185. The Tom Fazio–designed **Ridgefield Golf Club** offers a sporty front nine holes and a challenging back nine. ~ 545 Ridgebury Road, Ridgefield; 203-748-7008.

NORTHWEST CORNER   The nine-hole **Stonybrook Golf Club** is a scenic course with stone walls and brooks. ~ 263 Milton Road, Litchfield; 860-567-9977. New Milford's **Candlewood Valley Country Club** is reputed to have the most demanding back nine holes in the state. ~ Danbury Road off Route 7; 860-354-9359.

HARTFORD AREA   Of the many greens in the Hartford area, **Blue Fox Run Golf Club** is said to have the most beautiful course. ~ 65 Nod Road, Avon; 860-678-1679. Farmington's **Westwoods Golf Course** has a driving range and practice green. ~ Route 177, Farmington; 860-677-9192. The **Goodwin Park Golf Club** has a flat, nine-hole beginner course in addition to an 18-hole course. ~ 1130 Maple Avenue, Hartford; 860-956-3601.

NEW HAVEN AREA   The **Alling Memorial Golf Course** was designed with the classic features of a links course. ~ 35 Eastern Street, New Haven; 203-946-8014.

LOWER CONNECTICUT RIVER VALLEY   At Old Saybrook, you can tee off near the sea at the nine-hole **Fenwick Golf Club**. Bring your own clubs and a strong arm—there are no club or motorized cart rentals here. ~ 580 Maple Avenue; 860-388-2516. Further up the river is the course at **Leisure Resort at Banner**. The front nine holes are open and wide; the back nine are woodsy, with narrow fairways. There's also a driving range. ~ 10 Banner Road, Moodus; 860-873-9075, fax 860-873-1613.

MYSTIC AREA   Stonington's **Pequot Golf Club** features tight fairways and small greens. ~ 127 Wheeler Road; 860-535-1898.

NORTHEAST CORNER   In scenic Woodstock, the nine-hole **Harrisville Golf Course** has wide, forgiving fairways. ~ Harrisville Road; 860-928-6098.

TENNIS

There's no lack of tennis courts in the state—schools, universities, clubs, hotels and municipalities are well supplied—but many are out of bounds to visitors. Each local parks and recreation department has its own rules; try calling when you come to town or ask your innkeeper or hotel desk person to make arrangements for you.

HARTFORD AREA   Unlighted courts are open to the public at three of Hartford's parks. **Elizabeth Park West** offers four courts. ~ Prospect and Asylum streets. There are two courts at **Goodwin Park**. ~ South Street and Maple Avenue. **Keney Park** features four tennis courts. ~ Woodland and Greenfield streets. The city's parks and recreation department can be reached at 860-543-8876.

Outside the city, you can play at **Sycamore Hills Park** or **Avon Middle School**, with four unlighted courts apiece. ~ West Avon Road, Avon; 860-409-4332. Also check out the **Simsbury Farms Recreation Complex**. Their four lighted courts are open to the public. ~ 100 Old Farms Road, Simsbury; 860-658-3836.

NEW HAVEN AREA   In New Haven, you can play at **Edgewood Park**'s seven courts (Whalley Avenue), **East Shore Park**'s eight courts (Woodward Avenue) or **Cross High School**'s eight courts (Mitchell Drive). For information call the Recreation Division at 203-946-8022.

LOWER CONNECTICUT RIVER VALLEY   **Old Saybrook Racquet Club**, a private club open to nonmembers, has four indoor and four outdoor unlighted clay courts. Lessons can be taken from the club pro. Fee. ~ 299 Spring Brook Road, Old Saybrook; 860-388-5115. **Lyme Shores Racquet Club** has two outdoor unlighted courts and six indoor courts. A pro is available for lessons. Fee. ~ 22 Colton Road, East Lyme; 860-739-6281.

MYSTIC AREA   Farther east, you can play at **Toby May Field**, which has four lighted courts. ~ Ocean Avenue, New London. For more information call the Recreation Department at 860-447-5230.

Mitchell College features six lighted courts. ~ 860-443-2811. Two courts are available at **Farquhar Park**. ~ Route 117, Groton. **Fitch Senior High** also has six lighted courts. ~ Groton Long Point Road. For more information, call 860-536-5680. **Washington Park** has six lighted courts. ~ Park Avenue, Groton. For more information, call 860-446-4128.

NORTHEAST CORNER   Check out the two lighted courts at **Willimantic Recreation Park**. ~ Route 6 and Main Street, Willimantic; 860-465-3046; www.windhamrec.thinc.net. There are 20 courts at the **University of Connecticut**, several of them lighted. ~ Storrs; 860-486-2837.

BIKING

Much of Connecticut is ideal for bike touring. The relatively gentle terrain and scenic back roads lend themselves to this unhurried form of exploration—except for the hillier northwest corner, which requires some strenuous pedaling. The **Connecticut Department of Transportation** publishes a free bicycle map that indicates touring routes, loop routes and the Connecticut section of the East Coast bicycle trail. It also lists bicycle and repair shops in the state.

The suggested routes cover most of the state, avoiding city traffic and high-speed highways. ~ 2800 Berlin Turnpike, Newington, CT 06111; 860-594-2000; www.state.ct.us/dot.

HARTFORD AREA At **Stratton Brook State Park** in Simsbury, not far from Hartford, the old railroad tracks have been replaced by an extensive bike trail traveling along a scenic brook.

MYSTIC AREA At **Haley Farms State Park** in Groton, an eight-mile trail winds its way through the picturesque old shoreline farm.

Bike Rentals A few inns and hotels keep a small fleet of bicycles for their guests. Other than that, there are no bikes for rent around Connecticut. Best to bring your own, if pedaling is your pleasure.

HIKING

Although Connecticut is densely populated, a surprising amount of open space has been preserved and provided with trails suitable for hiking. The Connecticut Blue Trails System, established and maintained by the **Connecticut Forest and Park Association**, consists of more than 700 miles of cleared and well-marked woodland trails touching on every county. Contact them for a brochure describing the trails. ~ 16 Meriden Road, Rockfall, CT 06481; 860-346-2372; www.ctwoodlands.org, e-mail conn.forest.assoc@ snet.net.

In addition, a portion of the white-blazed Appalachian Trail crosses northwestern Connecticut, and many state parks and forests and nature preserves have created their own hiking routes. You may also call or write to the **Department of Environmental Protection, State Parks Division** for hiking maps and information. ~ 79 Elm Street, Hartford, CT 06106-5127; 860-424-3200; www.dep.state.ct.us.

All distances for hiking trails are one way unless otherwise noted.

SOUTHWESTERN CONNECTICUT In **Devil's Den Preserve**, 20 miles of interconnecting trails cover a variety of terrain, from wetland, stream and pond through mature forest to rocky knolls with wide-open vistas. Take Exit 42 from the Merritt Parkway, go north on Route 57 for five miles, then east on Godfrey Road for one-half mile; turn left on Pent Road and follow it to the end. No picnicking allowed. ~ 203-226-4991.

NORTHWEST CORNER In **Kent Falls State Park** a steep trail (.5 mile) leads up the south side of the falls, across a bridge and down more gradually on the north side, through dense woods and towering hemlock trees. The south side trail hugs the cascade itself, enabling hikers to view the falls from many angles. ~ 860-927-3238.

The blue-blazed **Housatonic Range Trail** (6 miles) follows the general route of an old Indian trail along the hills above the

Housatonic River. Along the way are several caves to explore; fine views of Candlewood Lake, the Housatonic and its verdant valley; occasional steep climbing; and some areas of rough scrambling over boulders. The moderate to strenuous trail begins one and a half miles north of New Milford on Route 7. ~ 860-672-6139.

> Tories' Cave, found along the Housatonic Range Trail, is said to have sheltered Loyalists during the Revolutionary War.

Macedonia Ridge Trail (7 miles) is a loop within Macedonia Brook State Park. The trail, which begins and ends near the parking area at the southern end of the park, crosses bridges and brooks, passes old charcoal mounds and climbs Pine Hill and Cobble Mountain, both with splendid views and demanding ascents. ~ 860-927-3238.

Undermountain Trail (2.6 miles) is a steep, rugged hike to the 2316-foot summit of Bear Mountain, which reveals a vast panorama of mountains, lakes and forests in three states, as well as of turkey vultures soaring along the edge of the plateau. Take the Undermountain Trail to the Appalachian Trail—it's .75 mile on the Appalachian Trail to the top of the mountain. This hike begins on Route 41, at a small parking lot three-and-two-tenths miles north of its junction with Route 44 in Salisbury. ~ 860-482-1817.

HARTFORD AREA Heublein Tower Trail (1.3 miles) is an easy walk along a section of the blue-blazed Metacomet Trail, which circles around a scenic reservoir and climbs steeply up to Heublein Tower in Talcott Mountain State Park. From the tower, you'll see the skyline of Hartford and, on the clearest of days, the distant mountains of Massachusetts and New Hampshire. Before setting out, check with a ranger for detailed directions. The park entrance is on Route 185 in Simsbury. ~ 860-242-1158.

Windsor Locks Canal Trail (4.5 miles) provides a level, easy hike along the towpath that follows a historic canal built in 1829 to bypass the Enfield rapids on the Connecticut River. The trail begins on Canal Road, off Route 159.

NEW HAVEN AREA Westwoods, a 2000-acre open space in Guilford, is crisscrossed with hiking trails. By taking the white circle trail out and the orange one back, you'll have walked six mostly level miles along marsh boardwalks, stands of hemlock and laurel, rocks, ledges, an abandoned quarry and Lost Lake, a scenic halfway point for a picnic.

Sleeping Giant, two miles north of Hamden, is a series of mountaintops resembling an oversized reclining man. More than 32 miles of trails traverse the titan's anatomy—head, chin, chest —affording distant views of hills and cities. For a strenuous, up-and-down circuit of the major peaks (6 miles round-trip), follow the blue-blazed trail from near the parking lot all the way to the giant's right foot, then back on the white trail, with a detour to the stone tower for the loftiest vista. ~ 203-789-7498.

LOWER CONNECTICUT RIVER VALLEY Devil's Hopyard Trail (15 miles) in East Haddam crisscrosses the state park of the same name, beneath ancient groves of hemlocks, across picturesque foot bridges and along Chapman Falls, which tumbles in a 60-foot cascade. This moderate to strenuous trail begins near the parking lot. ~ 860-873-8566.

MYSTIC AREA The easy **Bluff Point Trail** (1.5 miles), in Bluff Point State Park and Coastal Reserve, leads from the parking area to the bluffs. Wander along the rocky, pristine beach, then wind your way back on a different trail through woods and salt marshes that cover this rare, undeveloped peninsula on Long Island Sound. ~ 860-445-1729.

NORTHEAST CORNER Wolf Den Trail (5-mile loop) lies within Mashamoquet Brook State Park and takes you along varied terrain into Israel Putnam's celebrated cave. It also loops past a boulder known as Indian Chair and into diverse environments that include swampland and open fields, woods and streams and high ledges that offer fine vistas. The blue-blazed moderate to strenuous trail starts near the parking lot off Wolf Den Drive. ~ 860-928-6121.

Mansfield Hollow Trail (3.7 miles) is part of the popular blue-blazed Nipmuck Trail. This medium-difficulty trail starts in the parking lot of the Mansfield Hollow Dam Recreation Area and winds along the Fenton River, then veers steeply up a hillside to emerge at a cliff known as 50 Foot, a fine lookout with views of eastern Connecticut. ~ 860-928-6121.

▼▼▼▼▼▼▼▼▼▼▼▼
Transportation

CAR

Four major highways thread their way through the state. Route 95, the Connecticut Turnpike, runs along the shoreline, all the way from the New York state line to Rhode Island. At New Haven, it connects with **Route 91**, which heads north through Hartford into Massachusetts. **Route 84** enters the state at Danbury and runs northeast through Hartford to join with the Massachusetts Turnpike at Sturbridge. **Route 15**, the celebrated Merritt Parkway, winds its scenic way a few miles north of Route 95, then swings north at New Haven to join with Route 91. The major highways are all linked to each other by north–south roads set at convenient intervals.

Route 1, the old Boston Post Road, goes through the heart of all the coastline communities paralleling Route 95. Unfortunately, most of Route 1 has turned into a commercial strip, with just a few old buildings here and there to recall the historic roadway it once was.

AIR

The major airport in the state is **Bradley International Airport** in Windsor Locks, 12 miles north of Hartford. Airlines flying into Bradley include Air Ontario, American Airlines, American Eagle,

Business Express, Continental Airlines, Delta Airlines, Downeast, Midway, Northwest Airlines, Trans World Airlines, United Airlines and USAir.

Several bus and shuttle companies provide ground transportation from Bradley Airport. Call **Bradley Airport Information** for details. ~ 860-292-2000.

Taxi service is available 24 hours a day from the **Yellow Cab Company**. ~ 860-666-6666.

Three smaller airports offer limited service. **Groton–New London Airport**, on the southeastern coast, is serviced by USAir. At Bridgeport's **Igor Sikorsky Memorial Airport**, scheduled flights are offered by Express and USAir Express. **Tweed–New Haven Airport** is serviced by Continental Express, United Express and USAir Express.

Residents of the southwestern section of Connecticut tend to use New York City's two airports, **La Guardia** and **John F. Kennedy**. They are crowded and frantic, but all the airlines fly there; they are less than an hour's drive from the Connecticut line (more at peak traffic time) and connected by frequent limousine service. For information, call **Connecticut Limousine Service**. ~ 800-472-5466, fax 203-874-2416.

Two auto ferry lines operate daily, year-round, from points on Long Island in New York state across Long Island Sound, to the Connecticut shore. On the **Bridgeport and Port Jefferson Ferry**, the trip from Port Jefferson, New York to Bridgeport, Connecticut takes approximately an hour and 20 minutes. You'll need a reservation if you want to bring your car along. ~ Within Connecticut: 888-443-3779; elsewhere: 516-473-0286.

The **Cross-Sound Ferry**, form Orient Point, New York to New London, Connecticut takes about the same amount of time. You'll need a reservation if you want to bring your car along. ~ 860-443-5281.

FERRY

Greyhound (800-231-2222) and **Bonanza** (800-556-3815) bus lines provide scheduled interstate service for most points in Connecticut. Greyhound offers service from the following terminals: Bridgeport (203-335-1123), New Haven (203-772-2470), Hartford (860-522-9267) and New London (860-447-3841).

BUS

Metro North (New Haven Line) runs hourly trains (more frequent at commute time) from New York City's Grand Central Station to New Haven, with connecting service from Stamford to New Canaan, South Norwalk to Danbury and Bridgeport to Waterbury. ~ Reservations: 800-638-7646 in Connecticut. At New Haven, Metro North connects with **Amtrak**'s main line to Boston, with stops at Old Saybrook, New London and Mystic. Also at

TRAIN

New Haven, Amtrak links with service to Hartford. Amtrak's service from Washington to Boston makes Connecticut stops at Stamford, Bridgeport and New Haven. ~ Reservations: 800-872-7245.

CAR RENTALS

At Bradley International Airport, you'll find the following car rental agencies represented: **Avis Rent A Car** (800-331-1212), **Budget Rent A Car** (800-724-6203), **Dollar Rent A Car** (800-800-4000), **Hertz Rent A Car** (800-654-3131) and **National Car Rental** (800-227-7368).

PUBLIC TRANSIT

The **Norwalk Transit District** has city buses, some of which meet Metro North trains at the railroad station. ~ 203-853-3338.

Connecticut Transit Company operates frequent buses within the city of Hartford and offers service to the outlying towns of New Britain, Middletown, Manchester, Windsor and the Farmington Valley communities of Avon, Canton, Farmington and Simsbury.

Connecticut Transit Company also services the New Haven area with city buses as well as buses that go to East Haven, West Haven, Milford, Cheshire, Waterbury and Wallingford, and frequent commuter buses to the shoreline communities of Guilford, Madison and Clinton. ~ 860-525-9181, 860-727-8196 (TTY). **Dattco Bus Company** operates buses that go from downtown New Haven east along Route 1, making stops along the way to Old Saybrook. ~ 203-772-2072, 800-229-4879.

The **Southeast Area Transit District** runs buses that connect New London, Norwich, Groton, East Lyme, Jewett City, Montville and parts of Mystic. ~ 860-886-2631.

TOURS

In New Haven, visitors can tour the **Yale University campus** on guided walks that are conducted twice daily. ~ Visitor Information Office, 149 Elm Street; 203-432-2300.

Heritage Trails, offers daily scheduled tours of Hartford and vicinity, as well as less frequent visits to other parts of the state and dinner tours of historic Farmington sites. Reservations required. ~ P.O. Box 138, Farmington, CT 06034; 860-677-8867.

THREE

Rhode Island

Rhode Islanders don't think of their state as small; they see it as compact, easy to get around in. They point out with great pride that no place in the state is more than a 45-minute drive away from anywhere else. In fact, one of the quirky traits that set Rhode Islanders apart from the rest of us is their reluctance to drive "long" distances. (Any commute longer than ten minutes is considered grounds for changing either one's job or one's residence.)

It's not only the locals who benefit from all this cozy proximity. Rhode Island's easy-to-reach destinations make it an ideal state for visitors. In a single day, it's possible to swim in Narragansett Bay, lunch in Newport, tour a mansion or two and still be in Providence in time for dinner.

Rhode Island, as every schoolchild knows, is the smallest state in the union—a mere 1214 square miles to be exact. But crammed into this tiny package is an overload of good things. The state's statistics are impressive: 400 miles of coastline (and this in a state that measures only 48 miles from north to south) with over 100 public beaches, some 18,000 acres of parklands, 12 institutions of higher learning, as well as a statewide storehouse of historically significant spots.

Having mentioned some of the state's obvious attributes, let's peek at some of its hidden virtues. Perhaps the best-kept secret about Rhode Island is the immense diversity within its modest boundaries. Some of its sites are well known throughout the world. Surely everyone has heard of the glittering mansions of Newport, but how many tourists know it is also possible to hike through a natural "cathedral of forest" near the historic village of Hopkinton? And while probably every sailor on the East Coast has discovered the seaport haven of Block Island, how many have ventured north into Narragansett Bay to set sail for the solitary splendor of Prudence or Patience Islands?

Those travelers who seek an individual path could not have found a more appropriate state than this one founded on an individual search for religious freedom. Back in 1636 Roger Williams settled this territory after he could no longer tolerate the religious constraints of the early Boston Puritans. Migrating south with his wife and daughters, he stopped to settle with the friends he had made among the Narragansett Indian tribe. After years of setbacks and negotiations, in 1663 Williams succeeded in wresting a royal charter from England for his new territory, one that would also allow him to unite Providence with several other settlements nearby.

A truly enlightened clergyman, Williams' religious tolerance was universal; his new state embraced all faiths. Although Williams founded his own Baptist Church in 1639 (the building in Providence can still be toured), Quakers, Jews and any other group seeking religious freedom were wholeheartedly welcomed. (Touro Synagogue in Newport, built in 1763, stands today as the oldest Jewish house of worship in continental America.)

This sense of tolerance endured. Although Rhode Island did participate in the infamous "triangle trade" (slaves traded for molasses traded for rum), it was also the first colony to prohibit slavery. Rhode Island was also the first colony to declare independence from Great Britain. And at the end of the Revolutionary War, it was the last of the original 13 colonies to ratify the new Constitution, holding out until the Bill of Rights, guaranteeing individual liberties, was added.

America's industrial revolution began in Rhode Island in 1790, when Samuel Slater started operating the first water-powered cotton mill. That power was provided by the mighty Blackstone River, and the rest is American history. Other successful industrial endeavors in the state have included jewelry and silver manufacturing, both of which have drawn immigrants here from all over the world. The newcomers brought along ethnic riches that can still be found in the state's cuisine, architecture and even the spoken word.

During "La Belle Époque" right before the turn of the 20th century, the seaside town of Newport became the darling of America's newly rich and famous, a status-conscious group who lavished their untaxable millions on opulent "summer cottages." Folks like the Vanderbilts, the Astors and the Belmonts vied to one-up each other architecturally in the designs of these palaces, as well as with the opulent furnishings within. It was truly a gilded age, the spoils of which we can all still marvel over.

But palaces of the past are only part of the splendor of today's Rhode Island, much of it to be found away from the cities. One glance at a map reveals why Rhode Island is nicknamed the "Ocean State": its flamboyant coastline can only be the handiwork of a creative sea. While its interior boundaries are the work of man (they are pure New England—ruler-straight and right-angled), it's a different story along the coast, where the relentless surf has carved out a wild, exotic profile, etching miles of extravagant bays and barrier beaches into the shores, capriciously sprinkling the expanse with an explosion of islands.

South County's coastal villages reflect this watery whimsy. From the westernmost reaches of Watch Hill up to Greenwich in the east, each small town harbors its unique bit of history and maintains its individual personality, yet each is linked to the others by common bonds—silken beaches that edge the coastline and a dependence on the sea.

Thirteen miles off this coast lies Block Island, offshore but very much a part of the makeup of South County. Aggressively underdeveloped (the resident islanders intend to keep it this way!), Block Island is a haven in the true sense of the word, with no traffic lights, no fast-food places and no neon. Peace, quiet and nature are the touristic lures here, combined with some world-class fishing and sailing.

Connected to South County by bridges across the broad expanse of Narragansett Bay is Newport County, occupying the islands the Indians named Conanicut and Aquidneck. Today visitors travel to Jamestown on little Conanicut Island, and the big draw on Aquidneck is Newport.

Although Newport is famous for its mansions and breathtaking beaches, the town has another, little-known side—its close proximity to relaxed country life.

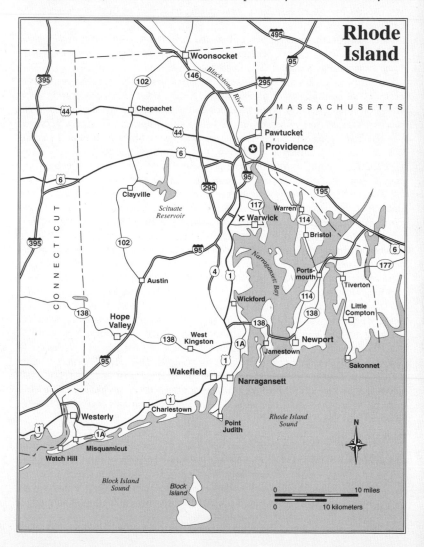

A mere ten-minute drive from all the glamour and the clamoring crowds of tourists along Bellevue Avenue stretch miles of bucolic farmlands, wilderness areas, deserted beaches and even a vineyard. A short drive to the postcard-perfect villages of Tiverton and Little Compton reveals a pastoral way of life that remains centuries removed from the glittering tourist passions of Newport.

Northwest of Newport, in the center of Rhode Island and representing its metaphysical heart as well, stretches the Greater Providence area. A get-acquainted visit to Providence helps first-time visitors establish a sense of place; the capitol building is here, as are Brown University and the Rhode Island School of Design, along with scores of historic buildings, some dating back two or three centuries to the original colony.

Providence combines the best of big-city/small-town; it's small enough for residents to know each other, yet large enough to support top-rate restaurants and one of the country's outstanding small museums.

Above Providence along the northern tier of the state, throughout the great rectangle of land known as the Blackstone Valley, folks have been gearing up to show off their special blend of treasures to the world. But for the moment, this densely forested river valley is yours to discover, its bounties still largely "hidden."

The Blackstone River itself is the key to this area. Its history includes a starring role in America's industrial revolution, and its future includes landmark status as a federally funded recreation heritage preserve. For the immediate present, the mighty Blackstone awaits your pleasure and your exploration.

Statewide, it is this appealing combination of big-city sophistication and country-style hospitality that makes Rhode Island such an intriguing place to discover. You'll note these qualities in the people you meet; they combine the best of both. Oh yes, and don't overlook their innate sense of independence—that legendary strength of will that surpasses even the rock-bound, generic version attributed to most Yankees. This rugged individuality—one of the principles on which Rhode Island was founded—comes naturally to the people of the Ocean State.

Weatherwise, temperate is the word. Much of the state lies near the ocean or Narragansett Bay, which plunges northward through Rhode Island's center. This watery influence results in light winter snowfalls and temperatures that reach the freezing mark only in January. In summers, the average temperature is around 72°.

Rhode Island has another nickname, "America's First Resort." We're confident you will enjoy discovering this state for yourself. The only question is whether or not you'll want to share the tales of your adventures in this newfound playground. You may decide you want to keep all these treasures hidden just a while longer, before the word gets out and Rhode Island becomes everyone's favorite place in New England.

▼▼▼▼▼▼▼▼▼ South County

Officially, this southern tier of the state—extending from Connecticut along Block Island Sound and reaching into Narragansett Bay—is called Washington County. But you will have trouble finding even one resident who calls it that. Rhode Islanders know this area as South County, and so should you if you want to be understood.

South County truly *is* resort country; beach lovers from all over flock here every summer. Even many native Rhode Islanders maintain vacation homes in this coastal area, which provides great seaside escapes from urban pressures.

The sometimes unpronounceable names of many of South County's villages and waterways—Misquamicut, Cocumscussoc, Pettaquamscutt—reflect the region's American Indian heritage. Roger Williams befriended the Indians when he settled Rhode Island and divided his time between Providence and North Kingstown (in South County), where he lived with his wife and two

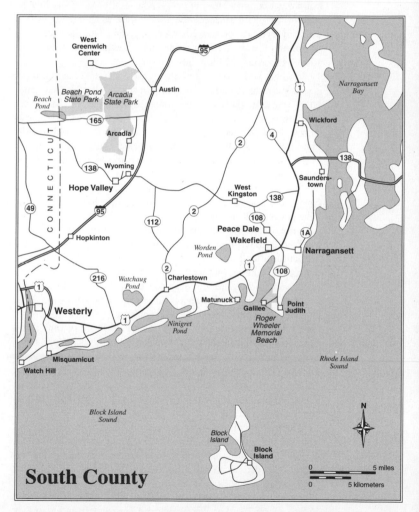

South County

children from 1644 to 1650. The rolling farmlands and white-sand beaches of today's South County—a bucolic landscape mercifully lacking in high-rise condos and fast-food stores—make this history seem ancient indeed.

SIGHTS   Among the more high-profile residents of South County's villages are those who live in **Watch Hill**. (This select group strives for seclusion and anonymity, but their lavish dwellings continue to pique the imaginations of outsiders.) Although there's no formal "sightseeing route," many visitors love to drive through Watch Hill's quiet country lanes to ogle the tastefully lavish summer estates of these rich and reclusive folks. It seems that every turn in the road reveals a more lavish, more imposing "summer cottage." Although most were built decades ago, there are one or two new additions to the "Millionaires' Colony."

In town, at the foot of Bay Street, the country's oldest **carousel** is still spinning its magic. Locals call it the "Flying Horse Carousel" because its gaily painted ponies are hung from chains that spin outward, so the horses "fly." Local custom decrees that as soon as a child's feet can touch the floor, he is too old to ride. Pint-sized riders still grab for the brass ring, squealing in triumph as they store less valuable rings on their horses' pointed ears for safekeeping.

In the nearby town of Westerly, **Wilcox Park**, a 14-acre haven right in the heart of town, has been an oasis for locals and visitors alike since 1898. Designed by a student of Frederick Law Olmsted, the park is listed in the National Register of Historic Places. In addition to strolling by the beautiful flower beds (with labeled horticultural collections), you can attend outdoor concerts here during the summer. ~ Tower Street, Westerly; 401-596-8590.

Inland from South County's coastal areas, along Route 138, lies the 1886 **Kenyon Grist Mill**. Run by the same family for years, Kenyon grinds the cornmeal that is the basic ingredient for proper Rhode Island johnnycakes. Proprietors Paul Drumm Junior and Paul Drumm III love to talk about their mill and its history. Drop by for a chat, a look around or for some tips, recipes or cornmeal from the mill's country store. The store is closed weekdays from September through May. ~ Village of Usquepaugh, Glen Rock Road, West Kingston; 401-783-4054, fax 401-782-3564; www.kenyongristmill.com.

The history of American Indians in South County stretches some 12,000 years; this whole area is rich in artifacts and trails. A four-page drive tour through some of the best sightseeing territory—complete with drive guides, detailed maps and historical commentary—has been assembled by the **Museum of Primitive Art and Culture**. There are also self-guided walking tours of Mill Village. Open Tuesday, Wednesday and Thursday from Labor Day

Author Picks

CHAPTER FAVORITES

I feel it's worth making reservations far in advance—and saving up—for a sojourn to **Hotel Manisses** on Block Island. Not only is it one of the finest Victorian grand dames on the island, but there's a touch of something magical sleeping in a room named after a princess. *page 136*

Of all the fabulous mansions in the Newport area, none brings a smile to my face like **Green Animals**, where topiary artists have devoted their full time to shaping bushes into birds, camels and bears. *page 146*

After a day of marveling at the old-fashioned opulence along Newport's Bellevue Boulevard, I'm ready to splurge on a five-course meal in one of the ostentatiously appointed rail coaches of **The Newport Dinner Train**. *page 152*

I was a little skeptical of the claim that the **Long Pond–Ell Pond Trail** is "the most beautiful walk in Rhode Island"—until I saw for myself on a walk through the cathedral forest. Now I'm a believer. *page 172*

to Memorial Day; Wednesday (by appointment only) the rest of the year. ~ 1058 Kingstown Road, Peace Dale; 401-783-5711.

Back along the coast, you may want to stop in at the **South County Tourism Council**, where the folks can help with maps, brochures and information on the entire county. Closed weekends. ~ 4808 Tower Hill Road, Wakefield; 401-789-4422.

From here the coast road starts winding north along Narragansett Bay. When you come to the village of Cocumscussoc north of Wickford, you'll find the building known as **Smith's Castle**. Although not a castle by fairy tale standards, this centuries-old woodframe house does harbor some impressive history, and 1.8 of its 23 acres are a National Historic Landmark. Roger Williams lived here and preached to the Indians in the mid-1630s, when the site was a trading post. Rebuilt in 1678 after a fire, it enjoyed celebrity as Updike Plantation and welcomed such famous guests as Benjamin Franklin and General Lafayette. Today, this grand era is memorialized by the 17th- and 18th-century household furnishings throughout the house. Closed Tuesday and Wednesday and from mid-October through April; open other times by appointment. Admission. ~ 55 Richard Smith Drive, Wickford; 401-294-3521.

On a newsworthy note: Experts at Brown University believe that America's oldest mass burial ground may lie beneath Smith's Castle property. In 1675, in the Great Swamp Fight with warring local Indian tribes, many colonists and Indians—including women and children—were killed. Archaeologists have conducted a dig at the site, where many of the colonists were buried.

Also near Wickford stands the **Gilbert Stuart Museum**. Sounds like an unlikely combination, but the famous "George Washington portraitist" was born here in this 1700 gambrel-roof house, next to where his dad owned and operated America's first snuff mill. Also on-site is a 1662 grist mill. Closed Tuesday and Wednesday and from mid-October to mid-April. Admission. ~ 815 Gilbert Stuart Road, Saunderstown; 401-294-3001.

Although Block Island is considered part of South County, this highly independent bit of territory 13 miles offshore marches to its own drummer. From its earliest days, when the native Narragansetts called it "Manisses," meaning "God's Little Island," this spirit has prevailed. (Dutch explorer Adriaen Block, in a 1614 visit, gave it his own name.) Many have compared Block Island's landscape to that of Ireland or Scotland. It's renowned for sightseeing of the natural kind; the island's remote location offers a unique closeness to nature. (See "Rhode Island's Favorite Island" in this chapter.)

LODGING

While visitors can always find one or two cookie-cutter chain hotels clustered near the larger towns, it is the rambling Victorians and out-of-the-way inns one remembers, and that tend to become a cherished part of the South County experience.

As with most New England resort areas, many lodgings here close for the winter. Rates, too, are seasonal; those indicated below reflect the heady rates of the peak summer season. Because of the crush of visitors, many places will also require two- or three-day minimum stays during high season and holiday weekends.

Personifying the genteel understatement of Watch Hill's old guard is the **Watch Hill Inn**, an 1890s white clapboard jutting out onto Little Narragansett Bay. The bay breezes cool the inn's 16 non–air conditioned rooms. Decor is simple—wood four-poster beds with puffy quilts, a few period antiques. Some rooms feature modernized baths with stall showers replacing the vintage clawfooted tubs. Guests can rock on the wide porch that overlooks the water. ~ 38 Bay Street, Watch Hill; 401-348-6300, 800-356-9314, fax 401-348-6301; www.watchhillinn.com, e-mail stay@watch hillinn.com. DELUXE TO ULTRA-DELUXE.

Not to be confused with the Watch Hill Inn, the **Inn at Watch Hill** is a stretch of 16 modern motel-type suites atop the stores on the town's main drag. While the decor of each unit is utilitarian rather than posh, the views from each open-air deck is pure New England; from your vantage point you can check out everything going on in town, while just beyond the bay, vistas stretch out forever. Specify "Bay View" when reserving; several (designated "Village View") have obstructed views of the water. Each suite has a private bath, air conditioning, TV and a kitchen area equipped with microwave, refrigerator and sink but without dishes or utensils. Closed October to May. ~ 118 Bay Street, Watch Hill; 401-596-0655, fax 401-348-0860. DELUXE TO ULTRA-DELUXE.

Guests at **Pleasant View House** get the full ocean treatment. The wide swath of beach unfolds like a carpet just at the edge of the hotel's manicured lawns. The rambling, white wood exterior is accented with sail-blue canvas fronting each private deck. The atmosphere is vintage seaside; dining rooms front the ocean, as do many of the rooms. Don't look for posh appointments; rooms are decorated in basic motel. But they're clean and comfortable, and the views from the private decks are well worth the price. There's also a jacuzzi and fitness room. Closed October to May. ~ 65 Atlantic Avenue, Misquamicut; 401-348-8200, 800-782-3224, fax 401-348-8919; www.pvinn.com, e-mail info@pvinn. com. DELUXE TO ULTRA-DELUXE.

The **Shelter Harbor Inn** looks exactly the way a seaside country inn should look: a spanking white clapboard main building with contrasting window shutters, well-manicured and welcoming. This 1800s farmhouse, its landscaped grounds defined by rustic stone fences, is an inn as well as a popular restaurant. There are nine guest rooms in the main building (each with private bath and some with private sun deck), ten more in the converted barn nearby and four in the coach house. In each room antiques gleam with care, and bedsteads complement the period decor. The public rooms include a cozy library just off the sun porch bar. Breakfast included. ~ 10 Wagner Road, Westerly; 401-322-8883, 800-468-8883, fax 401-322-7907. DELUXE TO ULTRA-DELUXE.

Not all of South County's inns reflect a Yankee heritage. **The Villa**, with its Italianate decor and colorfully decorated swimming pool, is decidedly Mediterranean in ambience. Rooms are chockfull, if not cluttered, with knickknacks. Enjoy a continental breakfast during the week or a full breakfast on weekends around the pool. No children or pets allowed. Gay-friendly. ~ 190 Shore Road, Westerly; 401-596-1054, 800-722-9240, fax 401-596-6268; www.thevillaatwesterly.com, e-mail villa@riconnect.com. DELUXE TO ULTRA-DELUXE.

Nestled in a wooded inland setting and thoroughly steeped in old New England is the **General Thurston House**. A lovingly restored 1763 Colonial, this bed and breakfast wraps its guests in cozy country living. Each of the three guest rooms has a fireplace and Early American antiques. A continental breakfast is included in the rates. ~ Old Route 3, Hopkinton; 401-377-9049. MODERATE.

Text continued on page 136.

Rhode Island's Favorite Island

When describing Block Island, some liken it to Ireland. Many choose to rhapsodize over its bucolic charms, while others see it as a Victorian time warp. Block Island is all these ideals—and more. A modest triangle of land lying 13 miles off the coast of Rhode Island, it measures a scant three miles wide by seven miles long. Yet captured within its 11 square miles are vistas that do indeed recall Ireland at its best: verdant, rolling hills, neatly defined by rambling stone fences; grassy meadows strewn with wildflowers; ponds—over 365 of them (one for every day of the year); and always, the wild Atlantic crashing just off-shore.

As you approach Block Island by ferry, you'll first spot the chalky cliffs that rise 200 feet in a straight vertical from the thundering waves of the sound. It was from these cliffs that the resident Narragansett Indians once dispatched a band of off-islanders who attempted to conquer them; in a now famous battle, they pushed a band of invading Mohegans over the bluffs onto the rocks below.

Although the Mohegans are long gone, Block Island does seem lost in a former time. As the ferry slides into Old Harbor, passengers are greeted by an imposing phalanx of ornate Victorian buildings that stand shoulder-to-shoulder, facing out to sea. These grande dame structures are really most welcoming, offering bed and board to the island's multitudes of summer visitors—the same throngs who swarm the sidewalks of Old Harbor, slurping up mountains of homemade ice cream, purchasing enough "I ❤ Block Island" T-shirts to clothe the entire population of an emerging nation, and generally soaking up the festive salt-air island mood.

Do not misunderstand: Block Islanders are not about to let their idyllic spot fall prey to tourist trappings. There are no fast-food chains and not a glint of neon anywhere. No traffic lights wink on this island; in fact, there is no traffic to speak of. Visitors can get around in local taxis, or they can rent bikes or mopeds. (Mopeds, however, are discreetly discouraged.)

This is an island for travelers who truly want to commune with nature. Just minutes (even by bike) from the bustle of Water Street in Old Harbor, the island's only town, lies a three-mile swath of sand known as **Crescent Beach**. As the island's most popular bathing and sunning beach, Crescent may become too "crowded" for a loner's tastes. No problem: simply pick up your towel and mosey a few yards to the north where an isolated stretch of sand awaits.

Bikers are delighted to find the island's rolling hills offer just the right amount of challenge. The quiet roads wind past a handful of weathered-shingle cottages and a clapboard Victorian or two. But mostly, it is nature that's on view: brushy bayberry and scrub pines, grassy moors punctuated by ponds.

An astute naturalist will observe that there are very few trees standing on this island. Once there were many. That was back in the mid-1600s, when the first white settlers arrived. They felled the island's forests for lumber for their houses and barns, and for fuel. When that ran out, they burned peat from the marshes. Life has never been easy for islanders anywhere; but these early island dwellers had to cope not only with stern New England winters but also with the resident Indians who took a dim view of the new arrivals.

The white settlers, however, met no fate as harsh as the would-be Mohegan invaders, forced off the high cliffs at the southern end of the island. Today, these **Mohegan Bluffs** are still an awe-inspiring sight, attracting hordes of visitors who peer down at the crashing Atlantic 200 feet below, or who brave the climb down wooden stairs to walk the rock-strewn sands that border the wild ocean.

You might also want to visit the **Southeast Lighthouse** or **North Lighthouse**. The Southeast Lighthouse features a museum as well as occasional guided tours. The North Lighthouse has been renovated and now houses an interpretive exhibit on Block Island.

History teaches that several explorers "discovered" Block Island, among them Italian Giovanni Verrazano, who named it "Claudia," in honor of the mother of his patron, Francis I of France. But it was the Dutch navigator Adriaen Block who, in 1614, claimed this bit of land as his own, dubbing it "Adriaen's Eylant."

Today's Block Island is available to visitors on a limited basis. We mainlanders will never really belong; that privilege is only for the handful whose ancestors first settled here. But we are welcome to enjoy the bounties nature has bestowed: the wildlife that inhabits the marshy ponds; the quiet countryside; the pebbly beaches that ring the coastline and the migrating birds that swarm here each spring and fall.

At the entrance to Rodman's Hollow, an ancient glacial crevice that is now a wildlife refuge, locals have posted a hand-carved sign that admonishes all visitors: "This land has been dedicated for preservation in its natural state ... please respect it so that all human, creature and plant life may share in its peace and beauty." A fitting sentiment that could easily be applied to all of Block Island.

The **Block Island Chamber of Commerce** can fill you in on anything else you want to know about the island. ~ Water Street, Block Island, RI 02807; 401-466-2982, 800-383-2474.

The Larchwood Inn sits on a hill above the country village of Wakefield, the quintessential manor house. Built in 1831, the three-story house shimmers with family history: one window in the dining room still bears the signature a daughter etched on the glass pane with her diamond engagement ring. Private baths can be requested, although some of the 12 guest rooms share facilities. There are also six additional units in the annex. Traditional dark wood headboards are brightened by country spreads and light streaming in through large windows. ~ 521 Main Street, Wakefield; 401-783-5454, 800-275-5450, fax 401-783-1800; www.xpos.com/larchwoodinn.html, e-mail larchwoodinn@xpos.com. MODERATE TO DELUXE.

Victorian is the word for most of the lodgings on Block Island. Imposing, gingerbread-trimmed structures dominate the island's ocean skyline. A word of caution: some "modernizations" may not please everyone. One such example might be the National Hotel's trendy front-porch scene. Although this place is well-known and located in the middle of the action, its amplified music and noisy camaraderie are not everyone's idea of an idyllic island vacation.

Presiding like a grande dame over all she surveys, the Hotel Manisses rules with Victorian splendor. Built in 1870 and restored by the Abrams family, innkeepers well known locally, the Manisses seems to personify Block Island's unique charm and individualism. In the wicker-appointed parlor leaded-glass windows rainbow the sunlight. There are a few surprises: several of the 17 guest rooms, like the Princess Augusta, feature jacuzzis; the Antoinette room opens directly onto the front porch; the Pocahontas has its own deck. ~ Spring Street, Block Island; 401-466-2421, 800-626-4773, fax 401-466-2858. ULTRA-DELUXE.

The 1661 Inn and Guest House combines Victorian charm with sweeping views of Old Harbor. Rooms with water views also sport private decks (the Ackurs room even has its own kitchenette). Guest quarters are antique-filled and sunny. The inn is known for its huge breakfast buffet, served overlooking the water. ~ Spring Street, Block Island; 401-466-2421, 800-626-4773, fax 401-466-3162. DELUXE TO ULTRA-DELUXE.

DINING   Everyone in Watch Hill eats at the Olympia Tea Room at one time or another; just sit in the old mahogany booths and watch the local world go by. Owners Jack and Marcia Felber stress a modern American cuisine with an emphasis on fresh seafood. It's a sort of back-to-the-future setting (waitresses wear formal black with white lacy collars and cuffs), but the menu is both homey and eclectic; the Olympia is as famous for its littleneck clam and sausage dish as for its dainty dessert pastries shaped like swans. Breakfast, lunch and dinner. Closed December through March. ~ 74 Bay Street, Watch Hill; 401-348-8211. MODERATE.

The ideal country dining experience is alive and well at **Shelter Harbor Inn**. Meals are served in several small rooms, with stone fireplaces, burnished wooden chairs and wildflowers at every table. The creative American cuisine reflects the local harvest, changing every season. Seafood, as you will have come to expect in this area, is fresh and excellent. Pasta dishes are well seasoned and imaginative. Try a wine from the local vineyards. And for dessert, sample the Indian pudding, which arrives warm and fragrant. Breakfast, lunch and dinner. ~ 10 Wagner Road, Westerly; 401-322-8883. MODERATE.

At **Ginger's Café and Bakery** you can dine inside, seated at tables dressed with snowy napery. Chef Ginger Neale serves breakfast (special frittatas, french toast made from challah), lunch (fresh homemade pastas, pesto chicken sandwiches) and dinner (fresh fish, tenderloin with hazelnut crust). For dessert, try the house specialty, tiramisu. Closed Monday in the winter. ~ 333 Main Street, Wakefield; 401-789-0914. MODERATE TO DELUXE.

Yearn for some Italian food that's good and won't dent the budget? Head for **Term's**. Nothing fancy here, just lots of families, with kids running around. Lots of enjoyment, too, as everyone digs into heaping plates full of seafood marinara, pastas and veal dishes. ~ 135 Boon Street, Narragansett; 401-782-4242. MODERATE.

Haute cuisine served in rarified surroundings greets visitors to **Basil's**. With striped awnings outside and delicate floral wallpaper inside, Basil's is a tiny gem of European-style dining. The service is formal, and guests tend to dress up for the occasion (unusual in a seaside area). The menu includes many usual Continental favorites (beef Stroganoff, scallops Provençal), but owner and chef Vasilios Kourakis has an inspired hand with herbs and spices, so old favorites tend to become new favorites at first bite. Closed Monday and Tuesday in the winter; closed Monday in the summer. ~ 22 Kingston Road, Narragansett; 401-789-3743. MODERATE TO DELUXE.

Eating at **George's of Galilee** has become a Rhode Island tradition. Diners at this casual, wood-paneled spot usually sit before huge windows that offer views of the fishing boat dock. Fare is a traditional mix of clam cakes, lobster, fish and pasta, plus beef and poultry items. Limited hours off-season. ~ 250 Sand Hill Cove Road, Narragansett; 401-783-2306. MODERATE TO DELUXE.

Most visitors to Block Island feel they have stepped back in time, into a gentler era. Among Block Island's bevy of Victorian mansions, the favored lodging is also the preferred dining spot. In summer the **Hotel Manisses** focuses its meal service on the flower-studded outdoor patio; when chill winds blow in off the Atlantic, the focus shifts indoors, where crackling fires warm the spirits. Seafood is featured, with seasonal variations. Appetizers include a selection of clams and oysters. The house-cured salmon is a perennial favorite. ~ Spring Street, Block Island; 401-466-2421, fax 401-466-2858. ULTRA-DELUXE.

Whether you fancy a sandy beach or a cliff-top ocean view, picnics will become an important part of your Block Island experience. Pick up your favorites at **Rebecca's Take Out**. Closed mid-October to mid-May. ~ 435 Water Street, Old Harbor, Block Island; 401-466-5411. BUDGET.

HIDDEN ►

Or stop by the **Old Harbor Take Out**, then hop on your bike and head for your wilderness pleasure. Closed mid-October to mid-May. ~ Water Street (above the ferry landing), Old Harbor, Block Island; 401-466-2935. BUDGET.

Late-fall and early-spring daytrippers who come over to Block Island for a few hours of biking or hiking are often surprised to find the hotels and restaurants closed for the season. No problem. Just join the locals who head for **Bethany's Airport Diner**, which serves basic breakfast- and lunch-counter meals all day, every day. Specialties are eggs Benedict and garden burgers. ~ State Airport, Block Island; 401-466-3100. BUDGET.

HIDDEN ►

SHOPPING

The **Sun-Up Gallery** introduces the wonderful world of dazzling and upscale made-in-America crafts, jewelry and wearable-art fashions to this staid and conservative community. They also have a paint-your-own pottery studio. ~ 95 Watch Hill Road, Avondale; 401-596-3430.

The **Hack and Livery General Store** is everything you ever dreamed a country store would be: more than 50 varieties of penny candy temptingly arrayed in glass canisters. Bet you can't walk out with only one of those tiny paper bags full of goodies. They also have a selection of collectibles. ~ 1006 Main Street, Hope Valley; 401-539-7033.

Antique lovers take heart; there are more than 25 traditional antique dealers in South County, including **Frink's Collectibles**, with glassware, china, silver, lamps and toys from the 18th, 19th and 20th centuries. Closed Tuesday and Wednesday. Call for hours. ~ Route 1, Dunn's Corners, Westerly; 401-596-2756.

Another antique dealer in the area is **The Artists Guild and Gallery**, which primarily conserves art, frames and furniture. Closed weekdays (except by appointment). ~ 5429 Post Road, Route 1, Charlestown; 401-322-0506.

For a brochure and map pinpointing every shop, contact the **South County Tourism Council**. ~ 4808 Tower Hill Road, Wakefield, RI 02879; 401-789-4422.

Near the waterfront, **Scarlett Begonia** is the place to go for quilts, pillows, jewelry, rugs and other handicrafts. Closed Christmas to Easter. ~ Dodge Street, Old Harbor, Block Island; 401-466-5024.

The **Windjammer** brings in big-city lights and stars for the under-
30 set (or anyone else who thrives on megadecibel rock). Live
bands perform every Friday and Saturday night in a room that
holds about 800 people. Closed mid-October through May. ~ Atlantic Beach Park, 321 Atlantic Avenue, Misquamicut Beach; 401-
322-9298.

In the summer, the **Colonial Theatre** offers drama and musicals on their main stage and free Shakespeare performances in
nearby Wilcox Park. Closed Monday. ~ 1 Granite Street, Westerly; 401-596-0810.

What began as a two-story farmhouse in the seaside village of
Matunuck back in 1891 is now the home of the famous **Theatre-
By-The-Sea**. In 1931, Alice Tyler converted her
farm's barn into a 500-seat theater, and the rest is   Several stars, including
show-biz history. Many vacationers plan their sched-   Marlon Brando, got
ules according to the theater's summer productions: their start at
Sound of Music, Grease and *Godspell* were part of one   Matunuck's Theatre-
bill. Theatre-By-The-Sea is part of both the state and the By-The-Sea.
National Register of Historic Places. Closed Monday and
from mid-September through May. ~ 364 Card's Pond Road,
Matunuck; 401-782-8587.

A handy addition to the farm-theater complex, the **SeaHorse
Grill and Cabaret** serves a popular (albeit incongruous) chicken
savannah as well as seafood favorites before the show; after the
show it offers entertainment and hors d'oeuvres to those who
yearn to stay up a bit later. Cover for cabaret shows. ~ 364 Card's
Pond Road, Matunuck; 401-789-3030.

There are 19 government-managed preserves, state parks, beaches
and forest areas in South County. The stretch of coastline from
Watch Hill to Narragansett is made up almost entirely of sandy
beaches.

NAPATREE POINT BARRIER BEACH 🏊 This Watch Hill spit   ◄ *HIDDEN*
of land evokes a true wilderness feeling; cars are barred from this
ecologically fragile, half-mile-long sandy fishhook, allowing the
many species of shorebirds and human visitors to enjoy a peaceful coexistence. ~ At the westernmost end of Watch Hill.

MISQUAMICUT STATE BEACH 🏊 One of the largest and most
popular beaches in New England, this is a good family beach,
with surf that is usually mild and a gradual drop-off. The wide
beach is equally good for lazing or walking, and the sand is of
fine quality, although August can bring in an excess of seaweed.
There are picnic tables, a pavilion, snack bars, restrooms, a bathhouse and changing rooms. Closed Labor Day to Memorial Day.
Day-use fee, $4 to $10. ~ Along Atlantic Avenue in Misquamicut; 401-596-9097.

NINIGRET CONSERVATION AREA (EAST BEACH) 🏖 A four-mile-long swath of broad, sandy barrier beach between Ninigret Pond and Block Island Sound, this is considered by many to be the most beautiful in the state because of its undeveloped expanse of dunes and scrub pines. (The 1938 hurricane blew away all houses, and the state now forbids any development.) The beach is usually not crowded because the state strictly limits parking in the entire conservation area. (Get there early in the morning on weekends for a parking spot.) The beach has a rocky bottom with a steep drop-off about three feet out. There is a lifeguard in a designated area, but this beach can be dangerous for small children. Because of drop-off, waves tend to break hard close to shore. There are portable toilets here. Closed November through April. Day-use fee, minimum $8. ~ At the foot of East Beach Road, off Route 1 in Charlestown; 401-322-0450.

▲ Permitted for four-wheel, camper vehicles only on barrier beach; $8 per night for residents, $12 for nonresidents; 401-322-8910.

ARCADIA MANAGEMENT AREA 🚶 🚴 🎣 🏇 🛶 🏊 🏕 🚤 ⛴ 🛶 Thousands of inland wilderness acres have been set aside in the northwest corner of South County and can be enjoyed by outdoor lovers at Rhode Island's largest recreation area. Because it lies along the Appalachian Trail, this park offers some excellent hiking opportunities. There's also boating and swimming along the sandy beaches of Browning Mill and Beach Pond during the summer months, and fishing in the freshwater pond and streams and rivers for trout and bass. You'll find picnic areas and lifeguards. ~ The main entrance is located off Route 165; 401-539-2356.

▲ The park has free hike-in tent camping and $15-a-night shelter camping. Camping requires a permit (free) available at park headquarters (260 Arcadia Road, Arcadia). If you don't find sufficient camping in the park, there's always **Oak Embers** (219 Escoheag Hill Road, West Greenwich; 401-397-4042), a private campground nearby. There are 50 seasonal RV sites with sewer hookups and 30 year-round RV hookup sites, both $18 per night, as well as tent sites ($16 per night).

EAST MATUNUCK STATE BEACH 🏖 One mile of nice shoreline, sand dunes and, on a clear day, a nice view of Block Island, are yours at this popular family beach. A gradual drop-off makes East Matunuck a good place to take the kids. Facilities include picnic tables, bathhouse, restrooms, concessions and lifeguards. Closed Labor Day to Memorial Day. Day-use fee, minimum $4. ~ On Succotash Road off Route 1 in South Kingston; 401-789-8585.

ROGER WHEELER STATE BEACH 🏖 Lying within the protective breakwater of Point Judith Harbor of Refuge, this wave-free spot known locally as Sand Hill Cove is an ideal swimming beach for families. The sand is fine and white, waters are calm and the drop-off is so gradual that it is often necessary to wade great distances just to reach waist-deep water. There are picnic tables, restrooms, bathhouse and showers. Open weekends in May and from Memorial Day to Labor Day. Day-use fee, minimum $4. ~ Off Sand Hill Cove Road in Narragansett, near Galilee.

NARRAGANSETT TOWN BEACH Voted the "best swimming beach in the state" by *Rhode Island Monthly* magazine, this swath is visible from every point in town and from every turn along the local stretch of scenic Route 1A. Just south of the elite Dunes Club, it's a quintessential New England beach with miles of fine white sand in a broad sweep from waterline to dune and rollers that can kick up enough to lure surfers in rough weather. The Northeast Surfing Championships are held here every fall; for wanna-be surfers, free lessons are given by the pros every summer Wednesday at noon. You'll find a bathhouse and lifeguards (seasonal). ~ On Route 1A, two miles east of Route 1; 401-783-6430.

Newport Area

You'll really understand just how much diversity Rhode Island crams within its tiny borders as you leave mellow South County and cross over Narragansett Bay to Newport, with its abundance of high-powered millionaires' yachts and extravagant mansions. These, of course, are the very elements that set Newport apart from other New England resort towns.

Modern-day Newport does retain its fair share of Colonial history and landmarks, however. Founded in 1639 by settlers from Providence, the town became an important shipbuilding center and seaport, a landing site for the infamous "triangle trade" in molasses, rum and slaves. By the time of the Revolution, Newport was already prospering.

That prosperity would reach staggering heights during the next century, when wealthy families from New York and Philadelphia started building their summer mansions in this idyllic spot. It is really the lavish excesses of these "gilded age" palaces that everyone flocks here to see; we want an insider's glimpse into the lifestyles of the long-ago rich and famous.

SIGHTS

The **Preservation Society of Newport County** maintains ten historic house museums, six of them among the most dazzling mansions along exclusive Bellevue Avenue. In each, the one-hour tours are well organized and quite thorough, given by guides who obviously love their work. You'll see examples of mind-boggling wealth and extravagance, holdovers from a pre–income tax era when vast fortunes could be squandered on palatial "summer cottages" for families with Vanderbilt-like reputations to uphold. The Society offers individual and combination tour tickets. Mansions are open daily from May through September, seasonal hours the rest of the year. ~ 424 Bellevue Avenue, Newport; 401-847-1000; www. newportmansions.org.

Hammersmith Farm offers a unique appeal: a down-to-earth look into the contemporary old-money lifestyles of the Kennedy-Auchincloss dynasty. Hammersmith was a working farm in 1600s. More recently the farm's cottage and its 50 waterfront acres (landscaped by Frederick Law Olmsted) served as summer home to young Jacqueline Bouvier and as a "Summer White House" to her husband, John F. Kennedy. Closed December 20 to April 1. Admission. ~ Ocean Drive, Newport; 401-846-7346; www.hammer smithfarm.com.

The name **Newport Casino** refers not to gambling but to the elegant resort built in 1880 that now houses the International Tennis Hall of Fame and the Tennis Museum, as well as famed championship grass courts and court tennis (the "sport of kings"). Admission. ~ 194 Bellevue Avenue, Newport; 401-849-3990; www. tennisfame.org.

Not *everything* in Newport has to do with gilded monuments and big bucks—the city is one of the oldest in the United States and has an intriguing history stretching back three centuries. One spot that has attracted a horde of historical theories yet remains a mystery is the **Old Stone Mill**. Some believe it was erected by Norsemen in the days of Leif Ericsson. Others date it to the 17th century or believe it to be the remains of a 17th-century windmill. ~ Bellevue Avenue and Mill Street in Touro Park, Newport.

America's oldest Jewish house of worship, **Touro Synagogue** dates back to 1763. The first members of Newport's Jewish community—Sephardic Portuguese whose families had fled to the New World to escape the Catholic Inquisition—had arrived in Newport a century earlier, drawn by Rhode Island's then-unique policy of universal religious tolerance. Although not large, the Georgian-style brick structure is considered the crowning achievement of Peter Harrison, 18th-century America's leading architect. It embodies features typical of Sephardic temples in Spain and Portugal, such as the seating arrangement and the massive columns, each carved from a single tree, that support the women's gallery. Twelve in number, they symbolize the twelve tribes of Israel. The synagogue is set at an angle on the property so that worshippers standing in prayer before the Holy Ark containing the Torah face east toward Jerusalem. On display on the west wall is a facsimile of George Washington's 1790 letter to the congregation, now considered the classic expression of religious liberty in America. ~ 85 Touro Street, Newport; 401-847-4794; www.tourosynagogue.org.

Across the street from the synagogue, the Newport Historical Society's **Museum of Newport History** provides a context for the city's architectural marvels. Artifacts, graphics, old photographs and audiovisual programs reveal the origins of Rhode Island's policy of religious tolerance and show the lifestyles of the wealthy, the artists, writers and architects and the diverse ethnic subcultures that shaped Newport's cultural heritage. Among the exhibits are model ships, Colonial silver and the printing press used by Benjamin Franklin to produce *Poor Richard's Almanack*. Computers offer a virtual tour of Bellevue Avenue's historic homes. ~ 82 Touro Street, Newport; 401-846-0813; www.newporthistorical.com.

The oldest library building in the United States, the **Redwood Library** was erected in 1748–1749 and today boasts an important collection of books and paintings, including several by Gilbert Stuart. ~ 50 Bellevue Avenue, Newport; 401-847-0292; www.redwood1747.org.

POINTS OF INTEREST
- Ⓐ The Astors' Beechwood
- Ⓑ The Breakers
- Ⓒ Chateau-Sur-Mer
- Ⓓ The Elms
- Ⓔ Hammersmith Farm
- Ⓕ Hunter House
- Ⓖ Kingscote
- Ⓗ Marble House
- Ⓘ Newport Casino
- Ⓙ Old Colony House
- Ⓚ Rosecliff
- Ⓛ Touro Synagogue
- Ⓜ Wanton-Lyman Hazard House

Newport

Mansions of Newport

It's not possible to tour all the mansions that are open to the public on the same day, since each one takes almost an hour. This walk lets you hit the high points in a day and covers about four miles, not counting the vast interiors of the mansions. Start around 10 a.m. at the **Preservation Society of Newport County** visitors center at 424 Bellevue Avenue (401-847-1000). Buy a $38/adult ($12/youth under 18) combination tour ticket for seven mansions (saving $28 over individual admission). You need not use the ticket at all houses on the same day; it's good for the entire season. Three-house combination tickets are also available.

CHATEAU-SUR-MER   From the visitors center, follow the sign to the nearby Chateau-sur-Mer with its distinctive mansard roofline. Built in 1852 for William Wetmore, who made his fortune in the China trade—hence the Chinese "moongate" in the south wall—the mansion incorporates most of the major design trends of the Victorian era. Its broad parklike grounds shaded by copper beech trees were the scene of "fêtes champêtres," elaborate picnics attended by as many as 2000 guests.

ROSECLIFF TO BELCOURT   Walking south on Bellevue Avenue, across Ruggles Avenue, you'll come to **Rosecliff**, architect Stanford White's version of the Grand Trianon at Versailles. It was completed in 1902 for the heiress to the Comstock silver lode, one of the richest silver finds in history. Next in line, **The Astors' Beechwood** (not one of the Preservation Society mansions—call 401-846-3772) offers living-history tours by costumed actors appearing as guides, gossipy servants, eccentric house guests and even an Astor or two. Beyond the Astor mansion, **Marble House** was the first of the Vanderbilt mansions in Newport (William Vanderbilt gave it to his wife as a present on her 39th birthday). Its interior boasts virtually no surface left ungilded, unmarbled or unembellished. It incorporates features from the Grand and Petit Trianons in Versailles and has a colorful Chinese teahouse overlooking the Atlantic. Near the south end of Bellevue, **Belcourt Castle** (not a

Nearby stands the **Friends Meeting House,** a Quaker worshipping place since it was built in 1699. The original large English Gothic structure received two Colonial-style additions in 1729 and 1807. The meeting house can be toured Tuesday through Saturday by appointment only. Admission. ~ Marlborough and Farewell streets, Newport; 401-846-0813.

Preservation Society mansion—call 401-846-0669) is a Louis XIII–style palace built in 1894 and filled with art treasures and antiques from around the world.

CLIFF WALK TO THE BREAKERS   Past the Belcourt estate, Bellevue Avenue makes a sharp right. Near the corner of Coggeshall Avenue, Cliff Walk goes off to the south toward a rocky point. From the point, the trail turns north and winds its sometimes precarious way above the crashing waves, providing "hidden" views of the front yards and facades of the great mansions you've visited so far. Keep to the inside of the path—erosion has weakened the outer edges in some sections. A little less than two miles along, you'll come to Ochre Point Avenue and **The Breakers**, the grandest of the Newport mansions. Cornelius Vanderbilt II commissioned architect Richard Morris Hunt to design this full-scale replica of a 16th-century Italian palace. After touring the Great Hall, with its 45-foot ceiling and the rest of the splendid interior, visitors can ramble through the 13-acre grounds overlooking the sea.

CHEPSTOW AND THE ELMS   Continue north on the Cliff Walk for another half-mile to Narragansett Avenue. Along the way you'll pass **Ochre Court**, a former summer home built in 1892 that now serves as the administration building for Salve Regina University. At Narragansett, turn inland to the two-story white Italianate **Chepstow**, which houses the art and historical document collections of the Morris clan, one of America's founding families. Continue on Narragansett back to Bellevue, then turn right to **The Elms**. The summer home of coal tycoon Edward Julius Berwind, it was modeled after the mid-18th-century French chateau d'Asniers and was famed for its classical gardens, which are now being restored.

ADDITIONAL HOMES   A Preservation Society combination ticket can also get you into **Kingscote**, a smaller early-19th-century residence that was among the first on Bellevue Avenue, as well as the **Isaac Bell House**, a restoration in progress, **The Breakers Stable and Carriage House** on Coggeshall Avenue, **Hunter House** (page 146) on Washington Street, and **Green Animals** (page 146) in Portsmouth.

The oldest restored home in Newport, the **Wanton-Lyman-Hazard House** dates to 1675 and has seen a wealth of history all by itself. Several Colonial governors called the place home, but its claim to fame was as the site of a riot following passage of England's infamous Stamp Act of 1765. It seems the stamp master lived in this house, which was nearly destroyed by a distraught

Sons of Liberty mob. Today the house features period pieces and a Colonial garden. Open by appointment only. Admission. ~ 17 Broadway, Newport; 401-846-0813.

A fine Colonial mansion dating to 1748, **Hunter House** was owned by Jonathan Nichols, the Deputy Governor of the time. Today it is a restored National Historic Landmark with an excellent collection of 18th-century Colonial furnishings, as well as paintings and other decorative objects. Open from May through September and weekends only in April and October. Admission. ~ 54 Washington Street, Newport; 401-847-1000.

A good stress-buster is **Viking Tours**, which helps you beat Newport's summer gridlock traffic. The bus tour leaves from the Gateway Center on America's Cup Avenue and stops at mansions of your choice and major attractions. Closed November through April. Fee. ~ 401-847-6921.

Newport County Convention & Visitors Bureau (Gateway Center) is a bustling hub of traveler's information: helpful staff; brochures, maps and guides; multimedia video; and bus, trolley and tourist train terminal. ~ 23 America's Cup Avenue, Newport; 401-849-8048, 800-976-5122; www.gonewport.com.

The towns of Middletown and Portsmouth share Aquidneck Island with Newport. In Middletown, the **Norman Bird Sanctuary** encompasses 450 acres of extraordinarily beautiful wilderness land. Wildlife (pheasant, nesting birds, rabbit and fox) inhabit the 30 acres of hay fields; there are woodlands, salt marshes and craggy ridges. An extremely active program includes guided trail walks, educational workshops, children's programs and themed hikes. Closed Monday from Labor Day to Memorial Day. Trail fee, $4. ~ 583 Third Beach Road, Middletown; 401-846-2577; www.normanbirdsanctuary.org.

In Portsmouth, **Green Animals** is a whimsical garden of more than 80 century-old trees and shrubs sculpted in the European manner to resemble dogs, camels, goats, roosters, bears and even a man on horseback and sailboats. It's a treat for kids, a mecca for horticulture buffs. A Victorian toy collection is housed inside the country estate's 19th-century white clapboard house. Closed October through April. Admission. ~ 380 Cory's Lane, Portsmouth; 401-847-1000.

To increase the fun of the excursion out to Green Animals, hop aboard the historic **Old Colony & Newport Railway**. During the eight-mile, one-hour roundtrip you'll pass a number of the island's maritime sites. There's ample time for viewing the animals before the return train departs. Closed Monday, Thursday and Friday during peak season; open Saturday from Columbus Day to mid-November, and Sunday from January through April. Fee. ~ 19 America's Cup Avenue at Bridge Street, Newport; 401-624-6951; www.ocnrr.com.

Across the Sakonnet River from Portsmouth lie the bucolic towns of Tiverton and Little Compton. Comparable to the fashionable bedroom communities found near any urban center, these towns have their fair share of power residents who share the country scene with gentlemen farmers. Everything is peaceful here; strict zoning laws and sky-high real estate prices conspire to keep things that way.

Sakonnet Vineyards is the oldest of Rhode Island's three vineyards. Established in 1975, Sakonnet now produces a southeastern New England selection including their popular chardonnay and vidal blanc. There are guided tours and winetastings. ~ 162 West Main Road, Little Compton; 401-635-8486, 800-919-4637.

◄ HIDDEN

Sakonnet's vineyards and its scenic acres are an altogether idyllic picnic setting. After buying a bottle of wine at Sakonnet's tasting room, stop by the **Provender at Tiverton Four Corners**, a gourmet food emporium housed in an old mansard-roofed general store, to assemble your dream lunch, complete with fresh-baked bread. Closed February; closed Monday in December, January and March. ~ 3883 Main Road, Tiverton; 401-624-8096.

In addition to the usual chain hotels, Newport has an abundance of small bed-and-breakfasts. As one islander observed, "In this town, almost everyone has an extra room or two to rent." Don't be fooled by that gem of Yankee understatement; we have observed that, in this town where extravagant landmark mansions are almost the norm, the bed and breakfasts tend to follow suit.

LODGING

The Wayside is a trim beige-brick Georgian mansion just across Bellevue Avenue from the famous Elms. Owners Dorothy and Al Posts have restored this sprawling 1896 home, creating a dozen guest rooms blessed with antique furnishings and majestic proportions—and each with its own private bath. There's even a heated pool in the back garden. ~ 406 Bellevue Avenue, Newport; 401-847-0302, 800-653-7678, fax 401-848-9374; e-mail wayside 406@aol.com. DELUXE.

The 1855 **Marshall Slocum Guest House** sits on a tree-lined, Norman Rockwell kind of street. An American flag flies overhead, and on the spacious front porch rocking chairs await your leisure. Inside, rooms are cheery and graced with antiques. Your gregarious innkeeper, Joan Wilson, who is creative both in the kitchen (fresh-baked quiches and muffins every breakfast) and in decorating, has chosen sunny yellows and marine blues to balance the house's original dark woods. Two of the five upstairs guest rooms have fireplaces and all have private baths. A full breakfast is served on the deck overlooking the sunny back garden in warm weather. ~ 29 Kay Street, Newport; 401-841-5120, 800-372-5120, fax 401-846-3787; www.marshallslocuminn.com, e-mail marshallslocuminn@edgenet.net. DELUXE.

The **Newport Marriott** is big, modern and close to the water. A number of the 317 rooms and seven suites command sweeping views of Newport Harbor. Glass-fronted elevators (often exasperatingly slow to arrive) seem to double as kinetic sculpture, providing space-age mobility to the lobby's plant-filled atrium design. Rooms feature pastel decor and the usual complement of electronic equipment. Among the definite pluses: a health club and indoor pool in the hotel; the Gateway Center (Convention & Visitors Bureau) next door; and shopping and waterfront browsing within easy walking distance. ~ 25 America's Cup Avenue, Newport; 401-849-1000, 800-458-3066, fax 401-849-3422. ULTRA-DELUXE.

Hotel Viking is Newport's grande dame, a 1920s National Historic Landmark in red brick trimmed in white. The understatement of the tidy four-column entrance is deceptive; inside, the hotel is a sprawl of rooms and levels. There are 184 guest rooms, numerous dining rooms and a health club and pool. Rooms are a bit cramped, crammed with heavy antique reproduction four-posters and furniture. In summer, dining at the Garden Patio Café offers a charming alternative to the somewhat overpowering hotel atmosphere inside. ~ 1 Bellevue Avenue, Newport; 401-847-3300, 800-556-7126, fax 401-848-4864; www.hotelviking.com. DELUXE TO ULTRA-DELUXE.

Castle Hill Inn & Resort sits on 40 acres of secluded peninsula overlooking Narragansett Bay. Built in 1874 for international naturalist Alexander Agassiz, this weathered, shingled inn today retains most of its original Victorian charm. Its rambling structure yields nine guest rooms of unique shapes, bursting with antique decor. Bedrooms are furnished with oriental carpets and Chinese antiques, authentic washstands and upholstered slipper chairs, and are paired with large, modern baths. Six more guest

SERVING TIME ... COMFORTABLY

For an overnight stay that will make a good story to tell friends later, spend the night in an 18th-century jail. Located in the heart of downtown Newport a block from the harbor, the **Jailhouse Inn** was built in 1772 as the town lockup. Beautifully renovated, the dining room and common areas are furnished with antiques for a homelike feel. The 22 guest rooms and suites emphasize the jailhouse motif with convict-striped bedspreads and upholstery. No jail cell was ever so spacious, though, as these rooms with their king- or queen-size beds, dormer windows and premium cable TV. Rates include afternoon tea and a continental breakfast buffet. ~ 13 Marlborough Street, Newport; 401-847-4638, 800-427-9444, fax 401-849-0605. MODERATE TO DELUXE.

rooms are found in cliffside harbor houses behind the main building, and beachfront cottages (closed in winter) draw repeat visitors every year (weekly rates in the summer, nightly rates in the spring). Individually decorated beach houses are their premier units, offering a large sitting area, kitchen, stone fireplaces, an entertainment center, two-person jacuzzi, and a private deck on the beach. Guests like to gather before the unique marquetry fireplace in the downstairs sitting room. ~ 590 Ocean Drive, Newport; 401-849-3800, 888-466-1355, fax 401-849-3838; www.castlehillinn.com, e-mail info@castlehillinn.com. ULTRA-DELUXE.

Built in 1880 as a summer home for Maryland governor Thomas Swann, the **Cliffside Inn** is ideally located—a block from Cliff Walk and within easy reach of the beach and Newport's mansions. But in this case, location is not everything. The inn is a beautiful Victorian building with 16 guest rooms, all furnished with antiques, some boasting fireplaces or whirlpools. At one point, it was home to artist Beatrice Turner, whose paintings can be seen throughout. No smoking and no pets. Children over 13 only; two-day minimum stay on weekends, three-night minimum on holidays. ~ 2 Seaview Avenue, Newport; 401-847-1811, 800-845-1811, fax 401-848-5850; www.cliffsideinn.com, e-mail cliff@wsii.com. ULTRA-DELUXE.

The Admiral Inns, three historic houses within a couple of blocks of Newport Harbor, are well-kept secrets among regular Newport visitors. Each has a fascinating history and distinctive characteristics.

The graceful Victorian **Admiral Benbow Inn** was built in 1855 by Captain Augustus Littlefield. Its 15 rooms have brass beds and private baths, and the entire inn is air-conditioned (which is welcome during Newport's steamy summers). ~ 93 Pelham Street, Newport; 401-848-8000, 800-343-2863, fax 401-846-8006; www.admiralsinns.com. MODERATE TO DELUXE.

The **Admiral Fitzroy Inn**, the largest of the three inns, has 17 rooms, each with a private bath, an elevator, and a roof deck with a harbor view. Admiral Fitzroy commanded the *Beagle* during Charles Darwin's *Origin of the Species* voyage to the Galápagos Islands. ~ 398 Thames Street, Newport; 401-848-8000, 800-343-2863, fax 401-846-8006; www.admiralsinns.com. MODERATE TO DELUXE.

During the Revolution, the **Admiral Farragut Inn**, built in 1702, housed two of the aides-de-camp of General Rochambeau, the French general who assisted George Washington throughout the war. The nine-room inn maintains its Colonial air, with wide plank floors, 12-over-12 paned windows, and original cave mouldings. ~ 31 Clarke Street, Newport; 401-848-8000, 800-343-2863, fax 401-846-8006; www.admiralsinns.com. MODERATE TO DELUXE.

Just three blocks from downtown Newport, **The Willows of Newport** is a small, seven-room inn that occupies two historic townhouses. The buildings were built 100 years apart—The John Roger House dates to circa 1740 and is a pre-Revolutionary Colonial while the addition, known as The Willows, is classic Greek Revival, circa 1840. Both the Colonial and Victorian eras are beautifully recreated in the inn, earning it a listing on the U.S. National Register of Historic Landmarks. In addition to its lovely interiors, the inn is known for its gardens. The chandeliered guest rooms offer fresh flowers and canopy bedframes draped in silks; two have jacuzzis. Breakfast in bed is served every morning. ~ 8 and 10 Willow Street, Historic Point, Newport; 401-846-5486, fax 401-849-8215; www.newportri.com/users/willows. ULTRA-DELUXE.

Within easy walking distance of the mansions is **The Hydrangea House Inn**, named after the blossoms so abundant in Newport. The six-room inn was built in 1876 and has been carefully restored. The guest rooms—which are all non-smoking—are variously decorated with antiques and original artwork. The rate includes a breakfast of fresh-ground coffee, just-squeezed orange juice, home-baked bread and granola, plus pancakes or scrambled eggs; the dining room is also a small gallery. The inn is right on Bellevue Avenue, about a five-minute walk to the waterfront. ~ 16 Bellevue Avenue, Newport; 401-846-4435, 800-945-4667, fax 401-846-6602; www.hydrangeahouse.com, e-mail innkeeper @hydrangeahouse.com. DELUXE TO ULTRA-DELUXE.

Spring Seasons offers three B&B accommodations situated in the heart of Newport. One suite features a two-person jacuzzi, a cathedral ceiling and a private deck. There is a regular jacuzzi in each of the other suites. All units in this 1840s Greek Revival building have air conditioning. ~ 86 Spring Street, Newport; 401-846-6810, 800-841-6810. ULTRA-DELUXE.

The **Ivy Lodge** is an eight-room inn housed in a large Victorian. All rooms are individually decorated in Victorian style. Six have their own bathrooms, a rarity at most bed and breakfasts, and a family suite is available. Breakfast is always a treat; you'll enjoy the homemade muffins and other baked goods. ~ 12 Clay Street, Newport; 401-849-6865, 800-834-6865; www.ivylodge. com, e-mail info.reservations@ivylodge.com. DELUXE.

Not everything in the Newport area is rarified and expensive. The **Newport Ramada Inn** offers clean, comfortable and affordable lodgings. The 147 guest rooms are large and decorated with modern furnishings. Amenities include no-smoking rooms, a lounge, a heated indoor pool and the Captain's Table Restaurant and lounge. ~ 936 West Main Road, Middletown; 401-846-7600, 800-556-6464, fax 401-849-6919; www.ramada.com. DELUXE.

As you might expect, the restaurant scene in this posh town can get quite fancy and expensive. For those who prefer a more laid-back approach, there are many waterfront places that specialize in seafood, harbor views and relaxed enjoyment.

Non-guests are welcome to enjoy the legendary Sunday brunch at **Castle Hill Inn & Resort**. This three-story, weathered-shingle 1874 Victorian, with its peaked roof and turrets, overlooks the bay from its own peninsula. Inside, the chestnut paneling shines in the glow of Tiffany lamps. Oriental rugs accent hardwood floors. Brunch, served on the lawn or indoors in a gazebo setting of green and white, combines just the right mix of formal and alfresco eating as you sit peacefully watching the sailboats on Narragansett Bay. The vast spread offers everything from breakfast items such as eggs Benedict to tempting entrées such as leg of lamb and whole poached salmon. Closed Monday through Wednesday. Closed November through April. ~ Ocean Drive, Newport; 401-849-3800. DELUXE TO ULTRA-DELUXE.

An atmosphere of elegance prevails at the **White Horse Tavern**, a restored 1673 Colonial landmark. Although it's America's oldest tavern, don't expect a typical pub scene; this is one of Newport's finest restaurants. The White Horse's interior, too, remains true to its Colonial heritage with huge fireplaces, exposed beams and lots of oil portraits of solemn-faced ancestors. While the menu varies with the season, you can count on always finding native seafood specialties like red snapper or terra-firma dishes such as beef Wellington and roast rack of lamb. Service is formal, lending additional panache to the upscale Continental cuisine. No lunch on Tuesday. ~ 26 Marlborough Street, Newport; 401-849-3600. ULTRA-DELUXE.

While not strictly hidden, **Canfield House and Patrick's Pub**   ◄ HIDDEN
are decidedly a couple of finds. Relying primarily on satisfied diners to spread its good word, Canfield maintains a discreet elegance. An unpretentious Victorian building tucked away in a tiny alley off the main street, Canfield began as a gambling casino, the joy and toy of Richard Canfield, a colorful figure in the gaming world of the early 1900s. Today's diners enjoy Continental classics in the main casino, under a vaulted ceiling of intricately carved cherry. Service is upscale-casual and attentive. Visitors and locals (many of whom come to celebrate special occasions) enjoy dressing up to complement the surroundings. ~ 5 Memorial Boulevard, Newport; 401-847-0416. DELUXE.

The biggest and freshest all-you-can-eat salad buffet in Newport is at the popular **Brick Alley Pub**. The casual downtown restaurant also serves an assortment of extra-lean, broiled hamburgers, sandwiches such as broiled chicken-artichoke and Cajun catfish, unusual pasta selections and a full range of seafood specialties including boiled lobster on a bed of steamed clams. The decor consists mainly of walls full of award plaques the restaurant has won since it opened in 1980. ~ 140 Thames Street, Newport; 401-849-6334; www.brickalley.com. BUDGET TO MODERATE.

A Newport classic and the town's oldest waterfront restaurant, **Christie's** is where the young and restless rub elbows with blue bloods just off their yachts. Diners can choose the main dining room, the Victorian Topside room or enjoy appetizers and pub grub at one of the two more casual outdoor deck eating areas— all with sea views. There's also a dockside raw bar where people gather for cocktails and live entertainment. Fresh lobster, of course, is the specialty, along with a menu of seafood, steak and chicken dishes. ~ Christie's Landing, off Thames Street, Newport; 401-847-5400. DELUXE TO ULTRA-DELUXE.

La Petite Auberge is a chef-owned French restaurant in a Colonial building that dates back to 1714. The five intimate dining rooms feature lace tablecloths. During the summer months you can also eat outside on the patio. There are two menus: a deluxe-priced formal menu and a moderate-priced bistro menu. The bill of fare usually includes some chicken dishes, seafood specialties, baby rack of lamb, trout and châteaubriand. ~ 19 Charles Street, Newport; 401-849-6669. DELUXE TO ULTRA-DELUXE.

Another worthwhile French restaurant, **Le Bistro** specializes in Provençal cooking, using lots of herbs and oils. Everything is made from scratch here including the sauces (which are lighter than traditional French sauces) and baked goods. Le Bistro is located on the waterfront, offering views of the water from the dining areas. The wine list won *Wine Spectator* magazine's Award of Excellence. ~ 19 Bowen's Wharf, Newport; 401-849-7778. MODERATE TO ULTRA-DELUXE.

If you've yearned to dine aboard the Orient Express, **The Newport Dinner Train** provides a handy American version. Two lavishly refurbished railroad cars roll sedately along tracks paralleling Narragansett Bay, making a three-hour journey to nowhere and back, allowing ample time for the four-course meal. Diners choose from entrées of ribs or pork and have the option to take part in a murder-mystery show on Friday evenings. The mood is festive, with many parties celebrating a special occasion. (The down side: Diners sometimes get very rowdy, and noise levels tend to magnify inside a space as small as a railroad car.) Reservations required. Closed January and February. ~ Newport Depot, 19 America's Cup Avenue, Newport; 401-841-8700, 800-398-7427. ULTRA-DELUXE.

A great little place for breakfast or a simple lunch, **Annie's** serves wonderful homemade muffins and delicious omelettes. The lunch menu includes sandwiches, soups, burgers and salads.

The restaurant—a cross between a diner and a bakery—has several booths and a counter area perfect for settling in with a meal and the newspaper. ~ 176 Bellevue Avenue, Newport; 401-849-6731. MODERATE.

Sea Fare Inn dazzles with festive opulence: chandeliers glitter, and tables (as well as patrons) are decked in Sunday best. The cuisine is American regional of the unabashedly haute classical variety—the kind that requires (and receives) similarly haute service and attention to detail. Whether you're seated in the large, formal, pillared dining room or in what once was the sun porch of this Victorian mansion, you'll catch the festive spirit of the place. Closed Monday. ~ 3352 East Main Road, Portsmouth; 401-683-0577. DELUXE.

The beachside line of people waiting to get into **Flo's Drive-in** is the first clue. A true "clam shack" and the best of the genre, this beachfront haven sells huge, puffy clamcakes, fried steamers and spicy "stuffies" (stuffed clams). Open Friday through Sunday from mid-March through September. ~ Park Avenue, Portsmouth. BUDGET.

◄ HIDDEN

In Newport even the shopping malls sport a nautical/historical air. **Bowen's Wharf** is a mix of 18th-century wharf buildings and 19th-century brick warehouses that make up today's complex of open-air restaurants, fashion boutiques and import shops. ~ Just off America's Cup Avenue, Newport; 401-849-2120.

SHOPPING

Brick Market Place is a three-and-a-half-acre complex of more than 30 shops and restaurants along a—you guessed it—brick road. The original building, which used to be the site of the market and granary built in 1762, is now a National Historic Landmark. It houses the **Museum of Newport History**. ~ Between Thames Street and America's Cup Avenue, Newport.

◆◆

YULETIDE FARMERS

Christmas trees are a $6 million-a-year business in Rhode Island, which has more Christmas tree farms than any other New England state. The industry has proved to be ideal for this tiny state, because the trees—balsam fir, Douglas fir, Fraser fir, noble fir, Scotch pine, Virginia pine and white pine—can be grown on relatively small farms on land that is only marginally productive for other crops. Besides being more profitable than timbering for lumber, Christmas trees are ready for harvest (six feet tall) in about seven years, compared to 20 to 30 years for timber. Most Christmas tree farms along Rhode Island highways welcome visitors, and as the holiday season approaches many farms let customers choose and cut their own trees.

Try **William Vareika Fine Arts** for 300 years worth of American paintings, prints and drawings—many of Newport and Narragansett Bay. It's a delight to shop in this museumlike setting. ~ 212 Bellevue Avenue, Newport; 401-849-6149.

If lace is your first love, don't miss **Rue de France**, where imported laces from France shape everything from window hangings to dainty camisoles. Some laces are sold by the yard as well. ~ 78 Thames Street, Newport; 401-846-2084.

A 1750s landmark shingle-sided farm complex called **The Old Almy House** houses several charming country stores that have everything from antiques and collectibles to a year-round Christmas store. ~ 1016 East Main Road, Portsmouth; 401-683-3737.

Tiverton Four Corners is a gathering of some very chic merchandise presented in attractive old-fashioned surroundings. On one corner, the 1829 Josiah Wilcox House is home to **Peter's Attic**, specializing in antiques, and the **Donovan Gallery**, featuring fine art. ~ 3879 Main Road, Tiverton; 401-624-4000. Nearby, **Provender at Tiverton Four Corners** purveys gourmet imports as well as fresh-baked goods and fancy take-outs. Closed February and closed Monday from September through May. ~ 3883 Main Road, Tiverton; 401-624-8096.

NIGHTLIFE   In summer, Newport's nightlife assumes world-class proportions with its famous festivals: the **August Jazz Festival** (401-847-3710), held the second week of August; the **Folk Festival** (401-847-3710), the first week in August; and the **Newport Musical Festival** (401-846-1133), the second and third weeks in July, which features classical concerts at some of the most spectacular mansions of Bellevue Avenue.

The **Newport Playhouse & Cabaret Restaurant** offers dinner theater and cabaret Friday through Sunday. ~ 102–104 Connell Highway, near the foot of the Newport Bridge, Newport; 401-848-7529.

Auld Mug Lounge features Saucy Sylvia Thursday through Saturday. Saucy plays the piano and parodies favorites of the '40s, '50s and '60s. Reduced hours in winter. ~ Newport Islander Doubletree Hotel, Goat Island; 401-849-2600.

Red Parrot Restaurant and Bar has live jazz in the downstairs restaurant on Friday through Sunday nights. ~ 348 Thames Street, Newport; 401-847-3140.

BEACHES & PARKS   Although not quite technically an island, Aquidneck Island has water along almost every inch of its four sides and an enviable selection of ocean, bay and river beaches.

FORT ADAMS STATE PARK   Built in 1824 to protect the entrance to Newport Harbor, Fort Adams stands now as a National Historic Landmark, its stone fortress open for tours (fee); its 21 acres of parklands offer a recreational haven for all. The park lies at the toe of Aquidneck Island's boot, facing Narragansett Bay. This vast grassy meadow—home to the Newport Jazz and Folk festivals and other summer concerts—matches great sounds with spectacular sights such as views of the bay and its active boating scene. Facilities include picnic groves with grills, restrooms and lifeguards. ~ Located at the end of Fort Adams Road on Ocean Drive; 401-847-2400.

EASTON'S BEACH (FIRST BEACH) This swath has a real public beach atmosphere, the only one you're likely to find in the area. A mostly young crowd comes here. This stretch of beach curves, with rougher waves for surfers on the outer edges and calmer waters on the broad inner arc. The sand is fine and very soft, the beach wide. There are restrooms, showers and lifeguards, as well as a concession stand, an aquarium and a boardwalk with amusements (miniature golf, bumper cars, carousel). Parking fee, $8 to $10. ~ Located along Memorial Boulevard, from the northern end of the Cliff Walk eastward to Middletown; 401-848-6491.

SACHUEST BEACH (SECOND BEACH) Its two miles of rolling dunes, fine sand and waves for surfing at one end make Sachuest the favorite local beach, and singles tend to congregate here. Beautiful views include St. George's School in the distance. There's surf fishing from the rocky coast. The beach abuts the 21 shoreline acres of the Norman Bird Sanctuary. Facilities include picnic tables, restrooms, showers, lifeguards and a concession stand. Parking fee, $10 to $15. ~ On Sachuest Way, Middletown; 401-849-2822.

▲ The campground (401-846-6273) offers 44 sites with full hookups. Some sites are available on a first-come, first-serve basis; others must be reserved. Daily fees are $25 to $30 per site, with weekly and monthly discounted rates. Closed October to mid-May.

PEABODY BEACH (THIRD BEACH) This spot is ideal for families because it fronts the calm waters of the Sakonnet River. Its profile includes high dunes and a beach that's more soil than sand. It's also popular with windsurfers. The view across the river includes Little Compton's sweep of rolling hills. Portable restrooms are the only facilities here. ~ Off Third Beach Road, Middletown.

Providence Area

At a glance Rhode Island seems comprised of water first and land second. The reason for this is Narragansett Bay. Twisting southward from Providence and the Blackstone River, the bay permeates the state's rocky landscape, then spills into the Atlantic at Newport. If you follow this waterway you will see that it defines Rhode Island. The communities it touches thrive on fishing, shipbuilding and sailing. From the busy port of Providence to the Herreshoff Boatyard in Bristol (builders of the first torpedo boat in 1887) to the resorts and beaches of Warwick, the Narragansett is a saltwater net that holds the state together.

Within the city limits of Providence are enough historical treasures to satisfy even the most insatiable culture buffs—from the architectural beauties of Benefit Street to the marble dome of the State House, which gleams like a beacon above the skyline. The lofty College Hill area is home to Brown University and to a resulting Cambridge-like neighborhood of bookstores, boutiques and trendy restaurants. Revitalized sections—such as Corliss Landing—are springing up like mushrooms almost overnight, bringing new life and lifestyles into forgotten parts of town. There's a vitality, a zingy balance of past and future, to this place.

This capital city of Rhode Island was also its first, established in 1636 by Roger Williams, founder of the Baptist Church, "in commemoration of God's Providence." Williams' religious bent extended even to the naming of local thoroughfares; visitors today walk along Benefit, Church, Benevolent, Hope and Friendship streets.

SIGHTS
Seven hills and the Providence River give the city its geographic complexity. Most fashionable addresses lie on the east side of town (not to be confused with the neighboring town of East Providence). College Hill is a steep incline dotted with many historic sites and crowned by the Brown University complex.

It is fitting to begin at the corner of Main and Waterman streets, site of Williams' **First Baptist Church**, built in 1775 (although his first congregation was founded in 1638). The 185-foot church steeple, visible from just about anywhere in town, was inspired by designs of Sir Christopher Wren. Actively used by its local congregation, the church opens its vast spaces every Memorial Day weekend for the commencement exercises of Brown University. Open to visitors Monday through Saturday, and by appointment only on Saturday from Columbus Day through Memorial Day. ~ 75 North Main Street, Providence; 401-751-2266.

Nearby is the **Museum of Art–Rhode Island School of Design**, considered one of America's finest museums of its size. Housed within a deceptively unimposing 1877 six-story, Federal-style brick structure, attached to the Daphne Farago Wing, are three floors of artistic masterpieces with dates ranging from the ancient Egyptian period to the present. Throughout the galleries, you'll encounter clutches of students studying and creating their own artworks; this museum is a treasured storehouse for RISD (pronounced Rizz-dee) students and faculty. Don't miss: the satiny Goddard-Townsend block and shell masterpiece (a 1760s mahogany desk and bookcase, one of only 12 still in existence, whose sibling piece fetched $12 million at a Christie's auction); the Babylonian lion bas-relief (605 B.C.); the impressionists (Manets and Monets); and the Rodin sculptures. Step into the Daphne Farago Wing for a look at the contemporary art collection, or wander through the museum's interior sculpture garden. Closed Monday; closed Tuesday from Memorial Day through Labor Day. Admission. ~ 224 Benefit Street, Providence; 401-454-6500.

If you're interested in seeing art by RISD students, head over to the **Rhode Island School of Design's Woods-Gerry Gallery**. Faculty as well as students show their work here in ever-changing exhibitions. It's located in the three-story Woods-Gerry Mansion, designed by Richard Upjohn in 1860. Opening times vary with semester schedules; best to call ahead for exact hours. ~ 62 Prospect Street, Providence; 401-454-6141.

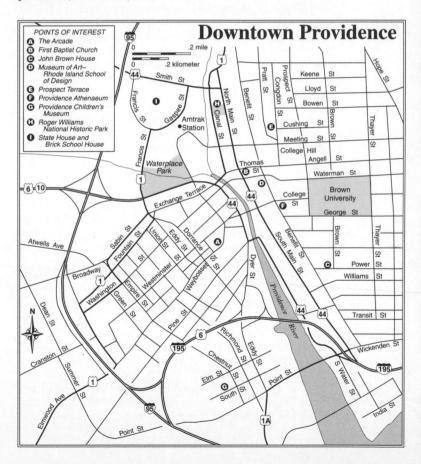

Downtown Providence

POINTS OF INTEREST

Ⓐ The Arcade
Ⓑ First Baptist Church
Ⓒ John Brown House
Ⓓ Museum of Art–
    Rhode Island School
    of Design
Ⓔ Prospect Terrace
Ⓕ Providence Athenaeum
Ⓖ Providence Children's
    Museum
Ⓗ Roger Williams
    National Historic Park
Ⓘ State House and
    Brick School House

Benefit Street, which traces a path across College Hill's vertical pitch, boasts a "Mile of History," regarded by scholars as the highest concentration of historic buildings anywhere in America. Along this miracle mile are restored Colonial, Federal and 19th-century buildings, all carefully maintained. They are also homes and businesses, for this is a street of *living* history as well. Every year, during the second weekend in June, a portion of Benefit Street—along with other historic areas—is open to the public for the "Festival of Historic Houses," a three-day celebration that includes tours, food events and sales. Contact the **Providence Preservation Society** for reservations or details; they also have maps and pamphlets. Closed weekends. ~ 21 Meeting Street, Providence; 401-831-7440.

One of Benefit Street's historic beauties is the **Providence Athenaeum**. Founded in 1753 as one of this country's first libraries, it sits in Grecian splendor, looking properly imposing and scholarly. The Greek Doric structure was completed in 1838. A wealth of rare and historic volumes is housed within, along with a bit of famous romantic history. It was here that Edgar Allan Poe met, loved and lost Sarah Helen Whitman, the inspiration for his "Annabelle Lee." Closed weekends in the summer. ~ 251 Benefit Street, Providence; 401-421-6970.

A few blocks south stands the **John Brown House**, built in 1786 for one of the famous Brown brothers. The name "Brown" is an integral part of Rhode Island history: the Browns were a merchant family who lived in Providence since the city's founding. This three-story brownstone and brick Georgian, which President John Quincy Adams once called "the most magnificent and elegant mansion that I have seen on this continent," houses an extraordinary collection of 18th-century furniture such as its nine-shell desk and bookcase, the latter considered to be the finest piece of American Colonial furniture in existence today. Closed Monday, and Tuesday through Thursday in January and February. Admission. ~ 52 Power Street, Providence; 401-331-8575.

Brown University is indeed king of the hill, the nation's seventh-oldest university, founded in 1764. ~ College Hill, end of College Street, Providence; 401-863-1000.

You'll feel the Ivy League influence throughout the sprawl of Gothic and Beaux-Arts structures and commons areas, dominated by the enormous **John D. Rockefeller, Jr., Library**, which houses Brown's general collections. ~ Prospect and College streets, Providence; 401-863-2167.

University Hall, a National Historic Landmark, served as a barracks and hospital for American troops during the Revolutionary War. ~ Prospect Street, Providence.

Before leaving College Hill, stop off at **Prospect Terrace**, the site of the Roger Williams Memorial, which overlooks downtown Providence. A tiny park is maintained here, making an ideal place for a picnic lunch. Enjoy the panoramic view while you digest all the history you've just seen and prepare to tour the city's other neighborhoods. ~ Congdon Street at Cushing Street, Providence.

Providence's downtown area is dominated by the **State House**, considered by some to be the most beautiful capitol building in America. The classic structure's white marble exterior dazzles in the sunlight. Its self-supported marble dome is the fourth largest in the world. A full-length portrait of George Washington, painted by Rhode Island's own Gilbert Stuart, hangs in the State Reception Room. Free tours of the capitol are given on weekdays. ~ Smith Street, Providence; 401-222-2357.

Several blocks south, you'll find **The Arcade**, an 1828 Greek Revival–style National Historic Landmark that is now a three-story shopping mall. Closed Sunday. ~ 65 Weybosset Street, Providence; 401-598-1199.

Nearby is the **Providence Children's Museum**, located in an enormous, old brick jewelry factory in the Jewelry District. Seven major exhibit areas include one called "Littlewoods"—appropriate for infants up to four years old. There, children learn all about the forest and its animals; they can climb trees and explore to their heart's content. Closed Monday. Admission. ~ 100 South Street, Providence; 401-273-5437.

For more information on this area contact the **Greater Providence Convention & Visitors Bureau**. ~ 1 West Exchange Street, Providence; 401-274-1636.

A short drive away is **Roger Williams Park Zoo**, Providence's favorite park since 1871, when Betsy Williams bequeathed her 102-acre farm to the city. Today this spacious parkland combines wilderness areas with such people pleasers as a zoo, complete with a community of penguins (admission), a lake and picturesque boathouse, a lakeside bandstand for concerts, a carousel, a nine-hole miniature golf course, paddleboats, bumper cars, pony rides and a greenhouse of exotic plants and flowers. All this amid landscaped, wooded parklands in the heart of the city. ~ 1000 Elmwood Avenue, Providence; 401-785-3510.

Also in the park is the **Roger Williams Park Museum of Natural History**, which has a planetarium, cultural and wildlife exhibits and a skeletal exhibit. Admission. ~ 401-785-9457; www.osfn.org/museum.

Across the Providence River, at the toe of the Bristol peninsula, nestles the serene haven of **Blithewold Mansion and Gardens**. Jutting spectacularly into Narragansett Bay, Blithewold dazzles with verdant acres and landscape gardens that border the water. A 17th-century-style manor house, all stone and turrets, plays centerpiece to this bucolic setting. Here lived the Van Wickle family from 1894 until the last heir, Mrs. Marjorie Van Wickle-Lyon, died in 1976 and willed the estate to the Heritage Trust of Rhode Island. Visitors today can tour some of the Van Wickle's private rooms and wander around their gardens. New England's tallest giant sequoia stands here, 90 feet tall, a century old and thriving far from its West Coast homeland. Tour the 33 acres of rose gardens, rock gardens and bosquets on your own, or join one of the guided tours. Even winter is special here, with the mansion decked in bows and baubles, its Victorian tree stretching past the balcony to the second-floor ceiling. House closed on Monday and Tuesday, and from January through April. Admission. ~ 101 Ferry Road, Bristol; 401-253-2707.

A short drive away, across the horseshoe cove of Bristol Harbor, is **Coggeshall Farm Museum,** a living history museum that represents a Rhode Island coastal farm in the 1790s. A costumed guide is often on hand to answer questions about the farm. The seasonal special programs—maple sugaring, 18th-century crafts demonstrations—are worth checking out. Admission. ~ Adjacent to the Colt State Park, Route 114, Bristol; 401-253-9062.

Across Narragansett Bay from Bristol lies Warwick, the second-largest city in Rhode Island. Home to the state's only commercial airport as well as to the largest concentrations of hotels and retail stores, it bills itself as "Rhode Island's Host City."

One of Warwick's most popular family attractions is the **John D. Florio Memorial Park.** Operated by a nonprofit children's charity, the park is known as the "impossible dream" to accentuate the positive. There are manual merry-go-rounds, a life-size doll house, a castle, a miniature golf course, children's train rides, swings and slides. Open spring through fall. Closed Sunday. ~ 575 Centerville Road, Warwick; 401-823-5566; www.warwickri.com.

FOURTH OF JULY EXTRAVAGANZA!

Nowhere in America is July 4th given such notice as in Bristol, where they've been celebrating since 1785, adding a bit more each year. Now, more than 250,000 visitors flood this tiny village in July (regular population: 21,625) to participate in its Independence Day celebration. The country's oldest parade marches along Route 114 (which features a red, white and blue stripe all year), and the festivities continue for days. For more information about this area, contact the Bristol County Chamber of Commerce. ~ 654 Metacom Avenue, Warren; 401-245-0750.

There are some large, urban hotels in the capital city, with several more under construction.

The **Westin Providence,** a 364-room, 25-story hotel, is a favorite among business travelers and others seeking all the amenities of a full-service hotel. There's a fitness center and a small indoor pool. Rooms are standard big-city hotel rooms with coordinated light and airy fabrics. ~ 1 West Exchange Street, Providence; 401-598-8000, 800-228-3000, fax 401-598-8200. ULTRA-DELUXE.

The **Providence Biltmore** has traditionally been the area's biggest and best. The 245 guest rooms are quite grand, with stately mahogany and dark green decor. The lobby's grand staircase and glass-cage elevator continue to impress, as does the view from the Grand Ballroom. ~ Kennedy Plaza, Providence; 401-421-0700, 800-294-7709, fax 401-455-3050; www.grandheritage.com. DELUXE TO ULTRA-DELUXE.

Judging from the number of briefcases and power suits, the **Providence Marriott** is a favorite site for local business meetings as well as a familiar setting for out-of-town visitors. The all-over design is classic Marriott, although the sprawling layout requires quite a hike to reach the guest room elevators. Rooms are standard issue, modern and clean, with no surprises either good or bad. The lobby bar tends to be very popular and noisy at night. The indoor/outdoor pool is also a gathering spot. ~ Charles and Orms streets, Providence; 401-272-2400, 800-228-9290, fax 401-273-2686. ULTRA-DELUXE.

The **Old Court Bed & Breakfast Inn** is an antique buff's delight. The building, which began as an Episcopal church rectory in 1863, was restored in 1985. Today each of its ten guest rooms is decorated in authentic treasures: four-poster beds, Victorian coverlets, period washstands. Reserve early; this inn is quite popular. ~ 144 Benefit Street, Providence; 401-351-0747, fax 401-272-4830; www.oldcourt.com, e-mail reserve@oldcourt.com. DELUXE.

The **Nathaniel Porter Inn** is a combination inn, restaurant and local success story. "Rescued" and painstakingly restored by the Lynch family, this red-clapboard Colonial house with jaunty yellow trim now has three guest rooms, each with a private bath, and a shared sitting room on the second floor. Everything, from the brick fireplaces to the four-poster canopy beds, is authentic and charming. A continental breakfast is included. ~ 125 Water Street, Warren; 401-245-6622, fax 401-247-2277. MODERATE.

Radisson Airport Hotel is the practicum facility for Johnson & Wales University, a hotel, tourism and culinary institute. Opened in 1989, this state-of-the-art hotel offers such wide-ranging facilities and amenities as concierge services, a restaurant, a lounge, a whirlpool and free airport shuttle service. Even better, guests can be sure that the entire staff will be trying extra hard to please; they're students, and they are being graded on their performance. Continental breakfast included. ~ 2081 Post Road, Warwick; 401-739-3000, 800-333-3333, fax 401-732-9309; www.radisson.com. DELUXE TO ULTRA-DELUXE.

Master Hosts Inn, a 103-room economy motel, offers excellent value. Guests can look forward to complimentary continental breakfasts and airport shuttle service. ~ 2138 Post Road, Warwick; 401-737-7400, 800-251-1962, fax 401-739-6483; www.masterhosts.com. MODERATE.

DINING

In keeping with its role as state capital, university town and business center, Providence has developed into a sophisticated dining arena. The many local yuppie types demand it, and visitors can enjoy it. Happily, the focus on upscale eateries has not banished the plentitude of casual, ethnic restaurants.

Overlooking a small lake called Spectacle Pond, **Twin Oaks** serves seafood, steak and Italian dishes in their classic Rhode Island eatery south of Providence. The restaurant offers two contemporary indoor dining areas with lake views, plus outdoor seating. Closed Monday. ~ 100 Sabra Street, Cranston; 401-781-9693. MODERATE.

Fine Continental cuisine with a creative twist fills the menu at **Rue de l'Espoir**. Along with traditional items, the restaurant serves a host of original sauces. Specials change nightly and might include entrées like pan-seared sushi-grade tuna and grilled chicken and pesto over three-cheese ravioli. Their "small plates," served with hot bread from the oven, are popular. The casual French-country decor features hardwoods and tables topped with red tile. Closed Monday. ~ 99 Hope Street, Providence; 401-751-8890. MODERATE TO DELUXE.

Al Forno was the inspiration of two local innovative foodies, George Germon and Johanne Killeen. Al Forno is renowned for its grilled pizzas (*al forno* means "from the oven"). The style is casual but the food is serious, hearty and, most of all, good. Closed Sunday and Monday. ~ 577 South Main Street, Providence; 401-273-9760. MODERATE TO DELUXE.

Next door, the **Hot Club**, housed in what was once a factory boiler room, serves lighter fare like grilled chicken breast sandwiches, hamburgers and grilled zucchini. When the Hot Club moved here, it caused the waterfront area of Corliss Landing to become gentrified, elevating it to the status of "in" spot. ~ 575 South Water Street, Providence; 401-861-9007. BUDGET.

The Fish Company, which shares a common outdoor boardwalk along the river with the Hot Club, is a casual, trendy and romantic spot at sundown for appetizers and predinner drinks on the deck, where you can watch the boats pass. ~ 515 South Water Street, Providence; 401-421-5796. BUDGET.

Adesso bills itself as a "California café" and specializes in mesquite grilling. Preferred seating is in the high, skylighted front room, but they also offer bar and lounge seating. Decor is minimalist, almost hard-edge. The wood-oven pizzas (topped with everything from barbecue chicken to smoked gouda) are popular favorites. ~ 161 Cushing Street, Providence; 401-521-0770. MODERATE TO DELUXE.

In a building that resembles a huge Rubik's Cube, **Hemenway's** serves what some consider the area's best seafood. The room's simple high-ceilinged decor does not detract from the cuisine, although the spectacular views of the river do tend to vie strongly for one's attention. ~ 1 Providence Washington Plaza, 121 South Main Street, Providence; 401-351-8570. MODERATE TO DELUXE.

Federal Hill, Providence's "Little Italy," is fairly bursting with wonderful ethnic restaurants; most are family-oriented with menus priced accordingly. A local favorite is **Angelo's Civita Sarnese Restaurant**. The decor in the front room is strictly luncheonette (and includes a photo-collage of celebrity customers) with more traditional decor in the back. The service is friendly and family-style and the cuisine is traditional, hearty and wholesome, with dishes like veal with roasted peppers and a variety of pasta specials. Closed Sunday from Memorial Day through Labor Day. ~ 141 Atwells Avenue, Providence; 401-621-8171. BUDGET.

For a more upscale venue in the same neighborhood, you might sample the fine Italian cuisine at **Camille's Roman Garden**. ~ 71 Bradford Street, Providence; 401-751-4812. MODERATE TO DELUXE.

Across the Providence River in Bristol County is the **Nathaniel Porter Inn**. Dine indoors in the restored 1750 Colonial's front parlors with their authentic stenciled walls and brick fireplaces or in an enclosed courtyard. Winner of the 1989 Grand Master Chefs

A GREAT PLACE TO RETIRE

Rhode Island's reputation for championing personal freedoms is once again evidenced in today's newest minority: senior citizens. The state is second only to Florida in its over-65 population. It's especially curious that many of these seniors have moved here from other states, choosing to move to a place far from the Sunbelt's climate. Whatever the reasons for the influx (state statisticians are still puzzling over this one), it becomes fairly obvious that Rhode Island's winters cannot be regarded as a negative factor.

of America award, the inn's menu of seafood and game specialties changes seasonally, although two favorites always remain: their award-winning seafood chowder and the "Autumn Harvest" apple pie, voted "best in New England" by the readers of *Yankee* magazine. ~ 125 Water Street, Warren; 401-245-6622. DELUXE.

HIDDEN ►

The tiny town of Warren is the "Clambake Capital of the United States." Local bakemasters take their titles very seriously around here; summer weekend **clambakes** are culinary poetry and all you can eat for $16. Reservations are a must: call retired police chief Robert Perry. ~ Warren; 401-245-1977.

SHOPPING Although there are a couple of vertical malls in downtown Providence, the best of the city's shopping is found in independent shops and boutiques all over town.

The Opulent Owl is typical of the innovative, trendy stores found in Providence. Here, nifty gift items—unusual frames, fine china—share space with handsome housewares and fine American crafts. Closed Sunday. ~ 195 Wayland Avenue, Providence; 401-521-6698.

The Arcade, which occupies three floors of an 1828 majestically columned marble National Historic Landmark building, bills itself as America's first shopping mall. It may be the oldest, but it's far from the nation's finest or most well-stocked. There are lots of small specialty shops to browse but nothing to lure the serious shopper. Closed Sunday. ~ 65 Weybosset Street, Providence; 401-598-1199.

The **Museum Gift Shop** offers a wealth of reproductions as well as jewelry, cards, textiles, sculptures, prints and books focusing on the art treasures exhibited throughout the museum. Closed Monday and Tuesday. ~ Museum of Art–Rhode Island School of Design, 224 Benefit Street, Providence; 401-454-6500.

NIGHTLIFE Two major theater experiences in town offer audiences both local repertory and touring company productions. **Trinity Repertory Company,** in operation since 1963, is going strong. This Tony award–winning repertory company supports a talented group of resident artists and also encourages audience participation. ~ 201 Washington Street, Providence; 401-351-4242.

Providence Performing Arts Center showcases national touring companies' road shows of Broadway and other hit productions. The PPAC is located in the landmark Loew's Theater, a 1920s beauty complete with vintage velvet seats and gilded ceiling. ~ 220 Weybosset Street, Providence; 401-421-2787.

An alternative gay and straight crowd frequents **Gerardo's,** a cavernous club with four bars, a dancefloor, pool tables, karaoke and an outside garden area. They specialize in theme parties that could include anything from a 1950s live band to a lingerie fashion show. Cover. ~ 1 Franklin Square, Providence; 401-274-5560.

Oliver's is a popular spot for Brown University students, offering a deejay Wednesday and Friday and karaoke on Thursday and Saturday. There are three pool tables and basic pub food. ~ 85 Benevolent Street, Providence; 401-272-8795.

Rhode Island is home to more than 20 percent of all Registered Historic Landmarks in the entire country.

Cable Car Cinema and Café show classic and foreign films in at-home comfort; half the regular theater seats have been replaced with overstuffed two-seater couches. A café serves sandwiches and pastries right in the theater building, with outdoor seating during good weather. ~ 204 South Main Street, Providence; 401-272-3970.

Providence Civic Center is the site of family shows, concerts and sporting events. ~ 1 La Salle Square, Providence; 401-331-6700.

COLT STATE PARK 🏃 🚲 🏇 🏕 ⚓ 🚢 ⛵ Formerly the private estate of the Samuel Pomeroy Colt family, this Bristol park now provides a 464-acre outdoor haven to all families. A three-mile shore drive traces Narragansett Bay, and a network of bike paths (which links up with the "East Bay Bike Path") crisscrosses the wooded park. There's excellent saltwater fishing. Visit the popular Chapel-by-the-Sea. In summer the Rhode Island Symphony gives occasional waterside concerts here. You'll find picnic areas and restrooms. ~ Along Route 114, Bristol; 401-253-7482; www.riparks.com.

BEACHES & PARKS

GODDARD STATE PARK 🏃 🚲 🏇 🏕 ⚓ 🎣 🛶 ⛴ ⛵ This beachfront park is beautifully maintained and provides outdoor recreation year-round. The old carousel building on the shore now serves as a performing-arts center for band and jazz concerts during the summer. Spread throughout the 500 wooded acres are 18 miles of bridal trails (no horse rentals in the park), an equestrian show area, a nine-hole golf course and a picnic gazebo. There are picnic areas, lifeguards, a bathhouse and concession stands. ~ On Ives Road about one mile south of East Greenwich; 401-884-2010.

To help pinpoint the Blackstone Valley area, visualize the state of Rhode Island as a layer cake: the Blackstone Valley forms the entire top layer. (And the icing, too, its fans would add.) The Blackstone River surges through the eastern portion of this layer with a force powerful enough to have altered the course of our country's history.

Blackstone Valley

America's industrial revolution began in the Blackstone Valley. In 1793, Samuel Slater harnessed the potential of mighty

Blackstone River (which subsequently became known as "the hardest working river in America"), creating the first factory in America able to produce cotton yarn by using water power.

Today this entire "top-layer" area is Rhode Island's undiscovered gem, a region dotted with historic industrial towns that lie within huge tracts of rural and forested wilderness areas. You'll drive along scenic country roads that meander past historic sites, charming villages, meticulously restored Colonial homes, antique stores and farm stands.

SIGHTS   The city of **Pawtucket**, located at the extreme southeastern edge of the region, is home to Mr. Slater's mill, the place where it all began. Fourth-largest city in the state, Pawtucket (an Indian term meaning "falls of water") sits at the upper tidewaters of Narragansett Bay.

Slater Mill Historic Site was the site of the 1793 mill and cotton factory, featuring the first water-powered cotton spinning mill in the U.S. Today, it is a National Historic Landmark. Visitors to this wooden building, resplendent in its original vivid yellow hue, can tour the museum, with its huge looms still intact. Next door is the original rubblestone 1810 Wilkinson building that houses the 16,000-pound waterwheel. The gallery upstairs has changing exhibits of textiles and other related topics. Closed Monday through Friday from January through April. Closed December. Admission. ~ 67 Roosevelt Avenue, Pawtucket; 401-725-8638; www.slatermill.org.

Nearby **Slater Memorial Park** is fun for children and adults. The oldest "stander carousel" in the world is located here. This gem is a genuine Charles Looff creation and one of the few that remain of this master craftsman's handiwork. Built in 1895, it was installed in Slater Park in 1910 and has been thrilling children ever since. The park has ball fields, bike trails, a pond full of ducks and even a regulation lawn bowling green. ~ Newport Avenue, Pawtucket; 401-728-0500 ext. 251.

At Diamond Hill Vineyards, you can design your own customized labels (complete with photos, personal messages or whatever else) to paste on gift bottles of their fruit wines or nonalcoholic ciders.

Also located within the park is the **Daggett House**, a 1685 farmhouse and the oldest home in Pawtucket. The Daggett House is open Saturday and Sunday from June through September as well as by appointment. Admission. ~ Newport Avenue, Pawtucket; 401-728-0500 ext. 251.

A few minutes drive north of Pawtucket is **Diamond Hill Vineyards**, which lies nestled in the beautiful Cumberland countryside. After a jostling drive over the private road that runs through fields of vines, you arrive at the trim, gray, 1780 home of the owners, the Berntson family, who welcome visitors and invite them to use the spacious porch and rolling front lawn for picnics. Inside there's a tasting room and gift shop. Closed Monday through Wednesday. ~ 3145 Diamond Hill Road, Cumberland; 401-333-2751, 800-752-2505.

While you're in the area, you might want to stop by the **Blackstone Valley Tourism Council** for maps, brochures and information about Blackstone Valley and its activities. ~ 171 Main Street, Pawtucket; 401-724-2200.

A bit farther north lies Woonsocket, whose residential North End holds an unexpected treasure—the **B'nai Israel Synagogue**. This house of worship has Milanese hand-blown glass chandeliers as well as a series of spectacular stained-glass windows designed by a disciple of Marc Chagall. It's listed in the *Encyclopedia Judaica* as one of America's premier synagogues. ~ 224 Prospect Street, Woonsocket; 401-762-3651.

Surprises await at the **Comfort Inn** in Pawtucket. There's an "Executive Section" where guest rooms are larger, more fashionably decorated and better appointed than in most chain hotels (including Nintendo video games in each room). The hotel also has a staff so courteous and helpful you'll be glad you stayed. Continental breakfast included. ~ 2 George Street, Pawtucket; 401-723-6700, 800-221-2222, fax 401-726-6380; www.hotelchoice.com. MODERATE.

LODGING

Wright's Farm Restaurant is the undisputed king of the "chicken family-style" dinners that are unique to the Blackstone Valley. This meal must always include macaroni, roast chicken, salad, french fries and dessert—served and served until you can't eat another bite. Wright's Farm's dining room can accommodate 1500, so expect busloads of fellow diners, groaning boards and low prices. Closed Monday through Wednesday. ~ 84 Inman Road, Harrisville; 401-769-2856. BUDGET.

DINING

This is *mill country*, birthplace of the mill-end and factory outlet concept. Among the many nearby, we especially like the **Slater Fabric Store**, where printed fabrics from well-known houses sell from $1.25 to $5 a yard. Store manager Christine Callahan remembers her goods and can locate a perfect match years after you've bought the original. ~ Industrial Drive, Cumberland; 401-727-9068.

SHOPPING

Contact the **Blackstone Valley Tourism Council** for a brochure listing all of the factory outlets. ~ 171 Main Street, Pawtucket; 401-724-2200.

There are about a dozen antique stores in the tiny village of Chepachet in the town of Gloucester, but the undisputed star of the group is the **Brown & Hopkins Country Store**. As country

◄ *HIDDEN*

stores go, this one is the genuine article; it's also one of the oldest continuously operated stores in America. Opened in 1809, Brown & Hopkins retains much of the old (the roll-top desk near the front door has been there since the Civil War era) while giving today's customers what they want (gourmet foods, hand-dipped candles, even penny candies). The antiques are displayed in room settings on the second and third floors. Owners Claudia and Joe Amaral also stock a popular 40-pound wheel of Vermont cheddar cheese. Closed Monday through Wednesday and for a few weeks in August. ~ 1179 Putnam Pike, Gloucester; 401-568-4830.

NIGHTLIFE **City Nights Dinner Theatre** presents a series of dinner shows as well as matinees. A typical season includes mostly musicals and comedies, as well as one drama. Performances are held Thursday through Sunday. ~ 27 Exchange Street, Pawtucket; 401-723-6060.

Chan's is, in addition to being a popular Asian restaurant, renowned throughout New England for showcasing international jazz artists. Host John Chan invites only the best to perform. Shows are usually on Friday and Saturday nights. ~ 267 Main Street, Woonsocket; 401-765-1900.

BEACHES & PARKS **LINCOLN WOODS STATE PARK** Over 600 acres of woodland make up this popular recreation area north of Providence. Visitors can swim in Olney Pond and hike or ride horses along the oak-bordered trails surrounding it. In the winter, people come here to skate, cross-country ski and snowmobile. Facilities include restrooms, a bathhouse, playing fields, lifeguards and a concession stand; horse rentals are available right outside the park at Sunset Stables. Picnic tables and sites can be rented for $2 a day. ~ Entrances are located on Great Road, Route 123, and Twin River Road off Route 146 in Lincoln; 401-723-7892.

DIAMOND HILL PARK This woodsy hill is skirted by a mile-long ledge of quartz, thus the park's moniker. The 373-acre spot, crossed by hiking trails, has a picnic area, restrooms and a ball field. ~ Located off Route 114 on Diamond Hill Road Cumberland; 401-728-2400 ext. 28.

PULASKI MEMORIAL STATE PARK A part of the 3500-acre George Washington Management Area, Pulaski has 80 acres of red pine, white pine and oak woods that skirt Peck's Pond, whose beach is a main attraction for visitors here. Fishing is good for bass, perch and trout; swimming is excellent. You can also hike or cross-country ski on trails through the forest area or get a game going at the ball field. You'll find a picnic area, restrooms, a changing room and lifeguards. ~ Located on Pulaski Road, off Route 44 six miles west of Chepachet; 401-568-2013.

Known as the Ocean State, Rhode Island is an angler's paradise. The New England Offshore **Outdoor Adventures** Sportfish Tournament is held here every summer, with weigh-ins at the Ram Point Marina in Port Judith. Local waters teem with tuna, bluefin, albacore, marlin and shark. Charter boats abound, sailing from every port along the coast. The best seasons to fish are summer and fall.

**SPORT-
FISHING**

SOUTH COUNTY **Snug Harbor Marina Booking Service** charters trips on Narragansett Bay or Block Island Sound. Offshore excursions for shark and tuna are also available. ~ 410 Gooseberry Road, Wakefield; 401-783-7766. On Block Island, **G. Willy Makit Charters** has trips on a six-passenger boat for codfish, striped bass and bluefish. ~ 401-466-5151.

While not every Sunday sailor gets to crew during Newport's famed America's Cup races, Rhode Island's bays, sounds and open ocean lure boating fans of all degrees of expertise. In fact, you don't even have to know how to sail: plenty of vessels come complete with their own crews.

SAILING

NEWPORT AREA **Newport Sailing School and Cruises Ltd.** and **Newport Sailboat Harbor Tours** offer lessons and popular harbor cruises. Closed November through March. ~ Goat Island Marina, Newport; 401-848-2266 (summer), 401-246-1595 (winter); www.newportsailing.com.

Paddling the inland waterways is an increasingly popular sport in Rhode Island. A number of places not only rent boats but offer instruction as well; some host group trips.

**CANOEING
& KAYAKING**

SOUTH COUNTY AREA The **Kayak Centre at Wickford Cove** offers kayak rentals and sales, instruction and harbor tours. ~ 9 Phillips Street, Wickford; 401-295-4400, 888-732-5292. **Snug Harbor Marina** offers guided nature and harbor cruises on a 53-foot pontoon boat. Available Labor Day through May by reservation only. ~ 410 Gooseberry Road, Wakefield; 401-783-7766.

NEWPORT AREA **Adventure Sports** rents everything from wave runners to sailboats and kayaks. They also offer fishing and charter trips. ~ 142 Long Wharf, The Inn on Long Wharf; 401-849-4820. **Kayak Center** offers guided tours of Newport's coastline. ~ 518 Thames Street; 401-848-2920. **Ten Speed Spoke** rents kayaks and offering guided tours. ~ 18 Elm Street; 401-847-5609.

PROVIDENCE AREA **Paddle Providence** has kayak and canoe rentals and tours in the Providence area, including an excursion on the Providence River right through downtown Providence. They also offer indoor classes in the winter. ~ Located at the Providence River dock in Memorial Park; 401-453-1633.

CROSS-COUNTRY SKIING
During winter months when areas in the state are blanketed by snow, cross-country skiing is a popular pastime. Though most ski centers are located in Eastern Massachusetts, several state parks have ungroomed trails that are available to skiers, including Lincoln Woods State Park and South County's Arcadia Management Area. The George Washington Management Area in Blackstone Valley has groomed trails.

WIND-SURFING
This sport, which requires both sailing and surfing skills to master, is also pretty to watch. All along Rhode Island's beaches the colorful sails of these water-skimming boards add to the beauty of the ocean views.

NEWPORT AREA   **Third Beach** in Newport is a popular windsurfing spot. If you'd like to give it a try, **Island Sports** offers lessons and rents and sells boards and gear. ~ 86 Aquidneck Avenue, Middletown; 401-846-4421, 888-639-7529.

GOLF
Throughout the state, many public courses welcome visitors.

SOUTH COUNTY   **Winnapaug Golf Course** is semiprivate and features an 18-hole course designed by Donald Ross. ~ 184 Shore Road, Westerly; 401-596-9164. Tee off at **Weekapaug Country Club**'s nine-hole course, but don't get stuck on their signature fourth hole, which shoots over a saltwater pond. Members only are allowed from 8:30 to 11:30 a.m. ~ 265 Shore Road, Westerly; 401-322-7870. In Hope Valley, try **Lindhbrook Country Club**, the only par-3 course in Rhode Island. ~ 299 Woodville-Alton Road, Hope Valley; 401-539-8700.

NEWPORT AREA   The semiprivate **Green Valley Country Club** has a course full of long and difficult par 4s and 5s. ~ 371 Union Street, Portsmouth; 401-847-9543. **Montaup Country Club** has an 18-hole course. ~ 500 Anthony Road, Portsmouth; 401-683-9882.

PROVIDENCE AREA   **Triggs Memorial Golf Course** is a beautiful, 18-hole, Donald Ross–designed public facility overlooking the Providence River. ~ 1533 Chalkstone Avenue; 401-521-8460.

TENNIS
Courts range from the modest playground variety to the grassy splendor of Newport's venerable Casino. Regardless of status, most require advance reservations.

SOUTH COUNTY   On Block Island, **The Atlantic Inn** has two courts. Fee. ~ 401-466-5883. **Champlin's Marine** also has two courts. Fee. ~ 401-466-2641.

NEWPORT AREA   At the **International Tennis Hall of Fame**, you can play on the world-famous Newport grass courts. Lessons available; reservations required to book one of the 13 courts. ~ 194 Bellevue Avenue; 401-849-3990.

PROVIDENCE AREA   Roger Williams Park has ten beautiful clay courts. ~ 1000 Elmwood Avenue; 401-785-9450.

Given Rhode Island's wealth of superb wilderness and park-lands, one might expect to find a similar abundance of stables of-fering horseback rentals, but there are relatively few.

RIDING STABLES

BLACKSTONE VALLEY   Guided rides in Arcadia Park are offered on the weekends at **Stepping Stone Ranch**. They also offer over-night camping trip rides. ~ 201 Escoheag Hill Road, West Green-wich; 401-397-3725. Lincoln's **Sunset Stables** also provides guided 45-minute weekend rides through Lincoln Woods State Park. ~ 1 Twin River Road, off Route 146, Lincoln; 401-722-3033.

Rhode Island is a biker's paradise. There are bike lanes every-where.

BIKING

SOUTH COUNTY   For strong cyclists who can handle the hills, Block Island can be biking heaven, with its pristine byways and incredible views.

NEWPORT AREA   In Newport, you can cycle the lovely 15-mile Bellevue Avenue and Ocean Drive route that hugs the Atlantic. Across the Sakonnet River, there are 25 to 35 miles of quiet routes that meander through the peaceful villages of Tiverton and Little Compton. As you travel the state's multitude of country lanes, you'll understand why so many Rhode Islanders are avid cyclists.

PROVIDENCE AREA   A special ten-foot-wide, 15-mile-long "East Bay Bicycle Path" runs from East Providence to Riverside along scenic shoreline routes and through several state parks.

Bike Rentals   Disappointingly few shops rent bikes in the state. However, the state's biking possibilities are superior enough to warrant bringing along your own cycle if you don't want to chance a rental.

In South County, **Narragansett Bikes** rents mountain bikes, tandems and hybrids. ~ 1153 Boston Neck Road, Route 1A, Nar-ragansett; 401-782-4444. On Block Island, visit **Esta's at Old Har-bor** for rentals, repairs and free maps of the island's dirt roads. ~ 53 Water Street, Old Harbor, Block Island; 401-466-5011.

In Newport, **Ten Speed Spokes** rents mountain bikes and hy-brids. ~ 18 Elm Street; 401-847-5609. **Adventure Sports** features mountain bikes and offers maps of popular bike paths. ~ 43 Main Street, Thames; 401-849-4820.

The entire state of Rhode Island holds wonderful surprises both for serious hikers as well as for those who simply enjoy meander-ing through the great outdoors. In the northern tier of the state, a unique two-state federal project, the Blackstone River Valley National Heritage Corridor, will develop miles of new trails along

HIKING

the banks of the river and the original tow paths along the canal. Even though not fully completed, this linear park offers endless opportunities to those who celebrate wilderness beauty. All distances listed for hiking trails are one way unless otherwise noted.

SOUTH COUNTY   The lowlands of South County are studded with great tracts of protected wilderness areas that are ideal for the hiking enthusiast.

Called "the most beautiful walk in Rhode Island," the **Long Pond–Ell Pond Trail** (4.5 miles) leads to three ponds through what locals call a "cathedral forest" of wild rhododendrons and hemlocks. Located in Hopkinton, this area is listed in the Registry of Natural Landmarks. Trailheads are located off North Road and off Cahouchet Road in Hopkinton.

Arcadia Park's **Yellow Dot Trail** (8 miles) can be followed via yellow spots painted on trees. It crosses much of the park's wooded wilderness. Call 401-222-1157 for a list of hiking paths within the Yellow Dot Trail.

In the 29-acre Kimball Wildlife Refuge near Charlestown, the **Orange Trail** (1.5 miles) leads through postglacial forests of oaks and maples to Toupoyesett Pond. This easy, leisurely walk is maintained by the Audubon Society for hiking, birding and photography. ~ 401-949-5454.

At Rudman's Hollow on Block Island, venture upon **The Green Way Nature Trail** (20 miles), a silent wilderness of intersecting trails where you'll encounter the "enchanted forest," rolling hills and open brush. Along the way you'll espy the foundation of an old mill and a cemetery—remnants of an old farm. The only sounds heard are bird calls; this glacial ravine provides sanctuary for over 200 species of migratory birds. The trail begins at Beacon Hill and is a moderate hike. For more information and trail maps, contact The Nature Conservancy. ~ P.O. Box 1287, Block Island, RI 02807; 401-466-2129.

NEWPORT AREA   The famous **Cliff Walk** (3.5 miles) in Newport must be counted as unique, if not the ultimate in hikes. Beginning at the Memorial Drive gate and winding its sometimes precarious way along and above the crashing waves, this scenic path provides "hidden" views of the front yards and facades of the town's great mansions, as well as sweeping views of Rhode Island Sound. Keep to the inside of the path because erosion has weakened the outer edges of some sections at the end of the trail.

There are a dozen varied trails through the 450 acres of the Norman Bird Sanctuary in Middletown, ranging from the brief **Woodcock Trail** (.5 mile) that leads through level shrublands and a forest of black cherry and black locust, to the 300-million-year-old Paradise Rock formation known as **Hanging Rock Trail** (1 mile), along a 70-foot-high rocky ridge that overlooks the ocean, Gardiner's Pond and the marshlands.

BLACKSTONE VALLEY   The **Blackstone River Valley National**   ◀ HIDDEN
Heritage Corridor encompasses both the canal tow paths as well as the river area itself. Covering over 45 miles in the region, the corridor will eventually contain miles of hiking trails. Although not yet a formal "hiking trail," a two-mile stretch of canal tow path in Lincoln provides a feel of what the finished park will offer. It's a flat walk bordered by flood plain meadows and dense forest; you will see great blue herons, woodchucks, rabbits and turtles along the way. ~ To get there, take Exit 10 off of Route 295 to Route 122S (also called Mendon Road). Continue on for about one and one half miles to Martin Street. Cross two bridges. Park in the pull-off at the second bridge. Skirt the orange guard rail and turn right. After one mile of hiking, you will see the old Captain Kelly house, the Ashton Mill and the dam. Turn back here.

Three marked trails crisscross the 77-acre Powder Mill Ledge Refuge in Smithfield. Owned by the Audubon Society of Rhode Island, this refuge is home to many species of birds, spotted turtles, ducks and some snakes in forests of shagbark and pignut hickory, butternut and chestnut trees. The **Orange Trail** (1 mile) and the **Blue Trail** (1.5 miles) are graded as "easy," while the **Yellow Trail** (2 miles) is a bit more difficult. In winter, all three are groomed for cross-country skiing. ~ 401-949-5454.

▼▼▼▼▼▼▼▼▼▼▼
Transportation

Route 95 traverses the state north and south, connecting Rhode Island to Connecticut and to the rest of New England. Along the coast, scenic **1A** hugs the ocean shoreline, a slower but more beautiful drive.

CAR

T. F. Green Airport in Warwick is the state's only commercial airport. Regularly scheduled service is provided by America West, American Airlines, American Eagle, Business Express, Continental Express, Delta Airlines, Northwest Airlines, TWA Express, USAir Express and United Airlines.

AIR

New England Airlines operates daily 12-minute commuter flights between Block Island and Westerly. ~ 401-596-2460.

Several limo and van companies link the airport to cities throughout the state: **Airport Taxi** runs to and from Warwick. ~ 401-737-2868. **Cozy Cab** runs daily shuttles to and from Newport. ~ 401-846-2500, 800-846-1502.

Ferry service between Block Island and Galilee, Newport, New London and Providence is provided by **The Interstate Navigation Company**. Cars and passengers are transported on a year-round

FERRY

basis from Point Judith, although the schedule is abbreviated during off-season. Reservations for cars are essential year-round. ~ Galilee; 401-783-4613.

BUS

Scheduled and charter bus services connect all points within the state. **Bonanza Bus Lines** operates out of Providence. ~ One Bonanza Way, Providence; 401-751-8800. **Pawtuxet Valley Bus Lines** is based in West Warwick. ~ 76 Industrial Lane, West Warwick; 401-828-4100. **Rhode Island Public Transit Authority** (RIPTA) operates throughout the state. ~ 265 Melrose Street, Providence; 401-781-9400.

TRAIN

Amtrak's (800-872-7245) Northeast Corridor service connects Rhode Island with Boston and New York. There is frequent service to and from Providence at Union Station (100 Gaspee Street; 401-727-7389) and less frequent service to Kingston Station (25 Railroad Avenue, West Kingston; 401-783-2913).

CAR RENTALS

Major car-rental agencies at the Warwick airport include **Budget Rent A Car** (800-527-0700) and **Hertz Rent A Car** (800-654-3131). Across the street from the airport are **Dollar Rent A Car** (1989 Post Road; 800-800-4000) and **Thrifty Car Rental** (2329 Post Road; 800-367-2277).

PUBLIC TRANSIT

Bus service throughout the state is provided by **Rhode Island Public Transportation Authority** (RIPTA). These buses can connect airport passengers with the Block Island ferry in Galilee, as well as direct service from Providence to Newport, Westerly and the South County beaches. ~ 401-781-9400.

FOUR

Boston

 A stately dominion of brick and brownstone, parks and trees, river and harbor, Boston has stood as the preeminent New England city for more than three and a half centuries. Holding fast to the tip of a tiny peninsula jutting into the Atlantic, the city grew and spread south and west through the centuries, but it's still compact and eminently walkable. Despite its tiny size, Boston has played a mighty role in history, a history etched in the minds of all Americans. For this is the birthplace of our nation, where Paul Revere made his dashing midnight ride, where "the shot heard 'round the world" was fired.

A city of fanatical Puritan roots, Boston has been mocked and scorned by more worldly others as dull, pious and provincial, no match for New York or Los Angeles in sophistication. Rich in artistic and intellectual life, Boston has still been notched down on the big-city scoresheet for its lackluster shopping, dining and hotel accommodations.

But Boston is changing its face. While still revering its history and roots, the city is searching for a new identity as a modern, stylish metropolis. In the 1980s, world-renowned chefs set up shop here, winning over Bostonians and food critics alike. The palatial shopping emporium Copley Place opened, anchored by flashy Dallas retailer Neiman Marcus, which would never have dared show its face here in the 1950s. A building boom pushed up skyscraping, first-class hotels like the Westin, the Boston Harbor Hotel and the Four Seasons, as well as gleaming Financial District office towers. At the same time, old treasures like South Station and the Ritz-Carlton Hotel received much-needed face-lifts. Change continued in the 1990s. In 1995, the Boston Public Library completed a $50 million, three-part restoration project. In September 1995 the FleetCenter, a $160 million contemporary sports arena, opened to replace the antiquated Boston Garden.

The push for class continues with a grand project called the "Big Dig" begun in the late 1980s, which involves carving a giant tunnel to place the ugly, elevated Central Artery expressway underground, as well as building a third tunnel to the airport. The project's completion will bring light and spaciousness to the downtown area. And the city's main eyesore—the burlesque district known as the Combat Zone—has all but disappeared. Several restaurants, cafés and shops have sprung up in Boston's efforts to demolish the Combat Zone and expand the nearby theater district. Boston's ambitious facelift includes the redevelopment of the Seaport District, a convention center, hotel, shopping and restaurant zone that will replace existing warehouses and will feature a harborfront walkway.

The city's Puritan past took root in 1630, when a small band of English Puritans led by Governor John Winthrop arrived and settled on the peninsula. The colonists found Boston waters teeming with cod and, by the 1640s, were shipping dried cod to the West Indies and the Mediterranean. In exchange, they received sugar, gold and molasses. By the 1670s, Boston dominated the West Indian shipping business, and by 1700 it was the third busiest port in the British realm, after London and Bristol.

But Britain resented this young upstart colony and began to impose trade and tax restrictions. The growing city resisted, and soon colonial anger erupted into riots. The British responded by sending troops to occupy the city in 1768. Anti-crown tensions climaxed in the Boston Massacre in 1770, a clash between British soldiers and colonists in which five American men were killed.

More signal events on the road to independence followed in rapid succession. In the 1773 Boston Tea Party, 200 men dressed as Indians tossed three shiploads of tea into Boston Harbor as a protest against the English tea tax. King George closed the port and sent more troops to Boston.

The Revolution began in earnest in and around Boston. The first shots were fired at nearby Lexington and Concord in 1775. In the Battle of Bunker Hill, the British drove off the heavily outnumbered Americans, but only after sustaining severe losses. When George Washington fortified Dorchester Heights in a single night, the British were ousted forever. They evacuated the city on March 17, 1776, and fighting never again touched Boston.

With the ink dry on the Declaration of Independence, thoughts turned to commerce. But lost British markets pushed the city into a depression, and Boston began looking toward the Far East for trade, bringing in silks, spices and porcelain.

The city grew and thrived in the years after the Revolution. Fortunes were made by Boston's more prosperous merchants, a group of influential families who came to be known as the "codfish aristocracy." They dubbed themselves Boston Brahmins, smugly adopting the title of India's priestly caste. This small group counted among them the names of Cabot, Lowell and Hancock. They ruled the city with an unapproachable elitism, letting it be known that "the Lowells speak only to the Cabots, and the Cabots speak only to God."

The Brahmins built brick monuments to their prosperity on Beacon Hill, an elite residential district that defined the social character of Boston throughout the mid-19th century. Beacon Hill was home to such intellectuals as Francis Parkman, William James, Henry Wadsworth Longfellow, James Russell Lowell, Bronson Alcott, Julia Ward Howe and Horace Mann.

In the 1850s Boston become the premier builder of clipper ships, sending these graceful crafts around the world. To accommodate the growing trade, the city built many wharves along its waterfront. But the clipper era was cut short by the rise of steam-powered ships, which conservative Bostonians did not trust and

Greater Boston

would not build. Merchants shifted their capital to manufacturing, and the harbor went into a long decline.

The mid-19th century also saw the founding of some of Boston's most famed cultural institutions, among them the Boston Public Library, the Boston Symphony Orchestra, the Massachusetts Institute of Technology and Boston University, the first to admit women on an equal basis. The cultural richness produced a new nickname for the city: "The Athens of America."

Into this bustling urban area swarmed thousands of immigrants, led in the 1840s by the Irish, who had been forced from their homeland by the potato famine. The influx of Irish changed the character of this Yankee city forever. First blatantly discriminated against by old-line Bostonians ("No Irish need apply"), they grew in numbers great enough to win political power. The first Irish mayor was elected in 1885.

The Boston Irish gave us such leaders as former Speakers of the House John W. McCormack and Tip O'Neill, James Michael Curley and the Kennedy clan.

Boston bloomed into an ethnic rainbow in the 1880s, when waves of Italians, Poles and Russians arrived, multiplying the population thirty-fold. At the same time, the city's area was itself multiplying. In the mid-19th century, Boston had begun filling in the bay between Beacon Hill and Brookline, a neighborhood now known as Back Bay. Other swampy land to the south was also filled and became the South End. By the turn of the century, Boston had tripled its size with landfill.

But soon after, Boston's economy suffered a tremendous decline that would last until the 1960s. The city lost its major port status to New York and Baltimore, and its textile, shoe and glass mills moved south in search of cheaper labor and operating costs. Population shrank in the 1940s and '50s, with Boston the only large city to decline in numbers during the postwar baby boom years. The city languished in the throes of this decline for decades.

Good times returned suddenly in the 1960s, as the Protestant elite and Irish Catholics finally cooperated in managing city affairs. Urban renewal projects created the new Government Center and the landmark Prudential and Hancock towers. The technological revolution of the 1970s and '80s enriched Boston's economy, with computer companies and think tanks springing up in Cambridge and Greater Boston.

With prosperity came urban problems. In the early 1970s, court-ordered busing among racially imbalanced schools sparked rioting and protests, particularly in South Boston and Charlestown. The crisis lasted several years. Racial strife eased somewhat in the 1980s and 1990s as African-Americans began to gain more power in local and state government and in private business.

Today Boston has a Democrat-controlled legislature and a reputation for liberalism, spearheaded by the reigning scion of the Kennedy clan, Senator Ted Kennedy. Breaking the Irish tradition, today's top city official—Thomas Menino—is the city's first Italian mayor.

Boston the city is home to a scant 650,000 souls. Many are under 30; thousands of students flood the city each September, injecting it with vitality and youthfulness. The weather is infinitely changeable, varying from warm, humid summers, when temperatures range from the 60s to the low 90s, to dry, crisp falls hovering in the high 40s (and the low 70s during Indian summer), to very cold winters, when temperatures dip to the 20s and 30s, occasionally falling below zero.

The nucleus of Boston proper is a pear-shaped peninsula. At its northernmost tip stands the North End, a small, Italian enclave clustered with shops, cafés and restaurants. The downtown area takes up most of the peninsula, winding between the waterfront and Boston Common from north to south and encompassing a Chinatown that is tiny yet rich in tradition.

High above Boston Common in regal splendor sits Beacon Hill, crowned by the State House and graced with bowfront brick homes, window boxes and hidden gardens. To the west of Beacon Hill lies its cousin, stately Back Bay, a place of wide boulevards and imposing brownstones. Back Bay also encompasses the architectural jewels of Copley Square: the Public Library, Trinity Church and the John Hancock Tower. Farther west is the Fenway, sprawling around its marshy gardens and home to baseball's famous Fenway Park.

A bit farther south lies the city's largest neighborhood, the South End, another 19th-century brick residential area in the process of gentrification. Cut off from eastern downtown by the Fort Point Channel, South Boston (not to be confused with the South End) is a primarily commercial area, home to the city's fish piers.

The residential neighborhoods, harking back to English architecture, have led to Boston's being characterized "America's most European city." But since Boston has added new space-age layers to the urban quiltwork of centuries, the city wears a more American and international face. Though the city took its time, it has come a long way from its Puritan roots and the days when books by male and female authors were separated on different shelves.

The North End

The North End is Boston's oldest, most colorful neighborhood. Today it's a tightly knit, homogeneous Italian community, established after a gradual takeover from pockets of Irish, Portuguese and Jewish residents starting in the late 19th century. The North End's mostly one-lane streets are crowded cheek-by-jowl with Italian restaurants and food stores. Many residents still greet each other in the language of the Old Country and hang their wash out between the alleys. All summer long, Italians celebrate their patron saints with picturesque weekend parades and street festivals.

On the roundish peninsula that is Boston, the North End juts north into Boston Harbor and is cut off from downtown by the elevated Southeast Expressway, which helps keep it a place unto itself. It's a spot where Boston history still lives.

SIGHTS

Probably no name evokes more romance in American history than Paul Revere. His famous ride warning of the British attack in 1775 has been chronicled the world over. The quiet little expanse of North Square, lined with cobblestones and black anchor

Text continued on page 182.

Three-day Weekend

Boston

DAY 1 • Explore historic Boston on the **Freedom Trail** (pages 190–91). This string of pre-Revolutionary buildings echoing with the footsteps of Samuel Adams and young Ben Franklin provides a good excuse to wander the streets of the city center. Along the way, you're sure to be sidetracked by other attractions such as the huge **Quincy Market** (page 190) near Faneuil Hall.

• Take a lunch break midway through your walking tour at **The Marshall House** (page 201), a hidden alternative to the usual Freedom Trail tourist haunts such as the Union Oyster House and Durgin Park.

• Continue under the freeway to the North End to see where Paul Revere rode. Today the North End is an Italian neighborhood boasting some of Boston's best restaurants. Why not try the *pollo all'Arrabbiata* ("angry chicken") at **Lucia's** (page 185), where the ceilings are covered with frescoes by local latter-day Michelangelos.

• Take in a play this evening at one of the city's fine theaters, then top off your history-packed day with a nightcap at the **Bell in Hand Tavern** (page 205), Boston's oldest bar.

DAY 2 • Learn more about some of the ethnic subcultures that have helped shape Boston's unique character. A good place to start is Beacon Hill, once the heart of the city's early-day free black community. Visit the **Museum of Afro-American History** and the **African Meeting House** (page 210).

• Next explore Boston's compact, bustling Chinatown, a very Asian enclave in the center of a Yankee city. Stop in for lunch at the best seafood restaurant in Chinatown, **Chau Chow** (page 203).

• This afternoon, head south to Columbia Point to visit the **John F. Kennedy Library and Museum** (page 235), celebrating the accomplishments of the 20th century's most famous Bostonian.

• Before returning to the city, enjoy a seafood dinner at **Jimmy's Harborside** (page 236), a long-established eatery that was a favorite of JFK and brother Bobby.

• Take your choice among the many nightclubs that have made Boston a music mecca.

DAY 3 • Cross the river to Cambridge and explore the hallowed halls of **Harvard** (pages 238–40), America's premier university.

• It's an amazing experience just to sit in Harvard Yard, read a book and watch students strolling by. To make a full day of it, visit some of the university's world-class museums. We recommend the **Peabody Museum of Archaeology** (page 240), the **Sackler Museum** (page 240) and the **Fogg Art Museum** (page 240).

• Complete your visit with a special dining experience **Upstairs at the Pudding** (page 244), steeped in Harvard tradition and one of greater Boston's finest restaurants.

chain, is where you come upon **The Paul Revere House**. This simple little three-story house with gray clapboards and leaded-glass, diamond-paned windows looks almost out of place in Boston today, and well it might. Built in 1680, it's the only example left in downtown Boston of 17th-century architecture. Revere lived here from 1770 until 1800, although not with all of his 16 children at the same time. Inside are period furnishings, some original Revere family items and works of silver. Closed Monday from January through March. Admission. ~ 19 North Square; 617-523-2338; www.paulreverehouse.org.

Next door to Paul Revere's house and entered through the same courtyard is the **Pierce-Hichborn House**. Built about 1711 for glazier Moses Pierce, it's one of the earliest remaining Georgian structures in Boston. It later belonged to Paul Revere's cousin, boatbuilder Nathaniel Hichborn. Closed Monday from January through March. Admission. ~ 29 North Square; 617-523-2338; www.paulreverehouse.org.

Also located in North Square are the **Seamen's Bethel** (12 North Square) and the **Mariner's House** (11 North Square). An anchor over the door announces the Mariner's House, a place where, since 1838, a seaman has always been able to get a cheap meal and a bed for the night. Said the sailor-preacher of the Seamen's Bethel, "I set my bethel in North Square because I learned to set my net where the fish ran." Once a place where sailors worshipped, it's now a rectory office.

On a street noted for "gardens and governors" lived John F. "Honey Fitz" Fitzgerald, one of Boston's Irish "governors," a ward boss, congressman and mayor. His daughter Rose Kennedy was born in this plain brick building at **4 Garden Court Street**.

The **Old North Church** is the one from which the sexton hung two lanterns the night of Paul Revere's midnight ride ("one if by land, two if by sea"). This beautiful church has Palladian windows and a white pulpit inspired by London designs. The four trumpeting cherubim atop the choir loft pilasters were taken from a French pirate ship. Replicas of the steeple's lanterns may be viewed in the adjacent museum. ~ 193 Salem Street; 617-523-6676; www.oldnorth.com.

Directly behind Old North Church in the **Paul Revere Mall** stands a life-sized statue of Revere astride his horse—one of the city's most photographed scenes.

On the other side of the mall you'll come to **St. Stephen's Church**, a brick Federal-style church designed by the man who established that style, Charles Bulfinch, America's first native-born architect. The only Bulfinch-designed church still standing in Boston, St. Stephen's has a bell and copper dome cast by Paul Revere. Inside are wedding cake–white fluted pillars, balconies

CHAPTER FAVORITES

Whether it's in Mexico or Marakesh, I am always drawn to the excitement of an open-air market—and that goes for Boston's centuries-old **Haymarket**, where fresh produce and seafood are weighed on ancient metal scales. *page 186*

I love the unpretentious air at **Wally's**, an old-time jazz club in the South End. You'll find a diverse crowd crammed in the small bar to hear free music 365 days of the year. And you won't find many tourists. *page 230*

Whenever my appetite is particularly voracious, I indulge at **Dalí**, a dining adventure involving Spanish fare—*tapas, paella* and Iberian wine–spiced with whimsical ambience. *page 245*

If, like me, you find a certain thrill in lying down with literary lions, then curl up with a volume of Henry Wadsworth Longfellow's poetry at **Longfellow's Wayside Inn**, which the famous 19th-century poet immortalized in 1862. *page 251*

Unable to resist the idea of walking to the **World's End**, I set out on the beautifully landscaped South Shore peninsula and was amazed by the diversity of meadows, wetlands and forest as well as the great view of the Boston skyline. I heartily recommend it. *page 262*

and Palladian windows, a pewter chandelier and an 1830s pipe organ. ~ Hanover and Clark streets.

Copp's Hill Burying Ground served as the cemetery for Old North Church in the 17th century. Set high on a little green knoll, it overlooks Boston Harbor and Charlestown, which was bombarded by British guns placed here during the Battle of Bunker Hill. Its simple gray headstones bear pockmarks from British target practice. Buried here are Increase and Cotton Mather, Puritan ministers who wielded considerable political clout. ~ Hull and Snowhill streets.

The widest street in all the North End is Hanover Street, a major center for shops and restaurants. Walking south on Hanover Street leads you straight to the **Haymarket–North End Underpass**, which leads under the Southeast Expressway to downtown. The underpass is lined with bright, primitive mosaics done by North End children, a kind of urban folk art. The walls of the underpass also sport the work of Sidewalk Sam, a well-known local sidewalk artist who paints brightly colored reproductions of works by the Italian masters.

Boston by Foot gives regular walking tours of the North End, as well as many other neighborhoods. Hour-

◄ HIDDEN

and-a-half tours take place each Saturday from May through October, rain or shine. Fee. ~ 77 North Washington Street; 617-367-2345, fax 617-367-3766; www.bostonbyfoot.com.

DINING

In the Italian North End, you can feast on pasta and regional dishes from one end to the other, stopping at little neighborhood "red-sauce" cafés, plush formal dining rooms or late-night espresso bars. Some of the best deals in Boston dining are here, with many restaurants offering moderate prices.

HIDDEN ►

Neighborhood regulars favor **Pat's Pushcart Restaurant**, which specializes in northern Italian dishes and also serves up a lot of red sauce. In its casual, speakeasy ambience, the sole homage paid to decor is red and white tablecloths. But who cares when you can get such wonderful dishes as chicken angelique, a juicy chicken breast stuffed with cold cuts and cheese, and spaghetti marinara at these prices? Dinner only. ~ 61 Endicott Street; 617-523-9616, fax 617-523-9616. MODERATE.

Mamma Maria's Ristorante is the queen of North End gourmet. Highly regarded, it's set in a ritzy townhouse bedecked with brass chandeliers, mirrors and peach-and-gray walls. An upstairs atrium overlooks Paul Revere's little house. Mamma Maria's menu is refreshingly free of red sauce, featuring the lighter, reduced-sauce dishes of Tuscany and Piedmont, which might include grilled swordfish on a bed of pesto garnished with shrimp and baby vegetables. Dinner only. ~ 3 North Square; 617-523-0077, fax 617-523-4348. DELUXE TO ULTRA-DELUXE.

Café Paradiso is a favored haunt of local Italians. There's an espresso bar decorated with hanging plants, mirrors and colorful Italian cakeboxes. The spumoni is handmade, and the gelato and *granite* are freshly churned. The café serves desserts and light Italian fare, including pizza, calzone and salad. They also feature a full bar. ~ 255 Hanover Street; 617-742-1768, fax 617-742-7317. BUDGET.

Upstairs, **Trattoria a Scalinatella** offers an intimate dining experience with exposed brick walls, a working fireplace, candlelit tables and three large bay windows. The authentic Italian menu is seasonal and may feature squid-ink ravioli stuffed with calamari, Texas wild boar, veal medallions or handmade pastas. Reservations recommended. Dinner only. ~ 255 hanover Street; 617-742-8240, fax 617-523-8865. MODERATE TO ULTRA-DELUXE.

Caffe Vittoria is the most colorful of the espresso bistros. It might have been shipped here straight from Italy, so Old World is it. A massive and ancient espresso machine stands in the window, and latticework, marble floors and a mural of the Italian coast add to the feeling. Here's the place to indulge in a late-night espresso, cappuccino or Italian liqueur, accompanied by gelato or cannoli. There's also a downstairs cigar lounge. ~ 296 Hanover Street; 617-227-7606. MODERATE.

If you can't visit the Sistine Chapel, you can still see its transcendent frescoes covering the ceiling at **Lucia's**. Art critics come to rave and art students to stare in awe. More magnificent ceiling frescoes show Marco Polo's visit to China, the 12 Apostles and the Last Supper. Lucia's chef hails from Abruzzi and prepares specialties from all over Italy, robust to light dishes, something for everyone. Try the *pollo all'Arrabbiata* or *maccheroni all'Arrabbiata* (angry chicken or angry macaroni). No lunch Monday through Friday. ~ 415 Hanover Street; 617-367-2353, fax 617-367-8952. MODERATE.

Pizza is all that's served at **Pizzeria Regina**, and that's fine with the loyal clientele who jam the doorway at lunch and dinner waiting for one of the few tables inside. When you get in, you'll sit on high-backed benches at long, battered, heavy wooden tables, where you'll eat slice after slice of pizza served with pitchers of beer, soda or house wine. The service is fast, if sometimes curt, but that's the North End style. ~ 11½ Thatcher Street; 617-227-0765, fax 617-227-2662. BUDGET TO MODERATE.

At **La Famiglia Giorgio's**, the portions are so big and the prices so small, you can't believe it. Locals do believe, and they pack the uproarious place nightly to feast on gargantuan helpings of spaghetti and meatballs, lasagna, linguine with clam sauce and a sautéed seafood platter. As the name suggests, the small, bright low-decor eatery is family-owned. Enjoy the reasonable prices *and* leave with leftovers. ~ 112 Salem Street; 617-367-6711, fax 617-367-6174. MODERATE.

SHOPPING

The North End is a food lover's shopping dream, chock full of wine and cheese shops and bakeries.

Since **Bova's Bakery**, at the corner of Salem and Prince streets, is open 'round the clock, it's a great place to satisfy late-night hunger pangs. It's also an ideal spot to hear local gossip. The well-connected Bova family owns shops and apartments all over the North End, and the bakery serves as an apartment-hunters' clearinghouse for folks who are in the know. ~ 134 Salem Street; 617-523-5601.

For a pungent whiff of Old World ambience, head for **Polcari's Coffee Shop**, a tiny shop brimming with open bags of cornmeal and flour, wooden bins of nuts and jars of coffee beans. ~ 105 Salem Street; 617-227-0786.

Tony Trio carries Italian cheeses and delicious homemade pasta and sauces in his shop, **Trio's Ravioli**, which is full of good smells. ~ 222 Hanover Street; 617-523-9636.

Mike's Pastry is a popular spot for North End–residing yuppies to pick up a boxful of pastries for their breakfast meetings downtown. A warning: The volume of goods available here far outweighs their consistent quality, so take your time to peruse the offerings. ~ 300 Hanover Street; 617-742-3050, fax 617-523-2384.

▼▼▼▼▼▼▼▼▼▼
Downtown

The downtown area comprises several distinct neighborhoods that sprawl around the peninsula and loop around Beacon Hill and the Boston Common. Although Boston's compactness makes it very easy to sightsee on foot, there is no convenient way to see these neighborhoods, and you'll find yourself doubling back more than once.

SIGHTS

The **Freedom Trail** (see "Walking Tour," page 190) is Boston made simple. But if you only follow the red line, you will miss many of Boston's riches. For visitors with more time and energy, the following tour provides an in-depth look at Boston, old and new. It loops northward from the North End to the old West End, back down through Government Center and Quincy Market, and out to the Waterfront. Then it goes up State Street, down through the Financial District to Chinatown and the Theater District, and finally back up Washington Street to Boston Common. Since all these neighborhoods are so small, there's no need to treat them as separate geographic areas. But when a sight lies within the boundaries of a particular downtown neighborhood, we'll be sure to let you know.

When you come out the North End Underpass, you'll be crossing Blackstone Street, home to **Haymarket** (covering several blocks of Blackstone Street), the country's oldest market, in operation more than 200 years. On Friday and Saturday, open-air vendors hawk fruits and vegetables, meats, fresh fish and crabs, crowding over several blocks. Ancient hanging metal scales are used to weigh purchases. Prices are good here, but don't try to touch anything without permission—the vendor will scream.

HIDDEN ►

You'll find the **Boston Stone** easily enough by looking behind the Boston Stone Gift Shop. A round brown stone embedded in the rear corner of the house and dated 1737, it was brought from England and used as a millstone to grind pigment. A tavern keeper named it after the famous London Stone and used it as an advertisement. ~ Marshall and Hanover streets.

Behind Marshall Street is the **Blackstone Block**, tiny alleyways that are the last remnants of Boston's 17th-century byways, the oldest commercial district. Their names, Marsh Lane, Creek Square and Salt Lane, represent the early topography of Boston's landscape.

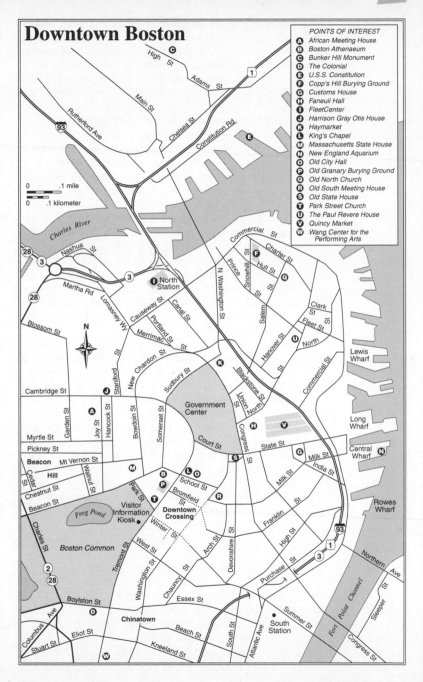

Downtown Boston

POINTS OF INTEREST
- Ⓐ African Meeting House
- Ⓑ Boston Athenaeum
- Ⓒ Bunker Hill Monument
- Ⓓ The Colonial
- Ⓔ U.S.S. Constitution
- Ⓕ Copp's Hill Burying Ground
- Ⓖ Customs House
- Ⓗ Faneuil Hall
- Ⓘ FleetCenter
- Ⓙ Harrison Gray Otis House
- Ⓚ Haymarket
- Ⓛ King's Chapel
- Ⓜ Massachusetts State House
- Ⓝ New England Aquarium
- Ⓞ Old City Hall
- Ⓟ Old Granary Burying Ground
- Ⓠ Old North Church
- Ⓡ Old South Meeting House
- Ⓢ Old State House
- Ⓣ Park Street Church
- Ⓤ The Paul Revere House
- Ⓥ Quincy Market
- Ⓦ Wang Center for the Performing Arts

The **Union Oyster House**, built in the 18th century, became a restaurant in 1826, making it the oldest continuously working restaurant in America. Here Daniel Webster drank a tall tumbler of brandy and water with each half-dozen oysters, and he rarely had fewer than six plates. Before it was a restaurant, exiled French King Louis Phillipe taught French here to wealthy ladies. Upstairs in 1771, Isaiah Thomas published *The Massachusetts Spy*, one of the first newspapers in the United States. ~ 41 Union Street; 617-227-2750; www.unionoysterhouse.com.

At the western edge of Boston's peninsula, stretching from the Southeast Expressway to Storrow Drive, is an area that used to be known as the West End. Once rich in many-quilted ethnic groups, it's now a mostly commercialized neighborhood. The area around North Station and the FleetCenter has begun to sprout new restaurants, while a few of the old-time sports bars have become trendy hangouts for a younger crowd.

Located next to the site of the hallowed Boston Garden is the state-of-the-art **FleetCenter**. With 19,000-plus seats, luxury suites, spacious concourses and air conditioning, the Center is a far cry from Boston's beloved but outdated Garden. Home to the Boston Celtics and Bruins, the shiny FleetCenter still sports the famous parquet floor and banners. ~ 1 FleetCenter; 617-624-1000, fax 617-624-1818; www.fleetcenter.com.

Not on the peninsula at all but out in the middle of the Charles River is the **Museum of Science**, reached via the Charles River Dam. The star of the museum is the Omni Theater, whose 76-foot domed screen and surrounding sound systems make you feel as though you're actually whizzing down Olympic slopes on skis, moving underwater through the Great Barrier Reef or breaking through the Antarctic's icy underwater depths. The museum also houses live animal exhibits, the Hayden Planetarium and changing displays on foreign cultures. Admission. ~ Science Park, O'Brien Highway; 617-723-2500, fax 617-589-0389; www.mos.org.

The **Harrison Gray Otis House** was the first of three Boston houses Charles Bulfinch designed for his friend Otis, a prominent

---

ADVERTISING—EARLY AMERICAN STYLE

Some say the **Steaming Teakettle**, a huge copper kettle hung outside the doorway at 65 Court Street at the edge of Government Center, is America's oldest advertising sign. It once announced the operations of the Oriental Tea Company, Boston's largest tea company. Made by city coppersmiths, it holds 227 gallons, two quarts, one pint and three gills. It gives you a warm feeling to see the teakettle steaming away, especially on a cold day. Ironically, it's now advertising a coffee shop.

lawyer and member of Congress. Built in 1796, the three-story brick house is classically symmetrical, with rows of evenly spaced windows and a Palladian window. Inside is one of the most gorgeous interiors in Boston, rich with imported wallpapers, opulent swag curtains and carpeting, gilt-framed mirrors, Adams mantels and Neoclassical motifs framing every doorway and window. Surviving abuse as a bathhouse, Chinese laundry and rooming house, the building became the headquarters of the Society for the Preservation of New England Antiquities in 1916. Closed Monday and Tuesday. Admission. ~ 141 Cambridge Street; 617-227-3956, fax 617-227-9204; www.spnea.org.

Right next door is the **Old West Church**, a handsome Federal-style brick building with a cupola and pillars on three stories. The British tore down its original steeple to prevent signaling across the river during the siege of 1776. Rebuilt in 1806, it houses a Charles Fisk organ; there are free organ concerts on Tuesday evenings. ~ 131 Cambridge Street; 617-227-5088, fax 617-227-7548.

A short walk up Cambridge Street brings you to **Government Center**, a sprawling brick plaza with multilevel stairs and fountains designed by I. M. Pei, an architect who was to change the face of the city in the 1960s, leaving his imprint on many key buildings. The plaza contains two of Boston's most important government structures, the **John F. Kennedy Federal Building** and **City Hall**, a modernistic-looking inverted pyramid. An abstract sculpture entitled *Thermopylae*, inspired by Kennedy's book *Profiles in Courage*, stands facing the JFK Building. A mass of twisting forms, it takes its name from a Greek battle in which the Spartans fought the Persians to the last man.

For a figure so flamboyant as **James Michael Curley**, one statue is not enough. The colorful but corrupt Curley dominated Boston politics for years, from 1914 to the late 1940s, serving as mayor, congressman and governor and figuring prominently in Edwin O'Connor's novel *The Last Hurrah*. This four-term mayor was loved by the poor and fond of calling Boston bankers the "State Street Wrecking Crew." Behind City Hall, two very life-like bronze statues immortalize Curley, one sitting on a park bench, the other standing right on the brick pavement with no pedestal. Tourists have been seen patting the stomach of the standing Curley, so temptingly portly is it. ~ Union and Congress streets.

If you walk down the stairs at the rear of Government Center and across Congress Street, you'll be entering Quincy Market, one of Boston's most popular destinations.

Faneuil Hall was the city's central market in the mid-18th century. The second floor of Faneuil Hall became known as the "Cradle of Liberty," as it resounded with the patriotic rhetoric of James Otis and Samuel Adams in the years leading to the Rev-

The Freedom Trail

This two-mile, one-way route, marked by a red brick or painted line on the side-walk, links 16 major historical places from downtown to Beacon Hill, the North End and Charlestown. It takes two to three hours to walk, though you can easily spend all day. Guided tours are also available, leaving every half hour from the National Park Service visitors center at 15 State Street opposite the Old State House.

BOSTON COMMON   Start your walk at Boston Common, one of the old-est public parks in the U.S., which has served during its 250-year history as a British army encampment, a cow pasture and the site of public hang-ings. Freedom Trail maps are available at the **Visitor Information Kiosk** on the southeast side of the park. ~ 147 Tremont Street; 617-536-1100. At the corner of the park, **Park Street Church** is often called the "church of firsts"; here, the first Sunday school in the U.S. was held, William Lloyd Garrison gave his first public anti-slavery speech and "My Country 'Tis of Thee" was sung for the first time. ~ Park and Tremont streets; 617-523-3383. Behind the church, governors, mayors and three signers of the Declaration of Independence lie in the **Old Granary Burying Ground**.

SCHOOL STREET   Walk northeast on Tremont, past the Granary Burying Ground, to School Street and turn east (right). **King's Chapel**, at the corner, was the first Anglican church in New England and the first church in Boston to have an organ (the Puritans didn't believe in music in church). ~ 617-523-1749. One block up the street, at the corner of Province Street, is the site of the **Boston Latin School**, the first pub-lic school in America, where Benjamin Franklin attended classes. The **Ben Franklin Statue** stands behind the school in Old City Hall Plaza. Another block up School Street, at the corner of Washington, the **Old Corner Bookstore** not only sold books but published them—in-

olution. On the fourth floor is a museum and armory of the **Ancient and Honorable Artillery Company**, the nation's oldest military group, founded in 1638. Look up to see the four-foot-long gilded copper grasshopper weathervane, a familiar Boston landmark and symbol. Closed weekends. ~ Off Congress Street; 800-233-2996.

Quincy Market is another historic marketplace, built in 1826 by Mayor Josiah Quincy to expand Faneuil Hall. In a move that has been imitated by almost every major city, Quincy Market, cluding *The Scarlet Letter, Walden* and the *Atlantic Monthly* magazine; it still operates as a bookstore under the ownership of the *Boston Globe* newspaper.

OLD HOUSES   Turn south (right) on Washington and walk one short block to the **Old South Meeting House**, where Samuel Adams and his co-conspirators plotted the Boston Tea Party. ~ 310 Washington Street; 617-482-6439. Across Milk Street is the house where Benjamin Franklin was born. ~ 17 Milk Street. Next, do an about-face and walk two blocks north to the **Old State House** (c. 1713), the oldest surviving public building in Boston, which is now a museum. ~ 206 Washington Street; 617-720-3290. Right next door, **National Park Service Visitor Information** has maps, tour books and brochures. ~ 15 State Street; 617-242-5642.

FANEUIL HALL   Turn east (right) on State Street and walk one block to the corner of Congress Street. Here, a circle of cobblestones marks the **Boston Massacre Site**, where British soldiers killed five colonists, triggering the Revolutionary War. Turn north (left) on Congress. Across the street from the present City Hall, Faneuil Hall has been a public market and meeting hall since 1742—and still is. Patriots gave speeches that inspired the American Revolution at Faneuil Hall. ~ 800-233-2996.

THE NORTH END   Follow the red tour route line carefully as it takes you about one mile north along Union, Marshall and Salem streets to loop around the North End. At the intersection of Salem and Tileston streets stands the **Old North Church** (c. 1723); its 191-foot steeple was the tallest structure in Boston when Robert Newman signaled the approach of British troops with his lanterns, launching Paul Revere's midnight ride. ~ 193 Salem Street; 617-523-6676. To find **The Paul Revere House**, follow Tilestone Street east past the Paul Revere Mall, take a little jog south on Hanover and Fleet streets, and go south (right) for one and a half blocks. The simple house is the only remaining residence in Boston dating back to the 17th century. ~ 19 North Square; 617-523-2338. To complete your tour, return to Salem Street via Richmond Street or catch any bus with a "Downtown" sign back to Boston Common.

along with its twin flanking arcades, the North and South Markets, was renovated in the 1970s into shops and restaurants that have become a major tourist draw for the city. The cobblestoned mall is a street festival by day, a lively nightspot in the later hours. It's wonderfully decorated during the holidays. ~ Off Congress Street.

If you walk out the rear of Quincy Market and under the Southeast Expressway across busy Atlantic Avenue, you'll arrive at the waterfront.

When Atlantic Avenue was built in the 1860s, it sliced right through the center of many of the great old wharves, including **Long Wharf,** the oldest existing one in Boston. Built in 1710, Long Wharf was named for its length—formerly 1800 feet. The British marched up Long Wharf when they occupied the city in 1768, only to retreat back down it when they were evacuated in 1776. Long Wharf also saw the departure of the first missionaries to Hawaii in 1819 and played a role in the 1850s California gold rush, when thousands of New Englanders departed for San Francisco.

Buildings imitating Renaissance palazzos and Greek temples were built in the 19th century along Rowes, India, Central, Long, Commercial, Lewis, Sargent's and Union wharves. **Lewis Wharf,** formerly Clarke's Wharf, was once owned by John Hancock. Nathaniel Hawthorne served as a customs inspector at Long Wharf. By the mid-19th century, the wharves were a center of clipper trade with China, Europe, Australia and Hawaii.

Some of the old wharf buildings, which once housed ships' chandlers and sail riggers, have been renovated into shops, offices and restaurants, including the **Pilot House, Mercantile Wharf** and **Chart House,** the only surviving late-18th-century building on the waterfront. ~ Off Atlantic Avenue.

Central Wharf is home to the **New England Aquarium,** just a short walk from Quincy Market. Bostonians like to congregate to watch the harbor seals in the outdoor pool. Inside, the Giant Ocean Tank is home to 95 species of exotic reef fish, sea turtles, sharks and moray eels. In the Aquarium Medical Center, you can observe medical check-ups of the sea life from behind a glass window. Sea lions perform next door aboard the Discovery, a floating theater. Admission. ~ Central Wharf, off Atlantic Avenue; 617-973-5200, fax 617-720-5098; www.neaq.org.

Waterfront Park is a neatly landscaped pocket park with brick walkways and benches that offers a lovely harbor view along with respite. Dedicated to the late matriarch of the Kennedy clan, the Rose Fitzgerald Kennedy Garden is a lovely spot at any time of year, but especially when it is in full bloom early in the summer. It's not far from Mrs. Kennedy's birthplace in the North End. ~ North of Long Wharf on Atlantic Avenue.

From the wharves, you can take cruises of Boston Harbor, a great way to while away an afternoon or evening and see the city skyline. One boat line there is **Boston Harbor Cruises.** ~ 1 Long Wharf; 617-227-4320; www.bostonharborcruises.com. Another servicing the harbor is **Massachusetts Bay Lines.** ~ 60 Rowes Wharf; 617-542-8000; www.massbaylines.com.

If you're into intrigue and humor, book passage with the **Boston Harbor Mystery Cruise.** These three-hour dinner cruises depart from Long Wharf and feature a comic murder mystery.

Closed November through April. ~ 264 Washington Street, Westwood, MA 02090; 800-697-2583.

From Long Wharf, walk up State Street. In a couple of blocks, you'll come to the granite Greek Revival **Customs House**, built between 1837 and 1847, where inspectors once examined all cargoes arriving at the wharves. Incongruously, this building also became Boston's first skyscraper in 1915, when the great clock tower was added. The clock, broken for many years, was restored in the late 1980s and its bright blue and gold face now glows handsomely at night, visible from great distances. ~ McKinley Square at State and India streets.

The **Cunard Building** was built in 1902 for the Cunard Steamship Line, owners of the ocean liner *Queen Elizabeth II*. Twin brass anchors flank its doors, festooned with dolphins and seashells. ~ 126 State Street.

The **Old State House** is a pretty little brick building dwarfed by the surrounding skyscrapers. The bronze lion and unicorn atop its gables stand as symbols of the English crown. Until the American Revolution, this was the seat of British government. A museum since 1882, the Old State House features winding galleries of exhibits on the building's history and architecture, early Boston and maritime history, including memorabilia, a model ship, paintings and prints. Admission. ~ 206 Washington Street, corner of State Street; 617-720-3290; www.bostonhistory.org.

Countless notables spoke at the Old South Meeting House, including Samuel Adams, John Hancock and, later, Oliver Wendell Holmes.

An outdoor flower market fronting the brick, Colonial-style **Old South Meeting House** adds to its charms. Built in 1729, Old South has high-arching Palladian windows, a white pulpit and candlelight chandeliers. Many crucial meetings leading to the American Revolution took place here, including the debate that launched the Boston Tea Party. Though Old South was repeatedly ravaged—the British turned it into a riding school complete with jumping bar, and it was forced to serve as a temporary post office after a devastating fire in 1872—it has been restored to its 18th-century look. Taped presentations re-create the famous Tea Party debate and others. This building offers historical and architectural programs and hands-on exhibits, and still serves as a public forum for community events. Admission. ~ 310 Washington Street, corner of Milk Street; 617-482-6439, fax 617-482-9621.

Milk Street leads into the heart of the Financial District, a warren of streets stretching south from State Street to High Street and east to Washington Street. Dominated by towering banks and office buildings, the Financial District was considerably built up in the 1980s with bold new buildings, provoking controversy over their design in tradition-minded Boston. One of these—the

BankBoston—is laughingly called Pregnant Alice because of its billowing shape. ~ 100 Federal Street.

In its marching devastation, the Great Fire of 1872 leveled 60 acres of downtown Boston. The spot where the fire was arrested on its northeastward path is noted on a bronze plaque on the front of the U.S. Post Office at Post Office Square, the corner of Milk and Devonshire streets.

HIDDEN ►

Two bonanzas await in the lobby of the **New England Telephone building**. One, a massive mural called *Telephone Men and Women at Work*, encircles the rotunda and depicts decades of telephone workers, from 1880s switchboard operators to later engineers, cable layers and information operators. The other reward is Alexander Graham Bell's Garret, a dark little corner filled with memorabilia surrounding the birth of the telephone in Boston in 1875. The garret looks much as it did when Bell worked in it at its original location at 109 Court Street. (A **bronze plaque** at Government Center in front of the John F. Kennedy Federal Building marks that spot, where sound was first transmitted over wires in the fifth-floor garret.) ~ 185 Franklin Street.

At 100 Summer Street stands a mobile that looks like a giant yellow lollipop tree, an ebullient surprise in a city where there is not much outdoor public art. Bostonians call it "the lollipops,"

HIDDEN ►

but its real name is **Helion**, one of a group of pieces called "wind-flowers" by sculptor Robert Amory.

Walk south down Summer Street until you come to **South Station**. South Station was a grand old station house in its day, in fact the largest in the world at the turn of the 20th century. After a thorough restoration completed in 1989, this pink granite beauty stands tall and proud. Ionic columns, a balustrade and a clock with eagle decorate the curved Beaux-Arts facade stretching for two blocks. South Station today serves as a transportation hub for subway, rail and bus connections. The interior, designed to resemble a European market square, sparkles with polished marble floors and brass railings and is filled with restaurants, shops and pushcart vendors. ~ Summer Street and Atlantic Avenue.

Across the street, you can tour the **Federal Reserve Bank**, which processes millions of dollars worth of currency every day. The Fed's unusual design—it looks like a giant white washboard, and there's a gap where the fifth floor should be—is intended to withstand downdrafts and wind pressures. The Fed, which boasts a lobby full of sculpture and murals, also hosts jazz and classical concerts and changing art and crafts exhibits. For a performance schedule, call 617-973-3454, 617-973-3453; www.bos.frb.org. The Fed is open to the public Monday through Friday; reservations are required for tours, held each Friday. ~ 600 Atlantic Avenue, corner of Summer Street; 617-973-3451.

A Taste of China

Compared to Chinatowns in other major cities, Boston's is geographically quite small, just a few blocks long, bounded by Essex and Washington streets and the Southeast Expressway. But this Chinatown was much larger decades earlier, before the expressway was built, cutting a wide swath through the district. The Tufts New England Medical Center, too, took a great chunk of Chinatown land when it was built. Now hemmed in by the Expressway and the Combat Zone, Chinatown has little room to grow. But don't be fooled by its physical size: Boston's densely populated Chinatown makes it the third largest Chinese neighborhood in the country.

The Chinese were first brought to Boston to break a shoe industry strike in the 1870s, coming by train from the West Coast. They settled close to South Station because of the convenience of the railroad. First living in tents, the Chinese eventually built houses or moved into places previously inhabited by Syrians, Irish and Italians.

Despite its small size and recent influx of Thai and Vietnamese immigrants, Chinatown is intensely and authentically Chinese. Signs are in Chinese characters, and the area is densely packed with Chinese stores and restaurants. Even the phone booths are covered with Chinese pagodas. For more information about this rich and unique area, visit www.boston chinatown.com.

The **Chinatown gates**, a bicentennial gift from Taiwan, stand at the intersection of Beach Street and Surface Road, marking the entrance to Chinatown. White stone with a massive green pagoda on top, they are guarded fore and aft by stone Chinese Foo dogs and sport gold Chinese characters on green marble. The classic characters are not readily translatable in modern Chinese, but they embody such moral principles as propriety, righteousness, modesty and honor.

At the corner of Harrison Avenue and Oak Street is the enormous **Unity/ Community Chinatown Mural**, painted in 1986, which depicts the history of the Chinese in Boston. Among its pigtailed Chinese figures are construction workers, a launderer and women at sewing machines. Other scenes show the Chinese learning to read, protesting to save their housing and gaining access to professional careers.

Although you may not want to take one home, you can see live chickens squawking in stacks of wire crates at **Eastern Live Poultry**, where locals line up to buy them "live or dressed." ~ 48 Beach Street; 617-426-5960.

HIDDEN ▶ **Winthrop Lane**, a tiny brick-lined channel between Arch and Devonshire streets, contains one of the most interesting pieces of public art in Boston, entitled *Boston Bricks: A Celebration of Boston's Past and Present*. In 1985 artists Kate Burke and Gregg Lefevre created bronze reliefs of various Boston personages, scenes and stories and placed them along this red-brick shortcut that's used by folks who work in the financial district. Take the time to peruse the bricks here; you'll recognize some things—the Red Sox, the swan boats in the Public Garden lagoon—and wonder about others.

Few people know that **Edgar Allan Poe** had a long history in Boston, so in 1989 a memorial bronze plaque was erected to his memory at the corner of Boylston Street and Edgar Allan Poe Way. Born here, Poe was the son of actors at the Boston Theatre. He published his first book, lectured and enlisted in the army in Boston.

HIDDEN ▶ The **Grand Lodge of Masons** is decorated with blue and gold mosaics of masonic symbols, and its grand lobby houses a small exhibit of masonic memorabilia. Closed weekends. ~ 186 Tremont Street, corner of Boylston Street; 617-426-6040.

Walk over to Tremont Street, and head south. In short order you'll be in the Theater District, centered on Tremont Street, Warrenton Avenue and Charles Street South. Boston has a lively and prestigious theater scene, with many tryouts moving on to Broadway. Among the half dozen or so nationally known theaters is the **Colonial**, the oldest continuously operated theater in America, built in 1900. At that time the sumptuously decorated Colonial was considered one of the most elegant theaters in the country, with its 70-foot Italian-marble vestibule and foyer rich with ceiling paintings, cupids, plate mirrors, bronze staircases and carved wood. George M. Cohan, Noel Coward, Fred Astaire, Katharine Hepburn and the Marx Brothers have trod its boards. ~ 106 Boylston Street; 617-426-9366, fax 617-880-2449; www.broadwayinboston.com.

A 1995 restoration gave the Colonial theater a refreshing facelift and brought back the original writing table, located outside the ladies' lounge, that Rodgers & Hammerstein used when they wrote *Oklahoma!*

Formerly the Metropolitan Theater, the splendid **Wang Center for the Performing Arts** was built in 1925 as a palace for first-run movies in the Roaring Twenties. Restored to its original grandeur, it is opulently decorated with gold leaf, crystal, mirrors and Italian marble, and was designed to be reminiscent of the Paris Opera and Versailles. This 3610-seat theater is one of the largest in the world, and has hosted a variety of artists including Yo-Yo Ma, Luciano Pavarotti, Robin Williams, Lauryn Hill and the Mark Morris Dance Troupe. The Center is listed on the National Register of Historic Places. ~ 270 Tremont Street; 617-482-9393, fax 617-451-1436; www.wangcenter.org.

The **Chinese Culture Institute,** opened in 1980, houses a gallery where rotating exhibits of Chinese paintings, sculpture, ceramics and folk art are shown. The institute also produces concerts, community plays, dance recitals and lectures on its stage. Closed Sunday and Monday. ~ 276 Tremont Street; 617-542-4599.

◄ HIDDEN

At the corner of Tremont Street and Charles Street South, **Eliot Norton Park** stands where Chinatown and the Theater District meet Bay Village. New lights and green lawns now brighten this once dark, dank and dangerous place. The park is appropriately dedicated to the dean of American drama critics.

Downtown Crossing is the heart of downtown shopping. Lunchtime shoppers crowd the brick pedestrian mall at the corner of Washington and Summer streets, fronting on Macy's and Filene's, one of Boston's oldest department stores. Downtown Crossing is street entertainment at its most diverse. Pushcart vendors and street musicians—one day a Peruvian folk band, the next a rock group—vie for space in the crowded mall. A one-man band is a permanent local fixture.

Old City Hall, a grand French Second Empire building, was renovated in the 1970s into offices and a French restaurant. As one of the first 19th-century Boston buildings to be recycled, it helped spark the preservationist movement. In front of Old City Hall stands the **Franklin Statue,** an eight-foot bronze tribute to Benjamin Franklin. Relief tablets at the base illustrate scenes from his career as printer, scientist and signer of the Declaration of Independence. ~ 45 School Street.

Bromfield Street, a short lane located between Washington and Tremont streets, is chock-full of tiny camera shops, jewelers and watchmakers, stamp traders, pawnshops and a couple of tiny cafés. There are some interesting historical buildings sprinkled along the street, including the home of Revolutionary War hero Thomas Cushing, who held meetings here with the Adamses, Thomas Paine and other cronies.

The **Omni Parker House** is the oldest continuously operating hotel in America, first opening in 1855. Soon after, it became a hangout of the Saturday Club, a literary group whose members included Nathaniel Hawthorne, Ralph Waldo Emerson, Henry Wadsworth Longfellow, James Russell Lowell, Oliver Wendell Holmes and John Greenleaf Whittier. This little group founded the *Atlantic Monthly.* ~ 60 School Street; 617-227-8600, fax 617-742-5729; www.omnihotels.org.

King's Chapel looks morosely like a mausoleum. Its steeple was never finished, so its Ionic columns flank a bare, squat granite building. The inside, however, is gorgeous, with carved Corinthian columns and pewter chandeliers. The first Anglican church in New England, King's Chapel eventually became the first Unitarian church in the United States. The chapel is open to the public Monday through Saturday from June through Labor Day. It is open Monday, Friday and Saturday the rest of the year. ~ Corner of Tremont and School streets; 617-523-1749, fax 617-227-4101.

Beside the church is **King's Chapel Burying Ground**, the oldest cemetery in Boston. It contains the graves of John Winthrop, the colony's first governor, and William Daws, the minuteman who helped Paul Revere warn the colonists the British were coming.

Park Street Church is one of Boston's most beautiful churches, with its white Christopher Wren spire and brick exterior. It was known as Brimstone Corner during the War of 1812 because gun powder was stored in its basement. ~ Park and Tremont streets; 617-523-3383, fax 617-523-0263; www.parkstreet.org.

Next door is the **Old Granary Burying Ground**, which took its name from a large grain storehouse the Park Street Church replaced. Buried here are Paul Revere, Boston's Mother Goose (Elizabeth Ver Goose, who became known for her nursery rhymes) and three signers of the Declaration of Independence, including John Hancock. You can't see exactly where each is buried, since the headstones were rearranged for the convenience of lawn mowing. Death's heads, skeletons and hourglasses were popular headstone motifs here.

Times have changed considerably at **Boston Common**, a large tract of forested green, America's oldest public park. In 1634, its acres served as pasture for cattle, training grounds for the militia and a public stage for hanging adulterers, Quakers, pirates and witches. A few steps from the visitor kiosk is **Brewer Fountain**, brought from Paris by Gardner Brewer in 1868 for his Beacon Hill home and later donated to the city. Notable among the statuary on the Common is the **Soldiers and Sailors Monument** high on a hill, whose figures represent history and peace.

Today, downtown office workers use the crisscrossing paths as shortcuts to work, and it's a popular spot for jogging, Frisbee tossing, dog walking, concerts and community events. You might wander into **Park Street Station**, the first station built on the nation's oldest subway, which opened in 1897.

Leaving the edge of Boston Common, you can walk up Park Street, which brings you to Beacon Hill.

LODGING   A small luxury hotel with 201 rooms, the **The Regal Bostonian** stands right next to Faneuil Hall and Quincy Market. In its lobby are two exhibits on early Boston firefighting. Besides one of the city's top-rated restaurants, the Bostonian has a multiple-story terraced atrium. A typical room might have a rose carpet and contemporary furnishings like glass-topped tables and white love seats. The bathroom is spacious, with double sinks and a large oval tub. Six rooms even have hot tubs and fireplaces. ~ North and Blackstone streets; 617-523-3600, 800-343-0922, fax 617-523-2454; www.regal-hotel.com/boston. ULTRA-DELUXE.

The **Boston Harbor Hotel** is the most visually stunning hotel to be built in Boston in many years. Set right on the harbor and designed in grand classical style, the brick structure is pierced with an 80-foot archway. The waterfront side is lined with Venetian-style piers and crowned with a copper-domed rotunda observatory. A cobblestone courtyard reaches toward the ornate marble-floored and crystal lobby. Many of the 230 guest rooms have magnificent water views and feature dark wood furniture, marble-topped nightstands and paintings of birds. The hotel has a health club and spa, sauna and lap pool, and an award-winning restaurant and bar. ~ 70 Rowes Wharf; 617-439-7000, 800-752-7077, fax 617-345-6799; www.bhh.com. ULTRA-DELUXE.

One of New England's top-rated hotels, the 288-room **Four Seasons Hotel** overlooks the Public Garden. Interiors reflect the Victorian residential character of Beacon Hill, with a grand staircase leading up from the lobby and, in the rooms, leather-topped writing desks, fresh flowers in the bathroom and marble-topped vanities. Duvets are handed out in winter, and there's a spa, whirlpool, exercise room, masseur and lap pool with a view of Beacon Hill. ~ 200 Boylston Street; 617-338-4400, 800-332-3442, fax 617-426-7199; www.fourseasons.com. ULTRA-DELUXE.

The **Hotel Méridien** is one of the country's most highly acclaimed hotels. It opened in 1981 in the former Federal Reserve Bank, built in 1922, a Renaissance Revival granite and limestone structure modeled after a Roman palazzo. Many original interior

GREENER PASTURES

Boston Common is the first jewel in Boston's **Emerald Necklace**, a seven-mile tracery of green that loops through and around the city, all the way to Jamaica Plain, Brookline and Fenway. It was designed in the early 1900s by famed landscape architect Frederick Law Olmsted, who believed that parks could provide a psychological antidote to the noise, stress and artificiality of city life. The Emerald Necklace also includes the Public Garden, the Commonwealth Avenue Mall, the Back Bay Fens, Olmsted Park, Jamaica Pond, Franklin Park and the Arnold Arboretum. The Boston Parks and Recreation Department (617-635-7383) conducts periodic walking and bicycling tours of the entire Emerald Necklace.

architectural details remain, including elaborate repoussé bronze doors, gilded, coffered ceilings and sculpted bronze torchières. The Julien Lounge is dominated by two massive N. C. Wyeth murals depicting Abraham Lincoln and George Washington. The hotel has 326 rooms, two restaurants, two bars, an indoor lap pool and health club facilities with whirlpool and sauna. The generous-sized guest rooms are elegantly cozy, with varied color schemes. A matching two-toned silver embroidered sofa and club chair contrast a black lacquer writing desk, and you will find granite vanities and marble floors in the bathrooms. ~ 250 Franklin Street; 617-451-1900, 800-543-4300, fax 617-423-2844; www.lemeridien.com. ULTRA-DELUXE.

Owned by a Swiss company, the 500-room **Swissôtel Boston** is run with legendary Swiss efficiency and hospitality. Conveniently located to everything, the hotel has every luxury you could ask for: 24-hour room service, bathroom telephones, spa, Olympic-size pool with outdoor terrace, sauna, an exercise room, one restaurant and a lounge, where tea and pastries are served in the afternoon. The decor mixes Colonial and European styles, with impressive antique furniture and paintings, Waterford crystal chandeliers and imported marble. Rooms are smartly finished in green, mocha or rose. ~ 1 Avenue de Lafayette; 617-451-2600, 800-621-9200, fax 617-451-0054; www.swissotel.com. DELUXE TO ULTRA-DELUXE.

Omni Parker House is a fabled Boston institution. Many celebrities have stayed here, from Charles Dickens and John Wilkes Booth to Hopalong Cassidy. Its lobby is decorated in the grand old style, with carved wood paneling and gilt moldings, a carved wooden ceiling, bronze repoussé elevator doors and candlelight chandeliers. In the heart of downtown, it's just steps away from Quincy Market. Rooms have writing desks and wing chairs, floral spreads and marble baths. ~ 60 School Street; 617-227-8600, 800-843-6664, fax 617-743-5729; www.omnihotels.com/bosparsf.htm. DELUXE TO ULTRA-DELUXE.

There are at least half a dozen bed-and-breakfast agencies in Boston, offering accommodations in host homes from downtown to Cambridge and the suburbs.

Bed & Breakfast Associates Bay Colony has rooms in 150 homes, most with continental breakfast and private bath, many offering Waterfront, Midtown, Back Bay or Beacon Hill locations. Accommodations range from a bow-windowed room with pine floors, antique brass bed and fireplace in a South End Victorian townhouse, to Beacon Hill and Back Bay homes close to the Public Garden. One of the best deals for the money. ~ P.O. Box 57166, Babson Park Branch, Boston, MA 02157; 781-449-5302, 800-347-5088, fax 781-449-5958; www.bnbboston.com. MODERATE TO DELUXE.

Breakfast is always included in rooms booked through **Greater Boston Hospitality**, which offers dozens of listings; many are in Back Bay, Beacon Hill and Cambridge. Host homes include a converted Georgian carriage house in Brookline and an 1890 Back Bay brownstone appointed with 18th-century mahogany furniture and floors. Gay-friendly. ~ P.O. Box 1142, Brookline, MA 02146; 617-277-5430, fax 617-277-7170; www.bostonbedandbreakfast. com, e-mail info@bostonbedandbreakfast.com. BUDGET TO DELUXE.

Downtown dining covers a wide spectrum, from traditional Yankee bastions to sprightly outdoor cafés and inexpensive ethnic eateries.

DINING

Haymarket Pizza fronts right on Haymarket, a weekend open-air food market, and the surrounding crowds make it hard to get in the door. But if you do, you'll find some of the best cheap pizza in Boston. ~ 106 Blackstone Street; 617-723-8585, fax 617-973-9576. BUDGET.

◄ HIDDEN

The **Commonwealth Brewing Co.** makes its own beer in the basement, serving nine styles of ale on tap. A vast hall lined with huge copper vats, beer kegs, copper-covered tables and a brass-railed bar, the dining room is popular with sports fans from the nearby FleetCenter where the Boston Celtics play. You can watch the beer being made behind glass walls. Chow down on hearty fare like three-alarm chili, steak and fish and chips. Tours are scheduled by appointment only. ~ 138 Portland Street; 617-523-8383, fax 617-523-1037. MODERATE.

Most tourists walk right by **The Marshall House** on their way to the picturesque Union Oyster House, the famous hostelry just down the street. Locals prefer this less crowded and less expensive alternative in this pocket of cobbles toned streets and brick sidewalks. Large portions of chowder, fish and chips, burgers and icy cold beer—all excellent—are served by friendly staff with thick Bahston accents. ~ 15 Union Street; 617-523-9396, fax 617-523-8163. BUDGET TO MODERATE.

◄ HIDDEN

You can't beat the **Union Oyster House** for historic atmosphere. In 1742 it was a dry goods store and in 1775 became a center for fomenting revolutionary activity. The restaurant opened in 1826, and Daniel Webster was fond of slurping down oysters at its U-shaped oyster bar, still standing today. Little alcoves with wooden booths and bare wood tables wend around the several wood-paneled dining rooms, and there are ship's models, a mahogany bar and antique wooden pushcarts in this casual and boisterous eatery. The menu features chowders, seafood and New England shore dinners. ~ 41 Union Street; 617-227-2750, fax 617-227-2306. MODERATE.

Noisy and chaotic, **Durgin Park** is legendary for its rude waitresses and community tables set with red-and-white-checked cloths. A Boston institution founded in 1827, it dispenses such solid and hefty Yankee fare as prime rib, corned beef and cabbage, franks and beans, corn bread and Indian pudding. ~ 30 North Market, Faneuil Hall; 617-227-2038, fax 617-720-1542. MODERATE.

Far above the crowded bustle of Quincy Market, you can dine in removed splendor at **Seasons**, one of Boston's top-rated restaurants. Widely spaced tables, designer show plates, mocha banquettes, crisp white napery and mirrored ceilings add to the mood. A creative New American menu is served, changing seasonally, which might include seared quail with polenta and sausage or roasted monkfish with lobster roe. ~ 20 North Street, Faneuil Hall, in The Regal Bostonian Hotel; 617-523-3600, fax 617-523-2593. DELUXE TO ULTRA-DELUXE.

For nonpareil French food, make reservations at **Maison Robert**. Actually, it's two restaurants. The formal main dining room beautifully incorporates elements of the French Second Empire-style architecture with contemporary furniture. Classical French cuisine is served on the main floor, while Le Café on the ground floor offers more casual, less expensive French fare. During the summer months, there's dining al fresco along with jazz nightly from 5:30 to 7:30 p.m. ~ 45 School Street; 617-227-3370, fax 617-227-5977. ULTRA-DELUXE.

The **Boston Sail Loft** stretches back and back, out onto the harbor for some wonderful views. Some of the best potato skins in town are to be had here, along with burgers, sandwiches, pastas and fish plates, in a nautical atmosphere. ~ 80 Atlantic Avenue; 617-227-7280, fax 617-723-3467. BUDGET TO MODERATE.

The **Chart House** is one of Boston's most historic restaurants. Set on cobblestoned Long Wharf, it was built in 1760 and served as John Hancock's counting house. His black iron safe is embedded in the upstairs dining room wall. The Chart House carries a marine motif all the way, with gilt-framed black-and-white pictures of ships, as well as model ships. Famed for its dense mud pie, Chart House also dishes up hearty steaks and seafood. Dinner only. ~ 60 Long Wharf; 617-227-1576, fax 617-227-5658. MODERATE TO ULTRA-DELUXE.

So, you want it kosher? You can get it at the **Milk Street Café**, a cozy Financial District cafeteria that dishes up some of the best inexpensive homemade food in the city with no meat or dairy: soups, sandwiches, salads, muffins, bread and desserts such as homemade brownies and cookies. No dinner. Closed weekends. ~ 50 Milk Street; 617-542-3663. BUDGET.

With its tall oak doors lettered in gold, **Tatsukichi** looks like a foreign consulate. The food is just as impressive: almost 50 kinds of sushi and the famed house specialty, *kushiage*, skewers of battered and fried meats and seafood. Dine Japanese-style in a light wood and beige tatami room, or at a Western-style table. ~ 189 State Street; 617-720-2468, fax 617-742-0757. MODERATE TO DELUXE.

Julien manages to be both sprightly and elegant with impossibly high rose-colored ceilings and massive crystal chandeliers. Wing chairs and rose banquettes guard your privacy, and softly shaded table lamps cast a romantic glow. When the waiter removes the silver cover from your plate with a *"Voilà!"* you'll find a light but vibrant hand has seen to the sauces. The seasonally changing menu emphasizes regional foods, which might include Long Island duckling with yellow root vegetables or roasted Maine lobster with a lemon, herb, butter and mushroom soufflé. Closed Sunday. ~ Hotel Méridien, 250 Franklin Street; 617-451-1900, fax 617-423-2844. ULTRA-DELUXE.

Five take-out restaurants with open kitchens surround a group of tables at the **Chinatown Eatery**. where the same type of chaos reigns as at a Hong Kong food market. Wall-mounted menus are hand-printed in Chinese, Vietnamese and English, and Asians predominate among the diners. Taken together, the restaurants offer some 400 items, covering Szechuan, Hunan, Mandarin, Cantonese Vietnamese and Thai cuisines. Open from 11 a.m. until 2 a.m. ~ 44 Beach Street, second floor. BUDGET.

◄ *HIDDEN*

The best Chinese seafood restaurant in Boston's tiny Chinatown district is **Chau Chow**. The decor is cafeteria-minimalist, and the well-meaning staff is practically non-English speaking, but Bostonians of all ethnicities ignore the communication problem—they queue up in long lines for fabulous shrimp, crab, sea bass and other delectables. ~ 52 Beach Street; 617-426-6266. BUDGET.

◄ *HIDDEN*

A thoroughly Chinese lobby greets diners at **Imperial Seafood** in the heart of Chinatown, with Chinese lanterns and gold dragons. Known for its dim sum, the restaurant also serves Mandarin cuisine to lots of appreciative locals. ~ 70 Beach Street; 617-426-8439, fax 617-889-1468. BUDGET TO MODERATE.

Representative of the Southeast Asian immigration to Chinatown is **Pho Pasteur**, an inexpensive Vietnamese restaurant that also serves Thai and Chinese cuisine. Choose from noodle dishes, a variety of soups and excellent seafood entrées. ~ 682 Washington Street; 617-482-7467. BUDGET TO MODERATE.

China Pearl specializes in Cantonese and Mandarin cuisine. Locals form long lines for their dim sum and seafood specialties. ~ 9 Tyler Street; 617-426-4338, fax 617-426-8417. MODERATE.

At **Ho Yuen Ting Seafood Restaurant**, no-frills service and decor don't diminish the excellent seafood specialties: shrimp, lobster, crab, clams, conch and snails. ~ 13-A Hudson Street, 617-426-2316. MODERATE.

Be sure to ask for a table by the window at **Aujourd'hui** so you will have a view of the Public Garden below. Tables are set with one-of-a-kind antique service plates, complemented by antique paintings and a display of porcelain. The regional American menu features game, poultry and seafood dishes. There's also a low-cholesterol menu. In addition to the regular menu, you can try the "Nightly Tasting Menu," either traditional or vegetarian, which offers five courses of the chef's evening specialties. One block from the theater district, this is a great place for *après*-theater. Dinner only. ~ 200 Boylston Street, in the Four Seasons Hotel; 617-451-1392, fax 617-351-2293. ULTRA-DELUXE.

A bright red railing leads upstairs to Boston's greatest culinary adventure at **Biba**, where chef Lydia Shire and sous-chef Susan Regis are unafraid to create from any palette: Chinese, French, Italian, Indian. Where else would you get lobster satay with green papaya and winter mint or beef short ribs with cumin seeds and cilantro? Her upstairs dining room feasts the eyes, too, with rich colors and primitive Mediterranean motifs set off by yellow walls. The menu is seasonal. ~ 272 Boylston Street; 617-426-7878, fax 617-426-9253. DELUXE TO ULTRA-DELUXE.

SHOPPING Next to the FleetCenter—the last place you'd expect to find a shopping mecca—is **Boomerangs**, a fundraising venue for the AIDS Action Committee that's chock full of recycled housewares and clothing. Brand-name quality goods are also donated by such retailers as Filene's Basement and Urban Outfitters. ~ 60 Canal Street; 617-723-2666, fax 617-723-4107.

The biggest tourist shopping bonanza in Boston continues to be **Quincy Market**, just a few steps from Faneuil Hall. A Boston marketplace since 1826, Quincy Market is the centerpiece of three shopping arcades filled with more than 150 shops and two dozen food stands and restaurants. Outside the market are a profusion of cheery flower and balloon stands, and under its glass-canopied sides are pushcart vendors selling novelty products. Flanking Quincy Market are two more arcades, the North Market and the South Market.

> Start with something sweet (jam, syrup) at Le Saucier before setting your tongue aflame—some sauces are so hot they're not sold to minors.

Feel the Irish eyes smiling at **Celtic Weavers**, an importer of Irish goods. You can set yourself up with clothing, jewelry and perfume, or take home some music, pottery and food. ~ Fanueil Hall, North Market; 617-720-0750, fax 603-887-6624.

Tantalize (or torture) your tastebuds at **Le Saucier**, the first store of its kind in the U.S., specializing in over 800 condiments from 37 countries: mustard, chutney, barbecue sauce. ~ Quincy Market, North Canopy; 617-227-9649, fax 617-474-9713.

For such a small area, Chinatown has more shops than you might imagine. If you've never experienced Chinese pastries, your mouth will water for them at **Hing Shing Pastry**, where you can see the bakers at work. ~ 67 Beach Street; 617-451-1162.   ◄ HIDDEN

Professional-quality Chinese cooking equipment is sold at **Chin Enterprises, Inc.**, including traditional Chinese chopsticks and two-foot-diameter woks. ~ 33 Harrison Avenue; 617-423-1725.

If there is such a thing as a vintage joke shop, **Jack's Joke Shop** is it. Open since 1922 and still run by the original family, the shop is festooned with dozens of elaborate Halloween masks and wigs, inflatable skeletons and glasses with noses and mustaches. ~ 38 Boylston Street; 617-426-9640, fax 617-338-8705; www.jacksjokes.com.

Downtown Crossing is the heart of downtown shopping. A brick pedestrian mall at Washington and Summer streets, it fronts on **Macy's** (formerly Jordan Marsh), one of Boston's oldest department stores. ~ 450 Washington Street; 617-357-3000. Down the street, **Filene's** has been one of its rivals since the mid-19th century. ~ 426 Washington Street; 617-357-2100.

No shopping tour would be complete without a visit to **Filene's Basement**, the country's oldest bargain store, founded in 1908, which has made a legend out of off-price shopping. In the 1940s, 15,000 women once stormed the doors to get the last dresses to leave Paris before the German occupation. Detractors say merchandise slipped during the 1980s, when the Basement opened 22 stores in six states. But the Basement is always crowded with women, who used to try on clothes in the aisles until dressing rooms were installed in 1989, and who don't mind the flaking paint and exposed piping when they can pick up designer dresses for less than ten percent of retail price after three markdowns. Or, on occasion, an $80,000 sable coat for $5000. ~ 426 Washington Street; 617-542-2011, fax 617-348-7915.

Boston's arts scene has rich centuries of history behind it and is expanding all the time. The **Bostix Booth** at Faneuil Hall offers half-price tickets for many performance events on the day of the show, cash only, first-come, first-served. ~ 617-723-5181.   **NIGHTLIFE**

THE BEST BARS   There's a Boston bar for everyone: young singles, bricklayers and stevedores, the State House crowd, Financial District workers, Cambridge academics, sports fans, the Irish.

The **Bell in Hand Tavern** is America's oldest tavern, opened in 1795, and retains a cozy, Colonial feeling. There's live music here Thursday through Saturday nights. Cover Friday and Saturday. ~ 45 Union Street; 617-227-2098.

Irish brogues roll so thickly at the **Black Rose** that it sounds like Dublin. Irish beers, Irish folk music and a rollicking good time are house specialties. Cover on the weekends. ~ 160 State Street; 617-742-2286.

Silvertone is a popular retro bar frequented by young urbanites. Fashioned after an art deco–era diner, the black-and-white photos on the wall herald the age of supper clubs and big band music. The raspberry martini is the signature drink of choice. ~ 69 Bromfield Street; 617-338-7887, fax 617-338-7890.

HIDDEN ►   The **Littlest Bar** is just that—Boston's smallest tavern. There are five stools at the bar and four tiny tables behind them. The noise from the television is often deafening, but this is a fun place to have a quick drink before dinner; most locals haven't heard of it, either. ~ 47 Province Street; 617-523-9766.

The Good Life specializes in retro cocktail drinks like cosmopolitans, Manhattans and sidecars. The drab '70s decor doesn't deter large after-work crowds or music enthusiasts who enjoy live jazz downstairs. Thursday through Saturday. ~ 28 Kingston Street; 617-451-2622, fax 617-292-9224.

NIGHTCLUBS AND CABARETS   **The Roxy** is a beautiful and elegant art deco–style club where people like to really dress up. Dress code. Closed Sunday through Wednesday. Cover. ~ 279 Tremont Street, in the Tremont House; 617-338-7699.

You can view the city from the 33rd floor of the prosperous **Bay Tower Room**, where a four-piece orchestra plays on Friday and Saturday nights. Closed Sunday. ~ 60 State Street; 617-723-1666.

In a Mardi-Gras setting, **Sugar Shack** offers up a mixture of house, funk, disco and R&B Wednesday through Saturday. Cover. ~ 1 Boylston Place; 617-351-2510, fax 617-351-2505.

The **Orpheum Theater** hosts nationally known rock artists. ~ One Hamilton Place off Tremont Street; 617-679-0810.

THEATER AND DANCE   Boston's theater district is tightly clustered on lower Tremont Street and several blocks west. Many of these host pre-Broadway tryouts and national touring companies. One such venue is the **Colonial Theatre**. ~ 106 Boylston Street; 617-426-9366. Popular contemporary plays are offered by the **Wilbur Theatre**. ~ 246 Tremont Street; 617-423-4008.

The opulent theater of the **Wang Center for the Performing Arts**, formerly a Roaring Twenties movie palace, sponsors extravaganzas in dance, drama, music and film. ~ 270 Tremont Street; 617-482-9393, fax 617-451-1436.

Also operated by the Wang Center, the **Shubert Theater** stages Broadway plays and community theater performances. ~ 265 Tremont Street; 617-482-9393.

The **Boston Ballet** performs classics like *The Nutcracker* and contemporary works at the Wang Center. ~ 19 Clarendon Street, Boston; 617-695-6950.

Musical comedies are the specialty at **The Charles Playhouse**. ~ 74 Warrenton Street. **Stage II** (downstairs) has been home to the country's longest-running nonmusical play, *Shear Madness*, a comedy whodunit. ~ 617-426-5225; www.shearmadness.com. On **Stage I**, the innovative Blue Man Group wows audiences with eye-popping performance art and fun-filled escapades. ~ 617-426-6912.

▼▼▼▼▼▼▼▼▼▼

Beacon Hill

Beacon Hill got its name from a beacon that stood atop it in 1634 to warn Colonial settlers of danger. "The Hill" used to be much taller; it was leveled by 60 feet to make way for residential building in the 19th century. After a building boom, Beacon Hill fast became the most elite section of the city, home to doctors, lawyers, writers and intellectuals. Oliver Wendell Holmes called it "the sunny street that holds the sifted few." The first formal residents of the neighborhood were John Singleton Copley and John Hancock. Later residents included Daniel Webster, Louisa May Alcott, William Dean Howells, Henry James and Jenny Lind.

SIGHTS

No single section of town is more elegant than Beacon Hill. This charming area still looks like a 19th-century neighborhood with its gas lamps, brick sidewalks and narrow, one-lane streets that wind up and down the hill. Its later brick rowhouses were designed in fine Federal style, with symmetrical windows, fanlight door windows, black shutters and lacy black iron grillwork. Beacon Hill residents love windowboxes and gardens, and many of the houses have beautiful hidden walled gardens. These are opened to the public during the **Hidden Gardens of Beacon Hill** walking tours in the spring, sponsored by the Beacon Hill Garden Club. ~ P.O. Box 302, Charles Street Station, Boston, MA 02114; 617-227-4392.

The crown of Beacon Hill, at its summit, is the **Massachusetts State House**, a grand replacement for the old State House downtown. After the American Revolution, state leaders wanted a more elegant home for the prosperous new government. Charles Bulfinch designed it for them in 1795 in Federal style, with a gold dome, brick facade, Palladian windows and white Corinthian columns and trim. A free, weekday tour of the interior is well worthwhile, but be sure to make advance reservations. An impressive rotunda, floors made of 24 kinds of marble, unique "black lace" iron grillwork stair railings, stained-glass windows and decorated vaulted ceilings are all part of the appointments. Don't miss the Sacred Cod in the House of Representatives, a wooden fish hung there in 1784 to symbolize the importance of the fishing industry to Massachusetts. ~ Beacon and Park streets; 617-722-2000, fax 617-727-4722.

The **Old Court House**, now the Suffolk County Courthouse, has a grand rotunda with vaulted ceilings decorated with gilt rosettes and figures of cherubs, urns, scrolls and trumpet-blowing figures. Stone caryatids line the rotunda, representing Justice, Fortitude, Punishment, Guilt, Reward, Wisdom, Religion and Virtue. ~ Pemberton Square.

Many come to admire **Louisburg Square** for its sheer beauty. The centerpiece of the square is a serene oval park with a tall black iron fence, ringed with brick bowfront houses. Louisburg Square looks so much like London that a British film company produced *Vanity Fair* here in the 1920s. Louisa May Alcott lived at number 20. ~ Between Mt. Vernon and Pinckney streets.

Tiny one-lane **Acorn Street**—just south of Louisburg Square between Cedar and Willow streets—is one of the few old cobblestone streets left on Beacon Hill, and a very picturesque one it is. Coachmen and servants for nearby mansions used to live here.

Although the **Rose Standish Nichols House Museum** was not fashionable for its time, it is a fine example of the late 19th-century rowhouse. Standish Nichols was quite a personage in her day. A noted landscape architect and pacifist, she traveled around the world and was a friend of Woodrow Wilson. Designed by Charles Bulfinch, her home is filled with rare antiques such as Renaissance Flemish tapestries, statuary by noted American sculptor Augustus Saint-Gaudens and unusual imitation leather wallpaper gilded with gold. Tours run frequently from May through October; call for reservations during the winter months. Admission. ~ 55 Mt. Vernon Street; 617-227-6993.

The house at **85 Mt. Vernon Street** was Harrison Gray Otis's second Bulfinch-designed home, while **45 Beacon Street** was his third, an unheard-of extravagance.

A grander library than the **Boston Athenaeum** would be hard to find. The interior features high, vaulted ceilings, pillared archways, scores of marble busts, solid wood reading tables and red-leather, brass-studded armchairs. Founded in 1807 by a group including the Reverend William Emerson, father of Ralph Waldo Emerson, it's one of the country's oldest independent libraries. Its picture gallery and sculpture hall served as Boston's first art museum, and the library still maintains an impressive collection of art today, including works by Gilbert Stuart, John Singer Sargent and Chester Harding. The library is also noted for its collections of 19th-century American prints, Confederate state imprints and books from the libraries of George Washington, General Henry Knox and Jean Louis Cardinal Cheverus. Public tours are given

Boston

.5 mile

.5 kilometer

N

Boston Harbor

North End

Commercial St

Nashua St

Charles St

Cambridge

Broadway

Main St

M.I.T.

Massachusetts Ave

Vassar St

Memorial Dr

Charles River

Storrow Dr

Commonwealth Ave

Boston University

Brookline St

Brookline

Beacon St

Park Dr

Riverway

Brookline Ave

Fenway

The Fenway

Back Bay Fens

Park Dr

Boylston St

Fenway Park

Back Bay

Beacon St

Boylston St

Commonwealth Ave

Arlington St

Berkeley St

Dartmouth St

Massachusetts Ave

Huntington Ave

Northeastern University

South End

Tremont St

Washington St

Shawmut Ave

Columbus Ave

Embankment Rd

Beacon Hill

Cambridge St

Stanford St

Government Center

Merrimac St

Court St

Congress St

State St

Atlantic Ave

Boston Common

Charles St

Park St

Summer St

Washington St

Tremont St

Chinatown

Dorchester Ave

Fort Point Channel

Dorchester Ave

South Boston

W Broadway

4th St

Congress St

Sleeper St

Northern Ave

Farge St

Summer St

93

93

93

90

28

2

3

2A

2

9

9

28

90

1

POINTS OF INTEREST

- Ⓐ Boston Center for the Arts
- Ⓑ Boston Tea Party Ship & Museum
- Ⓓ Chickering Piano Factory
- Ⓒ Children's Museum
- Ⓔ Isabella Stewart Gardner Museum
- Ⓕ Museum of Fine Arts
- Ⓖ Museum of Science
- Ⓗ Symphony Hall
- Ⓘ Union Park
- ➔ World Trade Center

by appointment Tuesday through Thursday. ~ 10½ Beacon Street; 617-227-0270, fax 617-227-5266; www.bostonathenaeum.org.

The **Appleton-Parker Houses**, twin Greek Revival structures alike in every detail, were built for two wealthy merchants. At number 39, Fanny Appleton married Henry Wadsworth Longfellow in 1843. Number 40 is now the home of the Women's City Club. ~ 39–40 Beacon Street.

At 63–64 Beacon Street you can see a few panes of the famous **Beacon Hill purple glass**, with hues caused by a reaction of sunlight. It acquired cachet, along with everything else traditional on "the Hill."

It is intriguing that while most people think of Beacon Hill as a Brahmin bastion, in the 19th century its north slope was the heart of Boston's emerging free black community. Blacks arrived in Boston as slaves in 1638. By 1705, there were more than 400 slaves, and a few free blacks, who settled in the North End. In the 19th century, most blacks lived in the West End, and on Beacon Hill, between Joy and Charles streets. The free blacks worked hard to provide decent housing and education for their own, and to help end slavery.

HIDDEN ►

A number of their houses and public buildings still stand, and you can see them on the 14-stop **Black Heritage Trail**. A guide leads daily scheduled trips.

Walking tour maps of the trail are available at the Boston Common Visitor Information kiosk and at the **Museum of Afro-American History**, a stop on the trail. The museum is closed on weekends. ~ 46 Joy Street; 617-739-1200, fax 617-739-1285; www.afroammuseum.org.

Among the public buildings on the Black Heritage Trail is the **African Meeting House**, the oldest standing black church in America. Built in 1806, it was known in the abolitionist era as the Black Faneuil Hall. It was here, in 1832, that the New England Anti-Slavery Society was founded, with black leader Frederick Douglass and abolitionists William Lloyd Garrison and Charles Sumner speaking from the platform. ~ 8 Smith Court.

A stirring tribute to the first black regiment recruited for the Civil War stands at the corner of Beacon and Park streets and marks the start of the Black Heritage Trail. A bas-relief sculpture by Augustus Saint-Gaudens, the **Robert Gould Shaw and 54th Regiment Memorial** shows the regiment on the march with their young white leader, Bostonian Robert Gould Shaw, and an angel flying overhead. The black military role in the Civil War won new recognition with the release of the film *Glory*, which chronicles the story of the 54th Regiment.

The trail also takes you to one of the first schools for black children and to homes built by free blacks, among them the

Lewis and Harriet Hayden House, which served as an Underground Railway station and was visited by Harriet Beecher Stowe. ~ 66 Phillips Street.

On an entirely different note, television history is also alive and well in Beacon Hill. Like homing pigeons, all tourists head for "Cheers," so we may as well get it out of the way. The setting for the television show was the **Bull and Finch Pub,** not to be confused with the impostor, Three Cheers, at 390 Congress Street. Even though the Bull and Finch has made such a big business out of all this—selling *Cheers* T-shirts, mugs and hats in the Hampshire House lobby upstairs—it's a bar with real atmosphere. Originally an English pub, it was dismantled and shipped here, complete with old leather and walnut paneling. ~ Downstairs at 84 Beacon Street; 617-227-9605, fax 617-723-1898; www.cheersboston.com.

Yet another point of television trivia can be found in Beacon Hill. Private eye Spenser of *Spenser for Hire* lived above a Boston firehouse, which he entered through a bright red door. The firehouse is right next to the Charles Street Meeting House on Mt. Vernon Street, at the corner of River Street.

Beacon Hill Bed & Breakfast, a pretty six-story brick rowhouse, is in a quiet residential neighborhood on the lower slope of Beacon Hill, just two blocks west of Charles Street. Each of three high-ceilinged guest rooms has a decorative fireplace and a private bath. Most rooms have a view of the Charles River; some look out over the lovely Gothic Revival Church of the Advent, across the street. ~ 27 Brimmer Street; 617-523-7376; e-mail bhillbb@aol.com. ULTRA-DELUXE.

LODGING

The **Eliot and Pickett Houses** is a bed-and-breakfast inn in two wonderful 1830s brick townhouses, with a total of 20 bedrooms (nine in Eliot House and eleven in Pickett House). Wall-to-wall carpeting, central air conditioning and rather generic Federal-style reproduction furniture make for a comfortable though not overly quaint inn. Guests may prepare their own meals in the houses' kitchens, and complimentary breakfast is served. Handicapped-accessible rooms are served. ~ 6 Mt. Vernon Place; 617-248-8707, fax 617-742-1364. MODERATE TO DELUXE.

A real find, far less pricey than downtown hotels, is the **John Jeffries House.** It offers 46 spacious studio apartments and suites, most with kitchenettes, in a renovated turn-of-the-20th-century house overlooking Charles Street. Guest rooms are furnished in tasteful pastels, with dark reproduction furniture, large windows and contemporary bathrooms. There is also a large, comfortable lobby. ~ 14 Embankment Road; 617-367-1866, fax 617-742-0313. DELUXE TO ULTRA-DELUXE.

DINING

Two steps from the State House, **The Black Goose** specializes in modern Italian cuisine. Take care not to load up on the home-baked *focaccia* bread or the *caprese* salad, a mound of plum tomatoes, mozzarella and basil. Save room for the tasty entrées; among the pastas and grilled meats and fish are lobster and crab raviolis, sautéed chicken Florentine and grilled tuna with a wasabi-ginger sauce. Contemporary dash has been added to the dining room, originally part of a historic hotel. ~ 21 Beacon Street; 617-720-4500, fax 617-720-0963. MODERATE TO DELUXE.

Along with its chic boutiques, Charles Street is lined with restaurants representing many ethnic cuisines.

Café Bella Vita is a great coffeehouse where you can linger over an espresso or cappuccino and feel welcome in a European way. Its café chairs are always crowded with young students munching on hearty Italian sandwiches. Specialties are desserts such as fresh gelato or chocolate cheesecake. ~ 30 Charles Street; 617-720-4505, fax 617-720-4505. BUDGET.

Step into a Tuscan village at **Ristorante Toscano**, whose dining room has exposed brick walls hung with paintings of the Italian countryside and antique Italian cookingware and pottery. Feast on Florentine cuisine including homemade pastas and game dishes. The *tiramisu* is a dessert standout. ~ 47 Charles Street; 617-723-4090, fax 617-720-4280. MODERATE TO ULTRA-DELUXE.

Good and spicy Thai food stars over the decor at **The King and I**. Start off your meal with satay and Thai rolls, then move on to dancing squids, seafood *panang* or any number of chicken, duck, beef, tofu and noodle dishes. ~ 145 Charles Street; 617-227-3320, fax 617-227-3320. BUDGET TO MODERATE.

HIDDEN ►

Surrounded by whizzing cars in a rotary, **Buzzy's Fabulous Roast Beef** looks unsavory, to say the least. Still, this take-out stand, open 24 hours, has the best steakhouse fries in Boston, as well as cheesesteak sandwiches, chili dogs and short ribs. ~ 327 Cambridge Street; 617-242-7722. BUDGET.

SHOPPING

At the foot of Beacon Hill, little Charles Street is thickly lined with antique shops, art galleries and specialty stores.

Quirky bargains lie in store at the **Beacon Hill Thrift Shop**, where Beacon Hill matrons bring their best silver along with bric-a-brac. Closed Sunday, Monday and Wednesday. ~ 15 Charles Street; 617-742-2323.

If you stop by **Rouvalis Flowers** you can take home an exotic plant or flower. The shop has a wonderful selection of topiary trees and orchids as well as unusual ginger and heliconia. ~ 40 West Cedar Street; 617-720-2266, fax 617-720-2636.

The retail outlet of a local paper manufacturer, **Rugg Road Paper Co.** carries virtually every paper product you can imagine, from woodblock-printed lampshades to stationery to hardbound books. ~ 105 Charles Street; 617-742-0002, fax 617-742-0008.

An amazing selection of beautifully colored and embroidered western-style leather boots awaits at **Helen's Leather**, along with leather coats, briefcases and belts. Closed Tuesday. ~ 110 Charles Street; 617-742-2077.

You ought to be able to find the perfect brass drawer pull at **Period Furniture Hardware**, which carries a full line of repro-duction hardware. ~ 123 Charles Street; 617-227-0758.

Despite its fame as the *Cheers* bar, **Bull and Finch Pub** is a wa-tering hole with character. The venerable English pub features big brews, burgers and an uproarious crowd. ~ Downstairs at 84 Beacon Street; 617-227-9605. **NIGHTLIFE**

The **Sevens Ale House** is a better Boston neighborhood bar than the nearby Bull and Finch Pub. Decorated in dark, mel-lowed wood and with photos of patrons finishing the Boston Marathon and other local events, The Sevens is small and lively, lacks tourists, and is blessed with some of the friendliest staff we've ever met. ~ 77 Charles Street; 617-523-9074.

Although it started life as a mud flat, Back Bay fast be-came a fashionable neighborhood. As the city grew, it started running out of room in its original peninsula sur-rounding Boston Common, so it began filling in the tidal flats of the Back Bay in 1858, the largest land reclamation project of its time. Some 450 acres of marshland were turned into usable land over 20 years. **The Back Bay**

Given all this room to plan, Back Bay is the only place in town laid out with any perceivable logic. Streets follow an orderly grid, with cross streets named alphabetically for palatial ducal man-sions: Arlington, Berkeley, Clarendon, Dartmouth, Exeter, Fair-field, Gloucester and Hereford.

The centerpiece of this grand reclamation project is **Common-wealth Avenue**. Patterned after the Champs Élysées, it's a wide boulevard with a grass strip mall that runs right through the heart of the Back Bay. "Comm Ave," as it's called by natives, is lined with stately brownstones and many historic buildings. New-bury, Beacon and Marlborough streets parallel Comm Ave. Sty-lish Newbury Street is lined with chic boutiques, expensive jew-elry, fur and clothing stores, art galleries, antique stores and loads of restaurants. Back Bay crosses Massachusetts Avenue, which natives shorten to "Mass Ave," and ends at Kenmore Square. **SIGHTS**

To the north, the Back Bay ends at the Charles River, where the wide, grassy Esplanade is a popular sunning spot in warm weather. Also on the Esplanade is the **Hatch Memorial Shell**, where the Boston Pops Symphony Orchestra performs summer concerts.

If Boston Common is Boston's Central Park, then the **Public Garden** is its Tuileries, the first botanical garden in the country. Lavishly landscaped with flowers and trees, it's home to the **Swan Boats**, which circle the weeping willow–draped lagoon in season. The famous boats were launched in 1877 by Robert Paget, who was inspired by the swan-boat scene in Wagner's opera *Lohengrin*. The same family continues to operate them. Also in the Public Garden is some notable statuary: George Washington on horseback and abolitionist Wendall Phillips. ~ Bordered by Beacon, Charles, Arlington and Boylston streets.

HIDDEN ▶   If you walk straight through the Public Garden gates at the corner of Beacon and Charles streets, you'll come upon **Mrs. Mallard and her brood of eight ducklings** stretched out in a row behind her, all heading for the pond. Placed here in 1987, the bronze, larger-than-life statues represent the ducks made famous in Robert McCloskey's children's story *Make Way for Ducklings*. Every Mother's Day, the ducklings are feted on Duckling Day with a parade and festival sponsored by the Historic Neighborhoods Foundation. ~ 99 Bedford Street; 617-426-1885, fax 617-426-5305.

Ever since opening in 1927, the **Ritz-Carlton** has catered to a select clientele. The 17-story brick building overlooking the Public Garden, while not particularly striking on the outside, is the epitome of old elegance inside, where the lobby is graced with a large curving staircase and antique touches such as an exquisite brass railing. The original owner would never permit a reservation without researching the client's reputation in the Social Register or business directories. Many notable people have lived at the Ritz, including Charles Lindbergh and Winston Churchill. Many more have stayed here, among them Rodgers & Hammerstein, Albert Einstein, the Duke and Duchess of Windsor, Tennessee Williams and John F. Kennedy—even Lassie and Rin Tin Tin. ~ 15 Arlington Street; 617-536-5700, fax 617-536-1335.

Down the street, the Georgian-style **Arlington Street Church** features a tall and graceful steeple fashioned in the style of Christopher Wren. ~ Arlington and Boylston streets.

The Beaux-Arts **Berkeley Building** looks like a wedding cake, so curlicued and beribboned is its frothy white bas-relief terra cotta molding. Tiers of windows are trimmed in sea green, and a black marble entrance sign is flanked with dolphins and sea serpents. Built in 1905 and beautifully restored in 1989, it formerly housed Boston's design center. ~ 420 Boylston Street.

There's no better way to view Boston than from the 60-story **John Hancock Observatory**, the tallest building in New England. From 740 feet up, you can see the State House, the White Mountains of New Hampshire and the South Shore. Besides the great view, there are exhibits, a film, photographs and a sound and light show on Boston history. Down on the ground, the Hancock's shimmering glass sides serve as a fantastic mirror, reflecting the surrounding buildings as clearly as a photograph. Admission. ~ 200 Clarendon Street, Copley Square; 617-572-6429; www.jhancockobs.com.

The **New Old South Church** is where the congregation of the Old South Meeting House moved in 1875, after they decided their Washington Street neighborhood had become too noisy to hear the sermon. The Gothic facade is dominated by a tower and carved stone rosettes. Inside are Venetian mosaics and 15th-century stained-glass windows depicting the Prophets, the Evangelists, the miracles and the parables. ~ Corner of Boylston and Dartmouth streets.

The heart of this area is gorgeous **Copley Square,** named for artist John Singleton Copley. Boston's religious and intellectual center at the end of the 19th century, the square is dominated by two architecturally imposing structures, Henry Hobson Richardson's Trinity Church and Charles McKim's Boston Public Library. ~ Boylston Street, located between Clarendon and Dartmouth streets.

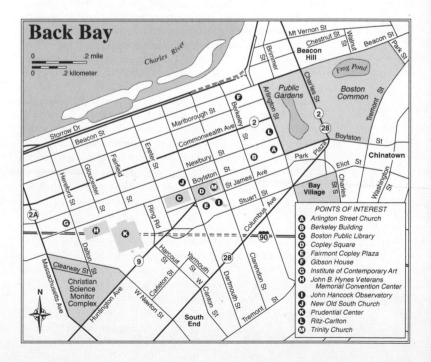

POINTS OF INTEREST

- Ⓐ Arlington Street Church
- Ⓑ Berkeley Building
- Ⓒ Boston Public Library
- Ⓓ Copley Square
- Ⓔ Fairmont Copley Plaza
- Ⓕ Gibson House
- Ⓖ Institute of Contemporary Art
- Ⓗ John B. Hynes Veterans Memorial Convention Center
- Ⓘ John Hancock Observatory
- Ⓙ New Old South Church
- Ⓚ Prudential Center
- Ⓛ Ritz-Carlton
- Ⓜ Trinity Church

The French-Romanesque, medieval-style **Trinity Church,** built in 1877, is visually stunning inside and out. One of Richardson's most brilliant creations, Trinity Church has an enormous tower reminiscent of the domes of Venice and Constantinople. Inside, rich colors and exquisite Moorish details cover the vaulted ceiling, rotunda and walls, and there are John LaFarge frescoes and stained-glass windows. Public tours run throughout the summer. Call for arrangements from October through April. ~ 206 Clarendon Street; 617-536-0944, fax 617-536-8916; www.trinity churchboston.org.

Much more than a library, the **Boston Public Library** houses art and architectural treasures. A wide marble staircase, Corinthian columns and frescoes grace its grand entrance hall (at the side door). Inside are murals by John Singer Sargent, paintings by John Singleton Copley, sculptures by Augustus and Louis Saint-Gaudens and bronze doors by Daniel Chester French. Inspired by Italian Renaissance palaces, it was opened in 1895. Take time to sit in the lovely central courtyard, where you'll find a fountain and benches. ~ 666 Boylston Street; 617-536-5400, fax 617-236-4306; www.bpl.org.

The grande dame of Boston's vintage hotels is the **Fairmont Copley Plaza,** built in 1912 in high Victorian style. It boasts a wide stone facade, whose curving center echoes the bowfront homes of Back Bay and Beacon Hill. Inside, marble and crystal appointments set off an elegant lobby topped with a trompe l'oeil painting of the sky. The internationally known Fairmont Copley Plaza has served as a resting place for a dozen presidents and European royalty. ~ 138 St. James Avenue; 617-267-5300, fax 617-375-9648; www.fairmont.com.

Like the Hancock, the **Skywalk Observatory** at the Prudential Tower gives you a bird's-eye view of downtown, this time a 360-degree one. Commonly called "the Pru," the Prudential Center was built in the early '60s as another piece of urban renewal. It houses shops and offices, and in front of it is a cast bronze statue called *Quest Eternal,* representing man reaching for the heavens. The tower is accessible for daylight or starlight viewing, from 10

THE SKY IS FALLING

When the John Hancock Observatory was built in the late 1960s, architects argued bitterly that the rhomboidal building designed by I. M. Pei would ruin the character of Copley Square. The blue glass windows of this landmark have become collectors' items ever since they fell out onto the sidewalk in the early 1970s. They were replaced at a cost of more than $8 million.

a.m. to 10 p.m. Admission. ~ 800 Boylston Street, Prudential Center; 617-859-0648, fax 617-859-0056.

The building at **314 Commonwealth Avenue** was created in the 1920s in an 1899 mansion modeled after a Loire Valley château. Its medieval-looking exterior has sculptured stone cherubs and gargoyles looking down from its battlements. Inside the building are spectacular bas-relief mahogany walls, gold-leaf carved ceilings, stained-glass windows and an ornately carved marble staircase.

Nowhere is the opulence of the Back Bay Victorians more amply evidenced than at the **Gibson House**, now a museum and location of the Victorian Society in America, New England chapter. Built for the prominent Gibson family in 1859, the Italian Renaissance Revival home is richly furnished with gold-embossed wallpaper and black walnut paneling, imported carpets and most of the Gibson family china and porcelain. Tours are available Wednesday through Sunday from May through October, and Saturday and Sunday the rest of the year. Admission. ~ 137 Beacon Street; 617-267-6338, fax 617-267-5121.

The **Institute of Contemporary Art** has won an international reputation for its wide-ranging artistic events, held here for more than half a century. Housed in an old Boston firehouse, the ICA often shows experimental or controversial works, among them art exhibits, films, videos, music events, lectures and literary readings. Open Wednesday through Sunday, with special guided tours on most days. Admission. ~ 955 Boylston Street; 617-266-5152, fax 617-266-4021; www.ica.org.

A major convention hall, the **John B. Hynes Veterans Memorial Convention Center** was extensively renovated and rebuilt in the late 1980s. Call for a schedule of the numerous conventions and expositions, including a college-fest weekend and a bridal expo. ~ 900 Boylston Street; 617-954-2000.

The vintage 1927 **Ritz-Carlton** sparkles after an extensive restoration. A standard room is spacious and airy, with a high ceiling, brown floral drapes and spread and French provincial furnishings. On the walls are prints of antique engravings of Boston and Bunker Hill. The bathroom has polished white marble floors and antique fixtures. Besides an in-house health and fitness facility with massage, the 278-room Ritz offers complimentary use of a full-service health club nearby. The hotel has three restaurants, an afternoon tea lounge and a bar. ~ 15 Arlington Street; 617-536-5700, 800-241-3333, fax 617-536-1335; www.ritzcarlton.com. ULTRA-DELUXE.

LODGING

The grande dame of Boston hotels is the **Fairmont Copley Plaza**, built in 1912. The hotel was famed for throwing such sumptuous affairs as an "Evening in Venice," with gondolas floating on the parquet floor, converted to the Grand Canal. Every president since Taft has stayed here, as well as royalty from eight countries. JFK was a regular visitor. The Fairmont Copley Plaza's elegant lobby is appointed with coffered gold ceilings decorated with a trompe l'oeil painting of the sky, marble columns and floors, crystal chandeliers and French provincial furniture. The hotel has two restaurants and a lively bar. The 379 bedrooms and 28 suites are decorated with dark period furniture and warm floral patterns, while bathrooms feature vintage marble and chrome fixtures. ~ 138 St. James Avenue; 617-267-5300, 800-527-4727, fax 617-247-6681; www.fairmont.com. ULTRA-DELUXE.

For less expensive lodging in Boston, rent a furnished room from Comma Realty, Inc. Units with kitchens, rented weekly, are plain but clean with twin beds and funky bathroom fixtures. ~ 371 Commonwealth Avenue; 617-437-9200.

Built in 1891, the vintage stone **Copley Square Hotel**, completely renovated, draws lots of families and Europeans to its cozy, friendly 143 rooms. Though the rooms are on the smallish side, they're comfortably appointed with modern furniture and fabrics in blues, greens and mauves. ~ 47 Huntington Avenue; 617-536-9000, 800-225-7062, fax 617-236-0351; www.copleysquarehotel.com. ULTRA-DELUXE.

Real working fireplaces add to the considerable vintage charms of the **Lenox Hotel**. Opening at the turn of the century, the 214-room Lenox was popular with such entertainers as Enrico Caruso, who pulled his private streetcar up to the door. The lobby wears its original Gilded Age elegance of soaring white columns, gold-leaf moldings, marble fireplace and handsome royal-blue decor. A typical room has a Colonial-style chandelier, a rocking chair, high ceilings and a Colonial ambience. The top floor, however, has been renovated in French provincial decor. ~ 710 Boylston Street; 617-536-5300, 800-225-7676, fax 617-236-0351; www.lenoxhotel.com. ULTRA-DELUXE.

Beacon Inn Guest Houses has 32 less-than-lovely rooms with twin beds. Still, these are reasonably priced rooms in the heart of Back Bay, with kitchenettes, air conditioning and private baths. ~ 248 Newbury Street; 617-262-1771, fax 617-266-7276; www.hotel-intl.com. MODERATE.

HIDDEN ► One of the city's smallest, most charming hotels, the **Eliot Suite Hotel** was built in 1925 by the family of Charles Eliot, a Harvard president. The hotel has a warm, welcoming feeling. Its soft green-colored lobby is set with Queen Anne chairs, sofas and crystal wall sconces. Rooms are furnished with antique-style furniture and chintz fabric. Some have kitchenettes. ~ 370 Commonwealth Avenue; 617-267-1607, 800-443-5468, fax 617-536-9114; www.eliothotel.com. ULTRA-DELUXE.

The first independent luxury hotel built in Boston since the 1950s, the **Colonnade Hotel**, opened in 1971, sparked the citywide hotel building boom a decade later. Recognized for its contemporary European atmosphere, the Colonnade has renovated its 285 rooms with classy mahogany and oak furnishings with copper or rose accents. The hotel has a restaurant as well as Boston's only rooftop pool. ~ 120 Huntington Avenue; 617-424-7000, 800-962-3030, fax 617-424-1717; www.colonnadehotel. com. ULTRA-DELUXE.

The **Ritz-Carlton Dining Room** offers one of the most serene and traditional dining spots in Boston. Overlooking the Public Garden, this sparkling, elegant place features cobalt-blue Dutch crystal chandeliers, French provincial–style furniture and blue-and-gold fringed drapes. The carving cart menu changes daily but might include such wonderful entrées as lobster in bourbon sauce, venison, pheasant or whole dover sole sautéed with pine nuts and lemon butter. There are almost 20 desserts, ranging from *bavorois à l'orange* to *crêpes Suzettes flambées*. ~ 15 Arlington Street; 617-536-5700, fax 617-536-1335. DELUXE TO ULTRA-DELUXE.

DINING

Though it emulates a Parisian bistro about as successfully as a McDonald's, the **Café de Paris** offers better fare than McD's: croissants, omelettes and the best chicken sandwich in Boston, with cafeteria-style service. ~ 19 Arlington Street; 617-247-7121, fax 617-247-9499. BUDGET.

Pignoli is more of a New York–chic restaurant than a Boston eatery. If the restaurant's main dining area hadn't been so carefully planned, the enormous paper balloons that float along the ceiling might make diners feel a bit claustrophobic. But they don't—the warm orangey-pink lighting and lightweight furniture expand the space, and the whimsical pig's tail–shaped flourishes scattered throughout Pignoli serve to further lighten the mood. Similarly, the menu is about as fun-loving as it is meticulously crafted. Northern Italian–based, it includes antipasto with more seafood than vegetables, and delectable meat dishes. No lunch on Sunday. ~ 79 Park Plaza; 617-338-7500, fax 617-338-7691. MODERATE TO DELUXE.

The **White Star Tavern** serves authentic global cuisine. Outstanding dishes include the shiitake and wood-ear stir fry, chilled lobster with a bloody mary cocktail sauce and lemon Thai aioli, and a seared wintergreen salad with duck confit. ~ 565 Boylston Street; 617-536-4477. MODERATE TO DELUXE.

Skipjack's Seafood Emporium boasts one of the biggest and most varied seafood menus in Boston—over two dozen kinds of fresh fish daily, ranging from tuna and salmon to lesser-known moonfish and parrot fish. The decor is far from traditional: glass block and glitzy red and blue neon, and changing exhibits by local artists. ~ 199 Clarendon Street; 617-536-3500, fax 617-536-4204. MODERATE.

Text continued on page 222.

Boston Area Bookstores

Boston is a book lover's delight, brimming with bookstores full of quirky personality, charm and the imprint of history. These shops display a colorful, individual stamp, with secondhand shelving, hand-lettered signs and perhaps a beat-up leather chair or two or a resident dog.

Rare and fine books are the specialty at **Booksellers at 355 Boylston Street**. Here you can get first editions, 19th- and 20th-century literature and private-press books. The shop is right in Back Bay at the corner of Boylston and Arlington streets. ~ 355 Boylston Street; 617-421-1880, fax 617-536-7072.

The **Brattle Book Shop** claims the title of being the successor to America's oldest continuous antiquarian bookshop, dating from the 18th century. Used books sit on battered gray steel shelving and range from fiction, humor and poetry to history, genealogy and heraldry. Old *Life* magazines dating to 1936 march up the stairway and through history, covered with the faces of Tallulah Bankhead, Betty Grable and Hedy Lamarr. Closed Sunday. ~ 9 West Street; 617-542-0210, 800-447-9595, fax 617-338-1467.

The intimate **Glad Day Bookshop** houses a comprehensive collection of gay and lesbian literature, magazines, newspapers, travel guides and music. The bookstore also hosts readings by authors. ~ 673 Boylston Street; 617-267-3010; www.gladday.com.

Good food and good books go hand in hand, and never more so than at **Trident Booksellers & Café**. Trident claims the prize for being funky: the province of young hippies dressed in black, a plethora of Third World, gay and alternative publications, and a menu of homemade soups and sandwiches tailored to a struggling writer's budget. It also sells bonsai trees, incense and myrrh, self-improvement videos and campy black-and-white postcards. ~ 338 Newbury Street; 617-267-8688, fax 617-247-1934.

An astonishing 25 bookshops surround Harvard Square. Established in 1856, **Schoenhof's Foreign Books, Inc.** is America's oldest comprehensive foreign-language bookstore. It carries reference books in over 240 languages, among them Swahili, Urdu, Tibetan, Navajo and classical Greek and Latin, whatever you need to complete a master's or Ph.D. Still, the shop is not too pedantic to sell children's favorites like *Le*

Petit Prince and *Babar*. ~ 76-A Mt. Auburn Street, Cambridge; 617-547-8855, fax 617-547-8551.

Where else but Cambridge could a poetry-only bookshop exist? The **Grolier Poetry Book Shop Inc.**, founded in 1927, is America's oldest continuously operating poetry bookshop, carrying more than 14,000 titles from all periods and cultures. Supported by friends of Conrad Aiken, who lived next door in 1929, the shop grew into a meeting place for such poets as Ezra Pound, Marianne Moore and T. S. Eliot. The shop sponsors an annual international poetry prize and a reading each semester. Closed Sunday. ~ 6 Plympton Street, Cambridge; 617-547-4648, 800-234-7636, fax 617-547-4230.

Many Harvard Square bookshops specialize in rare and out-of-print books. Among them is **James & Devon Gray Booksellers**, featuring rare books—in any language or on any subject—published before 1700. Among the obscure and hard-to-find volumes are a first edition of Edmund Spenser's *The Faerie Queene* and manuscripts by John Dryden. Closed Sunday and Monday. ~ 12 Arrow Street, Cambridge; 617-868-0752, fax 617-868-0853.

For new and used titles on history, philosophy and medieval times, visit **Starr Bookshop, Inc.** You'll also find a concentration of academic books from university presses. ~ 29 Plympton Street, Cambridge; 617-547-6864.

Seven Stars breathes New Age culture. Besides such titles as *Everyday Zen*, *The Biggest Secret* and *Passport to the Cosmos*, the shop sells tarot cards, incense and gorgeous chunks of amethyst and other crystals, which some believe have healing powers. ~ 731 Massachusetts Avenue, Cambridge; 617-547-1317.

A couple of miles out from Harvard Square, **Kate's Mystery Books** is a mecca for mystery lovers and writers. Opening on Friday the 13th in 1983, the store has a black cat logo and walls lined with several hundred black cat figurines. About 10,000 new and used titles range from Dashiell Hammett and Agatha Christie to Tony Hillerman and Robert Parker. A special section focuses on mysteries set in New England. Mystery Writers of America, New England Chapter, meets here, as does the Spenser Fan Club. Kate's hosts author readings and signings at least once a week. ~ 2211 Massachusetts Avenue, Cambridge; 617-491-2660.

This is just a sampling of Boston's bookstores, large and small. In this area of scholars and writers, there's a bookstore for everyone, with almost 300 listed in the Yellow Pages. That's one for every 2500 inhabitants.

Boston's only Hungarian restaurant, the **Café Budapest** has a romantic Old World ambience complete with pianist and violinist, crystal chandeliers, leaded-glass windows and a coat of arms over the fireplace. Try the iced cherry soup or wild mushrooms in paprika sauce for appetizers, followed by any of 38 entrées, including *wienerschnitzel à la Holstein*, sauerbraten, beef *gulyas* or beef stroganoff, and apple or cherry strudel desserts. ~ 90 Exeter Street, in the Copley Square Hotel; 617-266-1979, fax 617-266-1395. ULTRA-DELUXE.

Beautiful people dine at **Davio's**, a stylish Italian restaurant with primo service and real panache. Brick walls, white linens and soft lighting create an intimate milieu for superb creations such as cider-glazed crispy duck with smoked apple chutney and potato cake, and Tuscan marinated chicken breast with pepperoncini, kalamata olives, tomatoes and potatoes. ~ 269 Newbury Street; 617-262-4810, fax 617-437-0290. MODERATE TO DELUXE.

A cozy little basement restaurant, the **Kebab n' Kurry** smells of the spices of India. The tables are set with pink cloths and silk scarves embroidered with lion hunts and elephants. Authentic curries from North India, Bombay and South India include chicken, lamb, fish and shrimp and a wide variety of vegetarian dishes. ~ 30 Massachusetts Avenue; 617-536-9835, fax 617-536-9486. MODERATE.

If you're a fan of Indian curries but your dining companion tends to be unadventurous, try the smallish **Bombay Café**. There will be enough spicier selections to satisfy you, and your pal will probably be pleased with the milder items, such as stuffed *nan* or chicken *tikka*. ~ 175 Massachusetts Avenue; 617-247-0555, fax 617-247-0434. BUDGET TO MODERATE.

SHOPPING   Back Bay is another of the city's densest shopping districts, concentrated on fashionable Newbury Street, lined from end to end with chic boutiques.

Shreve, Crump & Lowe, a Boston jeweler since 1800, has always been the place to go for fine gold and silver jewelry. ~ 330 Boylston Street; 617-267-9100.

A gold swan sculpture over the door signals the **Women's Educational and Industrial Union**, founded in 1877 by a group of socially concerned women, the same year the Swan Boats set sail. Its shop sells upscale handmade gifts, jewelry, women's accessories, stationery, cards, children's clothing, even antiques. ~ 356 Boylston Street; 617-536-5651, fax 617-247-8826.

Alan Bilzerian is a chic shop filled with avant-garde clothing for men and women. The store carries designs by Issei Miyake, Yoji Yamamoto and Ann Demeule Meesler. ~ 34 Newbury Street; 617-536-1001.

Lou Lou's sells old and new tableware from planes, ships, hotels and restaurants. It's fun to browse through this funky store. ~ 121 Newbury Street; 617-859-8593.

London Lace specializes in reproduction Victorian lace patterns made on the only Victorian machinery left in Scotland. Items include lace curtain panels, table runners, tablecloths and antique furniture and accessories. ~ 215 Newbury Street; 617-267-3506, fax 617-267-0770.

The shopping jewel of this area is brass-and marble-bedecked **Copley Place** on upper Huntington Avenue, resplendent with indoor waterfalls and trees. The Copley Place complex also includes the Westin and Marriott hotels; the shopping mall is in between, connected to both hotel lobbies. A glass pedestrian bridge carries shoppers over Huntington Avenue to the Prudential Center.

The Society of Arts and Crafts is the oldest nonprofit craft organization in the United States, founded in 1897.

Opened in the mid-1980s, Copley Place holds 100 upscale stores, anchored by classy Dallas import **Neiman Marcus** (617-536-3660). Copley Place also houses outlets of **Polo–Ralph Lauren** (617-266-4121), **Gucci** (617-247-3000), **Enrico Celli** (617-247-4881), **Bally of Switzerland** (617-437-1910) and **Louis Vuitton** (617-437-6519).

Who would mind buying used clothing when it's as fashionable and "gently worn" as that at **The Closet Inc.**? Only the latest clothes in the finest condition are accepted. Closed Monday. ~ 175 Newbury Street, downstairs; 617-536-1919.

The **Society of Arts and Crafts** maintains two galleries where you can buy whimsical animal sculptures, ceramics, glass and furniture with real personality, as well as pottery and jewelry. The store's exhibits feature national artists. ~ 175 Newbury Street, 617-266-1810; and 101 Arch Street, 617-345-0033.

With its outrageous cards and T-shirts, screaming toy axes and other novelties, **In Touch** puts you in touch with strange gifts. ~ 192 Newbury Street; 617-262-7676.

Step into **Selletto** for handmade products, enhanced by piñon and cedar incense, from a worldwide network of artists. There are wreaths, dried flower arrangements and hand-carved marble peaches from Tuscany. ~ 244 Newbury Street; 617-424-0656.

Copley Place's much older cousin is the **Prudential Center**, anchored by **Saks Fifth Avenue** (617-262-8500) and **Lord & Taylor** (617-262-6000). The Pru's stylish interior includes a network of glass-roofed pedestrian streets lined with shops.

The **Nostalgia Factory** is a fun place to browse through old magazines, curios and kitschy souvenirs. Closed Sunday. ~ 51 North Margin Street; 617-720-2211.

NIGHTLIFE

For a special evening drink, head for the dark-paneled **Ritz Bar**, where tradition and Brahmin propriety rule. ~ 15 Arlington Street; 617-536-5700.

The **Boston Camerata**, formed in 1954, offers medieval, Renaissance, baroque and early American music concerts, both vocal and instrumental. ~ 140 Clarendon Street; 617-262-2092.

The **Lyric Stage Company of Boston**, Boston's oldest resident professional theater company, performs revivals and premieres. ~ 140 Clarendon Street, Copley Square; 617-437-7172.

The ornate **Oak Room**, was built in 1912; you can still sidle up to its original brass and wooden bar. Cabaret and jazz are performed regularly year-round. ~ 138 St. James Avenue, in the Fairmont Copley Plaza; 617-267-5300.

Theater-goers and other performing-arts fans may purchase half-price, day-of-show tickets at **Bostix**. Shaped like an enormous webbed wooden mushroom, the booth also serves as a full-service box office and Ticketmaster outlet for performing-arts events in and around Boston. ~ On the northwest corner of Copley Square.

Boston nightlife doesn't get more local than the **Pour House**, where an uproarious underground bar features blues and psychedelic music. ~ 909 Boylston Street; 617-236-1767.

Middle-class disco pleases the middle-class crowds at **Club Nicole** in the Back Bay Hilton's basement. Thursday and Saturday are international nights, while Friday is Asian night. Dress code. Closed Sunday through Wednesday. Cover. ~ 40 Dalton Street; 617-267-2582.

▼▼▼▼▼▼▼▼▼▼ The Fenway

The western side of Massachusetts Avenue edges over to the Fenway, the area surrounding the Back Bay Fens, another piece of the Emerald Necklace. Fens, from an Old English word meaning low wetlands or marshes, describes the area aptly. Along its sprawling length are several creeks and ponds, a rose garden and private garden plots, remnants of Boston's wartime "Victory Gardens."

SIGHTS

No one thinks of the Fenway without **Fenway Park**, the home of the Boston Red Sox and the Green Monster, the famous left-field wall. Fenway Park remains one of the homiest and most old-fashioned ballparks in the country. Built in 1912, it is one of the few baseball parks with a playing surface of real grass. The Green Monster is there to protect the ballfield from the Massachusetts Turnpike, and vice versa. Despite nostalgia, plans are underway to build a new park on the same site. ~ 4 Yawkey Way; 617-267-1700, fax 617-236-6640; www.redsox.com.

The campuses of two well-known Boston colleges are also in the Fenway—**Boston University**, along Commonwealth Avenue, and **Northeastern University**, south of Huntington Avenue.

Visible from Kenmore Square is the brightly lit, red-white-and-blue **Citgo Sign**, a gasoline advertisement and relic of the 1950s. It is the last of six similar signs in the United States.

Housed in a 15th-century-style Venetian palazzo, the **Isabella Stewart Gardner Museum** is a little jewel of a museum. It contains the personal collection of Mrs. Isabella Stewart Gardner, amassed over a lifetime of travel to Europe. "Mrs. Jack," as she came to be called, was considered somewhat eccentric and outrageous by proper Bostonians, and she collected what she liked. Her booty includes Italian Renaissance, 17th-century Dutch and 19th-century American paintings, as well as sculpture, textiles, furniture, ceramics, prints and drawings. Closed Monday. Admission. ~ 280 The Fenway; 617-566-1401, fax 617-232-8039.

The Boston University Bridge on Commonwealth Avenue is said to be the only place in the world where a boat can sail under a train traveling under a car driving under an airplane.

Not far from the Gardner Museum is the **Museum of Fine Arts,** world famous for its exceptional collections of Asian, Greek, Roman, European, Egyptian and American art. The MFA also holds impressionist paintings and works by such American masters as John Singer Sargent, John Singleton Copley and Winslow Homer. The MFA regularly attracts mega-exhibitions, such as traveling shows of Picasso and Monet works. Don't miss the Japanese gardens and the little first-floor café. Admission. ~ 465 Huntington Avenue; 617-267-9300, fax 617-247-6761.

LODGING

The Buckminster, a friendly lodging house with 100 rooms, is an inexpensive alternative to the higher-priced inns and hotels in nearby Back Bay. The hotel is on three floors of a nice old building in the heart of the vibrant Kenmore Square area. Rooms and suites tend to be large; all are furnished with reproduction furniture. The Buckminster's prime attraction is its thoughtful convenience to travelers who are staying for more than one night—each floor has a kitchen and full laundry facilities. If only there were hotels like this in every city! ~ 645 Beacon Street; 617-236-7050, 800-727-2825, fax 617-262-0068. DELUXE.

◄ HIDDEN

The best deal for budget-minded travelers in Boston just has to be **Florence Frances'** 1840s brownstone with four guest rooms that share baths. Florence has traveled around the world and decorated each room individually with an international flair. The Spanish Room, done in red, black and white, has a display of Spanish fans on the wall. The living and sitting rooms are beautifully furnished with antiques and a collection of Royal Doulton figurines. There is also a community kitchen. ~ 458 Park Drive; 617-267-2458. BUDGET TO MODERATE.

The **Boston International American Youth Hostel** represents the rock bottom of Boston accommodations, both in terms of price and amenities. Dormitory-style rooms hold six beds, with males and females kept separate. You must rent sheets, and no alcoholic beverages are allowed. Non-AYH members can stay here by paying a small extra charge for an introductory membership. The hostel can accommodate 190 people. There are laundry and kitchen facilities and a lounge with a piano and a juice machine. ~ 12 Hemenway Street; 617-536-9455, fax 617-424-6558. BUDGET.

The YMCA welcomes both male and female guests. Generously appointed, the YMCA has a comfortable wood-paneled lobby, an indoor pool, laundry facilities and cafeteria. But rooms are cell-like and furnished with Salvation Army–style furniture. Rooms are available from late June through early September. ~ 316 Huntington Avenue; 617-536-7800, fax 617-267-4653; www.ymcaboston.org. BUDGET TO MODERATE.

DINING   You'll halfway expect the girl from Ipanema to stroll into **Buteco**, so Brazilian and laid-back is it. Framed photos of Brazil line its white walls, Brazilian music plays softly and tables are simply set with oilcloth covers and fresh yellow primroses. A standout is the *feijoada*—the Brazilian national dish, a stew of black beans with pork, sausage and dried beef, served with rice (available on weekends only). There is also a wide variety of chicken and vegetarian dishes. Also try the homemade soups and desserts, among them caramel custard and guava paste. ~ 130 Jersey Street; 617-247-9508, fax 617-787-4357. BUDGET TO MODERATE.

The walls of **Bangkok Cuisine** look like a museum, lavishly covered with elaborate framed pictures of Thai motifs in gold leaf: a peacock, villagers with elephants, Buddhist figures. Warm orange lights and crystal-and-brass chandeliers add to the exotic flair. Entrées include deep-fried whole fish, hot and sour dishes, curry dishes, and rice and noodles. ~ 177-A Massachusetts Avenue; 617-262-5377, fax 617-247-1846. BUDGET TO MODERATE.

SHOPPING   The music of psychedelic '60s groups, '50s jazzmen and other performers of yesteryear rules at **Looney Tunes**, where you can buy used records on the cheap. ~ 1106 Boylston Street; 617-247-2238, fax 617-247-0821.

NIGHTLIFE   **Avalon**, one of the city's largest dance clubs, plays progressive and Top-40 sounds for avid dancers, and hosts names like Eric Clapton and The Artist Formerly Known as Prince. Closed Monday and Tuesday. Cover. ~ 15 Lansdowne Street; 617-262-2424.

Next door, one of the trendiest dance clubs is **Axis**, which features house and techno music. Sunday is gay night, though a mixed crowd turns out at both Axis and Avalon when the doors that separate the clubs are opened up. Closed Tuesday and Wednesday. Cover. Gay-friendly. ~ 13 Lansdowne Street; 617-262-2437.

The upscale **Karma Club** accommodates a number of musical tastes. On most nights, frenzied dance music pulsates through the club, where the sounds may be drum 'n' bass or acid house; international night is the draw on Tuesday. On most nights, you can fancy yourself a swinger with martini in hand while watching a Sinatraesque crooner in the Mambo Lounge. The dress code requires jackets for men and semi-formal attire for women. Cover. ~ 9 Lansdowne Street; 617-421-9595, fax 617-351-2562.

> Built around a beautiful flowered courtyard, the Isabella Stewart Gardner Museum offers weekly chamber music concerts from September through May.

A little farther out of the neighborhood are a couple more clubs. **The Paradise** draws SRO crowds for its national headliners who perform live rock music and dance. Cover. Closed Sunday. ~ 967 Commonwealth Avenue; 617-562-8800.

CLASSICAL MUSIC & THEATER Under the direction of Seiji Ozawa, the prestigious **Boston Symphony Orchestra** presents more than 250 concerts annually. ~ 301 Massachusetts Avenue; 617-266-1492.

The Symphony's **Boston Pops,** with the youthful Keith Lockhart as conductor, perform lighter favorites in spring and free outdoor summer concerts at the Hatch Shell on the Esplanade.

The **Handel and Haydn Society** is the country's oldest continuously active performing arts group, started in 1815. They perform instrumental and choral music, including Handel's *Messiah* at Christmas. ~ 300 Massachusetts Avenue; 617-266-3605, fax 617-266-4217.

The **Huntington Theatre Company,** Boston University's resident company, specializes in classics, comedies and musicals. No summer performances. ~ 264 Huntington Avenue; 617-266-7900, 617-266-0800.

The South End

Boston's largest neighborhood is also the least known. Like the Back Bay, it was built on filled land, preceding Back Bay by more than a decade. Victorian brick rowhouses rose apace as residences for the middle class and well-to-do. Today, the South End is listed on the National Register of Historic Places as the largest concentration of such houses in the United States.

After the panic of 1873, banks foreclosed on the area, and those who could afford to moved to Back Bay. The area was carved up into rooming houses and factories and became an immigrant ghetto of more than 40 nationalities, notably black, Syrian, Hispanic and Lebanese.

The South End languished for decades, but when Boston's economy rebounded in the 1960s, so did this neighborhood. Since 1965, an influx of middle-class professionals has renovated old rowhouses and partly gentrified the area. Not all of the South End has risen again, however, and there are still blighted, unsafe areas. But today the neighborhood is a vital center of creative activity, and many artists live here. Fashionable shops, restaurants and nightclubs line the main thoroughfares of Columbus Avenue and Tremont Street. The area along Columbus and Shawmut avenues between Massachusetts Avenue and Arlington Street is a largely gay neighborhood with many restaurants and nightclubs. For more information on this area, see "Boston Gay Scene" below.

SIGHTS

The South End stretches hundreds of blocks, bounded roughly by the Southeast Expressway, Herald Street, the tracks of the MBTA's Orange Line and Huntington Avenue. Although the South End is a massive area to explore on foot, annual house tours are given in October by the **South End Historical Society**. Admission. ~ 532 Massachusetts Avenue; 617-536-4445.

At the corner of Huntington Avenue and Massachusetts Avenue is the famous **Symphony Hall**. Designed in 1900, it's so acoustically perfect it's known worldwide as a "Stradivarius among halls." The Boston Symphony Orchestra celebrated its 100th anniversary here in 1981. Tours take place Monday through Friday. ~ 301 Massachusetts Avenue; 617-266-1492, 800-274-8499, fax 617-638-9436; www.bso.org.

Across the street is another handsome brick building. **Horticultural Hall** is the third home of the Massachusetts Horticultural Society, the oldest active incorporated society of its kind in America, founded in 1829. The society maintains the largest and finest horticultural library in the world. This 1901 Beaux-Arts building features limestone and terra cotta cornices and moldings ornately carved with fruits and garlands. Tours may be scheduled by appointment. ~ 300 Massachusetts Avenue; 617-536-9280, fax 617-262-8780; www.masshort.org.

The **First Church of Christ, Scientist** is the world headquarters of Christian Science, founded in 1879 by Mary Baker Eddy. The mother church is topped by an imposing dome and set in a brick pedestrian plaza with a reflecting pool designed by I. M. Pei. Take a walk through the echoing **Mapparium** in the Christian Science Monitor building, a unique 30-foot stained-glass globe with a footbridge through it, for a peek at how the world looked in 1935. Tours are available throughout the week and weekend; church services are also open to the public. ~ 175 Huntington Avenue; 617-450-2000, fax 617-450-3437.

The **Boston Center for the Arts** operates the Cyclorama, the center of South End arts activity. Built in 1884 to exhibit a huge cylindrical painting, *The Battle of Gettysburg* (now in Pennsylvania), it's also where Albert Champion developed the spark plug. Its large rotunda hosts art exhibits, plays, festivals and an annual antique show. ~ 539 Tremont Street; 617-426-5000, fax 617-426-5336; www.bcaonline.org.

Also part of the Boston Center for the Arts is the **Mills Gallery**, which specializes in exhibits by South End artists. These might include crafts, sculpture, oil paintings and gouache, and are always intriguing. Closed Monday and Tuesday. ~ 549 Tremont Street; 617-426-8835, fax 617-426-5336; www.bcaonline.org.

Once second in size only to the U.S. Capitol, the building that formerly housed the **Chickering Piano Factory**, now a craft guild, has been a Boston landmark since 1853. The pianos made here until 1929 were played not only in Victorian drawing rooms but in the concert halls of Europe and South America. Founder Jonas Chickering was said to be just like his pianos: "upright, grand and square." The building is now a living, work and exhibition space for artists and musicians. ~ 791 Tremont Street; 617-536-2622, fax 617-859-7794.

◄ HIDDEN

The **Berkeley Residence/YWCA** offers the most basic budget accommodations for women in the city. No men are allowed beyond the public areas. Rooms have twin beds with chenille spreads and floral decor, and bathrooms are down the hall. There are laundry facilities and a cafeteria. ~ 40 Berkeley Street; 617-482-8850, fax 617-482-9692. BUDGET TO MODERATE.

LODGING

Ever since yuppies began moving into the South End in the 1970s and 1980s, restaurants have been springing up left and right, from small inexpensive cafés to upscale eateries.

DINING

A popular, upscale eatery, **Icarus Restaurant** serves up contemporary American cuisine. There's a great bar to wet your palate, and appetizers to whet your appetite. Start with the parsnip soup or polenta with braised exotic mushrooms. Fare includes braised rabbit with porcini, leeks and red wine, pepper-crusted venison steak with pomegranate sauce, and halibut filet with stuffed lobster tail. Dinner only. ~ 3 Appleton Street; 617-426-1790, fax 617-426-2150. MODERATE TO DELUXE.

Don't look for silverware at **Addis Red Sea Ethiopian Restaurant**, the nation's first authentic Ethiopian restaurant. A very African decor features authentic basketweave straw tables in a bright geometric pattern, low, carved wooden chairs, and paintings of African villagers. Platters of food cover the entire table surface. Ethiopian *injera* bread is served with chicken, lamb, beef and vegetarian dishes. The chef uses all-natural herbs and spices. ~ 544 Tremont Street; 617-426-8727, fax 617-695-3677. MODERATE.

◄ HIDDEN

The heavenly scent of freshly baked pastries, breads, cakes and pies are the draw at **Garden of Eden**. This bakery/café was voted the Best of Boston neighborhood sandwich shop, serving scrumptious sandwiches (including the "Garden Of Eden" vege-tarian sandwich) on copper-topped café tables. The full gourmet market proffers unique cheeses and pâté. ~ 571 Tremont Street; 617-247-8377, fax 617-247-8493. BUDGET.

Decorated in Christmas kitsch, Elvis busts and retro parapher-nalia, the **Deluxe Café and Lounge** features a cheap, eclectic and tasty assortment of pub grub until 11:30 every night. Try the grilled chicken sandwich with homemade chutney, the shepherd's pie or the hot chili. Closed Sunday. ~ 100 Chandler Street; 617-338-5258. BUDGET TO MODERATE.

One of the South End's favorite breakfast and lunch hangouts is **Charlie's Sandwich Shoppe**. The walls are lined with photo-graphs of satisfied patrons—local politicians, famous actors and jazz greats of decades past. It's a delightful place for home-baked muffins, pancakes, sandwiches, burgers and conviviality, since you'll be sharing a table. No dinner. Closed Sunday. ~ 429 Columbus Avenue; 617-536-7669. BUDGET.

The charming **Claremont Cafe** is a cozy neighborhood estab-lishment featuring outstanding fare blending South American and Mediterranean cuisine. Entrées may include grilled marinated lamb chop with Tunisian coriander eggplant purée and braised cod with kalamata olives. The Claremont is also famous for Sunday brunch. They have a main dining room and a separate bakery store. Closed Sunday evening and Monday. ~ 535 Colum-bus Avenue; 617-247-9001, fax 617-437-0062. MODERATE.

SHOPPING   You can find things to decorate your nest with at **Fresh Eggs**, a home-furnishings store that carries furniture and kitchen appli-ances. In addition, it proffers high-end gifts handcrafted by local artists. Closed Monday. ~ 58 Clarendon Street; 617-247-8150.

Candle holders, picture frames, journals and other familiar gift items receive inventive makeovers at **Tommy Tish**. Even the gift bags and wrapping paper are flecked with dried flowers. ~ 102 Waltham Street; phone/fax 617-482-1111.

HIDDEN ►   Right next door is **Bibelot**, an antique store stocked with decorative accessories, collectibles and handmade arts and crafts. Bring home one of many Italian vases from the '20s or '30s. ~ 106 Waltham Street; 617-426-8477.

NIGHTLIFE   **Wally's Café** is everything that an old-time jazz club should be—small, smoky, dark and host to lots of talented musicians, in-cluding students from the Berklee School of Music, which is just a few blocks away. ~ 427 Massachusetts Avenue; 617-424-1408.

At the **Deluxe Café and Lounge** the cool crowd consists of rockers and artists, both gay and straight. The decor is funky, the drinks are cheap and the music ranges from Frank Sinatra to the Sex Pistols. Closed Sunday. ~ 100 Chandler Street; 617-338-5258.

Boston's gay community is continually growing, and its collection of gay spots is always expanding. **Boston Gay Scene** While gay activities and nightlife are found throughout Boston and Cambridge, the highest concentration is found in several blocks of the South End, one of the city's most diverse neighborhoods. Bounded by Columbus and Shawmut avenues, and Arlington Street and Massachusetts Avenue, this area is home to an array of gay restaurants, cafés, bars and nightclubs.

If this part of the South End reminds you of Beacon Hill, it's no wonder. The same hidden gardens and black iron grillwork decorate many facades. The oval-shaped **Union Park** resembles Beacon Hill's Louisburg Square. **West Rutland Square**, too, is a lovely little landscaped patch.

SIGHTS

If you're interested in learning more about Boston's gay history, stop by **Glad Day Bookshop** in the Back Bay. This comprehensive gay and lesbian bookstore also hosts community events and readings. ~ 673 Boylston Street; 617-267-3010, fax 617-267-5474; www.gladday.com.

At the very northeast corner of the South End lies **Bay Village**, which used to be known as South Cove. This cluster of narrow little streets displays the most charmingly antique character in the area. Gaslights stand on the sidewalks outside these Victorian rowhouses decorated with black shutters and windowboxes, black iron grilled doorways and hidden, sunken gardens in backyards. ~ Bordered by Arlington, Tremont and Stuart streets and Charles Street South.

Greater Boston Hospitality is a reservation service with dozens of bed-and-breakfast listings. It can help you find the perfect stay in Boston, many located in Back Bay, Beacon Hill and Cambridge. ~ P.O. Box 1142, Brookline, MA 02146; 617-277-5430, fax 617-277-5430; www.bostonbedandbreakfast.com, e-mail info@bostonbedandbreakfast.com. BUDGET TO MODERATE.

LODGING

A pretty streetside patio and stately brownstone facade greet guests of the **Newbury Guest House**. Besides its superb location on fashionable Newbury Street, the restored 1882 inn offers 32 guest rooms with pine floors, high ceilings and reproduction Victorian furnishings. Some have bay windows, and all have private baths, televisions and telephones—rarities in a small inn. A continental breakfast included in the room rate. ~ 261 Newbury Street; 617-437-7666, 800-437-7668, fax 617-262-4243. DELUXE TO ULTRA-DELUXE.

Popular with gays, **463 Beacon Street Guest House** also draws a mixed clientele. Twenty rooms, all with a microwave and refrigerator, make this turn-of-the-20th-century brownstone an excellent value. The five-story walk-up also offers short-term lodging in Back Bay, business services and a laundry. ~ 463 Beacon Street; 617-536-1302, fax 617-247-8876. MODERATE TO DELUXE.

The circa-1860 **Oasis** caters to a gay crowd but draws a mixed clientele. Some of its 16 rooms feature antiques and queen-sized beds. Located on a quiet street, the inn serves continental breakfast in the living room. ~ 22 Edgerly Road; 617-267-2262, fax 617-267-1920; www.oasisgh.com. MODERATE.

Although not everything matches, the tub may be chipped and hallways are narrow and dark, the **Chandler Inn** offers 56 rooms. Rooms are clean and appointed decently enough, in blues and greens and oak furniture, with all the basic amenities. The bar is a popular gay hangout in the South End. ~ 26 Chandler Street; 617-482-3450, 800-842-3450, fax 617-542-3428; www.chandlerinn.com. MODERATE.

DINING

The lesbian-owned **On the Park** is a cozy, casual American bistro that attracts both gay and straight diners with its tasty preparations of beef, seafood and poultry. Game hen stuffed with wild rice and apples, braised veal shank and mako shark are among the dishes to choose from. There's also a different vegetarian lasagna on the menu each week. Dinner only; brunch on the weekends. Closed Monday. ~ 1 Union Park; phone/fax 617-426-0862. MODERATE.

Geoffrey's Café & Bar looks like a Parisian-style bistro with crimson walls, oversized French paintings and large picture windows overlooking the street below. Breakfast is served daily until 3 p.m., and there's a wide selection of gourmet salads, sandwiches and tapas. ~ 578 Tremont Street; 617-266-1122. BUDGET TO MODERATE.

A local favorite for fresh, tasty food is the always-crowded **Jae's Café and Grill**. The health-conscious menu travels the Far East with selections from Korea, Japan and Thailand. Try the *karbi* (marinated barbecued beef spareribs), crispy *pad thai* noodles or a sampling of tidbits from the downstairs sushi bar. ~ 520 Columbus Avenue; 617-421-9405, fax 617-247-6140. MODERATE TO DELUXE.

Kick back in one of the booths at **Mario's**, a gay restaurant featuring inexpensive Northern Italian food. Steak and seafood specials are also served. ~ 69 Church Street; 617-423-6969, fax 617-542-2784. MODERATE.

Gays and straights alike head over to **224 Boston Street** to nosh on sandwiches, pasta, pizettas and salads in a lively setting. Entrées at this gay-owned restaurant include curried chicken stew; a combination of shrimp sausage, swordfish steak and salmon filet with shrimp beurre blanc; and honey-soy duck confit with butternut squash and smoked duck sausage. Dinner only.

~ 224 Boston Street, Dorchester; 617-265-1217, fax 617-825-4738. MODERATE.

At the top of the gay brunch scene is **Appetito**. The Sunday buffet includes eggs Benedict, fresh muffins, perfectly seasoned homefries, and cocktails. Reservations recommended. ~ 1 Appleton Street; 617-338-6777, fax 617-338-1962. MODERATE.

The **Glad Day Bookshop** in the Back Bay stocks an extensive selection of gay and lesbian literature, along with travel guides, magazines and music. ~ 673 Boylston Street; 617-267-3010; www.gladday.com.

SHOPPING

We Think the World of You is a great bookstore that carries mostly gay and lesbian titles. Come in to browse or pick up gift items like cards and music. ~ 540 Tremont Street; 617-423-1965, 617-574-5000, fax 617-350-0083.

For deejay-generated disco music in the theater district, gays head to **Chaps**. Women are also welcome at this high-energy club, which includes a separate lounge off the throbbing dancefloor. Cover. ~ 100 Warrenton Street; 617-695-9500.

NIGHTLIFE

The leather-and-Levis crowd likes to cruise down to **The Boston Ramrod**. There's a special two-stepping night at this primarily gay bar that also offers pool. If leather is not your scene, you can go dancing at **Machine**, which attracts all types. Cover Sunday. ~ 1254 Boylston Street; 617-266-2986.

Club Café, an avant-garde club, occasionally sponsors nationally known jazz musicians, attracting a gay and straight crowd. ~ 209 Columbus Avenue; 617-536-0972.

Fritz, located in the Chandler Inn, is a casual gay sports bar that's usually crowded with regulars. ~ 26 Chandler Street; 617-482-4428.

A gay video bar catering mostly to men, the **Luxor** specializes in comedy, classic Hollywood and alternative films. The bar is split into different rooms that you can choose from depending on what you like: dancing, talking or making out. ~ 69 Church Street; 617-423-6969.

You'll find buff bartenders, the latest deejay sounds and two dancefloors pulsating with sculpted bodies gleaming with sweat at **Buzz**, Boston's trendiest gay club. It's men-only on Saturday night, with a mixed crowd on Thursday and Friday. ~ 67 Stewart Street; 617-267-8969.

Jacque's has something for everyone, as long as you enjoy female impersonators mixed with your live rock. The clientele here is diverse—there are gay, straight and lesbian couples and groups of gawkers. Cover. ~ 79 Broadway, Bay Village; 617-426-8902.

▼ ▼ ▼ ▼ ▼ ▼ ▼ ▼ ▼ ▼
South Boston

Not to be confused with the South End, South Boston lies directly east of it. Despite its name, South Boston juts farther east into the Atlantic than any other point in the city, cut off from Boston by the Southeast Expressway and the Fort Point Channel. Everyone here calls it "Southie," especially the Irish who call it home.

The Irish poured into South Boston in the early 19th century, attracted by the work opportunities of the glass, iron and shipping industries. They stayed, and today this is the most predominantly Irish community in Boston, evidenced by the riotous St. Patrick's Day parade. The Irish are fiercely proud of their L Street Brownies, a local swim club that has won national publicity for swimming every day, even in January.

Though South Boston has historically been a conservative, family-oriented neighborhood, there has been a recent influx of young, single professionals to the area. Close to downtown with reasonably priced housing, this migration trend is sure to continue.

SIGHTS

Ideally positioned for shipping, the peninsula is lined with commercial fishing and shipping piers. The **Fish Piers**, near the World Trade Center and Jimmy's Harborside on Northern Avenue, are a lively scene at dawn, when the fishing boats return to port to unload their catch. The fresh catch is sold at a lively auction right off the boats to retailers.

Three bridges link South Boston with downtown: the Summer Street Bridge, the Northern Avenue Bridge and the Congress Street Bridge, with its Chinese lantern–style, wrought-iron lamps.

When you cross the Congress Street Bridge, you may not quite believe your eyes, but the first thing you'll see is a giant milk bottle. The 30-foot **Hood Milk Bottle** was a vintage lunch stand from the 1930s and sells snacks again today.

The Hood Milk Bottle signals the beginning of Museum Wharf, a mini-park of several museums. The Children's Museum is housed in a brick building, a former wool warehouse whose large windows and wool bays lend themselves nicely to exhibit spaces.

You don't have to be a kid to enjoy the **Children's Museum**, a gigantic toy box filled with four floors of hands-on fun where you can make giant bubbles or participate in a play production at the interactive theater. There's also a water play exhibit that re-creates the Fort Point Channel. Closed Monday from September through June. Admission. ~ 300 Congress Street; 617-426-6500, fax 617-426-1944; www.kidsorg.com.

Also on Museum Wharf is the **Boston Tea Party Ship & Museum**, a floating museum where you can board a two-masted brig and throw your own chest of tea into the harbor (it'll be retrieved by an attached rope for another visitor to heave). Displays are lively and informative, explaining the events surrounding the 1773 dumping of 342 chests of tea overboard, a tax protest that was one of many spurs to the American Revolution. Closed January and February. Admission. ~ Congress Street Bridge; 617-338-1773, fax 617-338-1974; www.historictours.com.

A spanking white building with a flag-lined boulevard, the **World Trade Center** replaced the drab old Commonwealth Exhibition Hall in the 1980s. It hosts many of Boston's biggest trade shows, including the Boston Boat Show. ~ 164 Northern Avenue; 617-385-5000, fax 617-385-5166; www.wtcb.com.

Four kinds of granite decorate the exterior of the **Boston Design Center**, New England's major design center. Architects and designers come here from miles away to search out the latest and chicest in interior designs. Outside the building stands an imposing cast of Auguste Rodin's sculpture *Cybèle*. Closed Saturday and Sunday. ~ 1 Design Center Place; 617-338-5062, fax 617-482-8449.

The work of painters, photographers, sculptors and others is on view at the **Fort Point Artists' Community Gallery**. You can also visit individual artists' studios by appointment. Look for them along the 200 to 300 blocks on Summer Street. Many gallery showings are free and open to the public. Call for showings and times. Closed Sunday. ~ 300 Summer Street; 617-423-4299.

> More artists live in the old high-ceilinged, industrial buildings of the Fort Point Channel area than anywhere else in the city.

Dorchester Heights Monument is where George Washington set up his guns and forced the British to evacuate Boston in 1776, never to return. The British were astounded to see these guns, which had been dragged 300 miles by oxen from Fort Ticonderoga. A 215-foot marble tower marks the spot. ~ 456 West 4th Street; 617-242-5642, fax 617-367-3539.

Out at the very tip of South Boston, **Castle Island** is a windswept place of green lawns and high granite ramparts, a fine spot for picnicking and exploring. A series of eight forts has stood here since 1634, making it the oldest continuously fortified site in North America. The island was held by the British during the Revolution until Washington forced them out, from his vantage point at Dorchester Heights. The current fort, the star-shaped **Fort Independence**, was built in 1851. ~ End of Day Boulevard.

On a peninsula just south of South Boston lies **Dorchester**, once the home of the country's oldest chocolate manufacturer, the Walter Baker Chocolate Factory, founded in 1780. Today Dorchester is a quiet, residential area known for its characteristic three-story houses called triple deckers.

Don't miss the **John F. Kennedy Library and Museum**, a stirring place to visit both inside and out. In a parklike setting by the ocean that JFK loved so well, the striking, glass-walled building was designed by I. M. Pei. The museum houses JFK's papers, photographs, letters and speeches, and personal memorabilia such as his desk and rocking chair, as well as an extensive exhibit on the former first lady, Jacqueline Kennedy. Also housed here are Ernest Hemingway's papers, which may be viewed by appointment. Admission. ~ Columbia Point, Dorchester; 617-929-4523, fax 617-929-4547.

The **Franklin Park Zoo**, once rated one of the country's ten worst zoos by *Parade* magazine, has made some dramatic improvements. The most impressive is an African Tropical Forest that opened in 1989. Inside the 75-foot-high bubble live tropical birds, antelopes, a pygmy hippo and gorillas, among other tropical denizens. You may also see snow leopards, lions and the Bongo Congo exhibit, as well as an exotic butterfly tent. Admission. ~ 1 Franklin Park Road, Dorchester; 617-541-5466, fax 617-989-2025; www.zoonewengland.com.

DINING

As you walk east on Northern Avenue, it becomes the Fish Pier, a crowded place of fish-processing plants and wharves. Not surprisingly, the Fish Pier is home to a spate of seafood restaurants, some of them among the city's finest.

Located right on the Fish Pier, two of Boston's most famous restaurants, Jimmy's Harborside and Anthony's Pier 4, have waged a decades-long battle for supremacy in harborside seafood dining. Both eateries offer a long list of fresh fish, from Boston scrod to steamed, boiled or baked lobster, as well as floor-to-ceiling windows with smashing views of Boston Harbor.

Albanian immigrant Anthony Athanas started life in Boston as a shoeshine boy and built the reputation of his **Anthony's Pier 4** with backbreaking work. The smiling Anthony has posed with Liz Taylor, Gregory Peck and Richard Nixon, whose photos gaze down from the walls. Despite its fame, Anthony's has its detractors, who say the seafood doesn't live up to its reputation, the dining halls process guests like a factory and the wait for a table is too long. Still, Anthony's has the largest wine list in Boston, and there is outdoor seaside dining on awninged terraces. ~ 140 Northern Avenue; 617-482-6262, fax 617-426-2324. MODERATE TO ULTRA-DELUXE.

We much prefer **Jimmy's Harborside**, founded in 1924 by Greek immigrant Jimmy Doulos, the "Chowder King," whose first customers were fishermen at a nine-stool cafeteria. Since then, President John F. Kennedy, Bobby Kennedy, Tip O'Neill and Bob Hope have dined here, leaving their autographed photos on the wall. The seafood here is served in a nautical decor where the bar is a boat and waiters wear gold-braided blue jackets. ~ 242 Northern Avenue; 617-423-1000, fax 617-451-0669. DELUXE TO ULTRA-DELUXE.

The Daily Catch helped pioneer the open kitchen. Its Sicilian menu offers more than a dozen fresh New England fishes and shellfish, as well as black pastas made with squid ink. Bare wood tables and paper placemats suit the Fish Pier's working-class ambience. The restaurant also has locations in the North End and Brookline. ~ 261 Northern Avenue; 617-338-3093. MODERATE TO DELUXE.

Largely undiscovered, the **International Food Pavilion** upstairs at the World Trade Center is one of the least expensive places to eat with a view in Boston. Grab a sandwich or slice of pizza to eat at the white tables overlooking the harbor. Breakfast and lunch. ~ 164 Northern Avenue; 617-385-5000. BUDGET.

◄ HIDDEN

The **No-Name Restaurant** not only has no name, it has no decor either. Famed for the freshness of its fish bought right off the boats, the No-Name always has long lines. ~ 15½ Fish Pier; 617-338-7539. BUDGET TO MODERATE.

Charlestown

▼▼▼▼▼▼▼▼▼

Across the river but still considered part of Boston, Charlestown is an area that has become increasingly popular among the yuppie set. This is the oldest part of town. It was founded in 1630 by a small band of Puritans who later abandoned it, moving across the river to Boston. Much of Charlestown was destroyed by the British in the Battle of Bunker Hill, so few 18th-century houses stand today.

SIGHTS

A walk over the river on the Charlestown Bridge brings you to the Charlestown Navy Yard, the berth of the **U.S.S. Constitution**, the oldest commissioned vessel in the world. It won its nickname of Old Ironsides when British cannon fire bounced off its sturdy oak hull in the War of 1812. While you can tour the decks and down below, lines are always long; try at lunchtime. ~ 617-242-5670.

Across the yard from Old Ironsides is the **Constitution Museum**, which houses exhibits on Old Ironsides' many voyages and victories, memorabilia and paintings. ~ Charlestown Navy Yard, Building 22; 617-426-1812, fax 617-242-0496.

◆◆◆◆◆◆◆◆◆◆◆◆◆◆◆◆◆◆◆◆

A handsome black-and-white frigate, the *Constitution* once required 400 sailors to hoist its sails.

Nearby is the **Commandant's House**, a handsome Federal-style brick mansion where Navy officers lived. ~ Charlestown Navy Yard.

The **Bunker Hill Monument** actually stands atop Breed's Hill, where the Battle of Bunker Hill was in fact fought. This encounter became legend with the words of Colonel William Prescott to his ammunition-short troops: "Don't fire until you see the whites of their eyes." The cornerstone of the 220-foot Egyptian Revival granite obelisk was laid in 1825 by General Lafayette, with Daniel Webster orating. There are 294 steps to the observatory, which affords a magnificent view of the city and the harbor. ~ 43 Monument Square; 617-242-5641, fax 617-241-5797.

Companion exhibits at the **Bunker Hill Pavilion** include a multimedia slide show with 14 screens re-enacting the battle. Admission. Closed mid-December through March. ~ 55 Constitution Road; 617-241-7575.

DINING   Mention Charlestown to a Bostonian and chances are you'll find yourself at **Olive's**. The food is New England with northern Italian and Mediterranean twists. Reservations are not taken for groups of fewer than six, so expect to wait for a table. Dinner only. Closed Sunday. ~ 10 City Square; 617-242-1999, fax 617-241-8497. MODERATE.

The **Warren Tavern** dates to 1780, and the small, clapboarded house with gaslights was patronized by Paul Revere and George Washington. The inside appears dark and Colonial, with a heavy beamed ceiling, wood planked floors, candelabra wall sconces, punched-tin lights and a roaring fire. The solid fare includes steaks, seafood and a tavern burger with fries. ~ 2 Pleasant Street; 617-241-8142. BUDGET TO MODERATE.

▼▼▼▼▼▼▼▼▼▼▼▼
Cambridge

Everyone thinks of Cambridge and Boston together, as if they were two sides of the same coin. While Cambridge is actually a separate city, it lies directly across the Charles River from Boston, and the lives of the two cities are very much entwined, linked by a series of foot and vehicular bridges.

Cambridge was founded in 1630, originally named New Towne, and was the colony's first capital. In 1638, two years after the founding of Harvard, the nation's oldest university, the city was renamed after the English university town where many Boston settlers had been educated.

Today Cambridge is still very much an intellectual center, home to Nobel Prize winners, ground-breaking scientists and famous writers, among them John Kenneth Galbraith, David Mamet and Anne Bernays. Cambridge became the heart of what came to be nicknamed "Silicon Valley East" when high-tech companies blossomed here during the 1960s and 1970s, as well as in outlying towns scattered along the Route 128 beltway. These think tanks and computer companies fueled a boom in the Massachusetts economy and its population.

Not all of Cambridge is serious or intellectual. It's given life and vitality by throngs of young students, ragtag protesters handing out leaflets, cult followers and street musicians.

SIGHTS   The heartbeat of Cambridge is **Harvard Square**, where life revolves around the many bookstores, coffeeshops, boutiques and newsstands. In the very center stands the **Out of Town Newspapers** kiosk, a Harvard Square landmark for many years, famous for its thousands of national and foreign periodicals. ~ 617-354-7777, fax 617-520-5005.

Right next to it you'll find the **Cambridge Office for Tourism**, which dispenses tourist information and walking maps. ~ 617-497-1630.

No one would come to Cambridge without taking a walk through **Harvard Yard**. A stroll of the yard's winding paths, stately trees, grassy quadrangles and handsome brick buildings is a walk through a long history of higher education. Six U.S. presidents have graduated from Harvard.

Enter the main gate by crossing Massachusetts Avenue. On the right, you'll see **Massachusetts Hall**, built in 1718, the college's oldest remaining hall. In the quadrangle of the historic Old Yard, on the left, tucked between Hollis and Stoughton Halls, is a little jewel of a chapel. **Holden Chapel**, built in 1742, has blue gables decorated with scrolled white baroque cornices, ahead of its time in its ornateness.

Cambridge

POINTS OF INTEREST
- **A** Busch-Reisinger Museum/ Fogg Art Museum
- **B** Christ Church Episcopal
- **C** Harvard Lampoon Castle
- **D** Harvard Museum of Natural History
- **E** Harvard Square
- **F** Harvard Yard
- **G** Hi-Rise Pie Co.
- **H** Holden Chapel
- **I** Longfellow National Historic Site
- **J** Massachusetts Hall
- **K** Memorial Chapel
- **L** Sackler Museum
- **M** Widener Library

Along the diagonal path that cuts across Old Yard is the **Statue of John Harvard** by Daniel Chester French, called the statue of the "three lies." Besides giving the wrong date for Harvard's founding, the statue is actually not of John Harvard at all, but of a student model instead; and John Harvard is not the college's founder but its first great benefactor.

Harvard's famed **Widener Library** stands in the New Yard, a massive building with a wide staircase and a pillared portico. With nearly three million books, Widener ranks as the third largest library in the United States, second only to the Library of Congress and the New York Public Library. Unfortunately, Widener is not open to the public, but its steps are still a popular spot for taking pictures.

Straight across from it is the **Memorial Chapel**, built in 1931 with a Bulfinch-style steeple in memory of the young men of Harvard who died in World War I. Their names are engraved on the walls.

Harvard is also home to a spate of museums known the world over for their esoteric collections, including three art museums (one fee is good for admission to all three museums; tours are offered Monday through Friday):

The **Busch-Reisinger Museum** is noted for central and northern European works of art from the late 19th and 20th centuries. Admission. ~ 32 Quincy Street; 617-495-9400.

The **Fogg Art Museum** showcases European and American art, with a notable impressionist collection. Admission. ~ 32 Quincy Street; 617-495-9400.

Ancient, Asian and Islamic art are the specialties at the **Sackler Museum**. Admission. ~ 485 Broadway at Quincy Street; 617-495-9400.

The Harvard Museum of Cultural and Natural History consists of four natural history museums. The **Harvard Museum of Natural History** holds the internationally famed handmade Glass Flowers, showcasing more than 700 species. At the **Museum of Comparative Zoology**, the development of animal life is traced from fossils to modern man. The **Mineralogical and Geological Museum** has a collection of rocks and minerals, including a 3040-carat topaz. ~ 26 Oxford Street; 617-495-3045. The **Peabody Museum of Archaeology** displays artifacts from the world over, including Mayan and American Indian relics. Admission. ~ 11 Divinity Drive; 617-495-3248.

Under the spreading chestnut tree/ The village smithy stands;/ The smith a mighty man is he/ With large and sinewy hands. These words from Longfellow's famous poem "The Village Blacksmith" were written about a real blacksmith who lived in a house in Boston built in 1811. It's now the **Hi-Rise Pie Co.** with an outdoor café in warm weather and upstairs seating in cooler weather.

Old World pastries and cakes are made here the same way they have been for decades. Brunch, lunch, and afternoon tea are served. Closed Sunday. ~ 56 Brattle Street; 617-492-3003.

Harvard Lampoon Castle, a funny-looking building with a round brick turret and a door painted bright red, yellow and purple, befits its occupants: the publishers of Harvard's longstanding satirical magazine, the *Harvard Lampoon*. ~ 57 Mt. Auburn Street at Bow Street.

Christ Church Episcopal, a simple gray-and-white structure with a squat steeple, is Cambridge's oldest church. George and Martha Washington worshipped here on New Year's Eve 1775. ~ Zero Garden Street; 617-876-0200; www.cccambridge.com.

Under an elm tree on the grassy **Cambridge Common**, General Washington took command of the Continental Army in 1775. A plaque and monument to Washington mark this spot. Nearby are three old black cannons, abandoned by the British at Fort Independence when they evacuated in 1776. ~ Massachusetts Avenue and Garden Street.

The **Longfellow National Historic Site** is where poet Henry Wadsworth Longfellow lived for 45 years and wrote most of his famous works. Painted a cheery yellow and accented with black shutters, the house was built in 1759 for a well-to-do Tory and years later was used by Washington as his headquarters during the siege of Boston. The house has many fine Victorian furnishings, among them Longfellow's desk, quill pen and inkstand. Closed Monday and Tuesday; closed mid-December to mid-March. The site will be closed to the public until early 2001. Admission. ~ 105 Brattle Street; 617-876-4491, fax 617-497-8718.

> The Longfellow National Historic Site contains Henry Wadsworth Longfellow's personal 10,000-book library and his 600,000-piece collection of family papers.

A handsome, slate-blue Georgian house with black shutters, the **Hooper-Lee-Nichols House** was built by a physician named Richard Hooper. Later it was the home of Joseph Lee, a founder of Christ Church, and then the home of George Nichols. Open Tuesday and Thursday. Admission. ~ 159 Brattle Street; 617-547-4252, fax 617-661-1623.

The western end of Brattle Street is called **Tory Row** because of the lovely homes built there by wealthy Tories in the 18th century. A fine example is at Number 175, the **Ruggles Fayerweather House**, first the home of Tory George Ruggles, later of patriot Thomas Fayerweather. The house served as an American hospital after the Battle of Bunker Hill.

Just down the street sits **Radcliffe College**, once a women's branch of Harvard but now fully integrated into the university. The gates to **Radcliffe Yard** are entered off Brattle Street, between James Street and Appian Way. As you walk the path, the four graceful brick main buildings of the campus will be in a semicircle to your right. First is **Fay House**, a mansion built in 1807, the administrative center. Next you'll find **Hemenway Gymnasium**, which houses a research center that studies women in society. Third is **Agassiz House**, fronted by white classical pillars, which holds a theater, ballroom and arts office. Last is the college's renowned **Schlesinger Library**, which contains an outstanding collection of books and manuscripts on the history of women in America, including papers of Susan B. Anthony, Julia Ward Howe and Elizabeth Cady Stanton.

A few miles east of Harvard Square lies Cambridge's other famous college, the **Massachusetts Institute of Technology** (M.I.T.). Offering a premier education in engineering and technology since 1865, M.I.T. draws students from all over the world, including China, Japan and Vietnam. In distinct contrast to the hallowed ways of Harvard, M.I.T. students are famed for their witty irreverence and contests they engage in to outdo each other in intellectual pranks. One of their episodes involved placing a car on top of a campus building. Fittingly, the campus looks modern and high tech, with geometrical buildings designed by Eero Saarinen.

LODGING   Set in an office tower and shopping complex, the 296-room **Charles Hotel** is just steps away from Harvard Square. Rooms are styled in grays and blues, with a Shaker-style bed, upholstered loveseat and armchair, and oak armoire; many have views of the river. The gray-tiled bath has a second phone and TV and pink-and-gray marble counters. There are three restaurants and one of the city's best jazz bars, as well as a health spa. ~ 1 Bennett Street at Eliot Street; 617-864-1200, 800-882-1818, fax 617-864-5715; www.preferredhotels.com. ULTRA-DELUXE.

A convenient place to stay in Cambridge is the **Harvard Square Hotel**. Although some rooms are on the smallish side, this 73-room private hotel has nicely appointed digs with contemporary furniture and floral spreads. ~ 110 Mt. Auburn Street; 617-864-5200, 800-458-5886, fax 617-864-2409; www.theinnatharvard.com. DELUXE TO ULTRA-DELUXE.

The **Inn at Harvard** is wonderfully situated only a couple blocks from Harvard Square. The label "inn" seems a little inappropriate, however, since it's more of a standard hotel (in fact, it's a Doubletree property). Even so, it has its charms; there's a wonderful atrium lobby area that's four stories high, open to balconies and guest rooms, very much like a Renaissance palazzo. The 113 rooms are well appointed with cherry furnishings and original artwork from the Harvard Fogg Museum. ~ 1201 Massachusetts Avenue; 617-491-2222, 800-458-5886, fax 617-491-6520; www.theinnatharvard.com. ULTRA-DELUXE.

Some of the least expensive, albeit plainest, accommodations are to be had at the **Irving House** near Harvard Square. This woodframe walk-up offers 44 plain but clean rooms. Your best bets are the top floor units featuring skylights, private baths and wall-to-wall carpets. ~ 24 Irving Street; 617-547-4600, 800-854-8249, fax 617-576-2814. DELUXE.

The stepped, pyramidal walls of the **Hyatt Regency Cambridge** sit right on the banks of the Charles River, offering splendid views of the Boston skyline from many rooms. The 14-story atrium lobby has a semitropical feeling, from the Australian finches in a glass cage to a large fountain and towering potted plants and trees. The 467-room hotel has two restaurants, a lap pool and a health club with sauna, whirlpool and steam bath. The fair-sized rooms have natural woods, contemporary furnishings and carpeting, plus marble vanities in the bathroom. ~ 575 Memorial Drive; 617-492-1234, 800-233-1234, fax 617-491-6906; www. hyatt.com. DELUXE TO ULTRA-DELUXE.

A 20-minute walk from Harvard Square, **A Cambridge House Bed & Breakfast Inn** is a special place to stay. A private home built in 1892 with a wide pillared porch, it's listed on the National Historic Register. Beautifully restored and richly furnished with floral print fabrics, patterned wallpapers, period antiques and oriental rugs, the living room, den and dining room offer guests luxurious spaces. Each of the 16 rooms is individually decorated with antiques; one room has a canopied bed with a white lace duvet and a working fireplace. No children under seven. ~ 2218 Massachusetts Avenue; 617-491-6300, 800-232-9989, fax 617-868-2848; www.acambridgehouse.com. DELUXE TO ULTRA-DELUXE.

◄ HIDDEN

DINING

A retrofit, '50s-style decor of diner stools, neon and a black-and-white-tiled floor enlivens the **East Coast Grill & Raw Bar**. The Southern grilled ribs, pork and chicken are served with coleslaw, baked beans, corn bread and watermelon, and hot drinks to match: blue, green and gold margaritas. Grilled seafood with a tropical twist are other specialties. Dinner only except for Sunday brunch. ~ 1271 Cambridge Street; 617-491-6568, fax 617-868-4278. MODERATE TO DELUXE.

It would be hard to find a friendlier place than the **Casa Portugal**, one of only a handful of Boston Portuguese restaurants. Imbibe the Latin mood set by black iron lanterns, red-vested waiters and folk-art murals. *Chourico* arrives in a small, flaming grill, followed by spicy dinners of marinated pork cubes with potatoes or mussels, *linguiça* and onions, and squid stew, all served with thickly cut Portuguese french fries. There's a good selection of Portuguese wines and beers. ~ 1200 Cambridge Street; 617-491-8880, fax 617-354-6832. MODERATE.

At **Magnolia's Southern Cuisine**, chef John Silverman, a former student of Cajun master chef Paul Prudhomme, serves up Southern-inspired creations like fried green tomatoes with tomatillo salsa. You can also order blackened tuna, grilled duck with orange-chipotle sauce, sweet-potato pecan pie and praline parfait. Dinner only. Closed Sunday and Monday. ~ 1193 Cambridge Street; 617-576-1971, fax 617-876-1879. MODERATE.

The family-owned **La Groceria Italian Restaurant** looks like an Italian trattoria, with its striped awning, lattice ceiling and exposed brick wall. Famed for its hot antipasti and homemade pasta, La Groceria does old-style Northern Italian dishes such as lasagna, eggplant parmigiana and a seafood marinara that must be eaten to be believed. Its splendid dessert case offers cannoli, *tartufo* and *tiramisu*. Ask for the Godfather Family room, a beaded alcove, if it's available. ~ 853 Main Street; 617-876-4162, fax 617-864-9566. MODERATE.

African folk art hangs on the walls of the green, black and white dining room of **Asmara**, one of the many Ethiopian eateries in Greater Boston. Chicken, lamb, beef, fish and vegetarian entrées are to be eaten without silverware, in the Ethiopian manner. ~ 739 Massachusetts Avenue; 617-864-7447, fax 617-628-0663. BUDGET TO MODERATE.

Upstairs at the Pudding is located at the home of a Harvard institution: the Hasty Pudding Club and Theatricals. The stairway and dining room walls are a gallery of old theatrical posters from Pudding productions dating to the 1800s. Despite its emerald green walls and pink tablecloths, the dining room has the casual feel of a historic college dining room. Upstairs at the Pudding offers one of the top contemporary American dining experiences in Greater Boston. The à la carte menu selections include fresh local seafood, rack of lamb and venison. No lunch on Saturday, but there's Sunday brunch. ~ 10 Holyoke Street; 617-864-1933, fax 617-864-4925. DELUXE TO ULTRA-DELUXE.

HIDDEN ►

Run by a group of transplanted Londoners, **Shay's** is a fairly authentic English-style pub right in the heart of Crimson territory, with a good selection of international draft beers and pub grub. ~ 58 John F. Kennedy Street; 617-864-9161. BUDGET TO MODERATE.

The **Algiers Coffeehouse** is one of Cambridge's most Bohemian eateries. With its 50-foot domed ceiling, white stucco walls and copper embellishments, it feels like a cross between a Moroccan palace and a mosque. The menu has a Middle Eastern flavor, with lentil falafel and *baba ganoosh*. An immense lunch buffet is available Monday through Friday. There are 16 kinds of coffees and hot beverages, teas, iced drinks and Arabic pastries. ~ 40 Brattle Street; 617-492-1557. BUDGET.

The café/bar area and dining room of **Casablanca** sport murals of Rick, Ilsa and the rest of the "As Time Goes By" gang. The Mediterranean flavor continues with several exotic seating options in the café—the "love baskets" curve up to form a roof and a cocoon-like feeling. For the most part, the food is quite good. The lunch and dinner menus include lots of pasta, seafood, lamb and beef dishes. ~ 40 Brattle Street; 617-876-0999, fax 617-661-1373. MODERATE TO DELUXE.

Tucked a few blocks away from busy Harvard Square, **Café Pamplona** is a tiny basement-level café that serves Spanish dishes, pastries and strong coffee. During the summer, there are a few tables outside on a brick patio. ~ 12 Bow Street; no phone. BUDGET.   ◀ **HIDDEN**

Shades of the Southwest pervade the **Cottonwood Café**, decorated in green-and-purple neon and spiky cactus plants. A Southwestern-style menu includes snakebites, a deep-fried jalapeño pepper stuffed with jack cheese and shrimp, enchiladas, Rocky Mountain lamb, grilled chicken or shrimp in barbecue sauce, and Hill Country mixed grill. Patio seating is available in spring and summer. ~ 1815 Massachusetts Avenue; 617-661-7440, fax 617-661-1988. MODERATE TO DELUXE.

Just over the Cambridge-Somerville line, in a somewhat scruffy neighborhood, **Dalí** is as flamboyant as the artist it's named after. Who would've guessed that inside this vibrant blue building awaits the best Spanish food in the metropolitan area. The interior, radiant with red hues, is eccentrically decorated (the clothesline here is strung with undergarments donated by patrons). Make a meal of several different *tapas* and a bottle of hearty Iberian wine, or dig into entrées such as braised rabbit, *paella*, and shellfish stew. Dinner only. ~ 415 Washington Street, Somerville; 617-661-3254, fax 617-661-2813. MODERATE TO DELUXE.   ◀ **HIDDEN**

Harvard Square offers a wealth of shopping, from eclectic boutiques to upscale chain stores. Most notable in this intellectual bastion are the many bookshops surrounding the square. (See "Boston Area Bookstores" in this chapter.)   **SHOPPING**

The **Harvard Coop** (pronounce it as in "bird coop" to avoid student ridicule), formed in 1882 by several Harvard students as a cost-saving measure. The Coop holds three floors of men's and women's clothing, calculators, computer software, games and toys, and an astonishing selection of art prints, posters and books. ~ 1400 Massachusetts Avenue; 617-499-2000, fax 617-499-2016.

Colonial Drug is like a European perfume shop, with more than a thousand fragrances. Closed Sunday. ~ 49 Brattle Street; 617-864-2222.

The product of Cambridge-area artists is for sale at the **Cambridge Artists Cooperative**, a treasure trove of whimsical and beautiful things: handmade paper, fiber animals, *raku* bowls, quilts and hand-painted silk scarves. ~ 59-A Church Street; 617-868-4434, fax 617-868-5966.   ◀ **HIDDEN**

Jasmine/Sola Shoes/Sola Men is the best source for up-to-the-minute clothing and shoes that are wearable as well as fashionable. The accessories selection is extensive, too, particularly the wall stocked full of women's hosiery. They also have huge gift and jewelry departments. ~ 37-A Brattle Street; 617-354-6043.

Little Russia sells authentic Russian lacquered boxes and nesting dolls, jewelry, illustrated Russian fairy tales and other diverse tchotchkes. ~ 99 Mt. Auburn Street; 617-661-4928.

Over in the Porter Square area, you'll find **Iris Handmade Arts**, with all sorts of handmade items that are reasonably priced, unusual and very creative. The pieces are primarily by American artists. ~ 1782 Massachusetts Avenue; 617-661-1192.

NIGHTLIFE **Grendel's Den** is a comfy pub in the basement of Grendel's Restaurant, with brick walls, plank floors, and a bar you can really lean on. Sunday brunch is served on the outdoor patio in good weather. ~ 89 Winthrop Street; 617-491-1160.

Just a couple of blocks from Harvard, the original **House of Blues** looks more like a home on the bayou than a successful restaurant and club. Though several larger clubs in this chain have sprouted up all over the country, the Cambridge venue maintains its genuine Southern feel. The intimate stage offers national acts nightly. Reservations recommended. ~ 96 Winthrop Street; 617-491-2583, 617-497-2229 (box office), fax 617-876-8330.

One of the best jazz showcases in Greater Boston, the **Regatta-bar** offers an intimate jazz experience in a sophisticated club environment. The Regattabar regularly features such headliners as Wynton Marsalis, Herbie Hancock and Sonny Rollins. Cover. ~ Charles Hotel, 1 Bennett Street; 617-661-5000.

Ever since 1969, **Club Passim** has been going strong as a showcase for acoustic folk performers, including Tracy Chapman, Jimmy Buffett and David Bromberg, in a clean-cut, no-alcohol basement coffeehouse. Reservations for performances are suggested. Cover. ~ 47 Palmer Street; 617-492-7679.

Harvard's professional theater company, **American Repertory Theatre** produces world premieres and classical works, often taking a nontraditional approach. Their **New Stages** initiative mounts innovative productions in more intimate venues throughout Cambridge and Boston. ~ 64 Brattle Street; 617-547-8300.

The **Plough and Stars** is that rare thing, an uncorrupted working-class bar where habitués are logo-capped, burly types

EXTRA! EXTRA!

The **Out of Town Newspapers** kiosk has been declared a National Historic Landmark. Set right in the middle of Harvard Square and surrounded by traffic, the kiosk carries more than 3000 newspapers and magazines from all over the world. ~ Zero Harvard Square; 617-354-7777.

who belly up for live, boisterous entertainment. Black-and-white caricatures of neighborhood regulars line a whole wall. Cover on weekends. ~ 912 Massachusetts Avenue; 617-492-9653.

You never know what you'll hear on open-mike nights at the **Cantab Lounge**, but the rest of the time it's soulful rhythm-and-blues or bluegrass bands in a let-it-all-hang-out playpen. Cover on weekends. ~ 738 Massachusetts Avenue; 617-354-2685.

For the last several years, the coolest area in metro Boston has been in Cambridge—Harvard Square's scruffy cousin, Central Square, which is about two-thirds of the way down Massachusetts Avenue from Harvard to M.I.T. *The* nightspot in this haven of coolness is the **Middle East**, which has three venues for live music: Upstairs, Downstairs and the Corner. There's a mix of music and clientele here—from Michelle Shocked to Morphine, for example, as far as national acts go—and you're as likely to see underage high school (and college) kids as graying rock fans. Cover on most nights. ~ 472 Massachusetts Avenue; 617-864-3278; www.mideastclub.com, e-mail info@mideastclub.com.

An industrial dance club with a flair for art, **Man Ray/Campus** serves up progressive and alternative music. Wednesday is goth night and Thursday is gay night. Creative attire is encouraged, but when in doubt wear black. Cover. ~ 21 Brookline Street, in Central Square; 617-864-0400, fax 617-864-0401.

Named for the carved wooden amphibians overlooking the bar, **Toad** teems with music lovers of all ages enjoying nightly live bands. Aimee Mann has even been spotted in this tiny no-cover hotspot. ~ 1920 Massachusetts Avenue; 617-497-4950.

Pat Metheny got his start at **Ryles**, which features nightly jazz, R&B, Latin music and swing in a casual atmosphere. Closed Monday. Cover. ~ 212 Hampshire Street; 617-876-9330.

Scullers is in an unlikely place—on the second floor of the Doubletree Guest Suite Hotel in one of the uglier buildings along the Charles. Don't let the location or the architecture dissuade you—this classy jazz club (with a terrific view of the Charles, by the way) has big-name acts. Cover. ~ 400 Soldiers Field Road, Brighton; 617-783-0090, fax 617-783-0897.

▼▼▼▼▼▼▼▼▼▼▼
Outlying Areas

Although many tourists never leave the bounds of Boston and Cambridge, there is much of interest in the surrounding towns, many of which serve as bedroom communities for Boston workers and have rich Colonial histories, too.

SIGHTS

Due east of the city and bordering the Fenway, **Brookline** is one of the more prestigious and wealthy residential surrounding towns. The architect of Boston's Emerald Necklace lived and worked in a little house in a quiet Brookline neighborhood, where he often took his work outside to a landscaped hollow.

HIDDEN ▶ At the **Frederick Law Olmsted National Historic Site,** you can tour the house and grounds and see many of his landscape plans, memorabilia and photographs. Closed Monday through Thursday. ~ 99 Warren Street, Brookline; 617-566-1689; www. nps.gov/frlaw.

President John F. Kennedy was born in Brookline in 1917, in a little house now restored to its period appearance as the **John F. Kennedy National Historic Site.** The house holds much JFK memorabilia, including his crib and some of his toys. Closed Monday and Tuesday, and from late October through early May. Admission. ~ 83 Beals Street, Brookline; 617-566-7937; www. nps.gov/jofi.

South of Brookline lies Jamaica Plain, which is technically part of Boston. The star of Jamaica Plain is the **Arnold Arboretum of Harvard University,** one of the more remarkable green strands in Boston's Emerald Necklace. The 265-acre preserve was established in 1872, and growing here are more than 15,000 scientifically labeled trees and plants from around the world. The arboretum has one of the oldest and largest lilac collections in North America, 200-year-old bonsai trees and rare specimens from China. A two-mile walk along a nature trail takes visitors through meadows and over valleys and hills, offering serene and secluded vistas in any season. ~ 125 Arborway, Jamaica Plain; 617-524-1718, fax 617-524-1418; www.arboretum.harvard.edu.

To the southeast, the working-class city of **Quincy** may look uninteresting, but it happens to be the "City of the Presidents"— birthplace of John Adams and his son John Quincy Adams, the second and sixth U.S. presidents. There are several sights surrounding the Adams family history.

At the **Adams National Historic Site** stands an elegant gray Colonial house built in 1731, home to four generations of Adamses. The house is set on several acres strikingly set off with formal gardens that create a beautiful profusion of color in spring and summer. Inside the house are many original furnishings, including portraits of George and Martha Washington, Waterford candelabra and Louis XV furniture. There is also a cathedral-ceilinged library with 14,000 original volumes. As the Adams family prospered, John and his wife, Abigail, who moved into the house in 1787, enlarged it from 7 to 20 rooms. The National Park Service gives excellent tours. Closed mid-November to mid-April. Admission. ~ 135 Adams Street, Quincy; 617-773-1177; www.nps.gov/adam.

Nearby and part of the same site are the **John Adams** and **John Quincy Adams Birthplaces,** a pair of simple saltbox houses where the two presidents were born, built in 1663 and 1681. Admission. ~ 133 and 141 Franklin Street, Quincy; 617-773-1177.

East of the Adams National Historic Site lies the **Quincy Homestead,** home to four generations of Edmund Quincys, the family of Dorothy Hancock. The fourth Quincy daughter, Dorothy married John Hancock, who was born in Quincy. A Colonial-style herb garden and authentic period furnishings embellish the 1686 house, and one of Hancock's coaches is displayed. Closed November through April. Admission. ~ 1010 Hancock Street, Quincy; 617-472-5117.

The 1872 Gothic Revival **Adams Academy** was founded by John Adams and is home to the **Quincy Historical Society**. Exhibits show the city's industrial history. Closed weekends. ~ 8 Adams Street, Quincy; 617-773-1144, fax 617-472-4990.

Dominating downtown Quincy Square is a beautiful granite church, **United First Parish Church**, designed by Alexander Parris and built in 1828. The church crypt holds the remains of John Adams, John Quincy Adams and their wives. ~ 1306 Hancock Street, Quincy; 617-773-0062.

Located across the street is **City Hall**, designed in 1844 in Greek Revival style by Bunker Hill architect Solomon Willard. Near City Hall is the **Hancock Cemetery**, dating to about 1640, where John Hancock's father is buried, as are Quincy and Adams ancestors.

A few miles south of Quincy lies one of the South Shore's most attractive coastal communities, **Hingham**, settled in 1635. Sailing yachts bob in its picturesque harbor, and the downtown retains the characteristics of a small village, with mom-and-pop shops, restaurants and a vintage movie theater surrounding Hingham Square. A drive along the long and wide **Main Street** rewards you with views of stately 18th- and 19th-century homes sporting neat black shutters. A number of them are on the National Register of Historic Places. These houses are private, but many are open to the public during the **Hingham Historical Society's** annual house tour in June, reputed to be the oldest historical house tour in the country, held since 1924. ~ Old Derby Academy, Hingham; 781-749-7721, fax 781-749-1851.

There are two private houses worth a drive by. One is the **Hersey House**, a handsome gray mansion in Italianate style, with a flat-roofed, pillared porch, which dates to the 1850s and was once home to John Andrew, the Civil War governor of Massachusetts. ~ 104 South Street, Hingham. The other is the **Joshua Wilder House**, a beautifully restored house that probably dates to 1760. ~ 605 Main Street, Hingham.

The Old Ordinary, a house dating to 1680, numbered among its many owners tavern keepers who provided an "ordinary" meal of the day at fixed prices. Halfway on the day-long stagecoach ride from Plymouth to Boston, the Old Ordinary did a brisk business. Additions were made to the house in the mid-18th century. Now a museum of Hingham history, the house has an 18th-century taproom, complete with wooden grill, pewter plates and rum kegs. There's also an 18th-century kitchen outfitted with large hearth and butter churn, and a library, dining room and front parlor. Upstairs are four bedrooms furnished in period style. There are some rare objects among the collection, including "mourning" samplers, made to honor the dead; chinoiserie; a 17th-century Bible box; an 18th-century Queen Anne mirror; and paintings of Hingham ships that sailed to China. Closed mid-September to mid-June. Admission. ~ 21 Lincoln Street, Hingham; 781-749-0013.

The Old Ordinary counted Daniel Webster among its patrons.

The Puritan congregation of the **Old Ship Church** gathered in 1635. Built in 1681, it is the oldest building in continuous ecclesiastical service in the United States. Unlike later New England churches with white spires and sides, Old Ship was probably built of somber gray, wooden clapboards in Elizabethan Gothic style. The original color is under dispute due to some recently analyzed paint samples. Crafted by ships' carpenters, the church has curved oak roof frames like the knees of a ship, and the unusual roof structure resembles an inverted ship's hull. ~ 90 Main Street, Hingham; 781-749-1679.

Surrounding the Route 128 beltway are several more towns of interest to the traveler. A large and urbanized town about 20 miles west of Boston, Framingham offers a lovely respite within the **Garden in the Woods**, the largest collection of native plants in the Northeast. You can meander along 45 acres of woodland trails, planted with some 1500 varieties of flora. Specially designed garden habitats include woodland groves, a lily pond, bog, limestone garden, pine barrens and meadows. Closed November to mid-April. Admission. ~ 180 Hemenway Road, Framingham; 508-877-7630, fax 508-877-3658; www.newfs.org.

HIDDEN ►

A few miles north of Framingham lie the endearing green Colonial towns of Sudbury and Lincoln, still quite rural in character. Just off the historic Old Post Road, **Longfellow's Wayside Inn** is a wonderful place to visit, or stay. Built around 1700, the inn was made famous by Longfellow's cycle of poems, *Tales of a Wayside Inn*, which includes "Paul Revere's Ride." Historic structures include an 18th-century grist mill and a little red schoolhouse. Restored in 1923, it's a fully functioning inn and restaurant. ~ 63 Wayside Inn Road, Sudbury; 978-443-1776, 800-339-1776, fax 978-443-8041; www.wayside.org.

Walter Gropius, founder of the Bauhaus school of art and architecture in Germany, had his family home in the rolling green hills of Lincoln. The first house he designed upon his arrival in the United States in 1937, **Gropius House** embodies the principles of function and simplicity that are the hallmarks of the Bauhaus style. The house has works of art and Bauhaus furnishings. Closed Monday and Tuesday. Open weekends only from mid-

October through May. Admission. ~ 68 Baker Bridge Road, Lincoln; 781-259-8098, fax 781-259-9722; www.spnea.org.

Set in a wooded, green, 35-acre park overlooking Flint's Pond, the **DeCordova and Dana Museum Sculpture Park** has a collection of 20th-century American art, including paintings, sculpture, graphics and photography. In addition to changing exhibits, there are lectures, films and special events. Outdoor summer concerts are given on the grassy lawn at the amphitheater. The museum café serves light fare. Closed Monday. Admission. ~ 51 Sandy Pond Road, Lincoln; 781-259-8355, fax 781-259-3650; www.decordova.org.

LODGING

There's a great deal of historic ambience to **Longfellow's Wayside Inn**, which the poet made famous in his *Tales of a Wayside Inn*. The innkeepers have kept some of the original rooms furnished with period items, including the bed chamber where Longfellow stayed in 1862. You are welcome to tour all these rooms, as well as several historic buildings on the grounds, including a grist mill and the little red schoolhouse of "Mary Had a Little Lamb" fame. Of the inn's ten rooms, only two are in the older part of the inn. Eight are in a modern addition and feature Colonial reproduction furniture, traditional colors of cranberry and green, and oak floors. The two rooms in the original inn have wide-planked floors and hand-hewn ceiling beams, but the bathrooms are tiny with cramped showers. The inn has a wonderful restaurant that serves traditional country fare. Full breakfast included. ~ 63 Wayside Inn Road, Sudbury; 978-443-1776, 800-339-1776, fax 978-443-8041; www.wayside.org. DELUXE TO ULTRA-DELUXE.

DINING

Don't be deterred by the strip-mall surroundings of **La Paloma**, complete with laundromat, sub shop and package store. La Paloma has won several awards from *Boston* magazine including six "Best Mexican Restaurant" awards. People line up outside the doors on weekends for the first-rate Mexican food, including Mexican paella and *gorditos* (fried tortillas topped with homemade sausage and sour cream). The dining room feels as warm and festive as a Mexican village, with dim lantern light, airy latticework, tiled floors and Mexican paintings and folk art. Closed Monday. ~ 195 Newport Avenue, Quincy; 617-773-0512, fax 617-376-8867. BUDGET TO MODERATE.

◀ *HIDDEN*

The British Relief is a welcoming spot indeed, housed in a red-brick storefront and modeled on a British soup kitchen. Vintage signboards and photographs following the soup kitchen theme hang on the walls. The homey furnishings include a massive carved oak table that seats at least ten, and ancient wooden booths. Cafeteria-style service dishes up hearty homemade soups, salads and sandwiches. The restaurant also operates a deli counter with gourmet take-out. Breakfast and lunch only, except for Thursday-night dinner. Closed Sunday. ~ 152 North Street, Hingham Square, Hingham; 781-749-7713. BUDGET.

Visions of Longfellow will come to mind when you enter **Longfellow's Wayside Inn**. Before lunch or dinner, you can tour the period rooms of the original inn and several historic buildings on the grounds. Ask for a table in the small and intimate Tap Room, which has a truly Colonial ambience, with two fireplaces, ladderback chairs and brown-and-white-checked tablecloths. The menu features hearty game and seafood dishes such as those an 18th-century wayfarer might have dined on: prime rib, rack of lamb, roast duckling, goose and sole. For dessert, there are deep-dish apple pie and baked Indian pudding. ~ 63 Wayside Inn Road, Sudbury; 978-443-1776, fax 978-443-8041. DELUXE.

NIGHTLIFE   Ballroom dancers from 18 to 80 love **Moseley's on the Charles** for its large ballroom and 1940s ambience. Closed Sunday. Cover. ~ 50 Bridge Street, Dedham; 781-326-3075.

BEACHES & PARKS

HIDDEN ►

BOSTON HARBOR ISLANDS 🏃 ⛵ 🚤 🚢 ⛴ Some 30 islands lie in Boston Harbor, scattered along the coast from Boston south to Quincy, Hingham and Hull, with eight of them comprising a state park. The Puritans used these islands for pastureland and firewood, and there are tales of buried pirate treasure and ghosts haunting old Civil War forts. Each island has a unique flavor and character.

Peddocks Island, a 113-acre preserve of woodlands, salt marsh, rocky beaches and open fields, has a turn-of-the-20th-century fort, a wildlife sanctuary and an old cottage community, as well as a visitors center with displays detailing the island's history.

Peaceful and primitive **Lovells Island** is characterized by long beaches and diverse wildlife, rocky tidepools and sand dunes. This is the only island where swimming is allowed.

The smaller **Georges Island**, the most developed in the park, is dominated by Fort Warren, a National Historic Landmark built between 1833 and 1869. Construction was overseen by Sylvanus Thayer, the "Father of West Point."

Other islands in the park system include **Gallop's, Grape** and **Bumpkin**. Swimming is permitted on Lovells Island only. Fishing is good from the rocky shores and public piers on all the islands except Peddocks; you'll find lots of flounder, cod, haddock, pollack and striped bass. Picnic areas, restrooms, park rangers, nature trails, fort tours, historical programs, boat docks and a concession stand are available on Georges Island. Closed Labor Day to Memorial Day. Information: Peddocks, Lovells and Georges islands are administered by the regional Metropolitan District Commission; contact the MDC's Harbor Region Office. ~ 98

Taylor Street; Dorchester; 617-727-5359. Grape, Bumpkin and the other islands are state-owned; contact the Boston Harbor Islands State Park. ~ 349 Lincoln Street, Hingham; 781-740-1605 ext. 201. Georges Island serves as the entrance to the park and provides free inter-island water taxis from Memorial Day to Labor Day; for information, call the Department of Environmental Management. ~ 781-740-1605. The islands are also accessible through **Boston Harbor Cruises.** ~ 1 Long Wharf; 617-227-4320. **The Friends of the Boston Harbor Islands** sponsors special boat trips and tours. ~ 781-740-4290.

▲ There are free primitive sites on Peddocks and Lovells islands (free MDC permit required), and on Grape and Bumpkins islands. No water or electricity; outhouses available.

BELLE ISLE MARSH 🏃 ⚓ This preserve holds 241 acres of   ◀ HIDDEN
one of the largest remaining salt marshes in Boston. Typical of the wetlands that once lined the shores of the Massachusetts Bay Colony, Belle Isle Marsh is a special place where you can see lots of wildlife and salt marsh plants, a rare experience in an urban area. Facilities include nature trails and an observation tower. ~ At Bennington Street in East Boston; 617-727-5350.

NANTASKET BEACH 🏊 🎣 ⚓ 🚣 Once a classy mid-19th-century resort with grand hotels rivaling those in Newport, the Nantasket Beach area later declined into a tacky strip of bars, fast-food stands and Skeeball arcades. Still, this three-and-a-half-mile barrier beach is one of the nicest in the area, with clean white sand and a wide open vista of the Atlantic Ocean. The water is always good for swimming, and after a storm there's enough surf to go bodysurfing or windsurfing. There are picnic areas, restrooms, lifeguards, shade pavilions, a boardwalk, restaurants and snack stands. Parking fee, $3. ~ On Nantasket Avenue, at the terminus of Route 228 in Hull; 781-925-1777.

WOLLASTON BEACH RESERVATION 🏊 🚣 Come high tide, the beach virtually disappears, so narrow is this two-mile stretch of sand. The beach is backed by a wide seawall and a parking strip along its entire length. Here people like to sunbathe in lawn chairs or draped across the hoods of their cars, and to walk their dogs, giving this beach a distinctly urban feel. The sand here is gravelly and often crowded, but the beach does have a splendid view of the Boston skyline. You'll find picnic areas, restrooms, bathhouses and a playground; snack bars and restaurants with great fried clams are across the street. ~ On Quincy Shore Drive, south on Route 3A from Neponset Circle, Quincy; 617-698-1802.

BLUE HILLS RESERVATION 🏃 🚴 🐎 🚶 🏕 🏊 ⚓ 🚣 🚣 This 7000-acre park is the largest open space within 35 miles of Boston. Great Blue Hill, the highest point on the Massachusetts coast south of Maine, is the site of the oldest weather station in North America. The reservation comprises dozens of hills, forested land and several lakes and wetlands, as well as 150 miles of hiking, ski touring and bridle trails. There's the **Trailside Museum** (admission), a natural-history museum with live animals and exhibits, and 16 historic sites, including the 1795 Redman Farmhouse. ~ 1904 Canton Avenue, Route 138, Milton; 617-333-0694.

Houghton's Pond, with its calm waters and sandy bottom, offers particularly good swimming for children. Ponds are stocked with trout, bass, bullhead, perch and sunfish. Facilities include picnic areas, restrooms, lifeguards, a snack bar, tennis courts, a golf course, a small downhill ski run with rentals and ballfields. ~ Reservation headquarters are on Hillside Street next to the police station in Milton, where maps are available; 617-698-1802.

▲ The Appalachian Mountain Club operates 20 cabins and 2 campsites on Ponkapoag Pond (781-961-7007); camping rates are $12 to $16 per night, cabin rates are $83 to $112 per week (there are only weekly rentals in the summer). Reserve these well ahead of time. There are outhouses; no water or electricity.

MIDDLESEX FELLS RESERVATION 🚶 🚲 🏇 🏕 🎣 "Fells" is a Scottish word meaning wild, hilly country, which aptly describes the 2000-plus-acre terrain of this reservation. These rugged highlands were first explored in 1632 by Governor Winthrop, first governor of the Massachusetts Bay Colony. They were acquired as public parkland in 1893, and a 19th-century trolley line brought in droves of picnickers. The region has been used for logging, granite quarrying, ice harvesting and water power for mills that manufactured the first vulcanized rubber products. Fifty miles of hiking trails and old woods roads run through the Fells. For anglers, Fellsmere, Doleful, Dark Hollow and Quarter Mile ponds hold sunfish, catfish, perch, pickerel and bass. Horses are allowed, though there are no stables. Biking trails are seasonal. Facilities include picnic areas, a skating rink and a swimming pool. ~ Six miles north of Boston, off Exits 32, 33 and 34 from Route 93; 617-727-5380.

▼▼▼▼▼▼▼▼▼▼▼▼▼▼▼
Lexington & Concord

Just outside of Cambridge, the two towns of Lexington and Concord are forever linked by the historical events of April 19, 1775, when the first battle of the Revolutionary War took place. The British planned to advance on Concord from Boston to seize the colonials' military supplies. Warned by Paul Revere the night before, farmer/soldier Minutemen had mustered early before dawn on the Lexington Green.

About 77 men at Lexington Green, and hundreds more at Concord, fought off 700 highly trained British regulars. With heavy casualties, the British retreated back to Boston. "The shot heard 'round the world" had been fired, launching the American Revolution.

Between the two towns you can spend a couple of days visiting battle sites and monuments. When you arrive in Lexington, a few miles north of Lincoln off Route 128, stop first at the **Lexington Visitors Center** for maps and brochures, and to see a diorama of the battle. ~ Lexington Green, 1875 Massachusetts Avenue, Lexington; 781-862-1450; www.2000.lexington.com.

SIGHTS

Across from Lexington Green, in the center of town, stands the **Minuteman Statue**, a simple bareheaded farmer holding a musket. The statue's rough, fieldstone base was made of stone taken from the walls the American militia stood behind as they shot at the British. This statue has become symbolic of Lexington history. ~ Battle Green, intersection of Massachusetts Avenue and Bedford Street, Lexington.

On the green next to the Visitors Center is the yellow, woodframe **Buckman Tavern**, built in 1709. This is where the Minutemen gathered to await the British after Revere's warning. Smiling elderly ladies wearing mobcaps and long skirts guide you through the house, with its wide-planked floors and 18th-century furniture and musket displays. Admission. ~ Lexington Green, 1 Bedford Street, Lexington; 781-862-5598.

About a quarter mile north of the green is the **Hancock-Clarke House**, where Samuel Adams and John Hancock were staying that fateful night. Revere stopped here to warn them. John Hancock's father built this pretty little woodframe house with 12-over-16 windows around 1700. Admission. ~ 36 Hancock Street, Lexington; 781-861-0928.

The little red **Munroe Tavern**, built in 1695, served as British headquarters and housed wounded British soldiers after the battle. The tavern has been maintained as it was, and there are mementos of a 1789 visit by George Washington. Admission. ~ 1332 Massachusetts Avenue, Lexington; 781-674-9238.

The **Jonathan Harrington House**, now a private residence, was the home of Minuteman fifer Jonathan Harrington, who died in his wife's arms after being fatally wounded in the battle. ~ Harrington Road, Lexington.

The **Museum of Our National Heritage** has changing exhibits on American history in four galleries. Past programs have included retrospectives on Ben Franklin, Paul Revere and the USS *Constitution*, plus exhibits of clocks, furniture and swords from different periods. There are also permanent exhibits on the American Revolution and Masonic lodges. ~ 33 Marrett Road, Lexington; 781-861-6559, fax 781-861-9846; www.mnh.org.

Within the 750-acre **Minute Man National Historical Park** are several more sites involved in the Battle of Lexington and Concord. In this peaceful, sylvan spot, it's hard to picture the bloody carnage of the historic battle. A wide, pine-scented path leads to the site of the **Old North Bridge** spanning the Concord River, a 1956 replica of the bridge where Concord Minutemen held off the British. Another **Minute Man Statue** stands across the river, made of melted 1776 cannon, designed by Daniel Chester French. This one shows a farmer with gun and plow in hand. ~ Route 2A, Concord; 978-369-6993, fax 978-371-2483; www.nps.gov/mima, e-mail mimainfo@nps.gov.

At the **Battle Road Visitors Center** are a film and exhibits. ~ 174 Liberty Street, Concord; 781-862-7753.

Concord is also famed as the home of four great literary figures of the 19th century: Nathaniel Hawthorne, Ralph Waldo Emerson, Henry David Thoreau and Louisa May Alcott.

The **Old Manse** was home not only to Emerson but also to Hawthorne, who lived there with his wife for two years while writing *Mosses from an Old Manse*. The restored house is filled with Emerson and Hawthorne memorabilia. Closed late October to mid-April. Admission. ~ 269 Monument Street, near North Bridge, Concord; 978-369-3909, fax 978-287-6154; www.thetrustees.org.

The Alcott family lived at **Orchard House** for almost 20 years. Here Louisa May Alcott wrote her most famous novels, *Little Women* and *Little Men*. Closed first two weeks in January. Admission. ~ 399 Lexington Road, Concord; 978-369-4118, fax 978-369-1367; www.louisamayalcott.org.

Ralph Waldo Emerson House is where Emerson lived for almost 50 years, with Thoreau, Hawthorne and the Alcotts as his frequent guests. Almost all furnishings are original. Closed Monday through Wednesday and from late October to mid-April. Admission. ~ 28 Cambridge Turnpike, Concord; 978-369-2236.

The **Concord Museum** contains Revolutionary War artifacts, literary relics and other historic items associated with Concord. Emerson's study was reconstructed and moved here, and the Thoreau Room holds the simple furniture Thoreau made for his cabin at Walden Pond. Admission. ~ 200 Lexington Road, Concord; 978-369-9609, fax 978-369-9660; www.concordmuseum.org.

Few places have been more indelibly stamped by the presence of one individual than **Walden Pond State Reservation**. "I went to the woods because I wished to live deliberately, to front the essential facts of life, and see if I could not learn what it had to teach, and not, when I came to die, discover that I had not lived," wrote Thoreau in his famous account of his two years spent in a little cabin in these woods, beginning in 1845. Thoreau occupied himself studying nature, fishing and hoeing his bean crop. Today, Walden Pond offers less solitude—it's almost always crowded.

Lexington
& Concord

POINTS OF INTEREST

Buckman Tavern
Concord Museum
DeCordova and Dana
  Museum Sculpture Park
Hancock-Clarke House
Lexington Visitors Center
Minute Man Statue
Minuteman Statue
Munroe Tavern
Museum of Our
  National Heritage
Orchard House
Ralph Waldo Emerson
  House
The Wayside

But you can swim or fish in the pond, or perhaps try a little boating. Nature trails wind around the pond, and there are picnic tables. You can also visit the little cairn of stones that marks the cabin site. Admission. ~ Route 126 off Route 2, Concord; 978-369-3254, fax 978-371-6438.

Concord is also known for **Concord grapes**, developed and cultivated here by Ephraim Wales Bull.

LODGING   If you're looking for an inexpensive place to stay right in the middle of Lexington, you might stop at the **Battle Green Motor Inn**. The 96 rooms in this L-shaped motel surround two courtyards graced with tropical plants and a heated swimming pool. Inside, guest rooms sport blond furniture and Colonial decor. ~ 1720 Massachusetts Avenue, Lexington; 781-862-6100, 800-343-0235, fax 781-861-9485; www.battlegreeninn.com. MODERATE.

Concord is greener and more rural than Lexington, making it a more restful place to stay. You can't stay there without stumbling over history.

The **Hawthorne Inn**, built around 1870, is situated on land that once belonged to Emerson, the Alcotts and Hawthorne, and stands across the street from the Hawthorne and Alcott houses. This homey inn has seven rooms, three furnished with canopied, antique four-poster beds covered with handmade quilts, as well as Colonial-patterned wallpapers and oriental rugs. The private baths are large and nicely redone. Rates drop significantly during the off-season. Continental breakfast and afternoon tea are included. No smoking. ~ 462 Lexington Road, Concord; 978-369-5610, fax 978-287-4949; www.concordmass.com. DELUXE TO ULTRA-DELUXE.

Right on the town green, the **Colonial Inn** dates to 1716. The original part of the house was owned by Thoreau's grandfather. Although the inn has 49 rooms, few are in the historic old inn. Thirty-two rooms are in a newer wing added in 1961 and are comfortable but bland. The 15 rooms in the original part of the house are larger and have a more historic ambience, with wide-planked floors, hand-hewn beams and four-poster beds. The inn has a restaurant with two taverns. ~ 48 Monument Square, Concord; 978-369-2373, 800-370-9200, fax 978-371-1533; www.concordscolonialinn.com. ULTRA-DELUXE.

WAYSIDE WRITERS

The Alcotts and Nathaniel Hawthorne lived at **The Wayside**. The Alcotts lived there for several years while Louisa was a girl. Hawthorne bought the house in 1852 and wrote his biography of Franklin Pierce here. Closed Wednesday and from late October to mid-April. Admission. ~ 455 Lexington Road, Concord; 508-369-6975.

In nearby Bedford, the contemporary **Renaissance Bedford Hotel** occupies 24 piney acres, offering a bit of a resort experience. The 285 rooms are all decorated with modern furnishings. Facilities include indoor and outdoor tennis courts, a fitness center, a whirlpool and sauna. The hotel works well both as a family-friendly accommodation (rooms are child-proof) and as a business hotel (there are meeting rooms and a business center). ~ 44 Middlesex Turnpike, Bedford; 781-275-5500, 800-228-9290, fax 781-275-8956. ULTRA-DELUXE.

DINING

Yangtze River Restaurant specializes in Polynesian cuisine as well as Szechuan and Cantonese favorites. The dining room is noisy and casual, with a jungle of greenery and exposed brick walls. ~ 21–25 Depot Square, Lexington; 781-861-6030, fax 781-861-6213. MODERATE.

Styled after a Colonial country inn, the **Hartwell House** is actually two dining establishments in one. The casual bistro features familiar fare such as clam chowder, pizza and chopped sirloin burgers along with a limited choice of more elaborate chef's specials that change monthly. The more formal restaurant, where "smart" attire is required, serves a range of seafood, beef, fowl and pasta dishes including macadamia-crusted scrod, steak *au poivre* and grilled boneless maple leaf duck breast with brandied cherry glaze. ~ 94 Hartwell Avenue, Lexington; 781-862-5111; www.hartwellhouse.com. MODERATE TO DELUXE.

For some traditional Yankee fare in a historic setting, try the **Colonial Inn.** Built in 1716, the original part of the house was owned by Thoreau's grandfather. There are five dining rooms, each with its own Colonial-inspired decor. The menu includes prime rib, steak, scrod and lobster. ~ 48 Monument Square, Concord; 978-369-9200, fax 978-371-1533. MODERATE TO DELUXE.

A pleasant surprise from start to finish, **Aïgo Bistro** is in the middle of a pretty but sleepy suburban community, not the place you'd expect to find innovative cuisine. It's upstairs in the old Concord train depot. The menu is full of French- and Mediterranean-inspired delights arranged and served with quiet flair. Dinner only. Closed Sunday. ~ 84 Thoreau Street, Concord; 978-371-1333. DELUXE TO ULTRA-DELUXE.

Outdoor Adventures

SAILING

Sailing the blue waters of the Charles on a breezy day with views of both the Boston and Cambridge skylines is an experience to be savored. **Community Boating** rents windsurfers, kayaks and sonars to visitors who pass a test and buy a two-day membership. Closed November through March. ~ 21 David G. Mugar Way; 617-523-1038. You can charter captained sailboats at the **Boston Sailing Center.** Closed November to mid-April. ~ 54 Lewis Wharf; 617-

227-4198. Experienced sailors can rent 23- to 39-foot boats from the **Boston Harbor Sailing Club**. ~ 200 High Street; 617-345-9202.

WHALE WATCHING

Boston is within easy reach of Stellwagon Bank, a major feeding ground for whales. You can go whale watching from April through October with the **New England Aquarium**. ~ Central Wharf; 617-973-5277. **Boston Harbor Cruises** also offers day trips in the area around Stellwagon Bank. ~ 66 Long Wharf; 617-723-7800. **A. C. Cruise Line**'s full-day whale-watching charters travel 30 miles out to sea to spot humpback and finback whales. ~ 290 Northern Avenue; 617-261-6633.

JOGGING

Jogging is very big in Boston, where half the population seems to be in training for the Boston Marathon. The most popular running paths are along both sides of the green strips paralleling the Charles River; these run more than 17 miles. For information, call **USA Track and Field**. ~ 2001 Beacon Street, Brookline; 617-566-7600. Another safe place to jog is **Breakheart Reservation**'s two- and three-mile trails. ~ 177 Forest Street, Saugus; 781-233-0834.

ICE SKATING

Skaters have been tracing the curves of the lagoon in the Public Garden and the Boston Common **Frog Pond** for more than a hundred years. ~ 617-635-2197, 617-635-2120. The Charles River is almost never frozen hard enough for skating, but the MDC maintains 21 public indoor rinks, some with rentals available. Closed March through October. Admission. ~ 20 Somerset Street; 617-727-9547, fax 617-727-6059.

    The Skating Club of Boston has public skating and rentals. Admission. ~ 1240 Soldier's Field Road, Brighton; 617-782-5900.

SKIING

Cross-country skiers have a number of options. The **Weston Ski Track** has two kilometers of gently sloping trails that are machine generated and run over a golf course; lessons and rentals (including snowshoes) are available. They operate from December 15 through March 15. ~ 200 Park Road, Weston; 781-891-6575. The **Lincoln Guide Service** also offers lessons and cross-country ski rentals at Conservation Trail. ~ 152 Lincoln Road, Lincoln; 781-259-9204. The **Middlesex Fells Reservation** has a free six-mile trail, suiting a variety of skill levels, but you have to pay for the trail maps. ~ 4 Woodland Road, Stoneham; 781-662-5214. **Wompatuck State Park** has seven miles of relatively easy cross-country trails, with free trail maps at the park headquarters. ~ Union Street, Hingham; 781-749-7160.

GOLF

You can tee up at numerous public golf courses. In Hyde Park, visit the 18-hole **George Wright Golf Course**. Designed by Donald

Ross, the championship course rents carts and clubs. ~ 420 West Street; 617-361-8313. The **Presidents Golf Course** is an 18-hole, par-5 course. Their signature 15th hole lands even the most experienced golfers in the water. ~ 357 West Squantum Street; 617-328-3444. The 18-hole **Braintree Municipal Golf Course** is closed January and February. ~ 101 Jefferson Street; 781-843-9781. The public **Newton Commonwealth Golf Course**'s second hole is a difficult par 5 around a creek on an elevated green. ~ 212 Kenrick Street, Newton; 617-630-1971. The **Stow Acres Country Club** has two 18-hole courses. ~ 58 Randall Road, Stow; 508-568-8690. The **Colonial Country Club**'s course is surrounded by a natural marsh. ~ 1 Audubon Road, Lynnfield; 617-245-9300.

The Metropolitan District Commission (MDC) maintains 45 courts in the city and greater Boston. ~ 20 Somerset Street; 617-727-9547, fax 617-727-6059. Cambridge, too, has more than ten outdoor public courts. ~ Parks and Recreation: 617-349-6231.

TENNIS

There are numerous private clubs; one open to the public is the **Sportsmen's Tennis Club**, offering both indoor and outdoor courts. Pro-shop on-site. Fee. ~ Franklin Field Tennis Center, 950 Blue Hill Avenue, Dorchester; 617-288-9092.

Biking is popular around Boston's scenic waterways, including the Charles River, although we wouldn't recommend it in the narrow, congested downtown streets. The Charles River Esplanade, on the Boston side of the Charles River, has the well-marked, 18-mile **Dr. Paul Dudley White Bike Path**, which goes from Science Park through Boston, Cambridge and Newton, ending in Watertown. The **Stony Brook Reservation Bike Path** runs four miles through forests in West Roxbury/Hyde Park. ~ Turtle Pond Parkway, West Roxbury, Hyde Park; 617-698-1802, fax 617-727-6918. The **Mystic River Reservation** also has a nice bike path (3.5 miles) that runs from the Wellington Bridge in Somerville along the Mystic River to beyond the Wellington Bridge in Everett. Some of the best and least crowded biking in the area is at **Wompatuck State Park**, where 12 miles of trails cut through old forest groves. ~ Union Street, Hingham; 781-749-7160.

BIKING

If you're up for a really challenging route, try the 135-mile **Claire Saltonstall Bikeway**. The first segment runs from Boston to Bourne at the entrance to Cape Cod; continuing segments follow the Cape Cod Rail Trail all the way to Provincetown at the tip of the Cape.

For information on area biking, contact the **Massachusetts Bicycle Coalition** (MassBike). ~ 44 Bromfield Street, Room 207; 617-542-2453. You can also try the **Charles River Wheelmen Bike Club**, which organizes weekend rides. ~ 1 Belnap Road, Hyde Park; 617-325-2453.

Bike Rentals   **Community Bike Shop** has mountain bike and hybrid rentals. ~ 496 Tremont Street; 617-542-8623. Near Copley Square, **Back Bay Bike and Board** rents mountain bikes, hybrids, cruisers and tandems and offers maps of trails. ~ 617-247-2336

HIKING

Scant miles outside the urban clamor of downtown Boston, Massachusetts turns to rolling green hills, river valleys and pine and hardwood forests. A surprising number of parks and wildlife sanctuaries can be found in these rural country towns, where you can hike scenic trails, short or long. All distances for hiking trails are one way unless otherwise noted.

OUTLYING AREAS   The **Quincy Quarries Footpath** (2.5 miles), an easy, moderate hike, leads past steep quarry walls, the first commercial railway in America and an 1898 turning mill, used to cut and polish the Quincy granite columns and slabs that went into many famous buildings in America.

HIDDEN ►   The main path at **World's End** (4.5 miles) winds uphill and down over a little peninsula extending north from Hingham into Massachusetts Bay. Its beautifully landscaped, gently curving roads were laid out by landscape architect Frederick Law Olmsted for a housing development that was never built. The wide, grassy path meanders through meadows and marshland, past rocky glacial drumlins, through avenues of English oaks, pine and red cedars, and up a steep knoll with a knockout view of the Boston skyline, one of the best on the South Shore.

The **Ponkapoag Trail** (3.5 miles) in the Blue Hills Reservation circles Ponkapoag Pond, passing through wetlands and a golf course. From it, the Ponkapoag Log Boardwalk crosses a floating bog filled with highbush blueberries, blue flag iris and Atlantic white cedar.

Little known and little used, Stony Brook Reservation allows you to walk in solitude among peaceful woods along the **Bearberry Hill Path** (3 miles). The trail leads into the woods toward Turtle Pond, then returns via the east boundary asphalt bicycle path past a swampy thicket and a golf course.

The **Skyline Trail** (6.8 miles), in the Middlesex Fells Reservation, is a strenuous trail that climbs many rocky knobs running between two observation towers. Scenery varies considerably along the way, from a pond with water lilies and frogs to volcanic-rock hills, wild hardwood forests, an old soapbox derby track, carpets of Canada mayflower and swampy areas.

LEXINGTON & CONCORD   Although you will be accompanied by crowds of others, you can walk the shores Thoreau walked at **Walden Pond** in Concord. A 1.7-mile circuit trail winds through woods along the crystal-clear waters of the pond. At the cabin site where Thoreau lived for two years, travelers from all corners of the globe have piled up stones in memoriam.

If you arrive in Boston by car, you'll have to watch closely for road markings; routes change numbers and names frequently. Also, roads will be tied up by a major project designed to construct a third harbor tunnel and to depress the Central Artery underground. This project, known as the "Big Dig" now has an estimated completion date of 2004. For more information on its current impact on traffic in the city, visit www.bigdig.com. No one in his right mind would want to bring a car to downtown Boston, where narrow, confusing streets are ruled by legendarily homicidal drivers. Save the car for touring the suburbs of Greater Boston or outlying areas.

Transportation

CAR

From the north, **Route 95** follows a curving, southwesterly path to Boston, changing to **Route 128** as it forms a beltway around the city. **Route 93** runs directly north–south through Boston; its downtown portion is called the Central Artery, and it's known as the John Fitzgerald Expressway and the Southeast Expressway between Boston and Route 128 in Braintree. **Route 90**, the Massachusetts Turnpike, heads into and through Boston from the west. From the south, you can reach Boston by Route 95, **Route 24** or **Route 3**.

AIR

Logan International Airport, the busy and crowded main airport serving Boston, is two miles north of the city in East Boston. Numerous domestic and international carriers fly in and out of Logan, including Aer Lingus, Air Atlantic/Canadian Air, Air Canada, Alitalia Airlines, America West, American Airlines, British Airways, Continental, Delta Airlines, Icelandair, Lufthansa Airlines, Northwest Airlines, Sabena Belgian World Airlines, Swissair, TAP Air Portugal, Trans World Airlines, United Airlines, US Airways and Virgin Atlantic Airways.

Limousines and buses take visitors to numerous downtown locations, including **Carey Limousine** (617-623-8700), **Commonwealth Limousine Service** (617-787-5575) and **Peter Pan Bus Lines** (800-237-8747).

You can also take the subway from the airport by taking a free Massport bus to the Blue Line stop. The slickest way to get downtown is to hop the **Airport Water Shuttle**, bypassing traffic altogether for a scenic seven-minute ride across Boston Harbor. ~ 617-330-8680.

BUS

Greyhound Bus Lines has bus service to Boston from all over the country. The main downtown terminal is at South Station. ~ 720 Atlantic Avenue; 800-231-2222. **Bonanza Bus Lines** serves Boston from Cape Cod. ~ 700 Atlantic Avenue; 617-720-4110, 800-556-3815. **Peter Pan Bus Lines** runs between Boston and New York, New Hampshire and Cape Cod. ~ 700 Atlantic Avenue; 800-237-8747. **Concord Trailways** runs from points in New

Hampshire only. ~ 700 Atlantic Avenue; 617-426-8080, 800-639-3317.

TRAIN

Amtrak services many destinations from Boston including San Francisco, Chicago and New York. ~ South Station, Summer Street at Atlantic Avenue; 617-482-3660, 800-872-7245.

CAR RENTALS

Parking grows scarcer and ever more expensive, and you can easily see Boston on foot, but if you must rent a car, you can do so in the airport terminal at **Alamo Rent A Car** (800-327-9633), **Avis Rent A Car** (800-331-1212), **Budget Rent A Car** (800-527-0700), **Dollar Rent A Car** (800-800-4000), **Hertz Rent A Car** (800-654-3131), **National Car Rental** (800-227-7368) and **Thrifty Car Rental** (800-367-2277).

Used-car rentals in the area include **U-Save Auto Rental** (617-254-1900) and **Adventure Rent A Car** (617-783-3825).

PUBLIC TRANSIT

Boston's subway system is operated by the **Massachusetts Bay Transportation Authority**, MBTA, popularly called the "T." The T has four lines, the Red, Blue, Green and Orange, which will get you almost anywhere you want to go quite handily. The basic fare is 85 cents. Special multiple-day discount passes can be bought at many T stations and the visitor booths throughout the city.

The MBTA also operates a fleet of buses providing extensive coverage of Boston and Cambridge. Exact change is required for the 60-cent fare. ~ 617-722-3200.

TAXIS

Several cab companies serve Logan Airport, including **Boston Cab** (617-536-5010), **Cambridge Taxi Company** (617-492-1100), **Checker Cab** (617-497-1500) and **Town Taxi** (617-536-5000).

FIVE

Cape Cod and the Islands

Every year starting in June, close to 3.5 million people invade this foot-shaped peninsula, grappling with horrendous traffic and crowded beaches just to be on their beloved Cape Cod. It's easy to understand why.

The Cape has it all: silver-gray saltbox cottages, historic villages, sports, seafood, art, first-rate theater and more. But those attributes aren't the real reason people come here. It's the land itself. With its ethereal light, comforting woodlands and 300 miles of majestic, untamed shoreline, Cape Cod reaches deep into the soul. Formed 12,000 years ago from an enormous glacier that left in its wake a unique and magical landscape of sand dunes, moors, salt marsh and ocean vistas, the Cape has a staggering number of utterly beautiful beaches and natural parks.

Linked to the Cape in the minds of many travelers (although definitely *not* in the minds of residents) are the nearby islands of Martha's Vineyard and Nantucket, wealthy enclaves where celebrities find retreat and make their homes along quiet or dramatic seascapes, beside purple heath or in museum-perfect villages dotted with historic buildings. Following in the footsteps of Lillian Hellman and Dashiell Hammett, folks like Walter Cronkite have moved to Martha's Vineyard. Smaller Nantucket has one lovely town filled with museums, galleries and history, plus great wild beaches and backroads. Everyone calls Nantucket and Martha's Vineyard "the Islands"—except the people who live there. Don't even *suggest* that the "islanders" are connected to the Cape unless you want to start a row.

The Cape's first visitors were the Pilgrims, who landed near Provincetown just long enough to write the Mayflower Compact before heading off to Plymouth. As Massachusetts thrived after the Revolution, Nantucket and Martha's Vineyard joined other coastal areas as major whaling ports.

In the 1800s, artists and writers such as Henry David Thoreau discovered the Cape. Tourists were soon to follow, and these once-isolated fishing communities were never the same again.

Tourism has taken its toll. The Cape has a commercial side, complete with tired-looking shopping malls, pizza parlors, video arcades, tract houses and ugly motels. But it's easy to avoid all that if you know where to go.

The 70-mile-long Cape projects out into the ocean in an east–west direction for about 35 miles, then becomes narrower and turns northward. Practically everything worth seeing here lies along the shore, so an ideal way to explore is to follow the northern coast along Cape Cod Bay to the tip in Provincetown, then go back down along Nantucket Sound to Falmouth and Woods Hole. This is the route we will take.

We have labeled the first segment the North Cape, which follows scenic Route 6A along the north shore past some of the Cape's most charming historic villages. Route 6A eventually joins with busy Route 6 and soon arrives at Eastham. Here begins the Outer Cape area, the region known for sand dunes, rolling moors, impressive beaches and the bohemian and tourist enclave of Provincetown. Route 28 runs back along South Cape past a couple of attractive villages and some of the region's less scenic commercial areas (including Hyannis, home to the Kennedy clan). This section ends at the scientific community of Woods Hole, noted for its oceanographic institute. We then journey to those two pearls off the Cape's southern coast, Martha's Vineyard and Nantucket.

Touring this area, perhaps you'll understand what inspired Thoreau to write *Cape Cod*. There's something here, though, that can't be put into words—a special chemistry and charisma that draw people back year after year, generation after generation.

▼▼▼▼▼▼▼▼▼▼▼▼ The North Cape

Hugging Cape Cod Bay along Route 6A are the beautiful historic villages of Sandwich, Barnstable, Yarmouth, Dennis and Brewster. Once known as Olde Kings Highway, Route 6A is a tree-lined road that dips and turns past lovely old homes, sweeping lawns, stone walls, duck ponds, museums, elegant restaurants and antique stores.

SIGHTS

Sandwich, the first town we reach, is very green, woodsy and English looking. It dates back to 1639 and has a 17th-century grist mill. Sandwich has more sights than any town on the Cape except Brewster. Maps are available at the **Cape Cod Canal Region Chamber of Commerce**. The information booth is closed mid-September to mid-May. ~ 70 Main Street, Buzzards Bay; 508-759-6000; www.capecodcanalchamber.org.

Near the heart of the village stands **The Hoxie House**, one of the oldest houses in Sandwich. Built around 1675, this modest saltbox structure has furnishings that are impressive in their simplicity and ingenuity. A 1701 Connecticut blanket chest with inlay is spectacular; chairs turn into tables and benches into beds. Closed after Columbus Day to mid-June. Admission. ~ Water Street (Route 130), Sandwich; 508-888-1173.

A few doors down is the **Thornton W. Burgess Museum** dedicated to the author of *Old Mother West Wind* and other children's tales. This three-quarter Colonial building overlooking the idyllic, Canadian geese and swan–friendly Shawme Pond contains a large collection of books by Burgess, beautiful old book illustrations and a gift shop with children's books. Closed November through March. Admission. ~ 4 Water Street, Sandwich; 508-888-4668.

Heritage Plantation has a 1912 carousel, an antique car collection (including a stunning Dusenburg once owned by Gary Cooper), a military museum and an art museum. If cars, folk art or military history interest you, you'll be impressed. The military museum features 2000 hand-painted miniatures and all sorts of replica flags and firearms. The art museum includes an impressive collection of antique weathervanes, early American primitive and western art including many Currier and Ives lithographs, and cigar-store carved figures. The plantation's 76 acres of gardens are so perfectly manicured they look artificial. Closed mid-October to mid-May. Admission. ~ Pine and Grove streets, Sandwich; 508-888-3300; www.heritageplantation.org.

In the heart of Sandwich village is the **Sandwich Glass Museum**. The museum's collection includes everything from jars, nursing bottles and tableware to saucers, vases and candlesticks. A lot of

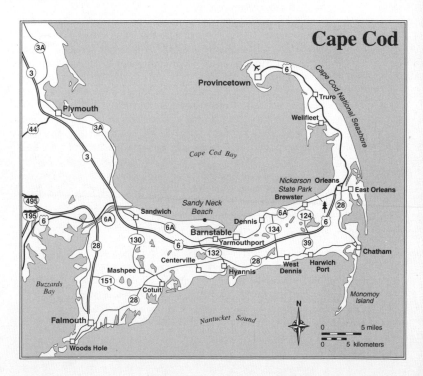

the glass is displayed on shelves in front of large picture windows. Sun illuminates the glass, and it lights up the museum in a kaleidoscope of sparkling colors. Closed Monday and Tuesday in November; closed in January. Admission. ~ 129 Main Street, Town Hall Square, Sandwich; 508-888-0251.

A few steps away from the Glass Museum you'll find **Yesteryears Doll Museum**, two floors packed with every antique doll and accessory imaginable—princesses, nurses, Indians, doll furniture, houses, paper dolls, baby buggies, parasols and much more. Closed Sunday; closed mid-October to mid-May. Admission. ~ Main and River streets, Sandwich; 508-888-1711.

The Green Briar Nature Center and Jam Kitchen and the **Old Briar Patch Conservation Area** are east of the center of town. "'Tis a wonderful thing to sweeten the world which is in a jam and needs preserving," wrote Thornton W. Burgess to Ida Putnam. As a boy Burgess roamed the woods around Ida's jam kitchen. Today, the Burgess Society produces natural jams, pickles and jellies from Ida's recipes. Nestled deep in the woods next to a pond, the old-fashioned kitchen looks like an illustration from one of Burgess' books. Peter Rabbit and his animal friends would have loved it here. ~ Discovery Hill Road, Sandwich; 508-888-6870; www.thorntonburgess.org.

East of Sandwich lies the popular resort town of **Barnstable**, where some of the Cape's most beautiful inns and tempting restaurants and shops are located. You'll find the **Donald Trayser Memorial Museum**, a brick structure built in 1856, which was once a custom house, then a post office. Named after a local patriot and historian, the museum includes a potpourri of artifacts related to Cape Cod life and history, such as Indian tools and ships in bottles. Next to the museum stands the oldest wooden jail in the United States (circa 1690), whose walls are covered with graffiti written by seamen. Closed Monday, and from mid-October to mid-June. ~ Route 6A, Barnstable; 508-362-2092.

Farther along Route 6A, Yarmouthport is the site of two historic homes with impressive antiques. A white Greek Revival

CRYSTAL CLEAR

In 1825 Deming Jarves, a Bostonian, built a glass factory in Sandwich because of its convenient water access to Boston and abundant wood supply for the furnaces, and also because he thought his employees wouldn't squander their money on city temptations, as they had in Boston. His formula worked, and in no time Sandwich became renowned for its glass. For a sparkling display of Sandwich glassware, visit the Sandwich Glass Museum.

home with black shutters, **Captain Bangs Hallet House** is fur- ◄ HIDDEN
nished with elegant settees, tables and chairs, and many classic
old toys such as a rocking horse with real animal hide and hair.
Open Thursday in July and August; open Sunday from June
through October; closed November through May. Admission. ~
11 Strawberry Lane, Yarmouthport; 508-362-3021.

The 1780 **Winslow Crocker House,** a shingled Georgian with
handsome wood paneling and an impressive walk-in fireplace,
has a rare 17th-century wooden cradle and blanket chest, a Windsor writing chair and many more valuable antiques. Open weekends only; closed mid-October through May. Admission. ~ 250
Route 6A, Yarmouthport; 508-362-4385; www.spnea.org.

Brewster has a couple of sights for children and history buffs.
The **New England Fire and History Museum** displays hand- and
horse-drawn fire equipment that makes you wonder how they ever
put out fires, and a full-scale model of Ben Franklin's first Philadelphia firehouse. Kids like all the bells and fire alarms that are
constantly sounding off here. Also on the premises are a blacksmith and an apothecary. Open weekdays only from late May to
Labor Day; open weekends only from Labor Day to Columbus
Day. Admission. ~ 1439 Main Street (Route 6A), Brewster; 508-
896-5711.

The **Cape Cod Museum of Natural History** has a working beehive and occasional guided walks through the salt marsh behind
the museum. The hands-on exhibits are popular with both children and adults. Admission. ~ Main Street (Route 6A), Brewster;
508-896-3867; www.ccmnh.org.

The Cape has some of the most beautiful inns in the country, plus   **LODGING**
hundreds of other accommodations in every price range, location
and style imaginable. If you plan to stay for at least a week, think
about renting a house, apartment or condo; it's usually less
expensive than a hotel. Contact the **Cape Cod Chamber of Commerce** for names of realtors handling rentals in a particular area.
~ Junction of Routes 6 and 132, Hyannis; 508-362-3225; www.
capecodchamber.org.

Located in the heart of Sandwich village, **The Village Inn** is   ◄ HIDDEN
a renovated 1830s Federal-style house. Without sacrificing historic details, the owners have made everything look fresh and
new. The eight soothing, uncluttered guest rooms have lace swag
curtains, Colonial armoires and pickled four-poster beds. All of
the wood furniture is custom made. A wraparound front porch
is a good spot for people watching. Breakfast included. ~ 4 Jarves
Street, Sandwich; 508-833-0363, 800-922-9989, fax 508-833-
2063; www.capecodinn.com. MODERATE.

The **Daniel Webster Inn** is a full-service hotel on Main Street.
The Federal-style, 47-room inn is so much bigger than the other

buildings in Sandwich, it looks a little out of whack. But the inside is very warm and cozy. Guest rooms are done in muted shades like smoke and rose, and are decorated with reproduction Colonial furniture and wing-back chairs; some beds have canopies. Brick paths lead through graceful flower gardens to a gazebo and pool area. The hotel has four dining rooms, a gift shop and a bar. ~ 149 Main Street, Sandwich; 508-888-3622, 800-444-3566, fax 508-888-5156, www.danlwebsterinn.com. DELUXE TO ULTRA-DELUXE.

The **Seth Pope House 1699 B&B** is a tiny, three-room bed and breakfast thoughtfully run by owners Beverly and John Dobel, two midwestern transplants. Unlike many bed and breakfasts there is a sense of privacy here since all three guest rooms have private baths. Each room is individually decorated with beautiful antiques, including a pencil-post bed in the Colonial Room—sneak a peek at it if you can. Comfort is important here; the beds are big with an abundance of pillows. A full breakfast is served each morning in the keeping room. Closed late October through March. ~ 110 Tupper Road, Sandwich; 508-888-5916, 888-996-7384; www.sunsol.com/sethpope. MODERATE.

The **Beechwood** is one of the prettiest inns on Route 6A. An ancient weeping beech tree shades a good portion of this buttery yellow, gabled Queen Anne Victorian and its wraparound porch. The entire house is furnished with fine antiques. In the Cottage Room you'll find a rare 1860 hand-painted bedroom set, while the third-floor Garret Room has steeply angled walls and a half-moon window overlooking Cape Cod Bay. It doesn't matter where you stay—all six guest rooms are wonderful. They all have private baths and air conditioning. A full breakfast is served in the wood-paneled dining room and tea on the porch. ~ 2839 Main Street, Barnstable Village; 508-362-6618, 800-609-6618, fax 508-362-0298; www.virtualcapecod.com/market/beechwood. DELUXE.

We'd heard from friends that innkeeper Evelyn Chester runs an unusual bed and breakfast, but nothing prepared us for how unique **Cobb's Cove** truly is. Guests follow a path of phosphorescent crushed white seashells up a slope, where they enter another world. Beds of lilies, wildflowers and herbs border the patio. Painted pottery, bird feeders and a zoo of birds vie for attention. Thick, rough timbers form a sparse wooden web overhead. The common areas are furnished with furniture and art from all styles and periods. In the winter, radiant heat under the tiled floors makes every room cozy. The six rooms (all with private baths) have magnificent views of the north side of the Cape and Cape Cod Bay. ~ Powder Hill Road, Barnstable Village; phone/fax 508-362-9356; www.bestofnewengland.com/cobbs coveinn. DELUXE TO ULTRA-DELUXE.

Built in 1812, the **Wedgewood Inn** sits on a little hill overlooking historic Route 6A. Surrounded by stately elm trees and

Author Picks

CHAPTER FAVORITES

Even during my first visit to Cape Cod, I felt an air of nostalgia surrounding its beaches and islands. One place that's sure to evoke this feeling is the **Thornton W. Burgess Museum** in Sandwich, filled with the children's books that my grandparents read to my parents. *page 266*

It took some searching among the trendy nouveau cuisine and northern Italian restaurants that are the norm on Cape Cod today, but I finally found timeless New England cooking in an equally classic setting at Falmouth's **Coonamesset Inn**. *page 295*

Speaking of nostalgia, after much searching for the empty beach where those classic, bittersweet photographs of the solitary John F. Kennedy might have been taken, I've decided that while the **Cape Pogue Wildlife Refuge** on Chappaquiddick Island may not be the place, it feels like it. *page 311*

If, like me, you harbor dreadful memories of wading through *Moby Dick* in school, you may feel more favorably disposed toward Melville after a stay at the **Jared Coffin House** in Nantucket, the town where the great white whale's legend originated. *page 316*

stone walls, the Colonial inn makes a lasting impression. Nine air-conditioned rooms sport handcrafted cherry wood pencil-post beds, antique quilts, private baths and wide-board floors; some have private decks and working fireplaces. The decor is an elegant interpretation of formal country style. A full breakfast, afternoon tea and fresh fruit in each room are included in the rate. ~ 83 Main Street (Route 6A), Yarmouthport; 508-362-5157, fax 508-362-5851; www.wedgewood-inn.com. DELUXE TO ULTRA-DELUXE.

Located in Yarmouth Port's historic district is **Gull Cottage**, a guest house that has a predominantly gay male clientele. The three guest rooms with shared bath are on the lower level of this 1790s house and are decorated mostly with antiques. The cottage is a mile from the beach and five miles from the boat docks. Closed January through March. ~ 10 Old Church Street, Yarmouthport; 508-362-8747. BUDGET.

A rambling white 1875 Victorian close to the beach, the **Four Chimneys Inn** is the kind of place where you can plop down on the living room couch in front of the fire and settle in for a good read selected from the study. Homey and low-key, the eight guest rooms (three with decorative fireplaces; all with private baths) are large and airy with high ceilings. A big yard with gardens surrounds the house, which sits well back from the road. Full breakfast included. Closed mid-December to mid-February. ~ 946 Main Street, Dennis; 508-385-6317, 800-874-5502, fax 508-385-6285; www.virtualcape cod.com/fourchimneys. MODERATE.

The **Isaiah Clark House**, an 18th-century sea captain's home, is surrounded by five acres of gardens, fruit trees and wild berry patches. Impeccably appointed with Shaker and Colonial antiques, many of the seven guest rooms have stenciled walls, canopy beds, sloping pine floors and fireplaces. Breakfast is served in an appealing room with an enormous fireplace—guests linger here all morning. Pre-dinner get-togethers are included. ~ 1187 Main Street, Brewster; 508-896-2223, 800-822-4001, fax 508-896-2138; www.isaiahclark.com. MODERATE TO DELUXE.

Situated on a high bluff right in Brewster's Historic District is the aptly named **High Brewster Inn**. The two guest rooms in the main house (built in 1738) are largely decorated with antiques, while the three cottages flaunt a combination of antiques and newer, traditional furnishings. The Pond Cottage, a summer cottage with lots of wicker, has just one room with a screened-in porch and a deck; the other two cottages have two bedrooms each plus kitchens and fireplaced living rooms. The inn overlooks a scenic pond and has one of the best restaurants in town. Closed December through March. ~ 964 Satucket Road, Brewster; 508-896-3636, 800-203-2634, fax 508-896-3734. MODERATE TO ULTRA-DELUXE.

A large turn-of-the-20th-century gray-and-white house, the **Old Sea Pines Inn** used to be a girls' finishing school. The spacious lobby and 23 guest rooms are comfortably furnished with antique brown wicker, slipcovered chairs and sofas; some rooms have private baths. Each of the suites can accommodate a family of four. A porch with rockers, perfect for reading or snoozing, overlooks a yard shaded by pine and oak trees. Breakfast is served in a bright sunporch with many skylights. Closed December through March. ~ 2553 Main Street, Brewster; 508-896-6114, fax 508-896-7387; www.oldseapines.com. MODERATE TO DELUXE.

Located in the former parsonage of the historic Unitarian Church, **The Inn at the Egg** is a gay-owned inn with five rooms (including one suite that welcomes children). It's right in the center of the village of Brewster, about a five-minute walk to the beach on Cape Cod Bay. Each room is individually decorated and has a private bath. Every morning, a full breakfast with candlelight and crystal is served in the dining room. ~ 1944 Main Street, Brewster; 508-896-3123, 800-259-8235, fax 508-896-6821; www.innattheegg.com. MODERATE TO DELUXE.

DINING

The **Daniel Webster Inn** is so Colonial looking, you expect it to serve traditional New England fare, but the menu is rather diversified. While the menu changes yearly, specials change every four to six weeks and cover a wide range of tastes. The award-winning restaurant boasts an extensive wine cellar. Meals are served in the very formal Webster Room with peach walls, mahogany chairs and brass chandeliers; in the intimate Heritage Dining Room, featuring a fireplace; the Music Room, which has a grand piano for music on the weekends; or in the greenhouse conservatory overlooking a garden. The Tavern at the Inn offers casual, reasonably priced meals that include wood-grilled pizzas, sandwiches, burgers and salads. Breakfast is also available. ~ 149 Main Street, Sandwich; 508-888-3622. BUDGET TO DELUXE.

The place to go for breakfast in Sandwich is **Marshland**. A diner-cum-bakery, it's locally famed for its reasonably priced, hearty and reliably good food. It has all the customary breakfast dishes plus lots of daily specials like pancakes, omelettes and hash. Be sure to order a home-baked muffin; they're celestial. No dinner on Sunday and Monday. ~ 109 Route 6A, Sandwich; 508-888-9824. BUDGET.

Barnstable Tavern serves traditional lunch and dinner fare such as mussels marinara, shrimp scampi and pasta. Located in a small complex of shops, the restaurant creates a pleasant Early American feeling with Windsor chairs, folk art, brass light fixtures and blond wood floors. The friendly bar is a good place for a drink. ~ 3176 Main Street (Route 6A), Barnstable; 508-362-2355. MODERATE TO DELUXE.

Mattakese Wharf, a quintessential summer resort eatery that's literally on the wharf in Barnstable Harbor, is a bit overpriced, but the million-dollar view will be well worth the cost of a meal. Try to get here before sunset and linger over cocktails while you watch fishermen and waterskiing families come and go in this quiet, lovely harbor. Entrées include large swordfish steaks, hamburgers, generous portions of mussels and boiled lobster, naturally. Closed November through April. ~ 271 Mill Way, Barnstable; 508-362-4511. MODERATE.

Abbicci serves up contemporary Italian cuisine in an 18th-century Cape Cod cottage on one of the prettiest stretches of historic Route 6A. A good spot for a special lunch or dinner, the restaurant has an imaginative, occasionally changing menu. Dishes have included grilled veal chop with a porcini madeira sauce, pistachio-crusted rack of lamb, and pan-seared halibut with lemon caper anchovy sauce. Cozy yet sophisticated, it has a number of small dining rooms with low ceilings, Windsor chairs and white tablecloths. ~ 43 Main Street (Route 6A), Yarmouthport; 508-362-3501. DELUXE TO ULTRA-DELUXE.

Gina's By The Sea, a sweet little white-shingled restaurant within walking distance of Chapin Beach, is far more sophisticated than it looks. The predominantly Italian menu features   ◄ HIDDEN daily specials as well as a regular menu; entrées include shrimp scampi, mussels marinara, chicken, veal and pasta dishes. Ruffled curtains, white tablecloths and plain wooden chairs create a casual elegance. Dinner only. Closed December through April. ~ 134 Taunton Avenue, Dennis; 508-385-3213. MODERATE TO DELUXE.

HIDDEN ▶   The food's hearty and predictable, the service fast and friendly at **Marshside Restaurant**, a glorified coffee shop popular with locals. Omelettes, bagels, pancakes and french toast are some of the breakfast offerings. Lunch items include lobster salad, quesadillas and fried clams. At dinner it's stuffed shrimp, steak, chicken piccata and daily specials. The decor is kitchen-cute with fake Tiffany lamps, bentwood chairs and ruffled curtains. The back room has a spectacular view of a salt marsh meadow. ~ 28 Bridge Street, East Dennis; 508-385-4010. BUDGET TO MODERATE.

The **Bramble Inn** is one of those restaurants people always rave about. Housed in two Greek Revival farmhouses on scenic Route 6A, the place offers a prix-fixe menu that changes every three weeks. Dinner is served in five small dining rooms complete with Queen Anne chairs, fresh flowers and antiques. Innovative dishes have included grilled seafood in curry sauce, smoked bluefish pâté, and rack of lamb with garlic and rosemary. Dinner only. Closed Monday and from November to mid-May. ~ 2019 Main Street (Route 6A), Brewster; 508-896-7644. ULTRA-DELUXE.

HIDDEN ▶   The blond wood floors, floral drapes, ceiling fans and cloth napkins of the **Brewster Fish House Restaurant** creates a quaint and casual atmosphere. Its small, imaginative menu features dishes such as calamari with tomato-red aïoli and grilled Atlantic salmon with prosciutto and a mild Dijon mustard sauce. Closed late November through March. ~ 2208 Main Street (Route 6A), Brewster; 508-896-7867. MODERATE TO DELUXE.

If you're in the mood for a quiet, special dinner, make reservations at the **High Brewster Inn**. This lovely old inn (the building dates to 1738) has three dining rooms, all with low ceilings, open beams and wide plank floors. The cuisine is contemporary American; the four-course, prix-fixe meal includes dishes such as rack of lamb and tenderloin of beef plus some of the best local seafood you'll find. The catch of the day varies with the season. Dinner only. Closed December through March. ~ 964 Satucket Road, Brewster; 508-896-3636. DELUXE TO ULTRA-DELUXE.

Elegant and expensive, **Chillingsworth** has been repeatedly praised by the *New York Times* and *Esquire*. The menu changes daily, utilizing seasonal and fresh ingredients. The food is French American, with dishes such as loin of veal with sun-dried tomatoes, risotto and sage, and free-range chicken with greens, chili brown sauce and sweet potato chips. Located in a tree-shaded, 1689 Colonial house, the restaurant has dining areas combining modern and traditional decorative touches such as contemporary artwork, antique mirrors and white tablecloths. The seven-course dinner is served at two seatings. The main dining room, closed on Monday, is ultra-deluxe. Bistro dining in the garden is moderate to deluxe. Closed Monday and Tuesday from Labor Day to late November and from Thanksgiving through Memorial Day. ~ 2449 Main Street (Route 6A), Brewster; 508-896-3640. MODERATE TO ULTRA-DELUXE.

SHOPPING

Some of the Cape's best shopping is along Route 6A, which is lined with antique stores and artists studios selling pottery, weavings, handcrafted furniture and more.

With its sloping wood floors and wainscotting, **The Brown Jug** looks like an old general store. Along with antiques from the late 18th- through early-20th-centuries, it sells high-quality, hand-pressed glass. Many of the pieces were made in Sandwich in the 19th century. Closed January and February. ~ 155 Main Street (Route 6A), Sandwich; 508-833-1088.

The **Blacks' Handweaving Shop** has beautiful handwoven coverlets, throws, place mats, hats, gloves and wallhangings in lush colors. The store is in a large barnlike room where you can watch owners/designers Bob and Gabrielle Black working at one of the many looms. ~ 597 Main Street (Route 6A), West Barnstable; 508-362-3955.

Design Works specializes in antique Scandinavian pine armoires, mirrors, chairs, settees, and white linen and lace napkins, tablecloths and bed accessories. ~ 159 Main Street (Route 6A), Yarmouthport; 508-362-9698.

Originally a general store that also housed a church on its second floor, **Parnassus Book Service** has a wealth of marine and Cape Cod book titles. ~ 220 Old King's Highway (Route 6A), Yarmouthport; 508-362-6420.

One of the nicest sights on Route 6A is the vibrant display of fresh produce and flowers at **Tobey Farm Country Store**. Stop here in the summer for fresh native corn, peaches and plums, and in the fall for pumpkins and apples. The white clapboard farm also sells reasonably priced dried wreaths. Closed January to mid-April. ~ 352 Main Street (Route 6A), Dennis; 508-385-2930.

Even if you can't afford anything at **Kingsland Manor**, stop and browse through its labyrinth of beautiful rooms and gardens filled with exquisite American and European antiques. ~ 440 Main Street (Route 6A), West Brewster; 508-385-9741.

NIGHTLIFE

Heritage Plantation Concerts offers a diverse program for Saturday evenings and Sunday afternoons, including jazz, ethnic and folk music, banjo music, Scottish pipe bands, chorale groups and big bands. Closed late October through Mother's Day. ~ Pine and Grove streets, Sandwich; 508-888-3300.

Established in 1926 and America's oldest summer theater, **The Cape Playhouse** presents well-known plays and musicals such as *The Sound of Music, Ain't Misbehavin'* and *Noises Off*, performed by Hollywood and Broadway stars. Lana Turner, Gregory Peck and Henry Fonda have been on stage here. Nostalgic and romantic-looking, the Playhouse is in an 1838 meetinghouse surrounded by graceful lawns, gardens and a Victorian Gothic ticket booth. Closed mid-September to late June. ~ Route 6A, Dennis; 508-385-3911.

Bette Davis, during her stint as an usher at The Cape Playhouse, was plucked from her job to fill a small role as a maid in a play here.

The Cape Museum of Fine Arts' **Reel Art Cinema**, on the grounds of The Cape Playhouse, shows quality films, both new and old, such as *Henry V* with Laurence Olivier, *Ginger and Fred* and *House of Games*. Films are shown all year long. ~ Route 6A, Dennis; 508-385-4477.

Barnstable Comedy Club Community Theater, founded in 1922, is the oldest amateur theater group on the Cape. Throughout the year it gives major productions and workshops. Kurt Vonnegut, an alumni of the Club, acted in many of its earlier productions. ~ Route 6A, Barnstable Village; 508-362-6333.

BEACHES & PARKS

North Cape beaches are on protected Cape Cod Bay. They tend to be quiet and calm, with gentle surf and scenic vistas of soft sand dunes and salt marsh.

SANDY NECK BEACH & THE GREAT MARSHES 🏃 🏊 This area has all the ecological treasures for which the Cape is known. Very straight and long, beautiful Sandy Neck Beach (also known as Horizons Beach) offers a 360-degree view of the ocean and rippling sand dunes bordered by the Great Marshes, 3000 acres of protected land harboring many species of marine life and birds. The sand is ideal for beach-combing, and trails meander through the dunes and marsh. There are restrooms and a snack bar. Parking fee, $8 (Memorial Day to Labor Day only). ~ Take Sandy Neck Road off Route 6A in Sandwich to the beach in Barnstable.

GREY'S BEACH 🏊 ⛵ 🛶 This small, quiet beach is perfect for children. But the main reason people come here is to stroll along the long, elevated walkway stretching across the marsh that skirts the beach. The walkway permits a close-up view of marsh flora and fauna, and from a distance it appears to be floating in grassy water. This area is quite beautiful, especially at sunset. Facilities include picnic tables, playground, restrooms, lifeguards and a pier for fishing. ~ Off Route 6A on Centre Street, Yarmouth; for information, call the Yarmouth Chamber of Commerce, 508-778-1008.

CHAPIN BEACH 🏊 🎣 🛶 The sand-strewn road leading to Chapin Beach passes gentle sand dunes and small, unpretentious, summer cottages. A pleasant spot for walks along the shore, the thin, slightly curved, dune-backed beach has soft, white sand ideal for clean, comfortable sunbathing. During nesting season, dogs are not allowed on the beach. Chase Garden Creek at the back of the beach is fun for canoers; you can shore fish for striped bass. Facilities are limited to portable toilets. Parking fee, $10 (mid-June to Labor Day only). ~ Off Route 6A on Chapin Beach Road, Dennis; 508-394-8300.

PAINE'S CREEK BEACH 🏃 🏊 There are better beaches nearby for sunning and swimming, but Paine's Creek is ideal for quiet walks through timeless scenery bathed in golden light. Weather-beaten skiffs are moored along the shore, and Paine's Creek, a gentle slip of a stream, winds through a salt marsh meadow down to a narrow strip of soft beach surrounded by tiny coves and inlets. Children love the tidepools that form when the water recedes. Parking fee, $8 (Memorial Day to Labor Day only). ~ Off Route 6A on Paine's Creek Road, West Brewster; for information, call the Brewster Chamber of Commerce, 508-255-7045.

NICKERSON STATE PARK 🏃 🚲 🐎 🏕 🏊 ⛵ ⛴ 🎣 🛶 🚤 🚣 ⛵ This 2000-acre park looks more like the Berkshires than Cape Cod. Dense pine groves, meadows and jewel-like freshwater ponds with beaches are home to abundant wildlife including red foxes and white-tailed deer. There is so much to do here—hiking, biking, motor boating, canoeing—it gets very crowded in the summer. Quiet beaches and hiking trails can be found around Little Cliff and Flax ponds. In winter there's cross-country skiing and ice-skating on the ponds. Catch-and-release fishing is excellent at Higgins Pond, which is stocked annually with trout; salmon can be caught for keeps at Cliff Pond. You can swim in freshwater ponds. There are canoe rentals, picnic areas, restrooms, showers, a ranger station and interpretive programs. ~ Off Route 6A, Brewster; 508-896-3491.

▲ There are 418 tent/RV sites (no hookups); 168 are available on a first-come, first-served basis; 250 require reservations six months in advance; $6 to $8 per night. Winter camping is allowed for self-contained RVs; $6 per night. Call 877-422-6762 for reservations.

Route 6A ends at Orleans, where it intersects with Route 6 and leads to Eastham. At this point the character of the landscape changes dramatically. The **The Outer Cape** woods disappear and the sky opens up to reveal towering sand dunes, miles of silver marsh grass and windswept moors. At the very tip is Provincetown, one of the Cape's largest communities.

About 50 percent of the Outer Cape is under the jurisdiction of the Cape Cod National Seashore, a natural playground with miles of bicycle paths, hikes and the Cape's most dramatic beaches (see the "Beaches & Parks" and "Hiking" sections in this chapter).

SIGHTS

HIDDEN ►

Fort Hill in Eastham offers a mesmerizing view overlooking Nauset Marsh that's so beautiful it doesn't seem real. Once productive farmland, the marsh today is laced with wavy ribbons of water that wind through downy, soft green-gold marsh grass past old farmhouses, stone walls and ponds complete with adorable ducks. Trails meander through this area, which is a special resting place for blue herons. ~ Off Route 6.

HIDDEN ►

Near the Fort Hill parking lot is the **Edward Penniman House**, a fairytale-like, red-and-yellow French Empire house with an enormous archway of whale jaw bones at its gate. Built by an eccentric whaler in the 19th century, the whimsical structure contrasts dramatically with the Cape's simple saltbox homes. ~ Off Route 6, Eastham.

After Eastham is **Wellfleet**, an unpretentious, wiggle-your-toes-in-the-sand kind of place with a surprising number of good art galleries and gourmet restaurants. On Saturday nights in the summer, many galleries have openings that feel like neighborhood block parties. Wellfleet has many year-round residents, and they all seem to know each other.

Before heading into town, stop at the **Wellfleet Chamber of Commerce** for a gallery guide. Closed Monday through Friday from mid-May to late June and from Labor Day to mid-October; closed from mid-October to mid-May. ~ Route 6; 508-349-2510; www.capecod.net/wellfleetcc.

On the way to Wellfleet is **Uncle Tim's Bridge**, a low wooden boardwalk that goes over a field of silvery marsh grass to a small wooded hill. A dreamy sort of place shrouded in delicate mist in the morning and soft mellow light in the afternoon, it's perfect for a picnic or quiet walk.

North of Wellfleet lies magnificent **Truro**, a vast treeless plain of rolling moors surrounded by water and some of the state's most impressive sand dunes. Named after an area of Cornwall, England, that's similar in appearance, Truro is a wonderful area for picture taking.

LODGING

HIDDEN ►

To capture the essence of Wellfleet, stay at the **Holden Inn**, a long, white farmhouse-style building. There's nothing fancy about the place, but like Wellfleet, it has an easy, casual feeling. Located on a shady country lane five minutes from the wharf, the inn offers 27 well-kept rooms (some with shared bath) with ruffled white curtains and floral wallpaper or wood paneling. Closed Thanksgiving to early May. ~ 140 Commercial Street, Wellfleet; 508-349-3450. MODERATE.

Restaurants on the Cape fall into three categories: expensive French/nouvelle cuisine, surf and turf, and coffee-shop fare. If you crave variety, head for the Outer Cape. Wellfleet has a surprising number of excellent, imaginative restaurants.

The noisy, friendly **Bayside Lobster Hutt** is a perfect spot after a day at the beach. Located on a country road leading to Wellfleet's galleries and harbor, this eatery looks like an old white schoolhouse. On the roof, a fisherman statue hauls an enormous red lobster into a boat. Everyone sits at long picnic tables. Buoys and fish nets decorate the walls. The menu features lobster, flounder, steamed clams, scallops and shrimp; you'll also find non-seafood items like chicken sandwiches. There's a raw bar as well as a take-out window where you can order clambake picnics. Dinner only. Closed mid-September through Memorial Day. ~ 91 Commercial Street, Wellfleet; 508-349-6333. MODERATE TO ULTRA-DELUXE.

Right on Wellfleet's pretty harbor, the **Bookstore Restaurant** lets you browse through regional titles while you wait for your order. The fare is almost entirely seafood, ranging from Cajun shrimp and steamed littleneck clams to broiled lobster and char-broiled swordfish. ~ Kendrick Avenue, Wellfleet; 508-349-3154. MODERATE.

The Lighthouse is a Wellfleet institution. If you want to mingle with the locals, come here in the morning for breakfast. The ambience is strictly coffee shop, as is the food, which includes french toast, bacon and eggs, fried seafood, sandwiches, hamburgers and the like. Located in the center of town, it has a kitschy miniature lighthouse on its roof that is impossible to miss. Breakfast, lunch and dinner are served. ~ Main Street, Wellfleet; 508-349-3681. MODERATE TO DELUXE.

Sweet Seasons is an exceptionally pretty restaurant overlooking an idyllic duck pond surrounded by rushes, flagstone paths, locust trees and woods. The pale gray and apricot restaurant serves dishes such as grilled swordfish, shrimp with feta cheese, tomatoes and ouzo, sliced island pork and lobster marsala. Dinner only. Closed Monday and from mid-September to late June. ~ 70 Main Street, Wellfleet; 508-349-6535. DELUXE.

FIRST ENCOUNTER BEACH This is where the Pilgrims first encountered the Wampanoag Indians, who were not exactly happy to see them. Six years earlier an English slave dealer had kidnapped some of them to sell in Spain. When the Pilgrims arrived a mild skirmish broke out, but no one was hurt and the Pilgrims made a hasty retreat. Sandy paths lead through dense green grass to this striking beach bordered by a vast marsh meadow and brilliant sky. The long, wide beach attracts a rela-

Text continued on page 282.

The Land of Lighthouses

Massachusetts' prominence as a shipping and fishing center made lighthouses essential early in its history. The first lighthouse in America was built in Boston Harbor on Little Brewster Island in 1716. During the years to follow, 60 more were built all along the coast.

The majority of lighthouses have been well preserved, and many are still in use, although the lighthouse keeper has gone the way of time. Today lighthouses are automated and unmanned. Lighted buoys, radio communications, radar and high-tech navigational equipment, electronic fog signals and the Coast Guard offer additional protection to seafaring vessels. Shipwrecks are practically unheard of these days.

A few beacons are privately owned, but most are maintained by the Coast Guard or local historic organizations. What follows is a guide to some of the most beautiful and historically significant lighthouses.

Built in 1797, **Highland Lighthouse Station** in Truro, Cape Cod, is better known as Cape Cod Light. It stands on clay bluffs overlooking an area once known as "the graveyard of ships" because hundreds of vessels went aground here before the lighthouse was built. Visible 20 miles out to sea, this classic white-and-black lighthouse is surrounded by scenic Cape Cod National Seashore and commands a magnificent view.

Located within the Cape Cod National Seashore, **Race Point Lighthouse**, built in 1816, guards the entrance to Provincetown Harbor. Surrounded by wild, windswept dunes, it is accessible only by four-wheel-drive vehicle or by foot. Even after the lighthouse was built, from 1816 to 1946 more than 100 shipwrecks occurred in this treacherous area.

Plymouth Lighthouse, established in 1768, is located on a beautiful bluff at the end of a peninsula that stretches from Duxbury to Plymouth Harbor. During the Revolutionary War, a British ship fired a cannonball at the lighthouse, but it barely made a dent. Destroyed by fire in 1801, it was rebuilt in 1843 and is one of Massachusetts' most scenic lighthouses.

On the road to Nauset Beach is **Nauset Light**, a classic red-and-white lighthouse, one of Cape Cod's most photographed sights.~ Off Route 6, at the end of Cable Road and along Nauset Light Beach Road, Eastham; 508-349-3785.

Scituate Lighthouse, built in 1811 on Cedar Point at the entrance to Scituate Harbor, is maintained by the Scituate Historical Society. It's no longer in use, but an event that took place here during the War of 1812 gave this lighthouse historic distinction. In September 1814, Rebecca and Abigail Bates, the lighthouse keeper's young daughters, were alone in the lighthouse when they spotted British war ships heading for the harbor. Frantic to do something, they started playing military songs on a drum and fife. The music made the British think the American Army was amassing, and they hightailed it back to the high seas. The girls became local heroes.

Minot's Lighthouse, which dates to 1850, is built on a ledge one mile offshore from Cohasset. The ledge can only be seen at low tide. Most of the time the lighthouse looks as if it's floating in water. Since it was built in a highly dangerous area, men working on the lighthouse were washed out to sea by strong waves and currents. In 1851 a ferocious storm destroyed the lighthouses and two keepers died. Because of these tragedies the lighthouse was thought to be haunted by the ghosts of those who perished at sea. A museum in Cohasset contains many artifacts and historical information on the lighthouse.

Annisquam Harbor Lighthouse is on Wigwam Point at the mouth of Annisquam River on the North Shore. Built in 1801, this lighthouse doesn't have historic significance, but it is one of the most scenic in all of Massachusetts. It's located off the beaten path: to get there, take Route 127 to Annisquam and turn right at the village church, then right into Norwood Heights and follow the road to the water.

Father out to sea, Nantucket has three lighthouses. Near the town of Nantucket, **Brant Point Light** was the second lighthouse built in America (1746); since then it has been rebuilt eight times. **Sankaty Head Light,** one mile north of Siasconset, dates back to 1850 but is now endangered because erosion is undercutting the cliff on which it stands. In 1987 this lighthouse was fitted with a modern airport beacon, and its original lens can now be seen in the Nantucket Whaling Museum. The **Great Point Light,** only ten years old, is a reproduction of an earlier lighthouse built in 1817. Its battery-powered light is recharged by solar cells. ~ The end of Wauwinet Road, off Polis Road, at the northeast end of the island.

tively quiet crowd in the summer. Facilities are limited to restrooms. Day-use fee, $5. ~ Take Samoset Road off Route 6, Eastham; 508-240-5972.

CAPE COD NATIONAL SEASHORE 🏃 🚲 ⛵ ⛵ ⛵ 🚤
This 27,000-acre ecological wonderland includes endless stretches of unbelievably beautiful beaches, 60-foot sand dunes, steep cliffs, wind-bitten moors, salt marsh, freshwater ponds and woodlands. Undisturbed and undeveloped, the area runs from Chatham to Provincetown and is laced with some of the Cape's finest hiking and bicycle trails (see "Cape Cod by Bike" and the "Hiking" section at the end of this chapter).

What follows are some of the National Seashore's most renowned beaches and ponds. For more information visit the **Salt Pond Visitors Center**. ~ Route 6, Eastham; 508-255-3421. The **Cape Cod National Seashore Headquarters** is also helpful. ~ Route 6, South Wellfleet; 508-349-3785.

COAST GUARD BEACH ⛵ 🏊 "On its solitary dune my house faced the four walls of the world," wrote Henry Beston of the place he built in 1927 on this extraordinary beach. In 1978 the house washed away in a storm, but Beston's experiences are chronicled in *The Outermost House*, available at most Cape Cod bookstores. Rugged and wild Coast Guard Beach goes on for as far as the eye can see. Bordered by cliffs, marsh grass and tributaries, a red-and-white coast guard station sits on a bluff overlooking the beach. The beach is ideal for long walks, sunbathing, swimming (although the sea can be rough at times) and surfing. There are restrooms, showers and lifeguards (summer only). Parking fee, $7 (mid-June to Labor Day only). ~ Take Doane Road off Route 6 near Eastham; 508-349-3785.

NAUSET LIGHT BEACH & MARCONI BEACH ⛵ 🏊 These impressive beaches—bordered by towering, shrub-covered cliffs—are right next to each other. Long, steep wooden stairways descend to the clean, white-sand beaches. The imposing cliffs and expansive vistas make you feel very small and in awe of it all. Walk north along the shore for a quiet spot in the summer, when the beaches get crowded. Swimming is excellent in the protected area, but watch the undertow. Facilities include restrooms, showers and summer lifeguards; Nauset Light is wheelchair accessible. Day-use fee, $7 per vehicle or $20 for a summer pass. ~ Nauset Light is off Route 6 at the end of Cable Road and along Nauset Light Beach Road in Eastham. Marconi is off Route 6 on Marconi Beach Road in Wellfleet; 508-349-3785.

HIDDEN ▶ **GREAT POND & GULL POND** ⛵ Wellfleet has some of the most idyllic freshwater ponds on the Cape. Less than a mile from wild-looking shoreline, these two offer a completely different nature experience. Densely wooded and pine-scented, they look like mountain ponds. The sparkling water is fresh and invigorating. Gull Pond has a lovely shaded grassy area with picnic tables, a small sand beach and a float in the water; there are paddleboat concessions here (508-349-9808). Great Pond is approached via wooden steps leading down from the parking lot overlooking the pond. It has a pretty sandy beach. Half-hidden houses lie along some of the shore. You must live or be staying in Wellfleet to go to either pond; nonresidents must purchase a permit. There are restrooms and picnic tables. ~ To reach Great Pond, take Calhoon Hollow Road off Route 6 in Wellfleet; for Gull Pond, take Gull Pond Road off Route 6 in Wellfleet. For information (late June through Labor Day only), call the Beach Sticker House, 508-349-9818; or call Wellfleet Chamber of Commerce, 508-349-2510.

Provincetown

Provincetown, at the Cape's outer tip, is nestled on a hill overlooking the bay. Everything good and bad about Cape Cod can be found here: elegant sea captains' mansions, a honky-tonk wharf, dazzling beaches, first-rate museums, schlocky galleries, hamburger joints and gourmet restaurants.

The people are equally diverse. Provincetown has a large gay population, as well as artists and writers, Portuguese fishermen, aristocrats, beer-guzzling rabble-rousers and plenty of tourists. Similarly, Provincetown's many attractions draw all types of visitors, but the town is particularly popular among gay travelers. The gay scene is everywhere, ranging from the beaches to the boulevards to the bars. Every hotel and restaurant in the area welcomes gays and lesbians and in many cases caters primarily to them, as is noted in the reviews below.

Of all the towns on the Cape, Provincetown has the most interesting history. The Pilgrims landed here in 1620 before going to Plymouth, and in the 18th and 19th centuries it was a prominent whaling and fishing port, attracting many Portuguese settlers who still fish the waters today.

Around the turn of the 20th century, artists and writers, such as Eugene O'Neill, started moving to Provincetown, and it became one of America's most renowned artists colonies. A renaissance period flourished until about 1945, when tourism evolved and many artists scattered for quieter parts of the world.

SIGHTS

To immerse yourself in Provincetown's artistic past, get a copy of *Walking Tours No. 2 and 3* from the Provincetown Heritage Museum, or contact the **Provincetown Chamber of Commerce**. These pamphlets list the name and address of every famous writer and artist who ever lived here. Their former homes aren't open to the public, but it's fun to walk by 577 Commercial Street and imagine what it was like when O'Neill rented a room there.

Closed January and February. ~ 307 Commercial Street, Mac-Millan Wharf; 508-487-3424; www.ptownchamber.com.

Provincetown Heritage Museum provides an overview of the town's historic and artistic past. The *Rose Dorothea*, the world's largest indoor model of a fishing schooner, fills up the entire second floor of the museum. Other exhibits include hand-painted Peter Hunt furniture featuring seascapes, photographs of artists at the turn of the 20th century and many paintings. Closed from Columbus Day through Memorial Day. Admission. ~ 356 Commercial Street; 508-487-7098.

Walk east on Commercial Street, the main drag, to the **Provincetown Art Association and Museum** for the best art on the Cape. The museum exhibits work by noted Provincetown artists. In the winter, the museum is open on weekends only. Admission. ~ 460 Commercial Street; 508-487-1750.

For a picture-postcard view of Provincetown and the surrounding seashore and sand dunes, visit the **Pilgrim Monument and Provincetown Museum**. The 252-foot granite tower was copied from the Torre del Mangia tower in Siena, Italy. The museum houses an eclectic collection that includes everything from antique dolls, Wedgwood china, primitive portraits and scrimshaw to figureheads, a captain's cabin from a whaling ship and the town's oldest fire engine. Closed December through March. Admission. ~ High Pole Hill; 508-487-1310; www.pilgrim-monument.org.

LODGING
The **Outermost Hostel** offers dorm-style accommodations in five cottages. Amenities are standard hostel: shared baths, common kitchen and lounge. One unique feature is the hostel's key system, which allows entry to your room during the day. Gay-friendly. Closed mid-October to mid-April. ~ 28 Winslow Street; 508-487-4378. BUDGET.

The **Brass Key Guesthouse** is one of the area's best gay-friendly inns. The owner's background in the high end of the hotel trade shows in his attention to the details that count—elegant yet comfortable furniture, sparkling clean bathrooms, meticulous landscaping and friendly staff. The Brass Key comprises 33 rooms in a sea captain's home and two other Victorian buildings, as well as three cottages. The large courtyard features a pool and hot tub. All rooms have private baths and air conditioning. Closed November through April (but open New Year's weekend). ~ 67 Bradford Street; 508-487-9005, 800-842-9858, fax 508-487-9020; www.ptown@brasskey.com. ULTRA-DELUXE.

When you see the carefully restored 18th-century sea captain's home that is the **Fairbanks Inn**, you might well expect high prices; however, you would be wrong. Despite the charming building and fairly extensive amenities (working fireplaces in most and air conditioning in all of the rooms, for example), the

13 guest rooms are reasonably priced, all year-round; one has a kitchen. Wide plank floors and wainscoting, large, airy rooms and four-poster beds complete the picture. An extended continental breakfast is offered in the dining room. Gay-friendly. ~ 90 Bradford Street; 508-487-0386, 800-324-7265, fax 508-487-3540; www.capecod.net/fairbank. MODERATE TO DELUXE.

With its dark wood shingles, sky-blue shutters and nursery-rhyme garden, the **Bradford Gardens Inn** looks like an illustration from a Mother Goose book. One of the most inviting cottages in Provincetown, the Bradford has 18 guest rooms and apartments, most with working fireplaces and all with private baths. An apartment on the side of the house with its own entrance has a sitting room, brick fireplace and garden view. A full gourmet breakfast is served by the cozy fireplace and all have private baths. Gay-friendly. ~ 178 Bradford Street; 508-487-1616, 800-432-2334, fax 508-487-5596; www.bradfordgardens.com. DELUXE TO ULTRA-DELUXE.

◀ *HIDDEN*

The gay-owned **Heritage House** offers great people watching and harbor views from the large upper veranda. This centrally located Cape Cod–style home, which dates from 1856, has 13 rooms furnished with an eclectic assortment of antiques. Guests are welcome to show their stuff on the baby-grand piano downstairs. Expanded continental breakfast buffet included. ~ 7 Center Street; 508-487-3692; www.heritageh.com. MODERATE.

Built in 1820, the **Watership Inn** is popular with gay men and women. Located on a quiet street yet close to everything, the inn features 14 guest rooms with arched beamed ceilings and antiques. Some have private decks. Two townhouses, each with private bath, kitchen, living room and deck, are available for week-long stays. Continental breakfast is served on an outdoor deck or in an attractive living room with vaulted ceilings and a bank of french doors leading out to a yard where volleyball is played in the summer. The inn offers terrific off-season bargains. ~ 7 Winthrop Street; 508-487-0094, 800-330-9413; www.capecod.net/watershipinn. MODERATE TO DELUXE.

Within easy reach of all of P-Town's attractions, yet a bit removed, is the **Ampersand Guesthouse**. Catering to a mostly gay male clientele, it's a Greek Revival house whose 11 guest rooms and one studio are decorated with a combination of antique and contemporary furnishings; most have private baths. Some have views of the water. There's a great sundeck with a view of the bay. ~ 6 Cottage Street; 508-487-0959, 800-574-9645; www.capecod.net/ampersand. MODERATE.

A short walk through the artsy East End brings you to and from **Windamar House**, a peaceful white clapboard guesthouse that caters mainly to women. Right across the road from Cape Cod Bay, the six rooms and two efficiency apartments (some with shared bath) vary from attractive to elegant, but the inn's prettiest areas are its spectacular gardens. Continental breakfast is provided in the common room, where guests are also welcome to watch television and videos or use the microwave to prepare snacks. Parking is available. Closed January to mid-February. ~ 568 Commercial Street; 508-487-0599, fax 508-487-7505; www. provincetown.com/windamar. MODERATE TO DELUXE.

DINING

Provincetown restaurants serve everything from Italian, French, vegetarian and Continental to nouvelle, meat-and-potatoes and bistro-style fare.

Ciro & Sal's is one of Provincetown's most legendary restaurants. Established in 1951 as a coffeehouse for artists, it grew into a full-fledged restaurant serving classic Italian food. In 1959 Sal left and opened his own restaurant (described below). Dripping with atmosphere, the basement dining room resembles an Italian wine cellar with a low ceiling, slate floor and candle-lit tables. An upstairs dining room overlooks a garden. Popular dishes include linguine with seafood in a plum tomato sauce, poached bass with clams and veal tenderloin with mozzarella and prosciutto. Dinner only. Closed Monday through Friday from November through May. ~ 4 Kiley Court; 508-487-8866. MODERATE TO DELUXE.

For a free directory of gay- or lesbian-owned hotels, restaurants, bars, shops and services, stop by the Provincetown Business Guild. ~ P.O. Box 421, Provincetown, MA 02657; 508-487-2313, 800-637-8696.

Sal's Place is cozy and intimate, with Italian ambience: Chianti bottles hang from the low-beamed ceiling, bay windows are draped with lace curtains and a Modigliani poster adorns a wall. The northern Italian menu includes 12 kinds of pasta, veal dishes and inventive seafood entrées such as *brodetto* (seafood medley) and broiled salmon with balsamic vinegar and capers. Try the heavenly homemade *tiramisu* or chocolate mousse for dessert. Dinner only. Closed November through April. ~ 99 Commercial Street; 508-487-1279. MODERATE TO DELUXE.

With its white cloths, salmon-colored walls and casablanca ceiling fans, Gallerani's Café attracts locals and out-of-towners alike. The prices are a bargain, the food is down to earth and so is the crowd. The room is bright and airy, and the long bar in back is a pleasant place for a drink. Gallerani's serves dishes such as baked stuffed lobster, filet mignon and a variety of pastas. Dinner only. Closed Monday and Tuesday from late September to mid-May. ~ 133 Commercial Street; 508-487-4433. MODERATE TO DELUXE.

Café Heaven is located on a part of Commercial Street away from the touristy hoopla. Housed in an old storefront with large picture windows, the restaurant is bright and uncluttered, with white wooden tables and wooden floors. Colorful paintings by nationally known artist John Grillo adorn one wall. The food is hearty and all American—bacon and eggs, Portuguese french toast, omelettes, tasty scones, lusty sandwiches, gourmet burgers and salads. This popular hangout for gays and lesbians is open for breakfast, lunch and dinner. Dinner only on weekends from mid-October through January. Closed January through March. ~ 199 Commercial Street; 508-487-9639. MODERATE.

The **Mews Restaurant & Café** has two levels of dining right on the waterfront. Elegant dinners and brunches are served downstairs, while upstairs is more casual. The cuisine is intercontinental, the fresh seafood especially good. Entertainment some nights. ~ 429 Commercial Street; 508-487-1500. MODERATE TO ULTRA-DELUXE.

SHOPPING

Marine Specialties sounds like a straightforward place, but it's not. Housed in a barnlike room, this eclectic shop is jammed with all sorts of reasonably priced oddball nautical and military items such as antique brass buttons, old-fashioned oars, bells, baskets, antique diving gear, fog horns and fishing nets. Even people who hate to shop love this place. Closed weekdays in January and February. ~ 235 Commercial Street; 508-487-1730.

Remembrances of Things Past is fun to explore even if you aren't in the mood to buy. It's full of nostalgic memorabilia from the '20s to the '50s—phones, jewelry, sports memorabilia and vintage photographs of Elvis, Marilyn and Lucy. Closed weekdays from November through March. ~ 376 Commercial Street; 508-487-9443.

NIGHTLIFE

Provincetown has first-rate gay and lesbian entertainment—everything from afternoon tea dances, cabaret and ministage productions to piano bars, discos, you name it. Here are some of the most popular spots, a few of which draw straights and gays alike.

The hottest gay bar and disco in town is the **Atlantic House**. You can join in on the "manhunt" on Wednesday or a specialty theme on Friday. Cover. ~ 4–6 Masonic Place; 508-487-3821.

During the summer a popular activity for gays is the daily afternoon tea dance at **The Boatslip Beach Club**, a full-service resort on the beach. Closed November to mid-April. Cover. ~ 161 Commercial Street; 508-487-1669.

The **Pied Piper** is a mixed gay bar with a waterfront deck and a big, open dancefloor. Locals say the best time to go is after 6 p.m. for the after-tea dances. Closed November through March. Cover from July through August and weekends in May. ~ 193-A Commercial Street; 508-487-1527.

Drag shows are a hit at the **Crown and Anchor** bar, housed in a historic waterfront building. This place attracts gays, lesbians and straights. Cover. ~ 247 Commercial Street; 508-487-1430.

The Post Office Cabaret is the spot for lesbians in the summer, when it presents noted female performers such as Teresa Trull. The café, located downstairs, is a good place to hang out; open year-round. Cabaret closed from Labor Day through Memorial Day. Cover. ~ 303 Commercial Street; 508-487-3892.

BEACHES & PARKS

RACE POINT BEACH & HERRING COVE BEACH 🏃 🚲 🏊

"Here a man may stand, and put all America behind him," wrote Thoreau in his book *Cape Cod*. Located at the end of the Cape, both beaches have magnificent 360-degree views of brilliant sky, ocean, dunes and a silver sea of beach grass. On cloudy days, the winds shift, the colors change and a minimalist environment unfolds. When the sun shines, everything shimmers. Both beaches offer long stretches of clean white sand surrounded by acres of untouched land. Bicycle paths and hiking trails are everywhere. Facilities include restrooms, showers, lifeguards and a snack bar (Herring Cove only). Day-use fee, $7 per vehicle (mid-June through Labor Day only). ~ To reach Race Point, take Race Point Road off Route 6; for Herring Cove, go to the end of Route 6 and follow the signs. Get information from Province Lands Visitor Center; 508-487-1256.

▼▼▼▼▼▼▼▼▼▼▼▼

The South Cape

This part of the Cape is a hodgepodge of scenic villages, inexpensive motels, mini-malls and gas stations. To explore it from Provincetown, head back on Route 6 to Route 28 in Orleans, a pleasant yet unassuming residential area. At Chatham, Route 28 swings around to the west and runs along the south shore of the Cape along Nantucket Sound.

SIGHTS

Chatham, one of the most stylish towns on the Cape, has exquisite inns, good restaurants and beautiful shops. It's a very Ralph Lauren kind of place where everyone looks as though they play tennis.

Chatham's **Information Booth** is in the middle of town. Closed mid-October to mid-May. ~ 533 Main Street, Chatham; 508-945-5199. For year-round information, you can stop by the **Bassett House**. ~ Intersection of Route 137 and Route 28.

At the end of Main Street, you run into **Shore Road**, lined with graceful oceanfront homes and a classic lighthouse across from the Coast Guard station.

Located nearby is the **Old Atwood House Museum**, an unassuming 1752 shingled house exhibiting antiques, seashells and Sandwich glass. Right next to the house, a barn displays compelling murals by realist painter Alice Stallknecht. The murals depict Chatham townspeople of the 1930s in religious settings, such as Christ preaching from a dory below the Chatham lighthouse. Open Tuesday through Friday from mid-June to late

September. Admission. ~ 347 Stage Harbor Road, Chatham;
508-945-2493; www.atwoodhouse.org.

Monomoy National Wildlife Refuge, two sandy, four-mile-
long islands immediately off the coast of Chatham, are home to
over 300 species of birds, many on the endangered species list.
More than 300 harbor and grey seals also inhabit this area. The
islands, which were actually one island
before it split in 1978, are accessible by private boat or by car via the dike. Parts of
them are off limits to the public. ~ Morris
Island, Chatham; 508-945-0594.

West of Chatham is Harwich Port, a lovely
residential area, followed by Dennis Port, West
Dennis, West Yarmouth and Hyannis, considerably less attractive spots. This stretch of Route 28
is mostly gas stations, coffee shops and cheap motels.
But if you've had it up to here with history and quaint
villages, this area is great for slumming. There are 11
miniature golf courses in the region, and one of the best is **Pirates
Cove**. The Trump Tower of miniature golf, it has an elaborate
pirate ship in a fake pond surrounded by terraced rock cliffs and
gushing waterfalls. Closed mid-November to mid-April. Admission. ~ 728 Main Street, South Yarmouth; 508-394-6200.

Because the Kennedys live in **Hyannis**, people usually expect
it to be glamorous and beautiful, but most of the town is very
commercial. The Kennedys live in the one nice area. People come
to Hyannis for three reasons: the airport, ferries to the Islands,
and spying on the Kennedys.

Six miles north of Falmouth, **Ashumet Holly & Wildlife Sanctuary** offers tours as well as nature trail walks through its 45
acres. A variety of holly and wildlife abound. Admission. ~ Off
Route 151 and Currier Road, East Falmouth; 508-563-6390.

At the western end of the South Cape is **Falmouth**, a large
and bustling town with a beautiful village green surrounded by
some of the Cape's loveliest historic homes. One of these homes,
which houses the **Falmouth Historical Society**, is a creamy yellow, hip-roofed 1790 Colonial building with a widow's walk. ~
Across from Village Green, 55 Palmer Avenue, Falmouth; 508-
548-4857.

The rest of downtown Falmouth isn't as scenic, but it does
have a number of beautiful, high-quality clothing and home fur-
nishing stores. The **Falmouth Chamber of Commerce** is located
right off Main Street. ~ 20 Academy Lane, Falmouth; 508-548-
8500, 800-526-8532; www.falmouth-capecod.com.

Immediately south of Falmouth is Woods Hole, a small, deeply
wooded, hilly village that's home to the **Woods Hole Oceanographic Institute**. The Institute isn't open to the public; it's strictly

Even though the Kennedy compound (near Ocean Street) is
surrounded by tall hedges, all
day long tour buses prowl
this area, hoping to catch a
glimpse of one of the clan.
Their efforts are almost
always in vain.

a research facility ranked in stature alongside Scripps Institute of Oceanography in California.

However, the nearby **National Marine Fisheries Service Aquarium** is open to the public year-round. Its sole function is to preserve regional species, hence everything in its 16 major display tanks is native to the area: cod, lobster, flounder. The aquarium also has a seal tank. Closed weekends from mid-September to mid-June. ~ Corner of Water and Albatross streets, Woods Hole; 508-495-2001; www.noaa.gov.

LODGING

A romantic, dark brown 1807 farmhouse, the **Nauset House Inn** is within walking distance of beautiful beaches. One of the inn's most memorable features is a magnificent 1907 conservatory with white wicker furniture, exotic plants and grapevines. Each of the 14 guest rooms is individually decorated, and may feature tiny floral-print wallpaper, stenciling and antiques such as a hand-painted Victorian cottage bed. Most of the guest rooms in the main house and carriage house have private baths. Full breakfast included. Closed November through March. ~ 143 Beach Road, East Orleans; 508-255-2195; www.nausethouseinn.com. MOD-ERATE TO DELUXE.

Chatham Bars Inn, one of Cape Cod's most luxurious grand resorts, looks like the kind of place where everyone should be wearing white linen and playing croquet. Built in 1914 as a hunting lodge, the horseshoe-shaped gray-shingled inn sits high on a gentle hill overlooking Pleasant Bay. An expansive brick veranda runs the length of the inn. The inviting lobby, luxurious rooms and comfortable cottages reflect the original beauty of this historic building with antique reproductions and period pieces like Vanderbilt Casablanca fans, authentic Victorian mantels and Hitchcock chairs. The 20-acre resort has a private beach, heated swimming pool, tennis courts, fishing, sailing, windsurfing, golf, magnificent theme gardens and three restaurants. ~ 297 Shore Road, Chatham; 508-945-0096, 800-527-4884, fax 508-945-5491; www.chathambarsinn.com. ULTRA-DELUXE.

HIDDEN ►

Port Fortune Inn is located two blocks away from the historic Chatham Lighthouse. The small, attractive, nonsmoking inn stands in an exclusive residential neighborhood of winding streets and impeccably restored oceanfront homes. Chatham village is about a five-minute walk. The inn's 13 rooms are decorated with traditional touches such as four-poster beds and antique furnishings. All have private baths and air conditioning; some have ocean views. A continental breakfast buffet is served in the private dining room. ~ 201 Main Street, Chatham; phone/fax 508-945-0792, 800-750-0792; www.capecod.net/portfortune. DELUXE.

Most of Chatham's hotels are expensive, but not the **Bow Roof House,** a real bargain. Located in the heart of the high-rent district, a five-minute drive from the beach, this cozy late-18th-century sea captain's house feels comfortable and casual. A patio overlooking a scenic, winding road makes an ideal spot for afternoon tea or cocktails. The six rooms are appointed with Colonial bedspreads and furniture, but they're far apart and private. ~ 59 Queen Anne Road, Chatham; 508-945-1346. MODERATE.

One of the best places for families in Chatham, the 24-room **Ridgevale Beach Inn Resort Motel** provides plenty of space for kids and parents, as well as an outdoor pool, barbecues and widely spaced picnic tables. Five cottages rent by the week. Closed November through March. ~ 2045 Main Street, Chatham; 508-432-1169, 800-244-1169, fax 508-432-1877. MODERATE TO DELUXE.

Motels aren't known for beautiful landscaping, but **Pleasant Bay Village Resort**'s beautiful landscaping will be a welcome surprise. It boasts impeccably maintained rock and flower gardens that are so lush you hardly notice the 58 nondescript guest rooms and apartments. It is, however, only one-eighth of a mile away from a warm-water bay beach. Closed November through March. ~ 1191 Orleans Road, Route 28, Chatham Port; 508-945-1133, 800-547-1011, fax 508-945-9701. DELUXE TO ULTRA-DELUXE.

Accommodations in Harwich Port are limited and expensive, but **Harbor Walk Guest House** is an exception. The white 1880   ◄ HIDDEN
B&B with gingerbread trim is within walking distance of the town's exclusive beaches. Six guest rooms (two with shared bath) are decorated with a mix of new and antique furnishings. A porch runs the length of this house overlooking the yard. A full breakfast is included. Closed November through March. ~ 6 Freeman Street, Harwich Port; 508-432-1675. MODERATE.

Augustus Snow House is one of the most beautiful inns in New England. Every inch of this magnificent Queen Anne Victorian is flawless. It's known for its fabulous wallpapers—some have ceiling borders of antique roses or clusters of fall flowers that look hand painted. Then there are the unbelievable bathrooms—one has an antique Victorian mahogany sink, another a black-and-white diamond tile floor and claw-footed tub. The dazzling public rooms are appointed with thick oak and mahogany paneling, moreen drapes, etched-glass french doors and period antiques. Located in a quiet, affluent town, the inn has five rooms, all with private baths, fireplaces and ceiling fans. A full breakfast is included. ~ 528 Main Street, Harwich Port; 508-430-0528, 800-320-0528; www.augustussnow.com. ULTRA-DELUXE.

On a very quiet street, with its own mile-and-a-half stretch of Nantucket Sound beach, **Dunscroft By The Sea**, a 1920 Dutch Colonial inn, offers eight rooms plus a cottage. All are romantically decorated in designer linens and each room has its own bath. Some feature fireplaces and jacuzzis. There's a sitting room and screened porch to be enjoyed by all. Children over 12 only. A full breakfast is included in the room rate. ~ 24 Pilgrim Road, Harwich Port; 508-432-0810, 800-432-4345, fax 508-432-5134; www.dunscroftbythesea.com. DELUXE TO ULTRA-DELUXE.

HIDDEN ►

Route 28 from Dennis Port to Hyannis is dotted with one indistinguishable motel after another. However, if you head south toward the beach you'll find some nice alternatives, like **The Lighthouse Inn**, a sprawling, 61-room, Old World resort. Located on the ocean, the inn is formed around a lighthouse that stood at nearby Bass River during the 19th century. The ambience is friendly and unpretentious. A children's director provides daily family activities, as well as day and evening babysitting. Guest rooms in the main inn are simply furnished, and separate cottages are also available. Full breakfast is included in the rates. Closed October through April. ~ 1 Lighthouse Inn Road, West Dennis; 508-398-2244, fax 508-398-5658; www.lighthouseinn. com. ULTRA-DELUXE.

Located in elegant Hyannis Port, the **Simmons Homestead Inn** was once a country estate. Built in 1820, this gracious inn is furnished with antiques, canopy beds, white wicker and brass. Sweeping porches overlook gardens leading down to Simmons Pond, where you can fish with a borrowed rod and reel. The inn also has bikes for guest use, as well as a billiards room. Unlike those in most old inns, the 12 guest rooms and one two-bedroom suite are fairly large. Full breakfast and evening wine are included in the rates, which drop on weekdays. ~ 288 Scudder Avenue, Hyannis Port; 508-778-4999, 800-637-1649, fax 508-790-1342; www.capecodtravel.com/simmonsinn. ULTRA-DELUXE.

Craigville Realty rents a wide variety of homes within a mile of Craigville Beach in Centerville. The houses, available by the week, are clean, well equipped and situated in quiet neighborhoods. ~ 648 Craigville Beach Road, West Hyannis Port; 508-775-3174, fax 508-771-5336. DELUXE TO ULTRA-DELUXE.

The **Village Green Inn**, a white clapboard house with green shutters and a picket fence, is typical of many of the homes in Falmouth's historic district. Guest rooms are decorated with antiques. Two of the five rooms have working fireplaces; all rooms have air conditioning, private bath and TV. One room has impressive wood inlay floors. Full gourmet breakfast included. ~ 40 Main Street, Falmouth; 508-548-5621, 800-237-1119, fax 508-457-5051; www.villagegreeninn.com. DELUXE TO ULTRA-DELUXE.

In 1849 Captain Albert Nye built **Mostly Hall Bed and Breakfast Inn** for his Southern bride, who refused to live in a traditional Cape Cod house. Typical of houses in New Orleans' garden district, this striking, raised Greek Revival mansion has ten-foot windows, louvered shutters, a wraparound veranda, wrought-iron fence and a 35-foot center hall—which is why it's called

Mostly Hall. The six guest rooms are spacious and airy, furnished with antiques, including canopied, four-poster beds. No smoking. Bikes are available for guest use. Full breakfast is included. Closed from January to mid-February. ~ 27 Main Street, Falmouth; 508-548-3786, 800-682-0565, fax 508-457-1572; www.mostlyhall.com. DELUXE.

DINING

A popular local hangout, especially on Saturday nights, **Land Ho** is a fish and chips place. The white clapboard restaurant has red-and-white checked tablecloths, dark wood walls and nautical decorative touches. The menu offers classic Cape Cod fare—fried and broiled seafood, hearty salads, fries and burgers. The bar is a friendly watering hole. ~ Route 6A and Cove Road, Orleans; 508-255-5165. BUDGET TO MODERATE.

Kadee's Lobster and Clam Bar is a colorful, inexpensive sea shanty draped with lobster traps and buoys. The menu includes steamers, lobster, corn-on-the-cob, kale soup and chowder; or try a burger, steak or chicken dinner. An outdoor patio shaded by umbrellas is the perfect spot for beer and fried clams after a day at the beach. Closed from Labor Day through Memorial Day. ~ 212 Main Street, East Orleans; 508-255-6184. MODERATE TO DELUXE.

On their days off, chefs from the Cape's most noted restaurants often dine at **Nauset Beach Club**, on the road to beautiful Nauset Beach. The small grey-shingled restaurant offers consistently good, reasonably priced Northern Italian fare such as saltimbocca, caesar salad, a wide range of seafood dishes such as grilled shrimp scampi, and a host of creative pasta dishes. Dinner only. Closed Sunday and Monday from mid-September through May. ~ 222 Main Street, East Orleans; 508-255-8547. MODERATE.

◄ HIDDEN

The **Impudent Oyster** is the place to go for traditional or exotic seafood in an informal setting next to a park. The lunch and dinner menus change seasonally. Many of the dishes have Chinese or Mexican ingredients, such as Szechuan beef and shrimp satay or mussels. There are also excellent non-seafood items, such as the chicken enchiladas *rojas* and steak *au poivre*. The cheerful restaurant has skylights, a cathedral ceiling and stained-glass panels. Prices are considerably lower during the winter. ~ 15 Chatham Bars Avenue, Chatham; 508-945-3545. MODERATE TO DELUXE.

In historic Chatham village, **Christian's** draws an attractive tennis and yachting crowd. The bar does as much business as the two restaurants combined. A formal, nonsmoking dining room on the ground floor is appointed with oriental rugs, dark wood floors and lace tablecloths; an informal, wood-paneled restaurant and bar is located on the second floor. Both serve dishes such as codfish with champagne hollandaise sauce, seafood sauté, veal chops and boneless split duck as well as pasta, quiche, burgers and sandwiches. The downstairs dining room is closed mid-

October through April. ~ 443 Main Street, Chatham; 508-945-3362. MODERATE TO DELUXE.

The **Chatham Bars Inn**, one of the Cape's most luxurious resorts, also has an excellent restaurant. The food, service and location are superb, the crowd elegant old money. The large dining room overlooking the water is decorated in soothing shades of beige, rose and navy. In the summer the restaurant offers a menu of healthful dishes such as steamed halibut, and raspberry torte, plus a regular dinner menu—grilled swordfish and beef tournedos. Reservations are required if you aren't a guest at the inn. Breakfast and dinner served from mid-June to mid-October; breakfast only from mid-October to mid-June. ~ 297 Shore Road, Chatham; 508-945-0096. DELUXE TO ULTRA-DELUXE.

Woods Hole is primarily a scientific community, and it looks and feels like a small university town, with a good bookstore, craft galleries and cafés. This is also where you can catch a ferry for the islands—Martha's Vineyard and Nantucket.

It looks like something out of a Popeye cartoon. Half of **The Lobster Boat Restaurant** is a gray-shingled Cape Cod cottage with cheerful red window boxes, and the other half is an enormous red, white and blue lobster boat that seems to have grown out of the restaurant's side. The dining room overlooks a small harbor, and the decor is very yo-ho-ho with captains chairs, dark wood and rope. The atmosphere is free and easy, and the menu features lobster as well as a variety of fried, sautéed and broiled seafood. Dinner only. Closed from late October to early April. ~ 681 Main Street, West Yarmouth; 508-775-0486. MODERATE.

HIDDEN ►   At **Mildred's Chowder House** you'll find a crowd of fanatical regulars. All the favorites are available: thick chowders, steamers and scrumptious lobster rolls. The restaurant looks like a coffee shop, but that's not the point. ~ 290 Iyanough Road (Route 28), Hyannis; 508-775-1045. BUDGET TO MODERATE.

Another great find in Hyannis is the **Roadhouse Café**. With four dining rooms, all with fireplaces, it can seat 200, but the restaurant has a small, intimate feel with lots of antiques, hardwood floors and oriental rugs. The menu features local seafood (whatever's in season), plus beef, veal medallions, chops and pasta dishes. Diners can choose from the regular dinner menu or a lighter bistro menu, for salads, sandwiches and thin-crust pizza. There's an impressive wine list and over three dozen types of beers, plus desserts—all made on the premises. Dinner only. ~ 488 South Street, Hyannis; 508-775-2386. BUDGET TO DELUXE.

Penguins Sea Grill serves classic New England–style dishes, such as baked stuffed lobster and grilled salmon, as well as Italian favorites, sushi and New York sirloin. Brick walls, mahogany chairs, natural-finish oak tables, linen napkins and waiters outfitted in long, black, bistro-style aprons contribute to the upscale ambience. Dinner only. Closed Sunday during winter and closed in January. ~ 331 Main Street, Hyannis; 508-775-2023. DELUXE.

An attractive, reasonably priced nouvelle Italian restaurant, **Gone Tomatoes** is in Mashpee Commons, an upscale outdoor mall that resembles an old-fashioned Cape Cod village. The clapboard restaurant has lofty ceilings, cream-colored walls, honeywarm wood and terra cotta floors. Fare includes thin-crusted focaccia pizza, pasta, grilled swordfish with basil butter, and veal chop with marsala and rosemary. A take-out counter sells desserts, pasta, salads, sandwiches and espresso. ~ 11-A Steeple Street, Mashpee; 508-477-8100. MODERATE.

The Regatta of Cotuit is considered one of the top restaurants on the Cape. Housed in a Federal-style mansion that dates back to 1790, it specializes in New American cuisine with European and Asian touches. Selections include a wild mushroom strudel with a sauté of five mushrooms in a phyllo basket, sesamecrusted swordfish steak and a house-smoked broiled salmon filet with a roasted pepper vinaigrette. They also do wonderful things with striped bass, lobster and shrimp. Eight intimate, candlelit dining rooms are warmed by fireplaces on cool nights. Dinner only. ~ Route 28, Cotuit; 508-428-5715. DELUXE TO ULTRA-DELUXE.

Set in an 18th-century, red-and-white inn on the edge of a duck pond, the **Coonamesset Inn** serves seafood Newburg, oysters on the half shell, quahog chowder, Indian pudding and other classic New England dishes. The Cahoon Room, one of three dining rooms serving lunch and dinner, features primitive paintings by artist Ralph Cahoon depicting life on Cape Cod. The inn and restaurant are tastefully decorated with Shaker and Colonial furnishings. ~ Jones Road and Gifford Street, Falmouth; 508-548-2300. MODERATE TO DELUXE.

Located on a winding country road, **Peach Tree Circle** is the ◄ HIDDEN
perfect place for lunch on a lazy summer day. A combination restaurant, farm stand, gourmet health food store and bakery, it is shaded by large graceful trees. Fresh flowers and vegetables are sold in front of the small grey building with nasturtiums climbing its walls. Lunch offerings include big, healthy sandwiches, quiche, chowder, garden salad, fruit and cheese. ~ 881 Old Palmer Avenue, Falmouth; 508-548-2354. BUDGET.

The Regatta of Falmouth-By-the-Sea is the mother restaurant to the Regatta of Cotuit. Set at the water's edge, it offers stunning views of Falmouth Harbor and Vineyard Sound from two large dining rooms. The cuisine is French with an emphasis on seafood. The menu changes monthly, but past entrées have included seared filet of summer sole and roasted buffalo tenderloin. The towering Nantucket oatmeal spice cake with warm rum-caramel sauce is heavenly. Lighter fare is offered on a special menu. Dinner only. Closed late September through April. ~ 217 Clinton Avenue, Falmouth; 508-548-5400. DELUXE TO ULTRA-DELUXE.

Locals come to **Fishmonger's Café** because it isn't as touristy as some of the other Woods Hole restaurants. The café serves California food—avocado tostada, tabouli, garden vegetable salad—and Cape Cod classics like fried clams, grilled fish and chowder. The atmosphere is casual, the decor salty dog. Paned windows overlook the harbor, and there's a counter where you can have lunch or a beer while you're waiting for the ferry. Breakfast, lunch and dinner are served. Closed on Tuesday from Labor Day through Memorial Day; closed from early December through February. ~ 56 Water Street, Woods Hole; 508-548-9148. MODERATE TO DELUXE.

The place to go for a raw bar in Woods Hole is **Shuckers Raw Bar**. It's a bustling little spot, on the water, with table service provided by college students. In addition to raw bar offerings, you can choose from a tempting selection of seafood dishes and lobster rolls that just hit the spot. Shuckers serves its own homebrewed beer, Nobska Light. Closed mid-September to mid-May. ~ 91-A Water Street, Woods Hole; 508-540-3850. MODERATE.

SHOPPING

HIDDEN ►

Aptly named **Bird Watcher's General Store** sells anything having to do with birds—field guides, binoculars, 25 kinds of birdbaths, bath heaters, birdfeeders and carving kits. It also has coffee mugs, T-shirts, stamps, floor mats and pot holders adorned with birds. ~ 36 Route 6A, Orleans; 508-255-6974.

For kitchen utensils and beautiful hand-painted dishes from all over the world, visit **Chatham Cookware**, a blue-and-white cottage-style store. Fresh and sweet, the shop also sells excellent bakery goods, deli items and coffee. ~ 524 Main Street, Chatham; 508-945-1550.

There are countless stores on Cape Cod selling nautical decorative items, but few are as classy as **The Regatta Shop**. Here you find silver nautical jewelry, sleek hand-carved house signs, painted furniture and a wide collection of museum-quality maritime posters. Closed Monday through Friday in January and February. ~ 483 Main Street, Chatham; 508-945-4999.

The Spyglass is a wonderful salty dog store filled to its dark brown rafters with antique telescopes, microscopes, opera glasses, barometers, nautical antiques, paintings and tools. Closed Sunday during winter. ~ 618 Main Street, Chatham; 508-945-9686.

NIGHTLIFE

Musical acts, comedies and plays are presented at the **Academy Playhouse**, in a former town hall built in 1837. ~ 120 Main Street, Orleans; 508-255-1963.

Duval Street Station draws a gay and lesbian crowd for dancing to deejay music Thursday through Sunday nights. During the summer you can gather around the baby-grand and sing along to your favorite showtunes. Cover charge on Friday and Saturday. ~ 477 Yarmouth Road, Hyannis; 508-771-7511.

Cape Cod Melody Tent, an enormous theater-in-the-round, hosts big names such as Willie Nelson, Tony Bennett, Kenny Rogers, Bob Newhart and Ray Charles. Closed after Labor Day through Memorial Day. ~ 21 West Main Street Rotary, Hyannis; 508-775-9100.

Don't be misled by the name—**Casino by the Sea** isn't a gambling joint, it's a fun, clamorous bar that's right on Falmouth Heights beach, in the heart of Falmouth's college-kid country. Live rock Friday and Saturday. Cover on Friday and Saturday. ~ 286 Grand Avenue, Falmouth Heights; 508-548-0777.

South Cape beaches are usually big and wide with huge parking lots and ample facilities. Located in residential neighborhoods, they're popular with college students and families. Because this is the ocean side of the Cape, the water tends to be rougher than on the North Cape.

BEACHES & PARKS

HARDINGS BEACH Big, straight and long, this popular beach attracts a gregarious crowd of kids. Expensive houses on a hill overlook Hardings, a spot good for swimming, sunning and hanging out with the neighbors. You can surf fish for blue fish and striped bass. Modest little sand dunes with paths running through them lead down to the beach. There are restrooms, showers, lifeguards and concessions open from July to Labor Day. Parking fee, $8 per vehicle (July to Labor Day only). ~ Take Barn Hill Road off Route 28 to Hardings Beach Road, Chatham; 508-945-5158.

WEST DENNIS BEACH The view at the end of this sprawling beach, where the Bass River empties into the Atlantic, is of old summer houses with green lawns spilling down toward docks dotted with boats. West Dennis Beach attracts big summer crowds; its parking lot can accommodate 1600 cars. Popular with windsurfers, families and teens, this wheelchair-accessible beach is bordered by flat salt marsh laced with tributaries from the river. Surf fishing is good for bass and blue fish. There are restrooms, showers, a boardwalk, lifeguards, swings and a snack bar. Day-use fee, $10. ~ Take School Street off Route 28 to Lighthouse Road, West Dennis; 508-398-3568.

ASHUMET HOLLY & WILDLIFE SANCTUARY A treat for bird- ◄ *HIDDEN* watchers and botany enthusiasts, this 45-acre reserve abounds with many varieties of holly grown by the late Wilfred Wheeler, who donated the land to the Audubon Society. You're definitely out in the wilds here, and nothing looks manicured or fussed over. An easy-to-maneuver trail goes past a pond, forest, dogwoods, rhododendrons and a grove of Franklinia, an unusual, fall flowering shrub discovered in Georgia in 1790. Wildlife includes catbirds, so named because they make a meowing sound, belted kingfishers and pond critters such as ribbon snakes, catfish and painted turtles with bright yellow heads and dark shells. Since 1935, a barn on the property has been a nesting site for swallows. Every spring up to 44 pairs arrive to nest, then depart in late summer. Day-use fee, $3. ~ 286 Ashumet Road, off Route 151 and Currier Road, East Falmouth; 508-563-6390.

OLD SILVER BEACH This spot, popular with a college-aged crowd and locals, doesn't look like a typical Cape Cod beach. A large, modern resort is situated on the north end, and most of the beach houses in the immediate area are fairly new. A lovely cove to the south is protected by wooded cliffs jutting down to the shore. The beach itself is somewhat rocky. Swimming is calm. There are restrooms, showers, lifeguards and a snack bar. Parking fee, $10. ~ Off Route 28A on Quaker Road, Falmouth; 508-548-8623.

Martha's Vineyard

With its museum-perfect villages, Gothic Victorians and scenery that mimics the coast of Ireland, it isn't any wonder that this enchanting island swells from around 12,000 year-round residents to more than 80,000 in the summer.

Discovered in 1602 by the English explorer Bartholomew Gosnold, it was named by him for its proliferation of wild grapes. Who Martha was is anybody's guess, but legend has it she may have been Gosnold's daughter or his mother.

An active whaling port in the 19th century, "the Vineyard," as it's often called, became a popular summer resort in the 20th century. Today it is a summer home to an impressive number of celebrities fiercely protected from ogling tourists by proud locals. Vacationing notables such as President Bill Clinton, Michael J. Fox and Spike Lee have also spent time on the Vineyard.

One way not to impress the natives is to rent a moped. In the summer these noisy motorized bicycles sound like swarms of angry bees. They're considered a menace on the road, and bumper stickers that read "Outlaw Mopeds" are everywhere.

Only 20 miles long and 10 miles wide, the Vineyard can easily be toured in a day. Ferries dock at Oak Bluffs or Vineyard Haven, or you can fly in (see the "Transportation" section at the end of this chapter). The Vineyard's three major towns—Vineyard Haven, Oak Bluffs and Edgartown—are on the northeast side of the Island. The western end, known as "up-island," is comprised of bucolic farmland, moors and magnificent beaches.

SIGHTS In the '30s, Lillian Hellman and Dashiell Hammett spent their summers in **Vineyard Haven**, and ever since writers have been coming to this friendly, unpretentious town. Vineyard Haven has never attracted tourists like Edgartown, the island's main resort town, and therein lies its charm. It has the best bookstore (Bunch of Grapes), attractive shops, restaurants and a handful of inns. It's also home to the **Martha's Vineyard Chamber of Commerce**. ~ Beach Road, Vineyard Haven; 508-693-0085; www.mvy.com.

One historical sight of note here is the **Martha's Vineyard Seafaring Center**, established in 1893 to provide spiritual guidance to seamen and a refuge to shipwreck victims. Today it is part of a larger organization, the Boston Seaman's Friend Society, that still offers social services and ministry to seafarers. A small museum houses a collection of seafaring artifacts. ~ 110 Main Street, Vineyard Haven; 508-693-9317.

Oak Bluffs is only a couple of miles away. A must-see here is the **Martha's Vineyard Camp Meeting Association**, also known as **Cottage City**, right off the main drag through town. In 1835, Methodist church groups started holding annual summer meetings in Oak Bluffs, with hundreds of families living in tents for the occasion. Over time the tents were replaced by tiny whimsical cottages with Gothic windows, turrets, gables and eaves dripping with gingerbread and painted in a riot of colors—pink, green and white; peach, yellow and blue. Called "campground Gothic Revival," this is the only architecture native to the Vineyard. In mid-August, on Illumination Night, a custom dating back to 1870, hundreds of colorful glowing oriental lanterns are strung up all over the cottages, creating a dazzling display of light. ~ Off Circuit Avenue, Oak Bluffs.

With the exception of Cottage City and Ocean Park—a genteel neighborhood of Queen Anne Victorians overlooking the

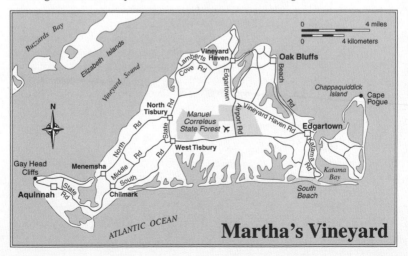

Martha's Vineyard

water on the road to Edgartown—most of Oak Bluffs is hamburger restaurants and T-shirt and souvenir shops. It has a funky, saltwater-taffy kind of charm. In the center of town is the **Flying Horses Carousel**, an antique, hand-carved wooden carousel still in operation. In the glass eye of each horse is a replica of a small animal. The carousel is closed from mid-October to Easter Sunday. Admission. ~ Lake Street at Circuit Avenue, Oak Bluffs; 508-693-9481.

Not far from Oak Bluffs is elegant **Edgartown**. With its narrow streets, brick sidewalks, graceful yachts and pristine Greek Revival and Federal-style architecture, it looks like a living museum. Prim, proper and perfect, Edgartown can sometimes appear a bit too perfect.

Edgartown has always been a town of considerable wealth and power. Prosperous whaling captains retired here, building magnificent homes along **North Water Street** that can still be seen today. Today's residents include many Boston Brahmin families. Life revolves around the formidable yacht club, where expert sailor Walter Cronkite reigns supreme.

The main thing to do in Edgartown is walk along its tree-lined streets window shopping and admiring the homes. The **Martha's Vineyard Historical Society**, tucked away on a beautiful side street, maintains a museum exhibiting scrimshaw, ship models, period costumes and whaling gear such as harpoons. Admission. ~ Cooke and School streets, Edgartown; 508-627-4441; e-mail mvhist@vineyard.net.

Operated by Martha's Vineyard Historical Society, the **Vineyard Museum** comprises several buildings, including the 1765 Thomas Cooke House, a fine example of pre-Revolutionary architecture that once served as a customs house. The house, which has undergone little renovation since the mid-19th century, contains relics of the Vineyard's whaling days, including scrimshaw and other artifacts. The original lens from the Gay Head Lighthouse is housed here; it's illuminated for a few hours each night. Open Tuesday through Saturday from mid-June to mid-October. Admission. ~ 8 Cooke Street, Edgartown; 508-627-4441; e-mail mvhist@vineyard.net.

WINERIES IN MASSACHUSETTS?

From Menemsha head back to Vineyard Haven via North Road and State Road, which goes by **Chicama Vineyards**. Massachusetts' first winery, it offers guided tours and winetastings in an appealing shop that sells wine, homemade jam, mustard and herb vinegar. Closed from Columbus Day through Memorial Day. ~ Stoney Hill Road, West Tisbury; 508-693-0309.

With exquisitely preserved details that include an enclosed cupola, roof and porch balustrades, shallow hipped roof, large window panes and a portico, the 1840 **Dr. Daniel Fisher House** is the Vineyard's best example of Federal-period architecture. Dr. Fisher was Martha's Vineyard's 19th-century Renaissance man— he was a doctor, whaling magnate, banker, merchant and miller. The house is now the headquarters of the Martha's Vineyard Preservation Trust, which saves, restores, and makes self-sufficient any important island buildings that might otherwise be sold for commercial purposes or radically remodeled. Dr. Fisher's House is open (and tours conducted) daily from mid-June to mid-October. Admission. ~ 99 Main Street, Edgartown; 508-627-4440; e-mail mvpt@vineyard.net.

Right off the coast of Edgartown is **Chappaquiddick Island**. Called "Chappy" by locals, it is accessible by ferry (see the "Transportation" section at the end of this chapter). There's not much to do here except go to the beach and take long walks. The island, of course, is noted for the tragic auto accident involving Senator Edward Kennedy that resulted in the death of a young woman. Chappaquiddick Road ends at Dyke Bridge, site of the mishap, which has now fallen apart and is off limits to cars and people. The island's only other road, Wasque Road, leads to Wasque Point, a beautiful natural area.

The up-island section of the Vineyard includes West Tisbury, Chilmark and Aquinnah, bucolic rural areas with lush green farms, meadows and scenic harbors. To explore this area from Edgartown, take the Edgartown–West Tisbury Road. It cuts through the middle of the island.

About the only thing in West Tisbury is **Alley's General Store**, where locals sit on the front porch drinking coffee and glaring at tourists. It's the oldest running store in Martha's Vineyard, first opened in 1858. ~ State Road, West Tisbury; 508-693-0088.

On Saturday mornings, the big social event is the outdoor produce market at **Agricultural Hall**, down the road from Alley's. ◄ *HIDDEN* Don't be fooled by the casual way the locals are dressed. Look closely and you'll see Rolex watches, $600 cowboy boots and maybe, if you're lucky, James Taylor. This area is where many accomplished writers, musicians and artists make their homes.

From West Tisbury, follow the road to **Chilmark**. At the center of Chilmark, **Beetlebung Corner** is an intersection of the main up-island roads: Middle Road, South Road, State Road and Menemsha Cross Road. The intersection was named for a grove of beetlebung trees, the New England name for tupelo trees, which are unusual in the northeastern United States. A very tough wood, tupelo proved to be excellent for making wooden mallets, or beetles, and plugs, or bungs, that stopped up the holes of the wooden barrels used to store whale oil.

At Beetlebung Corner, bear left onto South Road, heading toward Aquinnah. After a mile, you'll pass over a bridge. Nashaquitsa Pond, or Quitsa, depending on who's talking, will be on your right, and Stonewall Pond on your left. About one-tenth of a mile farther, the road heads up a hill. Halfway up the hill, pull over to the wide spot on the side of the road. This is called the **Quitsa Overlook**. Get out of the car to look out over Quitsa and Menemsha ponds. Past the ponds is the tiny village of Menemsha, then Vineyard Sound, the Elizabeth Islands and Woods Hole and Falmouth on the mainland.

HIDDEN ►

About half a mile farther along on the road to Aquinnah, there is another wide spot in the road with room on both sides for two or three cars to pull over safely. This is where the locals park their cars and bikes, then walk over to drink from a fresh, sweet **aquifer**. This water is considered an antidote for various afflictions, from stress to the common cold to the occasional hangover.

HIDDEN ►

The road ends at **Gay Head Cliffs**, towering ocean cliffs formed by glaciers over 10,000 years ago. Laced with multicolored bands of rust, lavender, wheat and charcoal, constant erosion over the millennia has washed away most of the vibrant hues. This popular tourist attraction is approached by a path lined with chowder and gift shops owned by the native Wampanoag people.

Leave the Gay Head Cliffs area via Lighthouse Road, then turn left onto State Road. When you get to Beetlebung Corner, turn right onto Menemsha Cross Road, which takes you to **Menemsha Creek** and **Dutcher's Dock**, a lovely fishing village of simple, weathered gray shingled houses and short, sturdy docks. The channel seems to be impossibly narrow to be a working harbor, yet it's nearly constantly used by hardworking fishing folks.

LODGING

Upon entering the **Captain Dexter House**, you are greeted by the inviting aroma of cinnamon, cloves and warm bread. This meticulously restored 1843 white clapboard inn has sloping wood floors, oriental rugs, fireplaces and antiques. It's luxurious but not pretentious. The eight guest rooms are appointed with contemporary furnishings, Colonial antiques and period reproduction wallpaper; some have fireplaces, air conditioning and four-poster beds with lace canopies. This is a very warm and comfortable place. Gay-friendly. ~ 92 Main Street, Vineyard Haven; 508-693-6564, fax 508-693-8448; www.mvy.com/captdexter. DELUXE TO ULTRA-DELUXE.

Crocker House Inn is tucked away on a quiet side street within walking distance of Vineyard Haven and the harbor. The eight country-cozy, air-conditioned guest rooms in this shingled Victorian are masterfully decorated; all feature private baths, entrances and decks. For serious getaways, try a room with harbor views and a balcony. ~ 12 Crocker Avenue, Vineyard Haven; 508-693-

1151, 800-772-0206, fax 508-693-1123; www.crockerhouseinn. com. MODERATE TO ULTRA-DELUXE.

A classic 1918 craftsman-style main house, a Cape Cod–style shingled carriage house and a private cottage make up the **Thorncroft Inn**, which rests on a quiet, tree-lined residential street. There is nothing very craftsman-like about the decor, which leans toward country Colonial. Catering to couples on romantic getaways, most of the 14 guest rooms have working fireplaces and four-poster lace-canopy beds; some have jacuzzis and hot tubs. One of the best things about Thorncroft is its enormous breakfast of buttermilk pancakes, bacon, french toast, quiche, Belgian waffles, stuffed croissant sandwiches and more. An even better option is having it served in bed. ~ 460 Main Street, Vineyard Haven; 508-693-3333, 800-332-1236, fax 508-693-5419; www. thorncroft.com. ULTRA-DELUXE.

◄ HIDDEN

The front lawn of **Martha's Place Bed and Breakfast** stretches down to a small beach that overlooks busy Vineyard Haven harbor. Guests enjoy their continental breakfast on a terrace overlooking this pretty vista. The six pleasant guest rooms vary in their amenities—all have private baths, some have working fireplaces and some have fine views of the harbor. ~ 114 Main Street, Vineyard Haven; 508-693-1646; www.marthasplace.com. DELUXE TO ULTRA-DELUXE.

Just up the road from the center of Oak Bluffs is the **Admiral Benbow Inn**. What makes it stand apart from many inns is that it has all the New England touches, but not a don't-put-your-drink-on-this-table attitude. The 1870s house is a beauty. All six rooms are attractively furnished with some antique pieces, big comfortable beds and private baths. Continental breakfast is served. Closed January through March. ~ 81 New York Avenue, Oak Bluffs; 508-693-6825. DELUXE TO ULTRA-DELUXE.

Right across the street from busy, picturesque Oak Bluffs Harbor, the **Wesley Hotel** is the last of the seven large oceanfront hotels that graced Oak Bluffs during the turn of the 20th century. The Carpenter Gothic–style building, a traditional Gothic design elaborately constructed with wood, is wrapped with a wide, welcoming veranda. The hotel's 82 fairly large bedrooms (some with shared bath) are comfortably furnished. Closed October through Memorial Day. ~ 1 Lake Avenue, Oak Bluffs; 508-693-6611, 800-638-9027, fax 508-693-5389; www.wesleyhotel.vineyard.net, e-mail wesleyhotel@aol.com. MODERATE TO ULTRA-DELUXE.

At the top of Circuit Avenue, you can't miss the **Oak Bluffs Inn**—it's the pink building on the left with an enormous cupola atop the third story. Guests are encouraged to climb up to the cupola to take in the view of Oak Bluffs' rooftops and the ocean beyond. The inn's guest rooms and common areas are filled with fine examples of cottage-style furniture, prints and wall coverings. All nine accommodations have private baths, air conditioning and views of charming Oak Bluffs. Continental breakfast served. Closed November through April. ~ Corner of Circuit and Pequot avenues, Oak Bluffs; 508-693-7171, 800-955-6235; www.oakbluffsinn.com. DELUXE TO ULTRA-DELUXE.

The shingled, gingerbreaded 1872 **Oak House** is appropriately named—there's oak, oak everywhere, from the walls to the ceilings to the antique oak furniture. The large wraparound veranda has wonderful rocking chairs and swings where many guests spend a lot of time relaxing and looking out across Seaview Avenue to the ocean. Many rooms have private balconies. All eight guest rooms and both suites have private baths and air conditioning. Continental breakfast and afternoon tea are provided. Closed mid-October to mid-May. ~ Corner of Seaview and Pequot avenues, Oak Bluffs; 508-693-4187, 800-245-5979, fax 508-696-7385; www.vineyard.net/inns. ULTRA-DELUXE.

The Arbor Inn is a quintessential New England cottage, fresh and white with a winsome vine-clad arbor, brick path and English garden. Close to Edgartown's shopping district, the inn offers ten guest rooms simply but attractively appointed with antiques and fresh-cut flowers as well as a one-bedroom house that is available for rent on a weekly basis. Continental breakfast is served in the old-fashioned formal parlor or in the garden. Closed November through April. ~ 222 Upper Main Street, Edgartown; 508-627-8137; www.mvy.com/arborinn. DELUXE TO ULTRA-DELUXE.

Built in 1840 by Edgartown's leading physician, Dr. Clement Frances Shiverick, the **Shiverick Inn** is a fantastic example of the high Greek Revival style. Inside, the common areas and ten guest rooms are furnished with fine antiques and pieces of art of the same period. All rooms have fireplaces and private baths; most have air conditioning and queen beds. The library on the second floor has a terrace that looks out over the Old Whaling Church. In the backyard, there's a small flagstone terrace and flower garden. An expanded continental breakfast is served in the Garden Room. Closed January. ~ 5 Pease's Point Way, Edgartown; 508-627-3797, 800-723-4292, fax 508-627-8441. ULTRA-DELUXE.

Edgartown Commons has 35 comfortably furnished efficiencies, from studios to one- and two-bedroom apartments. Outside, there are grills and picnic tables, a play area for the kids and an outdoor swimming pool. Closed late October to early May. ~ 20 Pease's Point Way, Edgartown; 508-627-4671, fax 508-627-4271. ULTRA-DELUXE.

The **Tuscany Inn at the Captain Fisher House** reflects the innkeepers' flair for balancing color, space and magnificent furniture. The result is an inn with an elegant, airy feeling. The eight bedrooms are all doubles with private bath (one detached), and many have whirlpool baths. Full breakfast is served in the tile-floored dining room or, in warm weather, on the flagstone terrace, with a fountain, iron benches and a hammock nearby. Closed January to mid-March. ~ 22 North Water Street, Edgartown; 508-627-5999, fax 508-627-6605; www.mvweb.com/tuscany, e-mail tuscany@vineyard.net. ULTRA-DELUXE.

If you want to stay in a Vineyard classic, choose the **Daggett House**'s three 17th-century buildings. Located on the water, this inn has 31 rooms furnished with numerous antiques; some have wonderful water views while others have kitchenettes. The main house has its own dock and a Chimney Room (circa 1660), said to have been Edgartown's oldest tavern; it's now used as a dining room for breakfast and dinner (open to the public). ~ 59 North Water Street, Edgartown; 508-627-4600, 800-946-3400, fax 508-627-4611; www.mvweb.com/daggett. ULTRA-DELUXE.

For an inn with such a prestigious address, the **Shiretown Inn** has pretty good prices. Some rooms are furnished with antiques and have private entrances and air conditioning; others, especially those in the carriage houses in the back of the inn, are quite plain, rather than quaint. A cottage rents weekly and features a full kitchen. All have private bathrooms. Closed October to mid-May. ~ 40 North Water Street, Edgartown; 508-627-3353, 800-541-0090, fax 508-627-8478. MODERATE TO ULTRA-DELUXE.

With its elaborate windows and dormers, **The Victorian Inn**   ◄ HIDDEN
looks formal from the outside, but it's an easygoing place located one block from Edgartown harbor. Guests enjoy the cool, private garden in the summer. The 14 guest rooms are sweet and tidy with canopy beds, floral wallpaper, antiques and some antique reproductions; a few rooms have private balconies. Full breakfast included. ~ 24 South Water Street, Edgartown; 508-627-4784; www.thevic.com. DELUXE TO ULTRA-DELUXE.

IT'S CHEAPER IN THE GREAT OUTDOORS

Paine's Campground has wooded campsites just a few minutes' walk from Cape Cod National Seashore and the ocean. Nearby, crystal-clear kettle ponds offer freshwater swimming. The campground is designed to accommodate the preferences of different types of campers. Toward the front are trailer and RV sites with water and 30-amp electric hookups. A family section has hookups and room for multiple tents or a tent and a camper. Quiet couples and single and young couples sections have tent sites without hookups, and there are very private lug-in tent sites reached by 25-foot to 100-foot paths. There are central restrooms, and water is available throughout the camp. Reservations are recommended. ~ 180 Old County Road, South Wellfleet; 508-349-3007, fax 508-349-0246; e-mail camping@capecod.net.

The **Charlotte Inn** is one of the most elegant inns in America. A sparkling white 1860 sea captain's house, it is nestled amid a profusion of flowers, lawns, wisteria and latticework. Twenty-five meticulous guest rooms are appointed with English antiques, hand-painted china and equestrian prints. Suites, located in separate buildings, are quite extravagant—one has its own English cottage garden, another a bedroom balcony and palladium window. A continental breakfast is served in the inn's dining room. ~ 27 South Summer Street, Edgartown; 508-627-4751, fax 508-627-4652. ULTRA-DELUXE.

HIDDEN ►

The homey, unpretentious **Summer House** is a place for vacationers who enjoy staying in a B&B that really is someone's home. There's a big, beautiful, very private front yard with a wonderful ivy-covered wall as a backdrop. The two large bedrooms have king-size beds. Continental breakfast is served. Closed mid-October to mid-May. ~ 96 South Summer Street, Edgartown; 508-627-4857. DELUXE.

Hostelling International—Martha's Vineyard is an ideal place to stay on the Vineyard if you want to spend a lot of time biking. It's on the edge of the Correleus State Forest, which is criss-crossed with bike paths. Sleeping areas are dormitory-style bunk beds and are separated by sex. Bring your own linens or rent them; blankets and pillows are furnished. Bathrooms are large, as they are shared by all (also segregated by sex). There's also a fully equipped kitchen as well as a common room with a fireplace. Hostels aren't for everyone, but if you know what to expect, this is a good one. Reservations recommended. Closed mid-November through March. ~ Edgartown–West Tisbury Road, West Tisbury; 508-693-2665, fax 508-693-2699. BUDGET.

HIDDEN ►

Talk about off the beaten path. **Lambert's Cove Country Inn** is down a long country road deep in the woods. Surrounded by vine-covered stone walls, expansive lawns and apple orchards, the white clapboard inn is appointed with Shaker and Colonial-style antiques. Some of the 15 guest rooms have private decks, and one has a greenhouse sitting room. Guests have access to Lambert's Cove Beach, one of the Vineyard's most beautiful private beaches. Full breakfast included. Three-night minimum stay in summer. ~ Lambert's Cove Road, West Tisbury; 508-693-2298, fax 508-693-7890; www.vineyard.net/biz/lambertscoveinn. ULTRA-DELUXE.

One look at the **Captain R. Flander's House** and you understand why it was featured in Martha Stewart's *Wedding Book*. The rambling, 18th-century farmhouse sits on a grassy knoll overlooking ancient stone walls, rolling meadows, grazing horses, a sparkling pond, ducks and woodlands. Chilmark is so peaceful and bucolic, it's no wonder the rich and famous have chosen to live here. The inn is simply furnished, but with scenery like this who needs decoration? Guest accommodations (some with shared bath) are comfortable and sparsely appointed with antiques and country-style furnishings. Two ultra-deluxe-priced cottages are available. Continental breakfast is served. Closed November through May. ~ North Road, Chilmark; 508-645-3123. MODERATE TO ULTRA-DELUXE.

The emphasis is on the luxury of spare decorations and peaceful surroundings at **Menemsha Inn and Cottages**, which is situated on ten and a half acres of tranquil forest in beautiful Menemsha. There are six luxurious suites in the Carriage House, nine smaller, bright and lovely rooms in the inn's main building, and 12 fairly spartan housekeeping cottages. All rooms and cottages have private bath, and each cottage has a screened-in porch, fully equipped kitchen, outdoor shower, barbecue and wood-burning fireplace. Closed late October to late April. ~ North Road between Menemsha Cross Road and Menemsha Harbor, Menemsha; 508-645-2521; www.menemshainn.com. DELUXE TO ULTRA-DELUXE.

> Carly Simon, James Taylor, Caroline Kennedy Schlossberg, Diana Ross, Beverly Sills, Walter Cronkite, Mike Wallace and Art Buchwald all have homes on "the Vineyard."

The nice folks at **Flanders Up-Island Real Estate** rent properties seasonally, biweekly or monthly for homeowners all over Aquinnah, Menemsha, Chilmark and West Tisbury. They have houses and prices to suit nearly everyone. ~ State Road, Chilmark; 508-645-2632, fax 508-645-3346. BUDGET TO ULTRA-DELUXE.

Duck Inn is a health-oriented bed and breakfast that offers a variety of luxuries, including massages, post-massage relaxation in the inn's outdoor hot tub, all-natural fibers on the comfortable beds, and delicious breakfasts that accommodate vegetarians, vegans and flesh-eaters alike. Some of the island's most spectacular beaches are but a few minutes' walk through the waving beach grass. The five guest rooms are furnished eclectically with a duck motif, oriental prints and funky old calendars and posters. The suite in the basement has a large fireplace; all rooms have private baths. In residence: the inn's mascot, Oralee, a black Vietnamese potbelly pig. Gay-friendly. ~ Off State Road, Aquinnah; 508-645-9018. DELUXE TO ULTRA-DELUXE.

◄ HIDDEN

The Outermost Inn is on a 20-acre piece of land that has the island's second-most spectacular ocean view. (For the best, walk a few hundred yards up the hill to the Aquinnah lighthouse.) The inn has six rooms and one suite, all with private bath and one with a private whirlpool. Teal-blue carpets in the halls, unpainted furniture, subdued colors and natural fabrics suit the inn's location perfectly; nothing detracts from the location or the views. This is one of the most romantic inns in coastal New England; it's worth the splurge. Closed October through April. ~ Lighthouse Road, Aquinnah; 508-645-3511, fax 508-645-3514; www.outermostinn.com. ULTRA-DELUXE.

DINING

Only Edgartown and Oak Bluffs serve liquor, but you can bring your own when you dine in other towns.

A grey-shingled saltbox overlooking the harbor, rustic **Black Dog Tavern** is a Vineyard institution popular with the yachting crowd. The best place to sit in the summer is an enclosed porch with beautiful ocean views. The changing menu is traditional—clams casino, codfish, roast duckling—with an emphasis on fresh seafood. Breakfast, lunch and dinner are served. ~ Beach Street Extension, Vineyard Haven; 508-693-9223. MODERATE TO ULTRA-DELUXE.

Café at the Tisbury Inn, a trendy establishment with deco light fixtures, grey industrial carpeting, and a Lambert's Cove beach-scene mural, attracts a young, stylish crowd. The menu features grilled meat, poultry and seafood with different sauces such as Mediterranean or marinara. Other dishes include grilled lemon-pepper chicken, seafood enchiladas and pastas. An awning-covered outdoor patio in front is a good spot for people watching in the summer. Closed November to mid-April. ~ Main Street, Vineyard Haven; 508-693-3416. MODERATE TO DELUXE.

It's a bit off the beaten track in busy Vineyard Haven, but maybe that's why the locals go to **Louis'** for pizza and take-out salads and pasta dishes. ~ 102 State Road, Vineyard Haven; 508-693-3255. BUDGET TO MODERATE.

Giordano's is a classic family-style restaurant, and there usually are a lot of large families here, with many diners gobbling up what some people insist are the Vineyard's best fried clams. There is also an Italian restaurant on the premises, serving traditional fare. Closed late September to late May. ~ Lake and Circuit avenues, Oak Bluffs; 508-693-0184. MODERATE.

The homey **Linda Jean's** serves fantastic, thick pancakes and other delicious breakfast items, as well as such lunch and dinner fare as baked stuffed chicken, pork chops, fresh fish and meatloaf. Check the blackboard for daily specials. Breakfast, lunch and dinner are served daily. ~ 34 Circuit Avenue, Oak Bluffs; 508-693-4093. BUDGET.

Papa's Pizza isn't your average pizza parlor. This place has class. Located in a bright red, white and green storefront, it has an enormous dining room with a tin ceiling and walls, antique brass light fixtures and long wooden tables. The counter in back is solid granite—an elegant touch. Papa's serves lasagna, pizza, pasta and subs. The portions are healthy and hearty. ~ 158 Circuit Avenue, Oak Bluffs; 508-693-1400. BUDGET TO MODERATE.

David Ryan's Restaurant is the kind of place where you stop for a drink and end up staying for hours. It's a restaurant/bar where you can order anything from a burger to a big bowl of pasta topped with tasty sauce. Entrées include seafood linguine, sesame tuna and rosemary lamb. Downstairs is informal with high stools situated around tall tables; upstairs has a selection of booths and tables. ~ 11 North Water Street, Edgartown; 508-627-4100. MODERATE TO DELUXE.

Intimate and candlelit, **Savoir Fare** is a perfect spot for dinner. The cooking is done in the open kitchen; pastas and breads are made on site. The contemporary American menu with European influences changes often, and might include *vitello tonnato* (grilled rib chop) and orange-crusted halibut with arugula pesto. Dinner only. Closed November through March. ~ Post Office Square, Edgartown; 508-627-9864. ULTRA-DELUXE.

The Charlotte Inn's **L'étoile**, one of the finest dining establishments in New England, is perfect for a special occasion. An incredibly beautiful restaurant, it's in a 19th-century conservatory with skylights, bowed windows, a flagstone floor and lush plants. In this romantic, fantasylike environment, contemporary French cuisine is served. The prix-fixe menu offers fresh game and seafood entrées. Sauces are light and aromatic, flavored with fresh herbs, exotic fruit, shiitake mushrooms and shallots. Dinner only. ~ 27 South Summer Street, Edgartown; 508-627-5187. ULTRA-DELUXE.

On the way to Aquinnah is the **Feast of Chilmark**, where you can indulge in American-style food such as roasted rack of lamb with a cognac glaze. The bi-level restaurant serves dinner only and doubles as an art gallery. Closed Columbus Day through Memorial Day. ~ Beetlebung Corner, Chilmark; 508-645-3553. DELUXE.

Even if you're not knocked out the by the surf-and-turf menu (steak, salad, lobster, etc.) at **Home Port,** come here for the mesmerizing view. The rustic, brown-shingled restaurant overlooks sand dunes, rolling green pastures and idyllic Menemsha harbor. An outdoor patio is available for summer dining. Dinner only. Closed mid-October through March. ~ Basin Road, Menemsha; 508-645-2679. DELUXE TO ULTRA-DELUXE.

Small, exclusive **Beach Plum Inn** is easy to miss. A tiny sign points the way down a dirt road to a building without a sign that looks like a private home with a terraced rock and flower garden. Once you've figured out where to go, you'll be glad you came. The intimate dining room has large picture windows overlooking Menemsha Harbor. Diners have a choice of five prix-fixe dinner entrées that must be ordered in advance when making reservations; the same dishes may also be ordered à la carte. The cuisine features items such as duck with honey-curry sauce, steamed lobster and rack of lamb. Breakfast and dinner served. Closed from the end of October to Memorial Day. ~ North Road, Menemsha; 508-645-9454. ULTRA-DELUXE.

Bunch of Grapes Bookstore is a writers' hangout. The best bookstore on the island, it has shelves well-stocked with quality fic-   **SHOPPING**

tion and poetry. The store regularly hosts autograph parties. ~ 44 Main Street, Vineyard Haven; 508-693-2291.

Linen, antique English pine furniture, knubby hand-knit sweaters and hand-painted coffee mugs can be found at **Bramhall & Dunn**. ~ 19 Main Street, Vineyard Haven; 508-693-6437.

Take It Easy Baby is a very hip used clothing store selling leather bomber jackets, Hawaiian shirts, designer women's wear and incredibly chic Canadian foul-weather gear such as flannel-lined sou'westers. This is a fun store for the terminally cool. Closed late December through March. ~ 35 Circuit Avenue, Oak Bluffs; 508-693-2864.

In the Woods, a cavernous red brick room, sells handsome hand-crafted wooden spoons, plates, bread platters, bowls, cutting boards, Christmas ornaments, tables and benches. Prices are reasonable, and the craftsmanship is superb. Closed mid-January through March. ~ 55 Main Street, Edgartown; 508-627-8989.

NIGHTLIFE Throughout the year, the **Vineyard Playhouse**, the Island's only professional theater, presents an interesting selection of new works and classics. ~ Church Street, Vineyard Haven; 508-693-6450.

Island Theatre Workshop is the Vineyard's oldest theater. Year-round it presents a wide range of plays, musicals and children's theater performed by Vineyard actors. With no permanent home, it stages productions at different locations throughout the island. ~ P.O. Box 1893, Vineyard Haven, MA 02568; 508-693-5290.

In 1998, the town of Gay Head and the Aquinnah Wampanoag tribe voted to change the town's name back to Aquinnah.

Atlantic Connection, a hopping dance and music club, has live bands and entertainment year-round. Deejay dancing happens on Friday and Saturday. Cover. ~ Circuit Avenue, Oak Bluffs; 508-693-7129.

Old Whaling Church Performing Arts Center offers cultural lectures, classic films, concerts and plays throughout the year. Set in an 1843 Greek Revival church, the center has featured stars such as Patricia Neal, Andre Previn and Victor Borge. Folk artists such as Arlo Guthrie have also graced the stage. ~ Old Whaling Church, 89 Main Street, Edgartown; 508-627-4442.

BEACHES & PARKS Beaches in rural West Tisbury, Chilmark and Aquinnah are dramatic, untamed and less crowded than beaches near the Vineyard's three towns. But the parking lots are for residents only, and in the summer guards check to see if cars have resident stickers. Nonresidents ride bikes to these beaches. Shore fishing is excellent from all south shore beaches.

FELIX NECK WILDLIFE SANCTUARY 🏃 A 350-acre haven for wild animals, birds, flora and fauna, the sanctuary has four miles of easy walking trails through salt marshes, thick forests and open meadows of wildflowers. The area is managed by the Massachusetts Audubon Society. There are activities for children and adults, including guided nature walks and bird-watching trips geared toward novices and experts alike. Facilities include restrooms, an interpretive exhibit center, a gift shop and a library. Admission (free for Massachusetts Audubon Society members). ~ Three miles from the center of Edgartown on the Edgartown–Vineyard Haven Road, off State Road, between Oak Bluffs and Edgartown; 508-627-4850.

NANTUCKET SOUND BEACHES 🚲 🦞 Strung together along protected Nantucket Sound are Oak Bluffs Town Beach, Joseph A. Sylvia State Beach, Bend-in-the-Road Beach and Lighthouse Beach. This is where the movie *Jaws* was filmed, but don't panic—this isn't shark country. The narrow, gently curved shoreline has clean sand and calm water. Swimming lessons are offered at some of the beaches, and bicycle paths run alongside the shore, which is bordered by ponds, salt marsh and summer homes. A stately lighthouse overlooks Lighthouse Beach. There are lifeguards. ~ Along Beach Road between Oak Bluffs and Edgartown; 508-627-6145.

SOUTH BEACH 🦞 🏊 🎣 Also called Katama South, this popular, mile-long, Atlantic-facing beach runs into Norton Point Beach on one end and a privately owned beach on the other. Wide, expansive and flat, it is surrounded by heath dotted with 20th-century homes—a rare sight in Martha's Vineyard. In the summer the air is soft and warm from southwesterly winds. The beach is ideal for swimming (watch undertow), and fishing is excellent; you might be able to surf or windsurf if the waves or wind show up. You'll find restrooms, changing rooms and lifeguards. ~ Off Katama Road, south of Edgartown. You may take a shuttle bus from the center of town; 508-627-6145.

FULLER STREET BEACH 🦞 🎣 A favorite among the many young folks who spend the summer in Edgartown, it's a quick bike ride away and a great place to take a break from other, more crowded beaches. There are no facilities or lifeguards. ~ At the end of Fuller Street near Lighthouse Beach; 508-627-6165.

CAPE POGUE WILDLIFE REFUGE & WASQUE RESERVATION   ◀ *HIDDEN* 🚶 🚲 🐎 🦞 🚣 🎣 🦀 If you want to get away from it all, take the two-minute car and passenger ferry from Edgartown to these wilderness areas on Chappaquiddick Island, an undeveloped peninsula of vast, empty beaches and moors. The refuge and reservation are adjacent to each other and form the northeastern tip of the Vineyard. Both offer an assortment of low dunes, ponds, tidal flats and cedar thickets. Wildlife abounds, including noisy least terns, piping plovers, common terns and

American oystercatchers. East Beach, part of the Cape Pogue Wildlife Refuge, is the best spot for swimming (although it is sometimes rough), and is a great spot to catch blue fish. Wasque Point is a world-renowned fishing area that teems with bonito, mackerel, striped bass and more. Motorized boats are prohibited. There are restrooms. Day-use fee, $3 per person; parking fee, $7. ~ Cape Pogue is at the end of Chappaquiddick Road on the other side of Dyke Bridge. Access to Cape Pogue is limited to four-wheel-drive vehicles with permits. Wasque Point is at the end of Wasque Road; 508-693-7662.

MANUEL CORRELEUS STATE FOREST Right in the center of the Vineyard lie over 5000 acres of towering evergreens, scrubland, ponds and streams. Laced with bicycle and horseback-riding paths, as well as hiking trails carpeted with soft, thick pine needles, the cool, hushed forest offers a peaceful respite from the Vineyard's wind-bitten moors and wide-open beaches. Beware of ticks in spring. ~ Off Airport Road between West Tisbury and Edgartown; 508-627-6165.

LONG POINT WILDLIFE REFUGE A never-ending, loosen-your-teeth dirt road is the only way to get to this mystical, magical wildlife refuge. The road forks here and there; just stay on the widest part and eventually you come to a small parking lot (seasonal parking with a fee). Shortly beyond lies an endless grass and huckleberry-covered heath that looks like a prairie with two enormous ponds. Tisbury Great Pond and Long Cove are home to black ducks, bluebills, ospreys, canvasbacks and swans. Beyond the ponds you'll discover a sea of silver beach grass and a white sand beach. Swimming and fishing are good, although the waters can get rough. Only rental canoes are allowed here. Facilities are limited to portable toilets and a fresh-water pump. Day-use fee, $3 per adult; parking fee, $7. ~ This place is very difficult to find. It's one mile west of Martha's Vineyard Airport off Edgartown–West Tisbury Road on Waldrons Bottom Road, a deeply rutted dirt road without a sign; look for ten mailboxes in a row and the sign for Long Point. It's best to ask locals for directions; 508-693-7392.

LAND BANK BEACH Adjacent to the multicolored Gay Head Clay Cliffs, a national landmark off-limits to the public, this long, flat, sandy beach is extremely popular in the summer. Land Bank is great for sunning, fishing for bluefish and bass, swimming and beachcombing, but be cautious of the surf. Although it is illegal, nude swimming is popular here. You can pay a hefty fee to park at the lot behind the dunes (508-693-7662), but you may be better off taking the Up Island Shuttle Bus that runs in the summer. Restrooms and snack bars are adjacent to the beach. Parking fee, $15. ~ At the western tip of the

Vineyard at the end of State Road, which is also called South Road in Aquinnah; 508-627-7141

CEDAR TREE NECK SANCTUARY 🏃 The raucous chirping of   ◄ *HIDDEN*
song sparrows and Carolina wrens is the first thing to greet you
at this 300-acre preserve. This is their kingdom, and what a spectacular place it is. Follow one of two well-marked paths through
hilly woods of beech, sassafras, red maple, hickory oak and beetlebung. Soon the sky opens up, and, out of nowhere, extraordinary
vistas appear of deep ponds, rolling sand dunes and the ocean
beyond. Paths lined with ferns, moss and mushrooms lead down
through the woods to an elevated catwalk and the shore. Unfortunately, picnicking is not allowed, and swimming is prohibited
in the sanctuary. ~ From State Road in West Tisbury, take Indian
Hill Road about two miles to a dirt road with a Cedar Tree Neck
sign. The road goes down a hill to the parking lot; 508-693-5207.

Thirty miles out to sea from Cape Cod, this magical, fog-   ▼▼▼▼▼▼▼▼▼▼
shrouded island is a study in contrasts. With its historic   **Nantucket**
homes and cobblestone streets, it looks like storybook
land, circa 1800. Yet it has sophisticated New York City/San
Francisco–style restaurants and Madison Avenue shops. Outside
of town, Nantucket is a bittersweet world of rolling moors, wild
roses and windswept saltbox cottages that appear to have
sprouted from the earth itself.

Nantucket was first sighted in 1602 by Captain Bartholomew
Gosnold on his way to Martha's Vineyard. English settlers and
Quakers farmed the land until the 1830s, when it was one of the
busiest whaling ports in the world, a fact noted by Herman Melville in *Moby Dick*. In the 1870s, when kerosene started to replace whale oil as a fuel source and whales were becoming
scarce, the industry started to decline and Nantucket lost 60 percent of its population. A depression followed, but around the
turn of the 20th century tourism blossomed and the island prospered once again.

Nantucket is so small and flat you can zip across it on a bicycle in about two hours or by car in 30 minutes. There are almost as many bicycle paths as roads, and bicycle rental shops
abound on the wharf where the ferries dock. Like Martha's
Vineyard, the only way to get here is by ferry or plane (see the
"Transportation" section at the end of this chapter). If you come
here in summer, you must have reservations beforehand—competition for lodging is intense, and anti-camping laws are actively
enforced.

There is only one town, Nantucket, but it can occupy you for   **SIGHTS**
hours or days if you enjoy historic homes, museums, fine restaurants, shopping and gallery hopping.

Historic Nantucket

This easy walk through the streets of old Nantucket takes in more than a dozen historic sites from the town's 18th- and 19th-century whaling heyday. It takes about two and a half hours to walk.

THOMAS MACY WAREHOUSE Start your walk at the Thomas Macy Warehouse (c. 1846) on the waterfront. Originally a storehouse for whale-ship supplies, it now houses the Nantucket Historical Association Visitor Center. Buy a handy visitors' pass covering the sites on this tour. All are open daily May through September. ~ Straight Wharf; 508-228-1700.

BROAD STREET Walk one block west to South Water Street, then north (right) two blocks to Broad Street and the **Whaling Museum**. A former candleworks with enormous cross beams, this rustic old building contains a 40-foot finback whale skeleton, a lighthouse lens, a whaleboat, a scrimshaw collection and relics from the *Essex*, the ship rammed by an enraged sperm whale that inspired Herman Melville's *Moby Dick*. ~ 5 Broad Street; 508-228-1736. Next door, the **Peter Foulger Museum** traces Nantucket's human history from American Indian habitation to the present. ~ 15 Broad Street; 508-228-1655.

MAIN STREET Leaving the museums, walk one block west on Broad Street and turn south (left) on Federal, then west (right) onto the picturesque, cobblestoned Main Street. A fire destroyed most of the town in 1846, and some buildings, such as the public library, have only recently been restored. Two blocks up on Main, turn south (left) on Fair Street and go one block to the **Friends Meeting House** (c. 1838), which has been preserved by the historical society for more than a century and is still used as a house of worship by the island's Quakers. An annex to the meeting house, the **Fair Street Museum** originally housed the Whaling Museum and now contains changing historical exhibits. ~ 7 Fair Street. Returning to Main Street, turn west (left) again and continue for

If you walk up Main Street past the shops, you'll find many elegant mansions built during the heyday of whaling. See "Walking Tour" for a historical overview.

Nearby stands the **Maria Mitchell Science Center**. Mitchell, a Nantucket native, was the first person to discover a comet with a telescope, and the first female member of the American Academy of Arts and Sciences. The center, named in her honor, includes a natural science museum with an impressive insect colanother block to Walnut Street. Turn north (right) and go one block to Liberty Street to the **Macy-Christian House** (c. 1740), a pre-Revolutionary merchant's home where a guided tour takes you through rooms of period furnishings. ~ 12 Liberty Street. Returning to Main Street, walk two more blocks west to tour the **Hadwen House** (c. 1845), one of the most elegant mansions on the island; the local garden club maintains period-style gardens here. ~ 96 Main Street.

MILLS AND MOORS   Turn south (left) on Pleasant Street and go four blocks to South Mill Street, then turn west (right) and climb the hill to the corner of Prospect Street to see the **Old Mill** (c. 1746), a Dutch-style sailed windmill with wooden gears. It still grinds corn into meal, which is offered for sale to visitors. ~ Mill and Prospect streets. Returning north on Pleasant Street, turn west (left) on Mill Street. Passing the private **Moor's End** mansion (c. 1839) and the **1800 House** (c. 1801, closed for restoration), continue one block to New Dollar Lane.

GARDNER STREET   Turning north (right), walk one block and turn west (left) onto Vestal Street. Continue for one and a half blocks to the **Old Gaol** (c. 1805), used to incarcerate prisoners for nearly 130 years before a rash of escapes prompted the town council to build a new jail. ~ Vestal Street. Returning the way you came, turn north (left) onto Gardner Street and walk two blocks, past the **Civil War Monument** at the corner of Main Street, to the **Hose-Cart House** (c. 1886), the last of several fire stations housing hand-pumped fire carts that were built throughout town after the devastating fire of 1846. ~ 8 Gardner Street.

JETHRO COFFIN HOUSE   From the corner of Gardner and Main, you can return to your starting point at the visitor center by walking six blocks east on Main Street. For a longer walk—ten minutes each way—continue north on Gardner Street, which becomes North Liberty Street; turn east (right) on West Chester Street, then north (left) onto Sunset Hill Lane to see the Jethro Coffin House (c. 1686), Nantucket's oldest house. ~ Sunset Hill; 508-228-1894. West Chester becomes Centre Street and returns you to Main Street three blocks from the visitor center.

lection, a library (open year-round), aquarium, observatory and the house in which Mitchell was born. The center conducts summer field trips, as well as bird and marine walks. Call for hours. Closed September to mid-June. Admission. ~ Vestal and Milk streets; 508-228-9198; www.mmo.org.

For a heady dose of Nantucket country life, visit **Siasconset**, a doll-sized hamlet of 17th-century pitched-roofed cod fisher shanties transformed into beguiling summer homes. In spring and early summer this endearing village looks as though it's been attacked by roses. Everywhere you look wild pink roses are climbing over fences, up sides of houses and over roofs, creating a dusty pink, grey and sage landscape.

Called "Sconset" by nearly everyone, the village lies seven and a half miles from Nantucket town on Milestone Road, which is bordered by a smooth, flat bicycle path. There isn't much to do here except enjoy the scenery and go to the beach. Sconset has a couple of restaurants, including renowned Le Chanticleer, and The Summer House, one of Nantucket's prettiest inns.

On the way back to town, take scenic Polpis Road. It goes past **Sankaty Lighthouse** and **The Moors**, magnificent, wind-bitten low-lying land that resembles a Persian carpet in the fall.

The road also passes the windswept **cranberry bogs**, where you can watch cranberries being harvested in the fall (see "Exploring Cranberry Country" in Chapter Six for information about cranberry growing on the South Shore).

The rest of Nantucket is all huckleberry-covered heath dotted with houses surrounded by spectacular beaches (see "Beaches & Parks" below).

LODGING   Nantucket has an astonishing number of inns and bed and breakfasts, but perhaps the most well-known is the **Jared Coffin House**. Built in 1845 by wealthy shipowner Jared Coffin, it features guest and public rooms appointed with antiques, oriental rugs, crystal chandeliers, period wallpaper, marble fireplaces and canopy beds. All guest rooms have private baths; some are air-conditioned. A busy, festive establishment, it feels like a big city hotel of the 19th century. Sixty guest rooms span four different buildings. Full breakfast included. ~ 29 Broad Street; 508-228-2400, 800-248-2405, fax 508-325-7752; www.jaredcoffinhouse. com. ULTRA-DELUXE.

Right down the street from the Jared Coffin House is one of the island's few bargain spots, **The Nesbitt Inn**. The white Victorian was built in 1872 and most of the original furniture still remains. One room has a wood-rimmed bath tub that accommodates two. There are 12 guest rooms, each with a sink and shared bath. The inn's front porch is a great place for people watching. Closed January and February. ~ 21 Broad Street; 508-228-0156, fax 508-228-2446. MODERATE.

Nearby in the historic district is the **Centerboard Guest House**, a restored 1885 Victorian residence with seven rooms, all decorated with period furnishings. At such an inn, it's surprising to find modern amenities such as air conditioning and refrigerators in each room. Breakfast included. ~ 8 Chester Street; 508-228-9696; www.nantucket.net/lodging/centerboard. ULTRA-DELUXE.

The House of Orange is a small gay-friendly guesthouse, also in Nantucket's historic district. Each of the four rooms, furnished with antiques, has its own bath and both a double and twin bed. Two of the accommodations have glass-enclosed porches. The house is a former sea captain's home. Closed October through February. ~ 25 Orange Street; 508-228-9287. ULTRA-DELUXE.

Anchor Inn, a narrow grey clapboard house with green shutters and window boxes, is typical of Nantucket's many bed and breakfasts. Old and quaint, with narrow halls and sloping wood floors, it offers 11 cozy guest rooms, some hidden under dormers and eaves in small irregular spaces. Each has a private shower and air conditioning. Once the home of the Gilbreth family of Frank Gilbreth's *Cheaper by the Dozen*, the Anchor is furnished with Colonial and Shaker-style antiques. A continental breakfast is served in a cheerful blue-and-white breakfast room or out on a brick patio. Closed January and February. ~ 66 Centre Street; 508-228-0072; www.nantucket.net/lodging/anchorinn. MODERATE TO DELUXE.

The **Woodbox Inn** is one of Nantucket's oldest and most delightful inns. Built in 1709, it exudes New England charm, with low-beamed ceilings, wood-paneled walls and walk-in fireplaces. The three guest rooms and six suites are furnished entirely in period antiques; all have private baths. Located in a quiet part of

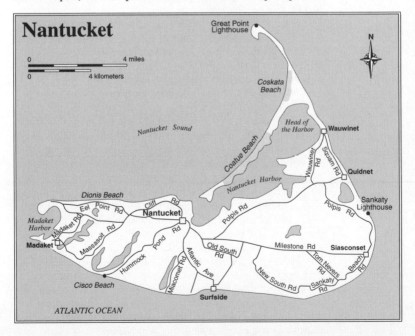

town away from all the hoopla, it has an excellent restaurant that can get a little noisy on weekends. Closed January through May. ~ 29 Fair Street; 508-228-0587; www.woodboxinn.com. ULTRA-DELUXE.

The Wauwinet, a lavish resort outside of town, is decorated to the hilt with country pine antiques, green wicker, primitive folk art, Victorian carpet runners, white wainscotting and pickled floors. The 25 guest rooms sport gentle sea-breeze colors like pale smoke, sage and cream; five cottages sleep up to six people each. White wrought-iron furniture sits prim and proper on a vast lawn overlooking Nantucket Bay, and cushioned wicker furniture lines a bayside porch. Guests are transported to and from town in a shuttle bus. The Wauwinet is one of the most expensive inns on the island, attracting a well-heeled young crowd. There's a full-service restaurant on the premises. Closed November to mid-May. ~ 120 Wauwinet Road; 508-228-0145, 800-426-8718, fax 508-228-6712; www.wauwinet.com. ULTRA-DELUXE.

HIDDEN ► If you haven't stayed in a youth hostel since you gave up your backpack, you might want to try it again when you see Hostelling International—Nantucket, also known as the Star of the Sea Youth Hostel. Located across from Surfside Beach, this historic wooden A-frame building looks like a cross between a Swiss chalet and a church. Originally a lifesaving station, it today attracts a lot of young people, Europeans, senior citizens and cycling groups. The rows of bunk beds inside remind most people of camp. As with most youth hostels, Nantucket's is closed to guests during the day. The dormitory-style rooms and restrooms are segregated by sex; there is also a good-sized kitchen, dining room and common room. Closed mid-October to mid-April. ~ 31 Western Avenue; 508-228-0433; www.tiac.net/users/hienec. BUDGET.

The Summer House, a rose-covered structure overlooking the ocean, is quintessential Nantucket, the kind of place you dream about but rarely find. Not surprisingly, it once graced the cover of *New York* magazine. Quaint little low-slung, vine-clad cottages surrounding the main house look as though they were designed by and for elves. But they're much bigger and lighter than they seem, and the decor blends just the right mix of rustic country charm. Guest rooms have features such as fireplaces, jacuzzis, rough-hewn beams, painted wood floors and hand-painted borders. There is a lively restaurant as well as an oceanfront pool. Closed late October to late April. ~ 17 Ocean Avenue, Siasconset; 508-257-4577, fax 508-257-4590; www.thesummerhouse.com. ULTRA-DELUXE.

DINING   Among Nantucket's astonishing number of sophisticated restaurants, one of the best is Le Languedoc. Elegant and hushed, the downstairs has bistro-style dining with yellow walls, contemporary art and dark carpeting that are strictly big-city, yet its navy-and-white checked tablecloths and Windsor chairs add a touch of French country; the upstairs resembles a pied-à-terre. Lobster hash, Boston glazed jumbo shrimp and jambalaya risotto can be found on the moderate-to-deluxe bistro menu, while the deluxe-to-ultra-deluxe upstairs menu may include pan-roasted lobster with garlic-thyme potatoes, soft-shell crab and porcini-dusted lamb tenderloin. A lot of care goes into the presentation. Advance reservations suggested for upstairs; no reservations accepted for downstairs. Lunch is served in the bistro September through December; dinner is served nightly. Closed Sunday in May and June; closed mid-December to mid-May. ~ 24 Broad Street; 508-228-2552. MODERATE TO ULTRA-DELUXE.

American Seasons serves American regional cuisine such as mesquite-smoked sweetbreads, tuna with dandelion greens salad, and herb-crusted root-vegetable gratin. The restaurant is in a white, two-story building with window boxes spilling a variety of seasonal blossoms. The folk-art-mural interior is romantically lit with hurricane lamps, and jazz plays softly in the background; the outdoor patio has copper tables. The crowd is young, happy and casual. Dinner only. Closed from mid-December to mid-April; closed Tuesday from mid-April to mid-May. ~ 80 Centre Street; 508-228-0397. ULTRA-DELUXE.

The Atlantic Café is on a street that should be called Hamburger Row. Every restaurant on this block serves the same thing —burgers, beer and rock-and-roll. You can smell the fried food before you get here. The restaurant attracts families with small children. The Atlantic is a clean-looking establishment with white walls, wood beams and a bar in the middle surrounded by wooden chairs and tables. Steak and seafood specials round out the menu. Closed from mid-December to early January. ~ 15 South Water Street; 508-228-0570. BUDGET TO DELUXE.

Espresso Café is good for a cappuccino and a brownie, picnic fixings or a casual lunch or dinner. There are paddle fans, a black-and-white tile floor, a tin ceiling and a tree-shaded brick patio. The food is trendy and hearty—cassoulet, soup, chili, pasta, thick pizza piled high with "yuppie" ingredients such as sun-dried tomatoes and goat cheese. Breakfast, lunch and dinner are served. ~ 40 Main Street; 508-228-6930. BUDGET.

One of Nantucket's most beautiful and versatile restaurants, the **Boarding House** has a shady brick patio that's perfect for people watching and a lovely bar and café with floor-to-ceiling windows. (A woman could come to the bar alone and feel totally at ease.) A formal dinner is served in the cellar, a grottolike, candlelit room with cream-colored arched walls. Dishes change frequently. Popular offerings include seared yellow-fin tuna with wasabi aioli and soy ginger glaze, and twin lobster tails grilled with champagne beurre blanc. A comprehensive wine list is featured. Lunch is served Thursday through Sunday (dinner nightly) from May through October; closed Sunday through Tuesday from November through April. ~ 12 Federal Street; 508-228-9622. DELUXE TO ULTRA-DELUXE.

Tiny **Sconset Café** has an enticing menu any time of day. The café's patrons are the lucky taste-testers of new recipes and variations on old favorites, which are best termed New American. Try the lamb Dijon or the baby vegetable risotto. Closed from mid-October through April. ~ Post Office Square, Siasconset; 508-257-4008. DELUXE TO ULTRA-DELUXE.

Le Chanticleer is one of New England's most romantic restaurants. In spring, the many-windowed, gray-shingled house is covered with climbing roses, and the garden is a riot of pink, white and lavender flowers. The menu features traditional French cuisine—foie gras, lobster soufflé, fresh figs in sweet white wine and herbs, trout with salmon mousse and lobster ginger sauce. Many locals prefer the restaurant for lunch; the prix-fixe dinner is a major production. Closed Monday and from November to mid-May. ~ 9 New Street, Siasconset; 508-257-6231. DELUXE TO ULTRA-DELUXE.

SHOPPING   **Hoorn-Ashby Gallery**, one of Nantucket's most beautiful galleries, sells American and European contemporary paintings, antique hand-painted blanket chests, French-country porcelain and more in a sun-filled room with wood-paneled walls, tall columns, wainscoting and high ceilings. Abbreviated hours from Columbus Day to mid-December; closed mid-December through May. ~ 10 Federal Street; 508-228-9314.

Many shops in Nantucket sell handwoven goods, but at **Nantucket Looms** the blankets, throws and shawls are a cut above the rest. Popular designs include voluminous, fluffy white throws with thin navy stripes, and blankets in all colors of the rainbow. Closed Sunday from late December through March. ~ 16 Main Street; 508-228-1908.

Four Winds Craft Guild specializes in the island's oldest crafts: antique and new lightship baskets and scrimshaw. The former are tightly woven, bowl-shaped baskets used as purses or decorative items; scrimshaw are items decoratively carved from whale bone and teeth. Both crafts were created in the 18th century by lighthouse keepers and sailors with idle time on their hands. Lightship purses are a status symbol among the island's conservative ladies. The older the basket, the better. ~ 6 Ray's Court; 508-228-9623.

Brimming with hidden delights, **Vis-A-Vis** offers an eclectic mix of goods ranging from hand-knit sweaters, bathing suits and antique hooked rugs, to quilts and jewelry. Women can find something to wear to the beach, a wedding or an evening on the town. Closed Monday through Friday in January and February. ~ 34 Main Street; 508-228-5527.

The **Nantucket Arts Council** presents classical music concerts in local churches and halls from September to June. ~ P.O. Box 554, Nantucket, MA 02554; 508-228-2190.

NIGHTLIFE

In summer, **Nantucket Musical Arts Society** gives classical concerts in the First Congregational Church located at 62 Centre Street. ~ P.O. Box 897, Nantucket, MA 02554; 508-228-1287.

Throughout the year, **The Theatre Workshop of Nantucket** stages plays such as *Arsenic and Old Lace* and *Don't Dress for Dinner*. ~ Bennett Hall, 62 Centre Street; 508-228-4305.

Actors Theatre of Nantucket has something for everyone: serious drama, light comedy (like Neil Simon's *Lost in Yonkers*), original youth theater productions and comedians. Watch for their summer benefit concerts, which have featured Judy Collins and Joan Baez in the past. ~ Methodist Church, 2 Centre Street; 508-228-6325.

For evening cocktails and live entertainment (summer only) in a comfortable old tavern, try the **Tap Room at Jared Coffin House**. ~ 29 Broad Street; 508-228-2400.

Fun, funky and informal, **The Chicken Box**, a bar with live entertainment, presents a variety of bands—rock-and-roll, reggae, rhythm-and-blues and others. They perform nightly in the summer, on weekends only in the winter. Cover for bands. ~ 4 Daves Street; 508-228-9717.

Bike paths go to Madaket, Dionis, Surfside and Siasconset beaches, and fishing is great from those on the south shore. Nantucket doesn't have parks, per se, but the Nantucket Conservation Foundation owns and manages more than 8400 acres of undeveloped land open to the public to explore. Foundation land is identified by roadside maroon posts topped with a wave and seagull logo. If you want to know more, stop in and talk to the foundation folks, a friendly group of people who are happy to discuss the island's flora and fauna. ~ Larsen-Sanford Center, 118 Cliff Road; 508-228-2884. The **Nantucket Park and Recreation Commission** oversees Dionis, Madaket, Cisco and Siasconset Beaches. ~ 2 Bathing Beach Road; 508-228-7213.

BEACHES & PARKS

Surfers take note: surfing is *not* permitted in lifeguarded areas. Furthermore, lifeguarded areas are subject to frequent change. Before dragging your gear out, you might want to call **Indian Summer Surf Shop** (508-228-3632) and ask where people are surfing.

DIONIS BEACH 🚲 🏊 If it weren't for a white rock on which the word Dionis is painted, you'd never find this beach, which faces the bay and is ideal for swimming, picnics and cookouts (fire permits available from the Nantucket fire station). Beyond the large dirt parking lot, a path leads through tall sand dunes to the beach. These are dunes protected from natural erosion and people by a fence. The beach has some rocks and seaweed. During low tide, a sand bar stretches out into the water quite a distance. There are restrooms and lifeguards in summer. ~ Three miles west of town off Eel Point Road, Dionis.

MADAKET BEACH One of Nantucket's most beautiful bicycle paths ends at this spectacular western-facing beach. Everything about this long, wide beach is just right. The sand is white and clean, the surf fantastic, the sunsets the best on the island. It's also one of the best spots on Nantucket to fish. You'll find portable toilets and lifeguards and a shuttle service, all in summer only. ~ At the end of Madaket Road, Madaket.

HIDDEN ►   **CISCO BEACH** The road to this out-of-the-way beach goes past scenic Hummock Pond and rolling heathlands. The wide-open beach is a free and easy place where you can walk for miles on white sand. It's popular with seasoned beach rats and young surfer types. ~ At the end of Hummock Pond Road in Cisco, four miles southwest of town.

SURFSIDE Narrow sand paths lace the moors leading to this massive beach. Because Surfside is only three miles from town, it gets very crowded in the summer. But it's a great beach—big, long and wide with small rolling dunes to explore and the best surf on the island. Surfside attracts families and college students. To get away from the crowds, walk east along the shore toward Siasconset and soon you'll discover long stretches of blissfully empty beach. There's a bike path. Summer facilities include restrooms, showers, lifeguards, a snack bar and a shuttle service. ~ At the end of Surfside Road, three miles south of town.

SIASCONSET BEACH This lovely eastern-facing beach seven miles from town is in the village of Siasconset. People make a day out of biking or driving here to explore the beach and the village; you can catch a shuttle bus from town in summer. Part of the beach is surrounded by grassy cliffs and dunes, then the land dips and becomes flat. To the left of the beach is Sankaty Lighthouse and the summer community of Quidnet. Walk south along the beach for an empty spot. Because of the wind, seaweed can be a problem. Keep an eye on small kids: this beach gets very deep about 20 feet out. You'll find lifeguards in the summer. ~ Seven miles east of town at the end of Milestone Road, Siasconset.

HIDDEN ►   **GREAT POINT, COSKATA & COATUE BEACHES** If you really want to leave civilization, consider exploring this narrow stretch of uninhabited land that wraps around Nantucket Harbor. It's like one giant sand dune surrounded by water. Driving through this desertlike landscape is an adventure, and those who make the trek can swim in calm waters lapping a deserted white-sand beach and view a nesting ground for piping plovers, clam and oyster ponds, the remains of a shipwreck, a century-old cedar forest and the Great Point Lighthouse. There's fantastic shore fishing for fluke, Spanish mackerel, bluefish and bass at Great Point, the northernmost point of land; swimming is calm on Nantucket Sound but not recommended on the Atlantic side, where the current and undertow are rough. Driving in this area requires an expensive permit ($20 per day for rental vehicles; $85 for the year) and a four-wheel-drive vehicle equipped with everything you need to dig yourself out of a deep sand rut. Permits are available at the Wauwinet Gate House on Wauwinet Road (508-228-0006). Tours and fishing excursions are advertised in the local paper. ~ At the northeast end of the island at the end of Wauwinet Road off Polpis Road.

SANFORD FARM 🏃 🚴 🏊 Owned by the Nantucket Conservation Foundation, this former dairy farm consists of 767 acres of classic Nantucket countryside. A magical place for quiet walks and private picnics, it has 6.6 miles of trails meandering through rare maritime heathlands that look like Scotland. Follow the trail past long and winding Hummock Pond down to the empty beach, which offers good swimming (but beware the undertow). No life-guards are posted. In spring and summer Sanford Farm is lush with wildflowers, but its most beautiful time is fall, when the land is a tapestry of burgundy, sage, rose, gold and ivory. Deer can be spotted early in the morning and at dusk. Turtles live in the pond. To minimize damage, visitors are urged to stay on the trails and roadways. ~ West of town off Madaket Road near the intersection of Cliff Road and Madaket; 508-228-2884.

◄ *HIDDEN*

Cape Cod, Martha's Vineyard and Nantucket offer a staggering number of opportunities for fishing, boating and other water sports, as well as cycling, golf, tennis and more.

▼▼▼▼▼▼▼▼▼▼▼▼
Outdoor Adventures

Bluefish, striped bass, tuna, cod and flounder are abundant. No license is required to fish, and tackle shops are everywhere. For detailed information on what to catch when, where and how, call the **Massachusetts Division of Marine Fisheries**. ~ 100 Cambridge Street, Room 1901, Boston, MA 02202; 617-727-3193.

FISHING

NORTH CAPE Among the hundreds of charter and party boat outfits on Cape Cod, one of the most reputable is **The Albatross**. This 52-foot boat holds up to 49 people. ~ Sesuit Harbor, East

Dennis; 508-385-3244. The 60-foot **Naviator** also comes highly recommended; sea bass, flounder and blackfish are common catches. ~ Wellfleet town pier; 508-349-6003. **Teacher's Pet** has a good reputation, offering bluefish and striped bass excursions. Closed November to mid-May. ~ Hyannis Harbor; 508-362-4925.

MARTHA'S VINEYARD Larry's Tackle Shop has shore guides and charter services. The four-hour trips can accommodate three to six people. ~ 258 Main Street, Edgartown; 508-627-5088.

NANTUCKET The **Albacore** will take you out for bluefish, bass, shark or tuna. Private charters only. ~ Straight Wharf, Nantucket; 508-228-5074.

WATER SPORTS

Cape Cod abounds with marinas and harbors where you can rent sailboats, windsurfing equipment, canoes and more. The bay and ponds around the area are good for canoeing and kayaking, while the ocean whips up some fine surfing waves.

OUTER CAPE Jack's **Boat Rental** has three locations for canoe, kayak, boogieboard and surfboard rentals. Closed Labor Day to mid-June. ~ Route 6, Wellfleet, 508-349-9808; Gull Pond, Wellfleet, 508-349-7553; and Flax Pond, Nickerson State Park, Brewster, 508-896-8556.

PROVINCETOWN Flyer's Boat Rental can outfit you with powerboats, sailboats and kayaks. Closed mid-October to mid-May. ~ 131-A Commercial Street; 508-487-0898.

SOUTH CAPE Cape Water Sports rents Hobie cats, canoes and kayaks. ~ Route 28, Harwich Port; 508-432-7079. They also have beachfront locations at Pleasant Bay in East Harwich and Ridgevale Beach in Chatham. The Pleasant Bay location offers sailing lessons.

MARTHA'S VINEYARD For sailboat rentals, as well as kayaking and windsurfing rentals or lessons, there's **Wind's Up**. ~ 199 Beach Road, Vineyard Haven; 508-693-4252. **Ayuthia Charters** has half- and full-day sails on a 48-foot ketch. Closed November through April. ~ Coastwise Wharf, Vineyard Haven; 508-693-7245.

NANTUCKET Nantucket Island Community Sailing rents windsurfing gear, kayaks and sailboats, and gives lessons. ~ North Beach Street; 508-228-5358.

WHALE WATCHING

April through October is the season to catch sight of humpbacks and minkes. **Hyannis Whale Watcher Cruises** guarantees whale spottings on the four-hour trip. ~ Millway Marina, Barnstable Harbor, Hyannis; 508-362-6088. In Provincetown, **Dolphin Fleet Whale Watch** also guarantees whales. A naturalist from the Center for Coastal Studies is on board one of three 100-foot boats to provide insight. ~ MacMillan Pier; 508-255-3857.

Lobsters, starfish, crabs and skates are common sights when diving in Cape Cod waters. Cape Cod Bay and Sandwich Town Beach are recommended spots.

East Coast Divers offers open-water certification as well as specialty classes, rentals and repairs. Shorediving and four-hour charter boat dives are among the options. ~ 237 Falmouth Road, Hyannis; 508-775-1185.

NORTH CAPE   Clientele primarily consists of club members and hotel guests, but nonmembers are welcome, at the semiprivate, 18-hole **Ocean Edge**. Carts are required. ~ 832 Village Drive, Brewster; 508-896-5911.

OUTER CAPE   Located on the Cape Cod National Seashore, **Highland Golf Links** is a nine-hole public course that requires tee times. You'll get views of Cape Cod Lighthouse as well as the seashore. ~ Lighthouse Road, Truro; 508-487-9201.

SOUTH CAPE   The **Harwich Port Golf Club** has a nine-hole course. ~ Forest and South streets, Harwich Port; 508-432-0250. The public 18-hole **Fairgrounds Golf Course** features a driving range, a pro shop, and a restaurant and lounge. A large sign at the driving range warns players to "Stop driving when planes approach." If you wait around for a while, you'll see why; the course is close to an airport that launches gliders. Sometimes the planes fly so low you can wave to the passengers. ~ 1460 Route 149, Marstons Mills; 508-420-1142.

MARTHA'S VINEYARD   You'll want to sink a few balls at **Mink Meadows Golf Club**, a semiprivate, nine-hole course featuring wooded, rolling terrain. ~ Golf Club Road off Franklin Street, Vineyard Haven; 508-693-0600. The 18-hole, semiprivate **Farm Neck Golf Course** offers beautiful scenery. ~ County Road, Oak Bluffs; 508-693-2504.

NANTUCKET   Tee off at the nine-hole, semiprivate **Miacomet Golf Club**, which also has a driving range and a practice putting green. ~ West Miacomet Road; 508-325-0333. Or play your nine holes at **Siasconset Golf Club**, one of the oldest courses in the country. This public links–style course resembles Scotland Yard. ~ Milestone Road, Siasconset; 508-257-6596.

NORTH CAPE   A privately owned club, **Mid-Cape Racquet & Health** has ten courts: nine lighted, one outdoors. They rent racquets and offer lessons. ~ 193 White's Path, South Yarmouth; 508-394-3511.

PROVINCETOWN   **Bissell Tennis Courts** is a privately owned facility with five clay courts. Pros here can show you the swing of things. ~ 21 Bradford Street Extension; 508-487-9512.

Text continued on page 328.

Cape Cod By Bicycle

Cape Cod, Martha's Vineyard and Nantucket are a cyclist's paradise. The flat landscape is laced with miles of smooth, paved bicycle paths that meander past sand dunes, salt marsh, woods and pastures. What follows is a modest sampling of some of the best rides. Local chambers of commerce can provide more comprehensive information.

Short Bike Rides, by Edwin Mullen and Jane Griffith (Globe Pequot Press) is a handy little book that describes 31 bike rides on Cape Cod, Nantucket and Martha's Vineyard.

NORTH CAPE   The Cape Cod Rail Trail, an eight-foot-wide bicycle path, runs about 30 miles along the old Penn Central Railroad tracks from Route 134 in South Dennis to six miles off Locust Road in Eastham, past classic Cape Cod scenery—ponds, forest, saltwater and freshwater marsh, cranberry bogs and harbors.

OUTER CAPE   Head of the Meadow, a moderately hilly bicycle path in the Cape Cod National Seashore in Truro, traverses some of the Cape's most dramatic scenery, including The Highlands' vast expanses of grassy knolls. The two-mile path starts at Head of the Meadow Road off Route 6 and ends at High Head Road.

PROVINCETOWN   Talk about dramatic scenery. The Province Lands Bike Trail dips and turns past towering sand dunes, silvery mounds of wavy beach grass, two magnificent beaches and the Province Lands Visitors Center. The five-mile loop starts at Herring Cove Beach parking lot at the end of Route 6 and includes many places where you can stop and picnic.

SOUTH CAPE   The Shining Sea bicycle path between Falmouth and Woods Hole is popular with experienced cyclists because it's hilly in some areas and very scenic. The 3.3-mile path runs along Palmer Avenue in Falmouth, then down a hill past deep woods and historic homes, ending at Woods Hole harbor.

MARTHA'S VINEYARD   The Oak Bluffs–Edgartown–Katama Beach bike path on Martha's Vineyard is smooth and easy, even though it's nine miles long. Departing from Oak Bluffs, the flat path runs along the shore past lovely old homes, beaches, ponds and salt marsh to historic Edgartown, then through heathland dotted with occasional houses to magnificent Katama Beach.

From Vineyard Haven, the hale and hearty can bicycle to Menemsha and Aquinnah via State Road to West Tisbury, then Middle Road to the end.

The ride is hilly in parts, but the scenery is breathtaking. The beaches in this area have residents-only parking lots, so bicycling is the only way a nonresident can enjoy them.

NANTUCKET Aside from the downtown hazards of cobblestone streets, narrow roads and heavy traffic, bicycling on Nantucket is a snap. Smooth, flat bike paths parallel the island's two main roads. The 6.2-mile Madaket bicycle path is the more scenic, dipping and winding past moors and ending at Madaket Beach, the western tip of the island. The 8.2-mile Siasconset path is a straight, flat line that goes past barren scrub pine and sandy scenery, ending at the village of Siasconset on the eastern end of the island. A 3.5-mile bike path leads to the ever-popular Surfside Beach and offers lovely scenery. The ten-mile Polpis Bike Path, an alternate route to Siasconset, features views of Nantucket Harbor.

Bike Rentals Practically every town on Cape Cod has a couple of bike rental shops. Most are closed November through April.

In South Yarmouth, **The Outdoor Shop** can outfit you with mountain or hybrid bikes, as well as helmets and locks. They also sell and repair bikes. ~ 50 Long Pond Drive; 508-394-3819. Along with sales and service, **The Little Capistrano Bike Shop** rents cruisers, hybrids and mountain bikes; helmets and locks cost extra. ~ Salt Pond Road, Route 6, Eastham; 508-255-6515. In Provincetown, check out Arnold's for repairs, sales or rentals (hybrids, kids' bikes, mountain bikes). Locks are included; helmets are extra. ~ 329 Commercial Street; 508-487-0844. Falmouth Heights' **Holiday Cycles** rents seven-speed cruisers, hybrids, mountain bikes, tandems and kids' bikes, as well as four-wheeled surreys. Repairs and sales are undertaken, and knowledgeable staff will direct you to a suitable bike path. ~ 465 Grand Avenue; 508-540-3549.

Martha's Vineyard has **Anderson's Bike Rentals** in Oak Bluffs. Choose from mountain and kids' bikes, hybrids and tandems; helmets and locks are included. Free road service for broken bikes is provided. You can also get the necessary repairs done here, or just buy a new bike. ~ 23 Circuit Avenue Extension; 508-693-9346. In Edgartown, there's **R. W. Cutler Bicycle Shop**. Rental bikes (mountains and hybrids) come with locks and helmets. They sell and repair bikes as well. ~ 1 Main Street; 508-627-4052.

Nantucket's wharf has many bicycle rental shops; one of the biggest outfits is the full-service **Young's Bicycle Shop**, whose rental bikes (tandems, hybrids, mountain, full-suspension) include helmets and locks. ~ 6 Broad Street, Steamboat Wharf; 508-228-1151.

MARTHA'S VINEYARD   Tennis is very popular on Martha's Vineyard. Municipal courts are at Church Street in Vineyard Haven, Niantic Park in Oak Bluffs, Robinson Road in Edgartown, Old Country Road in West Tisbury and the Chilmark Community Center on South Road.

NANTUCKET   Brant Point Racquet Club has nine outdoor clay courts and tennis pros ready to teach. They rent racquets and sell balls. Closed mid-October to mid-May. Fee. ~ 48 North Beach Street; 508-228-3700. Right near town, Jetties Beach Tennis Courts have six courts and plenty of lessons. Walk-ins are allowed during the off-season. ~ Bathing Beach Road; 508-325-5334.

RIDING STABLES

Liability insurance has gotten so high that only a few stables still rent horses.

SOUTH CAPE   Deer Meadow Riding Stable rents horses and ponies. Groups of up to 11 can saddle up for trail, sunset and pony rides. Deer and hawk sightings are common on this wooded, 30-acre farm. ~ Route 137, East Harwich; 508-432-6580.

MARTHA'S VINEYARD   Scrubby Neck Farms has trail rides through the forest for groups of four to six. There's horse camp for the kids, too, as well as pony and carriage rides. ~ West Tisbury–Edgartown Road, Martha's Vineyard; 508-693-3770.

HIKING

Otherworldly sand dunes, heaths that recall those across the Atlantic, sheltering forests and salt marshes are just a few of the environments available to hikers on Cape Cod and the Islands. You can trek through wilderness areas or stick to spots close to town. All distances listed for hiking trails are one way unless otherwise noted. For more information on hikes statewide, contact the **Massachusetts Department of Environmental Management Trails Program**. ~ 100 Cambridge Street, Boston; 617-727-3180.

NORTH CAPE   Talbot's Point Salt Marsh Trail (1.5 miles), off Old Country Road in Sandwich, offers excellent views of the Great Marsh. The trail winds through red pine forest, along the fern-filled marsh, and past cranberry bogs and the state game farm, where thousands of quail and pheasant are raised.

OUTER CAPE   Nauset Marsh Trail (1.2-mile loop) offers some of the Cape's lushest scenery. The trail starts at the Salt Pond Visitors Center in North Eastham and goes past the shoreline of Salt Pond and Nauset Marsh, then rises through pastoral farmland filled with beach plums, bayberries and cedars.

A mesmerizing view of salt marsh and the ocean beyond greets you at **Goose Ponds Trail** (1.4-mile loop) in the Wellfleet Bay Wildlife Sanctuary. The path leads through forest down a slight grade past Spring Brook to marshlands covered with wild lupine. A wooden boardwalk leads to secluded tidal flats. Among the many species of bird life are white-bottomed tree swallows nesting in bird houses throughout the sanctuary. ~ 508-349-2615.

Great Island Trail (about 3 miles, depending on the tide), a wind-bitten wilderness, is best in the morning when the sun isn't too intense. Starting at the end of Chequesset Neck Road in Wellfleet, this challenging trail borders tidal flats, grassy dunes, pitch pine forest, the ocean and meadows where purple marsh peas and fiddler crabs flourish. Great for solitary beachcombing, the trail offers a number of spectacular views.

PROVINCETOWN You'll find hikers and bikers on the moderately difficult **Beech Forest Trail** (1 mile), which winds to the Cape's most monumental sand dunes. Most of the trail wanders through cool beech forests and past freshwater ponds, and at one point it opens up to reveal the desertlike sand dunes. It starts on Race Point Road in Provincetown. ~ Information, 508-487-1256.

MARTHA'S VINEYARD **Felix Neck Wildlife Sanctuary Trail** (1.5 miles), off the Edgartown–West Tisbury Road, offers many opportunities to view ducks, swans, otters, muskrats, egrets, harrier hawks and other wildlife. The easy trail winds past waterfowl ponds, salt marsh, the tip of a peninsula, wetland vegetation and oak forest. It ends at the sanctuary's exhibit building, which has aquariums, wildlife displays, a library and a naturalist gift shop. Admission. ~ 508-627-4850.

NANTUCKET The island's only marked hiking trail is the **Sanford Farm–Ram Pasture Walking Trail**, offering 15 miles of wilderness. The Nantucket Conservation Foundation also owns parcels of wilderness the public can explore. For more on this, see the "Beaches & Parks" sections in this chapter. Following are two of the most scenic areas in which to hike:

Tupancy Links, off Cliff Road immediately west of town, is laced with paths that overlook Nantucket Sound. A former golf course, today this marked trail system traverses a big, open, grassy field offering dramatic views.

Alter Rock, off Polpis Road in the central moors, is crisscrossed by unmarked paths and rutted dirt roads. Dotted with kettle hole ponds, rocks and scrub oak thicket, the scenery is classic heathland. A four-wheel-drive is required if driving.

For more information on hiking trails on Nantucket, call the chamber of commerce at 508-228-1700.

Special note: For information on every conceivable way to get to Martha's Vineyard, Nantucket and Cape Cod short of walking on water, call the **Massachusetts Office of Travel and Tourism** and order a free *Getaway Guide*. ~ 100 Cambridge Street, 13th Floor, Boston; 617-727-3201, 800-227-6277; www.mass-vacation.com.

▼▼▼▼▼▼▼▼▼▼
Transportation

CAR   Route 6 cuts through the middle of Cape Cod, ending at Province-town. **Route 6A** runs along the north side of the Cape, and **Route 28** runs along Nantucket Sound. Both routes connect with Route 6 in Orleans.

AIR   Five airports serve Cape Cod and the Islands: **Logan International Airport** in Boston, Barnstable Airport and Provincetown Municipal Airport on Cape Cod, Martha's Vineyard Airport and Nantucket Memorial Airport.

Barnstable Airport in Hyannis is served by Business Express, Cape Air, Colgan Air, Continental Express, Delta, Island Air, Nantucket Airlines and USAir Express.

Cape Air services **Provincetown Municipal Airport**.

Flying into **Martha's Vineyard Airport** are Business Express, Cape Air, Continental Express, United Express and USAir Express.

Nantucket Memorial Airport is serviced by Business Express, Cape Air, Colgan Air, Continental Express, Delta, Island Air, Nantucket Airlines, United Express and USAir Express.

For ground transportation from Barnstable Airport to Logan Airport and areas throughout southern Massachusetts, contact ABC **Airport Coach**. ~ 508-747-6622.

Taxis and car rentals listed below provide ground transportation to all other airports except Logan.

FERRY & BOAT   Ferries and boats between Boston, Cape Cod, Martha's Vineyard and Nantucket require reservations during the summer. Throughout the year, the **Steamship Authority** transports cars and passengers from Route 28 to Woods Hole to Oak Bluffs and Vineyard Haven, as well as from Hyannis to Nantucket. ~ 509 Falmouth Road, Mashpee; 508-477-8600.

The following ferries and boats operate seasonally and do not transport cars: **Hy-Line Cruises** takes passengers to and from Hyannis, Nantucket (year-round) and Oak Bluffs on Martha's Vineyard. ~ Ocean Street Dock, Hyannis; 508-775-7185. **Martha's Vineyard Ferry** operates between New Bedford and Vineyard Haven on Martha's Vineyard. ~ 1494 East Rodney French Boulevard, Billy Woods Wharf, New Bedford; 508-997-1688. **The Island Queen** goes between Falmouth and Oak Bluffs on Martha's Vineyard. ~ 75 Falmouth Heights Road, Pier 45, Falmouth; 508-548-4800. The **Chappaquiddick Ferry**, universally known as the "Chappy ferry," travels between Edgartown and Chappaquiddick Island year-round. ~ Dock and Daggett streets, Edgartown, Martha's Vineyard; 508-627-9427.

BUS   **Greyhound Lines** offers frequent service to Newburyport and Boston. ~ 700 Atlantic Avenue, South Station, Boston; 617-526-1801, 800-231-2222.

Bonanza runs buses to and from Logan Airport, Hyannis, Woods Hole, Falmouth, Bourne, New Bedford, Fall River, Connecticut, Rhode Island and New York. ~ Depot Avenue, Falmouth; 508-548-7588, 888-751-8800.

Plymouth and Brockton Street Railway Company has year-round express service to and from Boston's Logan Airport and local service along Route 6 on Cape Cod from Sagamore to Provincetown. The Plymouth terminal is at 8 Industrial Park Road, Plymouth; the Hyannis terminal is at 17 Elm Avenue, Hyannis. ~ 508-746-0378, 508-775-6502.

Peter Pan Trailways offers service to Hyannis from Mount Holyoke, Springfield, Newton and Worcester. ~ 700 Atlantic Avenue, Boston; 800-343-9999.

Car-rental agencies at Barnstable Airport include **Avis Rent A Car** (800-331-1212), **Hertz Rent A Car** (800-654-3131) and **National Car Rental** (800-227-7368).

CAR RENTALS

Thrifty Car Rental (800-367-2277) serves the airport in Provincetown.

Martha's Vineyard Airport has **Thrifty Adventure Car and Moped Rentals** (508-693-1959, 800-367-2277), **All-Island Rent A Car** (508-693-6868), **Budget Rent A Car** (800-527-0700) and **Hertz Rent A Car** (800-654-3131).

Nantucket Memorial Airport agencies include **Budget Rent A Car** (800-527-0700), **Hertz Rent A Car** (800-654-3131) and **Nantucket Windmill Auto Rental** (800-228-1227).

Cape Cod Regional Transit Authority offers door-to-door mini-bus service (reservations required) and makes six daily round-trips between Barnstable and Woods Hole, Hyannis and Orleans, and Hyannis and Barnstable Harbor. ~ Old Chatham Road, South Dennis; 508-385-8326.

PUBLIC TRANSIT

On Martha's Vineyard, from late May to mid-October, **Island Transport** runs shuttle buses between Vineyard Haven, Oak Bluffs and Edgartown. Less frequent service is available up-island; call the above number for schedules. Nantucket doesn't have public transportation. Most people get around with rental cars or bicycles. ~ 508-693-1589.

Taxis serving airports on the coast are as follows: Barnstable Airport, **All Points Taxi** (508-760-0000), **Hyannis Taxi** (508-775-0400) and **Town Taxi of Cape Cod** (508-771-5555); Provincetown Airport, **Mercedes Cab** (508-487-3333); Martha's Vineyard Airport, **Adam Cab** (508-627-4462); Nantucket Memorial Airport, **All Points Taxi** (508-228-5779).

TAXIS

SIX

Massachusetts Coast

Immortalized by Herman Melville in *Moby Dick*, the Massachusetts coast today remains fertile territory for the imagination. This magnificent stretch of windswept coast abounds with historic seaside villages, vintage lighthouses, glorious beaches and history that reads like an adventure story complete with witches and pirates, authors and artists, Pilgrims and American natives, sea captains and Moby Dick.

An ethnic melting pot of Portuguese fishermen, Yankee blue bloods, old salts and the Irish (who seem to be everywhere), coast residents are very proud of where they live. North Shore loyalists wouldn't think of moving to the South Shore, and vice versa. What unifies everyone is the sea. Rich and poor alike have mini weather stations on their roofs to determine wind direction, and everyone reads tide charts. Kids learn how to fish, sail and dig for clams when they're five years old.

That all-encompassing sea is, of course, what lured Europeans to these shores in the first place. One hundred years before the Pilgrims stepped foot on Plymouth Rock, English adventurers fished the waters around the Massachusetts coast. Between 1600 and 1610, explorers Samuel de Champlain and Bartholomew Gosnold sailed to Gloucester.

Aboard the *Mayflower*, 102 Pilgrims landed in Plymouth in 1620, establishing the first permanent settlement in New England. By 1640, about 2500 of the new settlers lived in eight communities. Although they came to America to seek religious freedom, the Pilgrims persecuted Quakers and anyone else who didn't adhere to their strict Puritan religion. Their intolerant thinking helped fuel one of the most infamous pieces of American Colonial history—the Salem witch trials of 1692. Salem had been founded six years after Plymouth. Here the Puritans tried to impose their religious laws on rowdy fishermen who lived in nearby Marblehead, but adultery and drunkenness won out. The Puritans were more successful in their witch hunt—20 people, most of them women, were executed for practicing "witchcraft" in a single year.

The gruesome trials took place during a time when witchcraft was thought to be the cause for any unexplained event. Similar trials and executions occurred throughout New England and Europe, but Salem had the dubious distinction of executing the most women in the shortest amount of time.

Fortunately by the 1700s the focus was more on commerce than religion. Salem sailing vessels had opened routes to the Orient, thus establishing the famous China trade and Salem's reputation as a major port. When the Revolutionary War broke out in 1775, America didn't have a Navy, so Salem sea captains armed their merchant vessels and fought the British.

For the next 150 years, shipbuilding, the China trade and commercial fishing flourished along the Massachusetts coast, particularly in the towns north of Boston. Concurrently, New Bedford, near Rhode Island, became a leading whaling port.

All this maritime activity brought great prosperity to the coast. Fortune and adventure lay in wait for any man willing to risk his life on a whale boat or ship bound for the Orient to obtain ivory, spice, silver and gold. It was an exciting, swashbuckling time, filled with tall tales and tragedy. The widows' walks on many historic homes in towns such as Newburyport are a sad reminder of the men who never returned from the sea.

Evidence of the wealth gleaned during these years is apparent in the amazing number of 18th- and 19th-century mansions built by sea captains that dot the coast. Impeccably restored by a people in love with the past, these coast homes make up an architectural feast bulging with Greek Revival, Federal, Queen Anne, Victorian Gothic, Colonial and classic saltbox structures. Historic villages and buildings throughout the area enable visitors to see the evolution of America's unique architectural style.

By the mid-1800s everything along the Massachusetts coast started to change. Salem's prominence as a seaport was over. Its harbor was too shallow for the new, faster clipper ships, and railroads provided cheaper and more rapid shipping service. The whaling industry also started to decline as petroleum replaced whale oil and whales became scare. Eventually the entire industry vanished, plummeting New Bedford and other whaling ports into serious depressions.

The Industrial Revolution came along in the nick of time, and manufacturing businesses started to sprout along the Massachusetts coast and throughout New England. In the late 1800s, New Bedford and Fall River became leading textile manufacturers, but this prosperity was short lived. Prior to the Depression, union problems and cheaper labor in the South wiped out the textile industry.

While the coast economy was transforming itself in the mid-1800s, two other developments were evolving that would change the flavor of the coast forever. Tourism began to bloom on Cape Cod, and artists and writers discovered the inspirational charms of the coast.

Rudyard Kipling and Winslow Homer lived north of Boston in Rocky Neck, one of the country's oldest artist colonies. Nathaniel Hawthorne wrote about Salem, which he called home, in the *House of the Seven Gables*. Melville immortalized whaling in New Bedford. To this day, creative people are drawn to the Massachusetts coast, now supported by light industry, fishing and a tourist industry that just keeps growing.

We have divided the coast into two geographic areas. The North Shore (everything above Boston to the New Hampshire border) and the South Shore (Plymouth and the area from Cape Cod to the Rhode Island border). Cape Cod and the Islands have always attracted the lion's share of tourists, but the North Shore and South Shore offer more opportunities to discover hidden villages, inns, restaurants, beaches and more.

The North Shore wears many faces. Immediately north of Boston are the affluent commuter towns of Magnolia, Manchester and Marblehead, where prep schools, yachts and turn-of-the-century seaside mansions are a way of life.

Beyond these towns are Salem, known for architecture, witches and maritime museums; Gloucester, a major fishing port; Rockport, an artist-colony-turned-resort; Essex and Ipswich, pastoral areas with antiques and seafood; and Newburyport, a scenic 19th-century town on the New Hampshire border.

The South Shore is a patchwork of wealthy commuter towns, Portuguese neighborhoods, blue-collar communities and cranberry farms. Its three main towns include Plymouth, "America's Home Town," New Bedford and Fall River. You'll find Pilgrim lore, factory outlets, whaling museums, scenic ports, winding rivers and coastal pastures.

The coast has milder weather than the rest of the state. Summer temperatures range from the 60s to the 80s. Humidity can be a problem, especially along the North Shore, although ocean breezes keep things from getting too unbearable. In the fall temperatures range from the around 45° to 65°. Rain is unpredictable and can happen any time of year.

Traditionally the Massachusetts coast has been a summer destination, but more people are starting to visit in the fall, when prices decline along with the crowds. But no matter when you visit you're bound to be impressed. The scenery is unparalleled, the architecture magnificent, the history fascinating, the seafood plentiful.

▼▼▼▼▼▼▼▼▼▼▼▼▼▼
The North Shore

The North Shore is a real sleeper. Unspoiled and relatively uncommercial, it's a place where you can still discover hidden inns, restaurants, beaches and parks. An explorer's destination, it's perfect for people who like to go it on their own.

From Marblehead immediately north of Boston to Newburyport on the New Hampshire border, this craggy stretch of coast offers tremendous diversity. Marblehead has magnificent yachts; Salem means witches and maritime history; gritty Gloucester is filled with old salts; Rockport has art and beautiful inns; Essex offers antiques; Ipswich has the best seafood; and Newburyport displays 19th-century elegance.

The North Shore is a vacation area and bedroom community to Boston populated by investment bankers, Yankee blue bloods, fishermen, artists and history buffs. In the 18th and 19th centuries, the country's most magnificent ships were built in North Shore towns, bringing great wealth to the area.

SIGHTS

HIDDEN ►

In Marblehead, head directly to the Old Town historic district, where you'll find **Abbot Hall**, the Victorian town hall that houses the famous historic painting *The Spirit of '76* by Archibald

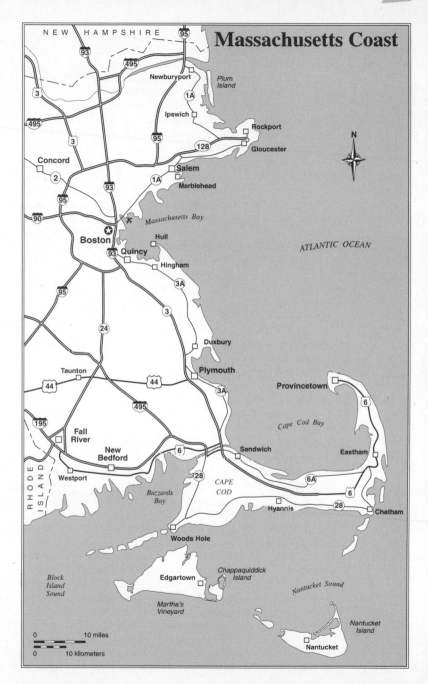

Massachusetts Coast

NEW HAMPSHIRE

Newburyport

Plum Island

Ipswich

Rockport

Gloucester

Concord

Salem

Marblehead

Massachusetts Bay

ATLANTIC OCEAN

N

Boston

Hull

Quincy

Hingham

Duxbury

Plymouth

Provincetown

Taunton

Cape Cod Bay

Eastham

Fall River

Sandwich

New Bedford

Hyannis

Chatham

Westport

CAPE COD

Buzzards Bay

RHODE ISLAND

Woods Hole

Block Island Sound

Edgartown

Chappaquiddick Island

Nantucket Sound

Martha's Vineyard

Nantucket Island

Nantucket

0   10 miles

0   10 kilometers

Willard. Visitors are free to wander in and view this dramatic work of art. ~ 188 Washington Street, Marblehead; 781-631-0528.

Right down the street is the **Jeremiah Lee Mansion,** a Georgian home built in 1768 for Colonel Lee, a Revolutionary War patriot. The guided tour is packed with entertaining anecdotes: We learn, for example, that the extra wide stairway in the entrance hall was designed by Mrs. Lee so women could swoop down the stairs in their enormous hoop skirts without knocking over their escorts. Closed November to late May. Admission. ~ 161 Washington Street, Marblehead; 781-631-1069.

Salem is so civilized and proper looking, it's hard to believe the 1692 witchcraft trials ever took place here. This macabre piece of American history began in a very innocent way. A group of teenage girls, who had learned black magic from a West Indian woman named Tituba, were diagnosed as bewitched. All hell broke loose, and everyone started accusing everyone else of being a witch. In the nine months to follow, 20 women were hanged and 150 imprisoned. The hysteria came to an end when the wives of prominent men were accused of being witches.

Salem's three witch exhibits are somewhat commercial, but kids love them. Every day in the summer, children wearing pointed black hats and capes purchased at nearby witch boutiques stand in long lines waiting to get in. The saving grace of the exhibits is that they are in historic buildings—not re-creations of haunted houses.

Salem Witch Museum is an audio-visual sound-and-light show. Life-size dioramas are spotlighted during the show to illustrate the events of the 1692 witch trials. Admission. ~ 19½ Washington Square North, Salem; 978-744-1692; www.salemwitch museum.com.

Witch House is the restored 1642 home of witch trial judge Jonathan Corwin, and the only structure still standing in Salem with direct ties to the witch trails. A narrated tour describes the style of life during this era and examines the process of the witch trials. Closed early December to late February. Admission. ~ 310½ Essex Street, Salem; 978-744-0180.

Witch Dungeon Museum re-enacts the witch trials. Admission. ~ 16 Lynde Street, Salem; 978-741-3570; www.cityofsalem.com.

To understand the real story of Salem, which was a major port in the 18th and 19th centuries, visit the **Peabody Essex Museum.** The Liberty Street site houses a treasure trove of objects acquired during Salem's active China trade days, such as an elaborate, moon-shaped, hand-carved wooden Chinese bed. A genealogy research library and original witch trial documents are some of the highlights. The Essex Street site consists of a history and decorative arts museum and four impeccably restored homes and gardens dating from 1684 to 1818. The houses are fascinating, especially if toured in chronological order, and the architecture and craftsmanship are superb. Anyone who has ever renovated an old house will appreciate a special exhibit about the painstaking efforts that go into museum restoration work. Since bright colors were a sign of wealth in the 19th century, the 1804 Gardner-Pingree House, a fine neoclassical building, holds a few surprises. The kitchen is deep salmon and green; one bedroom wears a vivid peacock blue hue, while another sports canary yellow. Admission. ~ East India Square, Salem; 978-745-9500, 800-745-4054; www.pem.org, e-mail pem@pem.org.

Chestnut Street is one of the most architecturally significant avenues in America. Many of its mansions were designed by Salem's famed Federal-period architect and woodcarver, Samuel McIntire. These brick and wood houses are simple in their design, yet the overall effect is graceful and elegant.

The North Shore

This 80-mile day trip from Boston provides a chance to explore the North Shore in all its diversity and quiet charm. Start by taking the Callahan Tunnel (Route 1A) north through the suburbs, where it becomes the McClellen Highway, then North Shore Road, and finally Lynnway before the divided roadway ends at East Lynn, a distance of ten miles.

MARBLEHEAD   Take the east fork in the highway and follow Route 129 for six miles to Marblehead, a small village of clapboard houses, hollyhocks and cobblestone streets. Marblehead is sailboat country. All summer long the harbor is alive with some of the most sophisticated racing vessels in America. A good place to picnic and watch them is high on a hill in **Crocker Park** at the western end of Front Street. Marblehead's **Old Town**, which surrounds the harbor, dates back to before the Revolution and is a pleasant place to stroll, with interesting shops and casual restaurants. The **Marblehead Chamber of Commerce** maintains a visitor information booth at Pleasant and Spring streets. ~ 62 Pleasant Street, Marblehead; 781-631-2868; www.marbleheadchamber.org.

SALEM   Salem, the largest North Shore town, is only ten minutes away from Marblehead on Route 114, which rejoins Route 1A just south of town. People come here for architecture, maritime museums, Nathaniel Hawthorne and, of course, witches. Tourist information is available at the **National Park Service Visitor Center**. ~ 2 New Liberty Street, Salem; 978-740-1650. Or contact the **Chamber of Commerce**. ~ Old Town Hall, 32 Derby Square, Salem; 978-744-0004; e-mail cc@salem chamber.org. An easy way to see historic sights is to follow **Salem's Heritage Trail**, a self-guided walking tour indicated by a red line painted on the street.

GLOUCESTER   Northeast of Salem, turn off Route 1A again onto scenic Route 127, which hugs the coast and takes you through the residential

Pickering Wharf, a short walk from Chestnut Street, is a new but made-to-look-old commercial development of tourist shops and chain restaurants. About a block east stands **Derby Wharf**— a good area for strolling along the harbor.

Even though it's often crowded with tourists, there's something romantic and compelling about the **House of Seven Gables**, located down the street from Derby Wharf. Built in 1668, the dark, almost black house is framed by ocean and sky. The tall, towns of Manchester and Magnolia, known for their old money, private schools and magnificent mansions. Right off Route 127, about 14 miles north of Salem, you'll spot **Hammond Castle** perched on the edge of a steep, windswept cliff, looking like the setting for a Gothic novel. Three miles beyond the castle is Gloucester, the oldest seaport in the United States. Home port to approximately 200 fishermen, it has a salty-dog ambience that brings you back to the real world after the castle. Overlooking the harbor stands the town's famed **Gloucester Fisherman** statue, *Man at the Wheel*, commemorating "They that go down to the sea in ships." There's not much to do in Gloucester; information on the town and local services is available at the **Cape Ann Chamber of Commerce**, the largest tourist information center on the North Shore, in the center of town. ~ 33 Commercial Street, Gloucester; 978-283-1601; www.cape-ann.com.

ROCKPORT   A short hop from Gloucester off Route 127 is **Rocky Neck Art Colony**, one of the country's oldest artist colonies, dating back to the 18th century. Winslow Homer and Rudyard Kipling lived here. Today it is a quainter than quaint seaside village with tiny houses, restaurants and galleries. Ten minutes farther along on Route 127 is Rockport, the quintessential New England seaside village and the North Shore's only resort town. Until the mid-19th century, Rockport was a quiet fishing village. Then artists discovered its scenic charm, and the proverbial seascape was born. Today tourists flock to Rockport in the summer. The town is rather commercial, but the beautiful harbor and windswept rocky coast that originally attracted artists are still here to enjoy.

BACK TO BOSTON   From Rockport, continue on Route 127 for nine more miles as it loops around the peninsula and joins Route 128, a divided freeway that connects to Routes 1 and 95 and can put you back in downtown Boston in less than an hour. Or, to extend your North Shore outing, leave Route 128 after four miles at Exit 14, detour through **Essex** and **Ipswich** (page 341) on Route 133, and return to Boston via Route 1A.

imposing gables look a bit like witch hats (although this thought probably wouldn't come to mind in another town). Inside, a labyrinth of cozy rooms with low ceilings, narrow passageways and secret stairs add to the ancient feeling of the place. The guided tour includes a good short film about how the house inspired Nathaniel Hawthorne to write his famous novel. Year-round guided tours are available. Admission. ~ 54 Turner Street, Salem; 978-744-0991; www.7gables.org.

HIDDEN ►

Northeast of Salem on the coastal Route 127 are the exclusive small towns of Manchester and Magnolia. Right off Route 127 is **Hammond Castle Museum,** a popular spot for weddings. Built by John Hays Hammond, Jr., creator of the radio remote control, the house features an eccentric collection of medieval artifacts. Closed Monday through Wednesday from Labor Day to the end of September; closed in October; open weekends only from November through Memorial Day. ~ 80 Hesperus Avenue, Gloucester; 978-283-7673.

HIDDEN ►

The **Beauport Museum** is a sprawling oceanfront English manor formerly owned by noted decorator Henry Davis Sleeper. From 1907 to 1934 Sleeper spent a fortune decorating all 40 rooms with a vast collection of American and European antiques, tapestries, wood paneling from abandoned old homes and much more. An informal pale green dining room has a worn brick floor and two long wooden tables set with a beautiful collection of colored glassware that reflects the light coming in from a bank of ocean-facing windows. Surprisingly, the overall effect is of an intimate English cottage. Closed mid-October to mid-May. Admission. ~ 75 Eastern Point Boulevard, East Gloucester; 978-283-0800.

Bearskin Neck, a narrow peninsula jutting out into the ocean, is one of Rockport's main tourist attractions. It's lined with Lilliputian-sized wooden fishermen's cottages transformed into restaurants and galleries selling everything from T-shirts and seascapes in every style imaginable to model ships made of cut-up beer cans. Overlooking the harbor, off Bearskin Neck, is Motif #1, a red lobster shack, so named because it has been painted by so many artists.

About two miles south of downtown Rockport is the **Rockport Chamber of Commerce.** ~ 3 Main Street, Rockport; 978-546-6575; www.rockportusa.com. The folks here can point out local sights such as the eccentric **Paper House.** At first it looks like a normal cottage, but it's made entirely out of newspaper. Even the furniture and fireplace are rolled paper. Elis F. Stedman, its creator, started the house in 1920; it took 20 years to complete. Closed from Columbus Day through March. ~ 52 Pigeon Hill Street, Rockport; 978-546-2629.

HOW DRY AM I . . . .
Rockport is a dry town, thanks to Hannah Jumper, a temperance supporter. In 1856 after a raucous Fourth of July celebration, Hannah convinced town fathers to outlaw liquor. Even today you can't buy it in a store or order it in a restaurant. But you can buy liquor in Gloucester, which is only ten minutes away, and bring it to any Rockport restaurant.

The rural villages of **Essex** and **Ipswich** are about 30 minutes north of Rockport. Essex is famous for its antique stores (see the "Shopping" section below), Ipswich for its clams. A pleasant day can be spent antiquing and enjoying fresh, affordable seafood at one of the many roadside eateries in this area.

This route takes you right past **John Whipple House**, a steeply pitched-roofed house built circa 1655 and occupied by the Whipple family for over 200 years. As did many colonists, the Whipples built their home in the post-Elizabethan style popular in England at the time. It has a lovely Colonial-style garden and is in a semi-rural area close to other historic buildings. Closed Monday and Tuesday and from mid-October to late April. Admission. ~ 1 South Village Green, Ipswich; 978-356-2811.

Just before the New Hampshire border, about 30 minutes north of Ipswich, lies the handsome 19th-century town of **Newburyport**. When the fog rolls in and the smell of brine and fish fills the air, you can walk along narrow streets bearing names like Neptune and imagine what it was like 100 years ago when this was a major shipbuilding center.

In the late 1970s the downtown area overlooking the harbor was renovated from top to bottom. Today, Newburyport's 19th-century brick buildings are so spit-and-polish clean, the town literally sparkles. As in many European towns, there's a central plaza overlooking the harbor where you can sit and watch the world go by. The shops and restaurants are quite tasteful; T-shirt and souvenir shops are the exception. **Greater Newburyport Chamber of Commerce** is in the heart of downtown. ~ 29 State Street, Newburyport; 978-462-6680; www.newburyportchamber.org.

For a healthy dose of the good life circa 1850, walk along **High Street** (Route 1A), which is lined with immaculate 19th-century Federal-style mansions built by sea captains. For a peek inside, visit **Cushing House Museum**, home of the Historical Society of Old Newbury. It has 19th-century antiques, plus a genealogical library, French garden and carriage house. Closed Sunday and Monday and from November through April. Admission. ~ 98 High Street, Newburyport; 978-462-2681.

LODGING

Many of the North Shore's accommodations are in the resort town of Rockport. A sprinkling of motels can be found along Route 127, but they're short on charm and expensive.

Pleasant Manor Inn, an 1872 Victorian, is located on a historic street surrounded by other impressive homes. A grand staircase leads to 12 good-sized guest rooms. Some furnishings are a bit drab, but the inn's wide hallways, tall ceilings and many fireplaces are impressive. The inn has a homey, laid-back feeling, which is perhaps why it attracts the serious sailors from around the world who come to Marblehead, a yachting center. A tennis court is located behind the house; each room has a coffeemaker, and a hearty continental breakfast is served. ~ 10 Liberty Lane, Marblehead; 781-631-5843. MODERATE.

HIDDEN ►

A modest-looking green clapboard house, **The Nautilus Guest House** doesn't have a sign outside. "People just know about it," says the owner. Four plain and simple guest rooms with contemporary furnishings occupy the second floor (no private baths). The house stands on a narrow street across from the busy harbor and the Driftwood, a colorful, sea shanty–style restaurant popular with fishermen and locals. ~ 68 Front Street, Marblehead; 781-631-1703. BUDGET TO MODERATE.

The **Stephen Daniels House** is like a trip back in time. Built in 1667 by a sea captain, it is one of the few bed and breakfasts around here furnished entirely with museum-quality antiques. The five guest rooms have enormous walk-in fireplaces, low beamed ceilings and age-worn pine floors. It's located on a quiet, historic street within walking distance of everything, although the sign outside is small and easy to miss. ~ 1 Daniels Street, Salem; 978-744-5709. DELUXE.

If you can't live without a telephone, color television, air conditioning and room service, stay at **The Hawthorne Hotel**. One of the few real hotels on the North Shore, this impeccably restored Federal-style building is located across from Salem Common. Eighty-nine guest rooms are tastefully decorated with reproduction Colonial antiques. Elegant public rooms have wood paneling, brass chandeliers and wing-back chairs. ~ 18 Washington Square West, Salem; 978-744-4080, 800-729-7829, fax 978-745-9842; www.hawthornehotel.com. MODERATE TO ULTRA-DELUXE.

The **Old Corner Inn** is a small, unpretentious and very casual inn in a building that dates back to 1865. It's within easy reach of Singing Beach and the village of Manchester. The nine rooms (six with private baths) are simply but comfortably furnished with some antiques. A couple of rooms have four-poster beds and working fireplaces; the bathroom of room number one has a ball-and-claw bathtub. Advance reservations are a must in the summer months since it's the only inn in Manchester. ~ 2 Harbor Street, Manchester by the Sea; 978-526-4996. MODERATE.

There's something inexpressibly lovable about the **White House**, a cross between an inn and a motel. Surrounded by a well-coifed lawn steps away from the heart of little Magnolia, it has a total of 16 rooms, six fitting beautifully into the charming-inn category (antique furnishings, all sorts of little Victorian touches), and another ten rooms that are traditional motel accommodations. The latter are actually quite comfortable, most with two big double beds, a television, a private entrance, a private bath and a parking spot—a welcome change from the inns that sometimes compromise on privacy. A continental breakfast is included. ~ 18 Norman Avenue, Gloucester; 978-525-3642. MODERATE TO DELUXE.

Beach lovers enjoy the **Blue Shutters Inn**, a lovely old house across the street from Good Harbor Beach, one of the North Shore's most beautiful strips of sand. It's situated on the outskirts of a secluded, affluent residential area overlooking the ocean and a vast expanse of scenic salt marsh. Blue and white throughout, the inn offers ten rooms and four individual apartments (weekly rental only), all with ocean views and sporting furnishings that are homey, simple and sparkling clean. Breakfast included. ~ 1 Nautilus Road, Gloucester; 978-283-1198. MODERATE TO DELUXE.

Only a ten-minute walk from Gloucester's famed fisherman statue, **The Manor Inn** has economical accommodations to satisfy all tastes. The main guest house, a lovely Victorian built in 1900, has 11 bed-and-breakfast-style guest rooms, some with turret-shaped ceilings and oversized beds. Next to the guest house are one-story motel units, some of which overlook the Annisquam River, a salt marsh and estuaries. The decor is plain and unobtrusive. Closed November through March. ~ 141 Essex Avenue, Gloucester; 978-283-0614. MODERATE TO DELUXE.

A 1791 Colonial bed and breakfast, **The Inn on Cove Hill** is a five-minute walk from Bearskin Neck, Rockport's main tourist attraction. Eleven guest rooms have wide pine-plank floors, beautiful restored moldings, antiques, queen-size canopy beds, country quilts and Laura Ashley–style wallpaper. In summer a continental breakfast is served in the garden; in spring and fall it's served in bed. Shared bath, budget; private bath, moderate to deluxe. Closed late October to mid-April. ~ 37 Mount Pleasant Street, Rockport; 978-546-2701, 888-546-2701; www.capeann. com/covehill. BUDGET TO DELUXE.

The **Old Farm Inn** looks like the original Sunny Brook Farm. ◄ **HIDDEN** Built in 1779, the barn-red inn is shaded by glorious weeping willow trees. Only ten minutes from downtown and within walking distance of Halibut Point State Park, it's a good place for getting away from it all without going to extremes. Four guest rooms in the main house (some featuring sitting rooms) have gun stock beams, wide pine-plank floors, fireplaces and antique quilts. Four large guest rooms in a newer building (some with kitchenettes) are decorated with country-style prints, but they lack the charm of the other rooms. Closed December through March. ~ 291 Granite Street, Rockport; 978-546-3237, 800-233-6828, fax 978-546-9308; www.oldfarminn.com. DELUXE TO ULTRA-DELUXE.

JFK and Jackie once slept at the **Yankee Clipper Inn**, one of Rockport's finest hostelries. The main inn, a stately white oceanfront mansion, has magnificent wood-paneled public rooms appointed with model ships, oriental rugs, paintings and elegant yet comfortable furniture. The Quarterdeck, a separate building built in 1960, has panoramic ocean views and a traditional look. The Bulfinch House, an 1840 Greek Revival building across the street, has fine period details but limited ocean views. Most of the 26 guest rooms are nondescript, but what they lack in decor is made up for by location. The inn has a good restaurant, saltwater swimming pool, gazebo and nature paths. Breakfast included. Closed late October to mid-March. ~ 96 Granite Street, Rockport; 978-546-3407, 800-545-3699, fax 978-946-9730; www. yankeeclipperinn.com. MODERATE TO ULTRA-DELUXE.

The **Peg Leg Inn**, a white clapboard Colonial, is only steps away from the beach. One of the inn's five buildings is on the ocean and commands the highest rates, but it has spectacular views, a large, sweeping lawn and a granite gazebo. The 33 guest rooms are furnished with chenille bedspreads, braided rugs and reproduction Colonial furnishings and wallpaper. A continental breakfast is included in the rates. Closed late October to mid-April. ~ 2 King Street, Rockport; 978-546-2352, 800-346-2352; www.cape-ann.com/pegleg. MODERATE.

Located on a quiet street in the center of town, the **Linden Tree Inn** has 18 rooms with private baths. Twelve antique-furnished rooms are in the main house; the rest are motel-style accommodations in the carriage house. The inn is named after an enormous linden tree on the grounds. Continental breakfast is included. ~ 26 King Street, Rockport; 978-546-2494, 800-865-2122, fax 508-546-2494; www.linden-tree.com. MODERATE.

Rockport's **Seaward Inn**, a rambling brown-shingle building, sits on a beautiful bluff overlooking the ocean. Surrounded by flower gardens, lawns and stone walls, it has a spring-fed swimming pond and bird sanctuary laced with nature paths. Cottages with kitchenettes and fireplaces, located behind the main inn, are ideal for families. Thirty-eight guest rooms, some with ocean views and fireplaces, are simply appointed with homey-looking Colonial-style furnishings. The Adirondack-style chairs on a grassy knoll overlooking the windswept shore are perfect for relaxing and reading. Rates include a full breakfast. ~ 44 Marmion Way, Rockport; 978-546-3471, 800-648-7733, fax 978-546-7661; www.seawardinn.com. DELUXE TO ULTRA-DELUXE.

A reasonably priced bed and breakfast in the heart of Rockport is hard to come by, but **Lantana House** fits the bill. The three-story cedar shake-shingled inn has seven charming guest rooms, each with distinctive decor. The third floor boasts a suite with a kitchenette. There are two decks where guests can enjoy breakfast or a quiet afternoon. Common areas are decorated with the innkeeper's artwork and book collections. Most rooms have private baths, and continental breakfast is included. ~ 22 Broadway, Rockport; 978-546-3535, 800-291-3535, fax 978-546-3231. BUDGET TO MODERATE.

Author Picks

CHAPTER FAVORITES

I'm intrigued by other people's eccentric lifelong projects, and one that ranks high on the list is the 1920 **Paper House** in Rockport—made entirely of newspaper and still standing. *page 340*

Witches aside, one of the best reasons I can think of to visit Salem is the **Stephen Daniels House**, among the oldest and most authentically antique-furnished B&B inns in the region. Huge fireplaces make it cozy on chilly autumn days. *page 342*

I find that when I'm traveling, a good breakfast is certainly the most important meal of the day—and often the hardest to find. That's why I appreciate "New England's largest breakfast menu" at **Persy's Place**, probably the only restaurant in Massachusetts where you can order catfish and eggs. *page 362*

The more chances I have to encounter whales up close, the happier I am that we humans are learning to interact with them instead of killing them. In fact, these days **whale watching** seems to be Gloucester's main industry. *page 366*

Guests at the **George Fuller House** will get the full Essex treatment. The house was built in 1830 by shipwrights who built many of the fishing schooners that plied Cape Ann's waters during the whaling era. Many of the original Federal-style details have been preserved, including the interior folding shutters, paneling and carved fireplace mantels. The seven rooms are furnished with antiques and reproductions; all have private baths, some have canopy beds and four have working fireplaces. The innkeepers serve a full breakfast every morning in the dining room, and tea is available on the porch or in the living room in the late afternoon. ~ 148 Main Street, Route 133, Essex; 978-768-7766, 800-477-0148, fax 978-768-6178; e-mail gfuller@ziplink.net. MODERATE TO DELUXE.

The **Clark Currier Inn** is a beautiful 1803 Federal home in the square style of the period. The woodwork and other details throughout the house are splendid, and the antiques and reproductions are, for the most part, true to the Federal period. The eight rooms are individually named for former owners or well-known visitors. Some rooms have canopy beds, and some have twin beds or are convertible to suites for parents who would rather have their children sleeping in an adjoining room. All rooms have private baths. The backyard boasts a lovely garden and a gazebo. ~ 45 Green Street, Newburyport; 978-465-8363, 800-360-6582. DELUXE TO ULTRA-DELUXE.

HIDDEN ▶   The **Morrill Place Inn**, a three-story, 1806 Federal-style mansion, stands on historic High Street, where wealthy shipbuilders lived in the 19th century. The inn's 12 spacious guest rooms are beautifully decorated. The Henry W. Kinsman room (named for a former owner) is a rich hunter green with an enormous white canopy bed, while the Daniel Webster room has a four-poster antique bed and sleigh dresser. Rooms on the third floor are less formal but charming in their own way, with Colonial-style antiques. Some rooms share baths; pets are allowed. Breakfast and afternoon tea are included. ~ 209 High Street, Newburyport; 978-462-2808, 888-594-4667, fax 978-462-9966. BUDGET TO MODERATE.

DINING   Rockport has the majority of restaurants on the North Shore, but few are outstanding. Restaurants with a steady local clientele in nearby towns are generally better.

HIDDEN ▶   **King's Rook**, a romantic café and wine bar, serves many varieties of hot chocolate, coffee, tea, imported beer and ale, wine, sherry, apéritifs and champagne. Also available are light entrées such as pesto turkey sandwiches, thin-crust gourmet pizza, pâté, cheese, sausage, soup and salad. The restaurant's low-beamed ceiling, soft peach walls, lace café curtains, candlelight and classical music create an intimate atmosphere favored by couples. ~ 12 State Street, Marblehead; 781-631-9838. BUDGET.

The **Driftwood Restaurant** is something of an institution. Homey, friendly and colorful, it attracts fishermen in the wee hours (it opens at 5:30 a.m.) and young professionals late on weekend mornings. The fare is traditional and plentiful: ham and eggs, pancakes, fried dough, clam chowder, burgers, fried seafood. The interior of this modest little establishment is plain and simple with red-and-white checked tablecloths. Tables are jammed close together, and there's a counter. No dinner. ~ 63 Front Street, Marblehead; 781-631-1145. BUDGET.

If the diner urge strikes, head for **Red's Sandwich**. Its booths and two horseshoe-shaped bars are always crowded with regulars who all seem to know one another. The menu includes all the diner favorites, from pancakes at breakfast to burgers for lunch. Outside there's a little courtyard area for warm-weather meals. No dinner. ~ 15 Central Street, Salem; 978-745-3527. BUDGET.

HIDDEN ▶   The North Shore has two first-rate gourmet delis perfect for unforgettable picnics. **Grange Gourmet** and **Bruni's** offer items such as breakfast pastries, leek soup, cucumber soup, homemade salsa and chips, tortellini primavera salad, chicken salad with green grapes and almonds, healthy sandwiches, gourmet desserts and baked goods. You can also pick up different types of coffee and tea, natural sodas and more. ~ Grange Gourmet: 457 Washington Street, Gloucester; 978-283-2639. Bruni's: 36 Essex Road, Route 133, Ipswich; 978-356-4877. BUDGET.

The Rudder is a quaint waterfront restaurant with low-beam ceilings and a natural wood decor that creates an atmosphere of casual dining. On any given night, you may find Hawaiian opakapaka or Australian shellfish featured. The fall menu boasts game meats such as venison and elk. Closed November through March. Dinner only. ~ 73 Rocky Neck Avenue, Gloucester; 978-283-7967. MODERATE TO ULTRA-DELUXE.

The Greenery, located near the entrance to Bearskin Neck, has sandwiches, a salad bar, bakery goods and desserts to go. The back dining room facing the harbor serves all these dishes plus entrées such as pesto pizza, lobster, crab quiche and grilled swordfish. The restaurant is appointed with blond wood, brass light fixtures and touches of green throughout. Closed November through March. ~ 15 Dock Square, Rockport; 978-546-9593. MODERATE.

Portside Chowder House is a good place for a cup of chowder on a cold, blustery day. Cozy and tiny, the dark wood restaurant has low-beamed ceilings, a fireplace and Windsor chairs. Specialties include New England and corn chowders, grilled sausage, crab and chicken. Lunch served year-round, dinner in summer only. ~ 1 Doyle's Cove Road, Rockport; 978-546-7045. BUDGET TO MODERATE.

Like many Rockport restaurants, the **Cutty's Harbour Café** serves classic entrées—Cajun-style shrimp, lobster linguine, fried calamari—but it prepares the food with more care than most of the competition. Sit at the upper-level dining room overlooking the harbor. A roaring fire adds to the romantic atmosphere of this eatery. Closed November through February. ~ 14 Bearskin Neck, Rockport; 978-546-2180. MODERATE TO DELUXE.

Follow Bearskin Neck as far as it goes (resisting the urge to stop for a lobster roll or bowl of chowder along the way) and you reach **My Place By-the-Sea**. Here the view of the ocean competes with the food for your attention. If the weather's nice, grab a table outside: this is Cape Ann's prettiest dining spot. For both lunch and dinner you'll find lots of seafood specialties, including lobster prepared several different ways. The lunch menu also includes an array of salads and sandwiches. Closed winter and early spring. ~ 68 Bearskin Neck, Rockport; 978-546-9667. MODERATE.

Downhome and fun, **Woodman's** hasn't changed anything except the prices since it opened in 1914. This roadside institution claims to have created the fried clam. The menu includes steamers, lobster, clam cakes, scallops and corn on the cob. Sit inside at old wooden booths or outside at picnic tables in back. There's a raw bar upstairs and a full liquor bar downstairs. Locals like to come here after a day at nearby Crane's Beach. ~ 121 Main Street, Route 133, Essex; 978-768-6451. BUDGET TO MODERATE.

Tom Shea's is a fine quality seafood restaurant with large picture windows overlooking Essex River—a perfect spot for watching the sunset. The wooden interior gives the restaurant an understated, nautical look. The fare is traditional—baked stuffed lobster, fried clams, stuffed sole, grilled teriyaki shrimp, pasta, Cajun dishes plus some beef and chicken dishes. ~ 122 Main Street, Route 133, Essex; 978-768-6931. MODERATE TO DELUXE.

HIDDEN ► **Chipper's River Café** serves casual fare in an idyllic setting overlooking Ipswich River. Tucked behind the Choate River Bar, the restaurant has a sign that's small and easy to miss. Chipper's imaginative, health-conscious menu, tile floors, natural wood, art prints and jukebox make it look and feel like a California restaurant. In the summer you can sit outside overlooking the river and quaint bridge. Dishes include grilled chicken breast with roast-garlic pesto, blackened filet mignon with a Cajun remoulade, and changing pasta dishes. Next to the restaurant is Chipper's Bakery, a good source for picnic treats. ~ 11 South Main Street, Ipswich; 978-356-7956. MODERATE TO DELUXE.

Classical music, candlelight, gold gilt mirrors and mismatched antiques give **Scandia** a romantic look. The menu changes with the seasons and the chef's whims. Entrées might include veal and lobster sauté with sweet butter or scallop chowder. The homemade salad dressings are excellent—fennel herb, maple curry, tomato cheddar and more. Reservations are a must. ~ 25 State Street, Newburyport; 978-462-6271. MODERATE TO DELUXE.

Fowle's Coffeehouse is a nostalgic, 1930s-style soda fountain and tobacco stand with authentic art deco decor. It features fresh pastries and freshly roasted coffee as well as soups served in bread bowls. The adjacent newsstand offers more than 3000 magazine titles. ~ 17 State Street, Newburyport; 978-463-8755. BUDGET.

Grog is a large, dark, woody college bar–type place in a non-college town. The burgers and Caesar salads are particularly good, and the cheerful staff may entice you into hanging out for longer than you'd planned. ~ 13 Middle Street, Newburyport; 978-465-8008. BUDGET.

SHOPPING Located in a former tavern, **Antique Wear** offers beautiful earrings, stick pins, broaches, pendants and tie pins made out of anHIDDEN ► tique buttons, some dating back to the 18th century. ~ 82–84 Front Street, Marblehead; 781-639-0070.

In Salem, the **Peabody-Essex Museum Gift Shop** offers a wonderful assortment of prints, shipbuilding kits and maritime souvenirs, as well as posters and regional history books. You'll also find children's books, Indian jewelry and ceramic plates from China. ~ East India Square, Salem; 978-745-1876.

Across from the House of Seven Gables is **Ye Old Pepper Candy Companie**. Established in 1806, it claims to be the oldest candy store in America. Specialties include gibralters, black jacks and other old-fashioned candies made on the premises. ~ 122 Derby Street, Salem; 978-745-2744.

Nearby you'll find the **Pickering Wharf Antique Gallery**, which at first glance looks like your garden-variety antique shop. Upon closer examination—walk to the back and turn left— you'll find an astounding arena for dozens of antique dealers. ~ Pickering Wharf, Salem; 978-741-3113.

◄ HIDDEN

One of Salem's biggest attractions is a witch shop owned by Jody Cabot, the city's most illustrious witch. **Crow Haven Corner** is filled with gargoyles, unicorns, crystal balls, magic wands and the full assortment of herbs, powders and seeds necessary for attracting good spirits or scaring off bad ones. ~ 125 Essex Street, Salem; 978-745-8763.

Don't leave Salem without stopping off at **Harbor Sweets**. Here you'll find sweet sloop chocolates (a combination of white and dark chocolate with almond butter crunch) that are frighteningly delicious. You can take a tour of the factory if you call ahead for an appointment. Fortunately, Harbor Sweets does mail-order, so before leaving fill out an address card to receive mailings. At Valentine's Day you can order a dozen tiny red boxes of sloops for all the loves in your life. ~ 85 Leavitt Street, Salem; 978-745-7648.

Hanna Wingate House sells American pine antiques, French country furniture and accessories. Closed weekends in January. ~ 11 Main Street, Rockport; 978-546-1008.

New England Goods specializes in wooden toys, salt-glazed pottery, Maine wind bells and other quality crafts made in New England. ~ 65 Main Street, Rockport; 978-546-9677.

Rockport has almost as many galleries as bed and breakfasts. The majority sell seascapes—some good, many bad. For an excellent selection of Cape Ann art, visit the **Rockport Art Association**. All the work on view is for sale. ~ 12 Main Street, Rockport; 978-546-6604.

Walker Creek, a real find, offers reasonably priced, finely crafted wood tables, hutches, four-poster beds, one-of-a-kind pieces and custom work loosely based on Shaker or Colonial designs. ~ 57 Eastern Avenue, Route 133, Essex; 978-768-7622.

◄ HIDDEN

Essex's 25 antique dealers run the price-range gamut. Always ask a dealer if you can do better on a price—you're expected to bargain. Don't hope for major savings, however. The **White Elephant** is bargain-basement heaven. ~ 32 Main Street, Essex; 978-768-6901. At the high end of the spectrum is **A. P. H. Waller & Sons**, which carries quality European antiques from the 18th and 19th centuries. ~ 140 Main Street, Essex; 978-768-6269. **The**

Scrapbook specializes in antique and decorative prints, as well as maps from the 16th to 19th centuries. ~ 34 Main Street, Essex; 978-768-7404. **Main Street Antiques** has antique wicker accessories, jewelry and textiles from the late-18th to the mid-20th century. ~ 44 Main Street, Essex; 978-768-7039. **North Hill Antiques** has 18th and 19th-century furniture. ~ 155 Main Street, Essex; 978-768-7365.

If you've ever spent a lengthy period of time in the British Isles and you miss such examples of British cuisine as Bovril, Ir'nbru or Smarties, you'll have a ball at **Best of British**, which imports a variety of English, Scottish, Irish and Welsh goods for Anglophiles who just can't do without 'em. ~ 22 State Street, Newburyport; 978-465-6976.

NIGHTLIFE

HIDDEN ►

Every Sunday afternoon Le Grand David and his Spectacular Magic Company perform a highly skilled magic show at the **Cabot Street Cinema Theatre**, featuring levitations, vanishing acts, comedy and song-and-dance routines, complete with outrageous costumes and sets. (The magic show is closed August to mid-September.) The rest of the week the theater shows first-rate foreign and domestic films. ~ 286 Cabot Street, Beverly; 978-927-3677.

Symphony by the Sea concerts take place in the Peabody Museum's spectacular East Indian Marine Hall and the Peabody City Hall Wiggen Auditorium on Lowell Street. Formal winter concerts are concluded by a reception with the musicians. ~ 181 Essex Street, Salem; 978-745-4955.

The **Gloucester Stage Company**, under the direction of playwright Israel Horovitz, stages first-rate plays in an old fish warehouse from March through December. ~ 267 East Main Street, Gloucester; 978-281-4099.

The **Rockport Chamber Music Festival** performs in the Hibbard Gallery of the Rockport Art Association from mid-June to mid-July. ~ 12 Main Street, Rockport; 978-546-7391.

From mid-July to mid-August, **Castle Hill** presents a wide range of summer picnic concerts (jazz, reggae, classical) in Castle Hill mansion or on the manicured grounds. ~ P.O. Box 563, Ipswich; 978-356-4351.

The Grog is an attractive restaurant and cabaret with live entertainment ranging from reggae, rock and rhythm-and-blues to oldies and dance bands. Cover. ~ 13 Middle Street, Newburyport; 978-465-8008.

BEACHES & PARKS

DEVEREUX BEACH 🏖 ⛵ On the causeway leading to scenic Marblehead Neck, Devereux is a small, clean beach. There's a lot to see here. The affluent town lies immediately behind the beach on a hill, while across the street lies a windsurfing cove and busy

Marblehead harbor. Devereux is popular with families and teens, yet, unlike most North Shore beaches, it isn't always packed on summer weekends. Swimming and fishing are good here. Facilities include picnic areas, restrooms, playground, lifeguard and a bike rack. Parking fee, $5. ~ On Ocean Avenue, to the south of Marblehead harbor; 781-631-3551.

SALEM WILLOWS Don't be thrown off by the tawdry-looking Chinese take-out joints and arcade you see when you enter the parking lot. Salem Willows holds some pleasant surprises, including a nostalgic old amusement park overlooking Salem Sound that is shaded with graceful willow trees planted in 1801 to provide a protected area for smallpox victims. Next to the park is a small beach. People come here to stroll in the park, admire the view, rent rowboats and fish from the shore or a short pier. The waters are a little rough, and may not be ideal for swimming. Locals swear by the popcorn and chop suey sandwiches sold in the parking lot. You'll find picnic areas, restrooms, lifeguards, a snack bar and rowboat rentals. ~ Located at the end of Derby Street in Salem; 978-744-0180.

SINGING BEACH This jewel of a beach, only a quarter mile long, has pristine sand that literally squeaks underfoot. Hidden away in a lovely affluent neighborhood, the beach is surrounded by steep cliffs and spectacular mansions. The crowd matches the conservative neighborhood—blond and preppy. The changing rooms and parking lot are for residents only, and parking in the immediate area is impossible. But that doesn't keep out-of-towners away. Bostonians like this beach so much, they take the commuter train to Manchester, then walk one long, sweaty half mile to the shore. Facilities include restrooms, lifeguards and a snack bar. Day-use fee, $1. ~ At the end of Beach Street, Manchester; 978-526-1242.

GOOD HARBOR BEACH Located in a spectacular natural setting outside of Gloucester proper, this sweeping, half-mile beach is all ocean, sand dunes, marsh grass and big sky. A small shrub-covered island, positioned between two rocky headlands and accessible at low tide, is fun to explore. The beach is raked clean every day in the summer. There are restrooms, showers, lifeguards and a snack bar. Closed early September through Memorial Day. Parking fee, $15. ~ On Thatcher Road, East Gloucester; 978-281-9790.

WINGAERSHEEK BEACH This gentle, sloping, fine-sand beach on Ipswich Bay is surrounded by rocks, tall marsh grass and homey summer cottages hidden in the woods. There are also tidepools to explore. The beach is quite close to downtown Gloucester and Rockport, but it feels as though it's far out in the country. Families with young children frequent this beach because it has good climbing rocks that aren't too slippery. There are restrooms, showers, lifeguards and a snack bar. Closed early September through Memorial Day. Parking fee, $15. ~ On Atlantic Street, West Gloucester; 978-281-9790.

ROCKPORT BEACHES Rockport has two small beaches right in the heart of town. **Front Beach**, a favorite with small children, has a parallel sidewalk that gives everyone in town a perfect view of the beach. **Back Beach** is on the other side of a small bluff and is much more private. There's a snack bar and restrooms; lifeguards are stationed on Front Beach. ~ Both beaches are on Beach Street in Rockport.

HIDDEN ▶ **HALIBUT POINT STATE PARK** This wild and rugged 54-acre oceanfront park, formerly the site of a granite quarry, has one of the most spectacular views on the North Shore. A walking path goes past the old quarry down a gentle incline to a vast, treeless plain of scrub thicket and wildflowers overlooking the ocean. The stark, rugged shoreline has tidepools and smooth granite rocks large enough for a group of people to picnic on. Swimming is permitted, but not recommended since the shore is covered with big, slippery rocks. Amenities include restrooms, walking trails and guided tours. Parking fee, $2. ~ Three miles north of Rockport off Route 127; 978-546-2997.

THE COX RESERVATION Formerly the home of famed muralist Allyn Cox, this 31-acre salt marsh farmland is now headquarters for the Essex County Greenbelt Association. Peaceful and pastoral, it has paths leading through gardens of perennials and roses, salt marsh, woods, orchards and open farmland down to winding Essex River. Artists come here in the late afternoon when the river and graceful marsh grass are bathed in a soft golden light, creating a dreamlike environment. It's easy to see why a muralist lived in this romantic and private place. ~ Off Route 133, Essex; 978-768-7241.

CRANE BEACH MEMORIAL RESERVATION This massive, four-mile, dune-backed beach is surrounded by over 1000 acres of salt marsh, shrub thicket and woods. In the off-season, the wide beach seems to go on forever. In the summer it's wall-to-wall people. Nature and beachgoers coexist peacefully, however. At certain times of the year, sections of the beach are fenced off to protect nesting birds. A boardwalk leading to the beach protects sand dunes and marsh grass. Facilities include restrooms, showers, lifeguards and a snack bar. Parking fee, $9 to $15. ~ Located on Argilla Road, Ipswich; 978-356-4354.

PARKER RIVER NATIONAL WILDLIFE REFUGE This magnificent oceanfront wildlife refuge on Plum Island is only about ten minutes from downtown Newburyport, but it feels very far away from civilization. One-third of Plum Island is covered with ramshackle summer beach houses; the rest is the refuge—4662 acres of bogs, tidal marshes, sand dunes and beach. It's a good beach for surf fishing, although a strong undertow discourages swimming. A boardwalk leads to the beach, and a trail meanders throughout the refuge. The abundant wildlife includes seals, geese, ducks, deer, rabbits and over 300 species of birds. Parker River is dearly loved by Newburyport residents. From April through August, most of the beach is closed to accommodate nesting piper plovers. Restrooms are available. Parking fee, $5. ~ On Plum Island in Newburyport; 978-465-5753.

▼▼▼▼▼▼▼▼▼▼▼▼
The South Shore

The South Shore is a mix of cranberries and Pilgrims, historic whaling ports, Portuguese bakeries, factory outlets, blue-collar workers and blue bloods. It is comprised of small scenic villages, pastoral farmland and three main towns—Plymouth, about 50 minutes south of Boston, and New Bedford and Fall River, next to each other and close to the Rhode Island border.

Each town has a different personality and history. Plymouth, of course, is where the Pilgrims landed. New Bedford, an active fishing port, was once the whaling capital of the world. Fall River, a factory-outlet mecca, was a leading textile manufacturer at the turn of the 20th century.

Sights, accommodations and restaurants are limited in Fall River and New Bedford. People usually visit these towns on their way to and from Cape Cod or Boston. Plymouth is much larger and draws over one million tourists annually. It has enough historic sights to occupy an entire weekend, although most people can't take more than a day of Pilgrim lore.

SIGHTS

To reach Plymouth from Boston, go south on Route 3 or take scenic Route 3A. It winds along the coast past beautiful, affluent commuter villages with lovely coves and harbors, old lighthouses, stately mansions and winding streets.

Right before Plymouth is wealthy **Duxbury**, an aristocratic residential area of elegant homes. Stop by **The King Caesar House**, one of the state's most beautiful historic homes, located off Route 3A on a winding coastal road. A fresh yellow-and-white, Federal-era mansion with green shutters, a sweeping lawn and climbing roses, the house stands across from a massive stone wharf where ships were once rigged. The house has finely crafted wood cornices, moldings, fanlights and balustrades, plus original hand-painted French wallpaper and fine antiques. Admission. ~ King Caesar Road, Duxbury.

◄ HIDDEN

From Duxbury head south for **Plymouth**. "America's Home Town" can't seem to make up its mind whether to be a tourist trap or a scenic, historic village. The town is a jarring mix of historic homes, cobblestone streets, '50s-style motels, souvenir shops, a tacky waterfront and tour buses everywhere you look. It's not particularly scenic in parts, yet the town is rich with historic sights.

Plymouth is small, and without trying you bump into everything there is to see here. The **Plymouth Area Chamber of Commerce** has walking-tour maps. ~ Water Street, Plymouth; 508-830-1620; www.plymouthchamber.org. So does **Destination Plymouth**. ~ 130 Water Street, Plymouth; 508-747-7525, 800-872-1620; www.visit-plymouth.com.

The first thing everyone heads for is **Plymouth Rock** on Water Street on the harbor. Believed to be the landing place of the Pilgrims, it is housed inside a Greek canopy with stately columns. Don't expect to see a big impressive rock; it's only large enough to hold two very small Pilgrims.

Right next to the rock is the **Mayflower II**, a brightly painted reproduction of the real *Mayflower* that looks like the pirate ship at Disneyland. The self-guided tour is worthwhile, even though there's occasionally a line to get in. The *Mayflower* is shockingly small. It's hard to imagine how 102 people ever survived 66 days at sea in such cramped quarters. Admission. ~ State Pier, Plymouth; 508-830-6013.

For more Pilgrim lore, head for **Pilgrim Hall Museum**, on the main drag. Continuously operating since 1824, the museum houses the nation's largest collection of Pilgrim possessions, including richly styled Jacobean furniture and the relic of a ship that brought colonists to America. Its hull is made out of naturally curved tree trunks and branches, a crude but effective design. Closed in January. Admission. ~ 75 Court Street, Plymouth; 508-746-1620; www.pilgrimhall.org.

Three miles south of Plymouth is **Plimoth Plantation**, a "living museum" where men and women in period costumes portray the residents of a 1627 Pilgrim village. This sounds contrived, but it's authentic and well-done. The re-created village, on a dusty, straw-strewn road overlooking the ocean, is comprised of many wooden dwellings with deeply thatched roofs. There's not a modern detail in sight—just the village, the ocean and settlers going about the daily tasks of the time, tending the vegetable garden or building a house with 17th-century tools. The villagers speak in period dialect, and you can ask them questions about anything—including the politics of the 17th century. There's also a Wampanoag Indian site that re-creates a typical native encampment with woven and bark dome-shaped dwellings. Closed late November through March. Admission. ~ Route 3A, 137 Warren Avenue, Plymouth; 508-746-1622; www.plimoth.org.

From Plymouth go west on Route 44, then south on Route 58 to rural **Carver**, cranberry capital of the world. In the fall the

HIDDEN ►

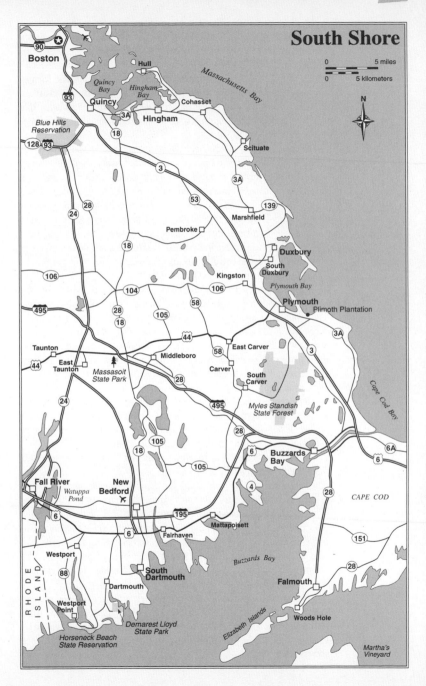

South Shore

0 _____ 5 miles
0 _____ 5 kilometers

N

Boston

Hull

Massachusetts Bay

Quincy Bay

Hingham Bay

Quincy

Cohasset

Hingham

Blue Hills Reservation

Scituate

3A

Pembroke

Marshfield

139

Duxbury

South Duxbury

Kingston

Plymouth Bay

Plymouth

Plimoth Plantation

Taunton

East Taunton

Massasoit State Park

Middleboro

East Carver

Carver

South Carver

Myles Standish State Forest

Cape Cod Bay

Buzzards Bay

Fall River

Watuppa Pond

New Bedford

Mattapoisett

Fairhaven

CAPE COD

Westport

South Dartmouth

Dartmouth

Falmouth

R H O D E   I S L A N D

Westport Point

Horseneck Beach State Reservation

Demarest Lloyd State Park

Elizabeth Islands

Buzzards Bay

Woods Hole

Martha's Vineyard

harvesting process, a breathtaking sight, can be witnessed from the road. There's also an antique train visitors can ride and a cranberry winery. (See "Exploring Cranberry Country" in this chapter.)

About a half-hour's drive southeast of Carver lies the former whaling town of **New Bedford**, which gained immortality in Herman Melville's *Moby Dick*. It still looks and feels a lot like a 19th-century whaling city, with a bustling waterfront and large Portuguese population.

Until the early 1980s the waterfront area was in disarray. Then, to attract tourists, the town restored more than 100 buildings. Fortunately New Bedford didn't go overboard with cute, contrived tourist attractions. Today it has a number of fine museums, restaurants, antique shops and galleries alongside the harbor. There's something genuine and tasteful about this miniature city.

The coast is dotted with majestic sea captains' homes, many of them now inns.

The New Bedford National Park Visitor Center offers brochures, maps and tours. ~ 33 William Street, New Bedford; 508-991-6200.

Rotch-Jones-Duff House and Garden Museum is a 19th-century Greek Revival with a picturesque rose garden that becomes a Christmas showplace during the holidays and is the site of summer concerts. Named for three families who owned the property, it features many of their fine antiques. This 28-room mansion is one of the region's best. Closed Monday from January through May. Admission. ~ 396 County Street, New Bedford; 508-997-1401.

For three sights that shouldn't be missed, begin with the Whaling Museum. Continue on to Seaman's Bethel, a church across from the whaling museum, and County Street, where wealthy sea captains built homes in the 19th century.

Start with **The New Bedford Whaling Museum**, then enter Seamen's Bethel, and New Bedford won't look the same again. The museum depicts whaling's profound impact on this town, telling the story beautifully with large, dramatic paintings of life aboard whaling ships and an enormous mural created in 1848. You can climb aboard a half-scale model of a fully rigged whaling ship housed in a large room with harpoons and figureheads. The museum is spacious, airy and absorbing. Admission. ~ 18 Johnny Cake Hill, New Bedford; 508-997-0046; www.whaling museum.org.

Across the street is **Seamen's Bethel**, where whalers prayed before setting out to sea. The pulpit of this plain, sturdy church is shaped like a ship's bluff bows. Its walls are covered with memorial tablets to men who died at sea. A visit to this church is a sobering experience.

"Nowhere in America will you find more patrician-like houses," wrote Herman Melville of **County Street**, located a few of blocks up a slight hill from the whaling museum. The impeccably restored Federal-style mansions and elaborate Victorians along this street illustrate how grand life was in 19th-century New Bedford.   ◄ *HIDDEN*

For a unique change of pace, consider visiting **Cuttyhunk**, an island 14 miles offshore from New Bedford accessible by ferry (see the "Transportation" section at the end of this chapter). It's part of the Elizabeth Islands, a chain of 16 tiny islands, 14 of them owned by the Boston Brahmin Forbes family. The island is practically all sand and scrub bushes with a rocky beach. It does have a general store, two restaurants and about 100 homes. Cuttyhunk is the opposite of busy, crowded Cape Cod—there's nothing to do but walk and fish—and therein lies its charm.   ◄ *HIDDEN*

Immediately southwest of New Bedford off Route 6 are the affluent rural communities of **Dartmouth** and **Westport,** where you'll find some of the most exquisite coastal farmland in all of Massachusetts. Like Kentucky bluegrass country, this area has miles of ancient stone walls, lovely old houses, shingled dairy barns, rolling pastures and elegant horse farms.

Off Slocums Road in South Dartmouth sits **Padanaram**, a fashionable yachting resort on Apponagansett Bay. It's home to the famous boatyard Concordia, where beautiful old wooden yachts are restored. The village is only two blocks long, but it has a number of fine restaurants and shops.

Not far from Padanaram is **The Lloyd Center for Environmental Studies**, a nonprofit organization that studies coastal and estuarine environments. Open to the public are an aquarium with an Interactive Touch Tank, five walking trails, a resource library and changing exhibits featuring such work as naturalist photography. The best thing here is the dazzling view from the observation deck, which overlooks winding Slocums River and miles of wetlands. Building closed Monday; trails always open. ~ 430 Potomska Road, South Dartmouth; 508-990-0505; www. ultranet.com/~lloydctr.   ◄ *HIDDEN*

Heading back to New Bedford, you can take Route 195 west to **Fall River** 15 minutes away. Factory outlets (see the "Shopping" section below) and Battleship Cove are this town's claims to fame.

At the turn of the 20th century Fall River had more than 100 textile mills, but in 1927 the industry sagged and the town went through serious hard times. Today its large granite mills are occupied by electronics and metals firms and factory outlets, but the effects of the depression still linger.

Text continued on page 360.

Exploring Cranberry Country

Hidden away in Carver, a scenic rural area ten minutes east of Plymouth, you'll find one of Massachusetts' most spectacular and least-known autumn attractions—**cranberry harvesting**. If you think fall foliage is a beautiful sight, wait until you see this dazzling display of color.

Cranberries are the state's number-one agricultural product, valued at $200 million annually. Around 500 growers, with 5500 employees, work more than 14,400 acres of cranberry bogs. Little Carver alone produces one third the nation's crop, while Cape Cod and Nantucket also have cranberry farms.

One of the few fruits native to North America, cranberries were known to Indians as sassamenesh. They ate the tart red berries raw and mixed them with venison and fat to make small cakes called pemmicans. The cranberry's slender, cone-shaped flower reminded early European settlers of the beak of a crane—hence the present name. Nineteenth-century sea captains sailing from New England ports supplied cranberries to their crews because it was the most readily available source of vitamin C to prevent scurvy.

The popularity of cranberries was limited to a harvest time until 1930, when a Massachusetts lawyer-turned-cranberry-grower joined with two other growers to form a marketing cooperative promoting demand for cranberry juice cocktails. The cooperative, which became Ocean Spray Cranberries, now has 915 members—more than 90 percent of all independent cranberry growers—and continues to explore ways to boost demand by touting the berries' health benefits and trying to popularize them in other countries. The co-op held a near-monopoly until the 1990s, when the Wisconsin-based Northland Corporation went public, raising investor capital to buy up bogs around Cape Cod, and quickly became the world's largest cranberry producer. Today, a "cranberry war" rages between the two companies, while cranberry surpluses have reached unprecedented levels.

Harvest time starts September 15 and continues until the first week of November. During this time, restaurants and bakeries in southern Massachusetts use the berry in a number of creative dishes, ranging from cranberry horseradish and salsa to cranberry soup, bread, muffins, sorbet and tarts. Other innovative recipes involve mixing cranberries with applesauce, wild rice and cole slaw. To experience the full range of creative cranberry cookery, head for the **Massachusetts Cranberry Festival**, held in South Carver on Columbus Day weekend.

To explore the cranberry bogs, from Plymouth take Route 44 east to Route 58 south. Bogs line both routes, and the harvest process is very easy to see from the road. Many farmers don't mind if you observe from the elevated dirt paths bordering the bogs, as long as you stay well out of their way.

The short, scruffy, dark green cranberry vines are grown in shallow bogs surrounded by deep woods. When the cranberries are ripe, they are picked by either dry or wet harvesting. Dry-picked berries are often sold fresh, while wet-picked fruit usually becomes canned or frozen cranberry sauce.

Dry-harvested berries are combed off the vine with a machine. But it's wet harvesting that's the real treat to watch. First the bogs are flooded with about 18 inches of water. Then farmers in bright yellow slickers cut the fruit off the vine with large water reels that look like giant eggbeaters stirring up a waterfall of crimson berries. The buoyant berries float to the water's surface, creating a scarlet sea surrounded by a fiery ring of woods ablaze with fall colors.

The wind blows the floating berries to one end of the pond, where they are corralled with wooden brooms. Giant vacuum cleaners then suck the berries into dechaffing machines. Helicopters and trucks transport the berries to packing houses, where they are graded according to size, color and quality.

It's easy enough to explore the bogs on your own, but if you want more information and an official tour, there are a number of options. Right in Plymouth is the **Cranberry World Visitors Center**. Operated by Ocean Spray, it has exhibits of harvesting equipment, historic and current photographs, two demonstrations of cranberry bogs and free cranberry juice. Guided tours are available. It's educational, but nothing compared to seeing the real thing. Closed December through April. ~ 225 Water Street; 508-747-2350.

Plymouth Colony Winery, off Route 44, is in a former berry-screening house in the middle of a ten-acre cranberry bog. It offers free tastings, plus a tour of the winery and bogs. Open weekends only in February and March. Closed in January. ~ 56 Pinewood Road, Plymouth; 508-747-3334.

Fall River's downtown has been spruced up, but there are so many "for lease" signs tacked to its grand 19th-century buildings that the town looks a little lost.

HIDDEN ► Columbia Street, the Portuguese section of downtown, is a colorful place to stroll, sample treats from the many good bakeries and discover the beautiful mosaic sidewalks. Television chef Emeril Lagasse grew up here, and can occasionally be spotted in the midst of this vibrant ethnic community. For travel information, call the Bristol County Convention and Visitors Bureau. ~ 70 North 2nd Street, Fall River; 508-997-1250, 800-288-6263; www.bristol-county.org.

Wealthy mill owners built their mansions on Columbia Street in the 1830s, but by the 1850s, immigrants began to settle here to be closer to the mills and the owners moved up the hill to Fall River.

There's also an information center at Battleship Cove, a harbor and park area right in town off Route 195 at Exit 5. Docked in the water at Battleship Cove are a World War II battleship, destroyer, attack submarine and PT boat that you can tour. Not surprisingly, these vessels, which are in excellent condition, are filled with children playing war. Hundreds of scout troops make pilgrimages to this John Wayne playground. Admission for boat tours. ~ Fall River; 508-678-1100; www.battleshipcove.com.

Next to the boats is the Fall River Heritage State Park Visitors Center. It has an attractive waterfront park and a building with exhibits about the town's former textile industry. A moving slide show documents the appalling working conditions, accidents and deaths suffered by children and adult immigrants who worked in the mills. ~ 200 Davol Street, Fall River; 508-675-5759; www.statepark.com.

LODGING   Plymouth has an abundance of very ordinary motels that attract families and tour groups. Accommodations are limited throughout the rest of the South Shore, but there is a sprinkling of hidden bed and breakfasts that is quite special.

HIDDEN ►   For a romantic getaway try the Windsor House Inn, 15 minutes north of Plymouth. This graceful old inn stands on a street lined with houses listed on the National Register of Historic Places, and it's next to a classic white-steepled church. Down the street are a few elegant little shops, a French bakery and a small wharf. Windsor House has two tastefully decorated guest rooms and a beautiful suite with pale blue wood-paneled walls and blue-and-white stenciling. All rooms are furnished with Shaker and Colonial-style antiques. A dark, cozy restaurant on the ground floor looks like an old seafaring tavern. ~ 390 Washington Street, Duxbury; 781-934-0991, 800-934-0993, fax 781-934-5955. DELUXE.

Route 3A in Plymouth is lined with indistinguishable motels, but the Cold Spring Motel is one of the most attractive. This

1950s motel is in pristine condition and beautifully landscaped. In the summer thick yellow marigolds border brick paths leading to the 33 guest rooms. These are spacious and simply appointed with standard-issue motel furniture. Closed December through March. ~ 188 Court Street, Plymouth; 508-746-2222, 800-678-8667, fax 508-746-2744; www.coldspringmotel.com. BUDGET TO MODERATE.

The **John Carver Inn**, a large, imposing, Colonial-style hotel, attracts tour groups and gets very crowded in the summer. But it's in the most scenic part of Plymouth, across the street from a row of 17th-century historic homes and a beautiful grist mill. Seventy-nine guest rooms are decorated in soft shades of beige and Colonial-style reproduction antiques. A full-service hotel, it has a restaurant, lounge, gift shop and an outdoor pool. ~ 25 Summer Street, Plymouth; 508-746-7100, 800-274-1620, fax 508-746-8299; www.johncarverinn.com. MODERATE.

Near the small town of Carver, the heart of cranberry country, **On Cranberry Pond** is a great place to stay if you want to get away from the crowds in Plymouth (which is just 25 minutes away). The house is surrounded by ponds, horse pastures, and cranberry bogs. The three high-ceilinged bedrooms are furnished with country decor. The enormous back porch is a great place to while away a morning or an afternoon. A gourmet breakfast is included in the rates. ~ 43 Fuller Street, Middleboro; 508-946-0768. DELUXE.

Off-the-beaten-path **Mattapoisett Inn** is in a scenic little seaside village of doll-sized clapboard houses with white picket fences and window boxes. The inn stands right across the street from the harbor. The village, which is only three blocks long, consists of a small dock, an art gallery, a coffee shop and the inn. The white-clapboard inn with black shutters has a restaurant and pub on the ground floor. Three spacious guest rooms upstairs all have balconies overlooking the ocean. The rooms aren't "decorated," but they're neat, clean, bright and comfortable. ~ 13 Water Street, Mattapoisett; 508-758-4922, fax 508-758-2528; www.mattapoisettinn.com. BUDGET TO MODERATE.   ◄ HIDDEN

A 1760 brown-shingle bed and breakfast, **The Edgewater** is so close to the water you'd swear you were on a boat when you look out the window. The inn seems miles away from civilization, yet it's only a five-minute drive from New Bedford's historic wharf district. A perfect spot for romance, the handsome house has soft taupe walls and crisp white arched moldings. The blue-and-white Captain's Suite, the best room in the house, has a sitting room, fireplace and spectacular views. The other four guest rooms are attractive and comfortable. All are appointed with contemporary and antique furnishings. ~ 2 Oxford Street, Fairhaven; 508-997-5512; www.rixsan.com/edgewater. BUDGET TO MODERATE.   ◄ HIDDEN

Salt Marsh Farm, an 18th-century farmhouse, is in the heart of pastoral South Dartmouth. A perfect retreat for nature buffs, the house is on a 90-acre preserve with trails leading through hay fields, woods and wetlands. Bikes are available to guests eager to explore the grounds. Salt Marsh Farm feels like another world and time. The floors are uneven, the doorways low and the rooms small, but it has comfortable, home-spun charm. Afternoon tea is served by the fireside in the common sitting room. Sunny guest rooms are furnished with antiques and fresh flowers, and a full breakfast is served in an attractive dining room with a beautiful old fireplace. ~ 322 Smith Neck Road, South Dartmouth; 508-992-0980; e-mail saltmarshf@aol.com. MODERATE.

DINING

For traditional New England–style fare, swing by **Isaac's**. They bake, they fry—they even prepare some Italian dishes such as chicken Milan. You'll also find steak, veal and seafood on the menu. ~ 114 Water Street, Plymouth Harbor; 508-830-0001. MODERATE.

Though a magnet for tourists, **The Lobster Hut** should not be avoided. Here you can feast on clam chowder, fried clams and lobster at outdoor picnic tables overlooking the harbor, or you can eat inside, though the atmosphere may be a bit too fast-food for your liking. Closed January. ~ On the Town Wharf, Plymouth; 508-746-2270. MODERATE TO DELUXE.

HIDDEN ►

A ramshackle red-shingle restaurant a few miles north of Plymouth, **Persy's Place** claims to have "New England's largest breakfast menu," and that's no joke. The menu takes about an hour to read, but some of its offerings include fish cakes, buttermilk pancakes, chipped beef on toast, catfish and eggs, hickory-smoked bacon, finnan haddie, no-cholesterol eggs, waffles and much, much more. The restaurant looks like a cross between a coffee shop and a country general store. No dinner. ~ 117 Main Street, Route 3A, Kingston; 781-585-5464. BUDGET.

HIDDEN ►

Hidden and lovely **Crane Brook Restaurant and Tea Room** is a must if you're touring cranberry country. Located in a former iron foundry, the cozy, antiques-filled restaurant overlooks a pretty pond and is surrounded by gardens and cranberry bogs. The restaurant started out serving only tea and pastries, but now it also offers lunch and dinner. A perfect place for a long, leisurely lunch, the Crane Brook has a changing menu of dishes such as grilled duck breast sandwich and imaginative salads; rack of lamb and spicy pork loin roast are offered for dinner. Closed Monday and Tuesday. ~ 229 Tremont Street, South Carver; 508-866-3235. MODERATE TO DELUXE.

Candleworks is housed in an 1810 granite candle factory half a block from New Bedford's major sights. A pink, atriumlike room in front is appointed with wooden tables and Windsor chairs.

The main dining room has a low-beamed ceiling and rich wood. The menu features Italian cuisine and a wide variety of American food including veal medallions sautéed with lobster and asparagus; chicken breast stuffed with prosciutto, provolone and roasted peppers and served with a pesto cream sauce; and grilled swordfish with lemon butter. ~ 72 North Water Street, New Bedford; 508-997-1294. MODERATE.

Bridge Street Café in the heart of Padanaram, attracts a young, well-dressed crowd. Clean and crisp, with slate floors, the café has an outdoor deck overlooking the town and harbor. Daily specials range from Creole-style grilled swordfish, scallops and pesto pasta, to soft-shell crabs, shrimp brochette and grilled sirloin. The house specialty is the grilled barbecue lamb. And you can't leave without trying one of Sally's outrageous desserts! Call for seasonal schedule. ~ 10-A Bridge Street, South Dartmouth; 508-994-7200. MODERATE TO DELUXE.

It may look like a coffee shop, but **Bayside** serves classic clam-bar fare as well as such specials as chicken burritos and eggplant parmigiana. More "in" than it seems, the restaurant has a clientele ranging from construction workers, senior citizens and families to yuppies and arty types dressed entirely in black. Bayside overlooks rolling pastures, salt marsh, stone walls and the ocean. ~ 1253 Horseneck Road, Westport; 508-636-5882. BUDGET TO MODERATE.

◀ HIDDEN

The South Shore is outlet country. Fall River has over 100 outlets, and New Bedford and Plymouth have quite a few, too. Until the 1980s these were novel, but today there are so many discount shopping places across the country that they don't seem unique. Choices are somewhat limited because the same brands are sold everywhere: Bass, Farberware, American Tourister, Jonathan Logan, Van Heusen and Vanity Fair to name a few.

SHOPPING

Cordage Park, housed in a former brick cordage rope factory, is an attractive marketplace with specialty shops and a weekend flea market. The lovely old building is surrounded by ponds,

DINE PORTUGUESE

There are many Portuguese restaurants in New Bedford, but one of the best is **Café Portugal**. A large, festive restaurant popular with Portuguese families, it features house specialties such as an enormous platter of succulent shrimp and marinated steak served with eggs on top. With its acoustical tile ceiling and plastic flower arrangements, Café Portugal looks a little bit like a banquet hall. Closed Monday and Tuesday. ~ 1280 Acushnet Avenue, New Bedford; 508-992-8216. MODERATE.

fountains, gazebos, rolling lawns and flower gardens. ~ Route 3A, North Plymouth; 508-746-7707.

Salt Marsh Pottery specializes in hand-painted pottery and tiles designed with wildflower motifs. ~ 1167 Russells Mills Road, South Dartmouth; 508-636-4813.

Driving the expressway in Fall River, you can't help but notice the mammoth, six-story granite textile mills transformed into factory outlets—**Fall River Outlets**. All the outlets are close together, and each building has between 50 and 100 retailers selling clothes, dishes, sheets, towels, jewelry, handbags and more. Prices are rock bottom, and the merchandise is pretty low-end. Natural fiber clothing is difficult to find. ~ To visit them from Route 195, which runs through town, take Route 24 south to the Brayton exit and follow the signs.

NIGHTLIFE   Free concerts at the **Village Landing Gazebo** range from swing bands to Irish balladeers to children's shows. ~ 182 Water Street, Plymouth.

Live bands can be heard free on Friday and Saturday at the **Sheraton Plymouth Pub**. ~ Village Landing, 180 Water Street, Plymouth; 508-747-4900.

Zeiterion Theatre presents a wide range of musical and dramatic performances—everything from *Guys and Dolls* to *The Nutcracker*. Located in historic downtown New Bedford, the Zeiterion is a masterfully restored 1923 vaudeville theater with gilded Grecian friezes, elaborate crystal light fixtures and a glamorous atmosphere. ~ 684 Purchase Street, New Bedford; 508-994-2900.

BEACHES & PARKS   **DUXBURY BEACH** 🏊 This five-mile stretch of clean white sand is one of the finest barrier beaches on the Massachusetts coast. The beach juts out into Cape Cod Bay and is bordered by a little harbor on one side and the Atlantic on the other. Stretches are dotted with salt marsh, and parts are accessible only by four-wheel-drive vehicles. Located in an affluent residential neighborhood, it attracts a well-heeled crowd. Facilities include restrooms, showers, a changing room, lifeguards, a snack bar and a restaurant. Parking fee, $8. ~ Off Route 3 on Route 139 in Duxbury, north of Plymouth; 781-837-3112.

MYLES STANDISH STATE FOREST 🚶 🚴 🐎 🗀 🕳 🍴 🚤 🚣 Locals joke that once you're in this 14,635-acre park, you'll never find your way out again. The park is enormous, and the roads winding through the forest and meadows seem to go on forever. Because of its size, it feels remote and peaceful even in the summer. Beautiful and clean, the park has 15 ponds with two beaches. You can fish most of the ponds and swim at College and Fearings beaches. Motorcycle, bicycle, bridle and hiking paths wind through the forest. Non-motorized boats are allowed. You'll find picnic areas, restrooms and interpretive programs. Day-use fee, $2. ~ Off Route 3 on Long Pond Road, Plymouth; 508-866-2526.

▲ There are 475 tent/RV sites (no hookups) with restrooms, hot showers, fireplaces and picnic tables; $6 per night.

PLYMOUTH BEACH 🏊 🚣 🦀 🚤 ⛵ Located in a half-rural, half-residential area, this straight, three-mile beach dotted with beach grass and clear stretches of sand serves as a nesting ground for migratory shore birds such as terns, plovers and sandpipers. The nesting area is fenced off for protection, but the birds are easily observed. In summer this busy beach attracts families and local kids. There are restrooms, lifeguards and a snack bar. Parking fee, $10. ~ Off Route 3A, three miles south of Plymouth; 508-830-4095.

HORSENECK BEACH STATE RESERVATION 🏃 🚴 🐎 🏊 🦀 🚣 🚤 ⛵ This vast, breezy beach is one of the state's most spectacular and least known. Bordered by fragile dunes that create a barrier between the huge parking lot and the beach, it has crunchy white sand and fine waves. From Labor Day to April, horseback riding is allowed. **Gooseberry Neck** is a narrow, mile-long stretch of land jutting out into the ocean and laced with paths. There's an abandoned World War II lookout tower at the end. Right before Gooseberry Neck is a clam bar, a small parking lot and a tiny beach popular with windsurfers. Facilities include restrooms, showers and lifeguards. Day-use fee, $2. ~ At the end of Route 88, Westport Point; 508-636-8816.

◄ *HIDDEN*

▲ Permitted in 100 RV sites (no hookups) on a first-come, first-served basis; $6 to $7 per night.

DEMAREST LLOYD STATE PARK 🏊 🦀 ⛵ This little-known state park has everything: natural grassy areas for picnics, rambling hills of beach grass, winding rivers, abundant wildlife—deer, hawks, egrets—and a fairly isolated beach. At low tide a long sand bar juts out into the calm, warm waters. Located in the bucolic Dartmouth area, Demarest is a real find. Closed from Labor Day through Memorial Day. You'll find picnic areas, restrooms, showers and lifeguards. Day-use fee, $2. ~ At the end of Route 88, east of Horseneck Beach in South Dartmouth; 508-636-3298.

◄ *HIDDEN*

▼▼▼▼▼▼▼▼▼▼▼▼
Outdoor Adventures

Bluefish, striped bass, tuna, cod and flounder are abundant on the Massachusetts coast. No license is required to fish, and tackle shops are everywhere. For detailed information on what to catch when, where and how, call the **Massachusetts Division of Marine Fisheries**. ~ 100 Cambridge Street, Room 1901, Boston, MA 02202; 617-727-3193.

FISHING

NORTH SHORE **Captain Bill's Deep Sea Fishing** has half- and full-day trips for cod and bluefish. ~ 33 Harbor Loop, Gloucester; 978-283-6995. Contact **Hilton's Fishing Dock** for full-day trips on the *Captain Lew*. ~ 54-R Merrimac Street; 978-465-9885.

SOUTH SHORE Half- and full-day cod fishing trips are available through **Captain John Boats**. ~ Town Wharf, Plymouth; 508-746-2643. **Captain Leroy Inc.** charters cabin boats for fishing and full-day party boat excursions. ~ Route 6, on the Fairhaven Bridge, New Bedford; 508-992-8907.

SAILING   Marblehead, on the North Shore, is sailboat country. **Coastal Sailing School**, the only rental outfit, has half- and full-day boat rentals. Lessons are available. ~ P.O. Box 1001, Marblehead; 781-639-0553.

WHALE WATCHING   The Massachusetts coast offers an enormous number of whale-watching excursions, some conducted by naturalists. The season starts in May and runs through October.

NORTH SHORE Gloucester is the North Shore's gateway to whale watching. **Yankee Fleet** is the oldest and largest whale-watching outfit, with trips to Stellwagon Bank and Jefferey's Ledge. Charter and fishing party excursions are also available. ~ 75 Essex Avenue; 978-283-0313. **Cape Ann Whale Watch** has a half-day trip to Stellwagon and a full-day trip from Gloucester to Provincetown. ~ 415 Main Street; 978-283-5110. The **Newburyport Whale Watch** runs half-day trips twice daily. ~ Hilton's Fishing Dock, 54 Merrimac Street; 978-465-7165.

SOUTH SHORE **Captain John Boats** goes to Stellwagon Bank to spot whales. ~ Town Wharf, Plymouth; 508-746-2643. **Cape Cod Cruises** books half-day trips on four 85-foot boats. ~ Town Wharf, Plymouth; 508-747-2400.

CANOEING & SEA KAYAKING   **NORTH SHORE** One of the most beautiful canoe trips in New England is along the Ipswich River, through the 3000-acre **Ipswich River Wildlife Sanctuary**. Here you can spot deer, beaver and fox, among other animals, on a naturalist-guided half-day trip. ~ Perkins Row, Topsfield; 978-887-9264. For canoe rentals, contact **Foote Brothers Canoes**. You can enter the Ipswich River on Route 97. ~ 230 Topsfield Road, Ipswich; 978-356-9771.

SOUTH SHORE South of New Bedford, near Dartmouth, are many rivers ideal for canoeing. The **Lloyd Center for Environmental Studies** organizes day-long guided canoe trips that focus on the natural history of local rivers. ~ 430 Potomska Road, South Dartmouth; 508-990-0505. **Palmer River Canoe** rents kayaks and canoes and provides half-day narrated trips. Shuttles are available. ~ 206 Wheeler Street, Rehoboth, or at the rear of Deans Plaza, Route 44, Raynham; 508-336-2274.

On the North Shore in Danvers, the brave and the bold bare the chilly waters with **New England Diving Adventures**, an outfit that teaches scuba diving, rents equipment, and runs half- and full-day trips off the coast. ~ 125 Liberty Street; 978-777-3483.

SCUBA DIVING

Ice sailing is a tradition on **Watuppa Pond** in Fall River. This graceful sport takes tremendous skill and specially designed sail-crafts. Rentals aren't available, but it's a delight to watch these lighter-than-air boats glide along the icy pond.

ICE SAILING

NORTH SHORE   Public golf courses are rare on the North Shore, but there is one beautiful semiprivate, 18-hole course surrounded by deep woods, the **Beverly Golf and Tennis Club**. The signature par-3 15th hole is called the Wedding Cake. ~ 134 McKay Street, Beverly; 978-927-5200. **Harwich Port Golf** is a nine-hole public course of par 3s and par 4s that offers pull carts. ~ Forest and South streets, Harwich Port; 508-432-0250.

GOLF

SOUTH SHORE   Golfing opportunities on the South Shore are limited. There aren't any public golf courses close to Plymouth, but about 30 minutes out of town is the par-71 **Pembroke Country Club**, a semiprivate 18-hole course. ~ West Elm Street, Pembroke; 781-826-0260. **Bay Point Country Club** is nearby and offers a full course with an island hole—completely surrounded by water. ~ Bay Point Drive, off Onset Avenue, Onset; 508-759-8802. Hilly **New Bedford Municipal Golf Course** offers golfers a challenging 18-hole course with several par 5s. ~ 581 Hathaway Road, New Bedford; 508-996-9393.

NORTH SHORE   A few municipal courts are available throughout the North Shore towns. The best spot here is the **Beverly Golf and Tennis Club**. It has eight clay courts open to the public; a tennis pro is available for lessons. Fee. ~ 134 McKay Street, Beverly; 978-927-5200.

TENNIS

SOUTH SHORE   Six clay municipal courts can be found in New Bedford's woodsy **Buttonwood Park**. ~ Rockdale and Hawthorne avenues. **Hazelwood Park**, a city park with playgrounds, has five lighted courts. ~ Brock Avenue, New Bedford; 508-991-6175.

Chipaway Stables, a mile north of New Bedford, has guided trail rides and hayrides through local woodlands. Call for reservations. ~ 600 Quanapoag Road, North Dartmouth; 508-763-5158.

RIDING STABLES

The North Shore and South Shore have limited bicycling areas, but a few choice spots are described below.

BIKING

NORTH SHORE   Cyclists in the area recommend scenic **Route 127** between Beverly, Manchester and Magnolia. The tree-lined road dips and turns past seaside mansions and historic homes. It's cool and peaceful in the summer.

SOUTH SHORE   The **Westport** and **Dartmouth** area on the South Shore doesn't have many cars, and the flat country roads wind past elegant horse farms, pastures and ocean. From Route 195, take Exit 12 and head south to Chase or Tucker Road. At this point it doesn't matter which road you take; they're all lovely, and as long as you head south you'll wind up at the beach.

Bike Rentals   On the North Shore, you can rent mountain bikes and hybrids at **Seaside Cycle**. Accessories and repairs are also available here. ~ 23 Elm Street, Manchester; 978-526-1200.

HIKING

The Massachusetts coast offers excellent opportunities to hike through salt marsh, forest, sand dunes and moors bordering freshwater ponds and the ocean. Many of these hikes are short and easy. The rest of the coast has a limited number of marked trails. All distances listed for trails are one way unless otherwise noted.

For more information on hikes throughout the state, contact the Massachusetts Department of Environmental Management Trails Program. ~ 100 Cambridge Street, Boston; 617-727-3160.

NORTH SHORE   **Art's Trail** (1 mile), in Dogtown Common, a 3000-acre park in Gloucester, winds through red oak forest past a highland of scrub oak, grey birch, blueberries and huckleberries. Several low areas flood in late winter and spring, forming frog-breeding ponds. Of moderate difficulty, the trail is rocky in parts and requires careful walking.

Also in Dogtown Common, **Whale's Jaw Trail** (4.5 miles) is a rugged, rocky, hilly hike starting at Blackburn Industrial Park off Route 128. The trail meanders through former grazing land and past Babson Reservoir, birch groves and cattail marsh. It ends at the top of a hill, where you'll see an enormous split granite boulder that looks like a whale's jaw.

SOUTH SHORE   **East Head Reservoir Trail** (3 miles roundtrip) starts behind the Myles Standish State Forest headquarters building in Plymouth. The best thing about this hike is that it covers the full spectrum of habitats in the 14,635-acre park. The relatively flat trail winds past deep forest, marsh, hardwood and softwood groves and a pristine pond. A pamphlet available at the start of the hike explains the flora and fauna of each environment. A couple of benches are located along the way.

The **Peter Adams Trail** (3 miles) in Massasoit State Park in East Taunton meanders through white-pine forest and hardwoods and past swamps and brooks. Skirting Lake Rico, it ends at a large, secluded sandy beach. Along the way, you might spot deer, fox, turkey and owls. To get a map, call 508-824-0687 (summer only) or 508-822-7405.

On the North Shore, **Route 128** is the main artery connecting Salem, Manchester, Magnolia, Gloucester and Rockport. **Route 95** is the major north–south artery to Essex, Ipswich and Newburyport.

Route 3 links Boston to Plymouth and ends at the Sagamore Bridge to Cape Cod. **Route 195** is the main east–west artery connecting Fall River and New Bedford.

Many people visiting this area come into **Logan International Airport** in Boston (see Chapter Four). Also serving the southern coastal area is the New Bedford Airport.

Cape Air flies into **New Bedford Airport**.

Ferries and boats between Boston, Plymouth, New Bedford, Cape Cod, Martha's Vineyard and Nantucket require reservations during the summer. The following ferries and boats operate seasonally and do not transport cars:

A. C. Cruise Lines goes between Boston and Gloucester from Memorial Day through Labor Day. ~ 290 Northern Avenue, Boston; 617-261-6633, 800-422-8419. **Captain John Boats** goes between Plymouth and Provincetown. ~ State Pier, Plymouth; 508-747-2400, 800-242-2469. **Martha's Vineyard Ferry** operates between New Bedford and Vineyard Haven on Martha's Vineyard. ~ 1494 East Rodney French Boulevard, Billy Woods Wharf, New Bedford; 508-997-1688. The **Cuttyhunk Boat Line** connects New Bedford and Cuttyhunk Island. ~ Fisherman's Wharf, Pier 3, New Bedford; 508-992-1432.

Greyhound Bus Lines offers frequent service to Newburyport and Boston. ~ 617-526-1801, 800-231-2222. **Bonanza** runs buses to and from Logan Airport, Hyannis, Woods Hole, Falmouth, Bourne, New Bedford, Fall River, Connecticut, Rhode Island and New York. ~ 700 Atlantic Avenue, South Station, Boston; 617-720-4110; 59 Depot Road, Falmouth, 508-548-7588.

Many Boston commuters live on the North Shore; hence **Massachusetts Bay Transit Authority** (617-222-5000) runs numerous buses from Boston's Haymarket Square and trains from North Station to Salem, Beverly, Gloucester and Rockport. **Cape Ann Transit Authority** (978-283-7916) provides bus service from Gloucester and Rockport.

Plymouth does not have public transportation. **South Eastern Regional Transit Authority** (508-997-6767) provides bus service throughout Fall River and New Bedford.

The New Bedford Airport is serviced by **Checker Standard Taxi** (508-997-9404) and **Yellow Cab** (508-999-5213).

▼▼▼▼▼▼▼▼▼▼
Transportation

CAR

AIR

FERRY & BOAT

BUS

PUBLIC TRANSIT

TAXIS

SEVEN

Central & Western Massachusetts

Take a good long breath once you arrive in this region, and prepare for a relaxing mix of the rural and the urbane: rolling hills and acres of cornfields, winding country roads that meander along rivers and streams, small museums, old houses, historic villages and college towns with maple-lined streets.

Don't bother to bring your high heels or tuxedo to central and western Massachusetts, unless you're spending a weekend in a fancy Berkshire resort. The mood here—and the dress code—is casual.

Culturally, economically and socially, this area has always been strongly defined by its landscape. The forests, fields and vistas of the Berkshire hills attracted poets and authors of a naturalist bent in the 19th century, and they in turn attracted the rich and famous, who built the elaborate estates of the so-called "Gilded Age." The majestic Connecticut River provided a transportation route as well as water power to generate the mills and factories in the last century. Those factories, along with the fertile soil along the Connecticut's shores, attracted immigrant mill workers and farmers, who helped make the area the breadbasket of New England for decades.

Europeans who first arrived here found primeval forestland as well as large, treeless stretches that had been settled by the Mohegan Indians, hunters who had journeyed from the Hudson River area, and by the Mohawks farther north.

Development first came to central and western Massachusetts in the early 17th century, as small forts like Deerfield were built and trading posts like Springfield sprang up along the Connecticut River. These settlements were significant to our nation's history, as they marked the first movement of the colonists into the interior of the Northeast and served as models for further exploration west.

In the 1800s, canals and mills were built in the southern end of the Pioneer Valley at South Hadley Falls. Within 30 years of its founding in 1850, the city of Holyoke, the first planned city in the country, would become the "Queen of Industrial Cities" and soon after "Paper City of the World."

Thousands of immigrants from Canada and Europe came to central and western Massachusetts in the late 19th century to work in the mills and factories, and to the east, Worcester was experiencing its historical pinnacle as a city where industrial innovation and forward thinking flourished.

As New England's manufacturing economy ebbed in the 20th century, so did the fortunes of the flourishing cities of Holyoke and Worcester, as well as the smaller rural mill towns. Other areas of the state found new economic life in high-technology industries, but for central and western Massachusetts, it's been a struggle. The area continues to rely largely on smaller manufacturing, education, agriculture and the service industries. As a result, there is a different standard of living in this region than in wealthier areas near Boston.

Today, though the three areas in this chapter are not so far apart geographically, each has its own identity. Central Massachusetts, with Worcester and Sturbridge as its hubs, is made up of small rural and mill towns. The Pioneer Valley, stretching up the Connecticut River, is shifting from an agricultural area into a bedroom community for Springfield and Hartford. The Berkshire area takes its influences more from New York City than from Boston, and it, too, is seeing changes as the manufacturing jobs that once served as the mainstay of the local economy have disappeared.

Many residents of eastern Massachusetts are unaware of just how rural this area is, and "westerners" often quip that the state ends at Route 495, which makes a large semicircle around Boston. Every once in a while a local politician brings up the idea of secession for central and western Massachusetts, partly because of the claim that the smaller cities and towns of the region don't get their fair share of state funds.

But it's also because people in this part of the state have a different way of thinking. There's a streak of high-mindedness and independence here that was already evident back in 1787 when Daniel Shays, a farmer from Hatfield, started the nation's first tax insurrection. It continues up to this day, with nearly a hundred citizens in the region who refuse to pay their taxes in protest of U.S. military policy.

Over the centuries, the region has drawn many writers: from Nathaniel Hawthorne (a Salem man who didn't like the Berkshires) and Herman Melville (a Pittsfield man who did). Comedian Bill Cosby has a home in the hills surrounding the Pioneer Valley, and Poet Laureate Richard Wilbur resides in Cummington, carrying on the tradition of poets William Cullen Bryant, who lived in the same town, and Emily Dickinson, who wrote in her home in the center of Amherst in the 19th century.

What all these people have found is a place that's close enough to city amenities and resources—New York is less than four hours away, Boston two—but far enough from the urban smog, crime and high cost of living.

Many current residents in this area first came here as students. In the 1960s, western Massachusetts was a haven for the "back to the landers," who found cheap land and stimulating political activities on the University of Massachusetts campus in Amherst. Like everyplace else, the area has mellowed, but for many, political activism remains an important part of life. Most municipal decisions, except in the cities, are made at traditional New England town meetings. The region is also rich with craftspeople and artists, drawn here for the area's natural beauty and solitude, and their works fill galleries and studios in even the smallest towns.

Education is big business in these parts: Worcester is home to Holy Cross, Clark University and Assumption College, while the Pioneer Valley boasts the so-called "Five Colleges"—the University of Massachusetts, Smith, Mount Holyoke, Hampshire and Amherst—as well as a number of prestigious private schools like Deerfield Academy and Northfield Mount Hermon. Williams College is in the Berkshire village of Williamstown.

This is a special place, taken best at a slow pace. Don't try to do too much here; take the time to loll in a sidewalk café in Northampton or to lose yourself in any of the fine museums of Springfield, Worcester or Williamstown. Though summer is the closest thing to paradise in this region, other seasons have their special pleasures as well. Spend an autumn day climbing a mountain to see the foliage colors, or a winter weekend cross-country skiing at a cozy inn in the Berkshires.

Mark Twain's adage "If you don't like New England weather, wait a minute" applies here, and the weather can vary in locations only 20 miles apart in the Berkshires. Expect anything in winter, from brilliant, 50° days after a snowstorm, to stretches when the thermometer doesn't get above 20°. Early spring—maple sugaring season—will bring warmer days and freezing nights, while summer generally offers 70° to 80° days and, oftentimes, thunderstorms in the early evening. Indian summer is truly one of the most beautiful times in this area, with crystal blue skies, stunning foliage and temperatures that range in the 50s and 60s.

A visit to this region can put you in touch with life's simple pleasures. Like the pleasure of being outdoors and listening to the silence. The exhilaration of a hike down a forested trail. The fun of getting onto a backcountry road and not knowing where you'll end up.

If you're looking for an area that combines the serene pleasures of country life with abundant recreational and cultural opportunities, you will want to return again and again to this scenic refuge.

Central Massachusetts

All too often travelers whiz through Central Massachusetts on the Mass Pike (Route 90) completely missing the attractions of the area. What a shame. This part of the state is home to several truly worthwhile attractions, including several museums in the city of Worcester (pronounced WUS-ter); Village, a living-history museum in Sturbridge; and the tiny town of Brimfield, which has been called the "flea-market capital of the world."

Thanks to Route 90, Central Massachusetts is a breeze to reach. In fact, Worcester is only an hour's drive west of Boston. People are often surprised to learn that Worcester's the second-largest city in New England. Perhaps even more surprising are its impressive contributions to education and commerce. It's home to a dozen colleges and was the birthplace of the ingenious machines that were the first to weave carpets and fold envelopes. The Valentine card was invented here, as were the cotton gin and the birth control pill. Abbie Hoffman, father of the Yippies, was born here, as was Clara Barton, mother of the Red Cross. Isaiah Thomas, publisher of the *Massachusetts Spy*, the country's first

Central & Western Massachusetts

newspaper, gave the premiere New England reading of the Declaration of Independence here in Worcester, and the American Antiquarian Society he founded was the first national historical society in the country.

Worcester's proximity to Boston hasn't helped its cultural image, and its recent economic history has not been quite as grand. Like its neighbor Springfield to the west, the city's fortunes faded with the manufacturing economy, and it is still struggling to redefine itself. There's not much doing here, but the downtown area is in the process of restoration and revitalization, and there are some interesting museums and sights spread throughout the city.

SIGHTS   The **Worcester Historical Museum** is housed in a Georgian Revival–style building and features a collection that details the settlement of the Worcester area. The library here has materials and books on local history for use by researchers. Closed Monday. ~ 30 Elm Street, Worcester; 508-753-8278.

Founded in 1812 by Isaiah Thomas, the **American Antiquarian Society** was this country's first national historical society. Its remarkable collection of printed material includes books, manuscripts, newspapers and ephemera produced in the United States before 1877. It also houses Thomas' printing press. Access to the library is limited, but tours of the collection and its conservation lab are offered on Wednesday. Closed Saturday and Sunday. ~ 185 Salisbury Street, Worcester; 508-755-5221, fax 508-753-3311; www.americanantiquarian.org.

The **Worcester Art Museum** has a fine reputation as one of the best art museums in New England and features a fine collection of European, Middle Eastern, Asian and early American works. Closed Monday and Tuesday. Admission. ~ 55 Salisbury Street, Worcester; 508-799-4406, fax 508-798-5646; www.worcesterart. org, e-mail wam@ultranet.com.

On the outside, the **Higgins Armory Museum** is a steel-and-glass art deco building, but inside it's a castle filled with dozens of sets of armor collected over the years by John Woodman Higgins, who was a local steel magnate. The museum details the history of armor from the year 2000 B.C. to the present and even features a set of armor made for "Hell-Mutt" the hunting dog. There's a children's room where kids can try on helmets and medieval costumes. Closed Monday. Admission. ~ 100 Barber Avenue, Worcester; 508-853-6015, fax 508-852-7697; www.higgins.org.

To the north of Worcester, the landscape opens up into the broad Nashoba Valley. It's worth the drive 20 miles north to visit

HIDDEN ►   the **Fruitlands Museums**. Fruitlands is an overlooked gem, with four small museums spread out on a hillside offering an expansive view of the valley. It was once the home of Bronson Alcott, father of Louisa May and founder of the transcendental movement of the 1840s, which espoused individualism and self-reliance, among other things, and included in its disciples Ralph Waldo Emerson and Henry David Thoreau. The **Fruitlands Farmhouse** has exhibits detailing the movement, while the **Shaker House** provides a look at Shaker life during the 19th century. The **Picture Gallery**, built by the museums' founder, Boston Brahmin Clara Endicott Sears, houses her collection of landscapes by several Hudson River School painters. The **American Indian Museum** has dioramas and artifacts relating to New England's Indians, including Thoreau's collection of arrowheads. The grounds here are quite spectacular, so bring a picnic lunch and spend the day if you can. Closed mid-October to mid-May. Admission. ~ 102 Prospect Hill Road, Harvard; 978-456-3924, fax 978-456-8910; www.fruitlands.org.

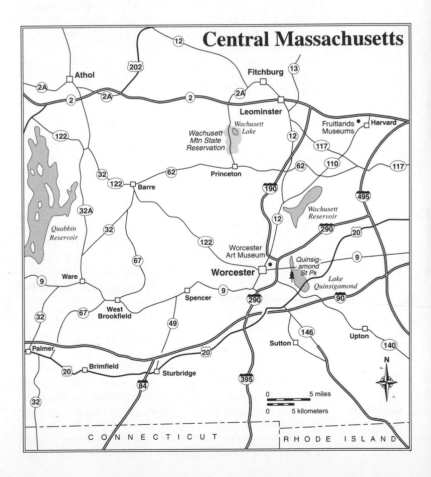

Central Massachusetts

Athol
Fitchburg
Leominster
Wachusett Lake
Wachusett Mtn State Reservation
Fruitlands Museums
Harvard
Princeton
Barre
Quabbin Reservoir
Wachusett Reservoir
Worcester Art Museum
Worcester
Quinsigamond St Pk
Lake Quinsigamond
Ware
Spencer
West Brookfield
Sutton
Upton
Palmer
Brimfield
Sturbridge

0   5 miles
0   5 kilometers

N

CONNECTICUT   RHODE ISLAND

West of Worcester, the land becomes less developed. You've now arrived in the real country. A good introduction to the history of this area comes in **Old Sturbridge Village**. Imagine a small New England village where time just stopped somewhere in the 1830s, and you'd probably conjure up a place like Old Sturbridge Village. It is a fascinating living-history museum that re-creates New England life of that period, from the shoes on the feet of the costumed interpretive guides to the rooftops of the 40-odd restored buildings.

Traveling the paths that wind through some 200 acres of the small village, gardens, farms and fields, you can learn how 19th-century potters, blacksmiths, basketmakers and other craftspeople created their wares. Every activity here is designed to bring the visitor back to the 1800s. They host a variety of special events, some of which are based on the seasons and include cider making, preparation and eating of special Thanksgiving dinners, and craft and antique conferences. A good place for families, this is a must stop on any tour of the region. Open daily from mid-February through New Year's Eve; open weekends January to mid-February. Admission. ~ Route 20, Sturbridge; 508-347-3362, 800-733-1830, fax 508-347-0375; www.osv.org.

Driving west from Sturbridge on Route 20, you're on the open highway, traveling past forests and ponds to the small town of Brimfield, home of the famous **Brimfield Outdoor Antique Show**, a week-long flea market extravaganza held three times a year, in May, July and September. Spread out along a mile-long stretch in the center of town, over 4000 dealers come here to sell their wares, from old postcards to fine European antiques. *The Brimfielder* is a guide to the different exhibitors, available at any local coffee shop or newsstand. For a schedule and detailed listing of exhibitors, send $5 to Quaboag Valley Chamber of Commerce. ~ P.O. Box 269, Palmer, MA 01069; 413-283-6149, fax 413-289-1355; www.quaboag.com, e-mail qvcc@mail.ccsinet.net.

For more information about the Worcester and Sturbridge area, contact the **Worcester County Convention and Visitors Bureau**. ~ 33 Waldo Street, Worcester, MA 01608; 508-753-2920, fax 508-754-2703; www.worcester.org.

LODGING

Worcester has its share of chain motels, but Sturbridge, 18 miles southwest, offers a better variety of accommodations.

Located near the busy University of Massachusetts Medical Center, the **Beechwood Hotel** is one of the town's newer hotels. The large round building has a lobby decorated with flagstone floors and light oak and lavender trim. The Beechwood offers 73 spacious guest rooms, including some fireplace suites, each decorated in pastels and wall-to-wall carpeting. The restaurant here has earned high praises from local food critics for its classic Ameri-

Author Picks

CHAPTER FAVORITES

My pick for the best sight in central Massachusetts is **Old Sturbridge Village**—a major tourist destination that could easily have been made hokey. The good news: it's not. Instead, it offers a true-to-life look at old-time New England. *page 376*

After visiting Old Sturbridge, I was glad that a fellow traveler suggested I head 15 miles up the road to continue my historical experience with a unique 1700-style drover's roast dinner at the **Salem Cross Inn** in West Brookfield. *page 378*

I couldn't resist stopping to dip into history—literally—at **Sand Springs Pool and Spa**, a natural swimming hole in the northwest corner of the state where people have been coming since 1762. George Washington might have swum here! *page 398*

Historic hotels are a passion of mine, especially in a region like New England that wears its history on its sleeve. One of the best is the **Historic Merrell Inn**, welcoming visitors to South Lee since 1794. *page 404*

can cuisine. ~ 363 Plantation Street, Worcester; 508-754-5789, 800-344-2589, fax 508-752-2060; www.beechwood hotel.com. DELUXE.

The **Old Sturbridge Village Lodges and Oliver Wight House,** located at the entrance to Old Sturbridge Village, offers a variety of lodging that includes the historic Oliver Wight House, the Dennison Cottage suites and Village units. The 1789 Oliver Wight House once served as a tavern providing food and lodging for farmers and travelers. The refurbished inn features ten large rooms decorated with Federal-style pieces, including big four-poster beds. The Dennison Cottage offers two luxury suites in a 19th-century country decor with stenciled walls. The Village units are decorated in an Early American motif, with Colonial reproductions. Though the service is friendly here, the atmosphere is motel-like, without the personal interaction you get at a country inn. ~ Route 20 West, Sturbridge; 508-347-3327, 800-733-1830, fax 508-347-3018; www.osv.org. MODERATE.

A local institution, the **Publick House on the Common** was originally founded in 1771 by Colonel Ebenezer Crafts. The original building, which is listed on the National Register of Historic Places, has 16 rooms plus several restaurants and shops. It's surrounded by other accommodations, including the next-door Chamberlain House (a four-suite building) and a 54-room motor lodge. ~ Route 131 on the Common, Sturbridge; 508-347-3313, 800-782-5425, fax 508-347-1246; www.public house.com. MODERATE TO DELUXE.

About a mile away is the **Colonel Ebenezer Crafts Inn**, which is in a farmhouse dating back to 1786. The rooms here—the most charming of all the Publick House accommodations—have canopy or four-poster beds, some antique furnishings and an all-around peaceful feeling. ~ Fiske Hill Road, Sturbridge; 508-347-3313, 800-782-5425; www.publichouse.com. MODERATE TO DELUXE.

Offering basic, modern motel rooms, the **Sturbridge Coach Motor Lodge** has nicely kept grounds and a swimming pool and is convenient to Sturbridge, Worcester and Brimfield. ~ 408 Main Street, Route 20, Sturbridge; 508-347-7327, fax 508-347-2954. BUDGET TO MODERATE.

Set on two acres and adjacent to a 100-acre park, **Wildwood Inn** is a late-19th-century Victorian. Nine rooms feature twin, queen and four-poster beds (seven of them have private baths). Down comforters and handmade quilts are supplemented by electric blankets for those cold New England nights. In the warm months you'll gravitate to the wicker furniture on the wrap-around porch. The country-casual parlor features antiques such as a spinning wheel and bed warmer as well as a fine library. Full breakfast and afternoon tea are delightful. ~ 121 Church Street, Ware; 413-967-7798, 800-860-8098. MODERATE.

Berkshire and Greater Springfield Bed and Breakfast is a reservation service that matches travelers with a number of small country inns in the Sturbridge area. ~ P.O. Box 211, Williamsburg, MA 01096; 413-268-7244, fax 413-268-7243; e-mail berkbb 33@javanet.com.

DINING   The Sunburst features natural foods for breakfast and lunch in a coffee-shop atmosphere. The muffins are excellent, as is the quiche and granola. Other items include fresh fruit bowls, sandwiches and "nogs," seasonal fruit mixed with milk and eggs. ~ 484 Main Street, Sturbridge; 508-347-3097. BUDGET.

A local dining institution, the **Salem Cross Inn** is a restored 1705 New England farmhouse filled with collections of antiques and photographs. The Salem family specializes in some unique eating events that include drinks in the old tavern downstairs, hayrides and sleigh rides through their 600-acre farm. In the summer, their Drover's Roasts serve up a large side of beef, slowly cooked as it was in the 1700s, over a fieldstone open pit. In winter, the weekend Hearthside Dinners feature prime rib cooked on a 1700s roasting jack in the fieldstone fireplace and apple pie baked in the inn's 1699 brick beehive oven. These meals are worth rearranging your schedule for, and reservations are recommended. Closed Monday. ~ Route 9, West Brookfield; 508-867-2345; www.salemcrossinn.com, e-mail salemxinn@aol.com. MODERATE TO ULTRA-DELUXE.

Spag's is a Worcester institution, with three large buildings and an assortment of tents filled with, well, stuff of all kinds, from small appliances to clothing to groceries. It's a warehouse-type operation where customers actually line up to get in the place. If you plan to do any heavy shopping, bring a tote or knapsack—vendors don't give out shopping bags. ~ Route 9, Worcester.

SHOPPING

The gift shop at the **Worcester Art Museum** is a great place to find small, quality gifts including reproduction jewelry, coffee-table books, calendars and toys. ~ 55 Salisbury Street, Worcester; 508-799-4406; www.worcester.org.

Another **Museum Gift Shop** and **New England Bookstore at Old Sturbridge Village** are two outstanding shops that feature crafts made at Sturbridge Village, as well as reproductions of early American items for the home. The bookstore features a wide selection of books about New England history, life and lore, including gardening and the home arts. ~ Route 20, Sturbridge; 508-347-3362, fax 508-347-0375; www.osv.org.

For a selection of reproductions of Shaker furniture, baskets, boxes and hand-cut stencils, visit the **Shaker Shop**. You can also buy authentic Shaker milk paint (yes, made with milk combined with lime and pigment). This old-fashioned product will not peel like modern paint mixtures. ~ 454 Main Street, Sturbridge; 508-347-7564, fax 508-347-2268.

The **Centrum Centre** is a 14,000-seat arena offering rock and pop music concerts, as well as hockey and basketball games and conference events. ~ 50 Foster Street, Worcester; 508-755-6800; www.centrumcentre.com.

NIGHTLIFE

Mechanics Hall, one of the finest pre–Civil War concert halls in the country, is especially noted for its fine acoustics. The hall draws folk, jazz and classical performers and has even been used for the recording of compact discs and records. ~ 321 Main Street, Worcester; 508-752-5608; www.mechanicshall.com, e-mail mechanicshall@mechanicshall.com.

When the warm weather comes, the **Worcester Forum Theatre Ensemble** presents off-Broadway shows and productions in an outdoor amphitheater. ~ 6 Chatham Street, Worcester; 508-799-9166; e-mail rrld@alternet.com.

Sh'boom's is a club with a '50s style, with disc jockeys and dancing Wednesday through Saturday. Also here is **Polyester**, a "classic dance" (read: disco) club accessible through Sh'boom's. Cover Thursday through Saturday. ~ 215 Main Street, Worcester; 508-752-4214, fax 508-831-1319.

The **Spencer Country Inn** draws locals in their 20s and 30s for its live Top-40 bands on the weekends. The place has a pub-type atmosphere, with cozy booths and lots of antiques, including a formerly horsedrawn carriage; there's a large dancefloor, and a big-screen TV for sports fans. Cover for bands. ~ 500 Main Street, Spencer; 508-885-9036, fax 508-885-9037.

VIP's Lounge has live bands with dancing on Friday and Saturday nights. ~ Sturbridge Host Hotel, Route 20, Sturbridge; 508-347-7393.

Those in search of more low-key nightlife should try the popular Ugly Duckling Loft, the loft of the Whistling Swan. The place has a warm and relaxed atmosphere amid brass and wood decor, with piano music Tuesday, Wednesday, Saturday and Sunday and a singing acoustic guitarist Thursday and Friday. ~ 502 Main Street, Sturbridge; 508-347-2321, fax 508-347-7262.

BEACHES & PARKS

PURGATORY CHASM STATE RESERVATION 🏃 This park offers 960 acres of forestland, including the dramatic and unusual Purgatory Chasm. The chasm itself is a quarter-mile-long granite fissure, a sharp valley filled with huge boulders that have detached from the walls. Geologists can't seem to agree on exactly how the chasm was formed, and its mystery adds to the allure of the place. There are hiking trails, including a difficult one through the chasm, as well as picnic areas and restrooms. ~ On Purgatory Road, off Route 146, Sutton; 508-234-3733.

QUINSIGAMOND STATE PARK 🏊 This 58-acre preserve is an urban park, offering a grassy, midday break for visitors to the Worcester area. There are several beaches, including Regatta Point and Lake Park. Crew teams from the area's colleges can often be found at Regatta Point, while Lake Park offers tennis courts and a track. Picnic areas and restrooms are found here. Weekend parking fee, $2. ~ On Lake Avenue off Plantation Street exit from Route 290; 508-755-6880.

▲ Nearby, at the Sutton Falls Camping Area (90 Manchaug Road, West Sutton; 508-865-3898), there are 100 tent/RV sites (hookups available); $15 to $18 per night.

▼▼▼▼▼▼▼▼▼▼▼
Pioneer Valley

The Pioneer Valley, actually a section of the Connecticut River Valley, stretches from the city of Springfield in the south to Brattleboro, Vermont, and beyond. Here you'll find an eclectic mix of old mill cities, semi-chic college towns and country villages, with tobacco, hay and cornfields in between. The farther north you travel from Springfield, the more country you'll find. Northampton and Amherst offer good restaurants and shops, while the towns in the surrounding hills are much more rural and relaxed, some with town commons and white-steepled churches, others with old iron bridges and brick factories along the rivers, remnants of the days when cutlery factories and paper mills fueled the region's economy.

Today, housing developments are starting to encroach on farmland, but the area is still remarkably rural in some parts. This area is known for its unique mix of Yankee stubbornness, ethnic influences and a '60s political outlook that remains even today.

THE LOWER VALLEY   Founded by fur trader William Pynchon in 1636, **Springfield** is the oldest settlement and the largest city in western Massachusetts, as well as the commercial hub of the region. Though it is a city that tries hard, Springfield's glory days

SIGHTS

Pioneer Valley

seem to lie in the past. It does have a good collection of museums, however, that makes it worth spending a rainy day here.

Overlooking the Connecticut River is the **Naismith Memorial Basketball Hall of Fame**. Basketball was invented here in Springfield in 1891, and this place is enjoyable even if you're not a sports fan. There are videos and plenty of interactive displays, including the Spalding Shoot Out, where visitors can shoot at baskets of varying heights while standing on a moving sidewalk. Admission. ~ 1150 West Columbus Avenue, Springfield; 413-781-6500, fax 413-781-1939; www.hoophall.com.

Court Square is a pleasant green space in the heart of Springfield bordered by the **Hampden County Courthouse**, the **Old First Church** and **Symphony Hall**. ~ Main Street, between Court and Elm streets, Springfield.

From here it's a short hike up the hill to **The Quadrangle**, which features four museums (one admission charge admits you to all four) and the Springfield Library. ~ Springfield Library and Museums Association, 220 State Street, Springfield; 413-739-3871, fax 413-263-6875; www.springfieldlibrary.org.

The **George Walter Vincent Smith Museum** houses a collection of Oriental art, as well as 19th-century European and American paintings. Closed Monday and Tuesday. ~ The Quadrangle, Springfield; 413-263-6800, fax 413-263-6807; www.quadrangle.org/gwvs.htm.

Across The Quadrangle is the **Museum of Fine Arts**, which features works from the early Renaissance to the 20th century. One gallery is devoted to impressionist, expressionist and early modern European works. Of special interest are the works of local 19th-century portrait artist Erastus Salisbury Field, whose gigantic *Historical Monument of the American Republic* is a mind-boggler. Closed Monday and Tuesday. ~ The Quadrangle, Springfield; 413-263-6800, fax 413-263-6807; www.quadrangle.org/mfa.htm.

The **Springfield Science Museum** offers exhibits in the natural and physical sciences, including a hands-on Exploration Center for children and the Seymour Planetarium. Closed Monday and Tuesday. ~ The Quadrangle, State and Chestnut streets, Springfield; 413-263-6800, fax 413-263-6807; www.quadrangle.org/ssm.htm.

The **Connecticut Valley Historical Museum** offers a glimpse of the social and economic history of the Connecticut River Valley. Closed Monday and Tuesday. ~ The Quadrangle, Springfield; 413-263-6800, fax 413-263-6807; www.quadrangle.org/cvhm.htm.

Up the hill from The Quadrangle, on the campus of Springfield Technical Community College, is the **Springfield Armory National Historic Site**, established at a spot chosen by George Washington in 1794. The Springfield Armory produced the first U.S. military small arms—the Springfield rifle—bringing skilled workers to the area and setting the scene for the valley's industrial growth. Closed Monday and Tuesday. ~ 1 Armory Square, Springfield; 413-734-8551, fax 413-747-8062; www.nps.gov/spar, e-mail spar_interpretation@nps.gov.

More information about Springfield is available from the **Greater Springfield Convention and Visitors Bureau.** ~ 1441 Main Street, Springfield, MA 01103; 413-787-1548, fax 413-781-4607; www.valleyvisit.com.

The venerable, if slightly shabby, old Riverside Park was taken over in 1999 by the Premier Parks Inc. conglomerate, given a complete facelift, and reopened in 2000 as **Six Flags New England**. The largest theme park in the Northeast, it features three new, bigger and faster-than-ever roller coasters including the 20-story Superman Ride of Steel, a freefall ride appropriately named Scream! and the tallest Ferris wheel on the East Coast. Batman stars in a live stunt show, and bigger-than-life versions of Bugs Bunny, Tweety and Sylvester and other Looney Tunes characters wander through the crowds. Admission. ~ Route 159, 1623 Main Street, Agawam; 413-786-9300; www.sixflags.com/newengland.

> The Mount Holyoke College campus was designed by Frederick Law Olmsted, designer of Central Park, who used a variety of rare trees to provide form, beauty and consistency.

Traveling north from Holyoke, you start to get into farm-and-college country. Gradually, the mills and tenements fade away and the land becomes more open. The small town of South Hadley is the home of **Mount Holyoke College**. Established by Mary Lyon in 1837, Mount Holyoke is one of the oldest women's colleges in the country. A maple-lined road leads the traveler through the 800-acre campus, between two campus ponds and up to the wooded Prospect Hill, which has bridle paths and a lawn for picnics. ~ 50 College Street, South Hadley; 413-538-2000; www.mtholyoke.edu.

On the Granby town line on Route 116 farther north is the funky and fascinating **Nash Dinosaur Land**, where 200-million-year-old dinosaur tracks were discovered in 1933. Geologist Carleton Nash and his son Cornell have built up a business over the past 50 years, excavating the tracks and building a small museum and shop to display the prints, some as tiny as chicken feet. The Nashes boast the largest footprint quarry in the world, as well as the largest footprints from the early Jurassic period; many pieces are for sale. Kids will love this place. Closed Monday through Wednesday from Columbus Day to Memorial Day. Admission. ~ Route 116, South Hadley; 413-467-9566.

◄ *HIDDEN*

THE UPPER VALLEY **Northampton** counts among its past residents Calvinist minister Jonathan Edwards and President Calvin Coolidge, who also served as mayor. Sylvester Graham invented the graham cracker here, and in the early 1800s the place was a thriving industrial center for wool, buttons, paper, and later, cutlery.

Today, it is perhaps the most cosmopolitan town in western Massachusetts (some locals say too much so), with its mix of restored old buildings, galleries, restaurants and trendy Main Street boutiques. The home of Smith College, the town is a pleasant and lively place year-round but especially nice in summer, when the students have gone home.

Smith College is located just outside the town's center. One of the so-called "Seven Sisters" (as is Mount Holyoke), Smith's campus is quintessentially old-money New England, with old Gothic buildings and beautifully tended gardens. Among its attractions is the **Lyman Plant House**, a rambling, old-fashioned greenhouse filled with hundreds of different flowers, plants and trees and open to the public. The annual bulb show in early spring is a favorite visitor destination. Another idyllic spot is **Paradise Pond**, framed by weeping willows and elm trees and ideal for an afternoon picnic.

The **Smith College Museum of Art** houses works by Picasso, Degas, Monet and Winslow Homer, as well as local sculptor Leonard Baskin and 19th-century local portrait artist Romanzo Elmer. The museum is being renovated; it is expected to re-open in fall 2002. ~ 76 Elm Street at Bedford Terrace, Northampton; 413-584-2700.

Calvin Coolidge, the nation's 30th president, attended Amherst College and settled in Northampton, where he practiced law and began his political career. Coolidge lived with his wife at **21 Massasoit Street**, and after his presidency the couple retired to The Beeches, a stately home located on Hampton Terrace. Both homes are private.

For an example of Gothic architecture, visit **The Academy of Music**, a former opera house built in 1891 that now serves as a movie theater with occasional live performances. ~ 274 Main Street, Northampton; 413-584-8435.

Historic Northampton operates three homes that highlight local history and daily life in Northampton over the past three centuries. The **Isaac Damon House** was built circa 1813 by Damon, a prominent New England architect of the day. The house includes an 1820 parlor display and changing exhibitions. A modern addition houses the Damon Education Center, which features the permanent exhibit, "A Place Called Paradise—The Making of Northampton Massachusetts." ~ 46 Bridge Street, Northampton; 413-584-6011, fax 413-584-7956.

The **Shepherd House** is furnished with the Shepherd family collection, including travel souvenirs from around the world. There is a museum gift shop located in a renovated 1820s barn on site. ~ 66 Bridge Street, Northampton; 413-584-6011, fax 413-584-7956.

Built in 1730, the **Parsons House** features an architectural tour; look inside the walls to see the various layers of wallpaper and paint from the 19th century. Guided afternoon tours are offered Saturday and Sunday, March through December. Admission. ~ 58 Bridge Street, Northampton; 413-584-6011, fax 413-584-7956.

For more information on the Northampton area, contact the **Greater Northampton Chamber of Commerce.** ~ 99 Pleasant Street, Northampton; 413-584-1900, fax 413-584-1934; www. northamptononcommon.com.

Follow Route 9 east across the Coolidge Bridge and you will reach Hadley, a farming town once noted for its asparagus and tobacco but now fast becoming a suburb. The **Hadley Farm Museum** is housed in a 1790s barn moved to the spot in 1929. The museum features a wonderful collection of farm tools, an 18th-century stagecoach, wagons and home utensils used during the 18th and 19th centuries. Closed Monday and from October through April. ~ Route 9, Hadley.

Amherst is a pretty college town with shops and restaurants spread out along a maple-lined town common. Though it has been influenced by the gentrifier's wrecking ball, there's still a spark of politics in its downtown area, with tie-dye clad students petitioning against U.S. military policy or in favor of animal rights.

Founded in 1821, **Amherst College** gracefully borders the southern side of the Amherst common. With about 1600 students, Amherst is one of the smaller Ivy League colleges, and its campus architecture includes a rich mix of old ivy-covered halls and newer buildings. ~ 413-542-2000, fax 413-542-2040; www.at amherst.edu.

One of the newer buildings houses the **Robert Frost Library**, named for one of the college's better-known faculty members. Open daily when school is in session. ~ 413-542-2373, fax 413-542-2662; www.amherst.edu/library.

The **Pratt Museum** houses a collection of approximately 10,000 mineral specimens, as well as the world's largest mastodon and

---

THE "BELLE OF AMHERST'S" FAMILY HOME

The **Emily Dickinson Homestead** was the family home of "The Belle of Amherst," reclusive poet Emily Dickinson. The large brick house built by Emily's grandfather in 1813 is now owned by Amherst College, and it has become a mecca for poetry lovers. The home is open to the public March to mid-December. Call ahead for hours. Admission. ~ 280 Main Street, Amherst; 413-542-8161; www.amherst.edu/~edhouse.

The Mohawk Trail

The Mohawk Trail is one of the region's oldest and finest touring roads, winding past farm towns, forests and some of the best scenic views in western New England. The trail is dotted with remnants of the 1950s heyday of automobile touring: cabins, old Indian souvenir shops and several spots with lookouts boasting multistate views. It is particularly popular in fall, when its hills offer spectacular foliage viewing. While the trail officially runs for some 60 miles across Massachusetts from Lexington to the New York state line, by far the most beautiful part is the 28-mile segment described here.

SHELBURNE   From the town of Greenfield on Route 5 or Route 91 Exit 26, drive west on Route 2. Six miles along, at the town of Shelburne, take time to visit the lovely **Bridge of Flowers**, a former trolley bridge across the Deerfield River that has been converted into an incredible flower garden in bloom three seasons out of the year. Across the bridge and down a side street, you'll find the **Glacial Potholes**, formed millions of years ago by "plunge pools" of waterfalls.

CHARLEMONT   Fourteen more miles bring you to the village of Charlemont, and a couple of miles farther on, the **Hail to the Sunrise Monument**, a 900-pound bronze statue depicting a Mohawk Indian with arms upraised to the east, memorializing the people who used this route for their annual migration in ancient times. A nearby pool contains 100 inscribed stones from tribes throughout the United States.

mammoth skeletons. Open daily when school is in session. ~ 413-542-2165; www.amherst.edu/~pratt.

At the other end of Amherst is the **University of Massachusetts**. With an enrollment of 24,000 students, it is one of the largest universities in New England. ~ 413-545-0111; www.umass.edu.

"UMass" has come a long way from its beginnings as an agricultural land-grant college in 1863, and its campus buildings reflect that stretch, from the classic-style **Old Chapel** to the 26-story **W. E. B. Du Bois Library** that stands beside it. The library, as well as the **Top of the Campus** restaurant at the **Murray D. Lincoln Campus Center**, offer fine views of the Holyoke range.

The Campus Pond is the center of fair-weather activities, and the **Fine Arts Center** presents varied performances in theater, dance and music. ~ 413-545-2511; www.umass.edu/fac.

As you travel farther, the curves deepen in the road as it enters the **Mohawk Trail State Forest** (page 394), one of the most scenic woodland areas in Massachusetts, where you can hike a portion of the original Mohawk foot trail.

FLORIDA   North of the highway near the town of Florida is the east entrance of the **Hoosac Tunnel**. One of the great engineering accomplishments of the mid-19th century, the railroad tunnel runs nearly five miles through the mountain and took 20 years to complete. Soon after passing Florida, Route 2 reaches the mountain pass the tunnel was designed to avoid—2272-foot **Whitcomb Summit**, the highest point on the Mohawk Trail, from which you can see parts of Massachusetts, New York, Vermont and New Hampshire. Descending the western slope, **Hairpin Turn** affords another breathtaking view of the Hoosac Valley and the Berkshire Hills. For more information, contact **The Mohawk Trail Association**. ~ P.O. Box 722, Charlemont, MA 01339.

NATURAL BRIDGE STATE PARK   Just before arriving in **North Adams** (page 397), the Mohawk Trail brings you to the intersection with Route 8 and Natural Bridge State Park, site of the only natural marble bridge in North America, formed by the raging waters of melting glaciers millions of years ago. Also interesting to look at are the carvings done by quarrymen and visitors, many dating back to the 1800s.

BIRTHPLACE OF SUSAN B. ANTHONY   To continue this drive as a scenic loop, from North Adams take Route 8 south for six miles to Adams and follow Route 116 back to Route 91/Route 5 at South Deerfield, a distance of 36 miles with few specific points of interest—other than the birthplace of Susan B. Anthony in Adams—but plenty of pastoral beauty.

For more information on the Amherst area, contact the **Amherst Area Chamber of Commerce**. ~ 409 Main Street, Amherst; 413-253-0700, fax 413-256-0771; www.amherstcommon.com.

Travel north on Route 116, and you'll leave the college towns behind. Here the landscape is punctuated by the long, faded red tobacco barns and cornfields whose crop will feed the area's dairy cows. Just off Routes 5 and 10 is **Historic Deerfield**. ~ Deerfield; 413-774-5581.

It's almost jarring to turn off the busy highway and onto the tree-lined main street of Deerfield because you have, in a sense, left the modern world behind. The mile-long main street of this late-17th-century village (it's just called "The Street") is flanked by a dozen restored Colonial and Federal-style houses, all painted in the muted reds, blues and greys of bygone days. Here you can get a sense of the emerging Connecticut Valley architecture, which was different from the styles in England as well as the coastal New England towns. And the interiors at Historic Deerfield are just as faithful to the past as the exteriors; the village's collection of decorative arts and architecture has been compared to that of historic Williamsburg and the Winterthur Museum in Delaware.

Surrounded by farmland and meadows, Deerfield began in the 17th century as a tiny frontier outpost. The town was massacred by French and Indian attackers in 1675 in the Bloody Brook Massacre and virtually destroyed by a later attack in 1704. Testimony to that fateful day still stands: there's a door with a hatchet hole in it at the **Memorial Hall Museum,** one of the oldest local historical museums in the country. Admission. ~ Memorial Street, Deerfield; 413-774-7476, fax 413-774-7070; www. deerfield-ma.org.

The town recovered, and Deerfield went on to prosper as a center for commerce and agriculture, as well as an exchange post for travelers between Boston and points west. In 1952, Mr. and Mrs. Henry Flynt established Historic Deerfield, Inc. to carry out the restoration of the town, one of the first such undertakings in the country.

The **Sheldon-Hawks House** is the best-preserved Deerfield building from the 18th century, and the dark-stained, clapboard structure is one of the oldest houses in town, dating back to 1740. The woodwork is intact, and some of the furnishings are original Deerfield pieces. The Sheldon-Hawks displays New England furniture, European brass and English ceramics, while the **Wells-Thorn House** features a series of period rooms that illustrate the influence of the local economy and changing styles in home life in Deerfield from 1725 to 1850. There is no admission fee to Historic Deerfield, but one admission fee is charged to tour all the individual houses.

The Connecticut River is the backbone of this region, and from June to mid-October, the **Quinnetukut II Riverboat** cruises a 12-mile section of the river, giving you a look at the geology, history and natural beauty of the area. Closed Monday and Tuesday. Admission. ~ Northfield Mountain Recreation and Environmental Center, 99 Miller's Falls Road, Northfield; 413-659-3714, fax 413-659-4460; www.nu.com.

If you're lucky enough to be in the area in the late summer or early fall, check out one of the region's many agricultural fairs. The **Eastern States Exposition** represents all six New England states and features music, food, agricultural contests, animal shows and much more. The exposition is held the third week of September in West Springfield. The **Cummington Fair** is another small-town beauty, held the last week of August. This fair's highlights are its old engine display, square dancing and fireworks. The **Northampton Fair** is held during the last week in August and the first week in September at the Tri-County Fairground on Bridge Street in Northampton. The **Franklin County Fair** is the first week in September, at the Franklin County Fairgrounds on Wisdom Way in Greenfield.

For a complete listing of agricultural fairs around the state, write to the **Massachusetts Department of Food and Agriculture.** ~ 100 Cambridge Street, Boston, MA 02202; 617-727-3018, fax 617-626-1850; www.massdfa.org.

If you're traveling the Mohawk Trail (see "Scenic Drive") in early spring, **Gould's Sugar House** is a tasty stop. You're likely to find Edgar Gould out in the back boiling sap to make maple syrup, while his wife and grandchildren are in the restaurant serving it on waffles and pancakes. (Dill pickles are served on the side to cut the sweetness of the syrup!) Open spring and fall; call for summer hours. ~ Mohawk Trail, Shelburne; 413-625-6170.

◄ HIDDEN

There are many opportunities for picnicking along the Deerfield River, and you may want to stop in Shelburne Falls for supplies. **McCusker's Market** has a good deli and a supply of health foods, oatscream as well as Bart's ice cream, local favorites. ~ State Street, Shelburne Falls; 413-625-9411, fax 413-625-6031.

The Springfield area offers a large selection of chain motels and luxury hotels, while accommodations in the upper Pioneer Valley include more motels, country inns and bed and breakfasts. Advance reservations are strongly recommended in June, when college graduations and the American Council Crafts Fair are held, and in September, when the Eastern States Exposition and fall foliage bring a flurry of visitors.

LODGING

The **Country Bed and Breakfast Association** offers information on eight small bed and breakfasts located in the farm and hill towns of the Pioneer Valley. ~ 181 School Street, Northfield, MA 01360; 413-498-2692, 800-498-2692.

The most elegant hostelry in the Pioneer Valley, the **Sheraton Springfield Monarch Place** has a plush lobby highlighted by marble, a 12-story atrium and amenities like an indoor pool with a sun deck. The 325 spacious guest rooms and suites are decorated in soft pastels. There are also two restaurants, a lounge and a health club with jacuzzi, weight room and sauna. Ask for a room with a view of the Connecticut River. ~ 1 Monarch Place, Springfield; 413-781-1010, 800-426-9004, fax 413-734-3249. MODERATE TO DELUXE.

The **Yankee Pedlar Inn** has 28 guest rooms in four separate buildings on a busy street in Holyoke. Rooms are individually decorated in Early American decor, with period pieces and antiques along with canopy and four-poster beds. The Pedlar has a Colonial-style tavern, an oyster bar and a restaurant. Although not an isolated country inn, this is a popular place for business travelers, and its location just off Route 91 makes it convenient to all parts of the Pioneer Valley. ~ 1866 Northampton Street, Holyoke; 413-532-9494, fax 413-536-8877. MODERATE.

Near downtown Northampton and right next to the Smith campus, the **Autumn Inn** is a simple, comfortable 30-room hostelry. Guest rooms are large, clean and individually decorated with wall-to-wall carpeting, Colonial reproductions, brass lamps, Hitchcock rockers and prints from the owner's collection. Extras include an outdoor pool and a dining room with a large fireplace. The place has attracted a regular clientele for its location and attention to detail. ~ 259 Elm Street, Northampton; 413-584-7660, fax 413-586-4808; www.autumninn.com. MODERATE.

The **Hotel Northampton** has undergone a facelift, converting a once semiseedy, middle-aged downtown hotel into something with a touch of class. There are 99 rooms here, including some with canopy beds and jacuzzis. The lobby is nicely decorated in a late-Georgian motif, and the hotel has become a favorite for Smith College parents for its accommodations and its proximity to the campus. Reservations advised. Continental breakfast is included. ~ 36 King Street, Northampton; 413-584-3100, 800-547-3529, fax 413-584-9455; www.hotelnorthampton.com. DELUXE.

Standing in the center of Amherst, the **Lord Jeffery Inn** has been a fixture in this college town for decades. Many of its 48 rooms are decorated with antiques, and some overlook the lovely town common. The inn has the sedate feel of an Ivy League faculty club, with an elegant dining room and tavern, as well as several cozy public sitting rooms, comfortable arm chairs and a fireplace. It's located within walking distance of the shopping area and Amherst College. ~ 30 Boltwood Avenue, Amherst; 413-253-2576, 800-742-0358, fax 413-256-6152; www.pinnacle-inns.com/lordjefferyinn.com, e-mail lordjefferyinn@pinnacle-inns.com. DELUXE.

HIDDEN ► The **Allen House** is a wonderful Victorian inn (seven rooms, all with private baths) that opened in 1991. The owners painstakingly restored it to its original form, earning it the Historic Preservation Award from the Amherst Historical Commission. It's set on three wooded acres within walking distance of town. A big country breakfast and afternoon tea are included. ~ 599 Main Street, Amherst; 413-253-5000; www.allenhouse.com. BUDGET TO DELUXE.

The **Campus Center Hotel** offers 116 rooms with standard low-cost hotel decor in a concrete highrise on the University of Massachusetts campus. The ambience is nothing special, but the hotel is convenient for visitors to the university, and the view of the Holyoke range and the campus is great. ~ University of Massachusetts, Amherst; 413-549-6000, fax 413-545-1210; www.aux.umass.edu/hotel. MODERATE.

One of the few elegant old country inns in the northern Pioneer Valley is the **Deerfield Inn**, built in 1884, which stands along a lovely, tree-lined street in Historic Deerfield. Its 23 rooms are decorated in antiques and Graeff fabric wallpaper. There's a comfortable sitting room with a fireplace to enjoy predinner drinks, and a good restaurant. The regular clientele from Boston and New York enjoy the ambience as well as the services of innkeepers Karl and Jane Sabo, themselves urban refugees. Breakfast and afternoon tea are included. ~ 81 Old Main Street, Deerfield; 413-774-5587, fax 413-775-7221; www.deerfieldinn.com, e-mail frontdesk @deerfieldinn.com. DELUXE TO ULTRA-DELUXE.

Berkshire and Greater Springfield Bed and Breakfast is a reservation service that matches travelers with small country inns in the Pioneer Valley, the Sturbridge area, Berkshire, and eastern New York. ~ P.O. Box 211, Williamsburg, MA 01096; 413-268-7244, fax 413-268-7243; e-mail berkbb33@javanet.com.

What the Pioneer Valley lacks in fancy eateries it makes up for with a solid roster of good, moderately priced restaurants, including a number of ethnic and vegetarian spots.

DINING

In downtown Springfield, **Tilly's** is a good choice for lunch or dinner, with an eclectic assortment of sandwiches, burgers, salads, quiches and pasta. In the old days, this would have been called a "fern bar," with a brick interior and a nice bar. The place used to be an old hotel. Closed Sunday. ~ 1390 Main Street, Springfield; 413-732-3613. BUDGET.

Traditional New England fare is served at the **Yankee Pedlar Inn**, including clam chowder, chicken pot pie, corned beef and cabbage, a large selection of seafood and grilled chicken teriyaki. The dining room is a handsome Colonial-style scene with wood-planked walls. Closed Monday. ~ 1866 Northampton Street, Holyoke; 413-532-9494, fax 413-536-8877. BUDGET TO DELUXE.

Joe's Café is a quintessential dive, with peeling paint and great Italian food: eggplant parmigiana, spaghetti and a marvelous vegetarian pizza primavera. Mingle with the locals and college students over pitchers of beer and try to figure out exactly what that mural on the wall means. Joe's is an oasis in an area fast succumbing to culinary gentrification. ~ 33 Market Street, Northampton; 413-584-3168. MODERATE.

At the other end of the Italian food spectrum is **Spoleto**, a local favorite. This place is a real find, with imaginative Italian dishes at reasonable prices. Dishes include a sublime chicken rollatini, homemade pasta served with shrimp, scallops, mussels and calamari, eggplant terrine and veal scallopine. Desserts are homemade, and the espresso is strong. ~ 50 Main Street, Northampton; 413-586-6313, fax 413-585-0978. MODERATE TO DELUXE.

Paul and Elizabeth's has a local following for its natural food lunches and dinners. You might be tempted by their salads—hummus, tabouli, spinach and egg—good soups, fish broiled with tamari, a vegetable and seafood tempura, sandwiches and pasta. Decor is light and airy; some nights the place can be bursting with vegetarian baby boomers and their vegetarian babies, but the staff always keeps its cool. ~ Thorne's Market, 150 Main Street, Northampton; 413-584-4832, fax 413-582-7999. BUDGET TO MODERATE.

> Pioneer Valley is noted for its craftspeople, who continue traditions started in the 17th century.

Judie's is an Amherst dining institution, noted for its sun-room view of the comings and goings of downtown Amherst, its chic clientele and wonderful desserts. The cuisine here is "nouvelle à la Judie" and includes some unusual dishes like paella and a chicken breast salad stuffed into an oversized popover. Desserts include chocolate truffle fudge cake and fried bananas and ice cream. ~ 51 North Pleasant Street, Amherst; 413-253-3491. MODERATE.

The dining room at the **Lord Jeffery Inn** is a good choice for a more formal meal (though in Amherst, a college town, *formal* means anything except jeans). It's a big Colonial-style room with a fireplace; tables are lit by oil lamps. Menu items include such dishes as grilled salmon filet, grilled New York sirloin and chicken prepared in a variety of ways, plus some house specialties, including a wonderful lemon-and-dill cured salmon as an appetizer and a Mediterranean vegetable pasta dish. There's live jazz during Sunday brunch. ~ 30 Boltwood Avenue, Amherst; 413-253-2576; www.pinnacle-inns.com/lordjefferyinn, e-mail lordjeffery inn@pinnacle-inns.com. MODERATE TO DELUXE.

SHOPPING **Tower Square** includes over 30 specialty food, gift and clothing stores. ~ 1500 Main Street, Springfield; 413-733-2171.

Holyoke Mall at Ingleside has over 185 specialty and department stores, including **Filene's Basement** (413-536-2777), **Lord & Taylor's** (413-534-5800) and **JC Penney** (413-536-3963). ~ Route 91 Exit 15, Holyoke; 413-536-1441; www.holyokemall.com.

A favorite Sunday excursion for locals is **Yankee Candle**, with its assortment of gifts and hundreds of hand-dipped candles along with a remarkable Christmas shop with ornaments and toys from around the world. A bakery and café offer light lunches, and afterwards you can wander through their candle-making museum. ~ Routes 5 and 10, South Deerfield; 413-665-8306, fax 413-665-4815; www.yankeecandle.com.

The Pioneer Valley is especially noted for the large number of craftspeople who make their home here, and their presence is reflected in several fine shops in Northampton and beyond. A few worth looking into include:

In Northampton, **Pinch** carries a wide variety of handmade pottery and ceramics from across the country and related gifts. ~ 179 Main Street, Northampton; 413-586-4509; www.epinch. com.

Thorne's Marketplace is an old department store renovated into five floors of shops and boutiques, including a record store, bead store, clothing stores and toy shops, as well as a natural-foods restaurant. ~ 150 Main Street, Northampton; 413-584-5582.

Check out the **Salmon Falls Artisans Showroom**, set in a late-19th-century post-and-beam granary overlooking the famous Bridge of Flowers. The works of nearly 200 artisans are showcased. ~ 1 Ashfield Street, Shelburne Falls; phone/fax 413-625-9833.

The town of Leverett offers **Leverett Crafts and Arts**. Approximately 20 local artists' studios are housed here. A gallery also features the works of other artists. ~ Montague Road, Leverett; 413-548-9070.

A list of members in the **Pioneer Valley Antique Dealers Association**, which guarantees authenticity of merchandise, is available by sending them an SASE. ~ c/o Donald Schimke, Secretary, Hadley Place, Hadley, MA 01035.

NIGHTLIFE

Concerts, entertainment and sporting events are held regularly at the **Springfield Civic Center and Symphony Hall**. ~ 1277 Main Street, Springfield; 413-787-6610; www.mccahome.com.

Stagewest, Springfield's resident theater company, presents comedies and dramas during its season from September to June. ~ 1 Columbus Center, Springfield; 413-781-2340.

For a wide array of folk, blues, African, Caribbean and Celtic music nightly in a coffeehouse setting, check out the **Iron Horse Music Hall**. There's a restaurant, a good dancefloor and a wide selection of imported beers at this intimate spot. Cover. ~ 20 Center Street, Northampton; 413-584-0610, fax 413-586-7488.

Northampton is also home to the **Academy of Music**—the oldest continuously operating theater in the country. ~ 274 Main Street, Northampton; 413-584-8435.

Pearl Street Night Club features local and nationally known rock, jazz, blues, reggae and funk performers in an art deco–style nightclub. Closed Sunday through Wednesday. Cover. ~ 10 Pearl Street, Northampton; 413-584-7771.

The **Fine Arts Center** at the University of Massachusetts offers concerts, plays, lectures and dance events during the regular school year. ~ Amherst; 413-545-2511.

BEACHES & PARKS

SKINNER STATE PARK 🏃 🖼 Located atop the Holyoke Range, this park offers a view of the Connecticut River that is reminiscent of Thomas Cole's painting *The Oxbow*, depicting an ancient bend in the river. Here the Summit House, a Victorian-style hotel built in 1851, has been restored as a visitors center. Birdwatchers can view hawk migrations in mid-April and mid-September. A picnic area and restrooms are available Memorial Day through October. Day-use fee on weekends and holidays, $2. ~ Off Route 47 on Mountain Road, Hadley; 413-586-0350, fax 413-586-5380.

▲ Nearby, at Daughters of the American Revolution State Forest (Route 112, Goshen; 413-268-7098), there are 50 tent/RV sites (no hookups); $10 per night for Massachusetts residents, $12 per night for non-residents. Reservations available through Reserve America, 877-422-6762.

MOUNT SUGARLOAF STATE RESERVATION 🏃 Jutting up out of the Connecticut River Valley farmland like a huge monument to nature, Mount Sugarloaf shows a red sandstone face and varied natural life. This forested, 652-acre reservation overlooks the Connecticut River from on high and is a foliage season favorite. You'll find picnic areas, restrooms and a lookout tower. Closed in winter. ~ Off Route 116, Deerfield.

MOHAWK TRAIL STATE FOREST 🏃 ⛺ 🏊 〰️ One of the state's well-kept secrets, this forest covers over 6000 acres spread along the Deerfield and Cold Rivers. The old Indian Trail used by Mohawks to travel from upstate New York to the Pioneer Valley is etched into the woods here, and open fields and meadows lead down to the river. Fish for trout on the Deerfield River and take a dip in a sheltered, sandy pool off the Cold River, or in the small waterfalls downstream. This park has a regular camping clientele because of its size and the number of activities available. Facilities include picnic areas, showers and restrooms. ~ Route 2, three miles west of Charlemont; 413-339-5504, fax 413-339-6682; www.reserveamerica.com.

▲ There are 56 tent/RV sites (no hookups), $10 per night for Massachusetts residents, $12 per night for non-residents.

▼▼▼▼▼▼▼▼▼▼▼▼
The Happy Valley

To its many inhabitants with alternative sexual orientations, the Pioneer Valley is fondly referred to as "The Happy Valley." Originally coined in the 1960s, the name was adopted by the gay community to describe this vibrant lesbian enclave. A scenic rural retreat with fine inns and restaurants, the Pioneer Valley is a relaxing vacation spot. With the second-largest lesbian population in the country (after the San Francisco Bay Area) and a sizable population of gay men, the Valley offers a rural version of the gay-friendly atmosphere found in such cities as New York or San Francisco.

A number of the Valley's happy denizens are spread out along quiet backroads and in the outskirts of towns, enjoying the peace of the country; many of the gay establishments, consequently, are also widely dispersed throughout the area. Northampton (or

"Noho" to locals) serves as the pulse of the Valley's gay scene. It's here that you'll find the concentration of gay clubs, restaurants and inns. You can pick up a copy of *The Metroline*, a free bi-monthly, at local cafés. Or you can get the Noho-based periodical, *The Lesbian Calendar,* at area bookstores for an update on local happenings. ~ 413-586-5514.

In addition to the places listed here, the Happy Valley's five colleges—especially Smith and the University of Massachusetts—sponsor gay dances and events just about every weekend. *The Five College Bulletin* (available in campus buildings and at bus-stop racks) is a good resource, or you can check flyers on campus to find out what's happening.

LODGING

On the outskirts of Northampton, the **Old Red Schoolhouse** provides a peaceful retreat. This Colonial-style building was the first schoolhouse in the area when it was built in the early 19th century. The entire inn, a suite with three guest rooms, a living room and a fully stocked kitchen, is available for one to six people. The decor is a combination of country antiques and art deco. One room has a fireplace, and the bathroom boasts a big, old claw-foot tub. Gay-friendly. ~ 67 Park Street, Northampton; 413-584-1228. MODERATE.

"For women and their friends," the lesbian-owned **Tin Roof Bed & Breakfast** has three guest rooms, each with double beds and a shared bath. This B&B, a 1909 farmhouse in a two-acre rural setting, is a short walk from the Connecticut River and a five-minute drive from downtown Northampton. It has a front porch with a swing, a large, peaceful yard with flower, vegetable, water and herb gardens, and a spectacular view of the Berkshires and the Holyoke Range. In the living room you'll find games, videos, a lesbian library and the resident cats. Continental breakfast is included. A two-night minimum stay is required on weekends and holidays. ~ P.O. Box 296, Hadley, MA 01035; 413-586-8665. MODERATE.

DINING

For gourmet vegetarian food, try lesbian-owned **Bela**. A lively, casual eatery that displays art by local artists on the walls, Bela features an eclectic variety of healthful entrées. This is a popular spot with the gay crowd. ~ 68 Masonic Street, Northampton; 413-586-8011. BUDGET.

The happening **Haymarket Cafe** serves coffee, tea and pastries and has a fresh juice bar. In addition, the kitchen whips up tantalizing vegetarian and vegan fare utilizing Eastern, Latin American and other ethnic flavors. It's always crowded with gays, lesbians and other alternative thinkers. Open for breakfast, lunch and dinner. ~ 185 Main Street, Northampton; 413-586-9969. BUDGET.

Named after the inventor of the graham cracker, Dr. Sylvester Graham, **Sylvester's Restaurant** is popular among both gays and straights. One wood-trimmed dining area sports a tin roof. The other is modern and airy with lots of windows. Lunch entrées include soups, salads and sandwiches. ~ 111 Pleasant Street, Northampton; 413-586-5343, fax 413-586-1552. BUDGET.

Healthful, organic food is the focus at **The Copper Angel Restaurant.** Choose between vegetarian, poultry and seafood dishes at this small, cozy restaurant decorated with heavenly creatures. For lunch, get a soup, salad or sandwich. For dinner try one of the seafood entrées such as pepper-seared scallops with basil-braised asparagus. Closed until December 2000. ~ 2 State Street, Shelburne Falls; 413-625-2727. MODERATE.

SHOPPING   One of the area's best bookstores, **Northampton Pride & Joy** has one of the best selections of feminist and gay/lesbian titles as well as gifts, clothing, jewelry, music, videos and locally made crafts. ~ 20 Crafts Avenue, Northampton; 413-585-0683.

You'll find the **Food For Thought** bookstore well stocked with gay/lesbian and progressive political material. ~ 106 North Pleasant Street, Amherst; 413-253-5432; www.foodforthoughtbooks. com.

NIGHTLIFE   **The Grotto** offers a gay/lesbian disco on Wednesday, Friday and Saturday; there is also karaoke one Thursday each month. Cover. ~ 25 West Street, Northampton; 413-586-6900; www.grotto.com.

Wednesday is gay/lesbian night at the industrial-looking **Club Metro.** Tuesday is gothic/industrial night; Sunday is salsa night. The club features dance music on Friday and Saturday. Cover. ~ 492 North Pleasant Street, Northampton; 413-582-9898; www. clubmetro.net.

The Berkshires

The lay of the land is different in the Berkshires. It's more rural than the Pioneer Valley and central Massachusetts, with more broad, open valleys and stretches of farmland and forest. There are three kinds of towns here: old mill towns like Dalton and Great Barrington, which have their own red-brick, utilitarian beauty; small country towns like New Ashford and Monterey, with tree-lined greens, a general store or two and a white church; and tourist towns like Lenox and Stockbridge, whose identities are closely tied to a plethora of cultural activities. Despite the tourism and second-home building boom of the 1980s, the area is still remarkably rural, and you can find yourself in a Lenox traffic jam one minute, and a few minutes later on the open road with nothing but lush green scenery around you.

The Berkshires have a noteworthy cultural heritage as well. For years, the hills' natural beauty and remoteness drew authors, poets and artists. The rich followed. At the turn of the 20th century, the area was nicknamed the "inland Newport" for the large number of wealthy families who built their ornate "cottages" (actually, they were 20-odd-room mansions!) here as summer retreats.

The gateway to the northern Berkshires, the city of **North Adams** **SIGHTS** was once a thriving manufacturing center of textiles and electrical components. Today, the old mills lie idle, and North Adams is a bit down-at-the-heels. The city may be on the comeback trail, however, thanks to the construction of the **Massachusetts Museum of Contemporary Art**. The town is in the middle of turning an abandoned 27-building mill complex into the world's largest contemporary art museum. The gallery opened in May 1999, and other buildings are still being renovated. The complex is listed in the National Historic Register. Closed Monday from November through May. ~ 87 Marshall Street, North Adams; 413-664-4481, fax 413-663-8548; www.massmoca.org, e-mail info@massmoca.org.

Natural Bridge State Park is the site of the only natural marble bridge in North America, formed by the raging waters of melting glaciers millions of years ago. Also interesting to look at are the many carvings done by quarrymen and visitors, a number of them dating back to the 1800s. Closed Columbus Day through Memorial Day. Parking fee. ~ Route 8, North Adams; 413-663-6312, fax 413-664-0033.

Traveling into downtown North Adams, you'll pass huge mills —monuments to bygone days. **Western Gateway Heritage State Park** has a fascinating exhibit on the construction of the four-and-three-fourths-mile Hoosac Tunnel between North Adams and Rowe. The tunnel opened rail traffic between Boston and Albany, and, at the time of its construction in the mid-19th century, was considered an engineering wonder. ~ Off of Route 8 at Furnace Street Bypass, North Adams; 413-663-8059, fax 413-664-0033.

West on Route 2 is the college and culture town of Williamstown. Established as the town of "West Hoosuck" by Ephraim Williams in 1750, Williamstown is the home of **Williams College**. The college has a rambling, classical campus with many fine buildings.

The **Williams College Museum of Art** is in an octagonal building inspired by Monticello and a wing designed by Charles Moore. The museum is one of the best college art museums in the country, with changing exhibitions as well as a strong collection of older and contemporary watercolors, oils, photographs, fabric art and sculpture. Works by Charles and Maurice Prendergast provide a look at 19th-century seaside New England. Closed Monday. ~ Route 2, Williamstown; 413-597-2429, fax 413-458-9017; www.williams.edu/wcma, e-mail wcma@williams.edu.

In summer, the **Williamstown Theatre Festival** draws crowds from around the country. One of the nation's finest summer theater offerings, the festival showcases productions that are weightier than the average summer stock, such as *The Legend of Oedipus* and works by Anton Chekhov and Tennessee Williams. Regulars include Joanne Woodward and Paul Newman, Dianne Wiest and Olympia Dukakis. The schedule is usually announced in mid-May, and it's a good idea to order tickets as early as possible. Season runs from mid-June to late August. ~ P.O. Box 517, Williamstown, MA 01267; 413-597-3400 (box office), 413-597-3399 (information line); www.wtfestival.org.

Just west of the center of Williamstown, you'll find another fine-art museum. The **Sterling and Francine Clark Art Institute**, housed in a classical white marble building, has an extensive collection of 19th-century impressionist paintings, including ones by Renoir, Monet, Degas, Pisarro and Sisley, as well as older masters and 17th-century prints and drawings. Closed Monday from September through June. ~ 225 South Street, Williamstown; 413-458-9545, fax 413-458-2318; www.clark.williams.edu.

For a cool dip in some naturally therapeutic waters, turn north onto Route 7 and take a right onto Sand Springs Road to **Sand Springs Pool and Spa**. This place has a casual, family feel to it. People have been coming here since 1762 to take the natural, 74-degree waters. There is a large hot tub, an Olympic-size pool and a toddlers pool. Closed Labor Day to Memorial Day. Admission. ~ Sand Springs Road, Williamstown; 413-458-5205; www.sweet wood.org/archive/swim.htm.

From Williamstown center heading south, Route 43 to Hancock is a pleasant country drive with open countryside and rolling hills dotted with tumbledown barns. **Caretaker Farm** is one of the area's most successful community-supported organic farms, and owners Sam and Elizabeth Smith invite visitors to walk through their fields and admire their diverse crops. It's a good idea to call ahead before visiting. Closed Saturday afternoon and Sunday and from November through April. ~ Route 43, Williamstown; phone/fax 413-458-4309.

If you love the furniture and crafts of the Shakers, you may also enjoy learning more about how they lived, with a visit to **Hancock Shaker Village**. Restored in the 1960s, the Shaker settlement at Hancock was the third of 18 communities to be established by the followers of Mother Ann Lee in the early 19th century. At its height in the 1840s, the population in Hancock reached 250 members, divided into six groups called "families." The Shaker economy was built on agriculture, including the growing, processing and selling of medicinal herbs and seeds, as well as the crafting of furniture for which they have become so well known. The guides stationed in the buildings are an excellent source of information on the Shaker way of life. Crafts demonstrations take place on a

The Berkshires

VERMONT

22
7
2
22

Williamstown
North Adams
100
Whitcomb Summit

2
43
Mt Greylock State Res
7
▲ Mt Greylock
Adams
2
Trail
Mohawk Trail State Forest

NEW YORK

TACONIC RANGE

43
New Ashford
8
116
8A
8A
Savoy Mtn State Forest
8A

Lanesboro
Pontoosuc Lake
8A
Windsor State Forest
116

22
20
7
9
8
9

Onota Lake
Pittsfield

Hancock Shaker Village

THE BERKSHIRES

Worthington
112

90

Lenox
8
Trail

22
20
Lee

Stockbridge
South Lee
Tyringham
8
20
90

7
Appalachian
8
Otis
23

71
Great Barrington
23
23

23
South Egremont
41
Monterey

Mt Everett State Res
Housatonic River
Otis Reservoir

Mt Washington State Forest
Bash Bish Falls State Park
41
Sheffield

0   5 miles
0   5 kilometers

8

7
Canaan
44

CONNECTICUT

regular basis in many buildings, and the village's round stone barn, originally built in 1826, is a real sight to behold. For horticulturalists there are daily tours (guided or self-guided depending on time of year), occasional workshops and special dinners. In June 2000, a new gallery will open containing a permanent exhibit of gift drawings from Hancocks's collections. Open year-round but call ahead in winter. (Note: Visitors coming from the north on Route 7 should be aware that Hancock Shaker Village cannot be reached through the town of Hancock. Keep heading south toward Pittsfield and take Route 20 west.) Admission. ~ Route 20, Pittsfield; 413-443-0188, fax 413-447-9357; www.hancockshaker village.org, e-mail info@hancockshakervillage.org.

With a population of about 50,000, **Pittsfield** is the largest city in Berkshire County but it's not the most attractive. One exception to Pittsfield's otherwise dull demeanor is the **Berkshire Museum**. Established in 1903 by Zenas Crane, a member of the Crane paper family, the museum has 18 galleries of permanent and changing exhibitions, including works by a number of Hudson River School painters and early American portraits by Bierstadt, Copley and Peale. There are also classic and modern sculptures as well as an aquarium with a touch tank. Open daily in July and August; closed Monday the rest of the year. Admission. ~ Route 7, Pittsfield; 413-443-7171, fax 413-443-2135; www. berkshiremuseum.org, e-mail burger@berkshiremuseum.org.

Pittsfield is also home to **Arrowhead**, the house where Herman Melville wrote *Moby Dick* while living here from 1850 to 1863. Headquarters for the Berkshire County Historical Society, the house displays historical exhibitions, antique furnishings and costumes, and a video presentation. There is also a gift shop. Open daily from Memorial Day through October, and by appointment the rest of the year. ~ 780 Holmes Road, Pittsfield; 413-442-1793; www.mobydick.org.

"The **Lenox and Stockbridge** region is Berkshire in its best dress suit and evening gown," wrote the authors of a Federal Writ-

NORMAN ROCKWELL AMERICANA

Though there are "Norman Rockwell museums" in other places around New England, the **Norman Rockwell Museum** is the only collection of original paintings authorized by the Rockwell family. The museum houses the largest collection of Rockwell art in existence, including selections from his *Saturday Evening Post* covers, early drawings for *St. Nicholas* magazine, portraits and advertising works and the famous Four Freedoms and Main Street at Christmas. Admission. ~ Route 183, Stockbridge; 413-298-4100, fax 413-298-4145; www.nrm.org.

ers Project book on the Berkshires in 1939. The writers were no doubt assessing the remnants of the so-called "Gilded Age" in the days before income taxes, when the Vanderbilts, Carnegies, Roosevelts and others frolicked at their famous "Berkshire Cottages."

These estates, with their ornate architecture, elaborate furnishings and lovely gardens hold an allure even for the staunchest of socialists. For your viewing pleasure are 20 to 25 summer mansions from the time when Lenox was known as the "Inland Newport." Among these estates are:

The Mount was the home of Pulitzer Prize–winning author Edith Wharton from 1902 to 1911. Wharton, in her day a recognized expert on interior design, designed the interior as well as the gardens. The white American Classical mansion has marble floors and fireplaces, elaborate molding and plaster ceilings, and beautiful grounds. During the summer, Shakespeare and Company at the Mount performs the Bard's plays as well as plays based on Wharton's books and on episodes of her life. Open daily from Memorial Day through October. Admission. ~ Plunkett Street, Lenox; 413-637-1899, fax 413-637-0619; www.edithwharton. org, e-mail admin@edithwharton.org.

Chesterwood is a Colonial Revival mansion that served as the summer estate of Daniel Chester French, sculptor of *The Minuteman* and the Lincoln Memorial. French traveled widely, and his home is decorated with a remarkable collection of European and American furnishings, antiques and sculptures gathered in his travels. The grounds feature country gardens and woodland walks, and his studio houses the small-gauge railroad track that French used to move his sculptures into the natural light for viewing. The plaster casts of the Lincoln statue were made here and, as you'll see, still dominate the interior. Closed November through April. Admission. ~ Off of Route 183, Stockbridge; 413-298-3579, fax 413-298-3973.

Naumkeag, designed by Stanford White, was built in 1885 for Joseph Choate, the ambassador to England. The stately home remains an excellent example of turn-of-the-20th-century design, in its architecture as well as its landscaping and furnishings. Though it is not the largest of the mansions, Naumkeag's collection of antiques and porcelain from the Far East make it worth a visit. And, like those of the other cottages, the gardens and grounds are magnificent. Closed Columbus Day to Memorial Day. Admission. ~ Prospect Hill Road, Stockbridge; 413-298-3239, fax 413-298-5239; www.thetrustees.org, e-mail westregion@ttor.org.

Route 7 south of Lenox takes you through another piece of lovely farmland, where you'll get a sense of just how rural this area is. Before too long you'll come to the town of **Stockbridge**, a pretty, if increasingly glossy, small town whose tree-lined main street is dominated by small shops and the rambling wooden Red Lion Inn.

Stockbridge has been immortalized in popular culture in two very different ways: as the setting for Arlo Guthrie's song "Alice's Restaurant" (now La Fête Chez Vous) and as the subject of works by its most famous former resident, artist Norman Rockwell.

Stockbridge center, with many shops and small galleries, is worth a stroll. An interesting stop is the **Image Gallery**, owned by photojournalist Clemens Kalischer. Closed Sunday and Monday. ~ Main Street, Stockbridge; phone/fax 413-298-5500.

The home of poet William Cullen Bryant, **Great Barrington** is a departure from the country-style villages of Stockbridge and Lenox. Its funky downtown looks as though it came straight out of an old Jimmy Stewart movie.

For a scenic country drive, take Route 23 east from Great Barrington to Monterey, and head north to the town of Tyringham.

Santarella, featuring contemporary paintings, sculpture and ceramics, is in a fairytale-like cottage built in the 1920s by sculptor Sir Henry Kitson. The place can only be described as magical, with an undulating, 80-ton thatched roof, large, jutting stones built into its walls, and a sculpture garden with a lily pond and nature trail. Closed November through April. Admission. ~ 75 Main Road, Tyringham; 413-243-3260, fax 413-243-9178.

For further information on the Berkshires, contact the **Berkshire Hills Conference Visitors Bureau**. Closed Sunday. ~ Berkshire Common, West Street, Pittsfield; 413-443-9186, fax 413-443-1970; e-mail bvb@berkshires.org.

LODGING   This area offers a large selection of elegant accommodations and small bed and breakfasts. Restrictions are common here, however, and some of the room rate cards are as complicated as life insurance policies. In a nutshell: rates are highest (and they do get high!) on weekends in summer and fall; most places close to Lenox require a two-night minimum stay on weekends during Tanglewood season, from mid-June to early September.

Budget lodging is virtually impossible to find in the Berkshires. One economical strategy is to make a home base in towns slightly away from the often-crowded and expensive Lenox-Stockbridge area. To the north, Williamstown offers a wider price range of motels and inns, with fewer restrictions. Just south of Stockbridge, the small towns of South Egremont, Sheffield and Great Barrington have many historic and pretty inns and bed and breakfasts.

A resort built around a country-inn motif, **The Orchards** offers 47 rooms individually decorated in English antiques and fancy bedspreads, some with fireplaces, refrigerators and marble-floored bathrooms. The ambience here is one of quiet elegance, despite the inn's incongruous proximity to the Route 2 commercial strip. Tea is served each afternoon in the graciously appointed lobby, and guests get a chocolate chip cookie with their turned-down beds each evening. On-site amenities include a pool, a sauna, concierge service and a restaurant. ~ Route 2, Williamstown; 413-458-9611, 800-225-1517, fax 413-458-3273; www.orchardshotel. com, e-mail the-orchards@worldnet.att.net. ULTRA-DELUXE.

The **Maple Terrace Motel** is a budget-conscious traveler's find. The 17 rooms are clean with standard motel decor, but the Maple Terrace, set back from the street, is a bit quieter than others along the highway. Behind the motel is a two-acre field with a spacious swimming pool, picnic tables, a playground and several large weeping willow trees. This is a good place for families and is within walking distance of the Williamstown Theater Festival, shopping and restaurants. Continental breakfast. ~ 555 Main Street, Route 2, Williamstown; phone/fax 413-458-8101; www.mapleterrace. com, e-mail stay@mapleterrace.com. MODERATE.

River Bend Farm is a historic bed and breakfast set in a tavern built in 1770 by Colonel Benjamin Simonds, one of the founders of Williamstown. The place has been meticulously restored and has shared baths and four rooms, each individually decorated in Colonial-style antiques. Its location makes it convenient to the Williams College campus. Expanded continental breakfast. Closed November through March. ~ 643 Simonds Road, Williamstown; 413-458-3121. MODERATE.

◄ HIDDEN

The Canyon Ranch in the Berkshires is an East Coast version of a famous Tucson fitness resort. It's housed at the 120-acre estate called Bellefontaine, one of the most ornate of the original Berkshire "cottages" and a replica of the French Petit Trianon built by Louis XV. The 126-room resort is geared for busy city folk looking for a bit of down time away from it all. There's a full fitness program, gourmet "spa cuisine," indoor and outdoor pools, walking trails and gardens. ~ Bellefontaine, Kemble Street, Lenox; 413-637-4100, 800-326-7080, fax 413-637-0057; www.canyon ranch.com. ULTRA-DELUXE.

A very homey Berkshire cottage, **Garden Gables Inn** is a lovely white clapboard house built in 1780. Though it is located within walking distance of downtown Lenox, the inn is quiet and relaxed, with nice gardens and a swimming pool. The inn's 17 rooms are individually decorated in a mix of styles, and all have private baths; some have jacuzzis or fireplaces, others balconies with a view of the pool. The inn has many regular long-term visitors. Full breakfast is offered in a small dining room. ~ 135 Main Street, Lenox; 413-637-0193, fax 413-637-4554; www.lenoxinn.com, e-mail gardeninn@aol.com. DELUXE TO ULTRA-DELUXE.

The **Village Inn** is an 18th-century hostelry with 32 rooms, all with private baths. All rooms are furnished with country antiques, some with working fireplaces and four-poster beds. This Federal-style building has served as an inn since 1775, and the innkeepers have restored and modernized it without destroying its integrity.

The low-beamed tavern downstairs offers a full bar. This place has a comfortable, homey feel despite its size and is conveniently located in the center of Lenox. ~ 16 Church Street, Lenox; 413-637-0020, 800-253-0917, fax 413-637-9756; www.villageinn-lenox.com, e-mail villinn@vgernet.net. MODERATE TO ULTRA-DELUXE.

Located right in the village of Lenox but on three very private acres, the **Walker House Inn** is a gay-friendly hostelry with eight rooms (all with private baths). It's a lovely house, built in 1804 with an addition built in 1906. The rooms are named after composers and decorated individually. There are lots of antiques around and fireplaces in many of the guest rooms. The parlor has a grand piano and another fireplace, and movies are shown on a 12-foot-wide screen in the library. ~ 64 Walker Street, Lenox; 413-637-1271, 800-235-3098; www.walkerhouse.com, e-mail phoudek@vgernet.net. DELUXE TO ULTRA-DELUXE.

Four miles north of Lenox is **Summer Hill Farm**, a late 1800s farmhouse on a 20-acre horse farm. Rooms are decorated with antiques and have their own baths; three have fireplaces. There is a one-bedroom cottage and a three-bedroom farmhouse available, both with full kitchens. The clientele is predominately straight, though Summer Hill is gay-friendly. A full breakfast is included in the price. ~ 950 East Street, Lenox; 413-442-2057, 800-442-2059; e-mail innkeeper@summerhillfarm.com. MODERATE TO DELUXE.

Red Lion Inn is a New England classic. Built originally in 1773 as a stagecoach stop, the inn was destroyed by fire and rebuilt in 1897. Today, the rambling wooden structure is one of the few remaining old wood hotels in the country. An icon of the Berkshires, the Red Lion serves as the centerpiece of Stockbridge Center. The lobby-parlor, with its fireplace, comfortable old couches and rich oriental rugs, is always full of visitors and diners. And there may be no finer place to enjoy a summer afternoon drink than from a rocking chair on the front porch. There are 110 rooms, including some suites with parlors, decorated with antiques and reproductions. Though it offers modern amenities like an outdoor pool, the Red Lion is an elegant old lady of a place that conjures up images of a bygone era. ~ Main Street, Stockbridge; 413-298-5545, fax 413-298-5130; www.redlioninn.com. ULTRA-DELUXE.

HIDDEN ► The **Historic Merrell Inn** wears its age well, having welcomed guests since 1794, when it was the next-to-last stop on a busy stagecoach route between northwestern Connecticut and the Berkshires. Original furnishings, such as the wooden birdcage bar in the dining room, the only complete and unmodified one of its kind in the country, adorn the inn. The ten guest rooms are luxurious and, for the most part, quite large, although a few of the bathrooms are small but adequate. Some beds have canopies, and four of the rooms have working fireplaces. The owners continually search for antique furnishings that complement the inn's historic past. Take a look at the book in the dining room that records the names of the inn's visitors and their horses on the corresponding date in the early 19th century. ~ 1565 Pleasant Street, South Lee; 413-243-1794, 800-243-1794, fax 413-243-2669; www.merrell inn.com, e-mail info@merrellinn.com. DELUXE TO ULTRA-DELUXE.

For a bed and breakfast that focuses on informal hospitality —the innkeeper calls it a "chintz-free zone"—spend a night or two at **Race Brook Lodge** in the southwestern corner of Massachusetts. It's a restored barn with a variety of rooms (all with private bath). It also has suites, which are perfect for a small group. The country decor—quilts, understated stenciling and hooked rugs on plank floors—allows the beauty of the building to speak for itself. Take a walk from the lodge to the Race Brook waterfall, then up to the Appalachian Trail. Or poke around in the nearby antique shops: Sheffield is a mecca for antiquing fiends from all over New England. ~ 864 South Under Mountain Road/Route 41, Sheffield; 413-229-2916, 800-725-6343, fax 413-229-6629; www. rblodge.com, e-mail rblodge@bcn.net. MODERATE TO DELUXE.

The **Egremont Inn** is a cozy country inn with 19 rooms decorated in 19th-century furnishings. A feeling of subdued elegance is conveyed by a long white porch where guests enjoy coffee and brunch during summer months. A Colonial-era tavern with a low, beamed ceiling adds to the ambience. The Egremont Inn has a full dining room, as well as a pool and tennis courts. Modified American plan offered on weekends, ultra-deluxe; bed and breakfast Sunday through Thursday. ~ Old Sheffield Road, South Egremont; 413-528-2111, 800-859-1780, fax 413-528-3284; www. egremontinn.com, e-mail egremontinn@taconic.net. MODERATE TO ULTRA-DELUXE.

Located in a late-18th-century New England home, the **Weathervane Inn** has 11 rooms, all with private baths, plus a swimming pool. This is a comfortable, informal place with a regular clientele. Modified American plan offered on weekends; bed and breakfast Sunday through Thursday. ~ Route 23, South Egremont; 413-528-9580, fax 413-528-1713; www.weathervaneinn.com, e-mail innkeeper@weathervaneinn.com. DELUXE TO ULTRA-DELUXE.

Days Inn offers proximity to southern Berkshire attractions in a motel setting, with a renovated pool area slated to open summer of 2000. For those who like to stay in places with televisions and no innkeepers to talk to, this is one of the few motels in the region. ~ 372 Main Street, Great Barrington; phone/fax 413-528-3150; www.newenglanddays.com/greatbarrington. MODERATE TO DELUXE.

The **Turning Point** offers a nonsmoking environment in a handsome, 1790s brick inn that served as a stagecoach stop in the 19th century. The inn has six rooms and a two-bedroom ultra-deluxe-priced cottage, with lovely grounds and hiking trails through the surrounding woods and fields. There are two chefs on the premises, so prepare to eat well. ~ 3 Lake Buel Road at Route 23, Great Barrington; 413-528-4777; e-mail ordeno@aol. com. MODERATE TO DELUXE.

Berkshire and Greater Springfield Bed and Breakfast can match you up with small country inns in the Berkshire area. ~ P.O. Box 211, Williamsburg, MA 01096; 413-268-7244, fax 413-268-7243; e-mail berkbb33@javanet.com.

DINING

There are many restaurants to choose from in the Berkshires, roughly divided into two classes: the expensive, fancy places that draw weekenders and visitors, and the places where locals eat, which are generally less expensive, casual and strong on all-American, meat-and-potatoes menus.

HIDDEN ►

Diner fans will adore **Miss Adams Diner**, a 1949 Worcester lunch car being restored to its original condition. Here the owners serve traditional diner breakfasts and lunches, along with some special touches, like cold blueberry soup and buckwheat flapjacks. Great homemade pies! Closed Monday. ~ 53 Park Street, Adams; 413-743-5300; e-mail mdiner777@aol.com. BUDGET.

Church Street Cafe offers an eclectic lunch and dinner menu in a pleasant outdoor café or indoor setting in the heart of Lenox's shopping district. Lunch features sandwiches and burgers, as well as more exotic fare like Louisiana gumbo, tabouli salad and bean quesadillas; dinner features Thai beef salad, Jamaican "jerked" chicken and red chile pasta with corn, peppers, cilantro and jalapeños. Closed Sunday and Monday from Columbus Day to Memorial Day. ~ 65 Church Street, Lenox; 413-637-2745. MODERATE TO DELUXE.

Gateways Restaurant is one of the most highly acclaimed dining spots in Lenox. The restaurant is located on the first floor of the small and elegant Gateways Inn, built in 1912 as the summer mansion of Harley Procter of Procter and Gamble. The entranceway is graced with a sweeping mahogany staircase, rich tapestries and beautiful flower arrangements. Gateways offers southern Italian cuisine such as veal cutlet Milanese, (sliced thin, lightly coated with bread crumbs, and sautéed to a golden finish), and ravioli filled with fresh lobster, served in a light tomato crème sauce. ~ 51 Walker Street, Lenox; 413-637-2532; www.gatewaysinn.com, e-mail gateways@berkshire.net. MODERATE TO ULTRA-DELUXE.

Wheatleigh is a restaurant of some renown, within walking distance of Tanglewood. It's a special spot, known for fine food and formal service, located in a restored 19th-century Italian palazzo built for a countess. The decor recalls the splendor of the Gilded Age, with a fireplace and crystal chandeliers. Wheatleigh serves Americanized French cuisine in four-course and six-course prix-fixe meals, and the menu includes such imaginative items as citrus-marinated Scottish salmon on a wild-rice blini with Osetra caviar and seared breast of free-range duck with potato, vegetables and fresh black huckleberries. Reservations required; jackets for men are preferred. Open daily during the summer. Abbreviated hours the rest of the year. ~ Hawthorne Road, Lenox; 413-637-0610; e-mail wheatleigh@taconic.net. ULTRA-DELUXE.

The **Red Lion Inn** has a menu that is contemporary New England, serving roast turkey and prime rib. You can choose the Colonial-style formal dining room, with pink-and-rose wallpaper, Norman Rockwell prints on the walls, and fresh flowers on the table. Or try the more casual tavern, with its publike atmosphere, wide-plank floorboards and beamed ceiling. In good weather, meals are served in the courtyard. ~ Main Street, Stockbridge; 413-298-5545, fax 413-298-5130; www.redlioninn.com. DELUXE TO ULTRA-DELUXE.

Cheesecake Charlie's is a café with a split personality. It specializes in both health-food and decadent desserts. You can get everything from a vegetarian chili to a rich, creamy (you guessed it) cheesecake. Other healthy choices include tofu salads and organic turkey sandwiches. The bakery has all sorts of butter-heavy pastries as well as 55 varieties of cheesecakes. ~ 271 Main Street, Great Barrington; 413-528-7790. BUDGET TO MODERATE.

A great place to go for a good (but not ridiculously inexpensive) meal is **Jodi's**. You can take your pick of several pasta dishes or choose seafood, chicken, veal or lamb. The restaurant is in a mid-18th-century building and has lots of antiques and hardwood floors. ~ 327 Stockbridge Road, Great Barrington; 413-528-6064, fax 413-528-0634. MODERATE TO DELUXE.

The **Castle Street Cafe** is a lively bistro known for its creative pastas and grilled fish dishes. It's a handsome spot with an exposed brick wall. There's a full jazz bar in the back. Closed Tuesday. ~ 10 Castle Street, Great Barrington; 413-528-5244; www.castlestreetcafe.com, e-mail mballon@bcn.net. MODERATE TO DELUXE.

Once an old blacksmith's shop, and yes, even an old mill, **The Old Mill** is now one of the nicer restaurants in the southern Berkshires. The menu includes grilled salmon filet with over leek mashed potatoes with merlot sauce and *hericot vert* in addition to chicken, steaks and chops. The building itself is a handsome one, set on a river, with large beams, rough wood paneling and old tools decorating the interior walls. Closed Monday from November through May. ~ Route 23, South Egremont; 413-528-1421, fax 413-528-0007. DELUXE.

Serious antique hunters head to the southern Berkshires and the towns of Egremont, South Egremont and Sheffield. There are dozens of shops in this corner of the state, featuring pieces from Early American to European to deco to plain old junk.

SHOPPING

Text continued on page 410.

The Sounds of Music in Rural Massachusetts

It's said that New England has only two seasons, July and winter. That's not exactly true, of course, but folks here do try to pack as much as possible into the fleeting times of good weather. Case in point: the large number of concerts and music festivals held in this area during summer and autumn, many spreading out under the warm, open skies. In central and western Massachusetts, visitors have some rich choices when it comes to music, from Cuban jazz under the stars to chamber music in a church.

The undisputed king of the music festivals in this region, and perhaps in the whole country, takes place at **Tanglewood**, the 600-acre Lenox summer home of the Boston Symphony Orchestra. ~ Before mid-June, contact Symphony Hall, Boston, MA 02115; 617-266-1492. After mid-June, contact West Street, Lenox, MA 01240; 413-637-1600; www.bso.org.

Tanglewood takes its name from a story by Nathaniel Hawthorne, and, with its tall and stately pine trees, rolling lawns and nearby mountains, the place is renowned for its physical beauty as well as the quality of the musicians and composers who perform there. These have included Leonard Bernstein, John Williams, Yo-Yo Ma, Itzhak Perlman and jazz performers like Ella Fitzgerald and Ray Charles.

Weekend symphony concerts are held Friday through Sunday in July and August, and chamber music concerts take place most Thursdays and other selected weeknights. Saturday morning rehearsals are open to the public (admission), providing an opportunity to see music-making in a more relaxed setting. Seating is available in the Shed, a covered, open-air theater, or, more reasonably, on the lawn. The tradition on the lawn is to bring a blanket or lawn chairs and an elaborate picnic lunch or dinner, complete with candelabra and champagne.

Tanglewood is just one of many music series and festivals in this region, offering all types of music in some spectacular settings. A sampling of some others:

South Mountain Concerts, a chamber music series running from September to mid-October, takes place in the acoustically superb, 400-seat South Mountain Concert Hall, built in 1918 and listed in the National Historic Register. ~ Box 23, Pittsfield; 413-442-2106.

Stockbridge Summer Music Series includes light opera, classical music, cabaret and jazz concerts held in a turn-of-the-20th-century mansion (Seven Hills Country Inn in Lenox). A mix of prominent regional and international artists performs Monday and Tuesday in July and August. ~ 148 Summer Street, Lanesboro, MA 01237; 413-443-1138; www.baygo.com/ssms.

Mohawk Trail Concerts offers summer and fall chamber music concerts in the intimate setting of a charming old white clapboard Federated church on the Mohawk Trail in Charlemont. ~ P.O. Box 75, Shelburne Falls, MA 01370; 413-625-9511, 888-682-6873, fax 413-625-0221; www.mohawktrailconcerts.org, e-mail info@mohawktrailconcerts.org.

Bright Moments Music Festival is one of Amherst's biggest summer assets, featuring Pan-African and jazz concerts on the lawn by the campus pond Thursday through Saturday in mid-July.

Although it's always a good idea to reserve tickets ahead of time for most of these events, last-minute seats are generally available. Check out the local newspapers for concert dates and times, and bring a sweater for those summer evenings that can turn cool once the sun goes down. ~ University of Massachusetts; 413-545-2877; www.umass.edu/fac.

For 18th-and-19th century formal antique furniture and decorative accessories, stop by **Darr Antiques and Interiors**. ~ 28 South Main Street, Sheffield; 413-229-7773.

Or check out **Centuryhurst Berkshire Antique Gallery** for Early American clocks, Wedgwood, 1850s country furniture, and a large collection of Wallace Nutting photographs. Forget the bargains here, however; the area's proximity to New York City money has raised the antique ante substantially. ~ Main Street, Sheffield; 413-229-8131.

NIGHTLIFE   During the summer **The Orchards** features soft rock by a pianist in its pub. ~ Route 2, Williamstown; 413-458-9611.

Lenox is home to **Tanglewood**, where the Boston Symphony Orchestra performs through the summer months. For program and ticket information call 617-266-1492 (between October and June) or 413-637-1600 (between June and September). ~ Route 183, Lenox; www.bso.org.

Shakespeare and Company offers theatrical performances during the May-through-October season. ~ 2 Plunkett Street (off Route 7), Lenox; 413-637-1199; www.shakespeare.org, e-mail mccleary@shakespeare.org.

Jacob's Pillow Dance Festival produces summer dance performances featuring companies from a variety of distant lands, including Cambodia, Indonesia and India. Closed September to late June. ~ George Carter Road, Becket; 413-243-0745; www.jacobs pillow.org, e-mail jacobspillow@taconic.net.

The **Lion's Den** regularly showcases folk music with occasional bluegrass, blues and jazz. ~ Red Lion Inn, Main Street, Stockbridge; 413-298-5545; www.lionsden.com.

BEACHES & PARKS   **SAVOY MOUNTAIN STATE FOREST** 🏃 🚴 🐎 🛶 🚣 ⛵ 🚤 🎣 Nearly 11,000 acres, this popular retreat bordering on the Berkshire hills is favored by families. North and South ponds offer fishing and swimming, and campsites are in an old apple orchard. The park has miles of hiking trails, including a route to Tannery Falls. The dramatic set of cascading waterfalls that once powered small mills there is now one of the prettiest spots in western Massachusetts. There's good trout fishing in North Pond, and trout and bass are found in Burnett and Bogg ponds. North Pond and South Pond have swimming beaches. Non-motorized boats are allowed. There are picnic areas, restrooms and a nature center. Closed for repairs, the park will reopen summer 2000. Parking fee, $2. ~ Off Routes 2 and 116, Savoy; 413-663-8469, fax 413-664-8614.

▲ There are 45 tent/RV sites (no hookups); $12 per night for Massachusetts residents, $15 per night for non-residents; information, 413-664-9567. Closed mid-October to mid-May. There are also cabins available year-round that sleep up to four people

($25 per night); reservations are required and are taken six months in advance.

WINDSOR STATE FOREST 🏃 🏊 ⟋ This spot is known for the spectacular Windsor Jambs, a half-mile-long series of waterfalls that travel through sheer granite cliff gorges of up to 100 feet. There are many old roads and trails for hiking and a good 100-foot sandy beach on a dammed-up spot on the Westfield River. There's good trout fishing in the West Branch of the Westfield River. This is a popular place for families with small children. You'll find picnic areas and restrooms. Closed Labor Day through Memorial Day. Day-use fee, $2. ~ On River Road off Route 9, Windsor; 413-684-0948, in summer; 413-442-8928, in winter; www.magnet.state.ma.us.

▲ There are 23 sites, for tents only; $4 per night.

MOUNT GREYLOCK STATE RESERVATION 🏃 🚲 ⛺ If you have time for a visit to only one park on your tour of the area, this is the one to see. This 11,000-acre reserve is atop the state's highest mountain. Immortalized by Thoreau, Hawthorne and Melville, Mount Greylock is noted for the number of rare species of bird and plant life, and the views in all directions are truly breathtaking. Hiking trails—including a stretch of the Appalachian Trail—and Nordic ski trails are plentiful. Facilities include picnic areas and restrooms; Bascom Lodge (413-743-1591) has a snack bar and offers evening camp dinners by reservation. ~ Off Route 7 in Lanesboro or off Route 2 in North Adams; 413-499-4262.

▲ There are 35 sites; $6 per night.

MT. WASHINGTON STATE FOREST 🏃 🚲 🐎 ⛺ 🛶 🚣 ⟋ This 5000-acre expanse on the New York–Connecticut–Massachusetts border spreads out over mountainous, densely wooded land, and there's a feeling of isolation and solitude here. Even during daylight, watch for deer as you drive into the area; they seem to be everywhere. **Bash Bish Falls State Park**, within the state forest, is home to Bash Bish Falls, featuring 80-foot drops and cascading pools, along with a serene view of farmland. You can also angle for trout in brooks and streams. All this provides a great escape from the sometimes-madding crowds of Stockbridge and Lenox. Non-motorized boats only. There are picnic areas and restrooms. ~ Off Route 41, Mount Washington; 413-528-0330.

▲ There are 15 primitive, hike-in sites; no fee.

The large number of lakes, ponds and rivers in this region provide ample opportunities for paddlers.

Outdoor Adventures

CANOEING & KAYAKING

CENTRAL MASSACHUSETTS Canoe, kayak and rowboat rentals are available at **Fin and Feather Sports**. ~ Route 140, Upton; 508-529-3901.

PIONEER VALLEY Zoar Outdoors offers raft trips, canoe rentals, and canoe and kayak instruction on the Deerfield River. ~ Mohawk Trail, Charlemont; 413-339-4010; www.zoaroutdoor.com.

THE BERKSHIRES Canoe and kayak rentals are available through **Berkshire Outfitters**. ~ Route 8, Adams; 413-743-5900; www.berkshireoutfitters.com.

FISHING

A fishing license is required for all freshwater fishing in Massachusetts. You're likely to hook trout and bass in the numerous lakes and streams. The Deerfield, Connecticut and Westfield rivers are some of the more popular spots.

PIONEER VALLEY In Northampton, try **Jim's Flies & Supplies** for all your fishing equipment needs. ~ 90 King Street; 413-586-3650.

THE BERKSHIRES Freshwater gear is available at **Dick Moon Sporting Goods**. ~ 114 Fenn Street, Pittsfield; 413-442-8281.

SKIING

The downhill ski areas in this region are tame compared to their sisters to the north, but lift lines are often shorter, the ambience less pretentious and the lift tickets cheaper. Lessons and rentals are available at most of these sites; they're good places to take the family. Those who prefer cross-country will find some wonderful spots in the region, from open farmland to wooded state parks. Some state parks' trails are groomed by the ubiquitous (and noisy) snowmobile crowd.

PIONEER VALLEY In Princeton, hit the slopes at **Wachusett Mountain**, which has a 1000-foot vertical drop. Downhill and cross-country skiing as well as snowboarding are available on this ski area, serviced by 18 trails. ~ 499 Mountain Road, off Route 140; 978-464-2300; www.wachusett.com.

In Charlemont, **Berkshire East** has a 1180-foot vertical drop. Snowboarders share the runs with downhill skiers, though there is a half pipe on one slope, Exhibition. ~ Mohawk Trail; 413-339-6617; www.berkshireeast.com.

Twenty-six miles of wide, well-groomed Nordic trails crosshatch **Northfield Mountain**. ~ Route 63, Northfield; 413-659-3714; www.nu.com.

For a more rustic ski on narrower cross-country paths through the woods, try **Stump Sprouts Ski Touring Center and Guest Lodge** with 25 kilometers of trails. ~ West Hill Road, Hawley; 413-339-4265; www.stumpsprouts.com.

THE BERKSHIRES In New Ashford, try the runs of family-friendly **Brodie Mountain Ski Area**, known for being the highest skiing elevation in Massachusetts at 2700 feet. Four double chair lifts serve 30 percent beginner, 45 percent intermediate, and 25 percent expert trials. A snow park is open to boarders. ~ Route 7; 413-443-4752; www.skibrodie.com, e-mail brodie@vgernet.net.

In Hancock, test the slopes at **Jiminy Peak, the Mountain Resort**, with an elevation of 2380 feet and a vertical drop of 1140 feet, nine lifts, and more than 11 miles of trails. ~ Corey Road; 413-738-5500; www.jiminypeak.com, e-mail info@jiminy.com.

Two terrain parks cover **Butternut Basin**, which has an elevation of 1800 feet and a vertical drop of 1000 feet. Six chair lifts (and two surface lifts) carry skiers throughout the trails—rated 20 percent beginner, 60 percent intermediate and 20 percent expert. The season runs from late November to early April. ~ Route 23, Great Barrington; 413-528-2000; www.skibutternut.com, e-mail ski@bsm.net.

GOLF

Wide-open spaces make for several good golfing spots in the region. Club and cart rentals are available at these 18-hole courses.

CENTRAL MASSACHUSETTS Tee off at **Crumpin-Fox Club**, a semiprivate course. ~ Parmenter Road, Bernardston; 413-648-9101; www.sandri.com. The challenging **Green Hill Golf Course** is located at the second-highest point in Worcester. Golfers enjoy spectacular views of the city down below. ~ Marsh Avenue, Worcester; 508-852-0913.

THE BERKSHIRES The **Waubeeka Golf Links** is a public facility with a combination of flat and hilly terrain. ~ Routes 7 and 43, South Williamstown; 413-458-8355. **Skyline Country Club** has a public course with scenic views. ~ 405 South Main Street, Route 7, Lanesboro; 413-445-5584.

BIKING

The steep mountains of western Massachusetts make two-wheeled travel between regions difficult, but once you're settled in, bicycling is a great way to explore the country backroads.

PIONEER VALLEY The Amherst–Northampton area offers some fairly flat and easy rides. The **Northampton Bicycle Path** begins at the end of State Street and ends up 2.3 miles later in Look Park. Several local bicycle groups also offer weekend day trips, including the **Franklin Hampshire Freewheelers** of western Massachusetts and Connecticut. Overnight camping trips are also occasionally arranged. Schedules for the group's trips and events are available in local bike shops. ~ 413-527-4877; www.freewheelers.org.

THE BERKSHIRES **Brooks Country Cycling and Hiking Tours** offers weekend tours that include inn accommodations in the Lenox-Stockbridge area. Day trips through the Berkshires provide wonderful views of the countryside and rolling hills. Rental information is available. ~ 140 West 83rd Street, New York, NY 10024; 212-874-5151, 800-284-8954; www.brookscountrycycling.com, e-mail brookscct@aol.com.

Bike Rentals Bikes, repairs and accessories are found at each of these locations. No bike tours are offered; however, information about trips in the area is available. In the Berkshires, **Valley Bicycles** rents mountain and hybrid bikes. ~ 319 Main Street, Amherst; 413-256-0880. In the Pioneer Valley, **The Spoke** specializes in sales and repairs. ~ 618 Main Street, Williamstown; 413-458-3456. **Plaine's Bike Golf Ski** rents bikes by the day, week or month. ~ 55 West Housatonic Street, Pittsfield; 413-499-0294.

HIKING

There's no better way to experience the natural beauty of the hills and mountains of this region than on your own two feet—particularly during fall foliage season, when the highways can seem like parking lots. Hiking opportunities abound at any of the region's state parks and conservation areas.

Some private companies offer tours geared to the serious hiker. **New England Hiking Holidays** leads hiking tours of the Berkshires as well as other New England locales. Trips range from two to eight days. Lodging and meals are included. ~ P.O. Box 1648, North Conway, NH 03860; 603-356-9696; www.nehikingholidays.com. Nature photographer and tracker **Paul Rezendes** combines hiking tours with nature photography and animal tracking workshops. ~ Bearsden Road, Royalston, MA 01368; 978-249-8810; www.mossbrook.com/rez.

All distances listed for hiking trails are one way unless otherwise noted.

CENTRAL MASSACHUSETTS The **Mid-State Trail** (91 miles) travels from Mount Watatic at the New Hampshire state border through Worcester County to the Rhode Island border. The trail offers a mixed bag of central Massachusetts scenery, traveling along old cart roads, through forests and across open fields. You can pick up stretches of the trail at any of several spots in the Worcester area, including Douglas State Forest and Rutland State Park.

Wachusett Mountain State Reservation offers a comprehensive network of 18 trails (total 17 miles) through nearly 2800 acres, with some steep-going in parts. Trails wend through hardwood forests of oak and maple, past stands of mountain laurel, spring wildflowers, ponds and meadows. You may see wildlife on the mountain, and this area offers some good trails for fall foliage vistas. ~ Mountain Road, Princeton; 978-464-2987.

PIONEER VALLEY The **Laughing Brook Education Center** and Wildlife Sanctuary (Hampden; 413-566-8034) offers several short trails that take you along the Laughing Brook (named by author Thornton Burgess, a one-time resident), a pond and the surrounding forest. The Burgess home, the oldest residence in Hampden, may be toured during the summer.

At **Arcadia Wildlife Sanctuary** (413-584-3009; www.mass audubon.org) in Easthampton, the **Fern Trail** (1 mile) takes you past many different types of ferns and includes an observation tower for birdwatching. It is one of many self-guided trails that wind through some 600 acres of forests on an ancient oxbow of the Connecticut River.

The **Enfield Lookout Trail** (3 miles) at Quabbin Park leads up to the Enfield Overlook, from which you can spot eagles in the winter months. The trail is part of a 22-mile network that takes you through the state's largest piece of wilderness land.

At Northfield Mountain Recreation and Environmental Center (413-659-3714; www.nu.com), the **Hidden Quarry Nature Trail** (1 mile) offers a minicourse in the geology and natural history of the upper Pioneer Valley. The trail winds past the ancient beds of Lake Hitchcock, as well as porcupine dens, woods wildflowers and stands of eastern white pine.

THE BERKSHIRES   **Pike's Pond Trail** (.5 mile), at Pleasant Valley Wildlife Sanctuary (413-637-0320) in Lenox, cuts through fields and forest and ends up near beaver habitat on the pond and nearby Yokun Brook. Other trails at the sanctuary run past meadows, a hemlock gorge and a hummingbird garden.

One of the Berkshires' better-known hiking spots is Bartholomew's Cobble, a rocky-topped hill named for 18th-century farmer George Bartholomew. The **Bailey Trail** (1 mile) at the Cobble is a large loop that leads into the **Sparrow Trail** (1 mile). It's a gentle walk along the flood plain of the Housatonic River, through silver maple groves and rich deciduous woods and past an old oxbow. The Cobble offers wonderful views of the Housatonic Valley and, in late April and early May, a beautiful array of wildflowers.

This area is easily accessible from **Route 90**, the **Massachusetts Turnpike**, which runs the entire length of the state's southern half and has exits at Worcester, Sturbridge, Springfield and Stockbridge.

From Boston, **Route 2** offers a scenic highway route to the famed Mohawk Trail and the northern portions of central and western Massachusetts.

Transportation

CAR

AIR

Many people fly into Boston's **Logan International Airport** (see Chapter Four). The area is also served by **Bradley International Airport** in Windsor Locks, Connecticut (see Chapter Two), near Hartford, and **Worcester Municipal Airport**, a smaller but increasingly popular alternative to Logan, which is serviced by Continental Express and USAir Express. Those who are combining a trip to the Berkshires with a visit to Vermont may want to use **Albany County Airport** in Albany, New York.

Peter Pan Trailways (413-781-3320) provides regular shuttles between Bradley International and the Springfield Bus Terminal at 1780 Main Street.

There's no public transportation to or from the airport. **Worcester Airport Limousine** provides door-to-door van and minibus shuttle service between the airport and points in Worcester County, including Sturbridge. ~ 508-756-4834.

Taxis serving the Worcester airport include **Yellow Cab** (508-754-3211), **Arrow Cab** (508-756-5184) and **Red Cab** (508-752-5601).

BUS

All long-distance bus lines operate from terminals at 75 Madison Street, Worcester, and 1780 Main Street, Springfield.

Greyhound Bus Lines (800-231-2222) links Worcester and Springfield with the Berkshires, Boston and New York City. **Peter Pan Trailways** (800-343-9999) provides transportation to Boston; points west, including Springfield, Amherst, Northampton, the Berkshires and Albany; and points south, including Hartford and New York City. **Bonanza Bus Lines, Inc.** (800-556-3815) connects Springfield with the Berkshires, Albany and Providence, Rhode Island.

TRAIN

Amtrak serves the Worcester area from New York City and Albany. The "Montrealer" leaves New York City each day with stops in Amherst, and there are several trains daily between Springfield and New York's Pennsylvania Station. ~ 45 Shrewsbury Street, Worcester; 66 Lyman Street, Springfield; 800-872-7245.

CAR RENTALS

From the Worcester airport, you can rent a car from **Avis Rent A Car** (800-331-1212), **Hertz Rent A Car** (800-654-3131) or **National Car Rental** (800-328-4567).

PUBLIC TRANSIT

In central Massachusetts, **Worcester Regional Transit Authority** has bus service to local destinations within Worcester County. ~ 508-791-2389. In the Pioneer Valley, **Pioneer Valley Transit Authority** offers frequent service throughout greater Springfield, Holyoke, Northampton and Amherst. ~ 413-781-7882. During the school year, the free **Five-College Bus Service** links the campuses of the University of Massachusetts, Smith College, Mount Holyoke College, Amherst College and Hampshire College. ~ 413-545-0056. **Greenfield Montague Transportation Area** provides bus service throughout greater Greenfield, Amherst, Montague and Turners Falls. ~ 413-773-9478.

In the Berkshires, Berkshire Regional Transit Authority links Pittsfield with Williamstown, North Adams, Lenox, Lee, Stockbridge and Great Barrington. ~ 413-499-2782.

EIGHT

Vermont

Vermont offers a soothing dose of old-fashioned Americana, a carefully tended piece of pastoral utopia that's down-home, uphill and intrinsically genuine. Here, dreams are lived, farms are cultivated and children are raised the traditional ways. Vermonters are at peace with their land—and it shows.

Its candid beauty is unpretentious and beguiling, a patchwork of slumbering red barns, tangled country roads and old covered bridges riveted against a backdrop of emerald mountains that twist through the heart of the state. Forming the backbone of Vermont's terrain, those towering Green Mountains—New England's oldest range—burst forth some five billion years ago when the earth's crust trembled and buckled.

Though only 9528 square miles in size, Vermont explodes with soul-gripping tableaux—alpine ridges and surging rivers, sporadic flatlands and miles of untamed wilderness. Skinny at the bottom and wide on top, this New England wedge spans an easy 151 miles in length and ranges in width from 41 miles at the Massachusetts border to 90 miles at the Canadian line.

But more than just a spot to behold, Vermont is a place to *be*. For its magic persists not only in its glorious scenery but also in its illustrious history and fastidious Yankee ideals and uncomplicated mode of existence.

Vermont may be the only landlocked New England state (a detail many Vermonters remain quite touchy about), but travelers need only scan the shores of vast Lake Champlain to find a coastline whose beauty parallels any Atlantic Ocean vista.

It was, in fact, that extraordinary lake that seduced the state's first European explorers back in 1609. Frenchman Samuel de Champlain, accompanied by native Algonquian Indians, who told great tales of mysterious waters, led an expedition from Canada and instantly claimed the lake (modestly naming it for himself) and surrounding lands for France.

During the next two centuries, the French, British and Dutch grappled to control the waterway, the sixth largest freshwater lake in the United States. The scrap was finally settled during the War of 1812, when an American naval fleet won a battle off Valcour Island.

Vermont found itself entangled in a different kind of tug-of-war during the mid-1700s, when its territory was claimed by both New York and New Hampshire. England eventually ruled in favor of New York, prompting settlers who had come from New Hampshire to organize a Vermont military force known as the Green Mountain Boys. This troupe, led by Ethan Allen, harassed New York landholders and went on to defeat the British in several decisive American Revolution battles, including the Battle of Bennington.

A flamboyant patriot determined to conquer any who attempted to steal his precious state, Allen vowed to preserve the independence of Vermont or "retire with my hardy Green Mountain boys into the caverns of the mountains and make war on all mankind."

Though New Hampshire inevitably surrendered its claims to Vermont, New York persisted. In July of 1777, Vermonters called a convention in the town of Windsor, drew up a constitution and declared their independence.

Drafted by 72 delegates who met for seven arduous days in a town tavern, the constitution prohibited slavery and was the first to establish suffrage for all men. According to local lore, the Windsor document was nearly abandoned by the delegates, who were about to dash off to fight advancing British forces at the state's west border when a fierce storm arose and prevented their leaving.

Despite pleas to the Continental Congress for recognition as a state, Vermont was forced to remain an independent republic for 14 years because of boundary disputes with New York. Finally, in 1791, both sides acquiesced and Vermont became the 14th state.

Early 19th-century Vermont was a land of milk and honey, where cows outnumbered people and people took to fashioning grand Victorian estates and lobbying for abolition. But prosperous times turned tumultuous during the Civil War, as half of Vermont's young men headed for the battlefield. When it was all over, Vermont had lost a larger percentage of its men than any other state. The four-year war caused population and economic devastation that affected the state for more than 40 years.

Tourism eventually helped set things straight during the early 1900s, when word got out that Vermont was "The Switzerland of North America." Well-to-do New Yorkers set up fancy summer estates, developers threw up dozens of roadside attractions and interstate highways helped fuel the influx. Suddenly, the land boom was on.

By the 1950s, yet another new breed of visitors—the kind with skis—arrived en masse. Much to the dismay of firmly rooted Vermonters, dozens of ski runs were carved in the mountainsides, and resorts were planted where dense forests once thrived.

Today, ski resort areas remain the only real tokens of full-scale development in Vermont, often called the most rural state in the nation. Yankee conservatism has spawned a rigorous array of zoning and antipollution laws meant to stave off mass growth. Vermonters' sentiments toward development were summed up by former Governor Thomas P. Salmon in 1973 when he declared: "Vermont is not for sale."

Forests still cover 78 percent of the state, and a 1960s law banning all roadside billboards has worked wonders for Vermont's highways, which remain pristine and untainted by commercialism. In the 1980s, Vermont became the first state

to prohibit automobile air conditioners that use chlorofluorocarbons, chemicals known to damage the ozone layer.

Through the years, Vermont's feisty independence and great beauty have attracted dozens of national and international artists, writers and folk heroes, including Norman Rockwell, Dorothy Canfield Fisher, Robert Frost and Rudyard Kipling, to name a few.

Today's new artisans follow in the footsteps of those early protagonists of Vermont history, fleeing America's big cities for a simpler existence among the quiet mountains. Together with the die-hard Republicans, patriotic farmers, leftover hippies and well-heeled elite, they form a curious, independent populace, united by their laissez-faire attitudes and unwavering devotion to free living.

With a population just over 560,000, Vermont is the nation's third smallest state, though its exquisite forested mountains and shimmering lakes and rivers pack as much beauty per square mile as any of the other 49.

Best of all, the terrain reveals four distinct faces as the seasons change. Fall brings a sacred occurrence, and during the season—usually from mid-September to mid-October—the entire state is covered by resplendent colors, and the temperature hovers around a crisp 50° to 60°.

Winter delivers a Currier and Ives backdrop, with carpets of plush white snow that weave through the country and temperatures that plunge toward 0°.

Waterfalls thaw and gush forth in spring, and millions of maple trees give up their candied sap for that wonderful Vermont maple syrup. Summer is pure green, a panorama of verdant forests, lucid lakes and blissful, breezy days when the thermometer reads about 75°.

Vermont's enchantment exists not only in its fanciful seasons and scenery but in the 242 small towns that comprise the essence of this state. Sprinkled on hillsides and straddling mountain streams, these quaint villages often cling to the social values of times past and harbor historic legacies and colorful personalities. Their very structures spell tradition: each town will almost certainly have a Main Street, a village square, a general store and a cemetery where you're apt to discover tombstones from the 1700s.

Each region of the state maintains its own intriguing personality. Southern Vermont is a mingling of forests, ski resorts and small cities that have seen strong influences from neighboring New York, Massachusetts and New Hampshire. In central Vermont, "The Marble City" of Rutland has churned out tons of smooth stone for more than a century, its marble-plated buildings a testament to this vital industry. Nearby Woodstock is the state's center of prosperity, a summer playground of majestic estates, trendy shops and restaurants and total gentility.

Crawling through the upper center of the state, the Northern Mountain Region thrives as an alpine haven of ski centers and maple sugarhouses, obscure mountain hamlets and fields of wildflowers.

Gorgeous Lake Champlain wanders along the western border, edged by New York's Adirondack Mountains and Vermont's fertile Champlain Valley, and supports the state's largest city. Burlington—home to a mere 40,000 people—is a dynamic port and culture center whose well-groomed cityscapes and obvious lack of pollution make it a splendid place to tarry.

The Northeast Kingdom is undoubtedly Vermont's last stand, a 2000-square-mile piece of rural wonderland snuggled against Canada and New Hampshire. Here, craggy peaks hover above dozens of glacier-dug lakes, evergreen spires ache toward the clouds and man and nature exist together simply and peacefully.

But of all Vermont's jewels, perhaps none is so extraordinary as its people. Amiable, generous and always interested, Vermonters know how to make a person feel right at home.

In fact, visiting Vermont is a lot like coming home: Once you're there, you feel like you've always belonged. Once you leave, you'll yearn to go back.

Southern Vermont

Edged by New York, Massachusetts and New Hampshire, this southerly precinct serves predominately as a gateway for skiers, weekenders and other seekers of pleasure and solace. Here, spun into one fine geographical web, are all the components that typify the state of Vermont—wooded mountain corridors, lazy farmlands, bucolic villages and a cornucopia of history.

Two of Vermont's largest cities, Brattleboro and Bennington, anchor the state corners and bring culture, politics and manufacturing into the region. In between are several towns that were founded in the 18th century as frontier outposts.

SIGHTS

Nestled nicely between the Connecticut River and a string of western mountain ledges, **Brattleboro** debuted as a sparse colony in 1724, making it Vermont's first permanent settlement. Today, Brattleboro owes its importance to health care and educational centers, as well as wholesale distribution facilities.

The **Brattleboro Chamber of Commerce** carries helpful information. ~ 180 Main Street, Brattleboro; 802-254-4565, fax 802-254-5675; www.brattleboro.com, e-mail bratchmb@sover.net.

Every proper 1800s Brattleboro home simply *had* to have a parlor organ, and a few of those relics still remain at the **Brattleboro Museum and Art Center**. Located in a 1915 native stone railroad station, the museum has eight beautiful wood Estey organs, manufactured locally by the thousands until the plant shut down in the 1960s. You'll also encounter dynamic rotating exhibits of visual arts as well as historical programs. Closed Monday and from November through May. Admission. ~ Main and Vernon streets, Brattleboro; 802-257-0124; www.brattleboromuseum.org.

Back in 1892, Rudyard Kipling put down roots just north of Brattleboro in the village of Dummerston. Here, in an odd, ship-shaped house called **Naulakha**, he lived for four years with his wife, Vermont native Carrie Balestier, and penned *Captains Courageous* and two *Jungle Books*. Now available for week-long rentals, the dwelling is set back from the road and cloaked in tall trees. ~ Kipling Road, two miles north of Black Mountain Road.

Text continued on page 424.

Three-day Weekend

Vermont and New Hampshire

This itinerary showcases the diversity of the deceptively small mirror-image states of Vermont and New Hampshire in a spectacular driving tour that links half a dozen of the states' best sights and experiences.

DAY 1
- Coming from the Boston area, get an early start and take Route 95 north to Portsmouth, New Hampshire, a 66-mile drive that takes about an hour.

- Spend the morning exploring the historic homes of Portsmouth, including those of **John Paul Jones** (page 494) and **Daniel Webster** (page 496).

- Take a short drive down coastal Route 1A to Hampton for an atmospheric lunch at **Widow Fletcher's Tavern** (page 499).

- Head west on Route 101 for 43 fast miles, bypass Manchester and drive north on Route 93 for 76 miles. The long two-hour drive proves worth it as you turn off the freeway at exit 35 and soon find yourself in pretty Bretton Woods at the turn-of-the-20th-century **Mount Washington Hotel and Resort** (page 534), where the opulence surpasses that of any mansion you saw in Portsmouth this morning.

- Devote the remainder of the day to luxuriating in your elegant surroundings.

DAY 2
- In the morning, ride the **Mount Washington Cog Railway** (page 532) to the 6288-foot summit of New Hampshire's tallest mountain.

- Follow Route 302 south through the White Mountains and over Crawford Notch, stopping for a hearty Highlander lunch at the **Scottish Lion Inn and Restaurant** (page 537) in North Conway.

- From Conway, head west on the Kancamagus Highway (Route 112), the ultimate scenic drive through the White Mountains. The 60-mile trip joins Route 302 near the Vermont state line.

- Route 302 connects with Route 89 about 38 miles farther on at the outskirts of Vermont's capital, Montpelier. From there, continue for 14 miles on the interstate to Exit 10 at Waterbury and drive south on Route 100 to Waitsfield. You ought to arrive at just the right time to check in at the **Lareau Farm** (page 454) for a quintessential Vermont farmstay.

DAY 3
- Head back north to the interstate, stopping in Waterbury for a tour and tasting at **Ben & Jerry's Ice Cream Factory** (page 450).

- Drive south on Route 100 for about 60 miles along the eastern slope of the **Green Mountains**, one of Vermont's most beautiful excursions.

- When you reach the intersection with Route 4, turn west and drive seven miles to Mendon for an Alpine lunch at **Countryman's Pleasure** (page 444).

- Returning east on Route 4, turn off to the south on Route 100 for a visit to **President Calvin Coolidge State Historic Site** (page 440) in Plymouth Notch, an idyllic village that time seems to have forgotten.

- All good things must end. Return via Route 100A to Route 4, where a drive of 16 miles will return you to Route 89 near the New Hampshire state line. From there, a 131-mile, two-hour freeway drive will bring you back to Boston in time for dinner.

To experience the rural rhythms of this state, head north on Route 30 to **Newfane**. Settled in 1774, this beguiling village is a paradigm of Vermont culture, showcasing 40 exquisite buildings that harken back to the 1700s. White clapboard houses mingle with graceful maple and elm trees and vast green. The grand **Windham County Courthouse** (802-365-4257), a Greek Revival design with enormous pillars, edges the green and is the village focal point. Closed Saturday and Sunday. Across the green rests the **Old Newfane Inn** (802-365-4427), a venerable 1787 Colonial building trimmed in white lattice porches and chimneys.

A drive northward on Route 30 and then Route 35 will put you smack in the middle of back country, a piece of terrain laced with mountain brooks and meandering meadows, occasional farms and one-room schoolhouses.

If you're like Ulysses S. Grant and Oliver Wendell Holmes, you'll make a pit stop in Grafton at the **Old Tavern at Grafton**, an 1801 Colonial-style inn that's filled with marvelous antiques and Old World character. Once a popular stagecoach layover, the tavern also hosted the likes of Ralph Waldo Emerson and Rudyard Kipling. Closed April. ~ 92 Main Street at Route 121, Grafton; 802-843-2231

Some say **Grafton** got its name in a bidding contest—won with $5 and a flask of rum—back in 1791, though the village owes its existence to sheep farming (15,000 grazed here during the 1800s). Grafton now boasts two covered bridges, 650 residents and a network of well-preserved, white-frame buildings.

Exquisite views await back along Route 9, to the west of Brattleboro, where the road climbs 2350 feet to the top of **Hogback Mountain**. This captivating plateau, surrounded by lofty spires of spruce and fir trees, affords a 100-mile panorama across New Hampshire and Massachusetts' Berkshires.

The **Southern Vermont Natural History Museum** contains a vast collection of unusual birds and animals "stuffed" by taxidermist and naturalist Luman Nelson. The winged collection alone is staggering: more than 1000 different birds, including a large eagle and owl collection, the albino deer and skunks, and the extinct passenger pigeon and heath hen. If you tire of viewing immobile wildlife, visit the live hawks and owls exhibit. Closed weekdays from late October to Memorial Day. Admission. ~ Hogback Mountain, Route 9, Marlboro; 802-464-0048.

Continue through this forested mountain wonderland, traveling west on Route 9, and you'll descend into the town of **Wilmington**. Long a juncture between Brattleboro and western Bennington, this bucolic town of 1800 swells to 15,000 during winter when skiers pack nearby **Haystack Mountain** and **Mount Snow**. Of course, summer activities abound, too, and you can learn about these and other leisure pursuits at the **Mount Snow Valley Chamber of Commerce**. ~ Route 9 (Main Street), Wilmington; 802-464-8092, fax 802-464-0287; www.visitvermont.com, e-mail info@visitvermont.com.

Heading west toward Bennington, Route 9 cuts through the broad, verdant expanse of the **Green Mountain National Forest**. This sinuous, heady trail explodes with brilliant color during fall foliage season, though the views border on amazing the rest of the year, too. Keep an eye out for bears, coyotes and moose, which roam the area frequently.

You can see it before you get to Bennington, an intimidating limestone obelisk looming over the city like some celestial figure. The 306-foot **Bennington Battle Monument**, the region's geographical frame of reference, pays tribute to the 1777 Battle of Bennington, a decisive conflict during the American Revolution. Though American general John Stark organized his troops and supplies here in Bennington, the battle was actually waged 11 miles away on a New York hill. Closed November to mid-April. Admission. ~ 15 Monument Circle, Old Bennington; 802-447-0550.

Bennington is Vermont's southwesternmost city and the first town chartered in the state, though residents didn't arrive until 12 years later in 1761 because of fierce raids during the French and Indian War. Suffused with culture and Revolutionary War history, the city is flanked by the Green Mountains and the Taconic range, a setting that's nothing short of spectacular.

The downtown area is pretty but naturally quite commercialized, so you'll want to spend most of your time in **Old Bennington**. Draped across a hill on the city's west quadrant, this pristine borough harbors marvelous expressions of early American history. Here you'll find more than 80 well-preserved 18th- and 19th-century buildings, comprising a sort-of outdoor museum.

Before you start exploring, pick up a walking tour map from the **Bennington Area Chamber of Commerce**. ~ Veterans Memorial Drive, Route 7, Bennington; 802-447-3311, fax 802-447-1163; www.bennington.com.

American history becomes an enthralling experience at the **Bennington Museum**. This historic 1855 building—one of New England's finest museums—evokes America's past with American Revolution artifacts, the famous Bennington flag (one of the oldest Stars and Stripes in existence), the largest public collection of Grandma Moses paintings and a genealogical library. It also showcases the frame schoolhouse, moved from Eagle Bridge, New York, that Grandma Moses attended as a child. Adjacent to the museum is Hadwen woods with a nature trail and pavilion. Admission. ~ West Main Street, Bennington; 802-447-1571; www.benningtonmuseum.com.

West on Main Street rests Vermont's Colonial shrine, the **Old First Church**, erected in 1806 and now a much-photographed sight. Nestled on the green in Old Bennington, the simple white building has columns formed with single pine trees, arched Romanesque windows and well-preserved pine box pews. In this state of tradition, some of today's church members are descendants of the original founders. ~ Monument Avenue, Bennington; 802-447-1223.

Beside the church on a shady knoll, symmetrical rows of granite comprise the **Old Burying Ground**, where you can stroll peacefully among tombstones dating back to the 1700s. Many epitaphs are intriguing ruminations of early settlers and soldiers who toiled here under a more difficult life, but perhaps the most reflective endures on the grave of poet Robert Frost: "I had a lover's quarrel with the world."

Head north from Old Bennington on Fairview Street, cross one of three quaint covered bridges, and you'll arrive at **Bennington College**. A medley of Colonial designs, the campus lazes peacefully across 550 acres on a pretty hill overlooking mountains and valleys. ~ Route 67A, Bennington; 802-442-5401.

Since its founding in 1929, the tiny liberal-arts school has initiated some of the country's most progressive teaching styles, employing accomplished (and oftentimes renowned) artists, writers and musicians to act as both teachers and colleagues to students. Among the more famous who have graced these halls are dancer and choreographer Martha Graham and author Bernard De Voto. Rigorous scholastic and artistic exercises students must endure are often referred to as "The Bennington Experience."

Perhaps the most intriguing sight on campus is **Jennings Hall**, a grand three-story structure carved of solid granite. Built in the mid-1800s, the building was home to the Frederic B. Jennings family, who donated their estate to the college.

The cozy pastoral spirit and thoughtful personalities of **Arlington**, 16 miles north of Bennington off Route 7A, remain preserved on *Saturday Evening Post* covers, sketched by Norman Rockwell when he lived here during the 1940s and early 1950s. Rockwell's farm and studio are now the **Inn on Covered Bridge Green**, a ◄ *HIDDEN* scenic resting place nestled among apple orchards and dairy farms. ~ River Road at Covered Bridge Road, four and a half miles west of Route 7A, West Arlington; 802-375-9489, fax 802-375-1208; www.coveredbridgegreen.com, e-mail cbg@sover.net.

You can chat with some of the local people Rockwell painted if you stop by the **Norman Rockwell Exhibit**, a 19th-century church where several hundred *Saturday Evening Post* covers, illustrations and prints are displayed. Closed January. Admission. ~ Route 7A, Arlington; 802-375-6423; www.normanrockwell exhibit.com.

Meander north on Route 7A to Sunderland, then head west on **Skyline Drive** toll road for a hair-raising, five-mile trek to the top of **Mount Equinox**. At 3816 feet up, the panorama is inspiring, the air brisk and the feeling serene.

On the way down the mountain, stop at the **Southern Vermont Art Center** for a tryst with culture and nature. A beautiful early 1900s Georgian mansion holds ten galleries that display about 300 pieces (paintings, graphic art and photography) by contemporary artists. Set on 375 acres of forest and pastureland, the center also boasts a performing arts pavilion for indoor concerts, an extensive botany trail and a sculpture garden sprinkled with wildflowers. Closed Monday, May through October and Sunday, December through April. Admission. ~ West Road, Manchester; 802-362-1405; www.svac.org.

On Route 7A lies **Manchester**, which made its imprint in the 19th century as a thriving summer resort town and the 20th century as a nucleus for designer outlet stores. But its main claim to fame is a former resident, Robert Todd Lincoln, eldest son of Abraham Lincoln, who built a Georgian Revival mansion here in 1905 and called it **Hildene**. Possibly one of New England's finest historic scenes, Hildene offers a glimmer of the gilded, intriguing life of Robert Lincoln, an attorney, minister to Great Britain, and U.S. Cabinet member. Laid against 412 acres of beautiful formal gardens, evergreen trees and nature trails, the 24-room mansion is extremely well-preserved and filled with original furnishings and possessions including a grand 1908 Aeolian pipe organ once played by the Lincoln women. Closed November to mid-May. Admission. ~ Route 7A, Manchester Village; 802-362-1788; www.hildene.org.

Avid fishers—and even nonanglers—will get a kick out of the **American Museum of Fly Fishing**. Peruse more than 30,000 flies and 1000 rods and reels, tracing the history of this intriguing sport. You'll see what Dwight Eisenhower, Daniel Webster and Ernest Hemingway used to snag a fish, along with artifacts from famous rod-makers like Thomas and Orvis. A real treat for anyone fishing for fun. Admission. ~ Route 7A, Manchester Village; 802-362-3300; www.amff.com.

LODGING

Art deco in Vermont? Just check out **The Latchis Hotel**, a 1938 deco charmer in the heart of downtown. This four-story find sparkles with bright terrazzo floors and curved chrome designs and boasts 30 guest rooms in soft pastels offset by black lacquer furniture and restored 1930s pieces. The best part is that many rooms peek a view at the Connecticut River. There's also a movie theater and microbrewery on the premises. ~ 50 Main Street, Brattleboro; 802-254-6300, fax 802-254-6304; www.brattleboro.com/latchis. MODERATE TO DELUXE.

Something about the **Old Newfane Inn** makes you instantly feel as though you've come home. Perhaps it's the lazy wraparound porch with rocking chairs, the warm parlors with brick hearths or the wonderful old general store across the street. It could be the eight rooms, decorated without pretension in rich woods and country wallpapers, or the massive maple trees that stand across the front lawn. Whatever the reason, the magic is there—and has been since this venerable country inn opened way back in 1787. ~ Route 30, Newfane; 802-365-4427; www.old newfaneinn.com. DELUXE.

The sophisticated serenity of the **Four Columns Inn** has long drawn celebrities (Mick Jagger, Tom Cruise and Nicole Kidman among them) seeking a quiet reprieve from life's fast lane. Set amidst 150 forested acres, the 19th-century Greek Revival inn sports a swimming pool enveloped in flowers and a cobblestone path that wends across brooks and meadows. Its trademark is four majestic columns that stand astride the loggia—a marvelous place to mellow out and listen to birds chirp. The 15 guest rooms offer wide plank floors, lace curtains and a mix of canopy and four-poster beds. Four suites are also available. ~ 21 West Street, Newfane; 802-365-7713, 800-787-6633, fax 802-365-0022;

Author Picks

CHAPTER FAVORITES

"Right out of a Norman Rockwell painting" is a description so often used that it has become a cliché, but I can't help saying it about my stay at the **Inn on Covered Bridge Green**, a bed and breakfast that really was Rockwell's home. *page 431*

I'm living proof that you don't have to be a kid to love the largest folk-art collection in New England at the wonderful **Shelburne Museum**, with its miniature circus parade, a thousand duck decoys, a steamboat, a costume collection and countless other curiosities. *page 462*

Although I've yet to catch a glimpse of Lake Champlain's legendary monster, watching for it is all the excuse I need to while away a sunny afternoon on the secluded peninsula tip at **North Hero State Park**. *page 468*

Vermont does wonders for my sweet tooth, if not my waistline. Just when I think I've recovered from Ben & Jerry's world headquarters, along comes **Maple Grove Farms of Vermont**, the world's oldest and largest maple sugar candy factory. *page 470*

www.fourcolumnsinn.com. DELUXE TO ULTRA-DELUXE.

The Old Tavern is possibly the most renowned spot in Grafton, and rightly so, since guest rooms are scattered in eight different historic buildings across town. The main house is an 1801 Colonial design brimming with lovely antiques, pine floors and pewter and brass. Formerly a popular stagecoach stop, the tavern boasts a notable guest list that included Ulysses S. Grant and Ralph Waldo Emerson. Houses and rooms might feature braided rugs, Victorian furnishings and full kitchen. Closed April. ~ 92 Main Street at Route 121, Grafton; 802-843-2231, 800-843-1801, fax 802-843-2245; www.oldtavern.com. DELUXE TO ULTRA-DELUXE.

Tucked away in Andover, seven miles northwest of Chester, is **The Inn at High View**, a gay-friendly place that attracts a mixed clientele. It's a lovely 1789 vintage farmhouse, added onto over the years and completely renovated in 1987. The eight guest rooms are all decorated in a Laura Ashley style; some have canopy beds, and all have their own baths. It's a quiet place, perfect for relaxing, swimming in the inn's pool or hiking on nearby trails. In winter, you can cross-country ski right on the property or go downhill at nearby Okemo. ~ East Hill Road, Andover; 802-875-2724, fax 802-875-4021; www.innathighview.com. MODERATE TO DELUXE.

If you want to escape from absolutely everything, consider **The Hermitage Inn**. This 18th-century farmhouse is a hidden

◄ *HIDDEN*

treasure tucked down a piece of paved road and nestled against a rushing brook. The owner's love of hunting is evidenced by the English setters that roam the 40 acres, as well as hundreds of antique decoys found throughout the inn. There is even a court for clay pigeon shooting. Twenty-nine rooms—many with working fireplaces—are adorned in a hunting motif. Breakfast and dinner at the inn's exceptional gourmet restaurant are included in the price. ~ Coldbrook Road, Wilmington; 802-464-3511, fax 802-464-2688; www.hermitageinn.com. ULTRA-DELUXE.

Skiers seeking close proximity to the slopes should check out **Mount Snow Resort Lodge**, a lodge and a cluster of condominium buildings at the base of Mount Snow. There are 419 accommodations, ranging from hotel rooms to modern, apartment-style condos. Many rooms offer ski-to-front-door skiing, as well as use of tennis courts and pools. A golf course and a mountain biking school should please summertime guests. ~ 89 Mountain Road, Wilmington; 802-464-7788, 800-951-0311, fax 802-264-4192; www.mountsnow.com, e-mail msresoff@sover.net. DELUXE TO ULTRA-DELUXE.

Thirteen miles west of Wilmington, the **Greenwood Lodge American Youth Hostel** lolls peacefully in a picturesque wooded glen. Rustic but tidy, the mountain lodge has 20 beds in four rooms, some of them available for private use. There's a fireplace and community kitchen, plus fishing ponds, canoeing, swimming, boating and 40 wooded campsites. Closed late October to mid-May. ~ Route 9, adjacent to Prospect Ski Mountain, Woodford; 802-442-2547. BUDGET.

A gorgeous Victorian mansion cloaked in a sea of trees, the **South Shire Inn** is positively dazzling. The first floor is a series of parlors and sitting rooms with mahogany woods, etched-glass doors, high carved ceilings and a knockout staircase; one guest room with antique double beds is situated downstairs; upstairs, four guest accommodations are equipped with original fireplaces and decorated in period pieces. Four more contemporary-styled rooms with jacuzzis tubs and fireplaces are in the carriage house. All rooms have private baths. Full breakfast is included. ~ 124 Elm Street, Bennington; 802-447-3839, fax 802-442-3547; www. southshire.com. DELUXE TO ULTRA-DELUXE.

For homey in-town accommodations, consider the **Molly Stark Inn**, an 1890 Victorian house that's been carefully restored by an enthusiastic and artistic innkeeper. The six bedrooms are small but charming, featuring hardwood floors, clawfoot bathtubs, lace curtains, antique patchwork quilts, ceiling fans and wall stencils. There's also a wraparound front porch and nifty antique wood-burning stove in the living room. Three very private saltbox-style guest cottages with cathedral ceilings, skylights, jacuzzis and fireplaces are also available. A full gourmet breakfast is included. ~

1067 East Main Street, Bennington; 802-442-9631, 800-356-3076, fax 802-442-5224; www.mollystarkinn.com. MODERATE.

Surrounded by mountains and bordered by the Battenkill River, **Hill Farm Inn** is a gay-friendly B&B attracting both gays and straights. Its two vintage farmhouses have a total of 13 understated guest rooms, with quilts on every bed and flowered wallpaper. In the summer months, four cabins are also available. Some rooms have private baths while others are shared. Nearby, you'll find hiking, biking, canoeing, kayaking and fishing and (come winter) skiing and skating. ~ RR 2, Arlington; 802-375-2269, 800-882-2545, fax 802-375-9918; www.hillfarminn.com. DELUXE.

> Nearly half a million people flock to Vermont to witness the fall foliage.

"Who is there, I wonder, who doesn't want to escape from the speed and rudeness of today's living . . . ?" When Norman Rockwell penned those words, he likely had in mind his secluded farmhouse in West Arlington. Today, the 1792 timber house is the **Inn on Covered Bridge Green**, a beguiling bed and breakfast offering a glimmer of the rural cheer that Rockwell's paintings so cleverly depicted. The scenic Battenkill River runs in front of the five-acre grounds, surrounded in all directions by apple orchards and tranquil horse and dairy farms. There are four bedrooms (one of which is a two-bedroom suite) set off by broad pine floors and provincial antiques, and a tennis court that Rockwell built. ~ River Road, four-and-a-half miles west of Route 7A, West Arlington; 802-375-9489, 800-726-9480, fax 802-375-1208; www.coveredbridge green.com, e-mail cbg@sover.net. DELUXE TO ULTRA-DELUXE.

◄ HIDDEN

Ethan Allen and his Green Mountain Boys checked into **The Equinox** once for a little rest and relaxation. It was the late 1700s, and the hotel was *the* place to stay. Centuries later, the place still draws history-makers, as well as anyone seeking indulgent surroundings. A main four-story building, fronted by Greek Revival columns, features 183 rooms graced with white Vermont pine furniture and country-style accents. An adjoining building offers nine one- and two-bedroom suites with fully stocked kitchens and elegant country decor. There are indoor and outdoor pools, a country club, 18-hole championship golf course, spa, tennis and volleyball courts, horseback riding, croquet and several restaurants. For those interested in learning a new skill there is a falconry school as well as an off-road driving school. In the winter you can ice skate and go snowmobiling. All set on 2200 acres etched with cross-country ski trails. Who could ask for more? ~ Route 7A, Manchester Village; 802-362-4700, 800-362-4747, fax 802-362-4861; www.equinoxresort.com, e-mail reservations@equinox resort.com. ULTRA-DELUXE.

For close proximity to Manchester's factory outlet stores, consider **Barnstead Innstead**. Built in 1830, the post-and-beam hay barn has been converted with all its charm intact. Fourteen tidy bedrooms are outfitted with old-time furniture and wall-to-wall carpets, and there's a heated pool out back. ~ Route 30, Manchester; 802-362-1619, 800-331-1619. MODERATE TO DELUXE.

DINING

The diminutive venue of **T. J. Buckley's** is the last place you'd expect to find some of the city's finest gourmet fare. But here it is, served in an adorable Worcester diner with eclectic decor and only eight tables. Four entrées are offered nightly on an ever-changing menu. Selections might include diver scallops served with roasted fennel and buckwheat polenta, roasted Guinea hen breast in a saffron-pear stew, or beef tenderloin with an ancho-chile sauce and native mushrooms. Dinner only. Closed Monday and Tuesday. ~ 132 Elliot Street, Brattleboro; 802-257-4922. DELUXE TO ULTRA-DELUXE.

Climb a battered flight of stairs to the second-floor roost of the **Common Ground**, a venerable mecca of ethnic and organic creations. Formerly a mid-1800s fire station, the eatery has dusty plank and brick floors and a glass solarium overlooking the downtown hubbub. The open kitchen, a jumble of pots and chefs, is where all the vegetarian goodies get whipped up. Try the cashew burger, seaweed salad and fresh baked bread. No lunch on Thursday. Closed Monday through Wednesday. ~ 25 Elliot Street, Brattleboro; 802-257-0855. BUDGET.

HIDDEN ►

Things take on a subdued pace at **Peter Havens**, a tiny but sophisticated eatery obscured beneath streetside awnings. Continental fare focuses on fresh seafood, including curried shrimp, sea scallops Provençal and grilled swordfish with geneva butter. Linen tablecloths, original artwork and only ten tables make this a cozy spot for two. Dinner only. Closed Sunday and Monday. ~ 32 Elliot Street, Brattleboro; 802-257-3333. DELUXE.

A majestic country establishment built in 1787, the **Old Newfane Inn** possesses quite an impressive restaurant. The surroundings are pure Vermont: dark pine floors, high beamed ceilings and wallpapered walls sprinkled with beautiful antiques. The bill of fare includes an array of highbrow delights such as smoked goose pâté and frogs' legs Provençal. Dinner only. Closed Monday. Closed in November and April. ~ Route 30 on the village green, Newfane; 802-365-4427. DELUXE.

Charm and elegance embrace at the **Four Columns Inn** restaurant, renowned across the region for its exceptional native cuisine. Built in 1839 of hand-hewn timbers, the Colonial-style inn exhibits four grand columns across its loggia. Inside, candlelit tables are arranged cozily around a brick fireplace accented by windows draped in lace sheers. Try the Peking duck breast with sun-dried plums; seared venison loin in a zinfandel sauce; or salmon in a steamy New England bouillabaisse. Closed Tuesday. ~ 21 West Street, Newfane; 802-365-7713. DELUXE TO ULTRA-DELUXE.

The Old Tavern imparts a warm formality that reveals its rich heritage. Indeed, the inn's handsome pine floors and beam ceilings, which date back to the late 1700s, have seen the likes of Oliver Wendell Holmes and Henry David Thoreau. Two lavish dining rooms are decorated with antiques and American portraits, while a sunny greenhouse affords picturesque views of gardens. The menu focuses on local fare such as Green Mountain lamb, smoked pork loin and New England salmon. Closed April. ~ 92 Main Street at Route 121, Grafton; 802-843-2231. DELUXE TO ULTRA-DELUXE.

A down-home eatery with spectacular views, the Skyline Restaurant is a great place to while away the morning. Perched 2000 feet up on Hogback Mountain, the Skyline offers simple decor and a vista that stretches more than 100 miles. Breakfast is the highlight, with goodies like banana and coconut griddlecakes smothered in (what else?) Vermont maple syrup, bountiful omelettes and steamy oatmeal. For dinner, try pan-fried trout or sugar-cured ham. Closed Tuesday. No dinner Sunday through Thursday. ~ Route 9, Marlboro; 802-464-5535. MODERATE.

West Dover's Inn at Sawmill Farm is fashioned from a 1797 barn. The ever-changing Continental menu usually includes a variety of fresh fish dishes and a selection of meat, poultry and game dishes. It also has one of the most impressive wine lists in the northeast, with a 36,000-bottle cellar. ~ Crosstown Road at Route 100, West Dover; 802-464-8131. ULTRA-DELUXE.

Tucked down a washboard road on the mountainside, The Hermitage is a tribute to gracious country dining. Fashioned in cool blue and cream tones, two dining rooms are graced with picture windows, large hearths and hundreds of antique decoys collected by an owner who loves bird hunting. There's more evidence of his passion on the menu, which often features partridge, quail, pheasant, duck and venison. The owner has also garnered national recognition for his wine collection, which exceeds 40,000 bottles. An exceptional dining choice. Dinner is served nightly and there is a Sunday brunch. ~ Coldbrook Road, Wilmington; 802-464-3511. DELUXE.

◄ HIDDEN

You find plenty of local color at Poncho's Wreck, a pub-style eatery with nautical decor and stained-glass windows. The food is dependably good and ranges from Mexican fare and smoked meats to seafood. The mood is casual but festive, particularly during ski season. No lunch Monday through Friday. ~ South Main Street, Wilmington; 802-464-9320. MODERATE TO DELUXE.

When it comes to fabulous views, it's tough to surpass the Publyk House Restaurant. This remodeled 1940s barn is the perfect place to gaze upon Bennington's battle monument and beautiful

Mount Anthony. Carved wood doors, stained-glass windows and loads of greenery make for aesthetic surroundings. Expect interesting American-style fare including poultry, pasta, ribs, seafood and steak dishes served with salad and homemade bread. Wednesday night treat your tastebuds to dinner and your ears to acoustic music in the Carriage Lounge. ~ Route 7A, Bennington; 802-442-8301, fax 802-440-8199. MODERATE.

During the mid-1940s, Norman Rockwell took a fancy to the **Quality Restaurant**. Chances are you will, too. This downtown tradition, which has long served as the local socializing nest, reeks of character. Polished wood floors saunter up to a worn pine bar where Rockwell used to read the daily paper. Along a wall hangs a print of *War News*, in which the artist captured the bar's essence during World War II. Breakfast, lunch and dinner are all-American affairs, from blueberry pancakes to burgers to smoked salmon alfredo. ~ Route 7A, Manchester; 802-362-9839. MODERATE.

SHOPPING   For the most part, Vermont shops are down-home and unpretentious, a smattering of country gift marts, antique nooks and epicure emporiums with locally made cheeses and maple syrup. To assist with shopping excursions, the **Vermont Travel Division** has excellent brochures on where to find antiques, designer outlets, cheese and Christmas trees (in case you brought the car). ~ 134 State Street, Montpelier, VT 05602; 802-828-3236, 800-837-6668.

Pick up your brand-name outdoor clothes and supplies at reasonable prices at **Sam's Department Store**, a downtown institution housed in a ruddy brick building. ~ 74 Main Street, Brattleboro; 802-254-2933.

Little people will adore **Jeannie Mac**. This factory outlet sells cotton kids' clothes made exclusively in Vermont. Closed Tuesday through Thursday from Thanksgiving to Memorial Day. ~ Route 30, Townshend; 802-365-7040.

The fun and funky selections at **Bartleby's Books & Music** reflect the owner's love of fiction, history, Vermont, cooking, and classical music. ~ North Main Street, Wilmington; 802-464-5425.

Mountain Jeanery, once an 1800s blacksmith's shop, caters to thrift shop fans with an assortment of army/navy gear and vintage women's clothing. You can dress like Marilyn Monroe (or Madonna—take your pick) after a visit to **The Next Store**, a vintage clothing mart in the same building. You'll find elbow-length lace gloves, rhinestone sunglasses and Victorian and art-deco jewelry among other treasures. ~ South Main Street, Wilmington; 802-464-5818.

Now and Then Books has a top-notch collection of used and out-of-print books; there's also a small selection of new titles. Closed Monday and sometimes Sunday. ~ 439 Main Street, Bennington; 802-447-1470.

The outstanding **Bennington Museum Shop** features Grandma Moses prints, historical literature, salt-glazed pottery and works by local artisans. ~ West Main Street, Bennington; 802-447-1571.

Panache is equipped with contemporary women's clothing, gifts and accessories such as Indonesian and Pacific jewelry and wild art stationery. ~ 457 Main Street, Bennington; 802-442-8859.

A marvelous neighborhood bar with a vast draft beer selection including their own brewed on the premises, **McNeill's Brewery** features recorded jazz and contemporary music. ~ 90 Elliot Street, Brattleboro; 802-254-2553.

NIGHTLIFE

Locals go underground at **Mole's Eye Cafe**, a noisy, crowded nook with booths and occasional blues and rock bands. Cover on Friday and Saturday. Closed Sunday. ~ Main and High streets, Brattleboro; 802-257-0771.

Deacon's Den, near Wilmington, is a wood-and-glass tavern where skiers stop off for a cold brew. There's live rock-and-roll and blues on weekends during winter. Occasional cover. ~ Route 100, West Dover; 802-464-9361.

Smack in the middle of ski action, **The Snow Barn** draws huge winter crowds with live rock-and-roll. Cover. ~ In the Snow Lake Lodge, South Access Road, Mount Snow; 802-464-3333.

One of the most prestigious thespian groups in Vermont, **Oldcastle Theatre Company** stages dramas, comedies and musicals in their arts center from late May through October. ~ Performing in the regional Bennington Center for the Arts, Route 9 and Gypsy Lane, Bennington; 802-447-0564.

Lilly's, a worn sports bar with dusty wood floors and outdoor volleyball action, has canned and live rock music on weekends. Cover Thursday through Saturday. ~ 135 Depot Street, Bennington; 802-447-2139.

GREEN MOUNTAIN NATIONAL FOREST This colossal tract of greenery constitutes the spine of Vermont, uniting over 350,000 acres that slice through the center of the state. Technically, it's divvied into two big chunks, starting at the Massachusetts border and climbing to the town of Wallingford, then picking up again in Mendon and heading northward to Bristol. Dense, verdant and pristine, the forest provides asylum for thousands of animals and birds, including black bears, coyotes, moose, white-tailed deer, wild turkeys, raptors and the protected peregrine falcons. You can spot these intriguing inhabitants by exploring miles of nature trails and canoeing the waters.

BEACHES & PARKS

The trees themselves—those great sweeps of maple, beech and birch, intermingled with black cherry, white ash, balsam firs and occasional hemlock forests—are no less enthralling. Rivers gush forth from the mountains, giving rise to imaginative waterfalls

HIDDEN ►

and tiny, pebble-studded brooks perfect for wading. Swimming is excellent at several spots, including **Hapgood Pond** and **Grout Pond**, a developed but rustic site in Stratton on Kelley Stand Road, six miles west of Route 100. There's excellent fishing from 440 miles of rivers and tributaries. Anglers ply the Otter Creek for brook trout and the White, Deerfield and nearby Battenkill and West rivers for rainbow and brown trout. To see everything the park offers would take several weeks, though there are several choice spots perfect for an afternoon rendezvous. Non-motorized boats only. Facilities include picnic areas and restrooms; nature trails and ranger stations are dispersed throughout the forest. ~ Route 7 scales the west side of the forest, while Route 100 borders the east side. In between, Routes 73, 125, 9, 11 and 30 slice through the middle. Along these roads are all 32 access points for trails, waterfalls, ponds, rivers and campgrounds. Before you go, contact the Green Mountain National Forest (231 North Main Street, Rutland, VT 05701-2417; 802-747-6700) for maps and information on the huge forest network.

▲ Several good campsites exist, in five developed campgrounds; four accommodate RVs (no hookups). Most sites are on a first-come, first-served basis and are $5 per night; reserved sites (Hapgood Pond only) are $13 per night. Try Hapgood Pond, on Hapgood Road in Peru, five miles from the intersection of Routes 11 and 30; and Moosalamoo, a developed campground on Ripton-Goshen Road, 3.2 miles from Route 125 and one mile east of Ripton.The developed campgrounds are closed from Columbus Day to Memorial Day. Call for information on backcountry camping in winter.

HIDDEN ►

FORT DUMMER STATE PARK 🏃 Stashed along some sylvan back roads, this 217-acre, heavily forested park is named after the first white settlement in Vermont, established in 1724. There's a small shaded clearing for picnicking and a mile of nature trails that ramble through evergreens to views of the Connecticut River and peeks at the Vermont Yankee Power Plant. Picnic tables, restrooms and a playground round out the amenities. Closed September to late May. Day-use fee, $2. ~ From Routes 91 and 5 in Brattleboro, take Route 5 north one-tenth of a mile to Exit 1 and go to the first set of lights. Take a right here onto Fairground Road, then follow the road until it ends. Take a right to the stop sign. Here you'll see a sign for the park. Continue to the parks' entrance; 802-254-2610.

▲ Camping is permitted at 61 wooded sites, including ten lean-tos, with showers and fireplaces but no hookups. Rates are $11 per night for tent/RV sites, $15 per night for lean-tos. There is also a non-refundable $5 reservation fee per site.

TOWNSHEND STATE PARK 🏃 ⛵ 🏊 🚣 Resting amidst a slew of craggy green mountains, this fine park spans 856 acres and borders the scenic West River. For delightful views, take a hardy hike 1680 feet up to the top of Bald Mountain; for sunbathing, swimming and canoeing, take a one-mile trek down to **Townshend Dam Recreation Area** (802-365-7503), where an 1800-foot thread of tawny sand stretches lazily along the river. Try by the dam for brook trout, walleye and smallmouth bass. You'll also find nice nature trails near the dam. Picnic tables and restrooms are available. Closed from Columbus Day through Memorial Day. Day-use fee, $2. ~ State Forest Road, three miles south of Route 30 near Townshend; 802-365-7500.

▲ Permitted at 34 campsites (eight for RVs) with fireplaces and showers but no hookups. Rates are $11 per night for tent/RV sites, $15 per night for lean-tos. There is also a non-refundable $5 reservation fee per site.

LIVING MEMORIAL PARK As municipal parks go, this one is tops. Blanketing 53 acres of gentle hills, this shady sanctuary teems with recreational opportunities, including a swimming pool and ice-skating rink, outdoor tennis courts, an indoor rink for rollerblading and inline hockey and an expansive playground with some state-of-the-art equipment. Families love this place, and it's one of the few parks that manages to be packed (or even open) year round. There are picnic pavilions, lifeguards, a snack bar, softball fields, tennis and basketball courts, and sled trails. Swimming fee, $3. ~ Route 9 a quarter of a mile west of Route 91, near Brattleboro; 802-254-6700.

MOLLY STARK STATE PARK Magnificent stands of maple and birch blanket this pristine area, marked by beavers, deer and rabbits. There's a broad clearing that affords cool picnicking and a one-and-a-half-mile roundtrip hike to the summit of Mount Olga. Once you're there, climb the abandoned fire tower and be rewarded with a view into New Hampshire. Facilities include picnic tables and shelters. Closed from Columbus Day to the week before Memorial Day. Day-use fee, $2. ~ Route 9, about four miles east of Wilmington; 802-464-5460.

▲ There are 34 sites, including ten lean-tos, with showers and fireplaces (no hookups); $11 per night for tent/RV sites, $15 per night for lean-tos. There is also a non-refundable $5 reservation fee per site.

JAMAICA STATE PARK The arrow-straight, wide, rocky West River plows right through this beautiful park, creating a cool, 689-acre playground for outdoor lovers. A short cord of gravel forms a semibeach against the river, where you can swim or roll up your pants legs and explore. You can also cast a rod for walleye, trout and panfish. But the best part is a trail along an old railroad bed that leads to the Ball Mountain Dam, a monstrous structure that's unleashed twice a year for popular canoe and kayak races. There's also a wooded trail leading up to Hamilton Falls, where eons of torrential water flow have formed curious miniature bathtubs among slippery rocks. You'll find restrooms, picnic tables and a playground. Closed from Columbus Day to late April. Day-use fee, $2. ~ Off Route 30, Jamaica; 802-874-4600.

▲ There are 46 tent sites ($13 per night) and 18 lean-tos ($17 per night) with showers and fireplaces but no hookups. Some sites accommodate RVs. There is also a non-refundable $5 reservation fee per site.

WOODFORD STATE PARK 🏃 ⛵ 🚣 🛶 🎣 Certainly one of the most picturesque parcels in the state, this 400-acre mountain woodland teems with wildflowers and all sorts of wildlife, from moose, deer and bear to very active beavers. Much of the activity centers around Adams Reservoir, dotted with small boats and canoes and rimmed by a small beach with coarse grey sand. You can swim, though the water can be murky at times. When the reservoir is stocked, the trout are biting. At 2400 feet up, the setting is cool and serene. Facilities include picnic areas, boat and canoe rentals and a nature trail. Closed October 13 to May 15. Day-use fee, $2. ~ Route 9, ten miles east of Bennington; 802-447-7169.

▲ Some of the most extensive in the state, with 102 sites, including 20 lean-tos, with fireplaces and hot showers. A third of the sites accommodate RVs (no hookups). Rates are $13 per night for tents, $17 per night for lean-tos. There is also a non-refundable $5 reservation fee per site.

LAKE SHAFTSBURY STATE PARK 🏃 ⛵ 🚣 🛶 🎣 Situated along a fine, clear lake, this park possesses 101 acres sprinkled with evergreens and maple trees, nature trails and those industrious beavers. Locals fancy the 600-foot beach of fine, ginger-colored sand that allows great sunbathing and swimming. You can fish along parts of shore or from boats for bass and rainbow trout. Boat and canoe rentals and available, as are picnic areas. Closed from Labor Day to Memorial Day. Day-use fee, $2. ~ Route 7A, Shaftsbury; 802-375-9978.

EMERALD LAKE STATE PARK 🏃 ⛵ 🚣 🛶 🎣 True to its name, this body of water glistens with a green glow and is so clear you can see much of its sandy bottom. A choice thread of tawny sand forms a popular beach, while nature trails crisscross the hillside terrain. Here you'll also find some of the tallest (more than 100-feet) maple trees in Vermont. In the lake you can cast a rod for panfish, small- and largemouth bass and northern pike. Amenities include a playground, restrooms and canoe and boat rentals. Closed from Columbus Day to Memorial Day. Day-use fee, $2. ~ Route 7, Dorset; 802-362-1655.

▲ Permitted in 105 sites, including 36 lean-tos, with showers and fireplaces but no hookups. Lean-tos are $17 per night; all other sites are $13 per night.

Central Vermont

Sprawled across the lower waist of the state are a diverse lot of mining cities, picturesque mountain hamlets, ski areas and affluent riverside towns. Driving through this fertile area, you'll encounter a variety of lifestyles and people—fifth-generation farmers, descendants of European immigrants, small-time merchants and established aristocrats.

On the region's west side, Rutland and nearby villages are pocked with marble quarries that have churned the wheels of industry for two centuries. Eastward, Woodstock is a meld of tree-lined streets and gracious 19th-century architecture that owes its affluence and elegance to a line of wealthy partisans, including Laurance S. Rockefeller and railroad magnate Frederick Billings. Beyond Woodstock rambles the lazy Connecticut River, a natural divider between Vermont and New Hampshire.

SIGHTS

◄ HIDDEN

◄ HIDDEN

Just south of Rutland and off Route 7 is a mandatory side trip (via a few dirt roads) to **Shrewsbury** (North Shrewsbury Road, about eight miles east of Route 7), a quiescent village of 800 that seems buried at the end of the world.

The **Meadowsweet Herb Farm** is a joyous feast for the senses, a skein of luxuriant gardens and greenhouses radiating brilliant flowers and redolent herbs. You get "free sniffs" of herbs, plus a wonderful shop filled with potpourri, spices and dried-flower arrangements. Pack a lunch and picnic by the pond under the apple trees. Closed November through April. ~ 729 Mount Holly Road, Shrewsbury; 802-492-3565.

Northward lies **Rutland**, which earned the name "Marble City" during the mid-1800s when local marble mining exploded, though it was also the state's largest railroad junction. This commercial city—Vermont's second largest with 18,230 people—bears a handful of marble-plated buildings, but much of its marble was used for more than 250,000 headstones at Arlington National Cemetery in Virginia as well as the Lincoln Memorial in Washington, D.C., and the U.S. Supreme Court.

The **Rutland Region Chamber of Commerce** will assist with sightseeing in the area. ~ 256 North Main Street, Rutland; 802-773-2747.

The marble bridge, sidewalks and high school are a testament to more than a century of serious quarrying in nearby Proctor, where you can check out the **Vermont Marble Company Exhibit**, a series of intriguing marble displays with history to boot. Admission. Closed mid-October to mid-May. ~ 62 Main Street, Proctor; 802-459-2300.

A short (and very worthwhile) trip north on Route 7 will bring you to the town of **Brandon**, where you'll find one of the state's best expressions of 19th-century architecture. This fertile farming town, lined with serene, shady streets, was chartered in 1761 and was the birthplace of Stephen A. Douglas, the famous Illinois debater who lost the 1860 presidential race to Abe Lincoln. Excellent walking-tour maps are available at the **Brandon Area Chamber of Commerce**. ~ Central Square, Brandon; 802-247-6401; e-mail brandon@sover.net.

A sensational drive along Route 73, **Brandon Gap** cuts through precipitous mountains and miles of forest and gurgling brooks. While you're there, why not take a hiking or biking tour of the area? You can book reservations with **Country Inn Along the Trail**. They also offer wildflower and bird-watching walks in spring. ~ 834 Van Cortland Road, Brandon; 802-247-3300, 800-838-3301; www.innton.com

East of Rutland, **Killington** and **Pico** constitute the state's largest and perhaps most popular ski area, though the resort scene seems quite contrived when compared to the genuine quaintness of surrounding villages (as most any native Vermonter will quickly point out).

From Killington, go east on Route 4 to Route 100S, then it's just a few miles to **Plymouth Notch**. This gloriously remote mountain hamlet harbors the **President Calvin Coolidge State Historic Site**, where the 30th president was born and spent most of his life. The entire scene is quite striking, a thread of well-preserved white clapboard and stone buildings and gravel lanes set against stalwart trees and mountain peaks. There's a one-room schoolhouse, a general store operated by Coolidge's father, the 1924 Summer White House with all its original furnishings and the home where, following President Harding's sudden death, he took his 2:47 a.m. presidential oath. There is also a restaurant on the premises. Closed mid-October through Memorial Day. Admission. ~ Route 100A, Plymouth Notch; 802-672-3773.

A short drive east on Route 4 transforms you from bucolic byroads to overt affluence and centuries of prosperity in **Woodstock**. Superb red-brick and white clapboard buildings skirt the beautiful oval green, fashionable shops and restaurants line side streets and a chalkboard called the **Woodstock Town Crier** (Central and Elm streets) provides the scoop on local goings on.

For more detailed information, stop by the **Woodstock Area Chamber of Commerce**. ~ 18 Central Street, Woodstock; 802-457-3555; www.woodstockvt.com.

While some Vermonters bash Woodstock as bombastic, the community's attempts to preserve the natural surroundings shine through any pretensions that may exist. Power lines are hidden from sight, thanks to donations from resident Laurance Rockefeller, and rural beauty has been preserved at **Billings Farm and Museum**.

A railroad magnate and Rockefeller's grandfather-in-law, Frederick Billings established the farm in 1890, planted 10,000 trees and waged wars for agrarian protection. Today, exhibits take you through those early days of sidehill plows, corn planters and "nooning" (lunching) in the fields, providing an interesting reflection on 19th-century farming. You can even watch the cows being milked every afternoon. Open daily from May through October; open weekends only in November and December; closed January through April. Admission. ~ Route 12, Woodstock; 802-457-2355; www.billingsfarm.org.

Picturesque and subtly beguiling, neighboring **Quechee** lolls across the banks of the Ottauquechee River and claims a large concentration of resort estates. These grand mansions and sprawling country villas serve as summer homes for members of society's upper echelons and as eye-pleasing spectacles for passersby.

Even more inspiring than the resort estates is **Quechee Gorge**, a mammoth rocky chasm chiseled by the Ottauquechee River. Maple and fir trees skate down the rocky walls of the 165-foot-deep gorge, carved by glaciers during the Ice Age. It's a mile walk to the bottom, but the trek is scenic, cool and rewarding. ~ Route 4, ten miles north of Routes 89 and 91.

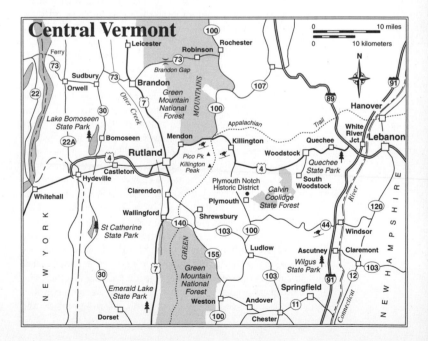

LODGING   There's plenty of room in the apartmentlike suites at **Best Western Hogge Penny Inn**, a modern hostelry just outside downtown. Set at the foot of the mountains, the medley of two-story frame buildings is accented by generous landscaping and a broad swimming pool. Expect one- and two-bedroom suites with vaulted ceilings, sectional couches, distinctive windows and kitchens with modern appliances. Motel rooms available. ~ Route 4, Rutland; phone/fax 802-773-3200, 800-828-3334. DELUXE TO ULTRA-DELUXE.

Nestled on a bank of rolling hills between Rutland and Killington, **The Vermont Inn** is a congenial 1840 farmhouse trimmed in chimneys and red-and-white awnings. The whole place is terribly cozy, a timeless structure of rubbed pine floors and cherrywood furniture. Bedrooms follow suit with eyelet quilts, private baths and fireplaces. ~ Route 4, Mendon; 802-775-0708, 800-541-7795, fax 802-773-2440. DELUXE.

Vermont supposedly acquired its name on top of Killington Peak in 1763 when the Reverend Samuel Peters ascended on horseback and proclaimed the area *Vert Mont*, French for "green mountain."

The Grey Bonnet Inn mixes new and old with 40 modern rooms decorated in country motifs and accompanied by amenities such as indoor and outdoor pools, tennis courts and an exercise room. Outside the two-story building wood shingles scale the walls and balconies, while inside the lobby is an intimate affair donned in carved wood beams, antique spinning wheels and a stately grandfather clock. Cross-country ski through the lodge's 25 acres, or take on Killington's slopes two miles away. The inn is closed from Columbus Day to Thanksgiving and from April to July. Complimentary breakfast. ~ Route 100N, Killington; 802-775-2537, 800-342-2086, fax 802-775-3371. MODERATE TO DELUXE.

Daniel Boone would have felt right at home in the **Inn at Long Trail**, a woodsy resting place with big country throw rugs, rustic furniture, pine tree pillars and a fieldstone fireplace. Vermont's original ski lodge, it has six fireplace suites with wood furniture, and 14 smaller rooms with private baths and cozy decor. But what ole' Dan would have liked best is the "relaxation room" fitted with a huge redwood hot tub. The inn is closed for a month after ski season, usually from late April to June. ~ Route 4, Killington; 802-775-7181, 800-325-2540, fax 802-747-7034; www.innatlongtrail.com, e-mail ilt@vermontel.com. DELUXE TO ULTRA-DELUXE.

Ski zealots will want to plant themselves at the **Mountain Green Ski and Golf Resort**, a maze of 216 alpine-style condominiums skirting the foot of Killington Peak. Here, convenience and amenities are stressed: lifts are within walking distance, and so are the heated outdoor pool and health spa. Accommodations range from studios to four-bedroom suites, all with fireplaces and modern designs such as vaulted ceilings and carpeting. ~ Killington Road, Killington Village; 802-422-3000, 800-336-7754, fax 802-422-2328. MODERATE TO ULTRA-DELUXE.

Despite its name, the large country-style **Cortina Inn** is actually a full-service resort. Its 97 rooms are individually decorated by the innkeepers. You'll find all the comforts here, including an indoor heated pool and fitness center with a hot tub and saunas. Some of the accommodations have fireplaces and some have decks. There are two restaurants on the premises. Killington Ski area is six miles away. ~ Route 4, Killington; 802-773-3333, 800-451-6108, fax 802-775-6948; www.cortinainn.com, e-mail cortina1@aol.com. MODERATE TO ULTRA-DELUXE.

About 16 miles north of Rutland, the lovely town of Brandon is a labyrinth of beautiful historic buildings, shade-giving maple trees and fine-trimmed lawns. Stashed away high in the mountains above Brandon, the **Churchill House Inn** is a fetching 1871 farmhouse known best to cross-country skiers, hikers and bikers. Three stories tall and fashioned in the Federal style, the inn features cozy sitting rooms with Early American furniture and Vermont casting stoves, as well as homey bedrooms adorned with pine plank floors and rocking chairs. Rates include homecooked breakfasts and gourmet dinners. Closed in April. ~ Route 73 East, Brandon; 802-247-3078, 877-248-7444, fax 802-247-0113; www.churchill museum.com. ULTRA-DELUXE.

The quintessence of Old World luxury exists at **The Canterbury House**, an elegant 1880 Victorian townhouse within walking distance of Woodstock's best sights and activities. Named after the *Canterbury Tales* (there's a Parson's Tale and Monk's Tale), eight air-conditioned bedrooms are decorated with refinement: antique spool and brass beds, pedestal sinks and old-fashioned clawfoot tubs. Within walking distance to restaurants and shops on the Village Green. ~ 43 Pleasant Street, Woodstock; 802-457-3077, 800-390-3077, fax 802-457-4630. DELUXE TO ULTRA-DELUXE.

Perhaps no other Vermont inn has received so much acclaim as the **Woodstock Inn & Resort**, partly because of all the luminaries who frequent the place. The other part is that it's just plain wonderful to look at and, of course, *be* at. Nestled against the village green, the grand, Colonial-style estate sports a ten-foot stone fireplace in its lobby and needlework rugs, solid wood beams and columns, and artwork from the Rockefeller collection. Most of the 144 rooms are furnished rather simply, but extensive amenities include a huge sports center, golf course, ski area and ski touring center. ~ Route 4 on the Village Green, Woodstock; 802-457-1100, 800-448-7900, fax 802-457-6699; www.woodstockinn.com, e-mail email@woodstockinn.com. ULTRA-DELUXE.

Run by a couple who fulfilled their dream of running away from their high-pressure New York City lives, the 28-room **Kedron Valley Inn** is a haven for other well-heeled escapees who need a shot of gentrified country life. Antique quilts adorn the guest rooms and common areas, and several rooms have furniture that has been handed down through the owners' families. Depending on the season, guests may stroll around the 15 acres, take a walk to nearby Woodstock, ski at one of the many nearby resorts, swim in the inn's enormous swimming pond or laze away a few hours on the front porch. Closed in April and the ten days immediately preceding Thanksgiving. Breakfast and dinner included. ~ Route 106, South Woodstock; 802-457-1473, 800-836-1193, fax 802-457-4469; www.innformation.com/vt/kedron, e-mail kedroninn @aol.com. ULTRA-DELUXE.

HIDDEN ►   **The Parker House Inn** is a meticulously renovated Victorian mansion with seven generously proportioned guest rooms (all with private bath) that are furnished with period antiques. One room has a (non-functioning) marble fireplace; another two rooms look out over the Ottauquechee River. Once the home of Senator Joseph Parker, this 1857 home is now a National Historic Site. Be sure to inspect the painstakingly preserved original stenciling on the plaster walls in the entrance hall. The restaurant features fresh produce, and guests may dine on the porch during warmer weather. Full breakfast included. ~ 16 Main Street, Quechee; 802-295-6077, fax 802-296-6696; www.theparkerhouseinn.com, e-mail parker_house_inn@valley.net. MODERATE TO DELUXE.

A sprawling 1793 farm that was home to Vermont's first lieutenant governor, **The Quechee Inn** radiates a spirit all its own. Relax in the rustic common room, complete with fireplace and grand piano, for a game or nightcap. Dine by candlelight on some of Vermont's own harvest in the restaurant. Retire to one of 24 rooms, each with private bath and air-conditioning, individually decorated with period furnishings. During the day, golf on one of two 18-hole, championship courses, play tennis, swim, canoe, bike or ski on the property that surrounds a scenic lake. Dinner is included. ~ 1119 Quechee Main Street, Quechee; 802-295-3133, 800-235-3133, fax 802-295-6587; www.quecheeinn.com, e-mail info@quecheeinn.com. ULTRA-DELUXE.

DINING   The surrounding Green Mountains make a perfect setting for the Austrian-style **Countryman's Pleasure**. Delicate pine chairs, pink draperies and straw wreaths complete this restored 1824 farmhouse-style interior, creating a soothing effect reminiscent of the majestic Alps. The impressive menu boasts roast duck with raspberry sauce and veal medallions with fiddleheads (a Vermont specialty), venison, grilled salmon and Jarlsberg. Closed occasionally on Sunday. ~ Off Route 4E on Town Line Road, Mendon; 802-

773-7141, fax 802-747-4959; www.countrymanspleasure.com, e-mail hentinter@aol.com. MODERATE TO DELUXE.

Just north of Rutland, **Swadi's Steak and Seafood** enjoys a longstanding reputation for serving thick, juicy, aged beef and fresh, no-nonsense seafood. The menu also features cajun-style entrées as well as nightly blackboard specials. Wood tables and chairs, dim lighting and a blazing fire make for a venerable Vermont atmosphere. ~ Route 7, Pittsford; 802-773-8124. MODERATE TO DELUXE.

For a bit of mountain funkiness, drop in to **Mother Shapiro's**, a joint that promises "Hot Food Till Last Call." Portions are large and range from kosher breakfasts and meat loaf to seafood salad and chicken soup. Popular with the après-ski set. ~ 1807 Killington Access Road, Killington; 802-422-9933. MODERATE TO DELUXE.

Beautifully prepared, innovative cuisine has garnered **Hemingway's** quite a reputation around these parts. Everything is fresh and scrupulously served among elegant surroundings of white tablecloths and crystal. The prix-fixe three- or four-course meal might include lobster and corn chowder with vanilla, sauté of pheasant with wild mushrooms or grilled striped bass with spring vegetables. The desserts are true works of art. Closed seasonally Monday and Tuesday. ~ Route 4, Killington; 802-422-3886, fax 802-422-3468; www.hemingwaysrestaurant.com. ULTRA-DELUXE.

Spooner's is a straightforward place that serves New York steak and mud pie. Situated in an old barn, the eatery bears a long brass bar, multiple archways and picture windows framing a pretty courtyard. Pickings are basic American, from burgers to sole. ~ Route 4, Woodstock; 802-457-4022. MODERATE TO DELUXE.

It began as a modest greenhouse that later took on a soda fountain. Now **Bentley's** is the local noshing post, an uptown eatery decked in antiques, lace curtains and fringed lampshades. You can show up in casual or dressy attire and feast on treats such as scampi pescatore, gourmet chili and fresh pasta. ~ 3 Elm Street, Woodstock; 802-457-3232; www.bentleysrestaurant.com, e-mail bentleys@bentleysrestaurant.com. MODERATE TO DELUXE.

Simon Pearce Restaurant affords an unusual blend of sophisticated cuisine and artistic talent. Glassblower Simon Pearce—who's quite well known around New England—has fashioned beautiful stemware and globes that rest on formal tablecloths. His creative Continental cuisine menu is a perfect accompaniment, highlighted by roast duck with mango chutney and sesame-crusted tuna with noodle cakes. The brick building—a story in itself—was an 1830s mill that produced the country's largest supply of wool flannel. ~ Main Street, Quechee; 802-295-1470, fax 802-295-2853. DELUXE TO ULTRA-DELUXE.

SHOPPING

HIDDEN ►

Chocolate peppermint, pineapple sage and lemon-scented marigold herbs create some fine smells (and tastes) at **Meadowsweet Herb Farm**, where several greenhouses and gardens make for merry shopping. They also sell wreaths, seasonings, herb plants and packaged herb seeds. ~ 729 Mount Holly Road, Shrewsbury; 802-492-3565.

Christmas is a year-round affair at **The Christmas Tree Barn**, a voluminous 1800s barn with every imaginable holiday item, plus potpourri, dried flower arrangements and oils. ~ 1481 Cold River Road, North Clarendon; 802-775-4585; www.christmas treebarn.com.

For unusual hand-crafted items, check out **Truly Unique Gift Shop**. Also available are various Vermont food products. ~ Route 4E, Rutland; 802-773-7742.

Woodstock's wealthy set fosters quite a posh shopping nest, centered downtown where strolling is very pleasurable. The **Vermont Workshop**, in an 1826 house, has an impressive cache of gifts, furniture and needlepoint kits. ~ 73 Central Street; 802-457-1400. Great kitchen treasures await at **F. H. Gillingham & Sons**, where you can pick up picnic baskets, costly wines and froufrou cooking devices. ~ 16 Elm Street, Woodstock; 802-457-2100. Indulge your eyes and nose together at **Primrose Garden**, a venerable assortment of fragrant potpourri and silk flowers, candelabras and blown glass. ~ 26 Central Street, Woodstock; 802-457-4049.

Vermont-style paraphernalia, from maple products and cheese to wicker baskets and country cookbooks, are all jammed under one big red roof at the vast **Quechee Gorge Village**. ~ Route 4W, Quechee; 802-295-1550.

NIGHTLIFE

Mother Shapiro's Restaurant houses a local watering hole with real character, featuring a piano player and jazz singer on Saturday nights in winter. ~ Killington Access Road, Killington; 802-422-9933.

During ski season, skiers jam into the **Pickle Barrel**, where you'll find late-night rock, a huge dancefloor and a barnlike environment. Closed May through September. Cover. ~ Killington Access Road, Killington; 802-422-3035; www.picklebarrelnight club.com.

The heart of trendiness, **Bentley's** is (and has been, forever) the town noshing spot, decked in lace curtains, antique lamps, and one long, polished bar. There's live music (in winter) on Friday night, and dancing to deejay music on Saturday night. ~ 3 Elm Street, Woodstock; 802-457-3232; www.bentleysrestaurant.com, e-mail bentleys@bentleysrestaurant.com.

BEACHES & PARKS

GREEN MOUNTAIN NATIONAL FOREST   See "Beaches & Parks" in the Southern Vermont section.

LAKE ST. CATHERINE STATE PARK With a three-mile shoreline, St. Catherine is one of Vermont's largest and most beautiful lakes. The 117-acre park borders only part of the lake, but its 250-foot beach draws large crowds, particularly on weekends. Swimming in the lake is exceptional and there are great opportunities to catch rainbow and lake trout, smelt, yellow perch, northern pike, bullhead and smallmouth and largemouth bass. There's also a trail where you're apt to see deer, raccoons and rabbits. Facilities include picnic areas, playground, concession stand and boat rentals. Closed from Columbus Day to Memorial Day. Day-use fee, $2. ~ On Route 30, three miles south of Poultney; 802-287-9158.

▲ There are 51 tent/RV sites ($13 a night) with hot showers, fireplaces and ten lean-tos ($17 a night); no hookups. There is also a non-refundable $5 reservation fee per site.

BOMOSEEN STATE PARK This vast area harbors Vermont's largest lake, Lake Bomoseen, along with an incredible stretch of forest sprinkled with dormant slate quarries. The park spans 2379 acres and contains yet another large freshwater body called Glen Lake. There's a nice long tawny beach on Bomoseen, plenty of surrounding nature trails, plus a visiting naturalist who conducts bird and wildflower walks and other programs. Swimming is good only in Lake Bomoseen, but fishing is exceptional at both lakes, with possibilities for panfish, yellow perch and bass. Facilities include picnic areas, a snack bar, and boat and canoe rentals. Day-use fee, $2. ~ Off of Route 4 on West Shore Road, about four miles north of Hydeville; 802-265-4242, 802-483-2001 (January–May).

▲ Permitted in 66 sites with hot showers, fireplaces and ten lean-tos but no hookups. Rates are $13 per night for tent/RV sites and $17 per night for lean-tos. There is also a non-refundable $5 reservation fee per site.

COOLIDGE STATE FOREST The 30th president spent most of his life in this incredibly scenic, remote swath of forest, which spans close to 17,000 acres and now serves as a nucleus for hiking, snowmobiling and relaxation. The dusky Black River and gurgling Broad Brook—great for wading and stone collecting—cut through dense, cool pine stands. Trails will lead you to magnificent views atop Shrewsbury and Killington Peaks. Within the forest is the 500-acre **Coolidge State Park**, where you'll find camping and hiking opportunities. There are picnic tables, restrooms, hiking and nature trails, and an extensive snowmobile network; the historic Calvin Coolidge Homestead is only two miles away. Closed mid-October to late-May. Day-use fee, $2. ~ Route 100A, two miles north of the intersection with Route 100, Plymouth; 802-672-3612.

▲ The state park has 25 tent/RV sites ($11 per night) and 32 lean-tos ($15 per night), with hot showers and fireplaces but no hookups. There is also a non-refundable $5 reservation fee per site.

CAMP PLYMOUTH STATE PARK 🚶 🚴 ⛵ 🎣 🏊 🚣 ⛵
There's gold in them there hills—at least in this park. Believe it or not, this 300-acre wooded spread attracts a sprinkling of gold diggers who wade ankle-deep and pan the silty bottom of the Buffalo Brook. Of course, no one has struck it rich lately, but who cares? This hilly park's other claim to fame is shimmering Echo Lake, which possesses a very pretty but small slice of cinnamon-colored sand. You can swim or try for smelt, trout, bass and yellow perch. Facilities include picnic tables, a playground, restrooms, a snack bar, volleyball, nature trails and boat rentals. Two cabins are available for rent. Closed from Labor Day to Memorial Day. Day-use fee, $2. ~ Off Route 100 just north of Ludlow in the town of Plymouth; 802-228-2025.

WILGUS STATE PARK 🚶 🚣 ⛵ This 100-acre park draws life from the very wide, very fertile Connecticut River. Most of the area is heavily wooded, but a small clearing allows for cool picnicking and nice views across the river to New Hampshire. There's no beach, but an opening in the steep river banks makes way for canoes. The strong currents discourage swimming. Facilities include picnic areas, restrooms, playground, canoe rentals and nature trails. Closed from mid-October to mid-May. Day-use fee, $2. ~ Route 5, south of Ascutney; 802-674-5422.

▲ There are 29 sites with nine lean-tos, including hot showers and fireplaces. Tent/RV sites are $12 per night and lean-tos are $16 per night. There is also a non-refundable $5 reservation fee per site.

QUECHEE STATE PARK 🚶 ⛵ This is one of the most visited parks in Vermont, and rightly so, since it provides access to the geological phenomenon called Quechee Gorge. Carved by glaciers during the Ice Age, the 163-foot gorge provides a cool, scenic milieu along the Ottauquechee River. Quite large, the 612-acre park mostly skirts calmer, flatter parts of the river and provides asylum for plenty of white-tailed deer. For anglers, this area is trout land. There are picnic tables, restrooms and top-notch nature trails. Closed from Columbus Day to Memorial Day. ~ Route 4, three miles west of Exit 189 in Quechee, six miles from White River Junction; 802-295-2990.

▲ There are 47 tent/RV sites ($12 per night) and seven lean-tos ($16 per night), with hot showers and fireplaces but no hookups. There is a non-refundable $5 reservation fee per site.

Seemingly limitless forests of maple trees, or "sugarbushes," have earned this region its image —along with a handsome maple syrup industry. Indeed, the entire region evokes a sense of ultimate Vermont charm, a place crisscrossed with valley farms and corn fields, winding country roads, hidden swimming holes and the whizzing Mad River that inspires virtually every part of local life.

▼▼▼▼▼▼▼▼▼▼▼▼▼
Northern Mountain Region

Most of the tranquil villages here can trace their roots to the early 1800s (some even further back), making them a delight to visit and investigate. Tiny, endearing Montpelier, the state capital, was established way back in 1805 after Vermont's legislature roamed for almost 30 years. Austria-like Stowe, its great alpine peaks forming a sea of green, harkens back to 1833 when it was a crossroads for travelers on horseback.

While longtime Vermonters surely appreciate the region's idyllic aura, it's the flatlanders—natives of New York, Massachusetts or any other place that's not Vermont—who have lately sought out the serenity of these vertical reaches. Typically owners of small businesses or bed and breakfasts, these "immigrants" have left the so-called good life in big cities for what they say is a better life among Vermont's Green Mountains.

Though the Sugarbush ski resort area churns up the most activity, the real local beauty lies in **Warren** (off Route 100 east of Lincoln Gap Road) and **Waitsfield** (northward along Route 100), a pair of pastoral towns with covered bridges, general stores and friendly, down-home folks.

SIGHTS

The region's alpine setting and excellent thermal currents make it a splendid place for **gliding**, also known as **soaring**. Ride the air currents 7500 feet up and secure a bird's-eye view of farmlands and mountaintop beaver ponds. Flights are offered at the **Warren–Sugarbush Airport**, where a pilot will take one or two passengers for rides lasting 15 to 30 minutes. Rides are offered from mid-May to the end of October only. ~ Airport Road off Route 100; 802-496-2290; www.sugarbush.org, e-mail soar@sugarbush.org.

East on Route 89 lies **Montpelier**. With a population of only 8500, Montpelier is the smallest state capital in the nation, though its grand old buildings and manicured cityscapes may well be the country's most charming. To direct you around town—and the state—the **Vermont Travel Division** provides an impressive array of information on sights as well as history, culture and economy. ~ 134 State Street, Montpelier; 802-828-3236, 800-837-6668.

Montpelier's sister city is **Barre**, though no two siblings could be less alike. Barre is the rough-and-tumble one of the pair, a working-class town put on the map by the granite industry. During the late 1800s, thousands of European and Canadian immigrant stoneworkers flocked to town, making Barre quite a bustling place and along the way producing frequent labor disputes and strong movements toward socialism.

Today, this self-proclaimed Granite Capital of the World harbors the largest monumental granite quarry in the world, known as **The Rock of Ages**. This colossal stony pit, which plunges more than 485 feet down and spans 50 acres, is strewn with mining equipment and boulders. Open May through October, weather permitting. Admission for tours. ~ Main Street, off Route 14, Graniteville; 802-476-3115; www.rockofages.com.

Some of the granite found its final resting place at the **Hope Cemetery**, a fascinating collection of memorial art. The delicate engravings of granite craftsmen (often designed for their deceased brethren) survive on everything from small headstones and ornate monuments to giant mausoleums. There are scrolls, hearts, religious sculptures and even a large soccer ball. ~ Merchant Street, Barre.

Remember those two crazy guys named Ben and Jerry who hit the big time with an ice cream recipe? Here's where you'll find them, smack in the middle of Vermont rural country, at **Ben & Jerry's Ice Cream Factory Tours**. The factory—the state's number one tourist attraction—is a lesson in American free enterprise. You'll see the creamy stuff being made, get free samples in their tasting room, watch a short film and learn about two guys who haven't let success stand in the way of having fun. Ben and Jerry are revered around this state, and not surprisingly, since one out of ten Vermont families bought stock in their ice cream corporation when they went public. Tours are offered daily, but no ice cream is made on Sunday and holidays. Admission. ~ Route 100N, Waterbury; 802-244-5641; www.benjerry.com.

Another fun stopover is the **Cold Hollow Cider Mill**, an old barn that houses a small apple cider mill and a vast country gift shop. You can watch the apple presses at work year-round. ~ Route 100, Waterbury Center, Waterbury; 802-244-8771, fax 802-244-7212; www.coldhollow.com, e-mail coldholl@together.net.

Northward along Route 100 lies picturesque, alpine **Stowe**, a country town augmented by a bustling ski resort area and set against a deep green necklace of mountains.

The busy "downtown" area, situated at the crossroads of Route 100 and Mountain Road, is a pleasing meld of 19th-century buildings and contemporary marts and restaurants. All the ski action awaits up Mountain Road, a seven-mile jog lined with hotels and inns, shops, pubs and eateries of every culinary calling.

Vermont's highest peak, **Mount Mansfield**, looms 4393 feet above the town and presents an incredible backdrop, its craggy profile resembling the silhouette of a human face. In the summer, you can take an auto toll road or gondola ride to the summit of Mount Mansfield then ride down the thrilling **alpine slide**. Admission. ~ Mountain Road; 802-253-7311, fax 802-253-3439; www.stowe.com.

The Stowe Land Trust was established during the 1980s by a group of Stowe citizens dedicated to preserving the rural quality of life in and around this picturesque mountain village. One of the trust's conservation projects is the **Wiessner Woods**, 80 acres of woods, streams and meadows that overlook the Stowe valley from Edson Hill. If you keep your eyes open and your conversation quiet, you're likely to see partridge, thrush, falcons and perhaps even an owl. From Mountain Road, turn right onto Edson Hill Road, three and a half miles from the village. Pass the entrance to the Stowehof Inn. Take the next drive on the right. Park on the left in the marked parking area. From here follow signs to the Wiessner Woods trailhead.

Several decades after the film *The Sound of Music* was released, Stowe visitors still keep asking the same question: how do we get to the **Trapp Family Lodge**? Certainly much of the town's appeal is bound to the history and beauty of this place, built as a singing camp during the 1940s by Maria Von Trapp and her

Northern Mountain Region

Montpelier's State Street

A casual walk down State Street, the main street along the north shore of the Winooski River, reveals the architectural charms of America's smallest state capital. Simply start at the **Vermont Travel Division Tourist Information Center** (134 State Street; 802-828-3236, 800-837-6668) by the Bailey Avenue Bridge and walk east.

CAPITAL BUILDINGS   The **State House** (c. 1836), with its gold-leaf dome resting dramatically against the evergreens of Hubbard Park, easily takes center stage. Modeled after the Greek temple of Theseus, the granite granddaddy sports a statue of Ceres, Roman goddess of agriculture. Take a free tour (mid-July to mid-October) or wander around and muse over the Civil War murals, Victorian decor and quotations by Theodore Roosevelt, Ethan Allen and other national legends. Closed Sunday in summer; closed Saturday and Sunday the rest of the year. ~ 115 State Street; 802-828-2228. Across the street, the **State Agriculture Building** (c. 1891), originally built as the home office of the National Life Insurance Company, features a Romanesque red brick facade, a conglomerate of roof styles, fanciful turrets and arched, convex windows. ~ 116 State Street. In contrast is another former insurance building, the symmetrical and stately **Vermont Department of Personnel** (c. 1870), an elegant Victorian with a mansard roof and Corinthian columns. ~ 110 State Street.

STATE STREET   The Pavilion Building, which houses the **Vermont Historical Society Museum**, is a modern reconstruction of the exterior of the Pavilion Hotel of 1876, an elegant Steamboat Gothic struc-

family. The baroness chose the spot because she said it resembled her beloved Austrian Alps. The Tyrolean-style buildings of the lodge sit high on a mountain, surrounded by 2500 acres of forest, ponds and pasture. Alpine ridges extend as far as the eye can see. During the summer, popular Sunday concerts are held in an adjacent meadow. Though Maria died in 1987, her family still runs the lodge. ~ 700 Trapp Hill Road off Mountain Road, Stowe; 802-253-8511, 800-826-7000, fax 802-253-5740.

There's no sign for **Bingham Falls**, but you won't want to miss this pristine look at nature's handiwork. A rocky footpath winds a quarter mile through the evergreen forest, culminating at a scenic gorge where rushing, gurgling water swirls around large boulture with inviting piazzas that provided lodging for legislators during sessions. The museum presents changing exhibits of fine and decorative arts, farm and industrial equipment and memorabilia that imaginatively traces the state's history. ~ 109 State Street; 802-828-2291. The three grand brick homes—one partly hidden by a service station—at **107, 99 and 89 State Street** are remnants of the vanished era of the 1820s, when the street was lined with high Federal style architecture.

SINNERS AND SAINTS   The Greek Revival **Washington County Courthouse** (c. 1844 and 1880), with its classic clock tower, is the county's third courthouse. After the second was destroyed by fire, this one was built from local granite. Its interior has been modernized, but the original wooden stairway remains intact. ~ 65 State Street. Behind the courthouse is the **Jailhouse Common** (c. 1857). The difference in brick between the first and second stories reveals that it was expanded in 1911. ~ 22–24 Elm Street. Across the street from the courthouse stands the Gothic **Episcopal Church** (c. 1867), more striking inside than out because its spire was removed for safety reasons after a fire and flood in 1927. ~ 64 State Street.

BUSINESS BUILDINGS   The simple-frame **Langdon Building** (before 1853) represents the kind of storefront that was typical in most Vermont towns before brick came into wide use in the mid-19th century. ~ 4 Langdon Street. The bank building at **41–45 State Street** (c. 1874), with its turn-of-the-20th-century mansard roof, has always been a bank, though its exterior has been modernized at least twice. Finally, the Italianate **Walton Block** (c. 1879), with its stamped sheet metal ornaments and cast-iron columns, typifies the style of storefronts in the late 19th century. It was the first structure in Montpelier to undergo historical restoration, beginning in 1967.

ders. A great swimming hole, if you don't mind chilly waters. ~ Off Mountain Road, about 100 yards north of The Lodge resort.

LODGING

The closest proximity to downhill skiing can be found at **Sugarbush Village Condominiums**, where you can choose from 150 condos (many ski-in and ski-out) sprinkled about the base of Sugarbush North and South. Most accommodations are modern apartment-style, though they vary widely from small studios and loft apartments to townhouses and four-bedroom condos. ~ Sugarbush Access Road, Sugarbush Village; 802-583-3000, 800-451-4326, fax 802-583-2373; www.sugarbushvillage.com, e-mail sugares@madriver.com. DELUXE TO ULTRA-DELUXE.

Set on a lovely hill, enveloped by terraced lawns, cobbled paths and winding streams, **Sugarbush Inn** is the plushest hostelry near the ski slopes. Inside the vanilla clapboard inn is a lobby done in dark, polished woods and rich blues, and 46 guest rooms adorned with country wallpapers, handloomed rugs and reproduction antiques. The Terrace restaurant, with its brick floors, French doors and mountain views, is a marvelous place for breakfast. An extensive health club, a golf course and 11 tennis courts make this the best resort choice in Sugarbush. ~ Sugarbush Access Road, Warren; 802-583-2301, 800-537-8427, fax 802-583-3209. ULTRA-DELUXE.

You can get a true feel for Vermonters and their lifestyles if you stay at **Lareau Farm**, a picturesque 67-acre spread hugging the Mad River. The owners are convivial and genuine, ready to show you their farming methods, local customs and all the town crazies. The 1832 farmhouse is quintessential New England: big gracious rooms with wide-plank floors, a living room with a fireplace, a fabulous gazebo-style porch overlooking the mountains and 13 very comfortable bedrooms with antique beds and plush quilts made by the owners. Closed early November and late April. ~ Route 100, Waitsfield; 802-496-4949, 800-833-0766, fax 802-496-7979; www.lareaufarminn.com, e-mail lareau@madriver.com. MODERATE.

Call it pastoral luxury or rural fancy, but the **1824 House Inn** is the place to indulge while soaking up the country. Set on more than 22 scenic acres in the Mad River Valley, this two-story gabled farmhouse is awash with beautiful antiques, oriental and dhurrie rugs, and a distinct air of elegance and precise design. Eight bright and airy bedrooms are done in different themes, plus a gracious dining room where guests get treated to fresh garden omelettes, huevos rancheros and fruit-filled baked pancakes. ~ Route 100, Waitsfield; 802-496-7555, 800-426-3986, fax 802-496-7559; www.1824house.com, e-mail 1824@madriver.com. DELUXE.

SMUGGLERS NOTCH

Perhaps the area's ultimate nature encounter occurs at **Smugglers Notch** (Mountain Road), a slender, sensational pass through the mountains with dramatic sheets of silver rock on either side. Used as a secret passage between Canada and the U.S. during the War of 1812, the notch harbors dozens of intriguing rock formations (check out the singing bird and elephant head) and a rock crevasse where the summer temperature hovers around 49°. Keep an eye out for rock climbers who navigate the cliffs and rappel down.

The most eloquent place to stay in the state capital is **The Inn at Montpelier**, a pair of stately antebellum buildings that breathe history. There are high ceilings and beautiful Victorian furnishings, ten fireplaces and an enormous wraparound porch dotted with hanging plants and fan-back chairs. Lavishly decorated, the 19 guest rooms feature mirrored armoires, Queen Anne and teak poster beds and polished pedestal sinks. Well worth the price. ~ 147 Main Street, Montpelier; 802-223-2727, fax 802-223-0722; www.innatmontpelier.com, e-mail mail2inn@aol.com. DELUXE TO ULTRA-DELUXE.

The prow-like roofline of the **Stowehof Inn and Resort** is deceptive: there's nothing remotely marinelike about this large, luxurious hotel. Perched on a hillside that overlooks the dips and swells of the Stowe valley, the Stowehof's generous spaces are attentively fitted out, with comfortable chairs in the lounge area and extra-thick drapes on the bedroom windows for guests to block out the bright morning light. Room decor varies: when you call for a reservation, ask about the range of rooms available during your visit (and unless you really want one, request a room without a mirrored wall). Although most travelers associate the Stowe area with winter sports, the Stowehof is a true four-season resort: in addition to the miles of cross-country trails and sleigh rides available right from the hotel during the winter, a swimming pool, four tennis courts, and stables and riding lessons are available for guests' use during warmer weather. Breakfast included. ~ 434 Edson Hill Road, Stowe; 802-253-9722, 800-932-7136, fax 802-253-7513. DELUXE TO ULTRA-DELUXE.

Butternut is one of those inns that tries to be homey and elegant at the same time—and pulls it off swimmingly. Wrought with dozens of beautiful country American antiques, the four-story lodge is nearly a museum. There's more refinement outside, where twinkling lights meander through evergreens, and a gazebo overlooks a swimming pool and perennial gardens. There are also four miles of lighted cross-country skiing trails lacing through the inn's eight-acre landscape. The fireside breakfasts, cozy game room, hot tub, river and mountain views, and warmly decorated bedrooms suggest quite a snug lodging experience. A full country breakfast is included. ~ Mountain Road, Stowe; 802-253-4277, 800-328-8837, fax 802-253-5263; www.butternutinnvt.com, e-mail inn stowe2@aol.com. DELUXE.

One of the best bargains in the area is **The Siebeness**, a straightforward country inn with comfy bedrooms. Count on a homelike setting with two floors of rooms adorned simply but tastefully in heavy wood antiques, downy, hand-stitched quilts and wall stenciling. Two cottage houses are also available, with jacuzzis and fireplaces. All units have private baths. There's a large pool and a hidden mountain stream out back, plus bountiful breakfasts that are extra special. ~ Mountain Road, Stowe; 802-253-8942, 800-426-9001, fax 802-253-9232; www.siebeness.com, e-mail siebeness@aol.com. DELUXE TO ULTRA-DELUXE.

Endless waves of mountains and evergreen valleys create a milieu that's nothing short of sensational at the **Trapp Family Lodge**. This peaceful, 2500-acre slice of nirvana was set up as a 1940s singing camp by Maria Von Trapp. Tyrolean in style, the enchanting buildings have flowerpots that brim with kaleidoscopic colors and 93 guest rooms simply adorned in dark woods and muted colors and featuring modern amenities. You can't miss the scenic pond, two swimming pools edged with lawn, greenhouse and gardens—and many more sightseers than guests. ~ 700 Trapp Hill Road, Stowe; 802-253-8511, 800-826-7000, fax 802-253-5740. ULTRA-DELUXE.

A serene French Provincial manor obscured down a winding mountain road, **Edson Hill Manor** offers 225 acres of solitude amid majestic surroundings. Featuring hewn-wood ceilings and oriental rugs, the main house offers nine spacious rooms—five with beautiful fireplaces—while a carriage house contains 16 guest rooms. You'll also find a terraced swimming pool, riding stables, nature trails and plenty of cross-country skiing possibilities. Full breakfast and dinner included in the rates. ~ Edson Hill Road off Mountain Road, Stowe; 802-253-7371, 800-621-0284, fax 802-253-4036; www.stowevt.com, e-mail edsonhill@stowevt.net. DELUXE TO ULTRA-DELUXE.

DINING

This is ski country, and most restaurants cater to those tired skiers with hearty appetites. Oftentimes, you'll find a cauldron of soup steaming over a blazing hearth and cushy chairs for snuggling.

The refinement and understated elegance of **The Common Man** has earned it a solid culinary reputation across Vermont. Situated in a 19th-century barn, the place is simply romantic. Pretty chandeliers hang from high beam ceilings, while well-spaced tables hug a large stone hearth. The cuisine is *très* gourmet, with an accent on native offerings. There's *faisan rôti* (Vermont pheasant), Vermont veal sweetbreads and *caneton* normandy (roasted duckling with apple glaze). Dinner only. Closed Monday during summer. ~ German Flats Road, Warren; 802-583-2800, fax 802-583-2826. MODERATE TO DELUXE.

Two miles down an unmarked dirt road rests the **Diner Soar Deli**, a splendid spot to observe all the local airplane activity. Nestled atop of a teeny building called the Warren-Sugarbush Airport, the Diner Soar affords exhilarating views of the surrounding Green Mountains and valleys. A diligent young owner serves inexpensive breakfasts, soups and deli fare, along with delicious baked desserts. It's a great place to hang loose. Closed November to Memorial Day. ~ Warren-Sugarbush Airport, Airport Road, Warren; 802-496-8831. BUDGET.

A charming 1850s inn and restaurant, the **Millbrook Inn and Restaurant** truly captures the flavor of Vermont. The decor is warm and inviting, with wide-plank floors, country antiques and paintings of local life. A congenial couple acts as manager and chef, serving hand-rolled pastas and very special pies. Entrées include two fresh fish specials every day, an "innkeeper's choice" of roast meat, *badami rogan josh* (lamb) and several curry dishes. Closed April, May and November. Open daily in winter and fall and closed Tuesday in summer. ~ Route 17, Waitsfield; 802-496-2405, 800-477-2809; www.millbrookinn.com, e-mail millbrkinn @aol.com. MODERATE.

If a place for steak is what you need, try **The Steak Place at Tucker Hill Inn**. The restaurant features Angus certified steaks as well as wood-smoked baby-back ribs, chicken, seafood and vegetarian meals. There is a lighter, late-night menu served in the pub for night owls. ~ Marble Hill Road, Waitsfield; 802-496-3983, 800-543-7841; www.tuckerhill.com, e-mail tuckerhill@tuckerhill. com. MODERATE TO DELUXE.

In Montpelier, the New England Culinary Institute operates three restaurants where you'll discover very vogue cuisine. The most upscale is the **Chef's Table**, which serves innovative and classical American cuisine in an intimate setting. The red walls, antique oil paintings and low lighting create a Baroque effect and a romantic atmosphere. The seasonal menu changes daily and features gourmet dishes such as warm goat cheese Napoleon and hickory-smoked duck. No lunch on Saturday. Closed Sunday. ~ 118 Main Street, Montpelier; 802-229-9202. MODERATE TO DELUXE.

For more casual surroundings, visit the Culinary Institute's **Main Street Grill & Bar** downstairs. This casual bistro offers hearty fare amidst eclectic country decor. There is a seasonal menu, but try the portabello mushroom sandwich or the herbed

---

BREAKFAST BRIGHT AND EARLY

To experience the true flavor of **McCarthy's**, get there just after dawn when local farmers arrive dressed in overalls and straw hats. This congenial breakfast and lunch café offers friendly service, huge portions and great prices. You'll find apple and blueberry pancakes with hot Vermont syrup, country eggs Benedict, sticky buns and pumpkin bread. Surroundings are modern and airy with Irish country touches. ~ Mountain Road, Stowe; 802-253-8626. BUDGET.

roast chicken with garlic mashed potatoes. The outdoor patio is open in the summer. ~ 118 Main Street, Montpelier; 802-223-3188. BUDGET TO MODERATE.

At **La Brioche Bakery and Café**, also run by the Institute, you can pick up puffy croissants, gourmet cookies, napoleons and other baked goodies. ~ 89 Main Street, Montpelier; 802-229-0443, fax 802-229-6462; www.neculinary.com. BUDGET.

The glistening gold-plated dome of the state capitol peeks through the windows of the **Horn of the Moon Café**, a bohemian habitat with bamboo shades and scuffed wooden floors. Politicians like to hobnob over the vegetarian inventory of imaginative soups, salads and desserts. Try the spinach tortilla wrap. Closed Monday. ~ 8 Langdon Street, Montpelier; 802-223-2895. BUDGET TO MODERATE.

HIDDEN ► For top-notch Tex-Mex fare, check out **Julio's**. This serene downtown niche, stashed up a rickety flight of stairs, offers up basic south-of-the-border entrées plus interesting selections such as Mexican pizzas and egg rolls. There's a shiny oak bar, brick archways and walls covered with Mexican prints and local art. No lunch on Saturday and Sunday. ~ 44 Main Street, Montpelier; 802-229-9348. BUDGET.

Jack's Backyard is a popular town rendezvous with real flair. The two-story, ranch-style eatery is flanked by wagon wheels and exhibits walls smothered in old license plates and farm tools. Popcorn is divvied up in tin pails for those with "drinking" appetites, but most opt for the potpourri of stacked sandwiches, chili, crêpes and salads. Lunch only. Closed Sunday. ~ 9 Maple Avenue, Barre; 802-479-9134. BUDGET.

Montpelier is the only state capital in the U.S. without a McDonalds.

The beautiful **Trapp Family Lodge** boasts one of the area's most renowned dining rooms. Situated in a marvelous mountain setting, the restaurant is simple yet elegant, with picture windows, draped hanging plants and light oak tables. The food is gourmet Continental with Austrian touches. Try the *zwiebelrostbraten* (Viennese onion steak) or the *wienerschnitzel* (breaded and sautéed veal cutlets). The menu is prix-fixe, with a five-course meal. ~ 700 Trapp Hill Road, Stowe; 802-253-8511, 800-826-7000, fax 802-253-5740. ULTRA-DELUXE.

Culinary aficionados won't want to miss **Isle de France**, a classic French restaurant with all the trimmings. The decor is terribly Parisian, accented by provincial furniture, impressionist paintings, huge, ornate mirrors and well-spaced tables designed for romance. The menu is an assortment of fresh seafood, steak, poultry, sweetbreads and frogs' legs, all draped in a variety of heady sauces and beautifully served. But here's the real scoop: dine in the lounge on similar but less expensive entrées from a revolving menu. After dinner retreat to the separate cigar bar for a smoke and a cordial in front of the fire. Dinner only. Closed Monday. ~ Mountain Road, Stowe; 802-253-7751, fax 802-253-9809. MODERATE TO ULTRA-DELUXE.

Absolutely don't miss **The Warren Store**, a former stagecoach inn that's like Grandpa's general store. The place starts with a jumble of fresh farm produce, jams, homemade honey and baskets, continues with a wonderful bakery, then finishes upstairs with clothing, jewelry and leather goods. ~ Main Street, Warren; 802-496-3864.

SHOPPING

Even if you leave empty-handed, don't miss a trip to **The Store**, a bi-level, cook's fantasy world of gourmet gadgets galore. They also feature accessories for the home, and American, English and Irish antiques. ~ Route 100, Waitsfield; 802-496-4465.

More than 50,000 books crowd **The Yankee Paperback Exchange**, where you'll find everything from old classics and out-of-print gems to volumes on religion, cooking and lifestyles. Closed Sunday. ~ 11 Langdon Street, Montpelier; 802-223-3239.

Outside of ski season, the main industry in Stowe appears to be the creation of quality arts and crafts. While galleries abound, the widest selection of work by local artisans can be found at the **Stowe Craft Gallery & Shimmering Glass**, where wares range from delicate crystal and Tiffany-style stained-glass lamps to Judaica jewelry and handmade furniture. ~ 55 Mountain Road, Stowe; 877-456-8388; www.stowecraft.com.

Women won't need to vacillate at **Decisions, Decisions**, where they can choose among beautiful sleepwear, lingerie and snug winter items. ~ 1056 Mountain Road, # 7, Stowe; 802-253-4183.

The Blue Tooth is an after-the-slopes place to hang loose and, on Saturday, listen to live contemporary music. Cover. ~ Sugarbush Access Road, Warren; 802-583-2656.

NIGHTLIFE

Local theater in Vermont tends to be high quality, and such is the case at **Valley Players Theater**, which focuses on drama, comedy and children's productions performed in a 200-seat, two-story, brick building. ~ Route 100, Waitsfield; 802-496-9612.

Politicians rub elbows at **The Thrush Tavern**, a tiny watering hole with framed old photos and occasional live folk music. ~ 107 State Street, Montpelier; 802-223-2030.

Tattered carpets lie before a worn pine bar at **Charlie O's**, a pool hall with live R&B on the weekend and a sound system that cranks. ~ 70 Main Street, Montpelier; 802-223-6820.

The **Main Street Grill & Bar** is a comfortable basement bar with exposed flagstone walls, original artwork and one of the state's largest collections of wine, beer and liquor. ~ 118 Main Street, Montpelier; 802-223-3188.

One of the hottest night spots in town is **The Rusty Nail**, with live bands and dancing on weekends; it's packed to the rafters during ski season. ~ Mountain Road, Stowe; 802-253-6245; www.matterhornbar.com.

The Matterhorn, Bamboo Bar and Oasis Grill, a voluminous rock-and-roll bar perched near the base of Mt. Mansfield, hosts big-name rock groups during the ski season. Cover. ~ Mountain Road, Stowe; 802-253-8198; www.matterhornbar.com.

BEACHES & PARKS

GREEN MOUNTAIN NATIONAL FOREST   See "Beaches & Parks" in the Southern Vermont section.

LITTLE RIVER STATE PARK 🏃 🚴 ⛵ ⛴ 🏊 🚤 🛶 A dense, bushy area within Mount Mansfield State Forest, this park spans 12,000 acres of maple, birch and fir forests and a big man-made body of water called the Waterbury Reservoir. There are two campers-only beaches—one in a wooded camping area and the other in a large picnic clearing. Nature lovers will revel in the excellent gridwork of trails. Swimming and fishing (for perch, rainbow trout, and small and bigmouth bass) are good all over the reservoir. Facilities include picnic tables, restrooms, a playground and boat rentals. Closed mid-October to mid-May. Day-use fee, $2. ~ From the junction of Routes 100 and 2, take Route 2 one and a half miles west to Little River Road and go north for three and a half miles; 802-244-7103.

▲ There are 101 sites with hot showers, fireplaces and 20 lean-tos. Fees are $13 per night for tent/RV sites (no hookups); $17 per night for lean-tos. There is also a non-refundable $5 reservation fee per site.

GROTON STATE FOREST 🏃 ⛵ 🏊 🚤 🛶 This 25,625-acre wonderland harbors several natural jewels. Fishing is good at the campgrounds, but the best place in the forest is Seyon Ranch State Park. One of the most popular forest activities is the hike to the summit of **Owl's Head Mountain** (802-584-3820), where incredible views stretch across Camel's Hump Forest. ~ Access points are located off Routes 302 and 232 northwest of Groton.

▲ Groton Forest has five camping areas, including primitive, group and developed campgrounds. All of the areas mentioned below have camping except Boulder Beach, which is day-use only. There is also a non-refundable $5 reservation fee per site at all the state parks.

Seyon Ranch State Park 🏃 ⛵ 🛶 There's outstanding flyfishing here; you'll find a trout pond and rowboat rentals. Closed November to mid-April. Day-use fee, $2. ~ Located just off Route 302 three miles west of Groton; 802-584-3829.

▲ The lodge here rents private and semiprivate accommodations. Meals are available.

Ricker Pond State Park 🛶 ⛵ 🚤 ⛴ This camping-only facility has a boat launch and rentals (canoes, kayaks, paddleboats). Anglers hook perch, bass and pickerel. Swim at your own risk—there are no lifeguards. Fireplaces, restrooms and showers are available. Closed Labor Day to week before Memorial Day. Visitor fee, $2. ~ Located on Route 232, three miles northwest of Route 302; 802-584-3821.

▲ Campers choose from 32 tent/RV sites ($13 per night), 23 lean-tos ($17 per night) and a cabin ($51 per night).

Boulder Beach State Park 🛶 ⛵ 🚤 ⛴ At this picturesque beach, bulky rocks dot the coarse, cream-tinted sand that edges Lake Groton. Small boats laze across the water, surrounded by mighty stands of evergreen trees. Swimming is excellent along a calm, shallow shelf at Boulder Beach. There are picnic areas, restrooms, boat rentals, a snack bar and a pavilion. Nearby is the **Groton Nature Center** (802-584-3827), which houses interesting displays of plant and animal life. Closed Labor Day to week before Memorial Day. Day-use fee, $2. ~ From Groton, go two miles west on Route 302, then six miles northwest on Route 232, then two mile east on Boulder Beach Road; 802-584-3823.

Stillwater State Park 🚶 🛶 ⛵ 🚤 🚤 ⛴ Facilities at Stillwater include picnic tables, fireplaces, boat rentals, dock, boat launch, playground and showers. Closed from Columbus Day to mid-May. Visitor fee, $2. ~ From Groton, go two miles west on Route 302, then six miles northwest on Route 232, then one mile east on Boulder Beach Road; 802-584-3822.

▲ There are 62 tent/RV sites ($13 per night) and 17 lean-tos ($17 per night).

New Discovery State Park 🚶 ⛴ New Discovery (on Osmore Pond) offers a scenic clearing for picnicking. You'll find picnic tables, restrooms, showers and pavilions. Closed Labor Day to week before Memorial Day. Visitor fee, $2. ~ On Route 232, nine and a half miles northwest of Route 302; 802-584-3820.

▲ There are 47 tent/RV sites ($13 per night) and 14 lean-tos ($17 per night).

SMUGGLERS NOTCH STATE PARK 🚶 🚲 Wedged at the apex of two stony, sheer mountains, Smugglers Notch offers idyllic surroundings of rock ledges and formations, fern grottos and damp caves for exploring. The park itself comprises 25 acres of shady, brookside picnic grounds, but you can walk to many choice sights outside the park grounds, including frigid Big Springs pool and the 6000-ton King Rock that broke from the mountain in 1910. Check out the great elephant head formation just above King Rock. There are picnic tables, restrooms and hiking trails. Closed from Columbus Day to mid-May. Day-use fee, $2. ~ On Route 108 (Mountain Road) in Stowe, about eight miles north of Route 100 junction; 802-253-4014.

▲ Small area with 21 tent/RV sites ($12 per night) and 14 lean-tos ($16 per night); hot showers and fireplaces but no hookups.

HIDDEN ►   **UNDERHILL STATE PARK** 🏃 Remote and rustic, this pretty park lies in the midst of back country, smothered in maple and birch trees and filled with moose, bear, deer, rabbits and raccoons. It lies within the 34,000-acre Mt. Mansfield State Forest and features four popular trails that ascend the western flank of Mount Mansfield. The park also holds rare, federally protected alpine tundra, which can only be viewed from specific trails. To get here, you'll have to tackle three miles of steep gravel road—but it's well worth it. There is a picnic shelter and restrooms. The park is closed from Columbus Day to Memorial Day. Day-use fee, $2. ~ From the town of Essex Junction, go nine miles east on Route 15, then four miles east on Pleasant Valley Road, then three miles east on gravel Mountain Road (there's a sign at this point); 802-899-3022.

▲ Camping is at a small primitive area with 11 tent sites ($12 per night) and six lean-tos ($16 per night). There is also a non-refundable $5 reservation fee per site.

Champlain Valley

A great big meeting of mountains, water and islands, the Champlain Valley is a prosperous, breathtaking region that ambles leisurely along Vermont's northwestern edge. Lake Champlain, the area's frame of reference, stretches 130 glistening miles and divides Vermont's flat, irregular lakefront border from New York's Adirondack Mountains. Back in 1609, French explorer Samuel de Champlain discovered the lake, named it for himself and laid the groundwork for its flourishing maritime history. Champlain Valley is also home to Vermont's most populated city, Burlington, which was founded in 1763.

SIGHTS   The state's most popular attraction lies in this region. Just south of Burlington, the **Shelburne Museum** is really a *collection* of buildings—37 to be exact. It takes two days to tackle this amazing 45-acre trek through Vermont and New England history. There's something for everyone here, from the 220-foot sidewheel steamboat and toy shop to the 1786 sawmill. Kids and adults will love the circus building with its carousel ride and remarkable 500-foot miniature circus parade that took 30 years to complete. The museum's Owl Cottage Family Activity Center has a children's dress-up exhibit, historical puzzles and toys. The Electra Havemeyer Webb Memorial Building contains artwork from Degas, Monet, Manet and Cassatt. A 168-foot covered bridge, built in 1845 and moved to the museum from Cambridge, Vermont, is the United States' only remaining two-lane bridge with a footpath. If snipes, loons and yellowlegs are your bag, stop in the wildfowl decoy exhibit, where an eye-popping 1000 specimens line the walls. A marvelous place to muse, the hat and fragrance textile gallery has hat boxes, costumes, perfumes, quilts and textiles dating back to the early 1800s. You'll also find the state's largest collection of folk art, divided among several buildings. Admission (good for two consecutive days). ~ Route 7, Shelburne; 802-985-3346, fax 802-985-2331; www.shelburnemuseum.org, e-mail museinfo@together.net.

Board a covered wagon for a tour of **Shelburne Farms**, a vast land empire that gives new meaning to the term "pastoral aristocracy." Sprawled across 1400 acres along Lake Champlain, the estate was designed back in the 1800s for Dr. William Seward Webb and wife Lila Vanderbilt, whose 24-room Queen Anne Revival farmhouse is still one of the largest in Vermont. The beautiful grounds—a series of free-flowing perennials, statues and fountains—were designed by Frederick Law Olmsted, architect of New York City's Central Park. There are extensive walking trails, scenic picnic sites and a children's farmyard. Closed mid-October to late May. Admission. ~ Bay and Harbor roads, off Route 7, Shelburne; 802-985-8686; www.shelburnefarms.org.

Five miles south of the Shelburne Museum is the **Vermont Wildflower Farm**, which sells more wildflower seeds than any other flower farm in the eastern United States. If you're not allergic to pollen, take an hour or so to wander along the paths that cross the six acres. The stupendous array of flowers are thoughtfully labeled with plaques describing the plants' provenance and, often, relating legends about the mystical powers attributed to them. Closed November to early May. Admission. ~ Route 7, Charlotte; 802-425-3500.

Just north of Shelburne, skirting the lake and reigning over the valley, is Vermont's Queen City, **Burlington**. With a population of 40,000, it's the state's largest city but one that manages to maintain an intimate milieu. Burlington's remarkable alliance of mountain and water vistas were lauded by none other than Charles Dickens when he landed here back in the mid-1800s. Today, art centers, innovative theater, a university and four colleges add to the cultural mix of this spirited, youthful metropolis. In the last couple of years, the waterfront area has flourished. A community boathouse provides boat rentals and a seven-mile path has been created along the lake shore for bikers, joggers and walkers. Restaurants and shopping abound, making the lakefront a very pleasant place for a stroll.

In fact, nearly half of Burlington's population is made up of college students, many of whom attend the statuesque hilltop campus of the **University of Vermont**. ~ Off University Place and Colchester Avenue; 802-656-3480.

The university's **Robert Hull Fleming Museum**, a grand Colonial Revival building, houses an excellent collection of European and American paintings, decorative artworks and costumes, and ethnographic objects from around the world. Closed Monday. ~ 61 Colchester Avenue; 802-656-0750, fax 802-656-8059; www.uvm.edu/~fleming.

To help get you started in the area, stop by the **Lake Champlain Regional Chamber of Commerce**. ~ 60 Main Street, Burlington; 802-863-3489, fax 802-863-1538; www.vermont.org, e-mail vermont@vermont.org.

The city's best side exists, naturally, on glittering Lake Champlain. Stroll along **Lake and Battery streets** and peer across the water to New York's Adirondack Mountains, then take a two-hour round-trip **ferry** from Burlington over to Port Kent, New York, while absorbing all the scintillating views. ~ Ferry: King Street Dock, King and Battery streets; 802-864-9804.

Most of the day and nighttime activity occurs on **Church Street Marketplace**, a thriving pedestrian mall jammed with outdoor cafés, trendy shops, strolling musicians and magicians and graced with 19th-century architecture. The effect is European, to say the least. ~ Church Street between Main and Pearl streets.

Northward, the **Champlain Islands** comprise Vermont's own "seacoast," a virgin outpost of apple orchards and dairy farms, rustic lakeside retreats and shores lined with anglers casting their nets. Though today there's a causeway linking these isles to Burlington, 19th-century residents had to make do with small skiffs and winter weather, when a frozen lake afforded the best access to the mainland. Route 2 traces a 30-mile path over water and land through this quiescent, largely undeveloped archipelago.

Revolutionary War veteran Jedediah Hyde, Jr., built a log cabin on the largest island, Grand Isle, back in 1783. Today the **Hyde Log Cabin** is thought to be the oldest log cabin in the country, a one-room alcove of rough-hewn beams held together by clay and straw. Amazingly, some of the original furniture and farm tools remain intact. ~ Route 2.

Up on Isle La Motte, 19th-century stone houses and a meandering rocky coastline form quite a beautiful tableau. The **St. Anne Shrine** denotes the site of Fort St. Anne—Vermont's earliest settlement—built in 1666 by Captain Pierre La Motte. ~ Off Route 129.

LODGING   Near the southern end of the Champlain Valley lies the vibrant college town of Middlebury. Here, the **Swift House Inn** reposes among enormous elm and maple trees and broods with New England history. The 1814 main house, a Federal-style building that

Keep your eyes peeled for "Champ," Lake Champlain's own Loch Ness Monster, whose bulky outline and distinct humps were first sighted by Samuel de Champlain and recorded in his ship's log.

was home to former Vermont Governor John W. Stewart, has ten rooms with poster beds and some marble fireplaces. An 1876 Victorian carriage house offers six cozy rooms with fireplaces and whirlpool tubs, while the gatehouse features five rooms with a mixture of reproductions and antiques. ~ Route 7 and Stewart Lane, Middlebury; 802-388-9925, fax 802-388-9927; www.swift houseinn.com. MODERATE TO ULTRA-DELUXE.

Occupying a choice 700 acres along Lake Champlain, the **Basin Harbor Club** has been a prime waterside getaway since 1886. Sprinkled along the lake banks and peeking across to New York's Adirondack Mountains are 38 rooms and 77 cottages with simple, cozy furnishings. This self-contained retreat boasts an 18-hole golf course, a swimming pool, tennis courts, a top-notch restaurant and an airstrip. Closed mid-October to mid-May. ~ Basin Harbor Road off Route 22A, Vergennes; 802-475-2311, 800-622-4000, fax 802-475-6545; www.basinharbor.com. ULTRA-DELUXE.

Perhaps the most distinguished lodging address in all the Champlain Valley is the **Inn at Shelburne Farms**. Formerly home to Lila Vanderbilt Webb, the 1899 brick manor has all the Vanderbilt trimmings: incredible Lake Champlain and mountain vistas, 24 guest rooms with opulent Queen Anne Revival furnishings and 1400 acres of lovely farmlands sprinkled with 19th-century buildings. Settle in, soak up the history of this fascinating place and pretend you'll never have to leave. Closed mid-October to mid-May. ~ Harbor and Bay roads, off Route 7, Shelburne; 802-985-8498, fax 802-985-1233; www.shelburnefarms.org. DELUXE TO ULTRA-DELUXE.

Burlington, Vermont's largest city, offers little in the way of homey bed and breakfasts and quaint inns but does have a smattering of motor lodges, motels and hotels.

Within easy reach of downtown Burlington and several ski areas, the **Inn at Essex** features 121 rooms, some decorated with 18th-century period-style furniture, some in an Ethan Allen country motif. Half the rooms have fireplaces. The suites have whirlpool baths. Dining is top-drawer: The inn is home to the New England Culinary Institute. In fact, the institute's kitchens and classes are right under the inn. ~ 70 Essex Way, Essex; 802-878-1100, 800-727-4295, fax 802-878-0063; www.innatessex.com, e-mail innessex@together.net. DELUXE TO ULTRA-DELUXE.

At the **Sheraton Burlington Hotel and Conference Center**, you will find 309 spacious rooms with contemporary furnishings, marble vanities and mountain views (though in the distance), as well as a health club with a removable glass atrium over the pool. There is also a large interior courtyard and a sundeck. ~ 870 Williston Road, Burlington; 802-865-6600, 800-677-6576, fax 802-865-6670; www.sheraton.com. MODERATE TO DELUXE.

Two miles northeast of Burlington, the **Days Inn** is a no-nonsense place where you can swipe a clean, modern-style room with a moderate price. The three-story design is generic motel, though the decor is a notch above, with cushy couches, designer draperies and cedar siding. Suites are more expensive. ~ 23 College Parkway, Colchester; 802-655-0900, 800-329-7466, fax 802-655-6851. MODERATE.

DINING

Woody's perches on the bank of Otter Creek in the middle of pretty Middlebury. The restaurant is three stories high, with floor-to-ceiling windows that make even the rainiest day seem bright to indoor diners. During warm weather, try to get a table on the outdoor deck. Fresh ingredients star in most dishes: the homemade soups are especially good. Some of our favorites include fajitas, caesar salad with grilled chicken and cheddar cheese soup. Closed Tuesday from November through April. ~ 5 Bakery Lane, Middlebury; 802-388-4182, fax 802-388-0813. MODERATE.

Burlington is Vermont's largest city and its restaurant capital, so not surprisingly, you'll find a medley of choice dining establishments. Some of the best can be found on Church Street's four-block Marketplace, a brick-lined pedestrian mall packed with outdoor cafés and college students.

A rare Vermont sushi bar is part of the **Marketplace at Sakura**, a simple but cheery restaurant with two tatami rooms and small wooden tables that peek out over the street. The sushi and sashimi are fresh and served on wooden trays with pretty designs. If you prefer a hot Japanese meal, opt for the *yakitori* (broiled chicken on skewers) or *gyoza* (meat dumplings) or select from the host of teriyaki and tempura entrées. ~ 2 Church Street, Burlington; 802-863-1988, fax 802-860-0496. BUDGET TO MODERATE.

The place for fresh New England seafood is the **Ice House**, a restored harborside building with a venerable seafaring aura. There's a wharf and ferry station a stone's throw away. Specialties include grilled swordfish and salmon, filet mignon and a shrimp, calamari and sea scallop combination. The place is draped in wood and stone and features two outdoor decks. ~ 171 Battery Street, Burlington; 802-864-1800, fax 802-864-1801. MODERATE TO DELUXE.

Located in nearby Essex, **Butler's** features New American cuisine prepared and served by students of the prestigious New England Culinary Institute. The menu changes nightly and usually includes a selection of fish and meat dishes with international influences. There is always a vegetarian dish. ~ Inn at Essex, 70 Essex Way, Essex; 802-878-1100, 800-727-4295; www.innatesse.com, e-mail innessex@together.net. MODERATE TO DELUXE.

Waterworks is a typical yuppie-style bistro with one very special attraction: water. The enclosed terrace here affords a sweeping view of the Winooski River, where waves of water rush and swirl across huge boulders, creating quite a commotion and a sublime dining environment. The cuisine is reliable and includes an assortment of chicken, seafood and steak dishes, as well as sandwiches. Inside, you'll find red brick walls, high ceilings and large windows for good water views. ~ The Champlain Mill, Winooski; 802-655-2044, fax 802-655-8005. MODERATE.

It nearly takes a miracle to find **Authentica African Imports**, but once you're there, it's worth it. More than just a shop, this place offers a look at African styles and customs, with jewelry from West, South and East African nations, Mali blankets, Ethiopian rugs, Zulu clay pots, fertility statues from Malawi and much more. ~ Greenbush Road about three quarters of a mile north of the Old Brick Store on Ferry Road, Charlotte; 802-425-3137; e-mail auth01@attglobal.net.

SHOPPING

◄ *HIDDEN*

Stroll Burlington's four-block **Church Street Marketplace** and you'll be rewarded with a bevy of fine, trendy shops. ~ Church Street between Main and Pearl streets.

Forests find their ways into clocks, homewares and furniture at **The Symmetree Company**. ~ 89 Church Street, Burlington; 802-658-1441.

The hottest night scene pulses in Burlington, where 16,000 college students feed a multitude of discos, progressive clubs and bebop joints.

NIGHTLIFE

The **Flynn Theatre for the Performing Arts**, a 1453-seat art deco palace and old vaudeville house, offers international and Broadway theater and major symphony and dance performances. ~ 153 Main Street, Burlington; 802-863-5966; www.flynn theatre.org.

A dark, smokey cubbyhole with a crowd predominantly in their 30s, **Nectar's** serves up top-notch live blues and rock. ~ 188 Main Street, Burlington; 802-658-4771. Upstairs at **Club Metronome** there's live music, including blues, funk, ska and hip-hop. Cover. ~ 802-865-4563.

The place to cut a rug is **Sh-na-na's**, where a sprawling checkered dancefloor is accented by pinups of Elvis and other '50s paraphernalia. With recorded music from the '50s through the '90s, this joint is often packed. Closed Sunday. Cover Friday and Saturday. ~ 101 Main Street, Burlington; 802-865-2596.

Sweetwaters is undeniably the area's upscale meeting place, where patrons linger around a shiny bar and watch all the street activity through large glass windows. ~ Church and College streets, Burlington; 802-864-9800.

Late-nighters flock to **The Vermont Pub and Brewery**, a spacious but cozy brew house with brick walls, archways, mirrors and hanging plants. There's usually live music Thursday through Saturday. ~ 144 College Street, Burlington; 802-865-0500.

The only gay bar for miles, **135 Pearl** offers deejay dancing on Tuesday, and Thursday though Saturday. Sunday there's a piano bar and on Wednesday, it's karaoke. Cover. ~ 135 Pearl Street, Burlington; 802-863-2343.

BEACHES & PARKS

MOUNT PHILO STATE PARK 🚶 Resting right on top of Mount Philo, this park rewards those who tackle its very steep but paved road with astonishing panoramas. From here, you can peer across Lake Champlain into New York's Adirondacks and farther. A total of 163 acres, most of the park is vertical and forested. There is a nice picnic area with tables, and the park's hiking trails are splendid. Closed from Columbus Day to a week before Memorial Day. Day-use fee, $2. ~ Off Route 7, six miles north of Route 22A near North Ferrisburg; 802-425-2390.

▲ There are eight tent sites ($11 per night) and two lean-tos ($15 per night), with hot showers and fireplaces (firewood is for sale). There is also a non-refundable $5 reservation fee per site.

SAND BAR STATE PARK 🏊 ⛴ 🚣 🏖 🚤 🍽 One of the flattest areas in the state, this ever-popular locale borders Lake Champlain and a waterfowl refuge. Families and college students crowd the coarse, mocha-colored sand and grassy areas lining the lake, while windsurfers and sailboats whiz along just offshore. The views across the lake of the Adirondack Mountains are exceptional. The water is waist-deep at least 100 yards out, and is popular with swimmers. Anglers catch perch, sunfish, salmon and bass. There are picnic facilities, a bathhouse, volleyball courts, boat and windsurfing rentals and a snack bar. Closed from Labor Day to Memorial Day. Day-use fee, $3. ~ On Route 2 in Milton, four miles west of Route 89; 802-893-2825.

NORTH HERO STATE PARK 🚶 🚴 🏊 🚣 🏖 🚤 🛥 🍽 From its perch on a thickly wooded peninsula, this 400-acre park captures a prominent view of Lake Champlain and glances backward on North Hero Island. Though it actually borders two miles of lake, the only real accessible shore is a small but pretty shale beach at the peninsula's tip, a secluded spot favored by Canadians and local sailboaters. Swimming is good, but you must wade out past a rim of slippery rocks. Immense Lake Champlain provides superb fishing opportunities, from bass and pike to perch, walleye and pickerel. You'll find picnic tables, restrooms, a playground, and rowboat and canoe rental; a store is four miles southwest on Route 2. Closed Labor Day to Memorial Day. Day-use fee, $2. ~ From Alburg, go ten miles south on Route 2 and cross the bridge to North Hero Island. Take an immediate left onto Bridge Road. Follow Bridge Road two miles to Lakeview Drive and take a left onto Lakeview. Go one mile on Lakeview, and the entrance will be on your left; 802-372-8727.

▲ Permitted at 117 sites with hot showers and fireplaces but no hookups. Rates are $12 per night for tent/RV sites and $16 per night for lean-tos. There is also a $5 non-refundable reservation fee per site.

▼▼▼▼▼▼▼▼▼▼▼▼▼▼

Northeast Kingdom

This vast rural outback could well contain the largest stretch of splendid scenery in all of Vermont. A broad land inhabited by log cutters, cattle drivers and mountain folk, it forms a fine skein of glacier-dug lakes, mellow ponds and rivers, untamed evergreen forests and abrupt alpine ridges. Fall foliage first peeks out its gorgeous head up here, snow falls early and huge bodies of water turn to compact ice.

Beginning in St. Johnsbury and extending northward to the Canadian border, the Northeast Kingdom could well be termed Vermont's last stand. Its thin population and lack of major industry perpetuate considerable unemployment (by Vermont's standards), though firmly rooted residents vow their rugged country living surpasses that in southern ski meccas any day.

SIGHTS

St. Johnsbury, the region's largest city, is a quaint, mostly blue-collar town located where the Moose and Sleepers rivers flow into the Passumpsic River. The local **Northeast Kingdom Chamber of Commerce** will provide walking-tour maps and regional information. ~ 30 Western Avenue, St. Johnsbury; 802-748-3678, fax 802-748-0731; www.vermontnekchamber.org.

A perfect spot to learn about local history is the **Fairbanks Museum and Planetarium**, where exhibits are imaginative and informative. The extensive wildlife collection includes stuffed condors and owls, pythons and chamois, and monstrous polar bears and Kodiaks. The building itself, with a barrel-vaulted ceiling and Romanesque designs of red sandstone, is marvelous. Admission. ~ 130 Main and Prospect streets, St. Johnsbury; 802-748-2372, fax 802-748-1893; www.fairbanksmuseum.org.

◄ HIDDEN

Tucked in the back of a beautiful 1871 library, one of 15 libraries that have been named National Historic Landmarks, the **St. Johnsbury Athenaeum Art Gallery** is a step back in time. The place bills itself as "oldest unaltered art gallery in the United States," and indeed, its collection has not changed since the mid-1920s. The 100-plus paintings feature numerous American landscape scenes by Albert Bierstadt and other famed Hudson River School artists. The library, a lovely Victorian-style masterpiece, has seen minimal architectural change over the century. Closed Sunday. ~ 1171 Main Street, St. Johnsbury; 802-748-8291, fax 802-748-8086.

Maple Grove Farms of Vermont house the world's oldest and largest maple candy factory. Founded in 1915 by two local women, the little farmhouse was converted into a factory in 1929. Tours take visitors through the factory, where vintage equipment from the 1930s is still in use and where large quantities of maple syrup are packaged by hand. The old sugar house now contains a maple museum, and a third building features an extensive gift shop. Admission. ~ 1052 Portland Street, St. Johnsbury; 802-748-5141, fax 802-748-9647; www.maplegrove.com.

Take Route 5A north to Route 105, then backtrack south on a splendid trek revealing yet another flawless meld of mountain and water. Gaze at the hilltop homes that scope out scenic views, at the farmers bailing hay and at old frame homes with laundry draped across their porches.

Soon you'll come to the town of Island Pond, where bait shops, log cabins and a gas station form an earthy setting. The town green overlooks the water and was the site of the first international railroad in North America. There's also a Civil War cannon and a World War II monument.

Head toward Canada again, traveling north along Route 111, and you'll quickly feel the French vibes of our northern neighbor. Enormous Lake Memphremagog shares its waters (nearly equally) with Vermont and Quebec.

Newport is a special town, resting on a procession of hills that skirt the lake and crowned by the spires of beautiful St. Mary's Star of the Sea Church. ~ 5 Clermont Terrace, Newport; 802-334-5066, fax 802-334-5067.

Downtown offers a nice array of shops and restaurants and a helpful Chamber of Commerce Information Booth that will load you up with information. ~ The Causeway, Newport; 802-334-7782; e-mail nekinfo@vermontnekchamber.org.

There are three dirt roads that lead to the valley hamlet of Brownington, though the less adventurous will opt for the one that's paved. Here awaits an enchanting museum called The Old

SWITZERLAND ON MY MIND

Travel north of St. Johnsbury on Route 5 to Route 5A and you'll arrive at what may be the state's single most stupendous vista. Lake Willoughby, an incredible expanse of water chiseled by glaciers, known as the "Lucerne" of the United States, shimmers peacefully beneath the craggy peaks of Mounts Pisgah and Hor. Rimmed with rocky shoreline, fine carpets of grass, and inns and lakefront cabins (not too many due to the foresightedness of local leaders), the lake dispenses all the beauty the eye can handle.

Stone House, built as a school dormitory in 1836 by the Reverend Alexander Twilight, the country's first black college graduate and legislator. Twenty-three rooms are filled with inspiring memorabilia that form endearing snapshots of early American life. Nearly everything here was donated by local families, including the 18th-century furniture, 19th-century military uniforms (worn by Brownington men) and a wonderful collection of 1800s newspapers. Admission. ~ Brownington Village near Orleans; phone/fax 802-754-2022; www.homepages.together.net/~osh.

A block from the Old Stone House is **Prospect Hill Observatory**, a wooden tower perched atop a grassy hill. Climb a short flight of stairs and be rewarded with a 360-degree panorama of rolling mountains and evergreen spires. A splendid way to remember Vermont, for sure. ~ Take a dirt road beside Brownington Congregational Church.

◄ HIDDEN

LODGING

A genteel Victorian house like **The Moonstruck Inn** seems so out of place at the junction of two major highways. But step inside and you'll discover an oasis of beautiful high ceilings, French windows, cherrywood banisters and oriental rugs. A hoppin' stagecoach stop during the early 1800s (there's still a dancefloor above the garage), the Moonstruck offers six rooms decorated with antiques; all have private baths. Rates include breakfast. ~ Routes 93 and 18, St. Johnsbury; 802-748-4661, 800-579-3644. MODERATE.

Children, animals and dramatic scenery abound at the **Wildflower Inn**, part of a 500-acre estate that's a great place to spend more than one night. All accommodations have private bathrooms and a mix of antique and reproduction furniture. Eight of the 22 units are suites; the honeymoon cottage is complete with a jacuzzi built for two. For the kids, there's a playroom with a chestful of dress-up clothes and, outdoors, a petting barn with several horses, ponies and cows. Breakfast and an afternoon snack are included. Closed part of November and in April. ~ Darling Hill Road, Lyndonville; 802-626-8310, 800-627-8310, fax 802-626-3039; www.wildflowerinn.com. DELUXE TO ULTRA-DELUXE.

Standing by Lake Willoughby, the **Willough Vale Inn** offers spectacular views and a rustic elegance. Though built in 1987, the Colonial-style inn harkens to yesteryear with stained-wood floors, antiques and oriental rugs. Most of the eight rooms snatch a lake view and are enhanced with simple oak and cherry furniture and country prints. There are four fully furnished lakeside cottages, each with a kitchen and living room, behind the inn. ~ Route 5A, Westmore; 802-525-4123, 800-594-9102, fax 802-525-4514; www.willoughvale.com, e-mail wvaleinn@aol.com. DELUXE.

Just getting to **Heermansmith Farm** is a joyous adventure. Truck two miles down a dusty washboard road, past grazing cows and romping dogs, then navigate a picturesque covered bridge and

◄ HIDDEN

you'll arrive at a prim whitewashed farmhouse. This country gem, enveloped by fields and total solitude, has been in the same family since 1807. The innkeepers are marvelous, the atmosphere congenial and the seven bedrooms very agreeable with antique beds, pitchers and basins and large closets stacked with well-thumbed paperbacks. Most of the rooms have private baths. Breakfast included in the rates. ~ Coventry Village; 802-754-8866; www.scene ofvermont.com, e-mail hersmith@sover.net. MODERATE.

The Inn on the Common is an impeccable inn in the impeccable little town of Craftsbury Common. There are a total of 16 rooms in three separate buildings, one of which is on the village green; the others are steps away. Several are furnished with antiques and attractive floral fabrics. At the back of the main building are formal gardens and a far-reaching view of the surrounding Northeast Kingdom countryside. Both breakfast and dinner are included in the room rate. ~ Craftsbury Common; 802-586-9619, 800-521-2233, fax 802-586-2249; www.innonthecommon. com, e-mail info@innonthecommon.com. ULTRA-DELUXE.

At the end of a long dirt road in the hilly Northeast Kingdom, the **Rodgers Country Inn** takes in a few visitors at a time. Once a working dairy farm, you can now take a walk through the pretty countryside, where you'll see that this corner of Vermont is a haven for family-run farms. There are five guest rooms; guests share three large bathrooms. In winter, you can cross-country ski or snowshoe on the property. Breakfast and dinner are included. Closed December. ~ Call for directions, West Glover; phone/fax 802-525-6677, 800-729-1704; e-mail jnrodger@together.net. MODERATE.

HIDDEN ►   **The Inn on Trout River** is a great find for travelers who find themselves in the Jay area of northern Vermont. Skiers will be especially satisfied with the flannel-sheeted queen beds, large bathrooms with claw-footed tubs, the publike bar and the substantial discount on lift tickets to Jay Peak. During the summer, visitors can take advantage of the excellent fishing in the area's many rivers and streams. Breakfast is included. ~ Main Street, Montgomery Center; 802-326-4391, 800-338-7049, fax 802-326-3194; www. troutinn.com, e-mail info@troutinn.com. MODERATE.

In Montgomery Center, at the base of Jay Peak, stands the 1882 **Phineas Swann and the Carriage House Suites,** a stunning gingerbread Victorian owned and run by gay men. Absolutely every inch of this house is beautiful—hardwood floors, canopy beds, Vermont antiques, hand-carved furniture. There are seven guest rooms, all with private baths. Breakfast is quite an event here, with all homemade dishes including homemade sausage and preserves from the blueberries and strawberries grown on the property. It's accompanied by big-band music and candlelight.

The room rate also includes afternoon tea with fresh-baked scones on the front porch. Gay friendly. ~ Route 118, Montgomery Center; phone/fax 802-326-4306; e-mail phineas@sover.net. MODERATE TO DELUXE.

The **Greenhope Farm** occupies a rural setting in the mountains. You won't find lace and antiques at this contemporary, six-room farmhouse, but you will find goats and horses. Riding lessons are available. There's also swimming, canoeing and, in winter, cross-country skiing on the grounds. Advance reservations are required. ~ Route 1, East Harwick; 802-533-7772; www.greenhopefarm. com, e-mail greenhopefarm@greenhopefarm.com. MODERATE TO DELUXE.

DINING

Cuisine here reflects the ruggedness of the land, and, though restaurants are far apart, they're certainly worth the scenic drive.

Nestled serenely on a glacier-carved lake, the **Willough Vale Inn and Restaurant** affords some of Vermont's most scintillating views. The dining room, which overlooks captivating Lake Willoughby, serves casual American fare. ~ Route 5A, Westmore; 802-525-4123. BUDGET TO MODERATE.

◄ *HIDDEN*

Locals know that to dine at **Heermansmith Farm Inn**, you must make reservations several days in advance. This 1807 farmhouse, concealed two miles down a washboard road, is an absolute find—the kind of place that instantly warms your blood. It's dinner only, served in a living room graciously adorned with antique lanterns, pine bookcases, a stone hearth and picture windows overlooking rolling meadows. The menu exhibits great flair with entrées such as roast duck masked in strawberry and chambord sauce, shrimp dijonaise and pecan chicken in a raspberry-butter sauce. A place worth finding. Closed Monday and Tuesday in the winter. ~ Coventry Village; 802-754-8866; www.scenesof vermont.com, e-mail hersmith@sover.net. MODERATE.

Lemoine's, located in The Inn on Trout River, offers a varied menu for all palates—fresh fish, leg of lamb, and good homemade soups, as well as an innovative "wholesome choices menu" for guests who need to restrict their fat intake. Try to sit near the fireplace; the carved fireplace mantel is intricate and worth a closer look, as are the mouldings and wainscoting throughout the inn. Dinner only. ~ Main Street, Montgomery Center; 802-326-4391, 800-338-7049; www.troutinn.com, e-mail info@troutinn.com. MODERATE TO DELUXE.

The **Miss Newport Diner** is one of those adorable town gossip spots that serves up great breakfasts and homestyle lunches. The 1947 Worcester diner bears five booths and a row of blue-and-silver counter stools where all the socializing gets done. The breakfast menu features eggs, omelettes and pancakes—most

Text continued on page 476.

Vermont Maple Syrup

It begins quite subtly during the first hint of spring: a tiny sprig of green sprouts, a bird chirps gaily and the sap inside a maple tree breaks free from its icy chamber and trickles ever so gently toward the warm ground.

Squirrels, rabbits and other forest dwellers scurry to lap up the sweet elixir, a welcome indulgence after a long, frigid winter. Along comes another mountain inhabitant, a farmer, who pierces the maple trunk with a plastic tap, drawing the sticky sap into a clear plastic tube. He does this hundreds, perhaps thousands of times, tapping trees and connecting them with little tubes until their sap trickles harmoniously down the mountain.

And so it goes. Each spring, millions of Vermont maple trees surrender their gooey, candied essence for the sake of that sought-after substance known as maple syrup. Called "sugarbushes" or "maple orchards," these grand stands of trees blanket the mountains with their stalwart trunks and burgeoning canopies of delicate toothed leaves.

Vermont is the country's largest supplier of maple syrup, producing an annual average of half a million gallons. Though the harvesting processes are fairly simple, they've changed quite a bit since American Indians cooked sap over an open fire back in the 1500s.

Today, most farmers use plastic tubes, drawing sap by gravity or with a vacuum system, but some still opt for the time-honored metal bucket system. In this method, sap drips from trees into large buckets, which are carted on sleds down the mountains.

Back at the sugarhouse, sap is boiled all day (and sometimes all night) in huge metal pans until it's reduced to a smooth syrup. It takes an average of 40 gallons of sap to net one gallon of syrup.

All the cooking takes place in hundreds of wooden sugarhouses—characterized by vented roofs to help steam escape—that dot verdant mountains and valleys. You can peek in on all the action by visiting large syrup mills, but for the most rewarding experience, stop in on a family-owned operation. Here, cordial folks will bring you up to snuff on the sweet stuff as well as share their lifestyles and family histories.

You'll discover small, family-owned farms all over the state, and while many display a small sign that says "Maple Syrup," others have no sign (these you can find out about at the local general store). More than 100 large and small operations are listed in *Maple Sugarhouses Open to the Public*, a dandy, free brochure published by the Vermont Department of Agriculture. Listings are by county and town and provide information on number of taps, size of sugarhouses, methods of operation and tours. ~ 116 State Street, Drawer 20, Montpelier, VT 05620; 802-828-2416.

The **New England Maple Museum** promises "The Sweetest Story Ever Told" if you visit its displays of maple sugar nostalgia. A great place to bone up on syrup history, the museum stocks old artifacts like wooden buckets and taps and horse-drawn sleds used for toting sap. The best part, though, is the free syrup tasting. Closed late December to mid-March. Admission. ~ Route 7, Pittsford; 802-483-9414.

Or, immerse yourself in syrupy activities at the **Vermont Maple Festival**, held each April in St. Albans, north of Burlington. Feast on pancakes smothered in syrup, take in the fiddlers' contest and savor the honeyed flavor of assorted syrup varieties. ~ Contact the Vermont Maple Festival Council, Box 255, St. Albans, VT 05478; 802-524-5800.

Plan to visit from late February (southern areas) through mid-April (northern areas). The choicest syrup, a fancy golden extract, is harvested first. As the season progresses, syrup turns a medium amber, then a dark amber and finally a bitter, murky consistency that's seldom edible.

Of course, the finer things in life always cost more, and such is the case with maple syrup. Usually double and triple the price of blended syrups, the real stuff can cost you from 40 to 60 cents per ounce.

But be forewarned. Those accustomed to blended syrup shall unwittingly be seduced by the pure maple kind, a victim of their own newly enlightened taste buds. Syrupoholics say it's sort of like switching from jug wine to fine wine: once you've tasted the good stuff, it's impossible to go back.

priced under $5. For lunch, there's meat loaf, fried chicken, ham steak and cheeseburgers. ~ East Main Street, Newport; 802-334-7742. BUDGET.

SHOPPING   Going fishing, perhaps? **The Great Outdoors of Newport** has loads of fishing gear, plus mountain bikes and skis. ~ 177 Main Street, Newport; 802-334-2831.

The Landing Clothing Company has not only men's formal attire but jeans and sportswear for both sexes. Reduced hours in winter. ~ 138 Main Street, Newport; 802-334-2953.

NIGHTLIFE   Other than a few motel lounges and pool halls, this remote mountain area is short on nightlife.

Have a drink by the lake at **The Eastside**. In the summer you can enjoy the views from the outdoor deck; in the winter, relax by the fire in the nautical-themed bar. Closed Monday evenings in winter. ~ Landing Street, Newport; 802-334-2340.

The Nickelodeon Café, a smart pub with Irish decor, is a nice spot for a cold brew. On weekends there are live bands. Cover for live music. ~ 41 Main Street, Newport; 802-334-8055.

Canada and the United States share the **Haskell Opera House**, a marvelous, ornate historic building that hosts major comedy, musicals and drama as well as symphony, jazz and ballet. A black line divides the building nationally, with two-thirds of the wooden seats in Vermont and the stage in Quebec. ~ Casswell Avenue, Derby Line; 819-876-2471 (Canada); e-mail haskell@together.net.

BEACHES & PARKS   **PROUTY BEACH** 🛶 ⛷ 🚤 ⛵ This popular municipal park corners the market on local views. Situated along tranquil Lake Memphremagog, Prouty preens across the water to the town of Newport, with its quaint downtown and historic church spires. A 100-foot sliver of tawny sand skirts the lake, protected by a row of weeping willows. Try from shore or on a boat for trout, salmon, pike and bass. And with tennis and basketball courts as well as football and soccer fields, who could get bored? Facilities include picnic pavilions and restrooms. Closed from Columbus Day to mid-May. Day-use fee, $3. ~ On Veterans Avenue in Newport; 802-334-7951.

▲ There are four tent sites ($15 per night) and 51 RV sites ($19 to $20 per night) with water and electrical hookups. Eighteen of those sites also have sewer hookups and are $20 per night. Amenities include washers, dryers and showers as well as a dumping station for RVs.

MAIDSTONE STATE PARK 🚶 🏊 ⛺ ⛷ 🚤 🎣 ⛵ Ringed with majestic mountain peaks and tucked in the middle of nowhere, this gorgeous preserve possesses a very special feature: the crystal clear, Maidstone Lake. It's enough to just sit and gaze at reflections of trees in the water, but the more adventurous might choose to sunbathe on a generous stretch of cream-colored sand. People swim here, though the water is quite chilly, even in summer. Fishing is excellent for lake and rainbow trout as well as salmon. You may see loons and moose while you're here. Don't be intimidated by the remoteness of this park. Once you're here, you'll be thankful you made the drive. Facilities include picnic tables, restrooms, boat and canoe rentals and a nature center. Closed from Labor Day to Memorial Day. Day-use fee, $2. ~ From Bloomfield, go south along the Connecticut River for five miles on Route 102, then turn southwest at the State Forest Highway (it's marked). This is a gravel road that extends six miles to the park; 802-676-3930.

▲ There are 45 tent sites ($13 per night) and 37 lean-tos ($17 per night); fireplaces and hot showers but no hookups. There is also a non-refundable $5 reservation fee per site.

BRIGHTON STATE PARK 🏃 🚴 ⛷ 🎣 🚣 🛶 🚤 ⛵ 🚗 Even ◀ HIDDEN
with the fiercest of competition, this has to be the prettiest park in all of Vermont. The setting is absolutely magnificent, the mood incredibly serene. Nestled along poignant Spectacle Pond, Brighton claims a sliver of crystalline tawny beach and 152 acres packed with spruce, firs, pines and many other very green, very big trees. There's also a nature museum and plenty of forested trails that scale the billowy terrain. There's excellent fishing for trout on Island Pond, bass on Spectacle Pond. Facilities include picnic tables, restrooms, showers, fireplaces and canoe rentals. Closed from Columbus Day to mid-May. Day-use fee, $2. ~ Off Route 105, two miles east of Island Pond; 802-723-4360.

▲ There are 63 tent/RV sites ($13 per night) and 21 lean-tos ($17 per night), but no hookups. There is also a non-refundable $5 reservation fee per site.

The thrills of downhill and cross-country skiing draw tens of thousands of enthusiasts to Vermont every year. Ski resort villages all over the state offer a variety of challenges and settings that cater to families, singles and the elderly.

Outdoor Adventures

SKIING

Before you go, send for the *Ski Vermont: Vermont Ski Area, Resort and Travel Guide* brochure from the Vermont Ski Areas Association. ~ P.O. Box 368, Montpelier, VT 05601; 802-223-2439.

The varied terrain of gentle hills and fields, old carriage roads and frozen ponds—combined with an excellent gridwork of trails —attract vast numbers of cross-country skiers to Vermont. In fact, tiny Vermont boasts more Nordic ski centers than any western state. Though many of the state parks are closed in the winter, most allow cross-country skiing on ungroomed trails. The best time for cross-country skiing is mid-December through March.

For a list of ski centers, write for the *Best of Cross-Country Skiing*, available from Cross-Country Ski Areas of America. The $3 charge covers postage and handling. ~ 259 Bolton Road, Hinsdale, NH 03451; 603-239-4341.

SOUTHERN VERMONT   **Haystack Mountain** is Vermont's southernmost ski resort area, with 44 trails and six lifts. It's a smaller and less expensive mountain than Mount Snow, so it attracts more families with children as well as college students. ~ Coldbrook Road, off Route 100, Wilmington; 802-464-3333, 800-245-7669; www.mountsnow.com.

Nearby, and owned by the same company, **Mount Snow** climbs 3600 feet and boasts a large array of alpine villas, condos and restaurants. Here you'll find 135 trails (many quite difficult), 26 lifts and a vertical drop of 1700 feet. Twenty percent of the trails are novice, sixty percent are intermediate and the rest are expert runs. The mountain has four terrain parks and two half-pipes. You may purchase a pass that allows you to ski both Mount Snow and Haystack Mountain. ~ Route 100; 802-464-3333, 800-245-7669; www.mountsnow.com.

CENTRAL VERMONT   The place to be in central Vermont is **Killington**, a sprawling, six-mountain network with 33 lifts and a vertical drop that plummets 3150 feet. Killington offers the Rams Head mountain, which is devoted to family activities, ten alpine and snowboard parks, and a gondola. The 212 trails are a third beginner, a third intermediate and a third expert. ~ Off Routes 4 and 100; 802-773-1330; www.killington.com.

NORTHERN MOUNTAIN REGION   **Sugarbush**, a six-mountain area with 115 trails, maintains a congenial atmosphere with its quaint shops and medley of fine restaurants and lodging. Its Family Adventureland comprises 22 novice and intermediate trails and an interactive fantasy terrain garden. Half of the Sugarbush area is intermediate, with more than a third rated advanced. Mount Rage is a trail designed for snowboarders but is also used by skiers; there's a half-pipe at the bottom. ~ Sugarbush Access Road, off Route 100, Warren; 802-583-2381; www.sugarbush.com, e-mail info@sugarbush.com.

Nearby **Stowe** harbors Vermont's highest peak, 4393-foot Mt. Mansfield, and a stunning alpine milieu with 47 trails and 10 lifts, including a terrain park with a half-pipe. Stowe also offers 35 kilometers of groomed cross-country trails and 40 kilometers of backcountry trails. ~ Route 108; 802-253-7311; www.stowe.com.

Several cross-country trails connect inns around Warren and Waitsfield in the Sugarbush area.

NORTHEAST KINGDOM   Vermont's best-kept ski secret is **Burke Mountain**, nestled in the outposts of the Northeast Kingdom. Here you'll find excellent skiing in an uncrowded (no lift lines!)

place, along with 42 trails, four lifts and a nice vertical drop of 2000 feet. ~ Off Route 114, East Burke; 802-626-3305; www. burkemountain.com.

Known as the "Longest Cross-Country Ski Trail in North America," the **Catamount Trail** will stretch 300 miles across the length of Vermont when it's completed (275 miles have already been blazed). The trail offers gentle, rolling slopes for beginners and challenging terrain for the most advanced, as well as inn-to-inn routes along old logging roads. For further information on the Catamount Trail, or to order a guidebook on the trail, call 802-864-5794; www.catamounttrail.together.com.

Another scenic route traverses the farmlands and forests between the **Craftsbury Nordic Center** near Craftsbury Common and the Highland Lodge in Greensboro. ~ 802-586-7767; e-mail crafts@sover.net.

Since **Jay Peak** regularly gets more natural snow than any other ski area in the northeast, you might well expect it to be packed—but it's not. The trek from any major city is a long one, and the weather can be pretty nasty up here; consequently, few New England skiers come, and lift lines are almost unheard of. Experienced skiers who are looking for a challenge should head for Jay's glade areas when the snow is deep enough. If it's not, the runs on the smaller of the two mountains are more challenging than the curving trails that descend from the tram, on the higher peak. ~ Route 242, Jay; 802-988-2611, 800-451-4449; www.jaypeakresort.com, e-mail jaypeak@together.net.

SLEIGHING

Sleigh rides afford wonderful opportunities to meet local folks and take in the beautiful countryside. They are usually offered from mid-December to mid-March.

CENTRAL VERMONT In Wilmington, **Adam's Farm** runs hour-and-a-half horsedrawn sleigh trips with a midway stop at a log cabin in the woods for hot chocolate. ~ Higley Hill; 802-464-3762. **Hawk Inn and Mountain Resort** has shorter sleigh rides. ~ Route 100, Plymouth; 802-672-3811. In Castleton, **Pond Hill Ranch** offers hour-long rides. ~ Pond Hill Road; 802-468-2449.

NORTHERN MOUNTAIN REGION The **Trapp Family Lodge** has short horsedrawn rides. ~ 700 Trapp Hill Road, Stowe; 802-253-8511, 800-826-7000.

NORTHEAST KINGDOM **Vermont Horse Park** offers one-hour sleigh rides in the Smuggler's Notch area. ~ Mountain Road, Jeffersonville; 802-644-5347.

FISHING

From salmon and trout to shad and walleye, Vermont's extensive network of streams, rivers and lakes teem with fine fishing opportunities. Ice fishing has become increasingly popular all over the state but particularly in the Northeast Kingdom, where northern pike, smelt and perch can be plucked from frozen lakes. The general fishing season, however, lasts from April to October.

To find out where the fish bite, contact the **Vermont Department of Fish and Wildlife**. ~ Information and Education Division, 103 South Main Street, Waterbury, VT 05676; 802-241-3700; www.anr.state.vt.us/fw/fwhome.

SOUTHERN VERMONT Half- and full-day flyfishing charters on the Connecticut River are available from **Strictly Trout**. ~ Off Route 121 just south of Saxton River Village; 802-869-3116; www.sover.net/~deenhome.

CENTRAL VERMONT Several outfits will set you up with rental boats and/or fishing equipment.

The **Vermont Fly Fishing School** offers early-morning and late-night guide service for flyfishing for trout and bass on the Connecticut River. ~ The Quechee Inn, Clubhouse Road, Quechee; 802-295-7620. **Duda Water Sports** rents small fishing boats and motor boats. ~ Creek Road, Hydeville; 802-265-3432. **Sailing Winds** rents poles, sailboats and rowboats and has fishing supplies. ~ Route 30, Wells; 802-287-9411.

NORTHERN MOUNTAIN REGION The **Fly Rod Shop** outfits four-hour trips, mostly on the Winooski and Lamoille rivers, for trout and bass. ~ Route 100, Stowe; 802-253-7346; www.flyrod shop.com.

CHAMPLAIN VALLEY In summer, **Yankee Charters** will take you on a half- or full-day trip for trout and salmon on Lake Champlain. ~ Route 7; 802-877-3318.

NORTHEAST KINGDOM Charlie's Northland Lodge rents 14-foot fishing boats—with of without motors—for use on the city bay. ~ Route 2, North Hero; 802-372-8822.

CANOEING Whether you're in it for sightseeing or for rugged adventure, canoeing through Vermont can be an idyllic experience. The season usually lasts from May through October.

SOUTHERN VERMONT Vermont Canoe rents canoes, kayaks and a rowboat. Closed in winter. ~ Putney Road, Brattleboro; 802-257-5008. You can also try **Battenkill Canoe** for canoe rentals and shuttle services along the Battenkill River. ~ Route 7A between Arlington and Manchester; 802-362-2800.

CENTRAL VERMONT In Wells, **Sailing Winds** rents canoes and kayaks. ~ Route 30; 802-287-9411. **Wilderness Trails** offers half- and full-day canoeing float trips down the White River joining with the Connecticut. ~ The Quechee Inn, Clubhouse Road, Quechee; 802-295-7620.

NORTHERN MOUNTAIN REGION Clearwater Sports rents canoes and kayaks for the Mad, Winooski and White rivers. Guided trips are also available and shuttles are provided. ~ Route 100, Waitsfield; 802-496-2708.

CHAMPLAIN VALLEY Hertz First Choice has 17-foot aluminum canoes. Closed Sunday. ~ 94 Harvest Street, Willison; 802-872-5300.

NORTHEAST KINGDOM In North Hero, **Charlie's Northland Lodge** has a canoe for rent. ~ Route 2; 802-372-8822. For canoes and kayaks, try **The Village Sport Shop**. ~ 511 Broad Street, Lyndonville; 802-626-8448.

You can tee off at numerous public courses across the state.

GOLF

SOUTHERN VERMONT The **Sitzmark Golf Course** is a par-3 executive course surrounded by woods. ~ East Dover Road off Route 100, Wilmington; 802-464-3384. There's a semiprivate course at the **Mount Anthony Country Club**. ~ Bank Street, Bennington; 802-447-7079.

CENTRAL VERMONT Surrounded by trees and brooks, the **Killington Golf Course** is a difficult Jeffrey Cornish–designed green. ~ Killington Access Road, Killington; 802-422-6700. **Neshobe Golf Club** has a course with rolling fairways. ~ Town Farm Road, Brandon; 802-247-3611.

NORTHERN MOUNTAIN REGION **Resort Sugarbush** has a Robert Trent Jones, Sr., mountain course. ~ Sugarbush Golf Course, Warren; 802-583-2301. The **Stowe Country Club**'s course has a view of Mt. Mansfield and Camel's Hump. ~ Cottage Club Road off Cape Cod Road, Stowe; 802-253-4893.

CHAMPLAIN VALLEY Don't land in the water on the fifth hole at **Kwiniaska Golf Club**. ~ Spear Street, Shelburne; 802-985-3672. **Marble Island Resort** has a nine-hole course. ~ 1223 Marble Island Road, Colchester; 802-864-6800.

NORTHEAST KINGDOM **St. Johnsbury Country Club**'s 18-hole course features lush fairways and marshlands. ~ Route 5, St. Johnsbury; 802-748-9894.

Tennis fans will find outdoor and indoor courts across the state.

TENNIS

SOUTHERN VERMONT **Mount Anthony Country Club** has three clay courts. Fee. ~ Bank Street, Bennington; 802-442-2617. **Manchester Recreation Area** has three courts. Fee. ~ Off Route 30, Manchester; 802-362-1439.

CENTRAL VERMONT Two courts are open to the public at **Vail Field**. ~ Route 106 behind the Woodstock Inn, Woodstock.

NORTHERN MOUNTAIN REGION The **Bridges Resort and Racquet Club** has two indoor clay courts, eight outdoor clay courts and two outdoor hardtop courts. Fee. ~ Sugarbush Access Road, Warren; 802-583-2922.

CHAMPLAIN VALLEY   Four lighted courts are open to the public at **Leddy Park**. ~ North Avenue, Burlington; 802-864-0123.

NORTHEAST KINGDOM   **Prouty Park** offers four lighted courts in Newport. Fee. ~ Veterans Avenue; 802-334-7951.

RIDING STABLES

What could be more exciting than tromping on horseback through the unspoiled Vermont countryside? Plenty of stables will provide horses and directions to the best trails.

CENTRAL VERMONT   Try **Kedron Valley Stables** for lessons and escorted trail rides in the woods. Overnight trips, with inn accommodations, are also offered. ~ Route 106, South Woodstock; 802-457-1480; www.kedron.com. **Pond Hill Ranch** provides guided trips on mountain trails. ~ Pond Hill Road, Castleton; 802-468-2449. The **Vermont Icelandic Horse Farm** offers trips on scenic back roads and mountain trails. ~ North Fayston Road, Waitsfield; 802-496-7141.

NORTHERN MOUNTAIN REGION   **Navajo Farm** has guided trail rides. ~ Route 100, Moretown; 802-496-3656.

CHAMPLAIN VALLEY   In Chittenden, **Mountain Top Inn Stables** leads one-hour guided excursions in the Green Mountain National Forest. ~ Mountain Top Road; 802-483-2311; www.mountaintopinn.com.

NORTHEAST KINGDOM   **Vermont Horse Park** has guided one-hour mountain trips. ~ Mountain Road, Jeffersonville; 802-644-5347.

BIKING

Vermont's mountains and abundance of back roads create a perfect environment for bicycling. The book *25 Mountain Bike Tours in Vermont* offers a wealth of information, including where to find emergency repairs. ~ The Countryman Press, P.O. Box 748, Woodstock, VT 05091; 802-457-1678, 800-245-4151.

NORTHERN MOUNTAIN REGION   In the **Sugarbush** area there's a 16-mile excursion along Route 100 and East Warren Road, winding through the scenic Mad River Valley and taking in the quaint towns of Warren and Waitsfield.

CHAMPLAIN VALLEY   You can take an easy but lengthy 51-mile trek through the fertile **Champlain Valley**, meandering among apple orchards and cornfields and skirting beautiful Lake Champlain. Stick to Routes 125, 17 and 23, picking up Lake Street along the lake.

Bike Rentals   In southern Vermont, **Brattleboro Bike Shop** has rentals, sales and repairs. ~ 165 Main Street; 802-254-8644. **Green Mountain Rentals** rents mountain bikes and sells accessories. ~ 158 North Main Street, Rutland; 802-775-0101. In the Northern Mountain Region, **Clearwater Sports** rents and repairs mountain bikes. ~ Route 100, Waitsfield; 802-496-2708. **The Ski Rack** has road, mountain, tandem and hybrid bikes; trail maps are available. ~ 85 Main Street, Burlington; 802-658-3313. Up in the Northeast Kingdom, **Village Sport Shop** provides road and mountain bike rentals and repairs. ~ 511 Broad Street, Lyndonville; 802-626-8448.

Bike Tours   To help get you started, **Vermont Bicycle Touring** offers tours with all levels of difficulty and will help build tours for groups of 12 or more. ~ Box 711, Bristol, VT 05443; 802-453-4811; www.vbt.com. For touring around the Champlain Valley, **Bicycle Holidays** rents mountain bikes for their custom-designed self-guided tours. ~ 1394 Munger Street, Middlebury; 802-388-2453. Bike Vermont hs tours for all levels that last up to six days. They'll rent you a bike, or you can bring your own. ~ P.O. Box 207, Woodstock, VT 05091; 802-457-3553; www. bikevt.com.

With more than 700 miles of splendid hiking terrain—including 512 miles on state and national forest lands—Vermont is a hiker's nirvana. The best time to go, of course, is early summer to late fall, avoiding the spring "mud season" from mid-April to late May.

HIKING

Vermont's hiking authority, **The Green Mountain Club**, can supply books, brochures and guidance on the subject, as well as information on biking, snowshoeing and Nordic skiing. ~ 4711 Waterbury-Stowe Road, Waterbury Center, VT 05677; 802-244-7037; www.greenmountain club.org.

All distances listed for hiking trails are one way unless otherwise noted.

The longest uninterrupted trek exists on **The Long Trail** (270 miles), a strenuous, primitive footpath that crawls along the crest of the Green Mountains from Massachusetts to Canada. Purists love the abundance of wildlife and foliage on this trek, which ambles through dense evergreen forests and shaded glens and alongside quiescent ponds and rivers. An inspiration for the Appalachian Trail, which links the mountains from Georgia to Maine, the Long Trail includes 175 miles of side trails and climbs as high as 4393 feet.

SOUTHERN VERMONT   Bald Mountain Trail (2.5 miles), off Route 9 in Bennington, makes a loop past an alder swamp and a cascading brook and through a hemlock forest. There are some fine mountain views along the way.

A nice, short hike in southern Vermont can be found along **Harmon Hill Trail** (1.7 miles) off Route 9 east of Bennington. There's a steep then moderate climb to the summit, where views of Bennington and Mt. Antone are fabulous.

A few miles north, **Baker Peak** and **Lake Trails** (3.3 miles), off Route 7 near Danby, wind through brooks and streams then scale Baker Mountain for a magnificent look at the Otter Creek Valley and marble quarry on Dorset Peak.

CENTRAL VERMONT   A dramatic crevice can be seen along the **Clarendon Gorge and Airport Lookout Viewing Area** (.2 miles), which picks up off Route 103 east of Route 7 near Clarendon. A path crosses a suspension bridge over the Mill River, then ascends steadily to a nice vantage point with views of the Otter Creek Valley and Bird and Herrick mountains.

For a history lesson capped by great scenery, take one of three trails at **Mt. Independence** past well-preserved remains of Revolutionary War fortifications built back in 1775. You'll also discover superb views of Lake Champlain, Fort Ticonderoga and surrounding valleys. The trail begins off Route 73A west of Orwell Village.

Abbey Pond Trail (1.9 miles) affords a close look at beautiful wilderness areas teeming with marsh plants, deer, rabbits, bear and other wildlife. Follow the trail from Route 53, near Forest Dale, past a series of cascades to a view of the twin peaks of Robert Frost Mountain.

The **Skylight Pond Trail** (2.5 miles) commences at Steam Mill Clearing, a pretty meadow and former logging camp, and meanders easily up Battell Mountain, then continues to picturesque Skylight Pond. Pick up the trailhead off Forest Road 59 seven and a half miles east of East Middlebury.

NORTHERN MOUNTAIN REGION   For a 180-degree view of the Champlain Valley and New York's Adirondack Mountains, opt for the **Battell Trail** (2 miles), a western-slope approach to the Long Trail. Hiking enthusiasts can continue 2.9 miles north to the Mt. Abraham summit for a look at the alpine vegetation. The entrance is located off Route 100 in the scenic Lincoln Gap.

Mount Mansfield is Vermont's highest peak (4393 feet) and naturally the most hiked. The easiest trek is via the **Long Trail** (4.6 miles), the most ghoulish endures along **Hell Brook Trail** (1.5 miles), a supersteep rocky climb recommended only for experienced hikers. Both trailheads begin off Route 108 in Stowe.

One of the most beautiful, secluded spots on the Long Trail is at **Devil's Gulch Trail** (2.6 miles), an interesting rock defile and fern grotto. The trailhead is along Route 118 five miles west of Eden.

CHAMPLAIN VALLEY   Take a hike to Lake Champlain on the **Red Rocks Park Trails** (2.5 miles), a series of short paths through cool pine woods that lead to vantage points on the lakeshore. The park is off Queen City Park Drive west of Route 189 in South Burlington.

Open only to campers using the campgrounds, the **Grand Isle State Park Trail** (.3 mile) is short on distance but long on views. The path cuts through a lush thicket and makes a loop over a low bluff to an observation tower. You can see Lake Champlain in the distance. The park is on Route 2 one mile south of Grand Isle.

Knight Point State Park Trail (1 mile) follows Lake Champlain's shoreline through a dense hardwood forest. You'll find the trail on Route 2 in North Hero.

NORTHEAST KINGDOM Mount Pisgah Trail (1.7 miles) crosses this 2751-foot mountain via thick forests and wooden walkways over beaver ponds. There are exceptional views packed into this trek, including a 60-mile panorama from Lake Memphremagog and Jay Peak to beyond Camel's Hump. The trail starts along Route 5A, about six miles from West Burke.

The remote Northeast Kingdom offers some glorious hikes, including the **Wheeler Mountain Trail** (1.3 miles), which creeps through meadows and woods and across open rocks to a 2371-foot summit. Along the way, you'll catch splendid views of Mount Mansfield and Lake Willoughby. The trail picks up off Route 5 east of Barton.

▼▼▼▼▼▼▼▼▼▼▼▼

Transportation

CAR

Automobile travel is quickest (though not very scenic) on **Routes 91 and 89**, Vermont's two interstate highways. Route 91 cuts in from Massachusetts and follows Vermont's eastern border, while Route 89 starts at the New Hampshire line and snakes across the northern center of Vermont to Quebec.

From New York, opt for **Route 7 or Route 4**, entering on Vermont's western edge. Though not a major highway by any means, **Route 100** is the picturesque thoroughfare slicing north–south through the center of the state.

AIR

Burlington International Airport, a small and easily accessible facility in Burlington, is the major air gateway for Vermont. Carriers serving it are American Airlines, Continental Airlines, Delta Airlines, Northwest Airlink, United Airlines and US Airways.

Burlington Airport Ground Transportation Desk provides service from the airport to anywhere in the state. ~ 802-863-1889.

BUS

Vermont Transit Lines provides extensive service throughout New England, with major Vermont stops. For general information, call 802-864-6811. Stations are in Brattleboro at the Junction of Routes 5, 9 and 91, 802-254-6066; in Bennington at 126 Washington Avenue, 802-442-4808; in White River Junction at Sykes Avenue, 802-295-3011; in Rutland at 122 Merchants Row, 802-773-2774; in Burlington at 135 St. Paul Street, 802-864-6811; in St. Johnsbury at Railroad Street, 802-748-4000; and in Newport at Coventry Street, 802-334-2132.

TRAIN **Amtrak** offers direct service from Washington, D.C., Philadelphia, New York, Connecticut and Montreal. The train stops in Vermont at White River Junction (Railroad Row), Montpelier (Montpelier Junction Road), Waterbury (Park Row) and Essex Junction Station (29 Railroad Avenue, near Burlington). ~ 800-872-7245.

CAR RENTALS If you arrive at Burlington International Airport, you'll find the following rental companies: **Avis Rent A Car** (800-331-1212), **Budget Rent A Car** (800-527-0700), **Hertz Rent A Car** (800-654-3131) and **National Car Rental** (800-227-7368). **Thrifty Car Rental** (800-367-2277) is located near the terminal and provides free airport transfers.

NINE

New Hampshire

New Hampshire. It's a heart-stopping collage of sculpted mountains, stony profiles, seamless country roads, expansive lakes and broad beaches. A place you yearn to clutch tightly, to safeguard and to proclaim.

A slender fragment of Yankee domain framed by Vermont, Maine and Massachusetts, New Hampshire is all this and much, much more. It is a region that seems not quite real when you first reach the state, yet you're certain you've been there before. New Hampshire's daunting landscape flirts with the imagination; its spirit roams wild around untamed timberland, wilderness expanses and riots of flowers.

Born of molten granite and giant glaciers, the state's geologic surface was but a labyrinth of smoke, dust and ice sheets some 300 million years ago. Hot rock hissed beneath the earth, forced its way up and drove the ground to buckle and split. Advancing ice sheets smoothed the rock, forming it into hills and mountains, then swiftly melted to create rivers and lakes.

Along the way, these icy torrents deposited thousands of granite chunks. All that stone gives today's New Hampshire a rugged veneer, as well as its moniker of "The Granite State." Boulders lie strewn across farmlands, jut out into the sea and loom atop mountains, their mystic profiles often evocative of some familiar face or object.

Human rumblings in this area go back at least 8000 years, when the Abenaki and Pennacook Indians roamed the lands. Members of Algonquin tribes, they fished the swift rivers, hunted forests for game and fruit and culled maple sugar from the trees. Their first European visitor, British captain Martin Pring, sailed up the Piscataqua River in 1603, though it was not until 1623 that the first settlement was founded at Odiorne Point in present-day Rye.

Several towns soon sprang up along the coast and river. Strawbery Banke, now Portsmouth, became the capital and commercial center of New Hampshire life as fishers, coopers and shipbuilders plied their trades there. In 1643, a greedy Massachusetts annexed the settlements into its Bay Colony, holding them for 36 years until England declared New Hampshire a royal province.

Thick forests, bitter winters and unforgiving earth made life difficult for those who tried to tame New Hampshire's interior. Even worse, previously friendly Indians came to resent white intrusion and exploitation, and a series of violent skirmishes ensued. In one infamous incident, Indians captured a settler named Hannah Dustin, a 39-year-old mother of 12, and took her to River Islet, near present-day Concord. During the night, Dustin killed and scalped her ten sleeping captors, escaping with her life.

In the mid-1700s, settlers struggled to cultivate the rocky soil that became bloodied by French and Indian conflicts. The French and Indian War finally settled the matter in 1763, though the subsequent American Revolution only brought more strife to a battered land.

New Hampshire entered the Revolution with a vengeance. In December 1774, when patriots received word from Paul Revere that British soldiers would soon be at Portsmouth, they stormed Fort William and Mary. Six months later, England's governor was driven from the colony.

After the war, people gave up on agriculture and turned to textile manufacturing. But an even more lucrative source of income was about to arrive: the stream of pleasure seekers who, lured by bewitching landscapes and a bevy of natural resources, started coming to New Hampshire in droves. Exclaimed one well-traveled visitor: "There is no doubt but the scenery of New Hampshire is more varied and beautiful than can be found in any other state in the Union."

Thousands of new arrivals, known as "summer people," converged on the land. Those with money built grand estates or lavish hotels, while the majority put up frame houses and white picket fences and settled on their front porches for the summer. All of a sudden, New Hampshire's first tourist industry was raging.

By the late 1800s, a different kind of industry had emerged. Virtually overnight, logging businesses penetrated the White Mountains and cleared thousands of acres of trees to feed a voracious lumber demand. Within 20 years, barren patches scarred the mountainsides and wildlife was dwindling.

It might have been the undoing of New Hampshire's precious mountains had not public outcry prompted Congress to halt the destruction. The Weeks Act of 1911 called for federal purchase of most of the state's forest lands, which today make up the 768,000-acre White Mountain National Forest.

Now forests cloak 84 percent of the state, while some 1300 lakes form pockets of beauty and intrigue. Shaped like a skinny triangle that points toward Canada, New Hampshire spans only 168 miles from top to bottom and 90 miles at its broadest point. Its 9304 square miles cover six geographic regions so disparate you might think they existed in separate states, though together they create a powerful display of nature.

The wind-whipped seacoast ambles a mere 18 miles from Massachusetts to Maine, though its dramatic jetties, swirling tidepools and generous stretches of sand pack a state-sized dose of beauty. Northern Portsmouth, one of the finest ports in New England, brims with culture and commerce and endearing remnants of history.

The Merrimack Valley crawls up the lower spine of New Hampshire, its old textile mills clinging to the shores of the Merrimack River. The valley claims its largest city, Manchester, and seat of government, Concord.

New Hampshire

Draped across the southwest corridor are lone mountains known as monadnocks. The Monadnock Region embodies a perfect canvas of rural New England, speckled with covered bridges, weathered barns and charming country towns that seem locked in the 18th century.

The state's midwestern edge, flanked by the Connecticut River, is graced with cornfields, subtle mountains and the culture of Dartmouth College. Nearby Lake Sunapee and its attendant sentinel, Mount Sunapee, are a year-round playground for lovers of the outdoors.

A tryst of twinkling azure water and gentle peaks, the Lakes Region is altogether captivating and soothing. A total of 273 bodies of water bundle together across New Hampshire's heartland. Their names—many were given by the Indians —conjure up romance and exotica. Lake Winnipesaukee, with 283 miles of coast and 274 habitable islands, is the sixth largest lake lying wholly in the United States.

Towering above the lakes are the White Mountains, overwhelming in appearance and massive in scope. Life slows down up here as people tend to small farms and businesses and raise their families. There are pockets of tourism, particularly ski resorts, nestled between canopies of evergreens and remote country roads.

In addition to its obvious aesthetic appeal, New Hampshire basks in the nation's political limelight every four years. Since 1915, it has secured the edge on presidential primaries, holding the first one in each election.

This claim to firstdom has yielded the tiny state considerable political clout, as candidates frequently gauge their campaigns according to New Hampshire's mood. In 1988, George Bush gained momentum after he trounced Robert Dole in New Hampshire. Back in 1976, a little-known Jimmy Carter earned credibility after a warm reception in the first primary. And since 1952, New Hampshire has chosen the candidate who would go on to be president, with the exception of Bill Clinton in 1992.

It's certain that New Hampshire aims to keep its first-primary position. Once, when Vermont mentioned it might hold elections earlier than its neighbor, New Hampshire quickly passed a law mandating that its primaries be held on the Tuesday before those of any other New England state. Wily Massachusetts once made the mistake of scheduling its primary on the same day as New Hampshire's. Indignant, New Hampshire pushed its elections up one week.

Indeed, politics is serious business in New Hampshire. The state legislature has 424 members—making it the third-largest governing body in the English-speaking world (behind Great Britain's Parliament and the U.S. Congress). The state tends to vote Republican.

"Live Free or Die" is New Hampshire's motto, as every native reminds you. It's emblazoned on state license plates, on not a few homes and across some businesses. But despite this constant assertion of autonomy, the state still sees fit to restrict itself in curious ways.

Nightclubs and bars standing alone are banned; they must be connected to a restaurant, sports club, bowling alley or similar business. You can purchase hard liquor only from state-run stores, many of which dot major highways and interstates. These cobwebbed laws have been in place since Prohibition and don't seem likely to change in the near future.

For the most part, freedom to New Hampshire inhabitants means no sales tax and no personal income tax. Not surprisingly, these particular freedoms have lured throngs of people who now live in New Hampshire but work in nearby states. Miffed at the situation, Maine responded by taxing its workers who live in New Hampshire—as well as their spouses who live and work in New Hampshire. Needless to say, the two states continue a classic Yankee feud.

Today's New Hampshire is home to a new band of artists, as well as the factory workers and bankers, innkeepers and small business people who run the general stores. Its thriving tourism and aesthetic surroundings make the state a desirable place to live for its 1.1 million residents.

Despite some apparent modernization, New Hampshire still clings to its founding principles. It is a world focused on clapboard houses and slender steeples, Yankee ingenuity and memories of Pilgrims, town halls and the freedom to worship and vote.

Over the years, New Hampshire changes—yet somehow stays quite the same. Lifestyles and customs are passed on through generations firmly rooted in its granite soil. With a seashore, mountains and lakes that remain poignant and timeless, this state is a glorious place under the sun.

The Seacoast

Despite its diminutive size—only 18 miles in length—New Hampshire's seacoast is one of the state's most revered possessions. And rightly so, for its alliance of pounding surf, rocky headlands and tidepools, stately mansions and nature preserves offers a wealth of beauty and continuous intrigue.

Naturally the dramatic seaboard is a driver's paradise, which explains why it remains perpetually clogged with traffic. Warm summer breezes and sunshine draw the most crowds—particularly on weekends—though locals claim that winter snow falling on the sand is truly a sight to behold.

SIGHTS

Just north of the Massachusetts line, whiffs of salty marsh air announce the town of **Seabrook**. Families favor this small oceanside nook for its amusement centers and pretty beaches, though the main attraction is **Seabrook Greyhound Park**. More than 1000 agile racing dogs call this fast track home, performing for bettors year-round. Admission. ~ Route 107, Seabrook; 603-474-3065.

Since 1976, Seabrook has received national attention because of the controversial **Seabrook Station Nuclear Power Plant**. Although citizens groups and the state of Massachusetts waged a long and costly battle to block the opening of the plant, it began operating in March 1990—three years after it was completed. The controversy continues today. For a closer look, the 1150-megawatt, $6.5 billion facility offers bus tours around the outside of its containment building, along with a ten-minute video of what's on the inside. Closed Saturday and Sunday. ~ Routes 107 and 1, Seabrook; 603-474-9521.

Traveling northward on Route 1A, you'll notice the scenery changing from marshlands to wide open beaches as you approach the seacoast's most animated stretch of sand, **Hampton Beach**. Mobbed by hundreds of thousands of vacationers every year, this heavily developed tract is one giant pleasure center, its nucleus an oceanside promenade that reels with constant activity.

Start out by walking the promenade, a three-mile human fiesta extending along Ocean Boulevard from Dumas Avenue to Hampton Beach State Park, taking in the well-strolled boardwalk jammed with trinket and T-shirt vendors, low-slung motels and the aroma of carnival food. This is people-watching at its best, a place where a whole spectrum of humanity—drifters, beach bums and the highbrow—converges on one long slab of concrete.

There's a constant hum of cars, joggers, bicyclists and curious sightseers who stop to ponder the **New Hampshire Marine War Memorial**, a tribute to soldiers lost at sea. The granite statue features a forlorn maiden draped in rolls of stone cloth and clutching a wreath. ~ Ocean Boulevard and Nudd Avenue, Hampton Beach.

Great Boars Head, a rocky bulkhead in the ocean, projects an imposing silhouette just north of Hampton Beach. Topped with grand old mansions and seaside homes, Boars Head is particularly intriguing at sunrise, when the day's first light and the ocean mist produce a surreal portrait. ~ Ocean Boulevard and Dumas Avenue.

To help get you organized with local sightseeing, stop by the **Hampton Beach Area Chamber of Commerce**, located a couple miles west of Hampton Beach and only open in the summer. ~ 180 Ocean Boulevard, Hampton; 603-926-8718.

A ten-minute drive west will land you in the rural respite of **Applecrest Farm Orchards**, where 20,000 apple trees and two pumpkin patches bask along the hillsides. Show up from Labor Day to mid-October and pick your own, or check out the applemart, an 1812 barn stocked with apple ciders, pies, butter, sauce and other great-smelling goodies. During the summertime, strawberries, raspberries and blueberries come ripe for pickin'. ~ Route 88 west of Route 95, Hampton Falls; 603-926-3721.

HIDDEN ► The best place to snag those plump, radiant raspberries is nearby **Raspberry Farm**. This 60-acre spread is a honey of a find. Wander through luxuriant patches, pluck your own berries (which also include strawberries, blueberries and blackberries) and receive harvesting facts from the friendly owners. Don't miss the market filled with pies, tarts and jams. Closed from late October to early June; call for hours. ~ Route 84 (also Kensington Road), three miles west of Route 1, Hampton Falls; 603-926-6604.

Hop back over onto Route 1A, heading north along this roving high road flanked on one side by a turgid ocean and on the other by regal New England mansions known as "Millionaire's Row" for the old-monied families who live here.

The largest tract of undeveloped coastline exists at **Odiorne Point State Park**, which wanders along two oceanfront miles and covers 327 acres. Back in 1623, New Hampshire's first white settlers landed here and found thick vegetation and whistling winds. The park includes grave sites, old stone walls, remains of a formal garden and several World War II bunkers. **The Seacoast Science Center**, located on the park's premises, offers a look at the area's natural and social history. (A separate admission fee is charged.) Admission during summer. ~ Route 1A, Rye; 603-436-7406 (park), 603-436-8043 (Seacoast Science Center).

From here you can peer out to sea and spy the stony profile of the **Isles of Shoals**, an archipelago that harbors great mysteries and torrid tales of pirates, treasures and wrecked ships. In 1614, Captain John Smith dubbed the isles "barren piles of rocks with a few scrub cedar," and they've seen minimal change since.

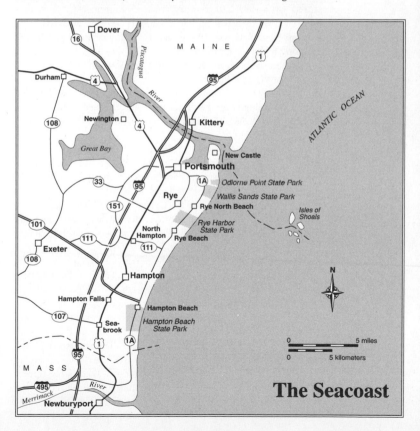

The Seacoast

Blackbeard and Captain Kidd supposedly stashed their loot among the rocky crevices, the former abandoning his wife there in 1723. Some say her spirit still roams the shores.

The isles later drew many artists and writers, including Nathaniel Hawthorne and Childe Hassam. Today, you can visit the islands via the **Island Cruises**, which offers narrated tours seasoned with history. Closed mid-October to early May. Admission. ~ Rye Harbor State Marina, Route 1A, Rye; 603-964-6446; www.uncleoscar.com.

Anchoring the northern end of the seacoast, **Portsmouth**, with its rich maritime history, has long played a critical role in the state's prosperity and development. Lying at the mouth of the Piscataqua River, the city seems like some profound old sage, locked in a bygone era yet quite vibrant and progressive at the same time.

Stone sidewalks and ivy-clad brick buildings, their walls holding two centuries of memories, gather stoically along the harbor. In central downtown, known as Market Street, immaculately restored 18th- and 19th-century enclaves mingle with sleek new highrises. Young artists and professionals continue to arrive from Boston, New York and Maine, polishing the cultural patina and dynamic night scenes of this port city.

There's so much to see here, and the best place to get organized is the **Greater Portsmouth Chamber of Commerce**. Pick up the *Harbor Trail*, a resource book featuring historical facts and a map outlining several self-guided tours. Closed Saturday and Sunday from September through May. ~ 500 Market Street, Portsmouth; 603-436-1118.

Built between 1716 and 1807, the houses vary architecturally and enjoy their own special museums and personalities. At the **John Paul Jones House**, a 1758 Georgian design, you'll find a room arranged with marvelous wedding gowns worn in the 1800s as well as the oldest piano in the United States. There's also a collection of Civil War guns, a nifty wooden bathtub, and oars and paddles from the South Seas. Admission. ~ 43 Middle Street, Portsmouth; 603-436-8420.

George Washington dropped by a party at the **Governor John Langdon House** back in 1789. According to memos he later penned, George found the home quite warm and its proprietor, future New Hampshire Governor John Langdon, very hospitable. Today, beautiful wood carvings and precious period furnishings adorn the interior. Closed Monday and Tuesday and from mid-October through May. Admission. ~ 143 Pleasant Street, Portsmouth; 603-436-3205.

One treat that goes with the Portsmouth Trail is the opportunity to meet the congenial docents (many are Portsmouth natives) who fill you with history and interesting anecdotes. Most of the trail homes close during winter and open only a few days

Author Picks

CHAPTER FAVORITES

I find ancient mysteries irresistible, and while **America's Stonehenge** may be a far cry from the lost cities of Atlantis, its 4000-year-old stonework walls, archaeoastronomical alignments and crystal mine provide plenty of strangeness to speculate about. *page 504*

When my budget isn't quite up to the grand inns that dot the landscape, a reasonable alternative for a quintessentially New England stay is in a modest farmhouse B&B like the well-hidden **Wyman Farm**. Finding it is entertaining in itself. *page 507*

As further proof that affordability need not be boring, I suggest **Patrick Henry's**, a long-standing favorite Dartmouth hangout where a dark, almost medieval atmosphere sets the stage for great pub grub. *page 519*

In October, I discovered, the most magnificent experience in New Hampshire costs nothing at all. See for yourself: forget about the bumper-to-bumper leaf-peeping traffic and hike the Appalachian Trail through **White Mountain National Forest** for the ultimate fall colors experience. *page 538*

each week the rest of the year, so call ahead.

To find out what makes Portsmouth tick, stroll southeast on Market Street down to the **docks**, where the Piscataqua River laps at the city's edge. Back in the 18th and 19th centuries, furniture makers, potters, coopers and shipbuilders gathered along the waterfront to ply their trades, while a flourishing sawmill industry provided Great Britain with thousands of ships' masts. Today, tugboats, fishing vessels and sailboats scoot across the dark waters that flow to nearby Kittery, Maine.

From here you can catch a harbor cruise or take a longer jaunt to the Isles of Shoals. **Isles of Shoals Steamship Co.** provides trips from June through October. Other stops include Portsmouth Harbor and Star Island. ~ 315 Market Street, Portsmouth; 603-431-5500, 800-441-4620. **Portsmouth Harbor Cruises** offers trips from May to mid-September. A tour of the inland rivers is also featured. ~ 64 Ceres Street, Oar House Dock, Portsmouth; 603-436-8084.

Follow the water northwest to Marcy Street, where you'll discover Portsmouth's most prized gem, **Strawbery Banke**, site of the original settlement. Sheltered within ten acres of rambling gardens and Colonial buildings is a wonderful lesson on New England architecture through 1943 and the struggles and lifestyles of America's founders. The area gets its moniker from the profusion of berries found here in 1630 by the city's first English settlers.

Thanks to the foresight of local leaders, the banke's 42 buildings, dating from 1695 to 1954, were spared demolition in the 1950s. Every place offers some fascinating historical insight, and it takes a full day to see it all. There's the **Daniel Webster House** (not open to the public), where Webster and his wife, Grace, lived from 1814 to 1816, as well as the boyhood home of author Thomas Bailey Aldrich, whose book *The Story of a Bad Boy* inspired Mark Twain to write *Tom Sawyer*. Closed November to mid-April. Admission. ~ Entrance off Marcy Street south of Court Street, Portsmouth; 603-433-1100; www.strawberybanke.org.

The 1766 **Pitt Tavern**, perhaps the banke's most historically significant building, was a meeting place for loyalists and then patriots. Revolutionary War strategies were devised within these walls, which now display ads from 1770s newspapers announcing those historic meetings.

Before you leave town, stop by the **North Cemetery**, purchased by the town for £50 in 1753. Buried on this unassuming grassy swell are John Langdon, former New Hampshire governor and signer of the Constitution, and General William Whipple, signer of the Declaration of Independence. ~ Maplewood Avenue and Russell Street, Portsmouth.

The coastline bustle takes on a gentler cadence as you head north of Portsmouth. **Dover**, a working-class mill town with charm, was founded by fishermen during the early 1600s and remained independent until 1642, when it joined the Massachusetts Bay Colony. Route 9 trundles right through town, flanked by huge mansions sporting multiple chimneys, many built in the 19th century by wealthy mill owners.

You can mull over the town's beginnings at the **Woodman Institute**, which houses an excellent display of New Hampshire memorabilia, wildlife and natural history. Closed Monday and Tuesday and February through March. Admission. ~ 182 Central Avenue, Dover; 603-742-1038; www.seacoastnh.com.

Travel south on Route 108 to the college town of Durham, where the **University of New Hampshire** provides a restful haven for strolling. A third of the campus' 2000 acres is a nature preserve, crisscrossed with walking trails and lakes perfect for winter ice skating. ~ Route 155A, Durham; 603-862-1234.

West on Route 108, **Durham Landing** recalls the venue of a bloody battle in 1694, when more than 200 Indians attacked about 100 settlers, destroying their houses and garrisons along the Oyster River.

In nearby Exeter, you'll find a constant drum of traffic and human motion caused by the presence of exclusive **Phillips Exeter Academy**. One of the oldest and most renowned preparatory schools in the country, the academy has aged beautifully. Founded in 1781, the school boasts lovely brick buildings that lay masked in tangled ivy and are edged by green lawns and maple trees. Through the years, its hallowed halls have seen students like Daniel Webster, historian George Bancroft and Booth Tarkington. ~ 20 Main Street, Exeter; 603-772-4311.

Toward the north (and somewhat quieter) end of Hampton Beach, the **Hampton House** offers very comfortable accommodations amid contemporary surroundings. A breezy lobby edges the busy beachfront street and comforts with soothing ocean views from the floor-to-ceiling glass windows. Three floors of spacious guest rooms feature wall-to-wall carpets, modern wood furnishings and private balconies that yield some fine ocean views and people-watching opportunities. ~ 333 Ocean Boulevard, Hampton Beach; 603-926-1033, 800-458-7058, fax 603-926-3473. DELUXE TO ULTRA-DELUXE.

LODGING

From the outside, you'd swear it's little more than a generic beach motel. But wander into the **Oceanside Hotel** and you'll enter a world of superb 19th-century Victorian designs. Handsome pine floors show off period furniture and braided rugs. Each of ten rooms (including two that face the ocean) is named after Hampton Beach settlers, with decor matching the pioneer period. ~ 365 Ocean Boulevard, Hampton Beach; 603-926-3542. DELUXE.

The Inn at Hampton possesses all the charm and detail of a fancy bed and breakfast. The guest rooms offer such personal touches as mirrored armoires, quilted headboards and dust ruffles, vaulted pine ceilings and scents of jasmine. Among the other niceties of this family-fun inn are an indoor pool and jacuzzi, an exercise room and, of course, a congenial staff. ~ 815 Lafayette Road, Hampton; 603-926-6771, 800-423-4561, fax 603-929-2160. MODERATE TO DELUXE.

For the charm of a country inn with the luxuries of a large hotel, consider the **Sise Inn**. Set in an 1881 Queen Anne home within walking distance of most downtown Portsmouth sights, the hostelry features a lobby that soars three stories and is highlighted by pretty butternut banisters and oriental rugs. Oversized guest rooms are suited with bay windows, four-poster beds, showers *and* tubs (some with whirlpools) and nice extras like VCRs. ~ 40 Court Street, Portsmouth; phone/fax 603-433-1200, 800-267-0525; www.someplacesdifferent.com/sise.htm; e-mail siseinn @cybertours.com. DELUXE TO ULTRA-DELUXE.

Resting on a shady knoll adjacent to a busy thoroughfare, the **Martin Hill Inn** will send you back in time. This gracious pair of 19th-century buildings, linked by a flower-lined brick path, lies awash in lovely antiques accented by bouquets of day lilies. The decor of the inn's seven rooms ranges from formal Colonial style to country Victorian. ~ 404 Islington Street, Portsmouth; 603-436-2287; www.portsmouthnh.com/martinhillinn. MODERATE.

The **Bow Street Inn** claims an unusual location: a second floor above a performing-arts center in central downtown. Not to worry—all nine guest rooms are nicely soundproofed and come with accoutrements like brass beds, plush carpets and ruffled curtains. A brewery during the 19th century, the ruddy brick building peers across the Piscataqua River. ~ 121 Bow Street, Portsmouth; 603-431-7760, fax 603-433-1680; www.bowstreetinn.com. MODERATE TO DELUXE.

In January 1776, New Hampshire became the first independent American state.

Around 1800, Christian ship captains—anxious to separate themselves from military captains—settled in modest homes west of downtown Portsmouth. Now the **Inn at Christian Shore** harkens back to those early days with simple, Federal-style design and sunny ambience. Five bedrooms are cheerfully outfitted with floral wallpaper and antique furniture. The dining room, with its low-slung beam ceilings and large fireplace, is quite cozy. Full breakfast included in the rates. ~ 335 Maplewood Avenue, Portsmouth; 603-431-6770, fax 603-431-7743; www.portsmouthnh.com. MODERATE.

Northwest of Portsmouth, the historic mill town of Dover maintains a handful of motels and B&Bs, including the **Silver Street Inn**. Built in the 1880s by well-to-do mill owners, the ornate mansion displays such Victorian indulgences as high carved ceilings, marble and slate floors, Spanish mahogany doors and Italian-tile hearths. There's a formal library and dining room and ten bedrooms ranging from simple to lavish. ~ 103 Silver Street, Dover; 603-743-3000, fax 603-749-5673. MODERATE.

Payne's Hill is a small bed and breakfast within walking distance of town. All four guest rooms in the 1888 New Englander are thoughtfully decorated with late-19th-century antiques and reproductions representative of the era. Guests can enjoy the music room (which has an upright piano, some guitars and other instruments) and the living room. The gazebo out back has lots of benches to lounge on. Gay-friendly. ~ 141 Henry Law Avenue, Dover; 603-740-9441; www.bestinns.net/usa/nh/payneshill.html. MODERATE.

DINING

For superb seafood amidst some hopping beach action, try the dining room **Ashworth by the Sea**. Lobster fiends will revel in the ten different lobster entrées such as baked stuffed lobster pie, lobster Newburg and a sinful baked lobster stuffed with extra lobster. For non-seafoodites, there's veal and chicken plus roast Vermont turkey. A breakfast buffet, lunch, dinner and a dinner buffet are served. ~ 295 Ocean Boulevard, Hampton Beach; 603-926-6762. MODERATE TO DELUXE.

Possibly the finest seafood restaurant on New Hampshire's 18-mile coast is popular **Ron's Landing**. Elegant yet quite relaxed, the restaurant sits across the street from the ocean; the Atlantic views are marvelous from its second-floor deck. Small tables draped in starched cloth and perfectly folded napkins create an intimate atmosphere. The Continental menu features a generous seafood selection plus interesting chicken, beef and pasta entrées. Dinner only, except for Sunday brunch. ~ 379 Ocean Boulevard, Hampton Beach; 603-929-2122. DELUXE.

The **Galley Hatch** is a bright, cheerfully modern restaurant offering something for every taste, from soup and salad to fresh-caught Downeast lobster. Also available are pasta, pizza, deli sandwiches including a succulent grilled vegetable sandwich on focaccia bread, and a full range of beef cuts from filet mignon with portobello mushrooms to a Thai-style marinated beef kabob. ~ 325 Lafayette Road, Hampton; 603-926-6152. BUDGET TO MODERATE.

Back in 1764, a 26-year-old grenadier named Thomas Fletcher reportedly died of fever after drinking a hot beer. Forlorn and eager for companionship, his widow turned their tiny frame home into a tavern. Today, **Widow Fletcher's Tavern** remains one of New England's supreme pubs, framed in hand-hewn wood beams and booths and wide plank floors worn to a perfect late-18th-century patina. Fare goes a step beyond standard tavern food, with entrées such as seafood linguine, broiled haddock, and a slew of excellent salads, sandwiches and appetizers. No lunch on Monday. ~ 401 Lafayette Road, Hampton; 603-926-8800. BUDGET TO MODERATE.

Paul's Carriage House provides a curious mix of Colonial and seaside ambience—and pulls it off swimmingly. The two-story casual nook rests across the street from Jenness Beach but looks like a mountain eatery. Early American wood tables and booths encircle a big hearth downstairs, while upstairs a smaller room promises great views of the beach. The Continental-style bill of fare offers gems like steak *au poivre*, roast Long Island duckling with raspberry and onion glaze, *frutti di mare* with shrimps, scallops and lobster over linguine. Dinner only. ~ 2263 Ocean Boulevard, Rye; 603-964-8251. MODERATE TO DELUXE.

Right off Portsmouth's Market Square, is **Metro**, where you can get pasta, seafood and a variety of steak, lamb and veal dishes. It's a lovely restaurant with wood paneling, stained glass and white tablecloths. On Friday and Saturday nights, there's live jazz. Closed Monday. ~ 20 High Street, Portsmouth; 603-436-0521. MODERATE TO DELUXE.

HIDDEN ▶

A departure from traditional New England fare can be found at **Porto Bello**. Here, southern and northern Italian cuisine is the order of the day. The menu includes such seasonal specials as farfalle with crab in a light cream sauce or center-cut veal chop. It's all served in a stylish second-floor dining room overlooking the river. Dinner only. Closed Monday. ~ 67 Bow Street, Portsmouth; 603-431-2989. MODERATE TO DELUXE.

The place for sushi is **Sakura**, a small but airy downtown nook that serves up fresh *maki* rolls and sashimi, tempura and teriyaki dishes, and interesting appetizers like soft-shell crabs. The decor borders on plain, with a small sushi bar, wood tables and railings, but it's as neat as a pin. Very popular with the business set. No lunch Saturday through Monday. ~ 40 Pleasant Street, Portsmouth; 603-431-2721. MODERATE TO ULTRA-DELUXE.

The **Harbor's Edge Restaurant** captures a superb view of the harbor amidst romantic surroundings. Decked in hues of emerald and rose, the eatery conveys an air of refinement with crystal and flower-topped linen tablecloths. Cuisine falls in the American and nouvelle categories, with seafood and mixed grill items. ~ In the Sheraton Portsmouth, 250 Market Street, Portsmouth; 603-431-2300. MODERATE TO ULTRA-DELUXE.

Portsmouth's famous old spaghetti house is **The Rosa**, a great family-style place that opened back in 1927. Adorned with dimly lit wood booths and old-time photographs, the restaurant serves up those heart-stopping, traditional Italian favorites like parmigianas and cacciatores, lasagna, ravioli, tortellini and thin-crusted pizza. ~ 80 State Street, Portsmouth; 603-436-9715. BUDGET TO MODERATE.

East of Hampton Beach, the town of Exeter is home to Phillips Exeter Academy, one of the country's most renowned and oldest preparatory schools. Here, the student population sustains a happy array of quaint street cafés, one of the best being **The Loaf and Ladle**. Everything is homemade and fresh, served cafeteria-style by friendly young people. There's black-bean soup, country pâté, stacked sandwiches and cheesecakes. ~ 9 Water Street, Exeter; 603-778-8955. BUDGET.

SHOPPING

For shopping in Hampton Beach, you can slum it on the boardwalk, bartering with vendors for jewelry, T-shirts and endless assorted souvenirs. The main action is along **Ocean Boulevard** from Nudd Avenue to Haverhill Avenue, where you can snag everything from leather jackets and tattoos to fake photo IDs and suntans (in tanning salons, of course).

North Hampton Factory Outlet Center is your place for discounted designer effects. There's a nice variety of items, from shoes and coats to furniture, crafts and ingenious kitchenware. ~ Route 1, North Hampton; 603-964-9050.

Bona fide mallaholics should head straight for **Fox Run Mall**, where over 100 stores and eateries provide quality browsing amid fashionable surroundings. ~ Fox Run Road off Spaulding Turnpike, Newington; 603-431-5911.

It's so much fun to stroll Portsmouth's colorful, funky shops that you'll likely forget you're spending money.

Spacious and entertaining, **G. Willikers!** has enough toys, stuffed animals, clothes and other kiddie paraphernalia to make a tot go crazy. ~ 13 Market Street, Portsmouth; 603-436-7746.

Handmade paper sneakers, Thomas Mann techno-romantic jewelry, papier mâché mermaids and Droll design–handpainted pottery are among the wonderfully crazy artwork at **Gallery 33**. ~ 111 Market Street, Portsmouth; 603-431-7403.

Another noteworthy art stop, **N. W. Barrett Gallery** proffers wood, handblown glass and other crafts by local and nationally acclaimed artists. On the second floor, there's a fine-art gallery with original and limited-edition prints, as well as unique wedding and engagement rings. ~ 53 Market Street, Portsmouth; 603-431-4262.

It's Raining Cats and Dogs is an animal lover's delight. Fake fire hydrants, doggie raincoats and cat-to-cat greeting cards are but a few of the crazy critter antics. ~ 13 Commercial Alley, Portsmouth; 603-430-9566.

The Dunaway Shop at The Strawbery Banke Museum has all sorts of gifts, including reproductions of museum items, pottery, books, candles, cards, toys and candy. ~ 64 Marcy Street, Portsmouth; 603-433-1114.

NIGHTLIFE

Despite its stringent liquor laws—which mandate that bars must be part of restaurants, ski lodges or similar businesses—New Hampshire manages an ample share of lively establishments.

The 1800-seat **Hampton Beach Casino Ballroom**, one of those great old big-band clubs built in the 1920s, headlines top-name rock-and-roll, jazz, country-and-western and comedy. The season runs from May to mid-October. ~ 169 Ocean Boulevard, Hampton Beach; 603-929-4100.

Nautical decor and contemporary tunes set the scene at **The Pelican Club**. Live music plays Friday and Saturday at this popular, upscale oasis. ~ Galley Hatch Restaurant, Route 1, Hampton; 603-926-6152.

You can hear a good jazz pianist and bass player at **Metro**, a bar/restaurant, on Friday and Saturday nights. ~ 20 High Street, Portsmouth; 603-436-0521.

Have a home-brewed beer (and watch it being brewed) at **Portsmouth Brewery**. Enjoy a laid-back evening downstairs playing pool or darts or just lounging in the oversized padded booths. ~ 56 Market Street, Portsmouth; 603-431-1115.

Nautical in style, **Dolphin Striker** resides above an underground tavern built around a spring-fed well. Hang out with the exotic fish that swarm the well, or relax to piped-in jazz or nightly live acoustic music. ~ 15 Bow Street, Portsmouth; 603-431-5222.

Set in a 19th-century brick brewery, the **Seacoast Repertory Theatre**, housed in the beautiful Bow Street Theatre, stages Shakespearean plays and other drama, major musicals and comedy in an intimate, under-300-seat pit theater. Closed Monday. ~ 125 Bow Street, Portsmouth; 603-433-4472.

BEACHES & PARKS

For the most part, New Hampshire's parks are open only for the summer, usually from Memorial Day through Labor Day. During the off-season, contact the **New Hampshire Division of Parks and Recreation**. ~ Box 1856, Concord, NH 03302; 603-271-3556.

HAMPTON BEACH STATE PARK One of the most popular parks in all New Hampshire, this place boasts a quarter mile of broad pewter-colored beach flecked with smooth stones. A jetty shoots several feet into the ocean, and there's a long row of sand dunes, some of the few remaining in the state. From here, you have tremendous views northward of Great Boars Head and an opportunity to fish from the jetty for flounder. You'll find a gazebo with picnic tables, restrooms, a bathhouse, a snack bar and lifeguards. Closed mid-October to early May. Day-use fee, $8. ~ On Route 1A at the southern tip of Hampton Beach; 603-926-3784.

▲ There's an RV campground with 28 full hookup sites; $35 per night.

HAMPTON SEASHELL STATE PARK This is *the* liveliest sand in New Hampshire. For six months a year, thousands jam a three-mile stretch of fine ashen grains whipped by waves and surrounded by street action. The boardwalk, with its sidewalk vendors, carnival food and trinket shops, follows the beach and creates constant activity. Despite the size of this beach, the crowds do follow a certain order: families cluster around the north end, older folks lay claim to the south tip and the skimpy-suited, let's-party group stakes out the middle near the Beach Patrol Station. There are restrooms, a playground, lifeguards, a pavilion, an amphitheater and a band shell. Closed November through April. ~ In Hampton Beach along Ocean Boulevard between M Street and Great Boars Head; 603-926-6705.

NORTH BEACH A thick seawall hides this beach from the roadway, though rough waves occasionally send salt water over the top and onto passing traffic. The narrow cord of hard-packed sand, stretching one and a half miles, is submerged during most high tides, when locals congregate atop the wall for prime wave watching. This is the most popular spot in New Hampshire to surf; it's best around Great Boars Head, a rocky bulkhead on the northern end of the beach. Restrooms are available. ~ In Hampton Beach along Ocean Boulevard between Great Boars Head and 19th Street; 603-926-2862.

PLAICE COVE BEACH Strewn with gray boulders and pebbles, this volcaniclike beach is encased in sand as silver as gunpowder. Small but picturesque, it rests before beautiful homes and appears to be a private beach. Locals know it as one of the quietest spots around and assemble here at low tide when the sand area is widest. Seagulls hang around the north end, scurrying about seaweed patches and constant ocean sprays. Swimming is okay at low tide during summer, though water is frequently quite rough. ~ Take the unmarked footpath that starts on Route 1A, across from Ron's Beach House restaurant just north of the intersection of Route 101C in Hampton Beach. The path leads between two houses down to the beach; 603-436-1552.

◄ HIDDEN

NORTH HAMPTON STATE BEACH Stretching 1000 feet along the ocean, this fine sliver of mocha sand covers a short lapse between seaside neighborhoods. Families favor the park for its subdued tone and gentle waves. Lovely Little Boars Head, a rocky ocean spur, looms to the north. You'll find restrooms and lifeguards. ~ Along Ocean Boulevard just south of Little Boars Head in North Hampton; 603-436-9404.

SOUTH RYE BEACH This so-called "beach" consists solely of millions of silvery pebbles (bad for the back but pretty to look at) that extend about one-quarter mile. Dedicated sunbathers set up lawn chairs and wear sturdy shoes, but the real action centers around surfing. Board toters call this beach "Rye on the Rocks" and arrive en masse anytime there's a whiff of wind. Stores are less than a mile away in Rye. ~ On Route 1A, south of Causeway Road in Rye.

RYE HARBOR STATE PARK Situated on Ragged Neck Peninsula, this park offers commanding views of Rye Harbor and a 200-foot jetty for prime fishing (flounder and pollack) and sightseeing. There's no beach, but a grassy lawn is flecked with trees. On a clear day, the historic Isles of Shoals hover in the distance. Picnic areas and restrooms are available. Closed Columbus Day through Memorial Day. Day-use fee, $2.50 per person. ~ Route 1A at Rye Harbor Road in Rye; 603-436-5249, 603-436-1552.

WALLIS SANDS STATE BEACH Wild and scenic, Wallis Sands boasts one of the coast's choicest swaths of copper-colored sand punctuated by a dramatic jetty. On windy days, waves slash the rocks, sending sprays as high as 60 feet. Only five acres in size, the park features soft patches of grass and a concrete walkway that edges the beach. Get there at low tide, when the beach spans up to 800 feet. When the tide comes in, the sand shrinks back to 150 feet—the only drawback of this beautiful place. Restrooms, lifeguards, a bathhouse, showers and a store are available to beachgoers. Day-use fee, $8. ~ Route 1A and Marsh Road, Rye; 603-436-9404.

ODIORNE POINT STATE PARK New Hampshire's first settlers landed amid these rocky headlands and marshes back in 1623. Today, the natural sanctuary accounts for 330 acres and three-fourths of a mile of shoreline—the largest undeveloped tract on the coast. You can spend days exploring all the goodies this place offers, including old grave sites and stone walls, three World War II bunkers, the remains of a formal garden, five miles of trails, two ponds, fishing for bass and flounder in spring and fall, dozens of tidal pools, and the Sea Coast Science Center with wildlife exhibits, bookstore and local history displays. Besides historical secrets, the park harbors a secluded beach on **HIDDEN ►** **Frost Point.** There's no sand here, only grass and pebbles and total seclusion. Just north of the point, sandy shores draw larger crowds. Facilities include a visitors center, restrooms and a bathhouse. Day-use fee, $2.50 per person. ~ There are two entrances on Route 1A in Rye. To get to Frost Point, park at the north entrance and take the rocky trail about one-quarter mile through the woods; 603-436-7406.

GREAT ISLAND COMMON Picturesque and serene, this municipal beach belongs to the tiny island of New Castle, near Portsmouth. Swampy meadows share the shoreline with hardpacked sand and several rocky beaches. There's a spacious grassy area for excellent picnicking and a series of jetties that offer interesting tidepooling. A lighthouse hovers in the distance, occasionally sounding its foghorn. You'll find picnic areas, restrooms and a playground. Day-use fee, $3 per adult. ~ Route 1B, New Castle; 603-431-6710.

▼▼▼▼▼▼▼▼▼▼▼▼▼
Merrimack Valley

For the last two centuries, towns have grown alongside the Merrimack River, their inhabitants making use of its swift waters first for fishing, then for running textile mills. Today many of New Hampshire's 1.1 million residents call the Merrimack Valley home, making the area a seat of commerce and the state government.

This industrial region takes in a string of sizable cities, including Nashua, often called a "suburb" of nearby Boston, as well as the metropolis of Manchester and the capital, Concord. Spiraling out from these cities are bedroom communities and fragments of endearing rural areas.

SIGHTS   Scenic Route 111 twists its way southwest from Exeter to one of the state's most peculiar phenomena. **America's Stonehenge**, also known as Mystery Hill, may seem like a big pile of rocks. To archaeologists and astronomers, who've pored over its contents for 50 years, it presents an unsolved puzzle. How old is it and where did it come from? Spread across 30 acres, the erratic stone walls and bizarre rock formations are reputed to be an astronomical site of an ancient civilization—some claim it goes back 4000 years. England's Stonehenge it's not, but it's worth a look. Call for hours in January and February. Admission. ~ Haverhill Road, off Route 111, North Salem; 603-893-8300; www.stonehengeusa.com.

A short drive northward will land you in **Manchester**, New Hampshire's largest city with a population of over 100,000. Get a feel for this predominantly industrial city by strolling Elm Street, the main drag, lined with tired brick buildings and coffee shops and crowded with businesspeople. The **Greater Manchester Chamber of Commerce** can point you to the best local sights. Closed Saturday and Sunday. ~ 889 Elm Street, Manchester; 603-666-6600.

The valley's other large city, **Concord**, is the state capital and probably best known for its Concord Coach. Drop by the **Museum of New Hampshire History** for a peek at the coaches that helped connect America's East and West during the 19th century. Closed Monday from October through November and from January through June. Admission. ~ 6 Eagle Square, Concord; 603-226-3189.

Pick up a copy of *The Historic Downtown Concord Walking Tour*, which will direct you to the city's choicest sites. It's available at the **Greater Concord Chamber of Commerce**, which also supplies general information on Merrimack Valley. ~ Carrigan Commons, 244 North Main Street, Concord; 603-224-2508.

Locals are fond of saying the carpets are rolled up at dusk in this very conservative city. The streets do clear out around dinner time, and except for a couple of watering holes, you'll be hard-pressed to find much activity around here.

RENAISSANCE PALACE

It's enough just to stand outside and ogle the **Currier Gallery of Art**, with its lustrous limestone facade and gorgeous mosaics that resemble a Renaissance palace. But step inside and your eyes will feast on a series of archways and carved ceilings, then trail off to a substantial collection of artwork ranging from the Romanesque and Byzantine eras to modern times. There's also a fascinating collection of glass and photography. The Currier ranks as one of the finest small museums in the country. Admission. ~ 201 Myrtle Way, Manchester; 603-669-6144; www.currier.org.

Of course, people who go to Concord looking for action will ultimately be sidetracked by the **State House**, a beautiful 1819 building coated in smooth granite and capped with a gold-plated dome. Inside this grand old edifice throbs the pulse of the city, setting the political, social and oftentimes cultural agenda for the entire state. It's the nation's oldest state house in which the legislature still occupies the original chambers. Closed weekends. ~ 107 North Main Street, Concord; 603-271-1110.

After you've roamed the capital streets, head north for the wilds of **Canterbury Shaker Village**. Stashed way out in an agrarian sanctuary, this insightful place will hold your attention for hours. Founded in the mid-1700s by one very progressive woman named Ann Lee, the religious sect lived in self-contained villages and aspired to create a utopia. Each of Canterbury's 24 buildings reflects principles of efficiency: drawers are built into walls and wall pegs eliminate floor clutter.

Exhibits highlight the Shakers' inventive ingenuity; the collection includes a bell cast by Paul Revere. Shakers believed in equal rights, shared work and celibacy, the last of which may have caused their virtual disappearance by the early 1900s. During April, November and December, the Village is only open on Saturday and Sunday. Admission. ~ 288 Shaker Road off Route 106, Canterbury; 603-783-9511.

LODGING   Small chain motels are the most frequent accommodations along New Hampshire's industrial combe, though you will find a few very special inns and bed and breakfasts.

One of the nicest chain motels, **Fairfield Inn by Marriott** mingles the new and old with its Federal-style red-brick design and its many modern amenities. There's a heated swimming pool out back and a lobby fashioned with reproductions of Victorian antiques and framed prints of hunting scenes. You'll find more antiques in the 116 guest rooms, along with designer wallpapers and a crisp, manicured feeling. ~ 4 Amherst Road, Merrimack; phone/fax 603-424-7500, 800-228-2800. BUDGET TO MODERATE.

Think about it this way: with rooms offering Italian marble whirlpool baths, big-screen televisions and gorgeous four-poster beds, how could you *not* adore **The Bedford Village Inn**. This vanilla-coated estate, a medley of Colonial-style buildings, barns and grain silos, is a lesson in ultra-indulgence, a place where staying in your room may well be preferred to venturing out. Wet bars, pine chests and huge bay windows are also standard accessories in the higher-end rooms, or opt for the two-bedroom apartment with a fireplace and six-foot whirlpool. ~ Village Inn Lane, Bedford; 603-472-2001, 800-852-1166, fax 603-472-2379. ULTRA-DELUXE.

Accommodation choices in Manchester are generally limited to motel and hotel chains. Nicely situated downtown, the **Center** of **New Hampshire Holiday Inn** caters mostly to business travelers and thus features plenty of extras like an indoor pool, sauna and a restaurant. Expect upscale motel decor in 250 rooms and 6 suites, including plush carpets and marble countertops. ~ 700 Elm Street, Manchester; 603-625-1000, 800-465-4329, fax 603-625-4595; www.holiday-inn.com. MODERATE TO ULTRA-DELUXE.

For exploring the state capital, the **Holiday Inn** provides prime proximity to downtown sights. The layout is classic motel, with a four-story, nondescript exterior and 122 comfortable rooms decorated with wall-to-wall carpets, formica dressers and headboards and standard conveniences. There's also an indoor heated pool, sauna, hot tub and a fitness room. ~ 172 North Main Street, Concord; 603-224-9534, 800-465-4329, fax 603-224-8266. DELUXE.

Standing amid acres and acres of rambling meadows and gardens and surrounded by mountain peaks, **Wyman Farm** is a place worth finding. Built back in 1783, the lovely farmhouse awaiting down a labyrinth of obscure country roads is the family homestead of one of the innkeepers. There are three suites warmly fashioned with old pine floors, sitting rooms or parlors, and oriental or hook rugs. For a real treat, request the room with the copper tub. Full breakfast and an evening tea tray are included. To get there, take Route 106 to the Clough Pond Road exit, then turn left on Flagg Road. Go eight-tenths of a mile on Flagg Road to Wyman Road, a dirt road. ~ 22 Wyman Road, Loudon; phone/fax 603-783-4467. MODERATE.

◄ *HIDDEN*

Just south of Manchester, **Hannah Jack Tavern** complements its round of warm dining rooms with marble fireplaces, stained-glass windows and New England wall murals. Locals show up for the homemade breads (the raisin nut brioche is divine), the 100-label wine list and the prime rib, cut daily at the restaurant. Hannah Jack's does something that more restaurants should do—it offers smaller portions of many entrées. ~ Daniel Webster Highway off the Everett Turnpike, Merrimack; 603-424-4171. MODERATE TO DELUXE.

DINING

In a world of Americanized Mexican restaurants, it's rare to strike authentic south-of-the-border cuisine. That, of course, is what makes **Hermanos** so very special. Here, surrounded by Aztec murals and paraphernalia, you discover hefty burritos, enchiladas, quesadillas and tostadas, served with verve and panache. The specials are interesting, too—try the *carne estufa* (spicy stew), Mexican pizza and *taco pastor* (soft-shelled tacos stuffed and wrapped in grilled corn tortillas). Enjoy live jazz in the lounge five nights a week. No lunch on Sunday. ~ 11 Hill's Avenue, Concord; 603-224-5669. BUDGET TO MODERATE.

Tucked away in the bucolic lull of Canterbury Shaker Village, **The Creamery** offers a leap back in time. Indeed, the village and

◄ *HIDDEN*

its 24 buildings have changed little since the early 1800s. Dine on heavy wood tables, surrounded by simple country decor. Menus utilize locally grown foods and may feature applewood-smoked pork loin with hard cider, pan-seared salmon on stewed white beans, hickory-smoked ham with maple-sugar mustard and peach oatmeal pie. The Creamery serves candlelight prix-fixe dinners on Friday and Saturday, with an option of a pre-dinner village tour on Saturday. Lunch is served daily. Closed January through April and weekdays in November and December. ~ 288 Shaker Road, Canterbury Shaker Village, Canterbury; 603-783-9511. ULTRA-DELUXE.

SHOPPING   **Pompanoosuc Mills** proffers handcrafted contemporary Shaker-style furnishings such as plush couches and silk arrangements and oak dressers. ~ 3 Eagle Square, Concord; 603-225-7975.

HIDDEN ▶   It's well worth a trip into the countryside to peruse the **Gift Shop** at Canterbury Shaker Village, an 1825 carriage house stocked with Shaker reproductions and literature, as well as cookbooks, potpourri, handmade sweaters and crafts. ~ 288 Shaker Road, Canterbury; 603-783-9511.

NIGHTLIFE   The best place to catch top-quality international and national plays is the **Palace Theatre**, an ornate, 883-seat downtown arena that also hosts musicals, ballet and concerts. ~ 80 Hanover Street, Manchester; 603-668-5588.

There's always a party going on at the **Stark Mill Brewery** in Manchester. At all times, six homemade brews are on tap. Wednesday through Saturday nights, you can hear live music—mostly blues and rock-and-roll bands. When hunger strikes, order anything from a burger, pizza or salad to a T-bone steak. ~ 500 Commercial Street, Manchester; 603-622-0000, fax 603-626-8820; www.starkmill.com.

An out-of-the-ordinary way to meet the locals is to attend one of the small-town dances held every week at the **East Concord Community Center**. ~ Eastman Street, Concord; 603-225-3547.

BEACHES & PARKS   **SILVER LAKE STATE PARK** 🏃 ⛵ 🛶 Locals mob this place on summer weekends for one reason: a very special sliver of sand. These toffee-colored granules extend 1000 feet along Silver Lake and churn up a storm of activity. The 34-acre lake itself is also quite stunning, sheltered by a cascade of grassy knolls and gracious pine trees. Facilities here include a picnic area, restrooms, lifeguards, a bathhouse, a play field and a refreshment stand. Day-use fee, $2.50. ~ Route 122, one mile north of Hollis; 603-465-2342.

PAWTUCKAWAY STATE PARK 🏃 🚴 🏠 ⛵ 🚣 ⛱ Tucked just outside the bustle of several major cities, this 5500-acre park has it all. There's 803-acre Lake Pawtuckaway with its broad mocha beaches and islands, a vast oak and hickory forest and hemlock ravine, 25 acres of wooded picnicking spots and the Pawtuckaway Mountains, surrounded by curious rock formations carved some 275 million years ago. There are extensive trails for hiking, snowmobiling and cross-country skiing. Swimming and bass fishing are excellent. You need to explore all three areas to get a good feel for this diverse park, so plan to spend some time. No pets are allowed. You'll find a picnic area, restrooms, a small store, a playground, boat rentals and a pavilion. Day-use fee, $2.50. ~ Off Route 156, three and a half miles north of Route 101 in Nottingham; 603-895-3031.

▲ Horse and Big islands and Neals Cove offer 192 tent sites, many right on the lake. Reservations are required for Horse Island. Most take RVs (no hookups); $16 to $22 per night.

BEAR BROOK STATE PARK 🏃 🚴 ⛱ 🎣 ⛵ This mammoth place covers 9600 acres and offers a slew of activities. Of the park's six ponds, Catamount Pond attracts the most activity with its wide beach, ball fields and picnic facilities for 1500 people. Cool, dusky Bear Brook snakes through the park, which is dense with red and white pines. You'll also find more than 30 miles of hiking trails, a physical fitness course, a snowmobile museum, a nature center, the Civilian Conservation Corps Museum, a family camping museum and two archery ranges. Fishing is excellent for trout, perch, bass and pickerel in lakes and streams. Archery Pond is reserved for fly fishing. You can swim in Beaver and Catamount ponds (restricted to campers only at Beaver Pond). Facilities include picnic areas, pavilions, snack bars, boat rentals, restrooms and bathhouses. Day-use fee, $2.50. ~ Off Route 28, five miles northeast of Hookset; 603-485-9874.

▲ Beaver Pond features 97 RV/tent sites (no hookups); minimum $15 per night; information, 603-485-9869. The campground is open from May 15 through Columbus Day only.

WINSLOW STATE PARK 🏃 After a 1820-foot climb (via auto) up Mount Kearsarge, the park rewards with magnificent panoramas that stretch into Vermont. The park was named for Civil War admiral John Winslow, and hang glider enthusiasts occasionally hurl themselves from the summit, landing (hopefully) in a parking lot below. A steep, one-mile hike takes you to the peak —2937 feet up. A picnic area and restrooms are available. Day-use fee, $2.50. ~ Off Route 11, three miles south of New London in Wilmot Flat. You can also take Exit 10 off Route 89 and follow the signs to Winslow State Park; 603-526-6168.

▼▼▼▼▼▼▼▼▼▼▼▼▼
Monadnock Region

Curled along the southwest bend of New Hampshire, the Monadnock Region makes up a collage of all the virtues one associates with New England. White steepled churches and old covered bridges, itinerant country roads edged by miles of wild woods and lazy lakes, and lovable Currier and Ives towns all mesh to give this domain a warm Yankee flavor.

SIGHTS

General stores, coffee shops and old-time pharmacies line the streets of **Peterborough**, founded in 1738 and believed to be the model for Thornton Wilder's *Our Town*. It's easy to see why Wilder may have taken to this mountain hamlet, which has spawned old saltbox homes and very congenial townsfolk.

At the **Peterborough Historical Society Museum** you can walk through exhibits of the town's heritage and commercial interests, including thriving agriculture and manufacturing industries and, lately, publishing. The museum also displays re-creations of Colonial kitchen and a Victorian parlor, along with a toy exhibit with items that date to the mid-1800s. Closed weekends. ~ 19 Grove Street, Peterborough; 603-924-3235.

South on Route 202, **Jaffrey** purports to be the only Jaffrey in the world but more important is home to **Mount Monadnock**, which looms 3165 feet over the region like an astute sentinel. This imposing butte has become world famous as the most-climbed peak; myriads ascend its 30 miles of trails each year.

Henry David Thoreau and Ralph Waldo Emerson scaled Monadnock, now part of **Monadnock State Park**, where you'll also find an environmental center with historical and geological displays. (See "Beaches & Parks" section below.) Admission. ~ Off Route 124, Jaffrey; 603-532-8862.

Just east of the park you'll encounter Jaffrey's grandest manmade structure, the **Colonial Meeting House**. Its huge clock and bell tower, built in 1773, are framed by Mount Monadnock, an arousing sight for sure. ~ Route 124, Jaffrey.

Behind the Colonial Meeting House rests a shaded cemetery and the graves of novelist Willa Cather and Amos Fortune, an African-born slave who purchased his freedom.

Some of Monadnock's choicest views can be had at **Cathedral of the Pines**, a wood and stone shrine built by local parents for a son who was slain in World War II. There are guided tours offering views of the precious artifacts donated from every U.S. president and from people around the world. A piece of the Rock of Gibraltar is here, along with a hunk from the Blarney Stone. You'll also see a holy ark carved in Portugal. When these carillon bells ring, they reverberate down the mountain and make melodies for miles. Closed from November 1 through April 30. ~ Off Route 119, Rindge; 603-899-3300.

Nature has surely blessed the Monadnock Region, and nowhere is it more evident than at **Rhododendron State Park**. Arrive in mid-July and be rewarded with 16 acres smothered in fields of wild rhododendrons. There's a one-mile trail through this riot of color. (See "Beaches & Parks" below.) ~ Rhododendron Road, off of Route 119, Fitzwilliam; 603-532-8862.

Nestled in a marvelous Currier and Ives setting, **The Birchwood Inn** oozes history and enchantment. Fashioned of deep red brick, the 1775 Federal-style building brandishes twin chimneys and lazes across from a white steepled church and a grassy hill topped with war memorials. Murals of itinerant artist Rufus Porter spread across dining room walls, while seven bedrooms exhibit different themes and eclectic decor. An "editorial room" features newsprint wallpaper, while a "music room" is arranged with musical instruments. Lose yourself in the 18th century at this place. Full breakfast is included. ~ Route 45, Temple; 603-878-3285, fax 603-879-2159. MODERATE.

LODGING

For up-to-date motel accommodations, consider **Jack Daniel's Motor Inn**. A single, two-story building covered with wood shingles, the inn maintains 17 quite modern guest rooms with plush carpets, high-back chairs, large showers and upstairs balconies. Some rooms overlook the pretty Contoocook River. ~ North Route 202, Peterborough; 603-924-7548, fax 603-924-7700. MODERATE.

The ultimate New Hampshire hideaway may well be **Woodbound Inn**, a captivating retreat stashed deep in a mountain forest. Here you have the trying task of choosing between several accommodations: Early American–style bedrooms housed in a 19th-century farmhouse; contemporary rooms with brass beds in the annex; or cozy lakeside cabins with fireplaces. It's easy to kick back in any of the three, or explore the inn's 165 acres thick with pines and firs. There are also a nine-hole, par-3 golf course, numerous cross-country ski trails, a clay tennis court and a superb restaurant. Full breakfast included. ~ East of Route 202 on Woodbound Road, Rindge; 603-532-8341, 800-688-7770; www.nhweb. com/woodbound/index.html. MODERATE TO DELUXE.

◄ *HIDDEN*

The Hancock Inn radiates an ancient aura, and rightly so— it's the state's oldest continuously operating inn. Braided rugs rest atop the 1789 floor, bouquets of fragrant flowers bask on old tabletops and walls sport early-17th-century Rufus Porter murals and Moses Eaton stencils. Upstairs in 15 bedrooms, sunlight streams in through rows of windows, and antique chests and beds provide a cozy demeanor. ~ 33 Main Street, Hancock; 603-525-3318, 800-525-1789, fax 603-525-9301; www.hancockinn. com. DELUXE TO ULTRA-DELUXE.

DINING

For quick, affordable Italian pies, try the **Jaffrey Pizza Barn**, a modest downtown cubbyhole with just four rows of orange formica booths. Thick- or thin-crusted pizzas come with a good selection of toppings (including steak and eggplant); there are hot and cold grinders, too. ~ Blake Street, Jaffrey; 603-532-8383. BUDGET TO MODERATE.

The Hancock Inn doles out some of the best Yankee cookin' around, dependable fare like Shaker cranberry pot roast and crab-cakes served with garlic mashed potatoes. Set in New Hampshire's oldest operating inn (circa 1789), the three dining rooms feature cultured country decor and face a rambling flower garden. Dinner only. ~ 33 Main Street, Hancock; 603-525-3318. MODERATE TO DELUXE.

About 20 minutes west of Keene on Route 9, the **Chesterfield Inn** has a very elegant, candlelit dining room looking out at the Green Mountains. The unfailingly good food is largely New England, but with some adventure to it. The dining room was an addition to an 1787 farmhouse inn. Dinner only. Closed Sunday. ~ Route 9, West Chesterfield; 603-256-3211, 800-365-5515, fax 603-256-6131. DELUXE TO ULTRA-DELUXE.

SHOPPING

Wanna feel better? **Maggie's Marketplace** supplies natural foods like organic corn chips and no-cholesterol ice cream, plus cookbooks. ~ 14 Main Street, Peterborough; 603-924-7671.

Your literary layover is **The Toadstool Book Shop**, a small-town shop with new and used books ranging from warship catalogues and world radio handbooks to New England journals. There's a coffee shop on the premises. ~ 12 Depot Square, Peterborough; 603-924-3543.

It's mall shopping 19th-century style at **Colony Mill Marketplace**. Located in a recycled 1838 mill, the aesthetic trading center houses a medley of stores offering clothes, gifts, cards, home decor items and books. ~ 222 West Street, Keene; 603-357-1240.

NIGHTLIFE

One of the most respected theater troupes in New England, the **Peterborough Players** perform in a marvelous converted barn from mid-June through August. ~ Hadley Road off Middle Hancock Road, Peterborough; 603-924-7585.

BEACHES & PARKS

MILLER STATE PARK 🏃 New Hampshire's oldest state park was settled back in 1891 and named for General James Miller, a hero of the War of 1812. It rests atop the 2300-foot summit of South Pack Monadnock Mountain, a one-and-a-half-mile semivertical drive with numerous hairpin curves. The Wapack and Marion Davis trails wander from the base to the summit of the mountain. Incredible vistas extend to the skyscrapers of Boston. Spring and fall are excellent times to view hawk migration from the summit.

Facilities include a picnic area and primitive restrooms. Day-use fee, $2.50 per person. ~ Off Route 101, three miles east of Peterborough across from Temple Mountain Ski Area; 603-924-3672.

CONTOOCOOK LAKE PUBLIC BEACH 🏖 It's a rare find indeed, this tiny but choice spot. Edging the shore of beautiful Contoocook Lake, a sliver of beach features glistening white sand as soft as talcum powder. During the summer, the town closes part of the road and spreads sand across it, making it a great spot for small children. There are picnic areas, restrooms, lifeguards and a concession stand in the summer. ~ From the junction of Routes 124 and 202 in Jaffrey, take Stratton Road southeast to Squantum Road. Head east on Squantum Road, and you'll soon arrive at the beach; 603-532-7863.

◄ HIDDEN

MONADNOCK STATE PARK 🏃 The lonely, imposing peak of Mount Monadnock has long inspired poets and intrigued all those who cast eyes upon it. Frequently called the world's most-climbed mountain, its barren granite pinnacle has been scaled by Mark Twain, Ralph Waldo Emerson, Henry David Thoreau and thousands of others. Today, the 5000-acre park remains a hiker's mecca, crisscrossed with 40 miles of trails enriched by views of every New England state. No pets are allowed. You'll find a picnic area, restrooms, a refreshment center and an environmental center. Day-use fee, $2.50. ~ Off Route 124, four miles west of Jaffrey; 603-532-8862.

▲ There are 21 tent sites; about half accommodate RVs (no hookups); $12 per night for two, $6 for each additional person.

RHODODENDRON STATE PARK 🏃 No doubt, this place is extra special. Arrive around mid-July and revel in the explosion of rhododendrons that form a pink-and-white canopy across 16 acres. A one-mile trail meanders up Little Mount Monadnock, ensuring a feast for the senses and lovely views of Mount Monadnock. Other jewels bloom here, too, including the jack-in-the-pulpit, trillium, mountain laurel and pink lady's slipper. The Wildflower Trail (.4 mile) offers views of stunning patches of wildflowers clearly marked by the Fitzwilliam Garden Club. No pets allowed. You'll find a picnic area and pit toilets. Day-use fee, $2.50. ~ On Rhododendron Road, off Route 119, two and a half miles north of Fitzwilliam; 603-532-8862.

The area north of the Monadnocks—edged on the west by the Connecticut River—is a long, lazy union of cornfields and hills and big tufts of wildflowers tossed against Vermont's western border. Bustling mill towns, Ivy League schools and Colonial hamlets bless this region. Inland, Lake Sunapee exists as a world unto itself, stretching ten glittering miles beaded with sylvan villages and a stat-

▼▼▼▼▼▼▼▼▼▼▼
Lake Sunapee–Dartmouth Area

uesque mountain crisscrossed with ski trails. Life here is lived slowly, a welcome pace for travelers seeking bona fide tranquility.

SIGHTS

In the summer of 1777, General John Stark, commissioned by New Hampshire's legislature, organized a military force in **Charlestown**, the first town we visit in this area. That 1500-man troop marched westward across Vermont's border and defeated British-German forces in the famed Battle of Bennington. Now a **historical marker** (Route 12) pays homage to these local heroes.

Of course, Charlestown had its own share of skirmishes, as you'll see over at **The Fort at No. 4**, a re-creation of the great log stockade village built by pioneers in 1744. The fort suffered a three-day attack in 1747 by French and Indian forces, who were staved off by a 31-man garrison. Today, a medley of log cabins, barns, blacksmith shop and saw pit are displayed alongside original 18th-century tools. A nice trip back in time. Closed mid-October through May. Admission. ~ Route 11, Charlestown; 603-826-5700; www.fortat4.com.

North of Charlestown, the industrial town of **Claremont** sustains a maze of centuries-old mills, weaving sheds and mansions. The folks in this blue-collar town are quite congenial. Stop by the **Claremont Chamber of Commerce** for a walking-tour map of the **Historic Mill District**, which is bounded generally by Main, Spring and Central streets. Closed weekends. ~ Moody Building, 18 Tremont Square, Claremont; 603-543-1296.

From here, the Lake Sunapee area presents an obvious side trip and promises panoramas of small towns, rocky coastlines, rhythmic beaches and distinguished lighthouses. Tourism has certainly hit this outdoor playground, but it's not yet overwhelming. Start by rounding the lake on Routes 11 and 103, gazing across pristine waters at the windsurfers and small boats and gentle backdrop of forest-covered Mount Sunapee.

The **M.V. Mount Sunapee II** offers narrated tours of the lake from mid-May through Labor Day. Go during fall foliage season to appreciate the area at its peak. Admission. ~ Sunapee Harbor, off Route 11; 603-763-4030.

Head back east to Route 12A and the hushed town of **Cornish**, where you'll find the country's longest covered bridge. Just in sight of the cornfields, the **Cornish-Windsor Covered Bridge** arches 470 feet across the Connecticut River, linking Vermont and New Hampshire. Built in 1866, it was the fourth at the site, the first two falling victim to raging floodwaters. An ancient sign still warns today's travelers to "Walk your horse or pay a two-dollar fine."

Cornish became a cultural mecca during the late 1800s and early 1900s when a series of noted artists, writers, poets, musicians and sculptors arrived and formed the Cornish Colony.

This mass migration was spurred by the 1885 arrival of Augustus Saint-Gaudens, one of America's foremost sculptors, whose works include the Admiral David Farragut statue in New York's Madison Square and the statue of Abraham Lincoln in Chicago's Lincoln Park.

Those artists and writers left Cornish long ago, but the **Saint-Gaudens National Historic Site** survives as a marvelous tribute to that great era. Saint-Gaudens' white brick house, his studios and beautiful formal gardens afford an endearing glimpse of a

Lake Sunapee-Dartmouth Area

prolific life. High hedges of pine and hemlock and birch-lined paths are a testament to Saint-Gaudens affection for gardening, while originals and copies of his sculptures reveal his gift of hand. Closed the end of October through Memorial Day. Admission. ~ Off Route 12A on Saint-Gaudens Road, Cornish; 603-675-2175.

Novelist Winston Churchill, poets Percy MacKaye and Witter Bynner, former *New Republic* editor Herbert Croly, landscape painter Willard Metcalfe and actress Ethel Barrymore all took up residence in Cornish.

North of Cornish throbs the valley's pulse, *the* reason why thousands pour into the region, and *the* place to go at night. Ivy League **Dartmouth College** exists in the archetypical New England college town of Hanover, although many would argue it *is* the town. ~ Hanover; 603-646-1110.

There's no other way to say it: this campus is absolutely beautiful. It at once impresses with masterful old buildings that seem to go on forever. Stately red brick Federal styles stand next to softer Georgian architecture, erected in the late 1700s and so unaffected by age or wars or government strife.

Dartmouth was actually started in Lebanon, Connecticut, in 1755 as a school for American Indians, called Moor's Indian Charity School. A donation of 3300 Hanover acres—plus a generous sum of money from England's second Earl of Dartmouth—put the school on its current site in 1769. Its charter, dated that year, can still be found in the hallowed halls of **Baker Library**, as can celebrated murals by Mexican painter José Clemente Orozco. ~ 603-646-2560.

The Hopkins Center for the Performing Arts is a must see. The exterior of Hopkins resembles the Lincoln Center in New York City, while inside, barreled ceilings, dramatic plant sculptures and abstract art combine to make this a work of great beauty. ~ Main Street, Hanover; 603-646-2422.

Next door at the **Hood Museum of Art**, you'll encounter a splendid small museum with a diverse permanent collection featuring works by American and European masters such as Whistler, Eakins, Paul Revere, Picasso and Dürer. There are also excellent examples of African, American Indian and Oceanic art, Assyrian reliefs and Chinese bronzes and ceramics. Closed Monday. ~ Wheelock Street, Hanover; 603-646-2808.

Dartmouth's distinguished life, combined with nearly 5000 students, spills over nicely into the town of Hanover. Gracious tree-lined streets, underground pubs and polished shops make the town a great place for strolling but awful for parking. For more information, stop by the **Hanover Chamber of Commerce**. (During the summer you can stop at the visitors booth on the Dartmouth College Green.) ~ 47 South Main Street, Hanover; 603-643-3115; www.hanoverchamber.org.

No signs even hint of **Goddard Mansion**. Pity those who bypass this camouflaged treasure, a European-style estate that exudes elegance and refinement. The expansive, ornate living rooms and parlors feature high-beamed ceilings, carved mantles and a baby grand piano. A breezy porch overlooks the manicured lawn, croquet court and tea house, and ten bedrooms are designed to gratify. Several rooms command views of mountains all the way to Vermont. ~ 25 Hillstead Road and Route 12, Claremont; 603-543-0603, 800-736-0603, fax 603-543-0001. MODERATE TO DELUXE.

LODGING

◄ *HIDDEN*

Lingering in the shadows of Mount Sunapee, **The Backside Inn** tenders home-style accommodations in an 1835 farmhouse-cum-inn. Resting on 120 acres, the inn is enveloped in pines; ten comfortable bedrooms featuring pretty antiques and wall-to-wall carpets or stenciled wood floors. A hot tub on the back deck offers beautiful sunset views. You can walk to a 49-acre pond or take the five-minute drive to sprawling Lake Sunapee. Closed April and November. ~ Brook Road off Routes 103 and 10, Sunapee; 603-863-5161; www.bsideinn.com. MODERATE.

Barely 12 miles from Lake Sunapee, **New London Inn** is one place that has grown beautiful with time. Built back in 1792, the three-story clapboard inn overlooking the town green and band-stand is surely the prototype of gracious New England sojourns. Spacious porches wrap around the lower floors, wood hallways lead to carpeted rooms, and beams crisscross ceilings. Twenty-six bedrooms have personality and flair, adorned with brass or wicker beds and lovely antique dressers and chairs. Full break-fast included. ~ 140 Main Street, New London; 603-526-2791, 800-526-2791, fax 603-526-2749. MODERATE TO DELUXE.

Its milieu is rural and unpretentious, but the history and intrigue of **The Chase House** is enough to liven your spirit. Within the walls of this modest 18th-century Colonial dwelling, Salmon P. Chase (as in Chase Manhattan Bank) was born and spent his early childhood. Chase was also a founder of the Republican Party and treasury secretary to Abraham Lincoln, among other things. Today, stacked firewood rests on the porch, and flower beds brighten the yard. The eight bedrooms—all with private baths—are heavy on country decor, including canopy beds and original softwood floors. Full country breakfast is included. Closed in November. ~ Route 12A, four miles north of Route 131, Cornish; 603-675-5391, 800-401-9455, fax 603-675-5010; www.chase house.com. MODERATE TO DELUXE.

◄ *HIDDEN*

Snuggled nicely against the upper Connecticut River, **The Sun-set** tenders simple accommodations. The configuration is standard motel L-shape, with 18 modest but clean rooms. Expect industrial-grade carpets and formica furniture; some rooms have splendid views across the river and mountains. ~ 305 North Main Street, Route 10, West Lebanon; 603-298-8721. BUDGET TO MODERATE.

The place to stay in Hanover is **The Hanover Inn**. For one, it's right across from (and owned by) Dartmouth College, thereby drawing all sorts of Ivy Leaguers. For another, it's one of those beautiful old buildings that absolutely commands respect. Graced in red brick and crowned by a sloping shingled roof, this grand-daddy has been accommodating the rich and prestigious since the late 1700s. Four floors of guest rooms reflect early Colonial designs but throw in amenities such as cable TV, air conditioning and a fitness room. ~ Main and Wheelock streets, Hanover; 603-643-4300, 800-443-7024, fax 603-646-3744. ULTRA-DELUXE.

A former stagecoach stop, **The Alden Country Inn** lounges under the shadows of the White Mountains and harkens back to the early 1800s with an unhurried pace and old-fashioned design. Indeed, the whole place is brimming with gorgeous antiques, from old clocks and handmade quilts to maple hutches and a pretty sleigh. There are no less than ten fireplaces, and 15 rooms and suites accented with stenciled wallpaper, wingback chairs and hooked rugs. Breakfast at the inn's excellent restaurant is included. ~ On the Common, off of Route 10, Lyme; 603-795-4404, 800-794-2296, fax 603-795-9436; www.aldencountryinn. com. ULTRA-DELUXE.

DINING

For standard American, family-style dining, **Dimick's** is your destination. The menu includes sandwiches—grilled chicken, tuna melt, roast beef—and entrées such as steak, pork chops, fried chicken and baked haddock. If available, ask for one of the three tables that overlook the Sugar River. No dinner on Sunday. ~ Lower Main Street, Claremont; 603-542-6701. MODERATE.

Depending on what's in season, the **Millstone** might be serving venison, pheasant, swordfish or even Bavarian schnitzel. Fashioned as a country inn, this congenial restaurant is embellished with bow-back chairs, linen tablecloths and local artwork. Freshness is the key word on this varied menu, and it keeps showing up in the seafood, game, vegetables, pasta and herbs. ~ Newport Road, New London; 603-526-4201. MODERATE TO DELUXE.

HIDDEN ►

You'll swear you've reached the outer limits of the universe by the time you arrive at **Home Hill Country Inn**. Stashed five mountain miles up a wooded sinuous road, the restored mansion conceals a French restaurant with a serious following. The dining room is intimate, with plank floors and blazing hearths. A prix-fixe menu changes seasonally, offering delights such as *daurade royale*, a Mediterranean fish entrée and veal in a morel mushroom sauce. Closed Monday and Tuesday. ~ River Road, off Route 12A, Plainfield; 603-675-6165. ULTRA-DELUXE.

Dartmouth students love to hang loose at **Patrick Henry's,** an underground habitat with great character and soul-warming grub. Zesty beef stew (some of the best anywhere) and fish chowder are definite favorites, but you can't go wrong with the stuffed potatoes or the picnic sandwich (grilled prosciutto and red peppers on focaccia). Wood beams criss-cross a low stucco ceiling, and knotty-pine booths are battered to a perfect college pub complexion. ~ 39 South Main Street, Hanover; 603-643-2345. BUDGET TO MODERATE.

It's hard to miss the big bubble windows of **Molly's Balloon,** a chic little nook that has "yuppie" written all over it. There's an expansive oak bar in the middle. Choose from seating in the cozy booths or the outdoor patio. The cuisine runs the gamut from stacked deli sandwiches and burgers, soups and salads to baby-back ribs and pasta dishes. ~ 43 South Main Street, Hanover; 603-643-2570. MODERATE.

SHOPPING

Powerhouse Mill Arcade is like a fairyland, adorned with barreled ceilings and colored strands of light. The more than 30 stores are imaginative and often feature a single theme. **Artifactory** (603-298-6010), for instance, leans toward the unusual with whimsical gifts like wizard-shaped candles, 14-karat gold jewelry and lava lamps. **HomeScapes** (603-298-6038) has furniture, glassware, rugs and other accessories for home styles ranging from Colonial to contemporary to high-tech. ~ Glen Road off of Route 12A, West Lebanon; 603-298-5236.

If cooking is your passion, stop in **Board & Basket** for the latest kitchenware gadgets, cookbooks and gourmet foods. ~ Powerhouse Plaza, West Lebanon; 603-298-5813.

NIGHTLIFE

The historic **Claremont Opera House,** with its arched stained glass and scrolled columns, is a superb place to see regional and national opera, orchestra, ballet and musicals. Pop and folk performances are also featured. ~ City Hall at Tremont Square, Claremont; 603-542-4433.

Dartmouth College nightlife sizzles on the underground circuit. Among the best below-ground pubs, **Five Olde Nugget Alley** features a long, battered maple bar, a round of maple tables and piped-in contemporary music. ~ Five Olde Nugget Alley, off Wheelock Street, Hanover; 603-643-5081.

Step down a flight of stairs to **Patrick Henry's,** a cozy establishment with high-back wood booths and a perpetual crowd of lively students. ~ 39 South Main Street, Hanover; 603-643-2345.

Dartmouth College's dazzling **Hopkins Center for Performing Arts** hosts major drama, musicals, concerts and films in two auditoriums. ~ Wheelock Street, Hanover; 603-646-2422.

BEACHES & PARKS

PILLSBURY STATE PARK 🚶 🚴 🛶 🎣 A 5000-acre wilderness of forests, ponds and subtle hills, Pillsbury was once a bustling village of sawmills and frame homes. Today there's no hint of that 18th-century activity as ducks, deer and other wildlife roam the moist hammocks and dense thickets. Hiking and picnicking are superb; nine ponds provide excellent stillwater canoeing and havens for serious fishers hoping to reel in bass, pickerel, or perch. There are 30 miles of hiking trails and 50 miles of biking trails, as well as picnic areas, canoe rentals and pit toilets. Day-use fee, $2.50. ~ Off Route 31, four miles north of Washington; 603-863-2860.

▲ There are 40 primitive sites bordering all nine ponds (2 accessible by canoe only); $13 per night. Warning: treacherous for big RVs.

MOUNT SUNAPEE STATE PARK 🚶 🚴 🎿 🛶 ⛷ 🎣 🚣 🎣 This ever-popular park is more like a resort (minus the accommodations), a year-round recreation haven that caters to swimmers and sunbathers, hikers and skiers, ice fishers and sightseers. Chair lifts cruise up 2743-foot Mount Sunapee for downhill skiing and lovely views of Lake Sunapee and the surrounding alpine mountains. There's a cafeteria up here and another at the mountain's base where you'll find a sun terrace and exhibition trout pool. Spring-fed Lake Sunapee is renowned for trout and salmon fishing. And there's more: the 2700-acre park claims a ski school and shop, a nursery and a lineup of events like state craft shows and sporting events. Across the street, **Sunapee State Beach** is a 900-foot ribbon of crystalline sand edging the lake. You'll find picnic areas, restrooms, bathhouses, lifeguards, cafeterias and snack bars. Day-use fee, $2.50. ~ On Route 103, three miles west of Newbury; 603-763-2356.

▼▼▼▼▼▼▼▼▼▼▼▼▼
The Lakes Region

Strewn across New Hampshire's heart like a strand of aquamarine beads, some 273 lakes range from sealike to pondlike. Skirted by olive hills and sheltered coves, the lakes weave about 39 towns and three cities and engender a slew of outdoor pursuits. Many of the lakes bear Indian names, including Kanasatka, Ossipee, Squam and Winnipesaukee, queen of them all.

SIGHTS

One of the westernmost—and least visited—lakes is **Newfound**, whose fine sandy shores are covered by spiraling evergreens, sand and chimney-topped cabins. It lies along Route 3A.

HIDDEN ►

The town of Hebron, on the northwest corner, harbors an unexpected treasure known as **Sculptured Rocks**. This geological treat comprises dozens of undulating rocks, carved into designs by thousands of years of swift water. There's a frowning face, a seal, a camel and other interesting sculptures. ~ Sculptured Rocks Road, a gravel road off North Shore Road, just southwest of Hebron town center.

Tucked away in North Groton you'll find a darling clapboard cottage that was the **Mary Baker Eddy Historic House**. Eddy, an astute woman who founded the Christian Science religion and *Christian Science Monitor*, lived here from 1855 through 1860. The house has been nicely maintained and features her old iron pot-bellied stove and bed strung with ropes. (Tours of this structure begin at Eddy's Rumney home.) Closed Monday and from November to May. Admission. ~ Hall's Brook Road, North Groton; 603-786-9943.

◄ **HIDDEN**

Eddy left North Groton in 1860 and moved to nearby Rumney, where her **Colonial frame house** rests behind a white picket fence. Here she penned the poem "Major Anderson and Our Country" in response to the Civil War and waged her own war against slavery. The late-1700s house is adorned with relics like a banjo clock, melodian piano and unusual wall drawers used to store ammunition. Closed Monday and from November to May. Admission. ~ Stinson Lake Road, Rumney; 603-786-9943.

◄ **HIDDEN**

From here, head east though the mountains and cut over to **Squam Lake**, speckled with fishing skiffs, sailboats and loons. Antique shops, decoy stores, rustic cabins and miles of tall trees give this area a peaceful milieu, a setting that no doubt attracted

Lakes Region

makers of the movie *On Golden Pond*, parts of which were filmed here.

Get close to those crazy loons at the **Science Center of New Hampshire**, a 200-acre wildlife preserve near Squam Lake. From the trails here you can spot whitetail deer, black bears and bald eagles, visit ponds and a turtle island and view otter and raptor (bird of prey) exhibits. Kids love the hands-on nature exhibits, games and puzzles. Closed November through April. Admission. ~ Route 113, Holderness; 603-968-7194.

South on Route 25, **Meredith** is a very lucky place. Resting on a finger of Lake Winnipesaukee, it also touches Lakes Wicwas, Waukewan, Pemigewasset and Winnisquam. The town bears a charming demeanor with cosmopolitan touches like small shopping malls, art galleries and numerous restaurants and motels.

The **Meredith Chamber of Commerce** has sightseeing information. ~ 272 Daniel Webster Highway, Meredith; 603-279-6121.

Drawing more people than any shopping mall, **Annalee's Doll Museum** stocks every doll imaginable (and even those you can't imagine). Displays are colorful and creative, featuring animals, presidents, Indians, spiders and witches, a Christmas section that would impress Santa himself, and much more. But more fascinating is the story of Annalee, a housewife who began making dolls at her kitchen table in the 1950s. Turned down for a loan because banks considered her business impractical, Annalee worked at home without electricity or running water and delivered dolls door-to-door from her VW Bug. Today, she's the area's largest employer. Closed from October through May. ~ Reservoir Road and Hemlock Drive, Meredith; 603-279-4144.

Lake Winnipesaukee (pronounced Win-a-peh-SAW-kee), which translates as either "the smile of the great spirit" or "smiling water in a high place," is by far the state's largest and most impressive lake, spanning 72 square miles with 283 miles of shoreline and 274 habitable islands. If you care to explore the big lake by train, show up at **Winnipesaukee Scenic Railroad** and catch the next choo-choo south to Weirs Beach. Of course, you can hop on at the Weirs Beach station (Lakeside Avenue) for the re-

COUNTRYSIDE CREATIVITY

The state's unswerving individualism, coupled with its bucolic settings, have enticed some of the country's most creative minds. Robert Frost, Nathaniel Hawthorne, Ralph Waldo Emerson, Thornton Wilder, sculptor Augustus Saint-Gaudens and many other talents employed New Hampshire's rural reaches as their studios.

turn trip. From mid-May to late June, the railroad is open only on weekends. Open daily from late June to Labor Day. Admission. ~ Route 3, Meredith; 603-279-5253.

At **Weirs Beach**, New Hampshire's own little Coney Island, a well-roamed boardwalk extends several blocks along Lake Winnipesaukee, sprinkled with arcades and bumper cars, pizzerias and souvenir shops. There's also a dock where you board the **M.S. Mount Washington**, a 230-foot passenger ship that glides across the lake on sightseeing excursions. Closed from mid-October to Memorial Day. ~ 603-366-5531.

Winnipesaukee's southeastern joints shelter miles of wooded estuaries and broad water vistas; you can wind your way around on Routes 11 and 28. You will soon land in **Wolfeboro**, a busy little town wedged between lakes Winnipesaukee and Wentworth. The village harkens back to 1763, when Governor John Wentworth built the country's first known summer resort here.

Scattered under some maple and elm trees, the **Clark House Museum Complex** is a trio of buildings that recall Wolfeboro's earlier years. There's a one-room clapboard schoolhouse built in 1805, a 1778 Cape Cod–style house with painted plank floors and marvelous antiques, and a late-1800s fire station with a shiny red fire engine. Open in July and August and by appointment the rest of the year. Closed Sunday. ~ South Main Street, Wolfeboro; 603-569-4997.

One local resident nicely catalogued Wolfeboro goings-on, and the results can be seen at the **Libby Museum**, a natural-history collection with a refreshing funky flavor. Here you'll find rows of stuffed birds, fish, animals and other native wildlife, relics from the long-destroyed Governor Wentworth mansion, and great Indian artifacts. Closed Monday and from Labor Day to May. Admission. ~ Route 109, Wolfeboro; 603-569-1035.

Tucked in a forest off the road, **Abenaki Tower** is one place   ◄ *HIDDEN* you can have all to yourself. The post-and-beam tower, erected by local townsfolk, will seduce you with stirring vistas of surrounding lakes and random wooded islands. ~ Route 109, about five miles north of Wolfeboro in Melvin Village.

Castle in the Clouds is an incredible place, cloaked in secrets and almost magical in design. Fashioned as a medieval castle and tangled in vines that droop from its awnings, it sits high on a mountain and gives the illusion that it's floating. The castle's maker, shoe magnate Thomas Gustave Plant, bought 6300 acres—including seven mountains—and paid $7 million to have his dream built between 1911 and 1914.

The 16 rooms and 8 bathrooms add to the mystique with their five- and eight-sided designs, doors of English lead, an enormous skylight, fluted windows and the curious absence of any nails. Plant had 12 closets and a secret reading room seen by others only after his death. At one time, he was worth $21 million. But on the advice of friend Teddy Roosevelt, Plant invested heavily in Russian bonds during the 1930s. In 1946, he died a penniless man. Closed Monday through Friday from mid-May to mid-June; closed mid-October through April. Admission. ~ Off Route 171, Moultonborough; 603-476-2352, 800-729-2468; www.castle springs.com.

LODGING

HIDDEN ►

Along placid Newfound Lake rests a grand old summer house and former stagecoach station called **The Inn on Newfound Lake**. Here you'll discover great vistas, fabulous sunsets, friendly inn-keepers and a completely unhurried pace. The 31 rooms are casually decorated and offer painted wood floors or carpets, some canopy beds and wicker chairs. During summer, there's a sandy lakefront beach across the street; during winter, the lake freezes and makes for splendid ice fishing, skating and skiing. ~ Route 3A, Bridgewater; 603-744-9111, 800-745-7990, fax 603-744-3894; www.newfoundlake.com. MODERATE TO DELUXE.

The Manor on Golden Pond took its moniker from the movie (not vice-versa), and its serene ambience does resemble the restful house depicted in the film. Stationed in a 50-acre wooded glen near Squam Lake—not on it—the graceful white clapboard house offers eight comfortable units enhanced by country decor with contemporary touches. Early American dressers and braided rugs contrast nicely with lace curtains and sleek bathrooms. Out back, a breezy lawn provides solace. ~ Route 3, Holderness; 603-968-7269. MODERATE TO DELUXE.

Shielded from a busy road by a string of giant rocks, the **Boulders Motel and Cottages** fits the standard motor court genre with one exception: every room claims a fabulous view of Squam Lake. There's also a small but pristine sandy beach out back, a great place to gape at passing boats. Accommodations range from 12 clean but sparse rooms to six efficiencies and three rustic cottages. Closed November through April. ~ Route 3, Holderness; 603-968-3600, 800-968-3601. MODERATE.

Lake views, dreamy Colonial architecture, shops and restaurants right outside your door. Sound enticing? Then **The Inn at Mill Falls** is where you want to be. Residing in a restored 19th-century mill, the spiffy resting place has 54 rooms done in rose chintz dust ruffles and draperies and designer shower curtains. Relax in the indoor pool, jacuzzi or sauna. A busy road is all that separates guests from Lake Winnipesaukee. ~ Route 3 in the Mills Falls Marketplace, Meredith; 603-279-7006, 800-622-6455, fax 603-279-6797; www.millfalls.com. MODERATE TO ULTRA-DELUXE.

HIDDEN ►

A short distance from the lake you'll happily discover **The Red Hill Inn**, a sublime country estate ringed with mountain vistas and a lovely herb path. Fashioned in 1904 as a summer retreat, the inn boasts 21 rooms, two old farmhouses and an unusual stone cottage. Rich colors and period furniture spell traditional elegance. Gay-friendly. ~ Route 25B and College Road, Center Harbor; 603-279-7001, 800-573-3445, fax 603-279-7003. DELUXE.

Greystone Motel has two very important virtues: It's hidden **◄ HIDDEN** down a scenic, little-traveled side road, and it's right on gorgeous Lake Winnipesaukee. There are two buildings with basic but clean accommodations ranging from motel rooms to waterfront apartments, and a glass solarium, though the name of the game here is boating, fishing and outstanding panoramas. ~ 132 Scenic Drive, off Route 11, Gilford; 603-293-7377, 800-470-7377. MODERATE.

Wolfeboro's premier lodging establishment is undoubtedly **The Wolfeboro Inn**, a rambling, Cape Cod–like manor resting beside Lake Winnipesaukee. The lobby is a fusion of wood beams, carpeted floors and velvet high-back chairs, while 44 rooms feature modern touches of sleek oak and pine furniture and pedestal sinks. ~ 90 North Main Street, Wolfeboro; 603-569-3016, 800-451-2389, fax 603-569-5375; www.wolfeboroinn.com. DELUXE TO ULTRA-DELUXE.

Wolfeboro is lucky enough to border three lakes, and you can catch views of two at **The Lake Motel**. Nestled on the picturesque corner of Lake Wentworth and Crescent Lake, the motor court takes advantage of its surroundings with an enormous lawn stretching to the shorelines. Some of the 30 rooms and five efficiency apartments offer water views and all are aesthetically furnished with textured wall coverings and wall-to-wall carpets. ~ Route 28, Wolfeboro; 603-569-1100, fax 603-569-1620; e-mail thelake@worldpath.net. MODERATE.

The Common Man enjoys a sterling reputation around the lakes, **DINING** undoubtedly for its steadfast, uncomplicated cuisine and nostalgic surroundings. Old farm tools and classic *Life* and *Saturday Evening Post* covers are parked on the walls of this two-story brick eatery, formerly an early-1800s home. Go for the steaks (the prime rib is heady stuff) or the fresh fish and seafood. There's also pineapple-ginger chicken stir-fry, rack of lamb and vegetable lasagna. ~ Main Street, Ashland; 603-968-7030. MODERATE TO DELUXE.

If you want to splurge on a special meal, consider making a reservation at **The Manor on Golden Pond**. In this mansion overlooking Squam Lake, you can feast on New England specialities (with quite a few international touches) in what was the original billiards room or in the very elegant original dining room. Prix-fixe meals are served nightly in the summer and Wednesday through

Text continued on page 528.

The Roads Less Traveled

They crisscross the state like a tangle of veins, concealing treasures that can be unlocked only by foraging through unfamiliar terrain. The **roads less traveled** may not be the shortest way to get there from here, but you can bet they're the most scenic.

New Hampshire's byroads exist everywhere, yet they are chosen by very few. They link towns and lakes, clamber up mountains, trundle through isolated villages and navigate miles of wild forest. They sometimes lead to nowhere, but they always harbor a special price: an 18th-century cemetery, a glistening pond or beach, a wildlife hollow or perhaps a vista to ignite your spirit.

To natives, these tireless country routes are known as "shunpikes," used to "shun" crowded main roads and highways. During fall foliage time, shunpikes are ripe with brilliant splashes of red and gold and purple leaves that form one incredible spectacle. They undoubtedly provide the best leaf- peeping seats in the house.

You'll discover glorious back roads in all of New Hampshire's six regions:

When you get tired of battling traffic on coastal Route 1A, take a jog on **Willow Avenue**, which starts just north of Little Boars Head, and relish a peaceful ride that explores grand 19th-century mansions and manicured lawns and gardens.

Few think of the seacoast in terms of fruit farms and old barns, but they're here, right along **Routes 88** and **84**. These roads twist through 1700s farmhouses and lonely stretches of pastureland, apple orchards and raspberry farms (where you can pick your own). Both begin in Hampton Falls. Take Route 88 from Route 1 to Route 101C; Route 84 starts at Route 1 and Wild Pasture Road.

New Hampshire's most populated region, the Merrimack Valley, manages to have some fine less-traveled roads. One of the best, **North Pembroke Road**, snakes through five miles of rural scenes between Route 28 near Allenstown and Route 106. It winds past a cornfield, wildflower farm, several log cabins, an old cemetery and a sap house where you can buy maple syrup.

The Monadnock Region shelters dozens of shunpikes, but perhaps the most beautiful is **Route 119**, which hovers near the Massachusetts border between Routes 202 and 10. Wend your way through the bucolic town of Rindge, then along remote Pearly Pond, where lakefront homes peek out from evergreen forests and reflect against the water. At sunset, bright orange light bands ignite the pond and make it appear to be on fire.

For unmatched views of Mount Monadnock, veer off Route 124 onto **Webb Depot Road** in Marlborough. Here you'll spy an old stone bridge and wonderfully clear vistas across open fields toward the vast summit.

Way out in the boondocks of the Lake Sunapee–Dartmouth area, **Stage Road** is one shunpike worth finding. It scouts out the soul of this fertile region, fording three brooks and a covered bridge and miles of hard-woods and idle hills. You'll find this gem between Route 120 in Meriden and Route 12A.

In the Lakes Region, seek out **West Shore Road** along the west side of Newfound Lake. A series of hairpin curves through patched tar and forest, the road frequently squeezes between the mountains and lake and dispenses unobstructed water vistas. With views of Squam Lake, **Route 113** and **Route 109** will take you past classic New England landscapes with villages, farms and old estates in Sandwich Notch.

Scenic Drive is like a secret pass along the west brink of Lake Winni-pesaukee. Prized by local residents for its peaceful, uncongested feeling, this shady bypass affords breathtaking panoramas of one of New England's most prominent lakes. It picks up just south of Weirs Beach.

In the White Mountains, **Bear Notch Road** is a cool, misty tryst with nature, a natural high of rock grottos, evergreen spires and tiny patches of blue sky. Keep your eye out for the pretty sandy cove along the Swift River, a solitary respite for those lucky enough to uncover it. The road runs from the Kancamagus Highway at Passaconaway to Route 302.

Route 116 from Jefferson to Franconia is the archetype of New England tranquility. Cows graze on grassy knolls, windmills twirl across hayfields and old farmhouses repose against the mountains. During fall foliage season, maple and elm trees flail their yellow and orange canopies across the road, truly a sight to behold.

Before you take the roads less traveled, get a good map, and when in doubt, ask for directions at a local general store. Shunpiking is primarily a summer and fall sport, since many byroads are jammed with snow the rest of the year. Don't be afraid to venture upon these foreign passages. It's virtually impossible to get lost, and if you do, there's always someone to set you straight again.

Sunday the rest of the year. ~ Route 3, Holderness; 603-968-3348. ULTRA-DELUXE.

The **Boathouse Grill** at the Inn at Bay Point is a more casual alternative, serving largely American cuisine and most popular for its steak and seafood. You can choose a booth or table amid boathouse decor. It's right on the water. ~ Route 25, Meredith; 603-279-2253. MODERATE TO DELUXE.

HIDDEN ► A splendid provincial manor in the grand style, **The Red Hill Inn** will make you forget life's worries. Set on the crown of an obscure country hill, the place has an outstanding restaurant adorned in period furniture and offering marvelous mountain views. The cuisine is unequivocally New Hampshire, sophisticated and heartwarming. Try the rosemary dijon rack of lamb, cedar-planked Atlantic coast salmon, or the country-style duck. No dinner on Monday. ~ Route 25B and College Road, Center Harbor; 603-279-7001. MODERATE TO DELUXE.

It's not hard to figure out why **West Lake Asian Cuisine** stays perpetually packed. Snuggled in a wooded area along Lake Wentworth, the eatery headlines over 100 different and delicious dishes that make choosing extremely difficult. You'll find seafood, poultry, beef and pork dunked in steamy sauces with garlic, chili or black beans, along with specials like mala lamb, and dragon and phoenix (whole lobster paired with chicken and scorched red peppers). Closed Monday from October through April. ~ Route 28, Wolfeboro Center; 603-569-6700. MODERATE.

The Chequers Villa is synonymous with outstanding Italian fare around the lakes, serving up a bright array of hearty, fresh dishes prepared with imagination. The place is warm and friendly, decorated in a medieval motif with stucco archways and oil lamps. Spaghetti entrées might feature a medley of seafood, tomatoes and herbs, or mounds of parmesan cheese and bacon in egg sauce. There's also lasagna blanca (layered with chicken breast, spinach and cheesy cream sauce) or linguine pollo Don Juan (with artichoke hearts and black olives). Dinner only, except lunch on weekends. ~ Route 113, Tamworth; 603-323-8686. MODERATE.

Lake residents frequently mob **The Yankee Smokehouse**, a modest cinderblock joint parked on the corner of a rural intersection. Smoke trundles out the top, and an old air conditioner hums away while diners scarf down massive portions of ribs and chicken that hang off plastic plates. Also known for its sliced beef and pork and killer barbecue sauce, the smokehouse offers summer outdoor dining on picnic tables. ~ Junction of Routes 16 and 25, West Ossipee; 603-539-7427. BUDGET TO MODERATE.

SHOPPING   Tucked in a 1700s roadside barn, **Dembiec Sportscards** is a gem of a place with '50s and '60s baseball cards and other fun collectibles. Call for hours. ~ Routes 3 and 25, Holderness; 603-968-3178.

Mill Falls Marketplace is a pretty lakeside complex where Christmas and bath shops mingle with sports stores, art galleries and candy kitchens. One of the largest stores here is **Country Carriage** (603-279-6790), a purveyor of American folk art, Yankee candles and other fine New England gifts. ~ Route 3, Meredith.

On Friday and Saturday summer nights, don't miss the one-man, six-piece band or live jazz and contemporary music at **The Common Man**, a lively place featuring comfortable couches, swag lamps and dart boards. ~ The Common Man restaurant, Main Street, Ashland; 603-968-7030.

NIGHTLIFE

The Barnstormers, the country's oldest summer professional theater group was formed in 1931. They perform a variety of summer comedy, mystery and drama from July through August. ~ Main Street off Route 113, Tamworth; 603-323-8500; www.theatre.com/bas.html.

Farm tools, wagon wheels and an American flag set a rustic tone at **Chequers Villa**, a friendly, crowded nook with saucy tunes and excellent pub grub. ~ Route 113, Tamworth; 603-323-8686.

BRISTOL TOWN BEACH 🏊 Sheltered by pine and maple trees, this pristine sandbox stretches like powdered cinnamon along Newfound Lake and opens onto a broad expanse of very clear water. It's packed on summer weekends. Crystal clear water and a sloping sandy bottom create perfect swimming conditions. A picnic area and volleyball nets can be found here. Parking fee, $5. ~ On West Shore Road, a quarter mile west of Route 3A in Bristol.

BEACHES & PARKS

◄ *HIDDEN*

WELLINGTON STATE PARK AND BEACH 🏊 Secluded pine coves, strings of granite boulders and a brow of chestnut sand amble around Newfound Lake at this ultra-scenic spot. Lying on a peninsula and framed by small peaks and isles of evergreens, Wellington has the views. The lake's white sandy bottom and gentle shores make it one of the best swimming holes in New Hampshire. Facilities include a picnic area, pavilions, bathhouses, restrooms and a playground. Closed October through Memorial Day. Day-use fee, $2.50 per person. ~ Off Route 3A, four miles north of Bristol; 603-744-2197.

WEIRS BEACH 🏊 This *is* the paradigm of summertime family vacations. It rests in an elbow of Lake Winnipesaukee and bears a half moon of amber granules bordered by grassy slopes. Though the lake views are pretty spectacular, the beach itself is nothing to write home about. Still, crowds flock here for the carnival mood stirred up by the adjacent boardwalk and amusement centers. There's also excellent fishing for lake trout and salmon. The monument called the Endicott Rock marks what used to be the most northerly point of Massachusetts before New Hampshire became a state. Facilities include a picnic area, restrooms, lifeguards and a playground. Closed after Labor Day to late June. Parking fee, $5. ~ Off Route 3 at Lakeside Avenue, Weirs Beach; 603-524-5046.

ELLACOYA STATE PARK AND BEACH 🏊 🚤 The only state park on Lake Winnipesaukee and one of its few parcels of public land, Ellacoya combines a 600-foot beach with birch groves and fabulous sunsets. Mocha-colored sand, flecked with pine needles and cones, weaves about the lake and courts sublime views of the Ossipee and Sandwich mountain ranges. Lake trout and salmon fishing is excellent. There are picnic areas, restrooms and bathhouses. Closed October through May. Day-use fee, $2.50 per person. ~ Route 11, Gilford; 603-293-7821.

▲ There's an RV campground with 38 full hookups; $30 per night. Closed October through May.

White Mountain Region

A bold sweep of compelling peaks hovers against New Hampshire's northern horizon. The White Mountains, which cover more than 760,000 acres, were named by 19th-century sailors for their brilliant crowns of snow framed by blue sky. Their drama—for centuries painted on landscape canvases—lies amid swift waterfalls, rocky gorges, rugged passes, granite silhouettes and one of the most stirring foliage displays in all of New England.

Towering above the region, broad Mount Washington is etched with jagged ravines and topped with rock-strewn grassy lawns. At 6288 feet, it's the highest peak east of the Mississippi and north of the Carolinas.

For the sightseer, the White Mountains ensure exploration at its height. Roads are scenic, usually remote and almost always dotted with hidden treasure. Even short distances can take a while to cover on mountain roads, so always allow extra travel time.

SIGHTS

Franconia Notch must be one of New England's seven wonders. At first glance, it is entirely overwhelming, offering dozens of natural phenomena and activities that could fill several days. A dramatic mountain gap caused by eons of glacial and river erosion, the notch lies within **Franconia Notch State Park's** 6500 acres and draws more than two million visitors annually. Off Route 93, Franconia.

Most sights can be accessed by scenic **Franconia Notch Parkway**, which *is* Route 93 for the eight-mile length of the park. The best place to start is **Park Headquarters**, which will help organize the numerous activities. ~ Tramway main building, Exit 2; 603-823-5563.

From the park headquarters, board the **Cannon Mountain Aerial Tramway** for a seven-minute cable car ride with panoramic views into Canada, Vermont, Maine and New York. The mountain, whose rocky profile resembles the barrels of a cannon, has the first engineered ski slopes in the United States. Closed November. Admission. ~ 603-823-5563; www.cannonmt.com.

Here also is the trail leading to pretty **Profile Lake**, headwaters of the Pemigewasset River. Pemigewasset, Indian for "swift waters," provides a reflecting basin for the granite profile of **Old Man of the Mountains**, his gnarled eyebrows and prominent chin looming 1200 feet up and keeping watch over the notch.

The Flume Visitors Center is a state-of-the-art complex with historic films and photographs of the park. It's also the entrance to The Flume (admission), a dramatic chasm that plummets 800 feet to the base of Mount Liberty. Carved before the Ice Age by the rushing waters of the Pemigewasset River, The Flume is banked in rare flowers and mosses and takes one and a half hours to visit fully. Closed late October to mid-May. ~ Franconia Notch State Park; 603-745-8391.

After you leave the park, head northward to the town of **Franconia**, a lovely mountain burg where you'll find **The Frost Place**. An old mailbox with the inscription "Frost" rests against a shady dirt lane, adjacent to the modest frame home where Robert Frost spent several years. Here he penned "Evening in a Sugar Orchard," "The Tuft of Flowers," "Mending Wall" and many other poems, gleaning inspiration from a backyard filled with sugar maples, an apple orchard and wildflowers. A Poetry Trail winds through the area, right by the Mending Wall. Closed weekdays from Memorial Day through June; closed Tuesday from July to Columbus Day; and closed from mid-October to Memorial Day. Admission. ~ Off Route 116, Franconia; 603-823-5510; www.frostplace.com.

Sugar Hill, Franconia's sister town, is just as charming and bucolic. The Abenaki Indians once hunted in this area, which today is sprinkled with whitewashed Colonial buildings and country stores. The **Sugar Hill Historical Museum** traces local ancestry to the late 1700s and has two barns filled with farm tools, old

A BATH FIT FOR A GODDESS

South on the Franconia Notch Parkway, turn off for a look at **The Basin**. Formed 25,000 years ago, this large pothole of whirling azure waters and smooth rock is bored 15 feet into the Pemigewasset River. It has long intrigued spectators, including Henry David Thoreau in 1839 and Samuel Eastman in 1858, the latter calling it "a luxurious and delicious bath fit for the ablutions of a goddess."

photographs and other juicy relics. Closed Monday through Wednesday and from late October through May. Admission. ~ Route 117, Sugar Hill; 603-823-8142.

Work your way eastward to Route 302, a picturesque mountain trail that crawls to Crawford Notch. A nice side trip from here, **Santa's Village** is a tot's fairytale world. The place is laid out like a fantasyland, with gingerbread houses and miniature trains, sleigh rides, a "Rudolph-Go-Round" carousel and "Frosty's Freezer" ice cream shop. Open weekends only from Labor Day through Columbus Day; closed from Columbus Day to mid-June (except for Thanksgiving weekend and days in December). Admission. ~ Route 2, Jefferson; 603-586-4445; www.santasvillage.com.

Then on to **Crawford Notch**. Moose hunter Timothy Nash discovered the pass in 1771, reporting his find to Governor John Wentworth. Nash could have a large piece of land, Wentworth said, if he took his horse through the treacherous notch. Nash and a friend got the horse through, sometimes hoisting him over ledges with ropes. In 1775, the first notch road opened.

The geographical pinnacle here is the big guy himself, **Mount Washington**. Sighted from the ocean back in 1605, the mountain soars 6288 snow-capped feet across the skyline. It's reputed to be the world's most dangerous small mountain, with wind-chill temperatures tantamount to those in Antarctica. The highest wind velocity ever recorded at a surface weather station (231 mph) was logged here.

Perhaps this fierce reputation only heightens the mountain's intrigue, as several hundred thousand people scale its slopes each year. One of the most popular ascents is on the **Mount Washington Cog Railway**, a three-hour round-trip with great vistas. Closed November through April. Admission. ~ Route 302, Bretton Woods; 603-846-5404; www.thecog.com.

The other easy climb is via **Mount Washington Auto Road**, a considerable drive east then north from the railway. The road takes a relaxed zigzag up the northeast ridge named for Benjamin Chandler, who died of exposure on the mountain in 1856. Closed mid-October to mid-May. Toll. ~ Route 16, Pinkham Notch in Gorham; 603-466-2222; www.mt-washington.com.

About 25 miles south, **North Conway** and **Conway** are the White Mountains' tokens of modern development. Actually it's the stretch of Route 16 *between* the two towns—jammed with outlet stores, fast-food joints, tacky tourist centers and condos—that seems so out of place in this earthy setting.

North Conway, which stays very crowded year-round, features quaint shops, restaurants and century-old buildings ringed with mountains. The **Mount Washington Valley Chamber of Commerce** is there to assist with your travels. Closed Saturday and Sunday. ~ Main Street, North Conway; 603-356-3171, 800-367-

3364, fax 603-356-7069; www.mtwashingtonvalley.org, e-mail info@mtwashingtonvalley.org.

Smaller Conway is the gateway for the **Kancamagus Highway**, one of the most inspiring treks in the White Mountains. Officially it's pronounced Kan-ka-MAW-gus, but don't worry if you get it wrong—locals are quite used to abuse of this Indian word for "the fearless one." Cool and evergreen, the road is rimmed with shaded glens, scenic overlooks, ponds, rocky gorges and lovely waterfalls.

The top half of the White Mountains region, for the most part, still belongs to nature. This is wild country, an unremitting stretch of land peppered with jagged hills, lucid ponds and very green, very tall trees. There's only a handful of people up here, including some old-timers so firmly rooted they seem part of the very earth.

Between civilization and Canada, several geographic points do stand out. **Dixville** is known for two things: its extremely remote location and as the first town in the nation to vote in presidential elections. The town lies within **Dixville Notch**, a stunning, narrow mountain pass formed by glaciers. Mention you've been to Dixville Notch and the likely response is: "You went all the way up *there?*"

Indeed, this area truly is "at the end of the world"—New Hampshire's world, that is.

LODGING

A rustic old-time air fills the **Woodstock Inn**, a homey kind of resting place that beckons to the late 1800s. Rosy wallpaper, pine floors and lacy Victorian draperies frame the 21 rooms, many of which face the Pemigewasset River and some of which share baths. Full breakfast. ~ Route 3, North Woodstock; 603-745-3951, 800-321-3985, fax 603-745-3701; www.woodstockinnnh.com. MODERATE TO DELUXE.

◄ HIDDEN

Wild winds whip through a slender valley, become trapped in a narrow opening and whirl backward to form what's known as a bungay jar. This explains the moniker of **The Bungay Jar**, a beautifully renovated 18th-century barn positioned at the mouth of just such a "tunnel valley." Set in a wooded mountain nest, this cozy bed and breakfast features seven rooms decorated with antiques; a separate cottage that can sleep up to five has a fireplace and jacuzzi. Stroll through the garden and see the water lily pond and stream. Guests enjoy the use of a small library, sauna and living room. ~ Route 116, just south of Sugar Hill Road, Franconia; 603-823-7775, 800-421-0701, fax 603-444-0100; www.bungayjar.com. DELUXE TO ULTRA-DELUXE.

You'll enjoy taking in the view from a wicker chair on the front porch of the **Ammonoosuc Inn**, on the western edge of the White Mountains. This nine-room B&B has been a tourist destination for nearly a century; along with that porch, guests love the spacious parlor and the sunny, roomy bedrooms (all with pretty coverlets on the beds, private bathrooms and claw-foot tubs). For summer visitors, there's a scenic nine-hole golf course. If you're here in the winter, the White Mountain ski areas aren't far away. Continental breakfast included. ~ Bishop Road, Lisbon; 603-838-6118, 888-546-6118, fax 603-838-5591; e-mail amminn@mail.com. MODERATE TO DELUXE.

HIDDEN ▶

Perhaps it's the dozens of nostalgic curios, or the cozy feel of the six bedrooms and one cottage, or even the hardwood floors that glide so smoothly under bare feet. Regardless of the reason, **The Hilltop Inn** is sure to make you feel at home. Situated along a secluded byroad, the inn is run by an amiable couple who loves to work around the house. The rates include a full breakfast. ~ Route 117, Sugar Hill; 603-823-5695, 800-770-5695, fax 603-823-5518; www.hilltopinn.com. DELUXE TO ULTRA-DELUXE.

Owned and run by lesbians, **The Highlands Inn** has four separate buildings with a total of 20 guest accommodations. Half the rooms are in the main inn; the rest are in the farmhouse, the annex and a cottage. Each room has its own identity and is thoughtfully decorated with antiques and special touches. It's a beautiful property sprawling over 100 mountain acres. There's a heated swimming pool, a hot tub and 15 miles of trails. Full breakfast. Women only. ~ Valley View Lane, Bethlehem; 603-869-3978, 877-537-2466; www.highlandsinn-nh.com. MODERATE.

By far one of New England's grandest summer retreats, the **Mount Washington Hotel and Resort** has been displaying its magical opulence ever since 1902. Set at the foot of the Presidential Range, the imposing, red-roofed mansion rests on 95 acres and is striking from miles away. Horse-drawn carriages meander through rolling manicured hills sprinkled with flower and rock gardens. Inside, an expansive lobby is heavy with archways, Doric columns and ornate chandeliers, and a rear porch seems to stretch for miles. The staff numbers 350, the rooms 205. Expect room decor ranging from simple to extravagant. ~ Route 302, Bretton Woods; 603-278-1000, 800-258-0330, fax 603-278-8838; www.mtwashinton.com. ULTRA-DELUXE.

In Mount Washington Valley, **The Notchland Inn** is a converted Victorian mansion with 12 rooms; all have fireplaces. In addition to ten rooms in the main house—built of granite in the 1860s—there's a converted schoolhouse with two suites. The inn is owned and run by gay men and welcomes a mixed clientele. The dining room is open to the public for dinner. Full breakfast included. ~ Route 302, Hart's Location; 603-374-6131, 800-866-6131, fax 603-374-6168; www.notchland.com, e-mail notchland@aol.com. ULTRA-DELUXE.

If you're traveling with children, the whole family will enjoy spending a night at **Rockhouse Mountain Farm Inn**, just south of Conway. The main attraction for kids is the old red barn, where swings hang from the rafters and kittens dart across the floor. They're also welcome to make friends with the farm's chickens, geese, peacocks, ducks, pheasants, horses, cows, pigs and llamas. Parents will enjoy the main house, where there are 15 rooms (some with shared baths), while the kids can spend the night in the bunkhouse that's available for all visiting kids to share. The farm's 450 acres boasts woods, fields, ponds and mountain trails to explore. Nearby is Crystal Lake, where you can launch a canoe, swim or laze away the day on the inn's private beach. Breakfast and dinner are included in the rates: meals incorporate fresh vegetables and fruit from the farm's gardens and eggs from the henhouse. Closed November to mid-June. ~ Off Route 153, Eaton Center; 603-447-2880. MODERATE.

Accommodations may be minimal, but you can't beat the price of the dorms at **Cranmore Mountain Lodge**, an independent hostel. ~ 859 Kearsarge Road, North Conway; 603-356-2044, 800-356-3596, fax 603-356-4498; www.cml1.com, e-mail c-u@cml1.com. If you have a Hostelling International card, you'll also find super-low-budget dorm beds at **Hostelling International—White Mountains**. ~ 36 Washington Street, Conway; 603-447-1001, fax 603-447-3346; www.angel.net/~hostel, e-mail hiconway@nxi.com.

Logs stay stacked on the stone porch of **The 1785 Inn**, a gracious old house that seems to say, "Do drop in." One of the oldest homesteads in Mount Washington Valley, the inn was built as a "publick house" by Revolutionary War veteran Elijah Dinsmore. These days, 17 guest rooms offer simple accommodations featuring country wallpaper, antique bed frames and ample mountain scenery. ~ Route 16, two miles north of North Conway; 603-356-9025, 800-421-1785, fax 603-356-6081; www.the1785inn.com. MODERATE TO DELUXE.

The **Inn at Thorn Hill** was designed by Stanford White in 1895. The main inn and private cottages are elegantly furnished with period pieces. There are 19 rooms with private baths plus a restaurant, pub and pool. Breakfast and dinner included. ~ Thorn Hill Road, Jackson; 603-383-4242, 800-289-8990, fax 603-383-8062; www.innatthornhill.com. ULTRA-DELUXE.

The quintessence of New England lodging exists at the **Christmas Farm Inn**, a tranquil place tucked high in the mountains. Resembling a quaint Colonial village, the inn includes a main house built in 1786, plus a cozy log cabin, a 1778 saltbox and a honeymoon cottage. Thirty-four rooms are carefully accented with canopy beds, vaulted ceilings, whirlpool tubs and beautiful quilts.

Congenial innkeepers make Christmastime here special, organizing caroling, eggnog breaks and visits from Santa. Breakfast and dinner included. ~ Route 16B, Jackson Village; 603-383-4313, 800-443-5837, fax 603-383-6495; www.christsmasfarminn.com. DELUXE.

The **Balsams Grand Resort Hotel** is one of those places that makes you wonder how guests can ever bring themselves to leave. This self-contained mini-city sprawls across 15,000 acres of exquisite landscape. This is escapism at its height, a reveling in alpine ridges, thick forests and spectacular lakes and rivers. Stashed way up in New Hampshire's northern boondocks, the rambling, castlelike resort boasts 226 rooms decorated in French provincial style. There's a movie theater, 27 holes of golf, an Olympic swimming pool, croquet and tennis courts, and an outstanding restaurant. The price includes meals and the use of facilities. Closed mid-October to mid-December and mid-March to mid-May. ~ Route 26, Dixville Notch; 603-255-3400, 800-255-0600, fax 603-255-4221; www.thebalsams.com. ULTRA-DELUXE.

DINING

A popular town spot that's just plain fun, **Truants Taverne** has pull-down wall atlases, library shelves and a menu that lists "electives," "detention delights" and "prerequisites." The decor is casual wood-lined pub, the food is basic, with items such as chicken parmigiana and chimichangas. ~ Main Street, North Woodstock; 603-745-2239. MODERATE.

HIDDEN ►

Stationed along a wooded mountain backroad, **Horse and Hound Inn** abounds in Colonial gentility. Lofty pine beams and large hearths are accented by a hunting motif in the 1832 farmhouse. The menu includes filling fare like veal marsala, lamb chops and roast duckling. On warm summer days, opt for the breezy outdoor terrace overlooking the forest. Dinner only. Closed Monday and Tuesday, closed mid-April to mid-May, and from mid-October to Thanksgiving. ~ 205 Wells Road off Route 18, Franconia; 603-823-5501. DELUXE.

GET IN HERE!

Mount Washington Valley's premier noshing post is **Horsefeathers**, a downtown pub with awnings that command "Get in Here!" There is an extensive menu with a focus on seafood dishes that changes twice a year. Items may include pan-blackened salmon and swordfish with black-bean and papaya salsa, as well as basic burgers, steaks and munchies. But the main reason you go here is to see and be seen. Get there early—lines are known to form at the drop of a "feather." ~ Main Street, North Conway; 603-356-2687. MODERATE.

Polly's Pancake Parlor was little more than a backwoods diner before the "Good Morning, America" crew wandered in one day. Ever since, the place has been invaded by tourists who line up outside the 1830 red-shingled carriage shed for home-style breakfast and lunch goodies. Polly's is still out in the boondocks, but views of the countryside are special. Ditto the griddle cakes, made from whole wheat and cornmeal batters and smothered in a choice of maple syrup, maple sugar or maple spread. From mid-October to December 1, and April 1 through Mother's Day, Polly's is open on weekends only; closed December through March. ~ Route 117, Sugar Hill; 603-823-5575. BUDGET.

The **Scottish Lion Inn and Restaurant** provides a nice change of pace with fare from the British Isles. There's a sandwich lineup for lunch, including Scottish bridie (puff pastry turnover), while dinner is strong on roasts and steaks. Hearty appetites should opt for the highland game pie (with venison, hare and pheasant). The three dining rooms are individually decorated with plaids and tartans. On Sunday, there's a brunch buffet. ~ Route 16, North Conway; 603-356-6381. MODERATE.

The views are superb, the surroundings intimate and the cuisine sublime at **The 1785 Inn**. The restaurant, a pretty glassed-in porch that scans a broad mountain range, resides in a venerable 18th-century inn. French dishes are served with flair and understated elegance and include appetizers like cinnamon-spiced shrimp and entrées like raspberry duckling and shrimp and scallop Provençal. Breakfast and dinner. ~ Route 16, North Conway; 603-356-9025. DELUXE.

Small gas lanterns flicker on linen tablecloths and beautiful valanced draperies hover across walls at the **Christmas Farm Inn**. The romantic mountain hideout purveys "French country" cuisine—exceptional dishes such as grilled mini-lamb chops with rosemary glaze, pork tenderloin, and veal medallion sautéed in red wine and tomato sauce. For breakfast, there are waffles with bananas in yogurt cream and corned beef hash. No lunch. ~ Route 16B, Jackson; 603-383-4313. MODERATE TO DELUXE.

SHOPPING

Conway and North Conway extend endless shopping opportunities. Quaint, eclectic marts line Main Street in North Conway, while Route 16 between the two towns is shoulder-to-shoulder with factory outlets and novelty stores.

North Country Angler will accommodate all your flyfishing needs. This is also your spot for expert local fishing advice, as well as guided flyfishing trips. Closed Monday from mid-October to mid-April. ~ Route 16, Intervale; 603-356-6000.

If it's nippy out, drop by **Jack Frost** for earmuffs, colorful sweaters, leather goods and skiwear. ~ Main Street, Jackson; 603-383-4391.

NIGHTLIFE The **North Country Center for the Arts,** located in a partially rehabbed 1800s paper mill, presents musicals and children's theater in the summer. ~ Route 112, Lincoln; 603-745-2141.

The **Red Parka Pub** is a wildly popular après ski bar that hosts rock-and-roll bands that keep things cranking. Live music is featured on Friday and Saturday. ~ Route 302, Glen; 603-383-4344.

If you're male, wear a kilt and a drink is on the house at the **Black Watch,** a mellow joint with a brick fireplace, candlelit tables and piped-in classical music. ~ Scottish Lion Inn and Restaurant, Route 16, North Conway; 603-356-6381.

Horsefeathers wins hands-down as the hippest mountain restaurant and neighborhood pub, a genuine rooting place with sports decor, crazy bartenders and a rough pine bar where patrons stand three deep. Live bands play soft rock, blues and jazz Thursday through Saturday in the Up Bar, the upstairs watering hole decked in leather and velvet. ~ Main Street, North Conway; 603-356-2687.

Looking like a low-slung barn, **Up Country Saloon** jams with live cover music from the '50s to '70s and mixes Tiffany lamps and greenery with a shuffle board and a rambling oak bar. Thursday is karaoke night; live music is featured on Friday and Saturday. Occasional cover on Saturday. ~ Route 16, North Conway; 603-356-3336.

> The state's most spectacular fall foliage displays occur in White Mountain National Forest, and one of the best places to see the changing colors is along the 34-mile Kancamagus Highway from Route 302 to Route 3A.

BEACHES & PARKS

WHITE MOUNTAIN NATIONAL FOREST 🏃 🚲 ⛷ 🛶 🎣 A colossal land mass draped across northern New Hampshire, the forest is New England's largest piece of public land and one of the country's most popular forests. It's so all-encompassing that you soon realize it *is* much of New Hampshire. Its 770,000 acres (45,000 lie in Maine) gobble up several state parks and 1200 miles of hiking trails, 50 lakes and ponds, 750 miles of fishing streams and 23 campgrounds. Most of the Northeast's highest peaks call this forest home, as do whitetail deer, black bear, moose, beaver and a host of other wildlife. There are endless possibilities for trout, salmon, bass, perch and cusk in ponds, lakes and streams. Some of the best are Basin Reservoir and Russell, Sawyer and Long ponds. Hiking trails, including part of the Appalachian Trail, are scattered throughout the forest. Picnic areas are found throughout. Day-use fee, $3 per vehicle. ~ The forest stretches more or less from Percy southward to Rumney, and from Benton eastward into Maine. Several main routes cut through, including Routes 93/3, 302, 16 and 112 (Kancamagus Highway); 603-528-8721, 603-447-5448, fax 603-528-8783.

▲ Permitted in 23 campgrounds, including primitive and trailer camps (no hookups); RVs can go into most of the sites. Fees range from $12 to $16 per night. Reservations: 800-280-2267.

FRANCONIA NOTCH STATE PARK This is the flagship of New Hampshire parks, the one that everyone raves about. A truly incredible place, Franconia blankets 6500 acres, hosts more than 2 million visitors a year and boasts a dizzying array of natural and manmade wonders that make it seem like the Disney World of parklands. Flanked by rocky peaks and riddled with rivers and lakes, the park encompasses the Cannon Mountain ski area and tramway, an intriguing rock pool called the Basin, a minicanyon known as the Flume, and the famous granite profile of **Old Man of the Mountains**. Then there are sandy beaches, miles of hiking trails, swimming and fishing (especially in Echo Lake; canoe and paddleboat rentals are available), beautiful fern grottos and some of the finest bike paths in New Hampshire. The best advice here? Plan to spend some time. (For more information, see the "White Mountains Region" sightseeing section in this chapter.) There are picnic areas, restrooms, a bathhouse, cafeterias, snack bars, bike rentals and the New England Ski Museum. ~ Located north of North Woodstock. Access all sights from Franconia Notch Parkway, which is also Route 93 for the eight-mile length of the park; 603-823-5563.

▲ Lafayette Campground (603-823-9513) has 97 sites, most accommodating RVs (no hookups), and includes showers; $16 per night. There are seven full hookups at Cannon Mountain State RV Park (603-823-5563); $24 per night. Closed Columbus Day through April.

CRAWFORD NOTCH STATE PARK A rugged mountain pass navigates some of the most untamed forest and rocks in New Hampshire. It forms a six-mile shear through the U-shaped Saco River Valley and harbors numerous ponds, trails and cascades, including Arethusa Falls, the highest in the state. Several log cabins commemorate the Willey Family, some of the area's first settlers who were killed in 1826 while fleeing a horrible landslide. Picnic areas, restrooms, a gift shop and a snack bar are available. Closed mid-October to mid-May. ~ Along Route 302, eight miles north of Bartlett; 603-374-2272.

▲ Dry River Campground features 30 tent sites (a few take RVs); $13 per night. Closed Columbus Day to mid-May. Call 603-271-3628 for reservations.

MOUNT WASHINGTON STATE PARK This 59-acre park wraps around the hood of Mount Washington, the highest peak in the northeastern United States. The summit—some 6288 feet up—tingles the spine as you peer across a cosmos of mountains and forests that seem to fall off the horizon. The mountain itself has long been the subject of curiosity and wonder. Its sometimes freakish weather can change from toasty to blizzardlike (or vice versa) in a matter of minutes, and its plant life is an unusual mix of sparse lichens, shrubs and rare wildflowers. Back in 1934, it endured the highest wind velocity (231 miles per hour) ever recorded on earth. You'll find more on this uncanny butte at the Observatory Museum (admission), parked right on the treeless, rocky crest. Amenities here include restrooms, a snack bar, a museum, a gift shop and a post office. Closed mid-October to mid-May. ~ On Route 16 in Pinkham Notch, off Route 302 north of Crawford Notch; 603-466-3347.

HIDDEN ▶   **COLEMAN STATE PARK** 🛶 ⛺ 🚤 ⛵ It's safe to say that this place is virtually at the end of the planet. Purists will find the surroundings heady stuff, a coalition of thick timbers, broad mountains and sparkling lakes. Much of the activity (though there's really not much) centers around Little Diamond Pond, sprinkled with small fishing boats and surrounded by rolling hills. You'll find a picnic area and a recreation building. ~ From Route 26 in Kidderville, take Diamond Pond Road north into the park; 603-237-4520.

▲ Permitted in 25 sites (most take RVs); $12 per night.

▼ ▼ ▼ ▼ ▼ ▼ ▼ ▼ ▼ ▼ ▼ ▼ ▼ ▼
Outdoor Adventures

SKIING

Downhill and cross-country skiing are pursued with a vengeance in New Hampshire. Ski centers are sprinkled along highways and a few rural roads, while backwoods trails exist everywhere. The length of the skiing season varies from December to April depending on the altitude.

For ski information, write to the **New Hampshire Office of Travel and Tourism**. A wintertime report on current ski conditions can be obtained by calling 800-258-3608 (alpine) or 800-262-6660 (Nordic). ~ Box 1856, Concord, NH 03302; 603-271-2343, 800-386-4664; www.visitnh.gov.

SEACOAST Though the region has no downhill facilities, you can ski through the countryside along the eastern corridor. One

HIDDEN ▶   of the best (and least-known) cross-country spots is **Applecrest Farm Orchards**, where 8 kilometers of trails cut through hills of apple orchards. ~ Route 88, Hampton Falls; 603-926-3721.

MERRIMACK VALLEY **Pats Peak**, just outside Concord, is the largest downhill ski facility in the valley. They offer 20 trails (half beginner runs) and a 710-foot vertical drop. There's a snowboard park. ~ Off route 114, Henniker; 603-428-3245. **Pine Acres Ski Touring Center** has 12 miles of groomed cross-country trails through 200 wooded acres. ~ 74 Freetown Road, Raymond; 603-895-2519.

MONADNOCK REGION Four lifts cover 1400-foot **Temple Mountain**, where the 16 trails are rated 40 percent beginner, 40 percent intermediate and 20 percent expert. ~ Route 101, Temple; 603-924-6949; www.templemountain.com. **East Hill Farm**'s six cross-country trails measure a total of 10 kilometers. ~ Off Route 12, Troy; 603-242-6495.

LAKE SUNAPEE–DARTMOUTH AREA Mount Sunapee Resort has 50 downhill trails and a 1510-foot drop. Its snowboard park has a half-pipe. ~ Route 103, Newbury; 603-763-2356. **Snowhill at Eastman**'s one double chair covers eight cross-country trails and three downhill trails. Open weekends and holidays only from December through March. ~ Off Exit 13 at Routes 89 and 10, Grantham; 603-863-6772, 603-863-4241 (winter). **Norsk Touring Center** has 16 Nordic trails. Guided moonlight tours are available. ~ Fairway Lane, off Route 11, New London; 603-526-4685.

LAKES REGION Gunstock features 46 trails, a 1400-foot vertical drop, a tubing park, and 50 kilometers of cross-country skiing. ~ Route 11A, Gilford; 603-293-4341; www.gunstock.com. One wooded, lakeside cross-country trail can be found at **Red Hill Inn**. ~ Route 25B, Center Harbor; 603-279-7001. **Nordic Skier** has 20 kilometers of trails. Lessons are available. ~ 47 North Main Street, Wolfeboro; 603-569-3151; www.wolfeboroxc.org.

WHITE MOUNTAINS REGION Five of the largest downhill ski centers run along the spine of Route 93. The **Waterville Valley Ski Area** has 52 trails served by 11 lifts. For snowboarders, there's a half-pipe on the Upper Valley run. Cross-country skiers can choose between 70 kilometers of groomed and tracked trails or 35 kilometers of backcountry trails. ~ 1 Ski Area Road off Route 49, Waterville Valley; 603-236-8311, fax 603-236-4344; www.waterville.com. **Loon Mountain**'s eight lifts serve 250 acres with 43 trails, nearly two-thirds rated intermediate. A 15-acre snowboard park sports a half-pipe. Cross-country skiers can trek on 35 kilometers of groomed trails. ~ Kancamagus Highway, Lincoln; 603-745-8111, 800-220-5666; www.loonmtn.com, e-mail info@loonmtn.com. In Franconia Notch State Park, **Cannon Mountain** has six lifts and 40 runs, with the range of difficulty divided equally between beginner, intermediate and expert. ~ Route 3; 603-823-7771; www.cannonmt.com. **Bretton Woods** offers some good slopes; nine lifts serve 64 trails. Also here are 100 kilometers of Nordic trails and a snowpark for boarders. ~ Route 302, Bretton Woods; 603-278-5000; www.brettonwoods.com.

Way up in the northern wilderness, the BALSAMS **Wilderness** is a marvelous setting with four lifts, 14 runs and a 1000-foot vertical drop. One run has a half-pipe. There are also more than 85 kilometers of cross-country trails. ~ Route 26, Dixville Notch; 603-255-3951, fax 603-255-3952; www.thebalsams.com.

FISHING   Aficionados of both saltwater and freshwater fishing will find a bounty of opportunities in New Hampshire. Angle for pollack, cod, mackerel and bluefish off the seacoast, or for trout, salmon, cusk, perch and bass in one of hundreds of ponds and lakes. Since lakes and ponds in this area freeze over in the winter, the best time for freshwater fishing is from April to October. Many tour companies only offer their services during these months; it is best to call ahead.

SEACOAST   Deep-sea fishing charters are offered by **Eastman's Fishing Fleet.** Excursions to Jefferey's Ledge will likely reel in cod and haddock. Closed November through May. ~ River Road, Seabrook Beach; 603-474-3461. **Al Gauron Deep Sea Fishing** provides half- and full-day charters. Closed November through March. ~ Hampton Beach State Pier on Ocean Boulevard, Hampton Beach; 603-926-2469, 800-905-7820; www.deepseafishing-nh. com. **Smith & Gilmore Fishing Pier's** two-hour, half- and full-day trips angle for pollack, cod, mackerel and bluefish. Closed October through March. ~ 3A Ocean Boulevard, Hampton Beach; 603-926-3503. In Rye Harbor, **State Marina Atlantic Fishing & Whale Watch** offers half- and full-day trips aboard an 80-foot boat. Closed Columbus Day to mid-April. ~ Route 1A; 603-964-5220.

LAKES REGION   **Landlocked Fishing Guide Service** books trips on Lake Winnipesaukee and at other prime fishing spots. ~ Lake Winnipesaukee, Center Harbor; 603-253-6119. Fish for landlocked salmon and trout on beautiful Squam Lake with **Squam Lake Tours.** Closed mid-October through April. ~ Route 3, Holderness; 603-968-7577; www.squamlaketours.com.

In Laconia, **Winni Sailboarders' School** rents boats of all varieties and offer instruction in windsurfing and kayaking. ~ 687 Union Avenue; 603-528-4110. **Fay's Boat Yard** rents boats from mid-April to October. ~ 71 Varney Point Road, Gilfords; 603-293-8000; www.faysboatyard.com. In Weirs Beach, there's **Thurston's Marina,** where you can rent boats from May through September. ~ Route 3; 603-366-4811; www.thurstonsmarina.com.

WHALE WATCHING   Humpbacks, finbacks, minke and other Atlantic whales are known to put on quite a show. **Eastman's Fishing Parties** has excursions to popular spots, such as the Stellwagon Bank, daily from July to Labor Day. ~ River Road, Seabrook Beach; 603-474-3461. In Hampton Beach, **Al Gauron Deep Sea Fishing** provides half- and full-day trips. Closed November through March. ~ Hampton Beach State Pier, Ocean Boulevard; 603-926-2469, 800-905-7820; www.deepseafishing-nh.com. In Rye Harbor, **New Hampshire Seacoast Cruises** offers expeditions from May through September. ~ Route 1A; 603-964-5545; www.whales-rye.com. In Portsmouth, **Oceanic Whale Watch Expeditions** offers five-hour cruises daily from mid-June through Labor Day. ~ 315 Market Street; 603-431-5505; www.islesofshoals.com.

Golf enthusiasts will happily take to New Hampshire's scenic greens. In general, depending on the weather, courses shut down from mid-November to mid-April. Most rent clubs and carts. **GOLF**

SEACOAST Visit **Sagamore Hampton Golf Club**, a walking course with 18 holes that is open to the public. ~ 101 North Road, North Hampton; 603-964-5341.

MERRIMACK VALLEY The **Deeryfield Country Club**'s terrain ranges from a hilly front nine to a flat back nine on a municipal course. ~ 625 Mammoth Road, Manchester; 603-669-0235; www.deeryfieldgolf.com. Or you can tee off at **Passaconaway Country Club**, a public 18-hole course that is flat and very lengthy. There's a putting green. ~ 12 Midway Avenue, Litchfield; 603-424-4653.

MONADNOCK REGION Try **Bretwood Golf Course**, with two 18-hole public courses. ~ East Surry Road, Keene; 603-352-7626.

LAKE SUNAPEE–DARTMOUTH AREA The semiprivate **Claremont Country Club** offers a hilly nine holes. ~ Maple Avenue, Claremont; 603-542-9550. The Sugar River meanders through the semiprivate, 18-hole **John H. Cain Golf Course**. ~ Unity Road, off Routes 11 and 103, Newport; 603-863-7787.

LAKES REGION Enjoy the scenic views of the White Mountains and Red Hill as you putt your way though the semiprivate 18-hole **Waukewan Golf Club**. ~ Waukewan Road, West Center Harbor; 603-279-6661.

WHITE MOUNTAINS REGION Surrounded by the White Mountains, **Waterville Valley Athletic Club** has nine holes open to the public. ~ Route 49, Waterville Valley; 603-236-4805. In Bretton Woods, **Mount Washington Hotel and Resort** offers a nine-hole and an 18-hole course, both with spectacular views of Mt. Washington. There's also a driving range. ~ Route 302; 603-278-1000.

SEACOAST You'll find seven outdoor public courts at **Exeter Recreation Park**. Lessons are available. ~ Sign up for courts at 32 Court Street; park is on Hampton Road, Exeter; 603-778-0591. Public courts in Portsmouth are on the **South Mill Pond**. ~ Junkins Avenue. **TENNIS**

MERRIMACK VALLEY **Memorial Field** has five outdoor public courts. ~ South Fruit Street, Concord; 603-225-8690.

MONADNOCK REGION **Wheelock Park**'s two outdoor courts are lighted. ~ Park Avenue, Keene; 603-357-9829.

LAKE SUNAPEE–DARTMOUTH AREA **Dartmouth College Athletic Complex** offers four clay and 18 hardtop outdoor courts. They're free from April through November. From October through May, play on one of four indoor courts for a fee. During the indoor months, you may want to call ahead for a reservation. ~ Wheelock and South Park streets, Hanover; 603-646-3074.

LAKES REGION Try one of the lighted public courts at **Prescott Park**. ~ Route 3, Meredith; 603-279-8197. **Moultonboro Tennis Courts** has four courts available to the public. ~ Playground Drive, Moultonboro; 603-253-4160.

WHITE MOUNTAINS REGION You'll find two courts at the **Mountain Club Fitness Center**. Lessons are available. Fee. ~ Route 112 at Loon Mountain, Lincoln; 603-745-8111 ext. 5280. Play on one of 18 outdoor clay courts or two indoor hardtop courts at **Waterville Valley Athletic Club**. Reservations are recommended for the indoor courts. Lessons are available. Fee. ~ Route 49; 603-236-8303.

RIDING STABLES

What better way to take in New Hampshire scenery than on horseback?

MERRIMACK VALLEY The trail rides at the **Winged Spur Ranch** take you along country roads where you may catch a glimpse of moose or deer. Highlights include Bear Brook Reservation. Lessons are offered, and there are day and overnight camps. ~ 24 Currier Road, Candia; 603-483-5960.

LAKES REGION **Castle in the Clouds** offers superb rides through hilly terrain; you'll see plenty of wildlife, including birds and deer. ~ Route 171, Moultonboro; 603-476-2352, 800-729-2468.

WHITE MOUNTAINS REGION The **Stables at the Farm By the River** leads one-hour guided tours through 65 acres located in the Mount Washington Valley year-round. Children's pony rides are also available. ~ 2555 West Side Road, North Conway; 603-356-4855. **Mount Washington Hotel and Resort Stables** offers trail rides over the cross-country ski trails at the base of Mount Washington. ~ Route 302, Bretton Woods; 603-278-1300.

BIKING

This state of grand mountains, vast lakes and rocky coastline is truly a bicyclist's nirvana.

SEACOAST One of the most popular routes in all New Hampshire, the 18-mile **Atlantic Shoreline** wends along the rugged seacoast on Route 1A from Massachusetts to Portsmouth. Caution: during summer months, traffic is extremely heavy.

Seven miles of rolling hills and apple orchards await along Route 88 between **Exeter and Hampton Falls**.

MERRIMACK VALLEY The 34-mile trek from **Milford to Concord** along Route 13 is lined with old red barns, rivers and streams, and superb vistas.

MONADNOCK REGION For a picturesque, less-traveled odyssey, take Route 149 from **South Weare to Hillsboro**. The 12-mile excursion slices through archetypical New England villages and rambling farmlands.

LAKES REGION   With its gorgeous water and mountain views, the 62-mile loop around **Lake Winnipesaukee** is a favorite among bicyclists. The terrain varies from flat to very hilly, and roads can be congested during the summer. Stick to Routes 28, 109, 25B and 11.

WHITE MOUNTAINS REGION   The strong at heart will opt for a very steep 10-mile journey on Hurricane Mountain Road from **North Conway to the Maine Border.** An easier mountain route that's just as scenic, Route 16 and Side Road follow the Androscoggin River for 29 miles from **Errol to Berlin.**

Bike Rentals   Because of high liability insurance rates, bike rental centers are scarce across New Hampshire. A full-service shop, **Piche's** rents mountain, road and hybrid bikes in the Lakes Region. ~ 318 Gilford Avenue, Gilford; 603-524-2068; www.piches. com. The **Adventure Center** rents, sells and services bikes. ~ Town Square, Waterville Valley; 603-236-4666, 800-468-2553. In Lincoln, call **Loon Mountain Bike Center,** which rents, sells and services bikes. Shuttle service to Franconia Notch is available; there you can take a self-guided bike tour and see refreshing waterfalls. ~ Kancamagus Highway (Route 112); 603-745-8111, 800-229-5666; www.loonmtn.com.

New Hampshire's vast timberlands and lakes, wide mountains and ravines make it a hiker's haven. Forests cover 84 percent of the state, and the White Mountain National Forest alone has over 1200 miles of trails. For information on many of these trails, contact the **White Mountain National Forest.** ~ 719 Main Street, Laconia, NH 03246; 603-528-8721.

HIKING

The Appalachian Mountain Club's **White Mountain Guide,** considered the hiker's Bible, is available through the club. ~ Box 298, Gorham, NH 03581; 603-466-2721. For inn-to-inn hikes and treks through Franconia Notch and Mount Washington, get in touch with **New England Hiking Holidays.** Tours are available from March through November. ~ P.O. Box 1648, North Conway, NH 03860; 603-356-9696, 800-869-0949; www.nehiking holidays.com.

The weather here can be highly unpredictable: you should always carry a flashlight and food essentials. Weather and trail conditions can be checked easily by calling parks ahead of time.

All distances listed for hiking trails are one way unless otherwise noted.

SEACOAST   Though you won't scale any significant peaks along the coast, you can explore some very scenic footpaths. One of the best spots is **Odiorne Point State Park,** where trails wander along gentle shoreline, rocky beaches and stands of pines, oaks and wild roses.

A few miles inland, the **University of New Hampshire's College Woods** offers a labyrinth of nature trails that crisscross more than 200 thickly forested acres. There's also the **College Brook Ravine** trail (1 mile), which follows a brook through a 15-acre ravine and offers peeks at 155 species of plants.

MERRIMACK VALLEY The **Uncanoonuc Mountain Trail** (.75 mile) cuts through a stone wall and hemlock forest and passes a small cave on the way to the summit, where views of Manchester await. To find the rather obscure trailhead, take Route 114 east from Goffstown to Mountain Road. Go south for a mile, then bear left for a mile and a half.

MONADNOCK REGION Isolated Mount Monadnock, often called "the world's most-hiked mountain," offers more than a dozen trails with all levels of difficulty. For detailed information, stop by the visitors center (off Route 124, four miles west of Jaffrey). **White Arrow Trail** (1 mile), one of the mountain's oldest footpaths, ambles across brooks, ledges and narrow gullies to the summit. It commences at the end of the mountain toll road.

Pumpelly Trail (4.5 miles) zigzags up Monadnock, following a ridge and passing a huge rectangular boulder and several glacial carvings. The trailhead starts on Old Marlboro Road off Route 101, just west of Dublin.

Hikers took the **Marlboro Trail** (2 miles) as early as 1850, tackling the steep nose of Monadnock's ridges to open ledges. Start on the dirt road located off Route 124, west of Monadnock State Park.

The popular **White Dot Trail** (2 miles), a steep and rocky course, is the most direct route to the summit.

Wapack Trail (21 miles) is a popular skyline trek along the Wapack Range, running from Watatic Mountain in Ashburnham, Massachusetts, across the Pack Monadnocks in New Hampshire. With many open ledges and beautiful views, it navigates a large spruce forest.

LAKE SUNAPEE–DARTMOUTH AREA The **Monadnock-Sunapee Greenway** (49 miles) crawls across ridgetops between Mounts Monadnock and Sunapee. You can also scale **Mount Sunapee** via its ski slopes (2 miles), which plow through heavy forests to gorgeous, secluded Lake Solitude and then go on to the summit.

LAKES REGION With its marvelous union of mountains and water, the Lakes Region provides some of the most scenic hiking in New Hampshire. On the north end of Squam Lake, a pair of low-lying mountains called the Rattlesnakes feature easy treks with unparalleled views.

Old Bridle Path (.9 mile), off Route 113 near Center Sandwich, meanders along an old cart road to the summit of West

Rattlesnake. **Ridge Trail** (1 mile) connects East and West Rattlesnakes, beginning northeast of the cliffs on the western mountain.

In the Red Hill area of Squam Lake, **Eagle Cliff Trail** (2.3 miles) ambles through a thicket and dense woods, scales the steep cliff and ends at the fire tower for great views from Red Hill. The trailhead is off Bean Road, 5.2 miles from the junction of Routes 25 and 25B in Center Harbor.

For excellent vistas of Lake Winnipesaukee, try the **Mount Shaw Trail** (3.5 miles), which travels through a hemlock forest and past several streams and brooks to an open knob. It starts at a dirt road on the north side of Route 171 west of Tuftonboro.

East Gilford Trail (2.1 miles) begins on Wood Road off Route 11A, climbs Belknap Mountain and affords several fine outlooks over Lake Winnipesaukee.

WHITE MOUNTAINS REGION Spectacular hiking is found everywhere in the White Mountains Region.

Offering splendid scenery, **Welch Dickey Loop Trail** (4.5 miles) follows rock outcroppings and gives you the feeling that you're above the timberline. The trailhead is beside the Mad River on Orris Road, off Upper Mad River Road from Route 49.

Along the beautiful Kancamagus Highway near Conway, you'll find **Boulder Loop Trail** (2.8 miles), a gradual climb with panoramas of Mount Chocorua and the Swift River Valley. The easy **Sabbaday Falls Trail** (.4 mile), a spur path off the **Sabbaday Brook Trail** (4.9 miles), wanders to a series of cascades in a narrow chasm. The Brook Trail offers easy grades, numerous brook crossings and views of the falls.

The Franconia Notch area is a maze of trails for all hiking levels. The more experienced hiker should check out the **Falling Waters Trail** (3.2 miles), which navigates lovely cascades and brooks, shady glens and narrow gorges, and offers great vistas of the notch. It starts at Lafayette Place.

The **Whitehouse Trail** (.8 mile) connects to the **Pemi Trail** (6 miles), which winds along the Pemigewasset River, making a nice trek through Franconia Notch State Park. Pick up the trail at the Flume Visitors Center.

Bald Mountain–Artists Bluff Trail (.8 mile) makes a panoramic loop in the notch, starting at Peabody Base on Route 18. Nestled in the mountains, **Lonesome Lake Trail** (1.6 miles) offers commanding views of surrounding peaks. It commences at the Lafayette Campground off Route 93.

Often overlooked, **Cascade Brook Trail** (5 miles) is a stroll through verdant foliage along Cascade Brook. The trail begins at the Whitehouse Bridge in Franconia Notch State Park and ends at the Kingsman Pond Shelter.

One of the state's most popular hikes, **Tuckerman Ravine Trail** (2.3 miles) is a rugged cirque with bare slopes and sheer cliffs on Mount Washington. A moderately difficult path, it starts at the Appalachian Mountain Club's Pinkham Notch Camp on Route 16.

Thompson Falls Trail (.8 mile) clambers up the south side of Wildcat Brook to cascades and views of the Presidential mountain range. The trailhead starts at Wildcat Ski Area on Route 16.

Transportation

CAR

The fastest means of road travel are the interstate highways. Route 93 scoots up the north–south center of the state, while **Route 95** cuts in from Massachusetts, follows the seacoast, then heads out into southern Maine.

On the west corridor, **Route 91** actually lies in Vermont but is used by many New Hampshire drivers as a major north–south artery.

There's no quick way to reach the state's northern wilderness, but **Route 16** and **Route 3** will take you there while skirting some spectacular scenery.

AIR

New Hampshire's air traffic flows through **Manchester Airport**, a small but quite convenient facility in Manchester. Several major carriers provide service, including Continental Airlines, Delta Airlines, United Airlines and USAir.

Boston's **Logan International Airport**, about 30 miles from New Hampshire's seacoast, is also a major air gateway for the state (see Chapter Four).

First Class Limousine transports passengers from Logan to most points in southern New Hampshire, including Nashua, Merrimack and Manchester. ~ 603-883-4807, 800-252-7754.

BUS

Concord Trailways operates a broad network across New Hampshire. Buses start from Boston's Logan Airport and stop in Manchester, Concord and smaller towns as far north as Littleton. ~ 603-228-3300, 800-639-3317; www.concordtrailways.com.

TRAIN

Train travel is practically nonexistent here, though **Amtrak** does provide service to Vermont's White River Junction and Bellows Falls, along New Hampshire's western border. The trains make direct routes from Washington, D.C., New York and Montreal to Springfield, Massachusetts; a bus connection will then take you into Vermont. ~ 800-872-7245.

CAR RENTALS

Arriving at Manchester Airport, you'll find the following rental companies: **Avis Rent A Car** (800-331-1212), **Budget Rent A Car** (800-527-0700), **Hertz Rent A Car** (800-654-3131) and **National Car Rental** (800-227-7368). **Thrifty Car Rental** (800-367-2277) is located near the terminal and offers free airport transfers.

TEN

Maine

Mention you're going to Maine and you get all sorts of envious looks. People automatically envision the Andrew Wyeth landscapes, the pine-scented woods, the candy-striped lighthouses, the huge platters of lobster and baskets of steamers. Over the years, its name has practically become synonymous with the word "vacation." License plates even read "Vacationland." Indeed, visitors can find many opportunities to vacate cluttered lived in this spectacularly scenic New England state.

Maine has the Ice Age to thank for its smashingly good looks. Massive glaciers left over 6000 lakes and ponds and 32,000 miles of rivers and streams in their wake as well as the towering peaks of Cadillac Mountain and Mt. Katahdin (the latter stretches about a mile high). The coast is made of a series of deeply cut indentations and narrow peninsulas and has more offshore islands than you can count. Measure the seaboard in a straight line and you come up with about 230 miles. Count every inch of shoreline and it's an amazing 3478 miles.

The state's name supposedly came from sailors' use of the term "main" for the mainland apart from the offshore islands. In later years, Maine was given the nickname "Pine Tree State" because nearly 90 percent of its land is covered with fragrant evergreens.

Maine's beauty, however, is not skin deep. The people who live here are really what make this state so special. Real Mainers—or State-of-Mainers as the most patriotic refer to themselves—are full of pride. They're also very individualistic and don't put on any airs. They are who they are, whether you like it or not. And they're tough. While carloads of tourists and summer residents pack up and head south at the end of the summer, they prepare for the long, cold winters ahead. Many Mainers also devotedly preserve the traditions of the past. You see crafts such as wooden boatbuilding, quilting and weaving still very much alive all over the state.

The biggest concentration of the population is clustered around the harbor-perched city of Portland, the state's commercial and cultural center. Established in 1624, Portland was destroyed four times, twice by the Indians in the 1600s, once by the British in 1775 and again by the great fire of 1866. Today the phoenix—the mythical Egyptian bird that rises from the ashes of destruction—is the city symbol.

A very progressive city, Portland has attracted people from across America as well as immigrants from Greece, Cambodia, Jamaica, Finland and a host of other countries. Maine's statewide residents are a mix of ethnicities as well. These include Abenaki Indians whose ancestors can be traced back 2000 years and Europeans whose forefathers settled along the coast in the beginning of the 1600s.

Most historians believe that Maine was sighted by Vikings as early as the year 1000, but since no real evidence can be found, the credit for discovering the area has been passed along to others. It is believed that John Cabot saw the Maine coast on his second voyage to the New World in 1498, thereby establishing all future British claims to the land. However, the first European colony was established at the mouth of the St. Croix River in 1604 by French explorers Sieur de Monts, Pierre du Guast and Samuel de Champlain. The colony didn't last very long, however. In 1605, England's King James I included the area in the land grant given the Plymouth Colony.

The years that followed were marked by territorial struggles between the English, French and Indians. In spite of its bitterly cold winters, Maine had an abundance of natural assets to fight over, including dozens of deep-water harbors, timber-filled forests, navigable inland rivers and waters teeming with fish. The fighting eventually led to the 18th-century French and Indian Wars. After the British were victorious, what would be the State of Maine became a part of the Commonwealth of Massachusetts. Not until 1820 was Maine admitted to the union as a free state.

About 50 years later, word got out that Mount Desert Island and its then-sleepy little fishing village of Bar Harbor was an exceptionally beautiful place. Indeed, with its rock-hewn shores and sky-poking mountains, it's certainly spectacular. Before long, the island became an exclusive retreat for wealthy and powerful American families who came by steamboat and train. Folks with names like Rockefeller and Vanderbilt built sprawling summer "cottages" on bluffs overlooking the sea. They hired locals to staff these homes and the well-appointed yachts on which they hosted glamorous cocktail parties. By the turn of the 20th century, there were over 200 magnificent mansions on Mount Desert Island. Other areas along the coast south of Bar Harbor started to become popular summering spots as well, as trains brought in the moneyed people looking to build by the sea.

These golden years did pass, however, their demise brought by the Depression and World War II. But the final blow to Bar Harbor's days of grandeur came when a fire broke out in 1947 and burned over a third of Mount Desert Island, including nearly 70 of its estates. The island was eventually rebuilt but in a less-opulent fashion. Affordable motels and hotels sprouted like mushrooms after a rain, making the area much more accessible to average tourists.

Maine's coastal beauty is still what attracts most travelers today. Dozens of little fishing villages here burst with character. Some have gone a little overboard trying to attract tourists and are a bit too gussied up. If you're interested in seeing places that haven't sprung into tourist hubs, you have to be willing to go an extra yard. Follow the little roads that turn off like stray thoughts. They may take you to a tiny village on the sea. Consider taking a boat trip out to an island you've

Text continued on page 554.

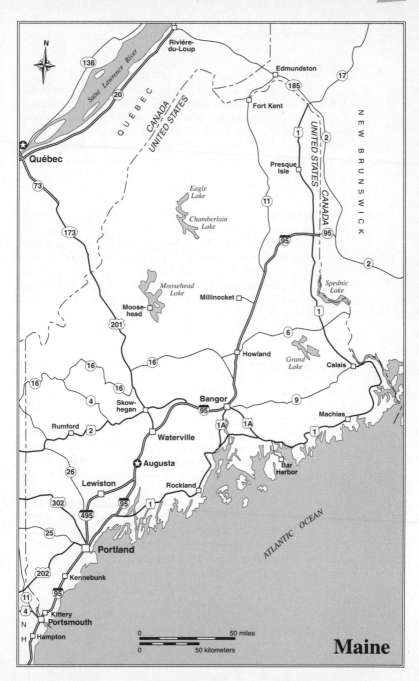

Maine

The Maine Art Museum Trail

Coastal Maine is a motorist's paradise, where Route 1 and countless small side roads provide access to more than 3000 miles of coastline. For generations, the scenery along this shoreline has attracted more painters than any other nonurban area of the East Coast, resulting in a rich artistic heritage to match its scenic beauty. You can explore both in a three-day weekend that connects Maine's seven major art museums.

DAY 1 • Leaving Boston early, take Route 95 north for about 75 miles to the Maine state line and get off at Exit 1, just before the Main Turnpike toll booth. Follow coastal Route 1 north for eight miles to Ogunquit, one of America's first art colonies, named for an Algonquin word meaning "beautiful place by the sea." Set in a beautiful location overlooking Narrow Cove, the **Ogunquit Museum of American Art** exhibits works by 20th-century artists including locals Marsden Hartley, Edward Hopper and Walt Kuhn. Closed October through June. Admission. ~ 183 Shore Road; 207-646-4909.

• After lunch in Ogunquit, continue up the coast to the city of Portland. It's a distance of about 50 miles on either Route 95 or Route 1 (which veers away from the coast on this segment), but you'll get a big dose of scenery by detouring along the coast on Route 9 and still arrive in Portland in time to visit the **Portland Museum of Art**, a five-story edifice that gives Maine native Winslow Homer top billing over such superstars as Degas, Monet, Renoir and Picasso. Closed Monday from late October to late June. Admission. ~ 7 Congress Square; 207-733-2787; www.portlandmuseum.org.

DAY 2 • From Portland, a 23-mile drive on Route 1 takes you to Brunswick and the **Bowdoin College Museum of Art**, which showcases Colonial and Federal portraits, including Gilbert Stuart's *Thomas Jefferson,* along with Roman and Greek artifacts and Winslow Homer memorabilia. The Winslow Homer gallery is open only in summer. Closed Monday. ~ Walker Art Building; 207-725-3275.

- From Brunswick, follow Route 196 inland through farm country for about 15 miles to Lewiston, Marsden Hartley's hometown. Here, the **Bates College Museum of Art** features not only a generous sampling of Hartley's work but also an exceptional collection of contemporary works on paper with a focus on pencil, pen and charcoal drawings. Free. ~ 75 Russell Street; 207-786-6185.

- Return to Brunswick the way you came. After lunch, rejoin Route 1 and drive north, crossing a number of inlets along 55 miles of the picturesque southern coast, to the touristy fishing village of Rockland and the **Farnsworth Art Museum**. One of the country's finest regional art museums, it has works by leading artists including the "first family" of Maine painting, with more than a thousand works by N.C., Andrew and Jamie Wyeth on rotating display. Admission. ~ 356 Main Street; 207-596-6457.

DAY 3 • From Rockland, drive 38 miles along the coast on Route 1. At Bucksport, turn north onto Route 1A and follow the Penobscot River for 27 miles to Bangor, where the **University of Maine Museum of Art** has a 5700-piece collection of regional and international, classic and contemporary works amassed with funding from Andrew Carnegie; what is remarkable here is the large number of pieces—20 percent of the collection—exhibited at one time. ~ 5712 Carnegie Hall, Orono; 207-581-3255.

- Returning south from Bangor on Route 95, a drive of 53 miles will bring you to Waterville, where the **Colby Museum of Art** has 13 galleries tracing the development of American art from the mid-18th century to the present. ~ Bixler Art and Music Center, Colby College; 207-872-3228. From here, the return trip to Boston takes about two and a half hours.

never heard of. And go north! The coast above Mount Desert Island is still largely undiscovered.

Bear in mind that Maine is enormous, so taking on a little piece at a time is all any visitor should do. We've broken it up into four areas, each of which might be seen in about a week's time. The coast is divided into two sections, the Southern Coast (between Kittery and Bucksport) and the Downeast Coast (from Castine to Calais). Maine's most visited area, the Southern Coast is well endowed with hotels, restaurants and other facilities geared for tourists. It's also home to some of the state's most beautiful beaches. Downeast Coast is not quite as busy and less developed, with the exception of Bar Harbor, an enormously popular vacation hub. This chapter follows Route 1 up the coast, taking you to the major tourist towns as well as the little-known villages and islands.

Our third section takes you through the northern woods, which Henry Thoreau praises endlessly in his book *The Maine Woods*. An area of unmatched wild beauty, it's home to the state's highest peak (Mt. Katahdin), the biggest state park (Baxter) and the largest lake (Moosehead). Its year-round residents include hearty-souled State of Mainers and a large black bear population, in addition to moose, bobcats and scores of birds.

Our final section—the western lakes and mountains—is an excursion to the White Mountains and the sprawling Indian-named lakes that are set in hills like precious gems. The woods that wrap around them teem with moose, deer and all sorts of songbirds. There are also several picture-perfect little villages crammed with antique and craft shops.

Like all the New England states, Maine has four distinctly different seasons. Summer—especially July and August—is the customary time to visit. That's when the bays swell with pleasure boats and towns open up like roses. Though the weather is predictably unpredictable (one day the harbor is bundled in mist, the next it's clear as a window), it's always lovely. Temperatures all over the state remain comfortable, hovering around 70° in the daytime. Nights, however, can get nippy, especially along the coast where the breezes off the sea can be chilling.

Some say autumn is the very best time to visit Maine. The summer-only residents have packed up and left. The partying vacationers are back at work and in school. The real full-time Mainers reappear. You're no longer one of many tourists but an appreciated guest. The weather is often phenomenally beautiful, with blue skies and sunshine. And, of course, you can see the fall colors. Spring, too, is appealing, as new life appears.

Winter brings on a whole array of snow-based activities, including great skiing, especially in the northern and western parts of the state. Maine's long and cold winters create a died-and-gone-to-heaven land for winter sports enthusiasts.

In this chapter, we introduce you to just some of Maine's attractions. In many ways, this is a very American state, but in others it feels almost like a foreign country. One visit and you'll inevitably feel compelled to return.

Southern Coast

Many people cross the New Hampshire border into the state of Maine expecting to find what they've always pictured: postcard fishing villages with salty characters, sprawling farms, pine forests. Well, dear readers, you have to look a little to find these pictures in southern Maine. What you are most likely to notice first along the Southern Coast—besides scores of factory outlets that line Route 1—is a profusion of hotels, motels, inns and every other kind of tourist accommodation conceivable, along with clam shacks and lobster joints broadcasting their low, low prices.

This is the gateway to the Vacation State. Just about everybody passes through the narrow southern tip on their way to the big tourist hubs like Boothbay Harbor and Mount Desert Island as well as the never-heard-of-before villages and hamlets that line the coast and lie scattered around the northern and western parts of the state. Interstate 95 can get you up north much faster, but we're going to take it slow, meandering up Route 1.

Southern Maine has an abundance of something the rest of the state can envy—sandy beaches. In fact, even though Maine boasts nearly 3500 miles of coastline, sandy beaches skirt fewer than 100 of those miles, and the majority lie below Portland. They start almost immediately around Kittery, Maine's southernmost town. As you drive along Route 1, don't hesitate to detour along shore roads and Route 1A, which lead right by the beaches.

SIGHTS

You can pull over at any time (why not, everybody else does—the traffic problem is part of the fun) to gaze out at the fury of the sea and the beach crowd. Beachgoers in this part of the world dress the gamut from string bikinis to down parkas and wool socks in August (the winds can really send chills racing through your body). If you want to take a swim, you can have your pick of beaches in Kittery, York, Cape Neddick, Ogunquit, Wells and other spots (see "Beaches & Parks" below).

These southern towns are also rife with worthwhile attractions. In **Kittery**, you might want to take a look around the **Kittery Historical and Naval Museum**. It's filled with naval relics from the Portsmouth Naval Yard and exhibits explaining the history of the Southern Coast. Closed late October through May. Admission. ~ Route 1, just north of the Route 236 Rotary, Kittery; 207-439-3080.

In **York**, several historic structures have been nicely restored. Guides take you through buildings including the **Old Schoolhouse**, the 18th-century **John Hancock Warehouse and Wharf** and the **Emerson–Wilcox House** (a tavern/family-dwelling-turned-general-store-turned-tailor-shop). Orientation and tours start at **Jefferds Tavern** on Route 1A. For more information, contact the Old York Historical Society. Closed late September to mid-June. Admission. ~ 207-363-4974.

One of the more intriguing of York's historic sights, the **Old Gaol** first opened its doors and dungeons in 1720. Today a museum, the gaol gives visitors a look at its gruesome relics—cramped cells, the disciplinary pit and jailer's quarters. You'll also find displays of Indian and pioneer artifacts. ~ Route 1A, York Street, York.

If you can drag yourselves away from the beaches in **Wells,** there are some good attractions for children, including the **Wells Auto Museum,** where over 80 antique cars are displayed. Closed Columbus Day through Memorial Day. Admission. ~ Route 1, Wells; 207-646-9064.

Birdwatchers can log in some remarkable sightings at Wells' **Rachel Carson National Wildlife Refuge.** See the "Beaches & Parks" section below. ~ Off Route 9, Wells. Another public preserve is the **Wells Research Reserve.** Parking fee, $2 per adult in July and August and weekends in September. ~ 342 Laudholm Farm Road, off Route 1, Wells; 207-646-1555.

Just north of Wells, you'll come to the Kennebunks—the commercial center of **Kennebunk** and the port town, **Kennebunkport.** Both towns were early shipbuilding and fishing settlements. The latter is now referred to as **Bush Country,** since it's home to former President Bush's summer home. The little town itself is a bit too gussied up for tourists (with prices to match), but it's a worthwhile stop nonetheless. Consider putting the car in a lot for a good part of the day and picking up a copy of the *Kennebunkport Walking Guide,* which is available at the **Kennebunkport Historical Society.** ~ 125 North Street, Kennebunkport; 207-967-2513, fax 207-967-1205; www.kporthistory.org. The **Kennebunk–Kennebunkport Chamber of Commerce** has reduced hours on weekends in the winter. ~ Yellow House, 17 Western Avenue, Kennebunk; 207-967-0857.

In summer months, there are walking tours of Kennebunkport's historical area on Thursday afternoon. They start at **Nott House,** a Greek Revival building that dates back to 1853. Closed mid-October through June. Closed Sunday and Monday. Admission. ~ Maine Street, Kennebunkport. The **Pasco Exhibit Center** offers more information and exhibits about Kennebunkport's history. Closed Tuesday and Friday; also closed Saturday from November through February. Admission. ~ 125 North Street, Kennebunkport; 207-967-2751, fax 207-967-1205; www.kport history.org.

If you want to get a glimpse of the former president's compound, take a drive along mansion-dotted **Ocean Avenue. Walker's Point** is the name of the Bush compound. It's a beautiful promontory surrounded by the horizonless waters of the Atlantic. The brown-shingled house is the centerpiece.

While you're in the neighborhood, you might want to stop at the **Seashore Trolley Museum.** Its comprehensive collection of antique electric trolley cars includes samples from around the world—Japan, Germany, New Zealand and Budapest. And visitors can hop aboard one trolley for a four-mile journey. Closed November through April. Admission. ~ Log Cabin Road, Kennebunkport; 207-967-2800; www.trolleymuseum.org.

Back inland, you can take an architectural walking tour of Kennebunk's **National Register District**. It includes **The Brick Store Museum**, a block of restored early-19th-century commercial buildings, including as 1803 Federal house. Closed Sunday and Monday. Admission. ~ 117 Main Street, Kennebunk; 207-985-4802; www.cybertours.com/brickstore.

One of the most well-known attractions in southern Maine is the **Wedding Cake House**. As the name implies, it's a yellow house with intricate white latticework that looks like lace. A local sea

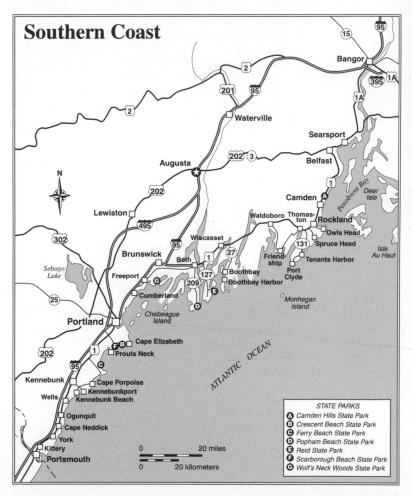

Southern Coast

STATE PARKS
A Camden Hills State Park
B Crescent Beach State Park
C Ferry Beach State Park
D Popham Beach State Park
E Reid State Park
F Scarborough Beach State Park
G Wolf's Neck Woods State Park

captain fashioned his house after cathedrals he saw in Milan, Italy. The public is not welcome inside, however. ~ Summer Street, Kennebunk.

As you continue north from the Kennebunks, you can either pick up Route 1 (at Kennebunk) or opt for the more scenic Route 9 from Kennebunkport. The latter takes you past several sun-soaked beaches. When you reach the town of Scarborough, turn right onto Route 207, which leads to **Prouts Neck**. This oddly shaped peninsula juts into Saco Bay about eight miles south of Portland. Much of its coastal scenery—steep cliffs, swirling surf and dwarfish rock-clinging trees—can be seen on the canvases of American painter Winslow Homer, who lived and worked here. His studio, a converted stable overlooking the ocean, is open to the public, by appointment, for touring. There's also the **Prouts Neck Bird Sanctuary** at the tip, where all sorts of exotic birds have been spotted.

Portland, Maine's largest city, is the next stop. Often called "The Little San Francisco of the East," it's a lovely city of hills surrounded by water. Many of Portland's streets are lined with beautifully preserved Victorian buildings. Very progressive, the city boasts a horde of museums, galleries, shops and restaurants.

Just down the street is the **Wadsworth Longfellow House**, where the poet spent his childhood. Guided tours available June through October. Admission. ~ 485 Congress Street, Portland; 207-772-1807.

One of the most interesting districts in the city is the **Old Port Exchange**, between Exchange and Pearl streets, on the waterfront. Here you'll see old brick and granite buildings that were erected during the early 19th century, when Portland was a major rail center and shipping port. Many now house restaurants, taverns and shops.

For exploring Portland's historic districts, consider stopping by the Portland Convention and Visitors Bureau's **Visitors Information Center**. Here you can pick up self-guided walking tours of the Old Port Exchange, **Congress Street** (Portland's most important commercial street since the early 1800s), **State Street** (a wealthy residential district with large Federal-style mansions) and the **Western Promenade** (a fascinating selection of architectural styles, including high Victorian Gothic, shingle-style and Italianate mansions). There are also guided tours of "Historic Portland" that leave from the same site (tours run July through September). Admission. ~ 305 Commercial Street, Portland; 207-772-5800.

For a wonderful view of the city and island-dotted Casco Bay, climb the 102 steps up the **Portland Observatory**, the last remaining 19th-century marine signal tower on the eastern seaboard, built in 1807. Closed in winter. ~ 138 Congress Street, Portland; 207-774-5561.

Author Picks

CHAPTER FAVORITES

I love Maine for its offbeat character, proudly out of the ordinary. Where else would you find a private museum like the **Musical Wonder House**? In this age of CDs and online audio, Danilo Konvalinka's vast collection of antique record players and the like seems stranger every year. *page 560*

The **Squire Tarbox Inn** on Westport Island has the nicest barn I've ever slept in. Fortunately, there are separate accommodations for the resident goats that provide the homemade cheese they serve at breakfast. *page 566*

Since I'd always associated Maine with lobsters, I was surprised to find that most are exported. Maine restaurants typically serve them—if at all—shredded into a stew, bisque or salad. A tasty exception is **Beal's Lobster Pier**, where you can eat 'em fresh or ship 'em home. *page 593*

I know of few experiences as sublime as canoeing silently through Maine's north woods. Although I daydream of paddling the 95-mile length of the Allagash Wilderness Waterway sometime, I'm glad to have had the change to canoe a stretch of the Moose River with a little help from **Wilderness Expeditions**. *page 614*

For a seal's-eye view of the bay, take a guided boat tour from Commercial Street during the summer. You can contact **Casco Bay Lines**. ~ Casco Bay Ferry Terminal, Commercial and Franklin streets, Portland; 207-774-7871, fax 207-774-7875; www.cascobaylines.com. **Bay View Cruises** operates tours from May through September. Admission. ~ Fisherman's Wharf, 84 Commercial Street, Portland; 207-761-0496.

For something completely different, spend a few days on **Chebeague Island**. One of the 365 Calendar Islands scattered across Casco Bay, Chebeague (pronounced "sha-BEEG") is a small forested island with only a few hundred hardy year-round residents. They earn their living from the sea or commute by ferry to the mainland and then on to Portland, which is approximately a half-hour's drive from the ferry parking area. Chebeague is a place for people who love to walk or bike along quiet roads. You can easily visit the island as a day trip. In Cumberland, call **Chebeague Transportation Company**. ~ 207-846-3700. In Portland, call **Casco Bay Lines**. ~ 207-774-7871.

◄ HIDDEN

About 20 miles north of Portland along Route 1 is the world-famous town of **Freeport**, home of the legendary **L. L. Bean**. The mall-like shop looks just like the catalogs: it's wall-to-wall camping gear, outdoor wear and sporting equipment. Aside from Bean's, the whole town has sprouted into a factory-outlet hub. You'll find all the big-name designers (Polo–Ralph Lauren, Calvin Klein, Laura Ashley) have set up shop here. This is definitely the place to come with your shopping lists. ~ Route 1, Freeport; 207-865-4761.

Bowdoin College is the spot where Harriet Beecher Stowe wrote *Uncle Tom's Cabin*, reportedly after seeing a vision.

A few miles down the road, Brunswick is home to **Bowdoin College**, founded in 1794. Such luminaries as Nathaniel Hawthorne and Henry Wadsworth Longfellow have walked the halls of this venerable school. ~ College Street, Brunswick; 207-725-3000; www.bowdoin.edu.

The next town along the coast is **Bath**, which holds in its borders a wealth of shipbuilding history. In the days of wooden ships, nearly half the world's seacraft came from Bath's shipyards. For a journey back to that era, stop by the **Maine Maritime Museum**. From June to October, visiting vessels are docked here and open to visitors. The museum's four venues, which are open year-round, also showcase marine artifacts, a working shipyard and a lobstering exhibit. Admission. ~ 243 Washington Street, Bath; 207-443-1316.

To glimpse a retail business that's dramatically different than the Freeport scene down the coast, pull off in Woolwich (just beyond Bath) at the **Montsweagg Flea Market**. One of the state's biggest flea markets, Montsweagg features hundreds of dealers peddling everything from old postcards to used trailers. Even if you're not in the market for anything, it's worth stopping just for the shot of local color. ~ Route 1, Woolwich; 207-443-2809.

Wiscasset is a very worthwhile stop as you travel north on Route 1. This lovely little village of sea captains' houses and beautifully maintained old brick buildings was a very prosperous shipping port between the years of the American Revolution and the War of 1812.

HIDDEN ►   **Musical Wonder House** has a collection of antique music boxes, musical automata, victrolas, talking machines and advertising icons such as the RCA Victor dog. Owner Danilo Konvalinka plays the rare Steinway player grand pianola, the classic boxes and other instruments during the tour. The museum, located in a 30-room sea captain's house, is one of the authentic treasures of the Maine Coast. Don't miss it. Closed late October through May 25. Admission. ~ 18 High Street, Wiscasset; 207-882-7163.

There's something incredibly lovable about the seaport of **Boothbay Harbor**, down a peninsula south of Wiscasset. Admittedly, it's about as overripe as a tourist town can be—and it's hit by around 500,000 visitors each summer. But Boothbay (which started life as a tiny lobstering and fishing town) definitely has a personality of its own.

If you've come to Maine for the serenity of the sea, you're best off totally skipping Boothbay. Though there are the customary seaside elements (soaring seagulls, lobster traps, bobbing buoys), this village leans more to manmade amusements. Just pause on the footbridge that stretches across the harbor and you'll hear bowling balls trundling down alleys, the ringing and dinging of pinball machines and the smack of a cue stick hitting a pool ball. The beauty of Boothbay, however, extends far beyond the footbridge. Walk into any restaurant, and you're sure to be served by a genuinely cheery college waiter or waitress whom—by the end of the meal—you'll know absolutely everything about.

Besides popping in and out of the dozens of shops and galleries that crowd around the hilly little streets, there are several ways to amuse yourself in Boothbay. One of the very best is by taking a boat trip. Several booths on the wharf sell tickets for anything from a one-hour sunset cruise to an all-day outing to nearby Monhegan (see the "Beaches & Parks" section in this chapter). If time is limited, at least go out on a short trip. You'll glide by tiny islands covered with spruce and fir trees, colonies of seals lounging around with their bellies up and the kinds of birds you've seen on the pages of *National Geographic*. If you're lucky, you'll spot a great blue heron standing in the water like a caryatid.

The sweet little village of **Waldoboro** is one of the next towns you'll come to as you continue up Route 1. It has several old homes and a Lutheran church that dates back to 1771. Farther out on that peninsula (following Route 220) is **Friendship**, a picturesque lobstering port. You have to go around the inlet and then out to the tip of St. George Peninsula to get to **Port Clyde**, launching site for the mail boat to Monhegan Island. You can head out to the island from here or take a boat from Boothbay Harbor. **Monhegan Island**, a mere smidgen on the map (less than two miles long and one mile wide), has been known as a popular artists and writers retreat for years. Its scenery is striking: steep cliffs thrashed by Atlantic surf and graced with pine forests and golden meadows. The lighthouse was built in 1824. The island's many hiking trails give the visitor on foot a chance to scout out its lovely terrain.

On your way back to Route 1, take time to visit the picture-perfect waterfront towns of **Tenants Harbor** and **Spruce Head**. Around this point of the coast—at **Penobscot Bay**—you start to see the Maine coastline everyone has always raved about. There are startlingly beautiful islands rising abruptly out of the choppy waters with sparkling sailboats gracefully skimming the waves.

Most beautiful, though, are the tall-masted **windjammers** that are famous in this area. You can spend three to six days on one, eating hearty home-cooked meals and flitting about from one gor-

geous island to another. The main departure points are located
in the Rockland, Rockport and Camden areas. ~ For further information, contact the Maine Windjammer Association, P.O.
Box 1144, Blue Hill, ME 04614; 800-807-9463; www.midcoast.
com/~sailmwa.

The towns of **Rockland** and **Camden** are fishing villages that
have been discovered by tourists. They are "cute" and can be
counted on for restaurants, shops and inns. Some say they're too
cute and have given in to the pressures of pleasing tourists, there-
fore losing their original charms.

One very worthwhile attraction in the area is the **William A.
Farnsworth Library & Art Museum**. Founded in 1948 with a
bequest from Lucy Farnsworth, the museum showcases American
art with a focus on the state of Maine. Among its holdings are
works by Thomas Eakins, Winslow Homer and Edward Hopper.
Two gallery buildings are devoted to the works of the Wyeth
family. Between them, they hold more than 4000 works by Andrew Wyeth and an extensive collection of works by N.C. Wyeth
and Jamie Wyeth. In addition to the art museums, the complex
includes the adjacent Farnsworth family homestead (one of the
finest Victorian-era residences on the East Coast) and the nearby Olson house, where Andrew Wyeth's masterpiece *Christina's
World* is on display. Closed Monday from Columbus Day through
Memorial Day. Admission. ~ Elm and Main streets, Rockland;
207-596-6457.

You should also visit the **Owls Head Transportation Museum**,
which houses one of the country's most impressive collections of
antique planes and cars, as well as engines, bicycles and carriages.
Here you can see an exact replica of the Wright Brothers' flier,
along with displays explaining the technological advances that
the brothers made. Admission. ~ Route 73, just south of Rockland; 207-594-4418.

As you continue up the coast, you'll come to **Searsport**, an old
shipping port with stately old sea captains' homes and a multitude of antique shops. **Bucksport** is next. It's home to the **Fort
Knox State Historic Site**, a very impressively constructed fort that
was manned during the Civil and Spanish-American wars. Tours
available in the summer. Closed November through April. Admission. ~ On Route 174, just off Route 1 west of the Waldo-
Hancock Bridge, Bucksport; 207-469-7719.

From there, you can take Route 15 right into **Bangor**, Maine's
third-largest city and a commercial and lumbering center. Take
time to stroll around the **West Market Square Historic District**
(a mid-19th-century block of shops) and the **Broadway Area**,
where you'll see one lumber baron's mansion after another lined
up as if contestants in a beauty contest. Then, jumping from the
sublime to the unusual, you can spot the huge—31-foot-tall,

3000-pound—statue of **Paul Bunyan** (Main Street), which com-
memorates the town's great logging past.

Maine accommodations come in all sizes and shapes, from con-
ventional sea-viewing motels to European-style inns. Most are
concentrated along the coast, predominantly in the southern and
midcoast regions. Many places are seasonal, open only during the
warm-weather months, so you should call ahead if you're traveling during the late fall or winter.

LODGING

You have two options at **Dockside Guest Quarters**. You can
stay either in the main house (a stately 19th-century building with
five guest rooms) or in one of the 20 modern shore-hugging units.
If it's charm you're after, go for the main house, where rooms are
individually decorated with antiques and floral fabrics. Two rooms
share a bath while the other three have private baths. Choose one
of the "units" for extra privacy. Though not exactly oozing with
charm, they're very separate. Open weekends only November
through May. Closed January. ~ Harris Island Road, York; 207-
363-2868, 800-270-1977, fax 207-363-1977. DELUXE.

Though right on Route 1, **Cape Neddick House** provides the
kind of hospitality and homeyness you'd expect to find in the deep
woods of Maine. There are five antique-furnished bedrooms in
this 1885 Victorian farmhouse, each named after one of the New
England states. You can't help but feel as if you're living back
in the 1800s when you stay here. The breakfast that comes with
a night's stay typically includes cinnamon popovers, strawberry
scones and fresh fruit. A five-course gourmet dinner is available
from fall through spring by advance reservation. ~ 1300 Route
1, Cape Neddick; 207-363-2500, fax 207-363-4499. MODERATE.

Located on a quiet street near Marginal Way (a footpath on
the ocean's edge), **The Heritage of Ogunquit** is a Victorian reproduction. A gay-friendly establishment, its clientele is predominately women. All five guest rooms have private baths. There is
an indoor hot tub and giant cedar deck plus a common room
with a refrigerator, cooking facilities, a VCR and a TV. ~ 14 Marginal Avenue, Ogunquit; 207-646-7787; www.one-on-onepc.
com/heritage. MODERATE.

The Inn at Two Village Square is an exclusively gay/lesbian
Victorian summer home propped up on a hillside. Of its 18
rooms, most have private baths and many offer ocean views.
Though there is plenty of privacy (the inn is on five acres), the
beach and gay bars are just a few minutes' walk away. There's
also a heated pool and hot tub. Closed mid-October through
April. ~ 135 Route 1, Ogunquit; 207-646-5779. MODERATE.

A former Catholic church, **The Haven** is now a delightful bed
and breakfast lovingly operated by John and Susan Jarvis. All
seven rooms have private baths, while the common areas include

a lobby with a three-story cathedral ceiling. You'll find a direct view of the ocean and a beach only 200 steps away. ~ Church Street, Wells; 207-646-4194. MODERATE.

Situated on three and a half acres two miles north of Kennebunk, **Arundel Meadows Inn** is a gay-friendly bed and breakfast. Seven guest rooms in this restored farmhouse (it dates back to 1827) are decorated with antiques and original artwork. Each has its own bathroom; three have fireplaces. There is a pool and jacuzzi. A full breakfast is served. ~ 1024 Portland Road, Arundel; 207-985-3770. MODERATE TO DELUXE.

One of the most wonderful things about the **Captain Lord Mansion** is that it successfully combines impeccably good taste with true comfort. Designed by Captain Lord, a wealthy merchant and shipbuilder, it's a stunning three-story Federal-style building that dates back to 1812. There is also a smaller 1807 house with additional guest rooms. Inside, it has all the hallmarks of a ship carpenter's craft, including a suspended elliptical staircase, blown-glass windows and mahogany doors with brass locks. Each of its 20 rooms has been decorated with period-reproduction wallpaper, exquisite antiques and four-poster and canopy beds. Most have gas fireplaces; all have private baths. ~ Pleasant and Green streets, Kennebunkport; 207-967-3141, fax 207-967-3172. ULTRA-DELUXE.

When George Bush was president, the **Cape Arundel Inn** was *the* place to be—it overlooks the Bush family compound. But even if you couldn't care less about what was once the Summer White House, it's a good choice. Propped up on cliff-hanging Ocean Avenue, it's just one of several eye-poppingly beautiful shingle-style buildings that line the road. From the wraparound porch and some of the 14 rooms of this 1895 Victorian house, you have a wide-angle view of Walker's Point and the Atlantic all around. Continental breakfast included. Closed January through March. ~ Ocean Avenue, Kennebunkport; 207-967-2125. ULTRA-DELUXE.

Back in the late 1800s when wealthy out-of-staters were flocking to Maine to build their summer houses, the **Black Point Inn** came into being. Like many of its neighbors, it's a massive shingled building complete with a front porch and far-reaching ocean views. The main house has 60 guest rooms, and there are another 20 in cottages on the grounds. Two meals. ~ Prouts Neck; 207-883-4126, 800-258-0003, fax 207-883-9976. ULTRA-DELUXE.

The **Inn at Park Spring** is the type of place that doesn't have to advertise. This elegantly furnished three-story Victorian rowhouse's six rooms are usually filled with found-it-by-word-of-mouthers. All rooms have private baths. A full breakfast of croissants, homemade muffins and more tops the bill. ~ 135 Spring Street, Portland; 207-774-1059, 800-437-8511; www.innatpark spring.com. DELUXE.

The **West End Inn** is a six-room bed and breakfast in a 19th-century brick townhouse that was built in 1871. There are two king and four queen-size (all four-poster canopies) guest rooms all with private baths and cable televisions. Each room is beautifully decorated in Waverly or Ralph Lauren decor. There is also a living room available for guests. The inn is located on the historic Western Prom minutes away from the old port. ~ 146 Pine Street, Portland; 207-772-1377, 800-338-1377. MODERATE.

Maine is home to some 1.2 million year-round residents, a startlingly small number when you consider it's as big as all of the other New England states put together.

The **Inn on Carleton** not only sounds like a place you'd find in London but looks like it, too. This townhouse in the Western Promenade part of town offers six rooms lavishly decorated with Victorian antiques; all have private baths. ~ 46 Carleton Street, Portland; 207-775-1910, 800-639-1779; www.innoncarleton.com. DELUXE.

If you want the big-city hotel experience, try the **Radisson Eastland Hotel**. It's certainly big (204 rooms) and offers all the typical metropolitan-hotel services and amenities, including a health club, a ballroom, restaurants and a cocktail lounge on the top floor. Rooms are conventionally furnished with wall-to-wall carpeting and soft earth tones. Many have delicious harbor views. The building itself is a landmark, originally built in 1927 as the Eastland Hotel. ~ 157 High Street, Portland; 207-775-5411, 800-333-3333, fax 207-775-2872. DELUXE TO ULTRA-DELUXE.

If peace and quiet in a remote country setting sounds good to you, spend a few days at **Chebeague Orchard Bed and Breakfast**. The 1876 Greek Revival home sits behind an impressive stone wall that borders a two-acre apple orchard. The five bedrooms and one apartment are comfortably appointed and tastefully decorated. Three of the rooms have private baths. The hospitable owners are only too happy to suggest walks or bike rides (rentals are available if you didn't bring your own); guests can play a game of croquet, relax on the swing, or look around in the organic flower and vegetable garden. A full breakfast is included. ~ Route 1, Box 453, Chebeague Island, ME 04017; phone/fax 207-846-9488. MODERATE.

If you want to be near L. L. Bean and the profusion of factory outlets that have taken over the once very New England (now almost mall-like) town of Freeport, consider booking a room at the **Harraseeket Inn**. This Colonial-style inn is within walking distance of all the shops and outlets. There are 84 guest rooms, some with jacuzzis, quarter-canopied beds and working fireplaces. Eight of the rooms are in the lovely older section of the building dating from the 1850s. There is a large banquet hall in one wing of the Inn. Rates include a full buffet breakfast and afternoon tea. ~ 162 Main Street, Freeport; 207-865-9377, 800-342-6423, fax 207-865-1684. DELUXE TO ULTRA-DELUXE.

Serenely situated on Westport Island, the **Squire Tarbox Inn** offers 11 guest rooms. Four of them are located in the main Federal-style house, the others, well, er . . . they're in the barn. But don't panic—it's a lovely barn dating back to 1763. And it's spanking clean. Meals in the Colonial dining room are a big part of any stay at the Squire Tarbox Inn. They usually are accompanied by goat cheese, fresh from the resident goats. Closed November through April. Breakfast and dinner. ~ 1181 Maine Road, Westport Island; 207-882-7693. MODERATE TO ULTRA-DELUXE.

Though the **Boothbay Harbor Inn** is clearly a motel (and not an inn as the name leads one to believe), it does have some personality. For one thing, it's smack-dab on the water. You walk into your room, roll open the glass doors and *voilà!* The bobbing buoys, the wooden fishing boats, the screaming gulls—you feel as if you've just walked into the postcard you bought down at the desk. Don't get your hopes up about the rooms, however. They are about as generic as motel rooms get. All 60 rooms have private baths, though. Closed November through April. ~ 37 Atlantic Avenue, Boothbay Harbor; phone/fax 207-633-6302, 800-533-6302; www.boothbayharborinn.com. ULTRA-DELUXE.

One look at the cluttered little streets of Boothbay Harbor and you'll be happy you're staying at the **Spruce Point Inn**. It's set apart from the ongoing carnival of town, on a 100-acre peninsula at the eastern end of the harbor. There's a main inn as well as a handful of cottages and lodges scattered around the grounds; some offer ocean views and private decks. Sports are big here, with two pools, clay tennis courts, a putting green, a playground and some lawn games. Closed mid-October to mid-May. ~ Spruce Point on Atlantic Avenue, Boothbay Harbor; 207-633-4152, 800-553-0289, fax 207-633-7138. ULTRA-DELUXE.

You can walk to the center of the village in minutes from the **Broad Bay Inn & Gallery**, a lovely Colonial house built in 1830 offering bed and breakfast. The five rooms are very New England with canopy beds and brightly polished antiques. There is a back deck and a garden with a hammock. Take time to stroll around the art gallery and art library, which is run by innkeeper Libby Hopkins. Several art classes are offered in the summer ~ 1014 Main Street, Waldoboro; 207-832-6668, 800-736-6769; www.midcoast.com/broadbayinn. MODERATE.

Set amongst the historic seaport buildings of Rockland is the **Captain Lindsey House Inn**, a nine-room inn that was built in 1837. All of the rooms are decorated with antiques and furnishings from around the world. Great attention is given to comfortable details including down comforters and European-style pillows on all the beds. There's a large living room with a fireplace and soft down couches plus a library with comfortable reading chairs and a computer port. ~ 5 Lindsey Street, Rockland; 207-596-7950, 800-523-2145; www.rocklandmaine.com. MODERATE TO DELUXE.

The **Blue Harbor House** in Camden is a restored 1810 New England Cape (and carriage house) with ten guest rooms. All are beautifully furnished with soft colors, country fabrics, comfortable antiques and hand-fashioned quilts. Some have canopy beds; all have private baths. Breakfast—which includes specialties such as lobster quiche, cheese soufflé and blueberry pancakes—are always memorable affairs. Dinner is also available. The inn is a short walk from the waterfront. ~ 67 Elm Street, Camden; 207-236-3196, 800-248-3196, fax 207-236-6523; www.blueharbor house.com. MODERATE TO ULTRA-DELUXE.

Choosing just one inn in Camden is like picking one chocolate out of a whole box. There are many you'll want to try. Be that as it may, you definitely won't be sorry if you stay at the **Edgecombe–Coles House**. Set back behind a tall private hedge, it's a beautifully maintained 19th-century house with half a dozen rooms. Three of them are especially blessed with views of Penobscot Bay, which sparkles like mica off in the distance. All the rooms are attractively decorated with Early American furniture, antique knickknacks and turn-of-the-20th-century art. A night's stay includes breakfast on the porch with a view of the bay and free bicycles for guests' use. ~ 64 High Street, Camden; 207-236-2336, 800-528-2336, fax 207-236-6227; www.camdenbandb.com. DELUXE TO ULTRA-DELUXE.

Many of the most beautiful houses in the state of Maine were once sea captains' homes. Such is the case with **Cap'n Am's**, a bed and breakfast right on the water. The rambling Cape-style abode, originally built in the late 1700s, has a wraparound porch. There are three guest rooms, two with far-reaching ocean views and all with shared baths. Closed from Labor Day through Memorial Day. ~ 77 Flood's Cove Road, Friendship; 207-832-5144. MODERATE.

For years, **The Trailing Yew** has been a favorite among artists   ◄ HIDDEN
visiting Monhegan. It's a friendly place where returning guests are welcomed as if family. Its 37 guest rooms—in four houses and one private cottage—are basic, with kerosene lamps and shared baths. Breakfast and dinner are hearty, home-cooked and served family-style. Special rates for children. Closed from Columbus Day to mid-May. ~ Monhegan Island; 207-596-0440. MODERATE.

The 19th-century **East Wind Inn** looks like something right out of Sarah Orne Jewett's *Country of the Pointed Firs*. Indeed, the author wrote the book in nearby Martinville. The inn is composed of a former sea captain's house, a sail loft and a more modern building. All of the 26 rooms are beautifully furnished with antiques and gaze out over the harbor. This view brings you the Maine coast just as you've pictured it—lobster traps piled high and wooden boats gently undulating with the tide. Closed December through March. ~ Mechanic Street, Tenants Harbor; 207-372-6366, 800-241-8439, fax 207-372-6320; www.eastwind inn.com. DELUXE TO ULTRA-DELUXE.

The beautiful, four-story **Phenix Inn** is located in the heart of historic Bangor. This 1873 brick structure, listed on the National Historic Registry, was lovingly restored and renovated. The European Victorian interior motif features mahogany and leather antique reproduction furnishings. ~ West Market Square, 20 Broad Street, Bangor; 207-947-0411, fax 207-947-0255; www.maine guide.com/bangor/phenixinn.com. MODERATE.

DINING

The **Cape Neddick Inn and Gallery** is a local legend of sorts, having been remarkably rebuilt after a fire damaged the original landmark building. The dining room is tastefully decorated with artworks. And though you are actually sitting in a gallery, there is a wonderful warmth to the place. The changing menu generally features lots of fish, lamb and duckling dishes accompanied by celestial sauces. ~ Route 1, Cape Neddick; 207-363-2899. MODERATE TO ULTRA-DELUXE.

The **Cape Neddick Lobster Pound** is not just lobster and clams. It boasts an array of other dishes such as reef and beef kebab, a mix of skewered shrimp, scallops, steak and vegetables. Its setting is fairly predictable in these parts—a shingled building right on the water. Closed October through April, depending on the season. ~ Shore Road off Route 1A, Cape Neddick; 207-363-5471. MODERATE TO DELUXE.

Follow your noses into **Pie in the Sky Bakery** if you're looking for a snack. Baker/owners John and Nancy Stern seem to be on a never-ending roll of creating one yummy treat after another, including breads, muffins and, of course, pies. Closed January; closed Tuesday from September through December, and Tuesday and Wednesday from February through April. ~ Route 1 and River Road, Cape Neddick; 207-363-2656. BUDGET.

For a quiet, elegant dinner in Ogunquit, try **Tavern at Clay Hill Farm**. It's a lovely New England restaurant located in an old farmhouse just west of the village. The menu is rather refined, with items like seared salmon with a dijon, caper and roasted pepper sauce, and roast duckling. A dreamy pianist provides the background music throughout dinner. Dinner only. Closed Tuesday through Thursday in January and February. ~ 220 Clay Hill Road, Ogunquit; 207-646-2272. MODERATE TO DELUXE.

Look for crowds outside **Barnacle Billy's**, a basic Maine lobster joint where you pull a number, wait to be called and then settle in for a feast. You can sit in the dining room, which has the air of a bustling fish house, or on the deck, where you can gaze out at boats while you eat. Closed mid-October to mid-April. ~ Perkins Cove, Ogunquit; 207-646-5575. BUDGET TO DELUXE.

A good spot to grab a sandwich is **Hamilton's Family Restaurant**. You can sit at the counter or grab a table and order up a pastrami sandwich, a bagel or any of the other traditional deli selections. The one big difference between Hamilton's and a real New York deli is the quality of the clam chowder. Here it's dense with clams and deliriously good. There's also take-out service. ~ 2 Shore Road, Ogunquit; 207-646-5262. BUDGET.

The menu is what drew us into the **White Barn Inn**, a barn-turned-restaurant. The cuisine is somewhat of a departure from the norm in these parts; the prix-fixe four-course dinners change seasonally and may feature Maine lobster and sweetbreads ragout, grilled tenderloin of beef with a carmel potato custard, and grilled vegetables with tomato coulis and basil oil. All this in a lovely candlelit barn. Closed January. ~ 37 Beach Street, Kennebunk Beach; 207-967-2321. ULTRA-DELUXE.

Expect perfection at the **Kennebunkport Inn**. This ultra-elegant restaurant prides itself on making sure everything is just right. The hushed Colonial dining room is a fitting background for a candlelight dinner of flawlessly grilled native salmon, traditional bouillabaisse or rack of lamb. In the summer months, you can opt to eat on the outdoor patio. There is also a turn-of-the-20th-century pub with a piano bar. Closed October through April. ~ 1 Dock Square, Kennebunkport; 207-967-2621. DELUXE TO ULTRA-DELUXE.

Windows on the Water has a major-league claim to fame. Its chef—John—was one of 52 who prepared food for former President Bush's inauguration. Admittedly, the food is right up there with the best, including dishes like lobster ravioli drizzled with drambuie cream and grilled prosciutto-wrapped shrimp. The *spécialité de la maison* is the lobster-stuffed potato, a concoction of fresh lobster, cream and Jarlsberg cheese fitted into one half of a hot baked potato. Scrumptious! The view almost one-ups the meal, however. Diners look out at the busy little port through the arched windows or from the terrace during warm-weather months. ~ 12 Chase Hill Road, Kennebunkport; 207-967-3313. DELUXE TO ULTRA-DELUXE.

For some real down-to-earth Maine dining, head to **Nunan's Lobster Hut**. Here you can stuff yourselves on ultra-fresh lobster and piles of steamers and top it all off with homemade apple or blueberry pie. It's a typically casual Maine restaurant, housed in a low-slung shed. Dinner only. Closed October 15 to May 1. ~ Mill Road, Cape Porpoise; 207-967-4362. MODERATE.

The **Back Bay Grill** is in a novel location: a restored 1888 pharmacy. But for the original pressed-tin ceiling, however, it retains no hint of its earlier incarnation. Now, it's a very elegant-looking restaurant (complete with white tablecloths). Local art adorns the walls, including a lively 22-foot mural of the restaurant in one dining room. One of the two dining areas is open to the kitchen. The New American menu is seasonal and has many offerings, including pasta dishes and fresh seafood. The kitchen does its own baking; try the crème brulée. The extensive wine list won the board of excellence from *Wine Spectator* magazine. ~ 65 Portland Street, Portland; 207-772-8833; www.backbaygrill.com. DELUXE TO ULTRA-DELUXE.

David's Creative Cuisine offers a range of food including seafood, such as lobster and salmon, vegetarian dishes, gourmet pizzas, filet mignon and their special cinnamon pork chops. Dinner only. ~ 22 Monument Square, Portland; 207-773-4340. MODERATE TO DELUXE.

If you want to combine dining with a bit of partying, find your way to the **Great Lost Bear**. This is one of Portland's most popular bar-cum-restaurants where you can count on getting the old standbys like chili, burgers, steaks and salads. It's located in the former Cameo Theater in Portland's tiny SoFo (Southside Forest Avenue) District. ~ 540 Forest Avenue, Portland; 207-772-0300. BUDGET TO MODERATE.

For Northern Italian cuisine, you can't go wrong with **The Roma**. Located in a Victorian mansion (circa 1885), it has six dining rooms—some with fireplaces. Especially good are the seafood dishes, including lobster. ~ 769 Congress Street, Portland; 207-773-9873. MODERATE TO ULTRA-DELUXE.

The owners of **Le Garage** have a good sense of humor. After all, this really is a 1920s-era garage-turned-restaurant. You'd hardly know it though, since they've gussied the place up and added on a glassed-in porch. The food is very good (predominately seafood, but lamb, steaks and chicken, too) and the value unmatchable. Closed January. ~ Water Street, Wiscasset; 207-882-5409. BUDGET TO DELUXE.

A two-story restaurant right in the pulsating heart of things, the **Black Orchid Restaurant** serves by-the-book Italian. In its dimly lit and somewhat cramped rooms, you can stuff yourselves on all the standard Mediterranean favorites such as fettuccine with fresh mushrooms and lobster in Alfredo sauce as well as a selection of local fish dishes. Save room for the *tiramisu*. Closed mid-October to mid-May. ~ 12 By-Way, Boothbay Harbor; 207-633-6659. MODERATE TO DELUXE.

Located on the wharf, the nautically themed **J. H. Hawk Restaurant and Pub** is a testament to the owner's sailing fanaticism. There's a casual dining room serving a diverse menu, from hamburgers with all the trimmings to Hawk's Haddock Royale: a haddock filet baked with a Maine lobster crumb topping and bernaise sauce. For dessert, try the chocolate hazelnut mousse. Piano music provides background delights in the evening, except Wednesday, when there are live bands. Closed November through April. ~ Pier 1, Boothbay Harbor; 207-633-5589. MODERATE TO DELUXE.

In spite of its magnet-for-tourists location, **Harborside Restaurant** attracts quite a few locals for all three meals. Lines form outside for the breakfasts, which are prefaced by large cinnamon rolls fresh out of the oven and dripping with a glassy icing. Lunch and dinner dishes are largely of the seafood variety, though you can get meat and poultry dishes as well. The restaurant is unimaginatively decorated, but the setting—inches from the water's edge—makes it enormously appealing. Closed mid-October to mid-May. ~ 12 Bridge Street, Boothbay Harbor; 207-633-4074. MODERATE TO DELUXE.

Any trip to Maine would not be complete without one meal at a diner. That's where you see the real characters, the perennial Mainers. One of our favorites is **Moody's Diner**. It's been passed down through the Moody family for generations. The decor is authentic dineresque. The menu is mainstream but good enough to make you want to go back several times—especially for breakfast! ~ Route 1, Waldoboro; 207-832-7468. BUDGET.

Tired of understated decor? Then make a beeline for the **Harbor View Tavern** where you'll find carriages hanging from the ceiling, airplanes built out of tin cans, nautical mementos, violins, trombones and enough mirrors to make a Caesar's Palace executive feel right at home. Graze on appetizers like fried mozzarella or the deep-fried calamari. Then move in on mussels in cream, scallops au gratin, sirloin or a shrimp boat. There's prime rib on weekends. Ask for a seat on the enclosed deck or open terrace and you'll enjoy a great view. ~ 1 Water Street, Thomaston; 207-354-8173. MODERATE.

The **Waterworks Pub and Restaurant** is locally famed for its super-fresh seafood and pub fare. Its long mahogany bar (where Maine-brewed ales, single malts, brandies and wines are served) is also a local favorite. The restaurant is part of a completely restored building that belonged to a waterworks company. The menu always includes the freshest seafood available as well as vegetarian dishes and plenty of meat dishes, including a delicious meatloaf. For dessert, the apple crisp served with cinnamon ice cream is not to be missed. ~ 5 Lindsey Street, Rockland; 207-596-7950, 800-523-2145; www.rocklandmaine.com. BUDGET TO ULTRA-DELUXE.

Even the most self-assured diners can't make up their mind what to order at **The Waterfront**. The dinner menu lists an inviting selection of specialties including crabcakes. And, of course, there are lobsters and steamers to further throw you into a tizzy. The setting—right on the harbor—is unmatchable. ~ Bayview Street, Camden; 207-236-3747. MODERATE.

Scooping up spoonfuls of clam chowder at **Cappy's Chowder House** is close to having a spiritual experience. But that's just the chowder. Cappy's is also famed for its seafood dishes, pasta, hamburgers—you name it. It's a pubby kind of place with nautical decor, always abuzz with both out-of-towners and salty locals. Closed Wednesday in the winter. ~ 1 Main Street, Camden; 207-236-2254. MODERATE.

One of the oldest family-operated restaurants in Maine (opened in 1940), **Pilot's Grill** serves up home-style American food, with an accent on local seafood: fried clams, broiled scallops and baked salmon. You'll also find steaks, roast beef, lamb chops and pasta dishes. The neat brick eatery has tables covered with linen cloths and fresh flowers. ~ 1528 Hammond Street, Bangor; 207-942-6325. MODERATE TO DELUXE.

SHOPPING   The most southern part of Maine, along Route 1, seems to be suffering—actually, prospering would be a more accurate term—from factory-outlet-and-mall-itis. Discount stores are everywhere. Unless you've come specifically to scout out bargains, you might be better off sniffing out the small shops, especially those that specialize in Maine arts and crafts. (See "State of the Artists" in this chapter.)

In York, stop by **The Old York Historical Society Museum and Gift Shop**. It offers a delightful array of traditional Maine crafts along with a large collection of Maine books. Closed Monday and from January through April. ~ 196 York Street, Route 1A and Lindsay Road, York; 207-363-4974.

R. Jorgensen Antiques is definitely worth stopping at, unlike some of the faux-antiques shops that have staked out prime tourist territory on the coast. There's a little bit of everything here, including genuine Americana and 18th- and 19th-century antiques and accessories. Closed Wednesday. ~ Route 1, Wells; 207-646-9444.

If you're in the market for some pottery, stop by **The Good Earth**. It's filled with decorative stoneware and cooking pieces in a fascinating array of designs—all produced by local potters. Closed December 25 through May 15. ~ Dock Square, Kennebunkport; 207-967-4635.

Some very attractive wood carvings, wooden boxes and other functional wares are found at **Gerard Craft Woodproducts**. They are all skillfully handcrafted by Gerry and Linda Laberge. Open by appointment or by chance. ~ 510 Mitchell Road, Cape Elizabeth; 207-799-3526.

In Portland, the best shopping can be found at the **Old Port Exchange**, along Fore and Exchange streets. For American crafts, make your way to **Abacus**. Over 600 of the country's craftspeople are represented here. (There are also galleries in Boothbay Harbor, Kennebunkport and Freeport.) ~ 44 Exchange Street, Portland; 207-772-4880.

The Maine Potters' Market is just as it sounds: a cooperative where you can shop for clay works created by local potters. In fact, it's the largest potters co-op in the state. You'll find more than a dozen artists displaying a wonderful selection of traditional pieces as well as avant-garde finds. ~ 376 Fore Street, Portland; 207-774-1633; www.mainepottersmarket.com.

Pick up sandwiches and other provisions at the **Island Market**, Chebeague Island's only store, where you're sure to meet the owner, congenial Chebeague native Ed Doughty. ~ South Road, Chebeague Island; 207-846-9997.

You'll find an amazing selection of wonderfully detailed maps of Maine (as well as other areas) at **The DeLorme Map Store**. ~ 2 DeLorme Drive, Yarmouth; 888-227-1656.

It's been called the preppy mecca, among other things. But love it or not, don't deny yourself the privilege of seeing **L. L. Bean**. Today, the quality of the rugged outdoor clothes and equipment is legendary, and the store—a huge mall-like building—is open 24 hours a day, 7 days a week, 365 days a year. L. L. Bean's success comes largely from marketing the image of Maine (outdoors, fresh air, healthy) and the Maine people (hard-working, rugged, independent). ~ Route 1, Freeport; 207-865-4761.

> L. L. Bean was started by an avid outdoorsman who built up a mail-order business for his Maine hunting shoe.

Right in the heart of the factory outlet town of Freeport stands the **Harrington House Museum Store**, a lovely Greek Revival house. It holds fine examples of the state's craftmanship, from handwoven baskets and reproduction cast-iron toys to 19th-century pieces. Limited hours in the winter. ~ 45 Main Street, Freeport; 207-865-0477.

Pop into the Boothbay Harbor branch of **Abacus** just to take a quick look around and an hour later, you realize you're still there. It has a captivating selection of crafts by a variety of American artisans. Check out the oak bentwood rocking chairs by Paul Miller. Closed November through April. ~ 8 McKown Street, Boothbay Harbor; 207-633-2166.

It may never have occurred to you that you needed a chowder mug. But one look at the selection of **Edgecomb Potters'** mugs and you can't live without one. But that's not all. The Potters' high-gloss, berry-colored pieces come in all sizes and shapes, from very attractive creamer and sugar sets to huge bowls. You'll also find

Text continued on page 576.

State of the Artists

L ike all beautiful places, Maine draws artists like a magnet. Along the shore, you'll spot painters studying the colors of the sea before easels firmly rooted in the sand. Shops often display watercolors, sculpture and jewelry by local artisans. Even in rural villages, you'll find artwork as impressive as that of sophisticated urban areas and European capitals. In fact, many resident Maine artists hold national or international reputations. Some of their studios and workshops are open to the public. Here's a sampling of what you'll find.

In Portland's Old Port District lies the **Maine Potter's Market**, a cooperative gallery featuring the work of 15 potters from the state of Maine. ~ 376 Fore Street; 207-774-1633.

Of course, you won't want to miss the prominent **Portland Museum of Art**, the state's oldest art museum. Its rooms are filled with the work of Maine natives Wyeth, Hopper and Homer. You'll also view pieces by Monet, Renoir, Degas and Picasso. Daily tours are available. Closed Monday from late October to late June. Admission. ~ 7 Congress Square; 207-773-2787.

It may be just a barn, but that building behind the **Broad Bay Inn and Gallery** features watercolor paintings and hosts several workshops during the summer. The gallery sells gift items such as puppets and books on Maine. Several art classes are also offered. Closed mid-October to late June. ~ 1014 Main Street, Waldoboro Village; 207-832-6668, 800-736-6769; www.midcoast.com/broadbayinn.

Maine Coast Artists, located in a historic firehouse, is a nonprofit gallery dedicated to promoting contemporary Maine art. During the summer they offer classes and workshops. Admission. ~ 162 Russell Avenue, Rockport; 207-236-2875.

A self-taught artist, Jud Hartman has created a series of bronze sculptures depicting the Amerindians of the Northeast. You can view them at the **Jud Hartman Gallery and Sculpture Studio**, along with watercolor paintings by William Bracken. Closed mid-September to mid-June. Also closed Sunday during the summer if it is sunny weather. ~ Main Street, Blue Hill; 207-374-9917 (from mid-June to mid-September only) or 207-359-2544.

Works by over 30 contemporary artists are on view at the well-known **Leighton Gallery**. The exhibit changes monthly, and the grounds also feature a sculpture garden. Closed mid-October to late May. ~ Parker Point Road, Blue Hill; 207-374-5001; www.leightongallery.com.

A large number of artists and craftspeople live and work on Deer Isle. For starts, you'll find **Ronald Hayes Pearson's Studio/Gallery**. This is definitely a high-risk zone if you're trying not to spend money; his sterling silver and gold jewelry pieces are stunning. Closed Sunday. ~ Old Ferry Road; 207-348-2535. The **Turtle Gallery** features works by regional artists and craftspeople. In the summer, the gallery offers two- and three-week exhibitions in a wide variety of media, including watercolors, oils, glassworks, collage, sculpture and clay. Closed October through April. ~ Just north of Deer Isle on Route 15; 207-348-9977.

On that same serene little island, at the end of a bumpy dirt road, you'll find the **Haystack Mountain School of Crafts**. Here artists from around the world gather to produce works in metal, textiles, wood, glass, pottery and paper. The school is housed in a series of studios designed by noted architect Edward Larrabee Barnes. Works created here are not for sale at the school, but you can purchase them at various studios and galleries around the island, including the Blue Heron Gallery and Studio in Deer Isle Village. A free tour of the school is conducted on Wednesday at 1 p.m. Call ahead for information. Closed September through May. ~ South of Deer Isle Village, turn left off Route 15 onto Sunshine Road and follow signs for about seven miles, Sunshine Village; 207-348-2306.

As one Eastport artist put it, "All great places are discovered—or rediscovered—by artists." Such is the case with this former sardine-canning town on the northernmost coast of Maine. Here, the painters and potters are the prominent citizens, and the works of around 20 artists are on display at the **Eastport Gallery**, two-story gallery. Closed January through April. ~ 69 Water Street; 207-853-4166.

With this list in hand, visitors will surely have a great deal of Maine art to choose from or simply to browse through. But travelers in these parts will undoubtedly find worthwhile art throughout the state, sometimes where they least expect it—in a hole-in-the-wall café, perhaps. Or you might discover the next Andrew Wyeth standing right next to you on a scenic stretch of beach, touching up his canvas.

a wide selection of jewelry, iron and glass products in the store. Closed mid-October to late May. ~ McKown Street, Boothbay Harbor; 207-633-4199.

A silver-mirrored disco ball hangs from the ceiling of **Enchantments**, casting confetti-like shadows as it twirls around. The floor is littered with colored metallic stars. This is the place to go for crystals and healing gemstones. It also has a book section that's broken into categories such as Findhorn, New Age, Astrology, Kabbalah, Runes and Fairies and Lore. ~ 10 Boothbay House Hill, Boothbay Harbor; 207-633-4992.

A delicious array of mohair, silk and cotton handwoven scarves, stoles and throws are the results of **Nancy Lubin Designs** hard work. A very worthwhile stop. Open by appointment or chance. ~ 13 Trim Street, Camden; 207-236-4069.

Étienne Perret and Company specializes in fine designer jewelry. Though somewhat pricey, they're cherishable works of art. Closed Sunday in the winter. ~ 20 Main Street, Camden; 207-236-9696, 800-426-4367.

Crafts, crafts and more crafts can be found at the **Maine Gathering**. Over 100 of the state's craftspeople and artisans are shown here. ~ 21 Main Street, Camden; 207-236-9004; www. mainegathering.com.

NIGHTLIFE   The **Ogunquit Playhouse**, which started in 1932, still brings in theater-goers from all over the country. It has a ten-week season every summer, usually with two musicals and three dramatic plays. ~ Route 1, Ogunquit; 207-646-5511; www.ogunquitplay house.org.

Portland is where you'll find the most to do after dark in southern Maine. It's rife with cultural diversions, including the **Portland Stage Company**, which puts on about half a dozen plays per season (September to May). ~ Portland Performing Arts Center, 25-A Forest Avenue, Portland; 207-774-1043.

For something a bit out of the mainstream, contact the **Mad Horse Theatre Company**. They put on four or five plays per season (October to July); most focus on social issues. ~ 92 Oak Street, Portland; phone/fax 207-828-1270; www.madhorse.com. The **Portland Players** have the distinction of being Maine's oldest community theater. The season's four or six productions are performed in an intimate community theater environment. Their season runs from September through June. ~ 207-799-7337, fax 207-767-6208. If musicals are your thing, the small **Lyric Theater** puts on four of them in a September-to-May season. ~ 207-799-6509 or 207-799-1421.

The **Portland Symphony Orchestra** offers classical, chamber pops and holiday concerts from October to July. ~ 477 Congress Street, Portland (administration); 207-773-6128; www.portland

symphony.com, e-mail psobox@portlandsymphony.com. **PCA Great Performances** puts on a variety of concerts—opera, jazz, chamber music and dance—from October through May. ~ 207-773-3150; www.pcagreatperformances.com, e-mail pcabox@pca greatperf.com. Both companies perform in the Merrill Auditorium, in the Portland City Hall at 20 Myrtle Street. For tickets, call PorTix. ~ 207-842-0800.

There's always something happening with the **Center for Cultural Exchange**. They put on numerous music and dance productions from September to June. Every Friday, be the star of your own dance production courtesy of Dance Friday, which features world music from various locations. ~ 1 Longfellow Square, Portland; 207-761-0591; www.artsandculture.org, e-mail portarts@ maine.rr.com.

Dance aficionados can try the **Ram Island Dance Company**. ~ Portland Performing Arts Center, 25-A Forest Avenue, Portland; phone/fax 207-773-2562; e-mail dmcneil1@maine.rr.com.

Portland has quite a few thriving nightspots, such as **Gritty McDuff's Brew Pub**, where you can chomp on fish and chips and down some beers brewed right on the premises. It's a rowdy spot, especially on Saturday nights, when you may have to scream your order across the copper-topped bar. ~ 396 Fore Street, Portland; 207-772-2739.

Another good pub is **Three Dollar Dewey's**, an English-style tavern that prides itself on its wide selection of draught beers and three-alarm chili. A large following of fanatical regulars really whoops it up here, knocking 'em down at long tavern tables. ~ 241 Commercial Street, Portland; 207-772-3310.

Alternative rock, dance and reggae music are all performed at **Bad Habits Live/Zootz**. They feature two full bars and weekend deejay dancing. Cover for live shows and on weekends. ~ 31 Forest Avenue, Portland; 207-773-8187.

The weekend lineup at **Raoul's Roadside Attraction** features live blues, folk or rock performed by local and national talent. Cover. ~ 865 Forest Avenue, Portland; 207-773-6886.

If your timing is right, someone famous—like Bonnie Raitt—will be putting on a show at the **Cumberland County Civic Center**. ~ 1 Civic Center Square, Portland; 207-775-3458, fax 207-828-8344; www.theciviccenter.com.

For additional entertainment suggestions in the Portland area pick up a copy of the *Casco Bay Weekly*. ~ 207-775-6601, fax 207-775-1615; www.cascobayweekly.com.

If you're in the Freeport area after dark, check out some of the **L. L. Bean** Outdoor Discovery Program's evening workshops and clinics at the Casco Street Conference Center and at other locations throughout New England. They offer a vast variety of programs including instruction in flyfishing, kayaking, canoeing, outdoor photography, wilderness survival and more, as well as an introduction to maps and compasses. Call ahead for details and reservations. ~ Casco Street, Freeport; 207-865-4761, 888-552-3261, fax 207-552-2094; www.llbean.com/odp.

From Thursday through Saturday, **Gilbert's Public House** has live bands playing mostly rock-and-roll but also R&B, jazz and pop in a maritime bar setting. There's karaoke on Sunday night. Cover on Friday and Saturday. ~ Sharp's Wharf, Bayview Street, Camden; 207-236-4320.

BEACHES & PARKS

RACHEL CARSON NATIONAL WILDLIFE REFUGE 🏃 This 5000-acre refuge spans approximately 50 miles of Maine's southern coast from Kittery to Cape Elizabeth. Each of ten divisions protects estuarine rivers that form salt marshes where they meet the Atlantic. The wheelchair-accessible Carson Trail (1 mile), located at the Wells headquarters, makes it easy to explore the coast and adjacent woodlands. You'll also find a picnic area and restrooms. This unit is also adjacent to the Wells National Estuarine Research Reserve/Laudholm Farm, a public facility offering seven miles of trails. ~ Headquarters is on Route 9E, west of Kennebunkport; 207-646-9226.

OGUNQUIT BEACH 🏃 🏊 🎣 🚣 Driving along Route 1, you can't help but pull over and gasp at the beauty of this spacious beach. It's utterly magnificent. You see the wild ocean crashing in, waves breaking in a series of prismatic explosions. On a good day, the sky's a beautiful blue punctuated with perfect white clouds. Wide and smooth, the beach stretches for three miles and divides into three main areas. You'll find the most popular expanse at the foot of Beach Street. The Footbridge Street area, slightly less crowded, is off Ocean Street. Moody Beach, off Eldridge Street, is even less peopled. Fishing and whale watching are popular activities here. Since the water temperature rarely exceeds 60° even in July and August, not all people would say swimming is good here. However, for northern Mainers and Canadians, it's tepid. There are restrooms in all three areas, and lifeguards are on duty in summer. ~ Near Ogunquit, off Route 1; 207-646-5533.

WELLS BEACH 🏊 Just north of the wave-slapped sands of Ogunquit Beach, this is similar in its natural beauty. The beach is wide and smooth and has great bodysurfing waves but, ooooh, is the water chilly. It does, however, go a bit overboard with the tourist clutter. There are motels, cottages, condos, lobster huts and restaurants lining the beach. Facilities include toilets, playgrounds, a parking area and lobster huts. ~ On Webhannet Drive in the village of Wells Beach.

GOOCH'S BEACH 🏊 🎣 🚣 🚤 🚣 One look at this beach and you'll understand why former President Bush lives nearby and why everyone else bought summer cottages in this area. It's wildly spacious, long and wide (some fine sand areas, some shingle patches) and smashed by waves that drown out any conversation you might try to have. Add a couple of diving gulls and an invigorating breeze and what more could you possibly want? There are portable toilets. Parking permit required. ~ On Beach Avenue, one and a half miles southwest of Kennebunkport; 207-967-0857.

ARUNDEL (COLONY) BEACH This small sandy pocket has a marvelous air of exclusivity in spite of its Bush Country location. It's backed by huge rocks that are fun for climbing on. It's also right down the coast from Walker's Point, where former President Bush's Summer White House is located. No lifeguards. You can catch a tour trolley (fee) to the beaches at designated stops starting at the head of Ocean Avenue. ~ Off Ocean Avenue, Kennebunkport.

FERRY BEACH STATE PARK Hugging the coastline, this 117-acre preserve is densely scenic. Along with patches of pines and other northern trees, there's a surprising stand of tupelo trees, which are rare at this latitude. The whole park is threaded with self-guiding trails that are wheelchair accessible. Guided nature walks are offered on Sunday. The beach—a sweep of white smashed by Atlantic waves—is perhaps its biggest attraction. Facilities include picnic tables, grills, toilets, changing rooms and lifeguards in summer. Closed October through Memorial Day. Day-use fee, $2 per person. ~ Off Route 9 on Bayview Road, between Camp Ellis and Old Orchard Beach; 207-283-0067.

SCARBOROUGH BEACH PARK Just before ◄ HIDDEN
following Route 207 out to Prouts Neck (a funny shaped little peninsula), you can turn off and find yourselves face to face with a gorgeous sandy beach that's backed by dunes and marshes. It's not big, and it's not heavily populated, thanks to limited parking. There are good bodysurfing waves and almost no undertow. You will find changing rooms, restrooms, drinking water, a snack bar and lifeguards. Day-use fee, $3 per person. ~ Take Route 207, three miles south of Route 1, from the town of Scarborough; 207-883-2416.

▲ There are two campgrounds near this park. Bayley's Camping Resort has 500 tent/RV sites (with hookups); $31.50 to $42 per night. ~ Route 9, Scarborough; 207-883-6043. Wild Duck Campground has 15 tent sites and 60 RV sites (with hookups); $19 to $25 per night. Closed Columbus Day to May 15. ~ Route 9, south of Scarborough; 207-883-4432.

CRESCENT BEACH STATE PARK Located in Cape Elizabeth, this 243-acre park is known for its sandy beach that sprawls on for a mile. It attracts lots of Portland-ers, especially during summer weekends. They come to swim in the sudsy surf and to soak up rays. There are also many water sports to enjoy, mostly at Kettle Cove at one end of the park. The beach is situated so that you're protected from the really cool Atlantic and northern breezes. Elsewhere in the park, you'll find a rocky headland, tidal pools, a freshwater marsh, a spruce and oak forest, and abundant wildlife and birds. Amenities include picnic tables, grills, changing rooms with showers, a playground and a snack bar. Closed Columbus Day to Memorial Day. Day-use fee, $2.50 per person. ~ Along Route 77, eight miles south of Portland; 207-799-5871.

WOLF'S NECK WOODS STATE PARK 🏃 🏕 You don't have to go very far from L. L. Bean's to try out your new hiking boots or cross-country skis. This 250-acre park is in Freeport, about five miles away. It's woven with five miles of well-maintained trails that offer achingly beautiful views of Casco Bay, its spruce and fir-covered islands and the coast's rocky shoreline. The park is largely covered with woods colonized by birds that belt out arias as if they were opera singers. Picnic tables, restrooms and nature programs are available here. Day-use fee, $2 per person. ~ On Wolf Neck Road, south of Freeport; 207-865-4465.

▲ Nearby **Recompence Shores** (Burnett Road, south of Freeport; 207-865-9307) has 100 woodsy or oceanfront tent sites, including eight RV sites with hookups; $14 to $25 per night.

POPHAM BEACH STATE PARK 🏊 🏄 🛶 Seemingly at the end of the world, this park offers an array of beachy pleasures. Along with a spacious sandy beach, there are tidal pools, smooth rocks to climb on and a sand bar to explore when the tide goes out. It's right at the mouth of the Kennebec River. You'll find bathhouses, freshwater showers and charcoal grills. No pets allowed. Day-use fee, $2 per person. ~ Off Route 209, south of Phippsburg; 207-389-1335.

▲ One half mile south of the park entrance is **Ocean View Park** (Route 9, Phippsburg; 207-389-2564), which has 48 tent/RV sites (with hookups); $23 to $24 per night.

REID STATE PARK 🏃 🏕 🏊 🎣 🛶 The centerpiece here is a great expanse of sand beach that stretches nearly a mile and a half and is backed by dunes and marshes. In addition to ocean swimming, there's a saltwater lagoon that is especially great for young children. Fortunately, the area never seems to get too crowded. There are also cross-country trails and ponds for fishing. Facilities include bathhouses with freshwater showers, grills and a snack bar. There are lifeguards. Day-use fee, $2.50 per person. ~ Off Route 127, 14 miles south of Woolwich; 207-371-2303.

RACHEL CARSON SALT POND PRESERVE 🏃 Named for the author of *Silent Spring*, this lovely Pemaquid Peninsula refuge offers a wide range of habitats to explore. Located a few peninsulas north of Boothbay Harbor, the one-quarter acre salt pond is encircled by rocks and home to a multitude of marine species, ducks and other waterfowl. ~ From New Harbor, follow Route 32 for about a mile and look for the entrance sign.

CAMDEN HILLS STATE PARK 🏃 🚲 🐎 A huddle of gentle hills, this park is always lovely whether bundled in mist or reflective as mica. It's laced with wooded trails that wrap around the hills like vines, offering beautiful views of Penobscot Bay, the wind-swept mountain scenery and the piney forests. There's a picnic area and restrooms. Day-use fee, $2 per person. ~ Two miles north of Camden on Route 1; phone/fax 207-236-0849.

▲ There are 112 tent/RV sites (no hookups); $17 per night.

Maine's Downeast Coast extends roughly from the east side of Penobscot Bay up to Calais on the Canadian border. Except in patches, it's not quite as built ▼▼▼▼▼▼▼▼▼▼▼▼ **Downeast Coast** up as the Southern Coast. The farther north you go, the more apt you are to find hidden places and Mainers (who, up here, are called Downeasterners) who are still genuinely curious about travelers. Don't expect to find lots of restaurants, nightlife and that sort of thing. The Downeast Coast—especially in the northern parts—is worlds away from big-city life. We continue up Route 1, veering off to several villages. Our first stop is Castine, poised on the tip of a peninsula about half an hour's drive from Bucksport.

If the state of Maine were to have a Tidy Village Award (like the Cotswolds in England), it would probably go to the village of **SIGHTS** **Castine**. The attraction here is the town itself: a community of ◀ *HIDDEN* 18th- and 19th-century Georgian and Federalist houses standing in impeccable condition. Most of these were originally erected in the mid-19th century when Castine was a prosperous shipbuilding town. Many have since been restored by people "from away" (in other words, big-city folks with money to invest). Much to the objection of some natives, the town is beginning to look and feel like an open-air museum. Like most of these small coastal villages, Castine is best seen *à pied*. For information call the **Town Office**. ~ Court Street, Castine; 207-326-4502, fax 207-326-9465.

From Castine, it's a short, steadily scenic drive over to the village of **Blue Hill**. You'll pass storybook farmhouses, ponies with tangled manes, shiny blue coves surrounded by firs and golden meadows rippling off in every direction. Blue Hill is not for everyone. In fact, many neighboring towns consider it snobby and pretentious. Indeed, it does have a big summer-home-owning community, and you're likely to see BMWs, Mercedes Benzes and Saabs with New York or Massachusetts plates.

The name Blue Hill comes from the hill that looms up behind, supposedly covered with blueberry bushes. The town itself is home to 75 buildings listed on the National Historic Register. Take time out to walk around and poke in the pottery and crafts shops for which Blue Hill is well-known (see the "Shopping" section in this chapter).

If you head southwest of Blue Hill, you'll eventually cut through a corner of Little Deer Isle and then climb an arching suspension bridge that takes you over to **Deer Isle**, a wonderful little island almost too beautiful to promote. Thanks to its seemingly end-of-the-world location, it gets only the serious Maine visitors. For a small island, it's well endowed with attractions—both man-made and natural.

HIDDEN ▶ Tops on our list of worthwhile stops on Deer Isle is the sweet little town of **Stonington** at the southern tip. In a state where once-quaint fishing villages turn into Disneyesque attractions seemingly overnight, this town is a welcome relief. It has everything you've been expecting in Maine—shingled houses, lobster traps piled high, seagulls screeching above, a harbor bundled in mist—but hasn't been completely colonized by the "Kennebushport" crowd. Ask one of the locals to point you in the direction of **Ames Pond**, about a two-minute drive east from the center of town. During the summer months, the rare pink lilies in the pond bloom, turning it into a meadow of pink blossoms.

Plan on arriving for the tour that starts at 1 p.m. at the **Haystack Mountain School of Crafts**. Dramatically situated amidst deep piney woods right on the water, the shingled buildings house artists' studios where you can observe devoted artisans skillfully manipulating clay, blowing glass or working in other media. Tours are given on Wednesday. Closed September through May. ~ South of Deer Isle Village, turn left off Route 15 onto Sunshine Road, and follow signs for about seven miles, Sunshine Village; 207-348-2306.

As you drive back in the direction of the mainland, go slow where you probably missed the turnoff on the way out to **Nervous Nellie's Jams and Jellies**, a jam and jelly kitchen surrounded by landscape sculptures by one of the owners. You're welcome to sample the jams and jellies. We took home a jar of blue-razz conserve and instantly became hooked. Thank goodness they do mail order. ~ Sunshine Road, Deer Isle; 207-348-6182, 800-777-6845, fax 800-804-7698; www.nervousnellie.com.

One of the nicest ways to enjoy Deer Isle is on foot or by kayak (see the "Outdoor Adventures" section at the end of this chapter). Think twice about riding bikes, though. With the narrow, shoulderless roads, it's not only dangerous, apparently the locals abhor bikers slowing down traffic.

Ever since the mid-19th century, **Mount Desert Island** has been one of Maine's most popular destinations. Once you cross the bridge connecting it to the mainland, it's easy to see why. The island (New England's second-largest) is home to **Cadillac Mountain**, at 1530 feet the highest point on the Atlantic coast of the United States. Looming all around are 16 other mountains that drop right down into the sea. Fortunately, most of the island

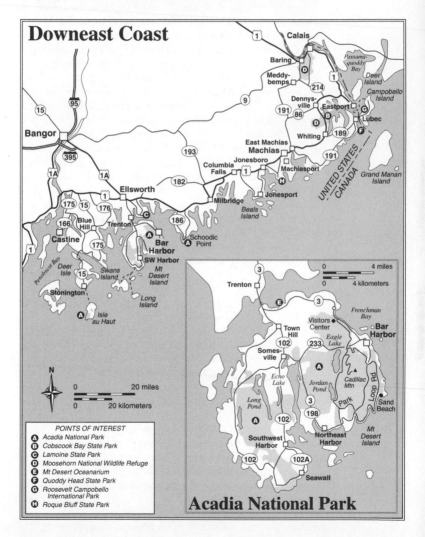

Downeast Coast

POINTS OF INTEREST
- Ⓐ Acadia National Park
- Ⓑ Cobscook Bay State Park
- Ⓒ Lamoine State Park
- Ⓓ Moosehorn National Wildlife Refuge
- Ⓔ Mt Desert Oceanarium
- Ⓕ Quoddy Head State Park
- Ⓖ Roosevelt Campobello International Park
- Ⓗ Roque Bluff State Park

Acadia National Park

(35,000 acres) is under the protection of **Acadia National Park**, which is threaded with miles of hiking, driving and biking trails.

Wherever your peregrinations take you, there's plenty to keep you enormously busy for at least a couple of days on Mount Desert Island. By the way, Mount Desert Island is pronounced like "dessert," the sweet course that follows a meal. It was given the name by French explorer Samuel de Champlain, who discovered the island in 1604. He named it *L'Isle des Monts Déserts* because of its bare, desertlike mountaintops.

Start by heading to **Acadia National Park's visitors center** to pick up a copy of the *Official Map and Guide to Acadia*. There's also a 15-minute introductory video and several racks of nature books. Ask for a copy of *Acadia's Beaver Log*, a park newspaper, if you're interested in finding out that week's naturalist activities. ~ Off Route 3 in Hulls Cove; 207-288-4932.

The **Park Loop Road** takes in the major sights of the park, including Frenchman Bay Overlook, a scenic lookout that faces Schoodic Peninsula; Sieur de Monts Spring, with its nature center; the Wild Gardens of Acadia, a lovely patch featuring local flowers, trees and shrubs; Sand Beach, made partially of the crushed shells of marine animals; the Abbe Museum of Stone Age Antiquities (admission), showcasing prehistoric artifacts of the area's original Indian tribes; and the summit of Cadillac Mountain. The road traverses approximately 27 miles up mountains, by the sea, through forests and past ponds and lakes, taking in the park's highlights (see "Beaches & Parks" below). For a closer look at the park's multitude of attractions, consider hiking along the many foot trails or signing up for a naturalist program. There are also boat trips, fishing opportunities and places to swim. In winter, there's cross-country skiing, snowmobiling, ice fishing and winter hiking. For more information, write: Superintendent, Acadia National Park, P.O. Box 177, Bar Harbor, ME 04609.

The island's main town is **Bar Harbor**, which, back in the late 1800s, was a thriving resort community for very wealthy and powerful American families. They built more than 200 enormous summer homes along the sea that were just as opulent as the Newport mansions. The Depression years and two world wars really took a toll on the community, however. And finally, the Great Fire of 1947 all but wiped it out. Many of the grand old hotels and about 70 mansions were destroyed.

Bar Harbor did recover, but it emerged as a more middle-class resort. Today, during summer months, it's crawling with tourists. The main street is a tangle of T-shirt shops, motels and restaurants busy with teeny-boppers and young families. We recommend visiting the **Bar Harbor Historical Society**, which features a collection of early photographs of the town before the big fire. Closed Sunday from June through October. By appointment only the rest of the year. ~ 33 Ledgelawn Avenue, Bar Harbor; 207-288-0000, 207-288-3807 (for appointments).

We also encourage a visit to the **Natural History Museum** which showcases taxidermied birds and animals from the area. It also features three complete whale skeletons and a marine touch tank. Closed Sunday and from Labor Day through May. Admission in summer. ~ College of the Atlantic, Route 3, Bar Harbor; 207-288-5015.

A quartet of other towns on the island—Northeast Harbor, Southwest Harbor, Seal Harbor and Somesville—are likely to appeal more to the traveler in search of hidden attractions. They're quintessential Maine fishing villages. One especially worthwhile stop to make is the **Thua Gardens**, a lovely spot devoted to azalea and Japanese gardens. ~ Route 3, near the junction of Route 198, Northeast Harbor; 207-276-5040.

You must also stop at the **Wendell Gilley Museum** if you're interested in seeing bird carvings. Closed Monday from May through October and Monday through Thursday from November to mid-December. Admission. ~ Corner of Harrick Road and Route 102, Southwest Harbor; 207-244-7555.

Families with children will want to stop at the **Mount Desert Oceanarium**, where you'll find plenty of hands-on exhibits, live sea animals and a touch-tank with sea snails, starfish and horseshoe crabs. Closed October to mid-May. Admission. ~ 172 Clark Point Road, Southwest Harbor; 207-244-7330.

Back on the mainland, in busy Ellsworth, try not to miss the **Colonel Black Mansion**, a startlingly beautiful 1820s Georgian estate filled with the original furnishings and decorative pieces of the Black family. Closed Sunday and from mid-October through May. Admission. ~ 81 West Main Street, Ellsworth; 207-667-8671.

Also worth visiting is the **Stanwood Museum and Birdsacre Sanctuary**, a 130-acre nature preserve centerpieced by an old homestead that dates back to 1850. Closed in the winter. ~ Route 3, Ellsworth; 207-667-8460.

DAY TRIP TO ISLE AU HAUT

From the dock at the corner of Sea Breeze Avenue and Bayview Street in Stonington, you can catch the mail boat, *Miss Lizzie* (207-367-5193), for a day trip over to elf-sized **Isle au Haut**. Since you've come this far, you might as well not miss it. Part of Acadia National Park, it has some mapped-out trails to explore and picnic areas. It's also home to a one-room schoolhouse and a general store.

As you work your way up the coast, you'll see less traffic, fewer commercial buildings and increasingly beautiful scenery (rolling farmlands, pine forests, glimpses of the sea). You'll also notice fewer tourists—here they're chiefly RV families and rugged outdoor sports enthusiasts en route to the dense wilderness of Baxter State Park. Your chances of meeting real, hard-working, homespun locals are much greater here than along the Southern Coast, where everyone grows up learning how to treat "people from away" properly so they'll come back. You'll find Downeasterners love to strike up a conversation with a "foreigner" and have a wonderful sense of humor.

HIDDEN ►

Continue to follow Route 1, veering off whenever a road looks appealing. There are several interesting detours to watch for, including **Jonesport** and **Beals Island**, which you have to squint to find on most maps. Ask any Maine aficionado which are their favorite coastal villages and they're sure to mention this little duet of lobstering and fishing towns at the end of Route 187. The two are connected by a bridge and in people's minds— rarely do you hear someone mention one without the other. Your best bet is to park in Jonesport and wander around aimlessly. You'll find a handful of restaurants, antique stores and other salty little shops.

Back on Route 1, don't miss the **Ruggles House**. Built for a wealthy lumber dealer named Thomas Ruggles in 1818, it's an extravagant Federal-style building with a flying staircase and meticulously carved woodwork throughout. Closed mid-October through May. Admission. ~ Columbia Falls; 207-483-4637.

Machias is one of the next towns you'll come to. It's worth pulling over and getting out to take a stroll around. An old commercial center, it now has a handful of shops and restaurants and is home to the **Maine Wild Blueberry Company**.

The Quoddy Head Lighthouse's claim to fame is that it sits on the easternmost point of the land in the continental United States.

Machias is supposedly an Indian word meaning "bad little falls," named because of the falls that run through the middle of town, where you'll also find a nice picnicking spot. Less than 15 minutes away is **Machiasport**, another photogenic village.

At East Machias, you can either continue on Route 1 or sidetrack to Route 191, taking in the little fishing village called **Cutler**. Consider taking a trip to see the puffins on **Machias Seal Island** (from May through August) on **Captain Norton's** excursions. Captain Norton has been taking visitors to the island since 1940. Fee. ~ Sea Street, Jonestown; 207-497-5933.

Next stop is **Lubec**, a once-very-active sardine-canning town. Today, it has sort of a lonely, end-of-the-world feel to it, but it's lovable nonetheless. It's the country's most easterly town and a stepping-stone to **Campobello Island** (506-752-7043), noted as the summer home of Franklin Roosevelt's family (which is actually in New Brunswick, Canada). You don't need passports, special papers or even toll change to cross the bridge and spend the afternoon visiting FDR's house. From late May to October, visitors can tour **Roosevelt Campobello International Park** (506-752-2922), the 34-room "cottage" where Roosevelt spent his boyhood summers from 1905 to 1921. Start by watching the excellent 15-minute movie. Then explore the house, which has been maintained exactly as the family left it. The grounds are landscaped with flower beds and woven with over eight miles of trails through piney woods and along the shore.

Back in Lubec, follow South Lubec Road to the end to get to the **Quoddy Head State Park**. You've undoubtedly seen the **Quoddy Head Lighthouse** before: the candy-striped, red-and-white tower is practically an emblem for the state of Maine. The perfect-snapshot lighthouse is at the end of a long bumpy dirt road. Signs warn visitors not to venture out when the tide is coming in. It rises five feet per hour and could leave you stranded for hours. There are some hiking trails to wander along as well as benches if you feel like sitting and waiting for the sun to come up.

Route 189 will take you back out to Route 1 and up through West Pembroke, where you can detour off to see Reversing Falls (see "Beaches & Parks" below).

You might also consider taking another detour along Route 214 to **Meddybemps**. The road stretches out like a canvas over one waterslide of a hill after another, edged by wheaty fields right out of an Andrew Wyeth painting. One little hill-clinging farm has a stand of vegetables with a self-service sign. Meddybemps itself is an adorable little village with a white church, white houses and a general store. There's also a pier on Meddybemps Lake and a small beach where you can swim.

It's worth arranging to spend a few days in **Eastport**, an intriguing port city set on Moose Island in Passamaquoddy Bay. For years, it's had a statewide reputation of being somewhat down and out, but actually it's quite charming and those who have discovered—or rediscovered—the spot keep it to themselves. At one time, Eastport was a bustling town with 18 sardine canneries. The population had reached 5300 by the turn of the 20th century. But between 1937 and 1943, it went bust. Canneries closed, and people moved out, leaving houses standing empty. Today, grand old Federal and Victorian houses remain as testimony to its better days. The skeletal population (maybe 2000) is a combination of old-timers remaining from the town's heyday, a thriving artist population and a small infusion of investment-seeking out-of-towners.

The best way to get acquainted with Eastport and the Eastporters is to wander along its streets. Water Street is the hub, with

◄ *HIDDEN*

more empty commercial space than filled. The town has been slowly upgrading and has completed a revival of the 19th-century storefronts on the waterfront. Unfortunately, few tenants have moved in. However, many say Eastport is the next frontier. The next Bar Harbor. We hope not. The star attraction is the **Eastport Gallery**, a highly respected and lovingly cared for showcase of local art. In addition to a changing ground-floor exhibit, upstairs you'll find an ongoing display featuring the works of 20 regional artists. Closed January through April. ~ 69 Water Street, Eastport; 207-853-4166.

One way to take in a big bite of this part of the coast is to drive the **Quoddy Loop**. Also known as "The Loop," it's a network of car-ferry services linking the New Brunswick mainland with Campobello Island, Deer Island (not to be confused with Deer Isle, farther down the coast), Lubec and Eastport. Ferry service is available late June to mid-September.

Calais (pronounced CAL-lus) is the last real stop along this stretch of coast, and actually it's set on the St. Croix River a little inland. It's a jumping-off spot for many outdoors sportspeople since it lies near **Grand Lake**, one of Maine's most beautiful and salmon-rich lakes. While in the area, stop at the **St. Croix Island Overlook** at Red Beach. It's a view of the island on which French explorers established the first European settlement in North America north of Florida (in 1604).

Another worthwhile stop in this area is the **Moosehorn National Wildlife Refuge**. Managed by the U.S. Fish and Wildlife Service, it's the northeast end of a chain of migratory bird refuges that extend all the way up the East Coast. Two areas make up the park, the largest (17,000 acres) in Baring, north of Calais, and the other (7000 acres) about 20 miles south near Edmunds. This is a wilderness area crisscrossed by hiking trails that can also be used for cross-country skiing and snow-shoeing. There are old logging roads that are suitable for biking, too. ~ Calais; 207-454-3521.

LODGING   If you're looking for the perfect New England inn in the perfect New England village, consider detouring off Route 1 to Castine and the **Castine Inn**. The 1898 bed-and-breakfast inn is ideally situated in town minutes from the water's edge. Its 19 antique-furnished rooms are bright, big and lovingly maintained by innkeepers Tom and Amy Gutow. Most have views of the sea. Full breakfast included. Closed mid-December through June. ~ Main Street, Castine; 207-326-4365, fax 207-326-4570; www.castine inn.com. MODERATE TO ULTRA-DELUXE.

Poised on Castine's stately Main Street is the main building of the **Pentagoet Inn**, a large old Victorian bed and breakfast. Guests can stay either in that house or at neighboring Ten Perkins Street, a late-18th-century building where all guest rooms have country antiques. Between the two, there are 16 rooms, all with private baths. Closed Columbus Day through Memorial Day. ~ Main Street, Castine; 207-326-8616, 800-845-1701, fax 207-326-9382; www.pentagoet.com. DELUXE.

Snugly set on 48 acres, **Blue Hill Farm Inn** seems to attract a healthy, life-loving crowd, including the occasional troop of Vermont Country Cyclers who come pedaling in on their inn-hopping tours. There are seven guest rooms in the farmhouse and seven in the renovated barn, all looking as though they might have been photographed for *Country Living* magazine. The rooms in the barn have private baths. The highlight every morning is breakfast: fresh-out-of-the-oven breads and muffins, homemade granola, fresh fruits and various cheeses. ~ Route 15, Blue Hill; 207-374-5126; www.bluehillfarminn.com. MODERATE.

The **Pilgrim's Inn** has found its way into travel and gourmet publications all over the United States and Canada. It's not surprising. Perched on a shiny millpond directly opposite Northwest Harbor, this 1793 house is impeccably maintained. Rooms—a total of 13, plus two housekeeping units in the neighboring guest cottage—are simply decorated with antiques and artwork and crafts by local artists, who are numerous in these parts. Tourists and Mainers from as far as Bar Harbor come for the dinners here, which are among the best in the midcoast area. Dinner is included. Closed mid-October to mid-May. ~ Deer Isle Village; 207-348-6615, fax 207-348-7769; www.pilgriminn.com. ULTRA-DELUXE.

As one totally satiated guest said while stretching his legs in a lounge chair and peering out at the fog-bundled sea with its hooting vessels, "This may not be luxurious, but you can't beat the setting." The **Inn on the Harbor** features 13 rooms of varying sizes, most of which are smack-dab on the water with ocean views. All are furnished with antiques and some feature private decks, sitting areas and fireplaces. Stepping out on the deck that hangs over the harbor is like walking right into a painting. Breakfast is included. ~ Main Street, Stonington; 207-367-2420, 800-942-2420, fax 207-367-5165; www.innontheharbor.com. MODERATE TO DELUXE.

Though many visitors take the mail boat out just to spend the day on Isle au Haut, you can overnight there. The **Keeper's House**   ◄ HIDDEN
is a stone lighthouse-keeper's-cottage-turned-inn that still uses kerosene and candles for its lighting. There are four large, airy and simply decorated bedrooms along with a dining room in the main cottage, a separate accommodation in the tiny Oil House with its own outdoor shower and an outhouse (there's no indoor plumbing in the Oil House). Three meals provided. Bicycles are available for guests' use. Closed November to mid-May. ~ Robinson's Point, Isle au Haut; 207-367-2261. ULTRA-DELUXE.

You can spend hours—no, days—roaming around the rooms of **Clefstone Manor**, which are filled with European bric-a-brac collected over the years. The house is a huge mansion built in 1894 as a summer home for James Blair, secretary of the Navy under President Lincoln. Its 16 ornately decorated guest rooms, with private baths, are named for British nobility, locations and writers. The grandly proportioned Romeo and Juliet room, with its wooden canopy bed, beamed ceilings, oriental rugs and fireplace, is worth taking a peek at if you happen to be staying in one of the others. However, all are jaw-droppingly impressive. Breakfast is included. Closed November through April. ~ 92 Eden Street, Bar Harbor; 207-288-4951, 888-288-4951, fax 207-288-2089. MODERATE TO ULTRA-DELUXE.

If you want to glimpse what life was like in turn-of-the-20th-century Bar Harbor summer cottages, consider staying at the **Ledgelawn Inn**. You can have your pick of rooms in either the main house or the Carriage House. There are 33 rooms, some with working fireplaces and verandas and, for a modern touch, whirlpool baths and saunas. All are handsomely decorated with beautiful antiques. Closed late November to late May. ~ 66 Mount Desert Street, Bar Harbor; 207-288-4596, 800-274-5334, fax 207-288-9968. ULTRA-DELUXE.

You have to book well in advance to get a room at **The Tides**. This marvelous Greek Revival manse is propped on a carpet of lawn with a stunning bay view. Classical music streams through the living room, a grand affair adorned with plush champagne carpets and a fireplace. There are just three guest rooms, all with king-sized beds. The master suite has a fireplace; the Ocean suite has a fireplace and a balcony. The innkeepers are extra-friendly and hospitable, preparing breakfasts that look like they might grace the cover of a gourmet magazine. ~ 119 West Street, Bar Harbor; 207-288-4968, fax 207-288-2997. ULTRA-DELUXE.

Listed in the National Register of Historic Places, the **Manor House Inn** is yet another summer cottage that has been restored and preserved. This lovely 22-room Victorian mansion, built in the late 1800s, has 14 guest quarters, all with private baths and Vic-

LEISURE READING

Try to get your hands on the Eastport edition of the Maine magazine called *Salt* (sold in various shops in town). It has beautiful essays about the town's wonderful characters. Another publication to pick up is the *Quoddy Tides*, a bimonthly newspaper highlighting all the area's goings-on, including the new titles the Lubec Library has added. Don't laugh. Some people love this little tabloid so much, they end up getting a subscription sent to their Park Avenue apartment.

torian furnishings, some with working fireplaces. A full breakfast is included in the price. Closed mid-November to mid-April. ~ 106 West Street, Bar Harbor; 207-288-3759, 800-437-0088, fax 207-288-2974. MODERATE TO ULTRA-DELUXE.

The big old hillside farmhouse at **Seal Cove Farm** is a three-room B&B that is also a working goat farm. The herd is a pampered lot, and they repay their caretakers with fine milk that is used to produce several highly respected varieties of cheese. Guests are welcome to take part in the daily chores of a working farm that is also home to pigs, chickens, turkeys, a horse and several vegetable gardens. The rooms are simply decorated with white curtains and comforters. Take a walk while you're here: the seaside views from the surrounding hills are stunning. ~ P.O. Box 140, Mount Desert, ME 04660; 207-244-7781. MODERATE.

Fortunately, some things never change. Such is the case with the **Claremont**, Mount Desert Island's oldest summer hotel (it dates to 1884). Of course, this grande dame (listed on the National Register of Historic Places) has been renovated—heavily. But it still manages to preserve the old Maine vacation traditions such as dressing for dinner (that means jacket) and socializing with fellow guests. The large, rambling, shingled building has a wide veranda lined with wicker rocking chairs. The view of Cadillac Mountain across Somes Sound is nonpareil. The food—lots of lobster and seafood—is unfailingly good. The rooms (a total of 43 units, 14 of them cottages) are homey and comfortable. On top of all that, guests can sample the many on-site sporting facilities, including clay tennis courts, bikes, rowboats, and croquet courts. Credit cards not accepted. Closed mid-October to May. ~ Claremont Road, Southwest Harbor; 207-244-5036, 800-244-5036, fax 207-244-3512. DELUXE TO ULTRA-DELUXE.

◄ *HIDDEN*

Many guests intending to spend one or two nights at the **Weston House** end up extending their stay. From what we could tell, it was the combination of the bed and breakfast itself (it feels very European) and the enormously interesting town of Eastport. There are five guest rooms and two baths on the upper level of the house, a stately old Federal built in 1810. All the rooms are thoughtfully furnished with comfortable beds along with tasteful antique pieces and little touches like fresh flowers in season. The house is within walking distance of everything. The breakfasts are unmatchable, featuring all sorts of inspired recipes. ~ 26 Boynton Street, Eastport; 207-853-2907, 800-853-2907. DELUXE.

The Inn at Eastport, a former sea captain's house, has five attractive rooms furnished with antiques. It's a good in-town base. The pièce de résistance is an outdoor hot tub with water views from the deck. Also, a real rarity in these parts, the inn provides evening turndown service. ~ 13 Washington Street, Eastport; 207-853-4307, fax 207-853-6143. BUDGET TO MODERATE.

DINING   In a little town as amphibious as Castine, it's surprising to find just one restaurant on the water. Fortunately, the food at **Dennett's Wharf**, a net-hung, bustling fish house, is just as appealing as the view of the sailboat-dotted harbor. It features 120 feet of float space out in front of the deck to accommodate visiting yachts. A lunch of freshly cracked oysters followed by a grilled crab sandwich and one of ten Maine microbrewed drafts on tap is deliriously good. Also try the mussels marinara, seafood linguine or one of the surf-and-turf specials. Dennett's is ultracasual, with waitresses sporting khakis. Don't forget to check out the ceiling covered with dollar bills. If you want to know how they got there, ask Gary. His response: "If you've got a dollar, I'll show you!" Closed mid-October through April. ~ Sea Street, Castine; 207-326-9045. BUDGET TO MODERATE.

The **Castine Inn** is elegantly accoutred with wall murals depicting harbor scenes and pretty table settings. The menu changes nightly, and features innovative entrées such as sweetbreads with a potato-leek cake and soy glaze or olive-crusted salmon with a grapefruit sauce. Be sure to try the crabcakes, grilled foie gras or any of the delicious desserts. Closed mid-October through April. ~ Main Street, Castine; 207-326-4365. DELUXE TO ULTRA-DELUXE.

The town of Blue Hill has a very sophisticated summer crowd who spend their evenings dining well and attending chamber concerts. However, there are still only a handful of truly commendable restaurants, including **Jonathan's**, with its two lovely dining rooms. The downstairs room is brick and yellow with handcrafted wooden booths and corkwood floors. The upstairs room has a more rustic feel, with exposed beams and oak tables. This "Maine bistro" offers Mediterranean-inspired recipes utilizing local ingredients. On the ever-changing menu you'll find lots of seafood dishes with imaginative sauces you'll beg to have the recipe for. Jonathan's also boasts one of the coast's best wine lists. Dinner only. Closed March. ~ Main Street, Blue Hill; 207-374-5226. MODERATE.

If you can't stay at **Pilgrim's Inn**, by all means do have dinner there. Your five-course prix-fixe meal—served in a converted timber-beamed barn—could be a butter-soft poached salmon with beurre blanc, tenderloin with cabernet, mushroom-leek sauce or perhaps glazed roasted duck. Among the other courses are wonderful bisques, chowders, salads (largely from the garden out back), home-baked breads and desserts. Closed mid-October to mid-May. ~ Deer Isle Village; 207-348-6615. ULTRA-DELUXE.

HIDDEN ►   The light-of-wallet but discriminating seafood eater won't find a better value than **Fisherman's Friend Restaurant**. Go when you are starving—the place prides itself on its generous servings of spanking fresh fish and seafood. The diner decor could use some gussying up, but with a platter piled high with clams, who cares? Closed November through March. ~ School Street, Stonington; 207-367-2442. MODERATE.

If you're in the mood for a warm and fuzzy experience, stop by the **Mountainville Cafe** at Nervous Nellie's Jams and Jellies. It serves coffee, tea, homemade scones and cookies plus a selection of the homemade jams and jellies. After a warming snack, plan to spend some time looking around the property, which is home to all sorts of sculpted critters and creatures created by the owner. All are made from native pine and dump "treasures" including vintage farm tools and old woodstove parts. Closed November through April. ~ Sunshine Road, Deer Isle; 207-348-6182, 800-777-6845, fax 800-804-7698. BUDGET.

We sat for hours at our window seat in the **Reading Room Restaurant** at the Bar Harbor Inn, mesmerized by the view. Breakfast and dinner are available at this expansive dining room with a circular view of the bay. The food is lovely, too, with specialties like fresh lobster pie and grilled mixed seafood. In addition, an outdoor waterfront terrace dining area offers lunch and light suppers. Closed November through March. ~ Newport Drive, Bar Harbor; 207-288-3351. MODERATE TO ULTRA-DELUXE.

When driving the Park Loop Road in Acadia National Park, you couldn't ask for a better place to stop for lunch, tea or dinner than **Jordan Pond House**. Along with a mountain view, it offers Maine specialties such as lobster stew and Maine crab cakes—in a setting of piano music warmed by the fireplace. Closed mid-October to mid-May. ~ Park Loop Road, Bar Harbor; 207-276-3316; www.jordanpond.com. BUDGET TO DELUXE.

Children are in their glory in the delightfully decorated **Route 66**. The restaurant is decorated with antique toys: everywhere you spot old toys, tools and other gadgets, each having a story of its own. The food is good old Americana, with standard favorites like grilled steaks and boiled lobster. And there are more innovative dishes as well, including shrimp fettuccine and baked stuffed sole. Closed mid-October to mid-May. ~ 21 Cottage Street, Bar Harbor; 207-288-3708. BUDGET TO MODERATE.

Certain restaurants tend to get everyone's recommendation, and such is the case with **Porcupine Grill**. This jewel of a place, tucked down a residential street, offers New American dishes with a Maine twist. The chef turns out inspiring creations such as caesar salad crowned with fried shrimp and sautéed lobster and mussels. Flickering oil lamps, a bar with a fireplace, art deco accents and big oak tables—placed far apart—make this one venue not to miss. Dinner only. Closed April. ~ 123 Cottage Street, Bar Harbor; 207-288-3884. MODERATE TO ULTRA-DELUXE.

Beal's Lobster Pier is another outstanding place to stuff yourself on clams or lobster. It's super casual, with picnic tables set outside in nice weather. They'll pack lobsters in ice to go and arrange air freight as well. Closed mid-October to mid-May. ~ Clark Point Road, Southwest Harbor; 207-244-7178. BUDGET TO ULTRA-DELUXE.

If hunger strikes while you're driving north on Route 1, stop in Milbridge at **The Red Barn**, a very casual, knotty pine–paneled spot with some counter seats, booths and separate dining rooms. It has a mainstream menu (pastas, burgers, steak, seafood) as well as some house specialties like the seafood stew, a delicious concoction of shrimp, scallops, haddock and crabmeat. ~ Main Street, Milbridge; 207-546-7721. BUDGET TO DELUXE.

The **Waco Diner** solves the pesky problem of wanting a shot of local color. Here you'll see all the local Eastport characters, including salty seafaring types and former sardine cannery workers. The food—standard diner fare—is nothing to get excited about, but that's not the point. You're here for the Eastport atmosphere. There is also a more upscale dining room overlooking the water that serves pasta, seafood, beef and poultry. Outdoor deck seating is available. ~ 47 Water Street, Eastport; 207-853-4046. BUDGET TO MODERATE.

One does not live by seafood alone. Try the salsa, enchiladas, burritos or Mexican pizzas at **La Sardina Loca** the easternmost Mexican restaurant in the United States. And on those cold Maine winter nights there just can't be a better place to sip a margarita than the cantina. The eatery is decorated with balloons, grandfather clocks and antiques. Dinner only. ~ 28 Water Street, Eastport; 207-853-2739. BUDGET TO MODERATE.

Before taking off for the northern woods, do yourself a favor and have a meal at **Chandler House Restaurant**. This warm and popular restaurant is well known in these parts for its prime rib and seafood dishes. All the baking is done right here. ~ 20 Chandler Street, Calais; 207-454-7922. MODERATE TO DELUXE.

SHOPPING   Though you probably won't find any bargains in the little shops and art galleries of Castine, you can find yourselves happily occupied looking at all the truly original fashions, the nautical gifts and the New England crafts and artwork. A bookstore-cum-art gallery, the **Compass Rose** has the best postcards in town. ~ Main Street, Castine; 207-326-9366. The **McGrath Dunham Gallery** showcases New England artists from May through October. Open year-round by appointment. ~ 9 Main Street, Castine; 207-326-9175. The **Water Witch** carries an exclusive line of handmade fashions that look like works of art. ~ 6 Main Street, Castine; 207-326-4884.

The village of Blue Hill is known in the area for its profusion of potters and artisans. For functional pottery, especially dinnerware, stop by **Rowantrees Pottery**. ~ Union Street, Blue Hill; 207-

374-5535. The family-aimed **Rackliffe Pottery** has been producing earthenware for three generations. ~ Route 172, Blue Hill; 207-374-2297. **Handworks Gallery** has pottery and diverse Maine-made items such as jewelry and furniture. Closed Christmas through April. ~ Main Street, Blue Hill; 207-374-5613.

The Blue Heron Gallery & Studio showcases the work of the Haystack Mountain School of Crafts' faculty. Closed October through April. ~ Route 15 and Church Street, Deer Isle Village; 207-348-2940.

William Mor Stoneware is a good source for good-looking—and functional—stoneware kitchen pieces. This is also the place for oriental rugs. Open mid-October through April by appointment or by chance. ~ Reach Road, Deer Isle; 207-348-2822.

Any visitor to Maine really ought to stop at **Nervous Nellie's Jams and Jellies**. Though it's actually a mail-order company, walk-in customers can sample the goods—hot tomato chutney, strawberry rhubarb conserve, cherry peach conserve, just to name a few—before deciding what to buy. In July and August, the company also serves as a café. The salesroom is closed from October through May, but Nellie's still sells jams and jellies right out of the kitchen. ~ Sunshine Road, Deer Isle; 207-348-6182, 800-777-6845, fax 800-804-7698; www.nervousnellie.com.

Bar Harbor is chockablock with shops, many of them purveying standard tourist goods—T-shirts that say "Baa-Haa-Bah" (the way Mainers pronounce it), multicolored wind socks (a craze here) and Maineana books, calendars and cards. However, there are some galleries and shops to make a point of finding.

Look for MDI **Workshop**, a showcase for Maine arts and crafts created by adults with disabilities. ~ Route 3, Bar Harbor; 207-288-5252. **Birdnest Gallery** has oils, watercolors, graphics and woodcarvings by contemporary New England artists. Closed November to mid-May. ~ 12 Mount Desert Street, Bar Harbor; 207-288-4054. **Island Artisans** is a cooperative with works by local artists. ~ 99 Main Street, Bar Harbor; 207-288-4214. **A Lone Moose** is the oldest gallery on the island. They offer wildlife sculptures in wood and bronze, pottery, watercolors, limited-edition wood blockprints, fine furniture and jewelry. ~ 78 West Street, Bar Harbor; 207-288-4229; www.finemainecrafts.com. Another interesting shop in the area is **The Woodshop Cupolas, Inc.**, where you can buy handcrafted cupolas and weather vanes. They're located on Route 3 in Trenton during the summer, and on Route 102 in Bar Harbor during the winter. ~ 207-667-6331 (summer), 207-288-5530 (winter).

The number of shops and galleries dramatically drops off as you go north of Ellsworth on Route 1. One worth looking out for is **The Sow's Ear**, which has a sweet selection of toys, some made-in-Maine clothes, jewelry and a good collection of books about Maine. Closed Sunday and the month of January. ~ 7 Water Street, Machias; 207-255-4066.

If you're interested in pottery, be sure to get to **Connie's Clay of Fundy** where you'll find museum-quality contemporary earthenware. If you're lucky, you may see the artist at work in her adjoining studio. ~ Route 1, East Machias; 207-255-4574.

Eastport is the salmon aquaculture capital of America. To sample this local specialty, stop by **Jim's Smoked Salmon**. ~ 37 Washington Street, Eastport; 207-853-4831.

For a selection of regional and American Indian titles visit **Fountain Books**, housed in a former drugstore. A reminder of that bygone era—when Eleanor Roosevelt frequented the store—is the old-fashioned marble soda fountain that brings in large summer crowds. ~ 58 Water Street, Eastport; 207-853-4519.

You may not find anything at **Border Crafts**, but it's worth browsing around. There are a lot of hand-sewn and knitted garments made by the "local ladies" who have lived there for decades, as well as so-called "antiques" that probably fall more aptly into the "second-hand" or "thrift" category. Like Eastport itself, this little shop is bursting with local charm. ~ Water Street, Eastport.

NIGHTLIFE   One look at Castine and it's clear: no neon-zapped discos here. Not even a sleazy bar. Most visitors plan their nights around a big, satiating seafood dinner.

The big night out in Blue Hill is attending concerts at the **Kneisel Hall Chamber Music Festival**. From late June to late August, string and ensemble performances are held on Friday evenings and Sunday afternoons. Kneisel Hall also features student and amateur concerts. ~ For information, write: P.O. Box 648, Blue Hill, ME 04614; phone/fax 207-374-2811.

Lights go off early on Deer Isle and Isle au Haut, as well.

In Bar Harbor, we managed to scrounge up a couple of things to do after dark. The hottest pub spot is **Geddy's**, a magnet for the young, hip and trendy. There are live acoustic performances Sunday through Friday and a DJ playing dance music every evening. This is also a good spot to pick up pizzas or burgers. ~ 19 Main Street, Bar Harbor; 207-288-5077.

Acadia National Park offers all sorts of nocturnal diversions, including ranger-led walks that focus on "Stargazing over Sand Beach" or learning about the nightlife of a beaver. There are also slide presentations in the amphitheaters at Seawall and Blackwoods Campgrounds. Programs are listed in the daily Ranger Activity Schedule. Closed mid-October through May. ~ 207-288-3338.

Like many parts of the Maine coast, Mount Desert Island has a flourishing cultural life. Check the local papers to find out what performances are on while you're on the island. The **Acadia Repertory Theatre** puts on four main stage plays and one children's production a season in the Somesville Masonic Hall. Their season runs from July to September. ~ Route 102, Somesville; 207-244-7260. The **Deck House Restaurant Cabaret Theatre** features outstanding summer cabaret shows in an ocean-view setting. ~ Southwest Harbor; 207-244-5044. Between mid-July and mid-August, the **Bar Harbor Music Festival** is in full swing with concerts of all strains—recitals, pops, tea, string and up-and-coming artists—performed at sites around town, including the outdoor amphitheater at Acadia National Park. There are also occasional jazz concerts. ~ 207-288-5744, 212-222-1026 (winter). Also from mid-July to mid-August, there's the **Mount Desert Festival of Chamber Music**, a series of chamber concerts. ~ Neighborhood House, Main Street, Northeast Harbor; 207-276-3988. The **Arcady Music Festival** draws a big crowd with summer performances ranging from small ensembles to baroque orchestras in locations throughout Bangor and Bar Harbor. ~ Phone/fax 207-288-3151.

Once you get north of Ellsworth, you'll find even less to do after the sun goes down. This is real Maine country, where going to the movies constitutes the big night out.

In July and August, there are a series of chamber music concerts hosted by the **Machias Bay Chamber Concerts**. ~ Centre Street Congregational Church, Machias; 207-255-3889.

In Eastport, check to see if there's anything going on at the **Eastport Arts Center**. In the summer they have a Friday night series of concerts and films that is a magnet for the intellectuals, artists and literati that have discovered the area. There is also a very active community theater that stages three or four productions each season. ~ Dana Street, Eastport; 207-853-4166.

ACADIA NATIONAL PARK

BEACHES & PARKS

One of Maine's most scenic areas, Acadia National Park encompasses a large portion of Mount Desert Island, the Schoodic Peninsula on the mainland and teeny Isle au Haut. For exploring on Mount Desert, consider driving the Park Loop Road. It hits the major highlights, including Frenchman Bay Overlook, a spectacular lookout point complete with interpretive signs pointing out the islands before you; the Wild Gardens of Acadia, a colorful wildflower garden; Champlain Mountain Overlook, another jaw-dropping view of the island-dotted Frenchman Bay area; Sand Beach, made up of the crushed shells of marine animals; and the summit of Cadillac Mountain, an above-the-clouds view of it all. The Schoodic Peninsula provides a good day-long side trip. A one-way road wraps around the peninsula, with sweeping views of Frenchman Bay, the Atlantic Ocean and the Mount Desert Mountains, while another climbs to the top of Schoodic Mountain. It takes a bit of planning to reach Isle au Haut, but once there, you can go hiking, birding and camping. To fish within the park, try Jordan Pond for salmon and lake trout; Long Pond for landlocked salmon; Eagle Lake for brook trout, salmon and lake trout; Echo Lake for brook trout and salmon; and Upper and Lower Hadlock Pond for brook trout. You can swim at Sand Beach or in freshwater Echo Lake. Among the many amenities are an information center, picnic areas, restrooms and souvenir shops. ~ The best way to approach Mount Desert Island is via Route 3 from Route 1 at Ellsworth. Isle au Haut is reached by a mail boat (fee; 207-367-5193) that makes regular trips from Stonington. The Schoodic Point peninsula is farther up the coast, off Route 186; 207-288-3338; www.nps.gov/acad.

▲ There are two campgrounds in the park. Blackwoods has 310 tent/RV sites (no hookups); free in winter, $16 per night in season. Seawall, open only in summer, has 212 tent/RV sites (no hookups); $10 to $14 per night. ~ For more information, contact: Superintendent, Acadia National Park, Box 177, Bar Harbor, ME 04609; 207-667-8550, 800-358-8550.

LAMOINE STATE PARK 🚶 🛶 🚤 ⛵ Located on Frenchman Bay, Lamoine State Park offers spectacular views of the dramatic peaks of Mount Desert Island. Its own 55 acres of woods and waterfront are popular for camping and picnicking. You can fish or swim (no lifeguard) in the cold water. There are picnic tables, restrooms, a dock and a boat launch. Day-use fee, $2 per person. ~ Follow Route 184 from Ellsworth to Lamoine.

▲ There are 61 tent/RV sites (no hookups) with flush toilets and hot showers; $8 to $17 per night. Information, 207-667-4778.

ROQUE BLUFFS STATE PARK 🚶 🛶 🎣 🏊 ⛵ Carved out of Englishman Bay, Roque Bluffs is a 300-acre park with both a saltwater and freshwater beach. There's a pebble beach on the ocean. The other beach is sandy and skirts the edge of a sheltered freshwater pond, ideal for fishing. There are four miles of hiking trails, perfect for spotting all kinds of wildlife, including eagles. Picnic and changing areas, toilets and a playground are the facilities here. Closed mid-October through Memorial Day. Day-use fee, $1 per person. ~ About six miles off Route 1; turn off Route 1 just beyond Jonesboro; 207-255-3475.

COBSCOOK BAY STATE PARK 🚶 🏂 🏕 🏊 🛶 🚤 An extremely scenic park, Cobscook (an Indian word that means "boiling tide") sits on the shores of Cobscook Bay, where tides can reach 24 feet. Its 888 acres are covered with spruce and fir trees and snaked by hiking and cross-country ski trails. It's also a good place to spot bald eagles. Fishing and clamming are permitted in the bay, but it is not an ideal spot for fishing as compared to surrounding areas. You'll find a picnic area and restrooms. Day-use fee, $2 per person. ~ Route 1, Dennysville.

▲ There are 106 tent/RV sites (no hookups); $8 to $16 per night; information, 207-726-4412.

QUODDY HEAD STATE PARK 🏃 Dramatically situated at the easternmost point of land in the continental United States, Quoddy Head State Park offers some magnificent views of the Atlantic Ocean and Grand Manan Island. The biggest attraction here is the red-and-white-striped lighthouse that surveys the Bay of Fundy, known for its extreme tides. Hiking trails ribbon through spruce groves; one skirts a high ledge along steep cliffs that drop into the sea. Picnic tables and fireplaces are available. Day-use fee, $1 per person. Closed October 15 through May 15. ~ From Route 1, take Route 189 to the town of Lubec and follow the signs; 207-733-0911.

REVERSING FALLS PARK 🏃 You're not alone if you're wondering what reversing falls are. This is definitely one of those go-see-for-yourself situations. The falls are actually a field of rapids dramatically galloping in the middle of the waterway. The Baltic scenery around it is part of a 140-acre park with hiking trails and picnic sites. Picnic tables and grills are available for the barbecue crowd. Restroom facilities are limited to outhouses. ~ Traveling north on Route 1, you'll pass the turn-off for Cobscook Bay State Park. Continue on for nine and a half miles and turn right at Antone's Triangle Store. Almost immediately, you'll turn right again at the red building. Follow that for three and a half miles, then turn right again. Follow for almost three miles, bearing left at the water. It's easier than it sounds, but none of these dirt roads have names.

▼▼▼▼▼▼▼▼▼▼▼▼

Northern Woods

Dense wilderness is what you'll find in this part of Maine. Mountains holding shiny blue lakes as if they were precious gems. Thick woods that seem to go on forever. Rivers roaring through canyons. The air here is invigoratingly fresh. Hiking, fishing, camping and other outdoor pastimes abound. For serious nature lovers, the northern woods provide the ultimate nirvana.

Not until you actually go to northern Maine can you understand how big the state really is. You can go for hours passing only an occasional farmhouse or two. You can't take anything (such as service stations and restaurants) for granted. Once you decide to travel up here, be sure to take a good map (you'll really need one, since there's often nobody to bail you out of jams). Your best bet is to pick a destination for the day and take your time getting there.

SIGHTS   Continuing on from Calais, you can stay on Route 1, which turns from a coastal road into an inland route and can be taken to **Aroostook County**, where lakes and forests reign. **Presque Isle** is the hub up in this region and also the commercial center of Maine's potato country.

We will, however, head for the Baxter State Park and the northern lakes area in the central northern part of the state. It'll take several hours to get to **Millinocket** (pronounced the proper Maine way, it's Mill-a-NORK-it), and there's not much in between. You can finally leave Route 1 at Topsfield, turning onto Route 6E and following the network of roads that eventually get you into the heart of Millinocket, where even one of the main streets is dirt. This town's biggest claim to fame is very big indeed. Being the home of Bowater Inc., it is one of the largest producers of newsprint in the United States.

Don't get your hopes up for anything more, though. Look at it as a good place to stock up on supplies and gas before heading off to the wilderness areas. In fact, do yourselves a favor and stop by the **Baxter State Park Headquarters** for some detailed maps. Millinocket is also a popular takeoff point for canoe trips to the Allagash Wilderness Waterway. This 95-mile passage comprises 200,000 acres of interconnected lakes and rivers than run from Telos Lake to the Canadian border. Before attempting to canoe the waterway, one should have some experience (see "Beaches & Parks" below). ~ 64 Balsam Drive, Millinocket; 207-723-5140.

You'll find the main entrance to **Baxter State Park** about 20 miles north of Millinocket. Sprawling majestically over 200,000 acres, this largest of Maine's parks is awe-inspiring. It was a gift to the state in 1931 by Percival Baxter, who, while serving as a legislator and as governor of Maine, urged creation of a park around Mt. Katahdin. Rebuffed, the governor bought the land with his own capital and deeded to the state of Maine the land "to be forever left in its natural, wild state." No overnight use from mid-October to December 1st and April to mid-May.

The centerpiece is, indisputably, **Mt. Katahdin**. At 5267 feet, it's the highest peak in Maine. It's also the northern terminus for the **Appalachian Trail**. Open mid-May to mid-October and December through March, the park has 45 other peaks and over 175 miles of well-marked trails. You can drive around the perimeter in less than three hours. (See "Beaches & Parks" below.)

As you continue west of the park, you'll come to **Ripogenus Dam**, where the mighty waters of several interconnected lakes are halted and washed out the other side in a narrow river that races triumphantly through a deep gorge. This is the departure point for several whitewater rafting trips. It's also the turnoff for those driving into the Allagash Wilderness Waterway.

A dirt road takes you south of Ripogenus Dam to **Kokadjo,** an adorable little complex of camps and a general store that was built as the headquarters for a lumber company in the early 1900s.

Continue south, stopping at **Lily Bay** (see "Beaches & Parks" below) and **Greenville,** a major New England seaplane base. You can stuff yourselves on local steamboat history at the latter's **Moosehead Marine Museum,** which displays local memorabilia and paintings as well as the restored steamship *Katahdin,* now a floating museum. Cruises are available. Closed Columbus Day through May. Admission. ~ Greenville; 207-695-2716.

From there, drive up the western coast of **Moosehead Lake** to the waterfront towns of Moosehead (a lumberman's depot and departure point for wilderness excursions) and Rockwood. The whole area is mesmerizingly beautiful, with mountains looming all around and evergreens perfectly reflected in the lake. It's very common to see moose in these parts.

Moosehead Lake is the center for the state's wilderness sports and the source of the Kennebec River. For more information, contact the **Moosehead Lake Chamber of Commerce.** ~ P.O. Box 581, Greenville, ME 04441; 207-695-2702, fax 207-695-3440; www.mooseheadarea.com, e-mail moose@moosehead.net.

LODGING

Before setting out into the wilderness of Baxter State Park, you can fuel up for a night by staying at **Pamola Lodge.** It's just as it sounds, a basic motor lodge with 30 generic motel rooms and efficiencies. ~ 973 Central Street, Millinocket; 207-723-9746, fax 207-723-9746 ext. 63. BUDGET.

Like a little nest hidden up in the trees, **Pray's Cottages & General Store** is a homey spot tucked away in the thick woods. It's the takeoff point for many bear-hunting groups and whitewater rafters, as well as a civilization-stopover for rugged campers desiring some hot water and electricity for a change. There are four one-bedroom efficiency units in a ranch-style building and two separate three-bedroom cottages. All are furnished with the kind of things you might have used to decorate your first apartment, but they're comfortable nonetheless. They also have all the modern kitchen conveniences. The general store is the hub of activity here, which is at its best around 6 a.m. during bear-hunting season, when the hunters congregate to swap eyebrow-raising stories before heading out again. Closed in winter after hunting season. ~ 101 Morgan Lane, Millinocket; 207-723-8880. BUDGET.

Anglers are the biggest fans of **Frost Pond Camps.** It's a group of ten campsites and eight rustically furnished housekeeping cabins set on Frost Pond, which is loaded with trout. It's also a great place for canoe groups, families and hunters (in the fall). Closed December through April. ~ Three miles beyond Ripogenus Dam near Baxter State Park; 207-695-2821, 207-723-6622 (winter). BUDGET.

HIDDEN ► The scenery around **Katahdin Lake Wilderness Camps** is gaspingly beautiful. There are ten log cabins (two to seven people can stay in each one) and a main lodge propped up on a bluff overlooking a lake. Each cabin is rustically furnished with the basic essentials (including kerosene lamps and a supply of firewood); some have gas stoves. There's no auto access to the camps, so you must arrange to be met by the owner with pack horses, or fly in from Millinocket Lake. In the winter, the facility is open only to cross-country skiers. Meals included; housekeeping is extra. ~ Three and a half miles off Roaring Brook Road; 207-723-4050. MODERATE.

Moosehead Lake is 40 miles long and 20 miles wide—the biggest of Maine's countless lakes.

Remotely situated within the Allagash Wilderness Waterway (50 miles north of Millinocket), **Nugent's Chamberlain Lake Camps** is a collection of eight rustic log cabins. The best way to reach them is to fly in (contact Folsom's Air Service, 207-695-2821). Otherwise, it's a five-mile boat (or snowmobile) trip up Chamberlain Lake. This is a year-round sporting camp with fishing, canoeing, Nordic skiing and snowmobiling. ~ Greenville; 207-944-5991. BUDGET TO DELUXE.

Try to get one of the two rooms that has a fireplace at the **Greenville Inn**. But if you can't, don't worry. All 12 guest rooms at this former lumber baron's 1890 home are wonderful. There are antiques scattered throughout the bed and breakfast, and in the common rooms cherrywood and mahogany panels warm up all the corners. Best of all are the views of Moosehead Lake and the encircling mountains from the porch and the dining room. Breakfast is included. ~ Norris Street, Greenville; phone/fax 207-695-2206, 888-695-6000; www.greenvilleinn.com. DELUXE TO ULTRA-DELUXE.

HIDDEN ► You can stay right in Chesuncook, a 19th-century lumberman's village that's on the National Register of Historic Places, at the **Chesuncook Lake House**. It's a beautifully maintained 1864 farmhouse with four rooms. The living and dining rooms have gas lamps. To reach it, you can be picked up by boat at Cushing's Landing or fly in. Three meals a day are included. Closed Labor Day through Memorial Day ~ Box 656, Route 76, Greenville; 207-745-5330. MODERATE.

If images of a palace and castles run through your head when you hear about **Chalet Moosehead**, forget them. It's just a motel with a bizarre name. It's ideally situated, however, overlooking Moosehead Lake. The "chalet" is also a very inexpensive way to settle into the area, with eight efficiencies, seven standard rooms and two cabins as well as a slew of diversions to keep you happily occupied (including a dock to swim off of, or dock your boat, and free use of canoes). ~ On Moosehead Lake, off Routes 6 and 15, Greenville; 207-695-2950, 800-290-3645; www.ctel. net/~mlodz. MODERATE.

Poised on the shores of Moosehead Lake, **The Birches** is a string of 16 log cabins privately spaced out in a grove of birch trees. All of them have porches and kitchens; some have wood-burning stoves or fireplaces. There's a main lodge with an open-timbered dining room where the fare is wholesome and good. Major pastimes include hiking, fishing, swimming, canoeing and boating. There's also tennis and golf nearby. In winter, there's more than 25 miles of cross-country trails. ~ Two miles from Rockwood; 207-534-7305, 800-825-9453. MODERATE.

Gazing over at Mt. Kineo on Moosehead Lake are the **Rockwood Cottages**. Eight cottages come with fully equipped kitchens, baths with showers and screened porches. There's a long list of activities to enjoy, including fishing, hunting, whitewater rafting, seaplane rides, tennis and hiking. Closed December through April. ~ Rockwood; 207-534-7725. BUDGET.

Maynards in Maine is one of Moosehead Lake's oldest established sporting camps. The centerpiece of it all is a grand old lodge filled with memorabilia from earlier hunting trips (such as stuffed fish and moose heads) and comfortable sofas and chairs that date back to the early 1900s. The dining room is always abuzz with outdoor lovers who congregate for three hearty meals a day. The camp has 13 cabins, with one to three bedrooms and full baths. Closed December through April. ~ Rockwood; 207-534-7703. MODERATE.

There are just six units at **Sundown Cabins,** so be sure to reserve yours early. Located on Moosehead Lake, these one-to-three bedroom kitchenette units are ideally located for water sports and fishing. ~ Route 15, Rockwood; 207-534-7357, fax 207-534-2285. MODERATE.

In this neck of the woods, you'll find most meals are included in the price at camps and lodges. They're often served family-style and consist of good solid home cooking. But there are a handful of restaurants you might want to try.

DINING

We were a little turned off when we saw the waitress/chef/cashier/store manager spray the grill with some aerosol and squeeze cheese out of a tube to make our grilled cheese at **Pray's General Store**. But hey, what can you say about a meal for under five bucks? And good luck finding another place to eat out in these woods. ~ 101 Morgan Lane, Millinocket; 207-723-8880. BUDGET.

One of the most elegant meals you can have in the northern woods is at the **Greenville Inn**. In its graciously decorated dining room, there's a good selection of Continental dishes, all enhanced

◄ *HIDDEN*

by festive sauces created by an adept kitchen. Dinner only. Closed November through April. ~ Norris Street, Greenville; 207-695-2206, 888-695-6000. DELUXE TO ULTRA-DELUXE.

If you're in the mood for a hamburger, lobster roll or a big bowl of chili, make your way to **Flatlander's Pub**. They serve heaping platters of Americana. It's a casual spot, attracting plain folks and backpacker types. Closed in April. ~ Pritham Avenue, Greenville; 207-695-3373. BUDGET TO MODERATE.

Housed in a barn, **Cangiano's** specializes in Italian-American cuisine. The lobster is especially popular here, as are the various fish dishes. ~ Routes 6 and 15, Greenville Junction; 207-695-3314. MODERATE.

Kelley's Landing is a great diner-style spot for breakfast. It opens at 7 a.m. and has a traditional American menu. ~ Greenville Junction; 207-695-4438. BUDGET TO MODERATE.

SHOPPING   There's not much in the way of shopping in the northern woods, unless you're into hunting gear and camouflage hats.

BEACHES & PARKS

BAXTER STATE PARK Maine's grande dame of parks, this 200,000-acre wilderness preserve is magnificent. There are over 75 miles of hiking trails that take you through pine forests, by rivers of rapids, alongside blue lakes and up mountains—including Mt. Katahdin (5267 feet), the highest in Maine. Katahdin is the northern terminus for the Appalachian Trail. Wildlife and birds are abundant here, as are a phenomenal variety of trees and plants. You can fish or swim (if you can stand the cold) in the park's streams and lakes. Once you're in the park, there's no food, fuel or supplies. Stock up in Millinocket. In the winter, roads are only plowed as far as Millinocket Lake. Closed to overnight use from October 15 to December 1, and from March 31 to May 15. ~ You can't miss this place. Look at any map, it's that huge green area in the central north section. The easiest approach is from Millinocket. Park headquarters: 207-723-5140.

▲ There are hundreds of sites in ten campgrounds. Two of the campgrounds are accessible only to backpackers. Among these are 72 lean-to sites, 80 tent sites and 21 cabins; prices range from $6 to $17 per night per person. Closed mid-October to mid-May. Permit and reservations are required; write: Reservation Clerk, Baxter State Park, 64 Balsam Drive, Millinocket, ME 04462; 207-723-5140.

AROOSTOOK STATE PARK Maine's northernmost park, Aroostook covers more than 600 thickly wooded acres on the shores of Echo Lake. It's an outdoor lover's paradise, with hiking and cross-country trails and secluded glassy coves for swimming. There's good trout fishing on Echo Lake. There are picnic sites, charcoal grills, changing facilities, paddleboat and canoe rentals, and a boat launch. Day-use fee, $1 per person. ~ Off Route 1, five miles south of Presque Isle; 207-768-8341.

▲ There are 30 tent/RV sites (no hookups); $8 per night for Maine residents, $10 per night for non-residents. For information, call 207-289-3824, 800-332-1501 (outside Maine).

ALLAGASH WILDERNESS WATERWAY 🛶 🚣 ⛵ Stretching for 92 miles from Telos Lake (north of Ripogenus Dam) to the far north near Fort Kent, this famous corridor of lakes and rivers is most well known for its flatwater/whitewater canoe trips. It's quite beautiful and known as "God's Country." The strip also boasts good fishing waters and snowmobiling in winter. You can swim the clear lakes as well, but there are no lifeguards or formal safety measures. If you plan to canoe, it's necessary to register at the gate when you enter the waterway, or write the Maine Department of Conservation, Bureau of Parks and Lands, 106 Hogan Road, Bangor, ME 04401. ~ Most of the Allagash Wilderness outfitters are in Allagash Village. If you're on your own, a good put-in point is Chamberlain Thoroughfare at the junction of Chamberlain and Telos lakes. You'll find rangers at Allagash Lake, Chamberlain Thoroughfare, Eagle Lake, Churchill Dam, Long Lake Thoroughfare and the Michaud Farm; 207-941-4014, fax 207-941-4222; www.state.me.us/doc/prkslands/alla.htm.

▲ There are 100 sites for tents only; $4 per night for Maine residents, $5 per night for non-residents.

LILY BAY STATE PARK 🚶 🛶 🚤 🛥️ ⛵ This is a beautiful wilderness area on the shores of 40-mile-long Moosehead Lake. The lake really does sparkle and is framed by evergreen forests and mountains that look like waves plastered against the sky. There is a hiking trail, but most of the activity revolves around the water—swimming, fishing or boating. Moosehead Lake is well known for its brook trout, salmon and lake trout. During the winter, snowmobiling and skiing takes over. There are two boat launches with berths. Closed mid-October through April. Day-use fee, $2 per person. ~ About nine miles north of Greenville on the eastern shore of Moosehead Lake.

▲ There are 93 tent/RV sites (no hookups); $12 to $16 per night. For more information, call 207-695-2700 (in season), 207-941-4014 (off season).

Stretching along the New Hampshire border right up to Quebec, the western lakes and mountains of Maine are unusually scenic. This area is home to dozens of lakes (in the Rangeley area alone there are about 40) and mountains (including Sugarloaf). The southern reaches—Waterford, Bridgton and the Sebago Lake

Western Lakes and Mountains

area—are within easy reach of Portland and other coastal destinations, and they attract lots of visitors, especially during the summer months. The northern parts such as Bethel and Rangeley take a bit longer to get to and feel as if they're worlds away. These areas tend to attract skiers in winter and wilderness-seeking vacationers in summer.

SIGHTS

The star winter attraction in the western region is **Sugarloaf/USA**, the state's second highest mountain and its biggest ski mountain (see the "Outdoor Adventures" section at the end of this chapter). At the top, you'll find New England's largest self-contained ski village, complete with hotels, restaurants, shops and a church. Below is **Carrabassett Valley**, home to the Carrabassett Valley Ski Touring Center, an enormous network of cross-country trails. The town of **Kingfield**, at the southern entrance to the Carrabassett Valley, was founded in 1816. It has a fine collection of shops, restaurants and inns.

Year-round, however, inland Maine is becoming more and more popular, especially the **Rangeley Lakes** region. Like the northern woods, this whole western area is almost solid wilderness punctuated with an occasional town (by town, we often mean a post office, a church and a general store). Moose, bear, wildflowers that look as strange as their Latin names, and birds who know a good thing when they spot one, are the most abundant residents. Some of the biggest lakes have names that are almost impossible to pronounce, but go ahead, try. They're Mooselookmeguntic, Kennebago, Aziscohos, Cupsuptic and Umbagog. Okay, we'll throw in a few easy ones: Rangeley and Richardson. They're all busy with boaters and anglers in summer months. And scattered along the shores are small camps with rustic log cabins hidden behind thick pine trees or in birch groves.

The town of **Rangeley** is evolving fast. Too fast, according to some old-timers. Seemingly overnight, it has gone from a sleepy backwoods town to an up-and-coming tourist center. Besides the little town of Oquossoc down the road, it's really the only place

---

TRAINS AND TIMBER

About 18 miles from Rangeley is the town of Phillips, where you'll find the **Phillips Historical Society**. There's an interesting collection of pictures from the area's early days when a narrow-gauge railroad connected nearby lumbering communities. Ask about the summertime rides on the Sandy River–Rangeley Lakes Railroad. Open first and third Sundays from June through September. ~ Pleasant Street, Phillips; 207-639-2881 or 207-639-3352, fax 207-639-5258.

where you'll find restaurants, a handful of shops, gas stations and, of course, ice cream parlors. The truth is, however, that Rangeley can't hold a candle to the real tourist towns on the coast. It's still a little town in the middle of the woods, no matter how many out-of-state license plates you count.

Rangeley does have some wonderful attributes on top of being one of the only signs of civilization for miles. It's *right* on the water. The silky ripples of Rangeley Lake practically slosh up onto the main street. It also has a landmark **library** (in the middle of town) that, according to one resident, "still smells the way it used to in the '40s."

As you move south of the Rangeley Lakes region, you come to the **Bethel** area, which is in the Oxford Hills, not far from the White Mountain National Forest on the New Hampshire border. Bethel itself is a lovely 19th-century village with a meticulously maintained green and stately old houses. Come winter, Bethel is a thriving cross-country skiing area.

One of the town's highlights is the **Moses Mason Museum**, featuring a restored Federal-style house displaying period furnishings and the Robinson House, which holds local historic exhibits. Closed Saturday through Monday and from September through June. Admission. ~ 14 Broad Street, Bethel; 207-824-2908. The **Gould Academy** is a very widely respected prep school. ~ 207-824-7700. The **Broad Street Historic District** is lined with historic homes.

The area south of Bethel (including Waterford, Bridgton and the towns near Sebago Lake) is loved mostly for its profusion of lakes and rivers (see "Beaches & Parks" below). In fact, from the summit of **Pleasant Mountain,** you can see about 50 lakes. These include crystal-clear **Sebago Lake,** Maine's second largest, popular with anglers and city folk from nearby Portland.

In addition to water sports, the area is rife with *terra firma* attractions, including the **Sabbathday Lake Shaker Community and Museum**, a complete Shaker settlement and one of the oldest in the United States. It features an exhibit on the lives of children in the community. Closed Columbus Day through Memorial Day. Admission. ~ Route 26, New Gloucester; 207-926-4597; www.shaker.lid.me.us.

The **Jones Museum of Glass and Ceramics** houses a collection of more than 7000 works in glass and ceramic. Tours available by appointment. There is also a research library as well as a gift shop with antiques, books and gifts. Closed mid-November to mid-May. Admission. ~ Off Route 107, Sebago; 207-787-3370, fax 207-787-2800.

LODGING

There are over 300 condominium units available through **Sugarloaf Mountain Corporation**. Each has its advantages. Some are close to the lifts, others to the restaurants and shops. They range from very modern accommodations with all sorts of new conveniences to ones that are older but more affordable. Some are bare-bones hotel rooms, others full-fledged homes. ~ Sugarloaf Mountain; 207-237-2000, 800-843-5623, fax 207-237-3052; www.sugarloaf.com. DELUXE TO ULTRA-DELUXE.

Nearby is the **Grand Summit Hotel**, a six-story building with one- to three-bedroom suites. ~ 207-237-2222, 800-527-9879, fax 207-237-2874; www.sugarloafhotel.com. DELUXE TO ULTRA-DELUXE.

HIDDEN ► You can stay near the Sugarloaf area at the **Widow's Walk**, an exceptionally friendly inn that attracts lots of skiers in winter and nature lovers in summer. Listed on the National Register of Historic Places, it's a beautiful 1892 Victorian house. There are six guest rooms, all with shared baths and basic New England furnishings. Full breakfast included. ~ Route 27, Stratton; 207-246-6901, 800-943-6995. BUDGET.

Fanatical skiers on a budget have a choice of bare-bones motels to choose from in this area, including **White Wolf Inn**, which actually is quite homey in spite of its generic looks. The ten rooms are ultra-basic but can accommodate between two and five guests. It's great for a pack of friends. ~ Route 27, Main Street, Stratton; 207-246-2922. BUDGET.

About 17 miles south of Sugarloaf Mountain stands **The Herbert**, an alternative to the mountain condos. It's a grand old hotel with 33 tastefully decorated guest rooms—all with jacuzzis in the bathrooms. The main lobby area offers a warm reprieve, and it's often filled with rosy-cheeked skiers who don't feel guilty about taking an afternoon off from the slopes to sit in front of the fireplace and listen to piano music. Continental breakfast. ~ Main Street, Kingfield; 207-265-2000, 800-843-4372, fax 207-265-4594; www.mainemountaininn.com. MODERATE.

Named after Amos Winter, the founder of the Sugarloaf ski area, the **Inn on Winter's Hill** is a Georgian Revival mansion with 20 charming antique-filled rooms in the main house and connecting barn. Registered as a National Historic Property, the Inn's lavishly decorated common rooms look as if they should be roped off like a museum, but actually they're very comfortable. Additional amenities include a pool, hot tub and tennis court. ~ Winter Hill Road, Kingfield; 207-265-5421, 800-233-9687, fax 207-265-5424; www.wintershill.com. MODERATE TO DELUXE.

Right on the water, the **Rangeley Inn and Motor Lodge** is a Rangeley landmark. The older building—erected in 1907—is a three-story shingled structure with 36 remodeled rooms. There's also a newer motel wing with 15 rooms, some offering fireplaces or wood-burning stoves, waterbeds and whirlpool baths. ~ Main

Street, Rangeley; 207-864-3341, 800-666-3687, fax 207-864-3634; e-mail rangeinn@rangeley.org. MODERATE.

Magnificently situated on a hill overlooking Rangeley Lake and surrounded by an 18-hole golf course, the **Country Club Inn** is a grand old summer resort built by a wealthy sportsman back in the 1920s. The living room is lavishly endowed with two immense fireplaces that face each other. The 20 rooms are nothing to get excited about though. They're rather ordinary for this extraordinary setting. Breakfast included; guests can choose to have dinner included. Closed mid-October to late December and April to mid-May. ~ Country Club Road, Rangeley; 207-864-3831. MODERATE.

Sunset Point Cottages could be in Sweden. As the name implies, Sunset Point is a sprig of land jutting into spectacularly scenic Mooselookmeguntic Lake. It's colonized by a quintet of housekeeping cottages (with one, two or three bedrooms), all inches from the water's edge. Though satisfyingly rugged (woodburning stoves, gas lights), the place provides real plumbing and hot showers (!) in one common bathhouse. All cottages but one have private bathrooms as well. Weekly rentals only. Closed mid-September through June. ~ On Mooselookmeguntic Lake, outside of Rangeley; 207-864-5387. BUDGET TO MODERATE.

◄ HIDDEN

Bald Mountain Camps are the woods of Maine just as you pictured them. They're right on Mooselookmeguntic Lake, surrounded by hundreds of miles of dense wilderness. Guests stay in cabins (there are 15, all with fireplaces) that are warm and homey. No fancy furnishings here—you never have to worry about the kids spilling things. Meals are taken in the log dining room, which is always alive with vacationers who come back to their same cabin year after year. Three meals included. Closed October to mid-May. ~ Bald Mountain Road, Oquossoc; 207-864-3671. DELUXE.

If you've never experienced a real Maine lodge, consider staying at the **Kawanhee Inn**. It has the works: exposed timber beams, an immense stone fireplace, woodsy smelling rooms. Guests can stay in one of ten rooms with basic furnishings in the main lodge or settle into a cabin (each accommodates two to seven people). All 12 cabins have their own fireplaces and screened-in porches. The setting is lovely—on a hill overlooking Lake Webb—and guests can use the small beach and boats. ~ Weld; 207-585-2000. MODERATE.

A lovely old Victorian house surrounded by five piney acres, **The Douglass Place** is situated in the small mountain town of Bethel. There are four guest rooms, all attractively furnished with antiques. Guests are welcome to use the common rooms as well, including the game room (with a piano, pool table and ping-pong table), living rooms, den and screened-in gazebo. Expanded continental breakfast included. ~ Bethel; 207-824-2229. BUDGET.

The **Bethel Inn and Country Club** is a large resort-type place that has everything. By everything, we mean 58 traditional rooms, 42 bedroom townhouses (all with their own telephones, TVs and bathrooms), as well as luxury rooms (with balconies) and suites, a well-respected dining room and an array of sporting options including golf on the 18-hole golf course, tennis, fishing, swimming, exercise rooms, sauna and cross-country skiing in winter. A huge, sprawling yellow building right on the town's common, it's impossible to miss. The individual rooms are decorated in a ho-hum style with all the modern comforts. The common rooms are formally attired in antiques. Breakfast and dinner are included. ~ On the Common, Bethel; 207-824-2175, 800-654-0125, fax 207-824-2233; www.bethelinn.com. ULTRA-DELUXE.

Within walking distance of the town's shops and restaurants, **L'Auberge Country Inn** is the kind of place you fall in love with and then hesitate to tell even your best friends about. Formerly a barn, it has seven guest rooms simply but elegantly furnished with country antiques. Guests are free to roam about the common rooms, which include a living room with a hearth, a baby grand piano and the kind of chairs and couches you sink into. During the winter months, you can cross-country ski right from the door. Country-style breakfast is included. Closed November and April. ~ Mill Hill Road, Bethel; 207-824-2774, 800-760-2774, fax 207-824-3108; www.l'aubergecountryinn.com. MODERATE.

Off in a world of its own is the **Speckled Mountain Ranch**, a gay-friendly bed and breakfast on 125 acres. It's a working ranch/ farm bordering the White Mountain National Forest with just three simply furnished accommodations. Baths are shared. Guests may use the living room and kitchen. Farmyard animals include eight horses, four dogs and six cats. Guided horseback rides are offered. ~ RR 2 Box 717, Bethel; 207-836-2908; www.speckled mountainranch.com. MODERATE.

The **Noble House** offers ten guest rooms in a turn-of-the-20th-century Queen Anne. Set on a hill, this bed and breakfast is comfortably furnished with antiques. The majority of the rooms and suites come with whirlpool baths and porches. You're welcome to play the baby grand piano or the pump organ. Explore the inn's private lake frontage with canoes or foot-pedal boats, or just watch the sunset from the comfort of your own hammock. Full gourmet breakfast included. Closed November through June 1. ~ 37 Highland Road, Bridgton; 207-647-3733. MODERATE TO DELUXE.

Surrounded by 34 lakeside acres, the **Tarry-A-While Resort** is a grand old summer hotel with 11 main-house rooms and another 17 in a quartet of cottages that punctuate the grounds. The innkeepers pride themselves on their unending hospitality. You almost feel as if you're guests in a private home. There's an array of diversions nearby, including water sports (two beaches plus canoes, rowboats, motorboats, sailboats and windsurfers), tennis and golf. Closed November to late May. ~ Highland Ridge Road, on Highland Lake, Bridgton; 207-647-2522, 800-451-9076, fax 207-647-5512. MODERATE.

DINING

For a quick but satiating meal between ski runs, try **Gepetto's**. You can warm up with a bowl of seafood chowder or a thick slice of pizza or settle in for fresh chicken and seafood dishes. From its windowed walls (it's the greenhouse style) you can sit and watch skiers schussing down the mountain. Dinner only. ~ Village West at Sugarloaf; 207-237-2192. MODERATE.

Julia's, an ornate dining room at The Inn on Winter's Hill, is as romantic and handsomely decorated as the rest of the historic building it occupies. The restaurant offers intriguing cuisine along with breathtaking mountain views. ~ Winter Hill Road, Kingfield; 207-265-5421. DELUXE TO ULTRA-DELUXE.

The area's most highly regarded restaurant is **One Stanley Avenue**. It's housed in a Queen Anne–style Victorian building and offers classic regional cuisine (maple-cider chicken, saged rabbit with raspberry sauce). Desserts can be counted on to elicit oohs and aahs. Open in the winter only. ~ 1 Stanley Avenue, Kingfield; 207-265-5541. MODERATE TO DELUXE.

In South Casco, you can visit Nathaniel Hawthorne's boyhood home on Hawthorne Road, where the 19th-century author spent his early years.

The antique-filled dining room is so pretty you'll want to linger for hours at **The Herbert**. A lovely spot for dinner, the changing menu offers a host of American dishes. ~ Main Street, Kingfield; 207-265-2000. MODERATE TO DELUXE.

The food at the **Country Club Inn** is almost upstaged by the view. From your table you can look out over Rangeley Lake, often as smooth as glass and interrupted only by a lone canoe. All around loom mountains that seem to change colors as often as you change courses. Fortunately, the food holds its own, with a selection of traditional American dishes along with some French recipes. Closed mid-October to late December and April to mid-May. ~ Country Club Road, Rangeley; 207-864-3831. MODERATE.

When locals want to celebrate birthdays or anniversaries, they usually go to the **Rangeley Inn**. It has a formal, late-19th-century dining room where you can feast on French or American specialties. Open winter weekends from Christmas through April. ~ Main Street, Rangeley; 207-864-3341, 800-666-3687, fax 207-864-3634; e-mail rangeinn@rangeley.org. MODERATE TO DELUXE.

If you just don't feel like cooking in your housekeeping cottage yet you're not in the mood to dress up for dinner out, pull up to the **Red Onion**. It's your basic pizza and subs kind of place that's crammed with locals and tourists alike. Don't be surprised if you have to wait a few minutes for a table to free up. Deck dining in summer months. ~ Main Street, Rangeley; 207-864-5022. BUDGET TO MODERATE.

If you're not staying at the **Bethel Inn**, at least treat yourself to dinner there. The fare at this lovely country resort is traditional New England served in the formal dining room (with views of the golf course and hills), in the Mill Brook Tavern downstairs or on the screened-in veranda during the summer. Closed November and April. ~ On the Common, Bethel; 207-824-2175, 800-654-0125. DELUXE.

If you get a craving for New American cuisine while hiking around these alpine hills, you're in luck. The **Tarry-A-While Restaurant** in the Tarry-A-While Resort serves such entrées as chicken *tortella*, a sautéed chicken breast filled with goat cheese, asparagus and sun-dried tomatoes in a rosemary and port wine demiglaze. While you take turns dunking homemade bread in the rich fondue, you can peer out at Highland Lake. Closed November through May. ~ Bridgton; 207-647-2522, 800-451-9076. MODERATE TO DELUXE.

True gourmands find their way to the **Oxford House Inn**, a 1913 house that faces the White Mountains. It has a lovely repertoire of dishes including a champagne-poached salmon with a fresh herb sauce and grilled pork tenderloin with a plum, cinnamon and port wine sauce. During the summer, cocktails are served on the piazza. Closed in the winter from Monday through Wednesday. ~ Main Street, Fryeburg; 207-935-3442. DELUXE.

SHOPPING If you lose your ski hat or mittens, head straight for **Sugarloaf Sports Outlet**, where you can find all sorts of great bargains. ~ Main Street, Kingfield; 207-265-2011.

The **Yarn Barn School** sells craft supplies for spinners, weavers, knitters and basket makers. Closed November to late May. ~ Bald Mountain Road, on Mooselookmeguntic Lake; 207-864-5917.

Bonnema Potters specialize in lamps, but they also have a beautiful assortment of functional stoneware pieces and porcelain pottery. Ask about seconds. ~ Main Street, Bethel; 207-824-2821.

If you're in the market for a handmade quilt, consider making your way to Bridgton in mid-July. At the annual **Quilt Show**, you'll find all sorts of wonderful quilts—both antique and new—and supplies for sale, plus demonstrations. ~ Location varies. Contact the Bridgton Chamber of Commerce, Portland Road, Bridgton; 207-647-3472.

In addition to artwork and crafts, Bridgton is a good place to shop for antiques. Its **Wales & Hamblen Antique Center** purveys the goods of more than 30 dealers. Closed end of December through Memorial Day. ~ 134 Main Street, Bridgton; 207-647-3840; e-mail waleshamblen@antiquesmaine.com.

The **United Society of Shakers** sells reproduction Shaker furniture, herbs, tea and handcrafted items. Closed Columbus Day through Memorial Day. ~ Route 26, New Gloucester; 207-926-4597; www.shaker.lid.me.us.

Nightlife in this area is also limited. In many towns, you're lucky if there's even a movie theater. **NIGHTLIFE**

However, if you're in the Rangeley Lakes region, you might be able to see a performance sponsored by **Rangeley Friends of the Arts**. They're put on throughout July and August at local churches, lodges and the high school. Contact the chamber of commerce for this year's program. ~ P.O. Box 317, Rangeley, ME 04970; 207-864-5364.

The **Sebago-Long Lake Region Chamber Music Festival** is a series of concerts held in July and August. Call for information. ~ Deertrees Theatre, Harrison; 207-583-6747.

RANGELEY LAKE STATE PARK This is unadulterated wilderness. Pine trees point to the sky, while white birch are perfectly reflected in the glassy lake. Moose are seen here frequently. The park covers 1000 acres, taking in lots of forest and the southern rim of Rangeley Lake. Anglers love to try for trout and land-locked salmon. People that know about the Rangeley Lake State Park usually keep it to themselves. Facilities include picnic sites, a bathhouse and a children's play area. Day-use fee, $2 per person. ~ Off Route 17 on South Shore Drive, south of Oquossoc; 207-864-3858. **BEACHES & PARKS**

▲ There are 50 tent/RV sites (no hookups); $13 to $17 per night.

MOUNT BLUE STATE PARK A 5000-acre park that encompasses Mount Blue and Webb Lake, Mount Blue offers one jaw-droppingly beautiful vista (mountains, lakes, more mountains) after another. There are plenty of hiking trails, as well as boating opportunities on Webb Lake. The lake also has good fishing for bass, perch, trout and salmon. The park offers guided nature walks in the summer. Facilities include a picnic area, a bathhouse, an amphitheater, a nature center and canoe, paddleboat and rowboat rentals. Day-use fee, $2 per person. ~ Off Route 156, Weld.

▲ There are 136 tent/RV sites (no hookups); $8 to $17 per night. Information, 207-585-2347.

GRAFTON NOTCH STATE PARK 🥾⛵ Over on the Maine–New Hampshire border, between Upton and Newry, is Grafton Notch. The 2000-mile Appalachian Trail passes through it on the way to its northern terminus, Mt. Katahdin. Throughout the park, you'll see waterfalls, caves and beautiful mountain scenery (it's at the end of the Mahoosuc Range). There are picnic tables, grills, toilets and a water pump. Day-use fee, $1 per person. ~ On Route 26, 16 miles north of Bethel; 207-824-2912.

▲ Nearby, Stoney Brook offers 30 tent/RV sites with hookups; $14 to $16 per night. ~ Route 2, six miles from Bethel; 207-824-2836.

SEBAGO LAKE STATE PARK 🥾🏊🚣🚤⛵ Some days, this gigantic lake shines like one huge sheet of tin foil. You'll find the water deliciously clear (it's Portland's main water supply). Many people come just for the day to swim and play on and off the sandy beaches. Some stay at the campsites that are spread out along the shores and in the woods on the northern end. You can fish for salmon and togue. Amenities include picnic sites with tables and grills, bathhouses, playgrounds, an amphitheater and lifeguards in season. Day-use fee, $2.50 per person. ~ Off Route 302, between Naples and South Casco; 207-693-6613.

▲ There are 250 RV/tent sites (no hookups); $13 to $17 per night.

▼▼▼▼▼▼▼▼▼▼▼▼▼
Outdoor Adventures

In a state where the sea, lakes and rivers sparkle like diamonds, you couldn't ask for a better way to explore than in a canoe.

CANOEING **SOUTHERN COAST** Rent canoes and motorboats from **Sally Mountain Cabins** for exploring Big Woods lake. ~ Off Route 201, Jackson; 207-668-5621. **Maine Sport** rents canoes and kayaks. Nice spots to boat in the area are Megunticook Lake and Penobscot Bay. ~ Route 1, Rockport; 207-236-8797, 800-722-0826; www.mainesport.com. **Acadia Bike & Canoe/Coastal Kayaking** leads sea kayak tours around Mount Desert Island. ~ 48 Cottage Street, Bar Harbor; 207-288-5483, 800-526-8615; www.acadia fun.com.

DOWNEAST COAST In Southwest Harbor, rent sailboats at **Mansell Boat Rental.** ~ Main Street; 207-244-5625.

NORTHERN WOODS Up in Millinocket, call **Katahdin Outfitters** to rent a canoe. ~ 207-723-5700, 800-862-2663; www.katah dinoutfitters.com. You can also rent canoes at **Allagash Wilderness Outfitters.** They will provide transportation to and from the Upper West Branch of the Penobscott or the Allagash rivers. Trips last three to seven days. Closed October through May. ~ 207-723-6622 (winter) or 207-695-2821 (summer). On Moosehead Lake, contact **Wilderness Expeditions** for sea kayaks, canoes, motor- and sailboats. They do not lead white-water rafting trips but will drive you to a put-in spot on a river and pick you up downstream several hours later. They do, however, lead kayak tours. Popular rivers in the area are the Penobscot (Class V) and Kennebeck (Class III and IV). ~ Rockwood; 207-534-2242, 800-825-9453, fax 207-534-8835; www.birches.com.

WESTERN LAKES AND MOUNTAINS Try **Saco River Canoe & Kayak**. ~ 188 Main Street, Fryeburg; 207-935-2369, 888-772-6573; www.sacorivercanoe.com.

Opportunities to get out on deep-sea fishing boats abound on Maine's coast.

SPORT-FISHING

SOUTHERN COAST **Seabury Charters** has trips on a 34-foot boat from June through October. Catches include bluefish, striped bass, tuna and shark. ~ Town Dock #2, York Harbor; 207-363-5675; e-mail lizzy@cybertours.com. From May through August, the **Ugly Anne** offers half-day fishing trips in search of cod and bottom fish. Cash only. ~ Ogunquit; 207-646-7202. The 33-foot **Devil's Den** cruises the ocean for striped sea bass, shark and tuna. Closed November through March. ~ DiMillo's Marina, Portland; 207-761-4466. **Charger Charters** goes out on half- and full-day trips for mackerel, shark, cod and whatever else the ocean yields. If you wish to go out on your own, they have three sailboats and two motorboats for rent. Closed January through April. ~ Tugboat Inn, Boothbay Harbor; 207-882-9309 or 207-557-2628.

DOWNEAST COAST **Seafari Charters** on Badger's Island offers private fishing charters up to 100 miles offshore. Catches range from cod, bluefish and stripers to sharks and giant bluefin tuna. ~ 7 Island Avenue, Badger's Island; 207-439-5068.

The central part of the coast is where you'll find Maine's largest concentration of golf courses.

GOLF

SOUTHERN COAST With a scenic course wandering through the Arcadia National Park, the **Kebo Valley Golf Club** is listed as one of the top 100 courses in the country. Its 18 holes will challenge even the most skilled golfer. ~ Eagle Lake Road, Bar Harbor; 207-288-3000. The Jordan River flows alongside the scenic, championship 18-hole **Bar Harbor Golf Course**. Watch out for the 18th hole; it has a reputation of being untouchable due to its 29-yard stretch. ~ Junction of Routes 3 and 204, Trenton; 207-667-7505. On Deer Isle, tee off at **Island Country Club**'s moderately challenging nine-hole green. ~ Route 15A, Sunset; 207-348-2379. In Hancock, the 18-hole **White Birches Golf Course** has two flags per hole. Two of the holes are over water and two others go through the woods. It is lighted for night golf. ~ Thorsen Road; 207-667-3621.

DOWNEAST COAST   Castine Golf Club's nine-hole, par-35 course was designed by Willie Park, Jr., who won the British Open in 1897. The green is fashioned in the old Scottish way, links-style. ~ Battle Avenue, Castine; 207-326-8844. In Southwest Harbor, the **Causeway Club**'s nine-hole course is located on the waterfront of Norewood Cove, affording beautiful water views. Watch out for the fourth, fifth and seventh holes—they are on the water. ~ Fernald Point Road; 207-244-3780. The **Northeast Harbor Golf Club** has an 18-hole course with stunning views of the surrounding mountains. The green is par 69, and their signature hole is the fifth, with a stream running through it. ~ Sargent Drive, Northeast Harbor; 207-276-5335. One of the nine holes at **St Croix Country Club** is on the St. Croix River. The seventh hole is their signature, featuring an eagle's nest above the green. ~ River Street, Calais; 207-454-8875. The quaint coastal **Grindstone Neck Golf Course** has nine holes right along the ocean, with the second green located on the rocks of the shore. ~ Grindstone Avenue, Winter Harbor; 207-963-7760.

SAILING   You'll find every kind of sailboat imaginable in Maine's waters, from simple Sunfish to tall-masted windjammers.

SOUTHERN COAST   **Saco Bay Sailing** can take up to six people in their 33-foot Freedom sailer, which explores the islands in the bay; they also do sunset sails. Call for reservations. Closed October through May. ~ Beach Avenue, Saco; 207-283-1624; www.sacobaysailing.com. You can book a charter or take a lesson with **Holladay Marine**. ~ West Boothbay Harbor; 207-633-4767. In Rockport, **The Schooner Timberwind** runs three-, four- and six-day trips as well as four-hour Sunday luncheon excursions. ~ Rockport Harbor; 207-236-0801, 800-759-9250; www.schoonertimberwind.com. If you're near Belfast, contact **Chance Along Sailing Center** for rentals or charters on one of the smaller lake sailboats, or on one of the larger sloops. ~ 207-338-6003, 800-286-6696. **Great Harbor Charters** will take you out for three-hour trips in a 33-foot sloop. ~ Municipal Pier, Northeast Harbor; 207-276-3993. Sailing lessons are offered by the **Camden Yacht Club Sailing Program**. ~ Bayview Street, Camden; 207-236-4575.

BOAT TOURS   Hundreds of boat companies along the Maine coast offer excursions that range from one-hour cocktail cruises to day-long whale-watching expeditions to week-long cruises on historic windjammers. You'll find the biggest concentrations of such companies in Kennebunkport, Boothbay Harbor, Rockland and Rockport, and on Mount Desert Island. Keep in mind that these are generally offered only in the summer months. Here are a few to try:

In Kennebunkport, go whale watching with **Cape Arundel Cruises** on the 65-foot Nautilus, which leaves from the Kennebunk port Marina. ~ Ocean Avenue; 207-967-5595; e-mail seahorse@ gwi.net.

Second Chance Cruiselines offers a scenic lobster cruise that glides by George Bush's summer home and past lolling harbor seals. The captain even provides a lobster-trapping demonstration. Its counterpart, **First Chance**, runs whale-watching cruises twice a day. ~ Kennebunkport; 207-967-5507, 800-767-2628.

Cap'n Fish Boat Trips is just one of many excursion companies competing for your attention on the Boothbay Harbor wharf. They offer sunset cruises and nature-viewing trips that spot seals, exotic birds and whatever else decides to fly or swim by. ~ Pier 1, Boothbay Harbor; 207-633-3244.

Tidal Transit offers guided kayak tours on the bay in Boothbay Harbor. Choose either the seal, lighthouse or sunset trip. They also provide rentals. ~ By the Footbridge; 207-633-7140.

Penobscot Bay is where you'll find Maine's tall-masted windjammers. You can spend three days or a week sailing on one, staying in comfortable cabins and eating like royalty. Contact the **Maine Windjammer Association** for a complete listing of all the possibilities. ~ P.O. Box 1144, Blue Hill, ME 04614; 800-807-9463; www.midcoast.com/~sailmwa.

For a scenic cruise to the legendary artist colony of Monhegan Island, head south from Thomaston to Port Clyde and board the **Laura B.** or the **Elizabeth Ann**. The cruises lead past seabird rookeries to idyllic Monhegan Island. Here you'll learn the fascinating story of renaissance man Rockwell Kent and see the summer home of artist Jamie Wyeth. There is also a lighthouse and nature cruise on Thursday, and a trip to watch the puffins on Wednesday. ~ 207-372-8848.

From Stonington, **Miss Lizzie**, Isle au Haut's mail boat, doubles as a sightseeing cruise boat. Ninety-minute cruises depart from the dock at the corner of Sea Breeze Avenue and Bayview Street (207-367-5193). **Palmer Day IV** also departs from Stonington and offers cruises around the waters of Penobscot Bay.

On Mount Desert Island, there are a number of boating possibilities, including whale watching with **Acadian Whale Watcher**. ~ Bar Harbor; 207-288-9776, 800-421-3307. There's also nature-viewing with **Sea Princess Naturalist Cruises**. ~ Northeast Harbor; 207-276-5352; www.barharborcruises.com/cruises.hotmail.

DOWNHILL SKIING

Maine offers a number of full-service resorts—including New England's biggest ski mountain—that'll keep you happily schussing the slopes. All facilities listed here rent equipment and offer lessons.

SOUTHERN COAST   Hit the slopes at **Camden Snow Bowl**, with a summit of 1200 feet and a vertical drop of 950 feet. Snowboarders and skiers are welcome on all 11 trails; Camden keeps boarders in mind by offering lessons for beginners. Equipped with one double lift and two T-lifts, seven miles of groomed trails are easily accessible. There's night skiing on over half the trails; the park tends to cater to the intermediate skier (only 10 percent of the trails are for beginners and 10 percent for experts). The season runs from approximately December to March. ~ Barnestown Road, Camden; 207-236-3438; www.camdensnowbowl.com, e-mail snowbowl@midcoast.com.

WESTERN LAKES AND MOUNTAINS Maine's downhill skiing revolves largely around **Sugarloaf/**USA, the biggest ski mountain in New England. With a base elevation of 1400 and a vertical drop of 2820 feet, there are challenges to be found on this hill for even the most experienced skier. Snowboarders will be thrilled with the 500-foot-long half-pipe and the snow park's jumps, rolls and spines. ~ Carrabassett Valley, Kingfield; 207-237-2000; www.sugarloaf.com, e-mail info@sugarloaf.com.

At a base elevation of 2500 feet, **Saddleback Mountain** has two lifts and three T-bars that cover 40 runs equally divided between beginner, intermediate and expert. The summit is at 4130 feet and the mountain has a vertical drop of 800 feet. A snow park features jumps and snow ramps for boarders. ~ Rangeley; 207-864-3380; www.saddlebackskiarea.com, e-mail saddleback@saddlebackskiarea.com.

Sunday River Skiway has 18 lifts servicing slopes that are 25 percent beginner, 35 percent intermediate and 40 percent expert. Snowboarders have a chance to test their skills on one of three half-pipes. The summit elevation of the resort is 3140 feet, with a vertical drop of 2340 feet. ~ Bethel; 207-824-2187; www.sundayriver.com, e-mail snowtalk@sundayriver.com.

Downhill skiers, telemarkers and snowboarders share **Shawnee Peak at Pleasant Mountain**, which has a base elevation of 500 feet and a vertical drop of 1300 feet. The resort has four lifts and one pony lift, with 38 trails crisscrossing the mountain. Night skiing is permitted on 17 of the runs. A terrain park keeps snowboarders busy with jumps, rolls and spines. Half the runs are intermediate. ~ Bridgton; 207-647-8444; www.shawneepeak.com, e-mail ski@shawneepeak.com.

CROSS-COUNTRY SKIING Gliding through Maine's miles and miles of pine-scented cross-country trails on skis is a compelling way to experience the essence of the state's winters. The season generally begins at the end of November and lasts well into April. The ski centers listed have rentals and lessons unless noted.

NORTHERN WOODS **Currier's Flying Service** offers scenic tours and charter touring trips in the Moosehead Lake area. ~ Greenville Junction; 207-695-2778. **Birches Ski Touring Center** has 25 kilometers of groomed trails, and offers rentals and lessons. ~

Rockwood; 207-534-7305; www.birches.com, e-mail wwld@
aol.com.

WESTERN LAKES AND MOUNTAINS   In Kingfield try the **Sugarloaf Outdoor Center**. With more than 90 kilometers of groomed
trails to explore, plus an ice-skating rink and a short track to
ski at night, there is plenty to keep the whole family happy. ~
Carrabassett Valley; 207-237-2000; www.sugarloaf.com, e-mail
info@sugarloaf.com. In Rangeley, snowboarders and downhill
and cross-country skiers share the mountain at the **Ski Nordic
Touring Center at Saddleback**. Some 20 kilometers of groomed
trails and 20 kilometers of backcountry trails are for the Nordic
skiers. ~ 207-864-5671; www.saddlebackskiarea.com, e-mail
saddleback@saddlebackskiarea.com. **Bethel Inn and Country
Club** has 120 kilometers of trails that wind through beautiful
woods and over brooks. Ice skating and sleigh rides are offered.
~ Bethel; 207-824-2175; www.bethelinn.com. Or you can try the
120 kilometers of trails at the **Sunday River Cross Country Ski
Center**. ~ Bethel; 207-824-2410; www.sundayriver.com.

The northern woods are laced with choppy-water rivers. **Wilderness Rafting Expeditions** leads one-day and overnight trips on
the Kennebec, Dead and Penobscot rivers. Levels of difficulty
range from beginner to experienced, and you can go down the
river in a raft, canoe or kayak. They also rent canoes, kayaks,
motorboats, pontoon boats and sailboats. ~ Rockwood; 207-
534-2242, 800-825-9453; www.birches.com. The experienced
guides at **Northern Outdoors, Inc.** lead one- or two-day trips
down the rapids of the Kennebec (Class II and III), Dead (Class
III and IV) or Penobscot (Class IV and V) rivers. ~ The Forks;
207-663-4466, 800-765-7238; www.northernoutdoors.com. For
an excursion down the Kennebec, Deerfield, Miller's or West
rivers, contact **Crab Apple White Water**. Take a full-day trip in
a raft; rapids range from Class I to Class V. They also offer half-
day funyak rentals. ~ The Forks; 207-663-2218.

**RIVER
RUNNING**

One of the best ways to see the coast is by pedaling along it. You
can pick a spot—any spot—and start riding; just watch out for
summer traffic.

BIKING

SOUTHERN COAST   A lovely 22-mile loop on Cape Elizabeth,
just south of Portland, starts and finishes at the **Scarborough
Public Library** on Route 207. It winds through Scarborough
Marsh, past several beaches (including Scarborough Beach and
Crescent Beach State Park) and through Lights State Park and
Prouts Neck Bird Sanctuary.

The **Boothbay Harbor** area is a lot more manageable on two
wheels than four. From Boothbay Harbor itself, try pedaling east
to East Boothbay and then south to Ocean Point (about 14 miles

roundtrip). Or do the loop around Southport Island (about 16 miles, starting and finishing in Boothbay Harbor).

DOWNEAST COAST   On Deer Isle, there are several bicycling possibilities. From the center of the village, you can ride through silent woods out to the Haystack Mountain School of Crafts (7 miles one-way) or to the little lobstering village of Stonington (6.5 miles one-way). Or take your bikes over on the mail boat to Isle au Haut and ride along the sea for a couple of miles.

There are more than 50 miles of carriage paths on **Mount Desert Island** to cycle on. One of the most exhilarating trips is the 28-mile **Acadia National Park Loop** (the car route with detours). The steep ascent of Cadillac Mountain, however, is not for everyone.

NORTHERN WOODS   You may find some pleasant inland trips though distances tend to be long and—in the western region— hilly or mountainous. A stunningly beautiful trip for big-time bikers can be had up at **Baxter State Park**. It's about 46 miles between Ripogenus Dam and Spencer Cove. You pass waterfalls, whitewater rivers and miles of majestically beautiful forest and you can see Mt. Katahdin looming on the horizon.

Bike Rentals   In Kennebunkport, the full-service **Cape-able Bike Shop** rents mountain, hybrid, children's and tandem bikes. ~ 83 Arundel Road; 207-967-4382. In Rockport, you can rent mountain and children's bikes, hybrids, baby trailers and tag-a-longs at **Maine Sport**. They also do repairs and carry biking maps. ~ Route 1; 207-236-8797. Mountain bike and hybrid rentals in Boothbay Harbor are found at **Tidal Transit**. ~ By the Footbridge; 207-633-7140. To rent 21-speed mountain bikes in Bar Harbor, contact **Acadia Bike & Canoe/Coastal Kayaking**. ~ 48 Cottage Street; 207-288-5483, 800-526-8615; www.acadiafun.com. At Moosehead Lake in the Northern Woods, mountain bikes are available at **The Birches**. ~ Birches Road; 207-534-7305.

HIKING   All distances listed for hiking trails are one way unless otherwise noted.

SOUTHERN COAST   The **Fore River Trail** (1 mile) goes through the heart of Portland's Fore River Sanctuary. It's an easy walk, weaving through woods and marshes to a 30-foot waterfall. Several other trails veer off the main loop.

The whole of Monhegan Island is prime hiking territory, but if time is limited, follow **Cliff Trail** (about 2 miles). It takes you through the most densely scenic part of the island, over the dramatic headlands and coves that make up the eastern shore. You'll probably spend about half the day following it, but the views (plunging cliffs, deeply indented coves, open sea) are worth it.

The hike to the top of **Bald Rock Mountain** (.5 mile) in Camden Hills State Park rewards trekkers with glorious views of Penobscot Bay, Blue Hill, Mount Desert Island and the islands anchored offshore. It's a fairly easy climb that passes through forests ablaze with wildflowers in the spring. To reach the trailhead, take Route 1 north of Camden to Lincolnville Beach. Turn left on Route 173 and take another left when you reach Young Town Road. The trailhead is near a fire road (Bald Rock Road).

DOWNEAST COAST   Duck Harbor Mountain (1 mile) is a delightful short hike on Isle au Haut. From its peak, you can see much of the island—it's largely covered with dense stands of spruce and fir, marshlands, streams and ponds and some spectacular cliffs.

From atop **Blue Hill** (1 mile) you won't be able to take your eyes off the view. Like a painting, the peaks of Mount Desert Island and the sailboat-dotted waters of the Blue Hill Bay spread out before you. On a clear day, you can see the villages of Penobscot and Castine and the Camden Hills. The trail itself passes through thick spruce and fir forests. To reach it, turn west on the Mountain Road opposite the entrance to the Blue Hill Fairgrounds; you'll see the trailhead about a mile down on the right.

Acadia National Park has an enormous network of hiking trails that attract hikers and rock climbers from around the world. The Visitors Center has an information sheet, profiling many of the trails, which range in difficulty from very easy paths to strenuous hikes.

The **North Ridge of Cadillac Mountain** (2.2 miles) in Acadia National Park is a moderate trail with some steep grades and level stretches. By and large, though, it's a gradual ascent with exhilarating views of the island-dotted bays, coastline and clouds—below you.

If you feel up to it, consider climbing **Acadia Mountain** (1.3 miles), also in Acadia National Park. It's fairly strenuous but offers achingly beautiful views of the mountains, the offshore islands (from the top they look like croutons floating in soup) and Somes Sounds, the only fjord of the eastern U.S. seaboard.

Another good, though strenuous, hike inside Acadia National Park is **Beachcroft Trail** (1.2 miles), whose trailhead is along Route 3 at the northern end of the Tarn. The trail takes you steeply up the side of an ice-carved valley where you can read the glacial record.

Beech Mountain (.6 mile) over in Southwest Harbor is our personal favorite. As you ascend, the land seems to fall off all around you, revealing increasingly magnificent views of the sea and islands. There's a fire tower at the summit, if you really want to stuff yourself on gorgeous scenery.

NORTHERN WOODS   Baxter State Park's Owl Trail (6.6 miles) begins gradually, passing through woods and by streams. However, it does get steep in patches, taking you through bouldery cliff areas. If you've got the physical fortitude, it's worth it for views of Katahdin. From the wind-slapped summit, you can see the lakes and streams that wash through this startlingly beautiful chunk of Maine. To reach the Owl Trail, start off on the Hunt Trail at the Katahdin Stream Campground. You'll see blue markers indicating where the Owl Trail turns off.

One of the most spectacular routes to Baxter Peak is the **Cathedral Trail** (1.8 miles). It is very steep and rocky, though, so be forewarned. Its name comes from the cathedrals you'll see—huge outcroppings of vertical rock slabs. To return, pick up the **Dudley Trail**, which is not as treacherously steep and easier to descend. Both trails begin and end at the Chimney Pond Campground in Baxter State Park.

Along the Allagash Waterway at Umsaskis Lake begins the trail up **Priestly Mountain** (3.5 miles). From the fire tower that crowns its peak (about 1900 feet), you'll have far-reaching views of the whole water-webbed Allagash area. To reach the trail, leave your canoe at the park ranger's camp about halfway down the western shore. You'll see a sign.

Two trails lead to the summit of **Mount Kineo**, which rises dramatically from the middle of Moosehead Lake. **The Indian Trail** (1 mile) is the tougher of the two, taking you along steep cliffs. The **Bridle Trail** (1 mile) is easier but not half as beautiful. Whichever way you choose, the views from the bald summit will make your heart throb. To reach the mountain, you have to boat in. There are motorboats for rent along the Moose River, in Rockwood, and on the western shore of Moosehead Lake; shuttle boats depart every other hour from Kineo House.

If you take just one hike while in New England, let it be at **Gulf Hagas** (8 miles roundtrip), otherwise known as "Maine's Grand Canyon." This area is perhaps the most scenic in the state, taking in the three-mile canyon, five major waterfalls and 40-foot-high vertical walls. The only catch is finding this place. It's east of Greenville and west of Katahdin Iron Works. Your best bet is to consult *The Maine Atlas*, where it's clearly indicated. If you're game for a hunt, follow these directions: From Routes 6 and 15 in Greenville, take a right on Pleasant Street and follow it for two miles. Pleasant takes a sharp right and becomes a dirt road; follow it for ten miles and you'll come to Hedgehog Check Point gate. The attendant will guide you from there.

The **Sally Trail** (3 miles) winds its way up Sally Mountain through forests of birch hardwoods and fir trees. From the summit, you can see island-dotted Attean Pond and other mountains that loom up all around. To reach the trail, drive two miles south from Jackman on Route 201 to Attean Road. Turn right and follow the road for about two miles to the Attean Lake Resort. The trail starts near the lake landing, by the railroad tracks. Look for signal post #770.

WESTERN LAKES AND MOUNTAINS   A good "starter" mountain in the Rangeley Lakes Area is **Bald Mountain** (1 mile), where the trail gradually ascends through hardwood forests. From the top at the observation deck, you can see portions of Mooselookmeguntic Lake and nearby lakes. You'll see the Kennebago Mountains to the north, the Azis cohos and Deer Mountains to the west and Saddleback Mountain to the east. To reach the trailhead, follow Route 4 from the Oquossoc Post Office for a mile and take a sharp left onto Bald Mountain Road.

The moderately tricky trail up **Little Jackson Mountain** (5.5 miles) climbs above the timberline through pretty woods and patches of blueberry and cranberry bushes. The view of the Weld area from the summit is worth the hike. To get there, follow the unmarked road that heads west out of Weld Corner. Stay on it until you see a cemetery. Just beyond that, turn right onto the bumpy dirt road.

Step Falls (1 mile) is a long, dramatic string of cascades and icy pools. During summer months (even late August), take along your bathing suit for a dip in the thrilling natural water slide. The falls are off Route 26, about 15 miles northwest of Bethel. There's no sign, but you'll see cars parked at the trailhead.

A simple walk recommended for young families is the trail to the summit of **Sabattus Mountain** (.75 mile), which passes through silent woods on gentle inclines. At the top, you'll find wide-angle views of the mountains. To reach the trail, follow Route 5 to just north of Center Lovell; turn right on the dirt road. When you come to a fork, stay right. Continue past a white house to the parking area.

▼ ▼ ▼ ▼ ▼ ▼ ▼ ▼ ▼ ▼

Transportation

CAR

The most common way to enter Maine is from the south, on **Route 95**, the interstate. It's the fastest way to reach Portland, Augusta and Bangor. It's also the quickest way to get to most of the coastal resort areas between the border of New Hampshire and Mount Desert Island, and to the edge of the northern woods.

An alternative to Route 95 is **Route 1**, which roughly runs along the coast from Kittery to Calais. At Calais, it turns north and follows the Canadian border all the way up to Fort Kent in the state's northern reaches. A word of caution: Route 1 is notoriously slow, especially in the south in the summer months, when tourists are traveling and stopping at the scores of factory outlets that line it. It's also hilly in parts (especially in the north), which makes passing quite dangerous.

You can easily reach towns in the southern half of the state on the well-maintained webwork of roads that cover it. The north is a bit more difficult, however. There are times when you may have to go north, south, north, south just to get from a western town to an eastern town. Fortunately, the scenery in these parts more than compensates. One more note about the north. Once you get north and west of Millinocket, you'll spend most of your time on dirt roads. Some are downright rough and rugged. And some are private and require permits.

AIR

There are two major airports in the state: the **Portland International Jetport** and the **Bangor International Airport**.

Portland is served by Continental Airlines, Delta Air Lines, United Airlines and USAir plus several regional airlines. Flying into Bangor are Delta Air Lines and United Airlines, as well as regional air carriers.

At both, you'll find plenty of taxis to take you into town. In Portland, you can bus in with the **Metro Bus Company** (207-774-0351). There are also small airports in Auburn/Lewiston, Augusta, Bar Harbor, Frenchville, Presque Isle, Rockland and Waterville—all serviced by either Continental Express or Valley Airlines.

FERRY

From Nova Scotia, Canada, you can ferry to Portland on one of the **Prince of Fundy Cruises**. Arrivals and departures are from 468 Commercial Street near Million Dollar Bridge. ~ 207-775-5616, 800-341-7540.

BUS

Concord Trailways cruises up Route 1, stopping in Brunswick, Bath, Wiscasset, Lincolnville, Waldoboro, Rockland, Camden and Belfast. ~ 100 Sewall Street, Portland; 207-828-1151, 800-639-3317.

CAR RENTALS

Unless you're planning to stay put in one hotel or in one city for the duration of your trip, you'll most likely need a car in Maine.

At the Portland and Bangor airports, you'll find **Avis Rent A Car** (800-331-1212), **Budget Rent A Car** (800-527-0700), **Hertz Rent A Car** (800-654-3131) and **National Car Rental** (800-328-4567). Serving Portland only is **Thrifty Car Rental** (800-367-2277).

PUBLIC TRANSIT

For getting around Portland on your own, there's a very good bus system called the **Metro**. It has regularly scheduled routes throughout the greater Portland area. ~ 207-774-0351.

TAXIS

Several taxi companies serve the Portland International Jetport, including **Town Cab Co.** (207-773-1711). In Bangor, try **Town Taxi** (207-945-5671).

Index

Lodging Index

Dining Index

HIDDEN GUIDES

Adventure travel or a relaxing vacation?—"Hidden" guidebooks are the only travel books in the business to provide detailed information on both. Aimed at environmentally aware travelers, our motto is "Adventure Travel Plus." These books combine details on unique hotels, restaurants and sightseeing with information on camping, sports and hiking for the outdoor enthusiast.

THE NEW KEY GUIDES

Based on the concept of ecotourism, The New Key Guides are dedicated to the preservation of Central America's rare and endangered species, architecture and archaeology. Filled with helpful tips, they give travelers everything they need to know about these exotic destinations.